£15

# Handbook of Child and Adolescent Sexuality
*Developmental and Forensic Psychology*

# Handbook of Child and Adolescent Sexuality
## Developmental and Forensic Psychology

Edited by

**DANIEL S. BROMBERG**
**WILLIAM T. O'DONOHUE**

Amsterdam • Boston • Heidelberg • London • New York • Oxford
Paris • San Diego • San Francisco • Singapore • Sydney • Tokyo
Academic Press is an imprint of Elsevier

Academic Press is an imprint of Elsevier

The Boulevard, Langford Lane, Kidlington, Oxford, OX5 1GB, UK
84 Theobald's Road, London WC1X 8RR, UK

Copyright © 2013 Elsevier Ltd. All rights reserved.

No part of this publication may be reproduced or transmitted in any form or by any means, electronic or mechanical, including photocopying, recording, or any information storage and retrieval system, without permission in writing from the publisher. Details on how to seek permission, further information about the Publisher's permissions policies and our arrangements with organizations such as the Copyright Clearance Center and the Copyright Licensing Agency, can be found at our website: www.elsevier.com/permissions.

This book and the individual contributions contained in it are protected under copyright by the Publisher (other than as may be noted herein).

**Notices**
Knowledge and best practice in this field are constantly changing. As new research and experience broaden our understanding, changes in research methods, professional practices, or medical treatment may become necessary.

Practitioners and researchers must always rely on their own experience and knowledge in evaluating and using any information, methods, compounds, or experiments described herein. In using such information or methods they should be mindful of their own safety and the safety of others, including parties for whom they have a professional responsibility.

To the fullest extent of the law, neither the Publisher nor the authors, contributors, or editors, assume any liability for any injury and/or damage to persons or property as a matter of products liability, negligence or otherwise, or from any use or operation of any methods, products, instructions, or ideas contained in the material herein.

**British Library Cataloguing in Publication Data**
A catalogue record for this book is available from the British Library

**Library of Congress Cataloging-in-Publication Data**
A catalog record for this book is available from the Library of Congress

ISBN: 978-0-12-387759-8

For information on all Academic Press publications
visit our website at elsevier.com

Printed and bound in the United States of America
13 14 15 16 17    10 9 8 7 6 5 4 3 2 1

**Working together to grow
libraries in developing countries**

www.elsevier.com | www.bookaid.org | www.sabre.org

ELSEVIER    BOOK AID International    Sabre Foundation

# CONTENTS

List of Contributors — xi
Preface — xv
Acknowledgements — xvii

## Part One: Ethical Issues Pertaining to the Sexuality of Minors

### 1. Choosing for Children — 3
Michael Lavin

The Rudiments of Consent — 3
Hot Button Case — 6
The Good, the Bad, and Best Interests — 10
Moral Disagreement — 15
Large Issues — 16
References — 18

## Part Two: Research Strategies: How Do We "Know" What We "Know?"

### 2. Research Methods: Current Strategies, Obstacles to Research, and Future Directions — 21
Daniel S. Bromberg and William T. O'Donohue

Why the Dearth of Research on Child and Adolescent Sexuality? — 22
Strengths and Shortcomings of Research Strategies Employed — 22
Research Strategies Utilized in Investigating Domains of Childhood Behavior Other Than Childhood Sexual Behavior — 25
Directions for Future Research — 34
Significant Dilemmas Impeding Advancement of Knowledge in the Field — 37
References — 38

### 3. Research Syntheses Related to Childhood and Adolescent Sexuality: A Critical Review — 41
Tania B. Huedo-Medina, Estrellita Ballester, and Blair T. Johnson

Introduction — 41
Systematic Reviews and Meta-Analysis: Evidence-Based Resources — 42
Systematic Review and Meta-Analysis Procedures — 47
Survey of Systematic Reviews of Child and Adolescent Sexuality — 57
Acknowledgement — 91
References — 91

v

## 4. Applications of Small-n Research Design in Child and Adolescent Sexuality — 97
Gregory S. Snyder and Stacy Shaw

| | |
|---|---|
| Introduction | 97 |
| Measurement | 99 |
| Withdrawal and Reversal Designs (AB, ABAB) | 101 |
| Multiple-Baseline Designs | 104 |
| Conclusions | 110 |
| Acknowledgement | 111 |
| References | 111 |

# Part Three: Child and Adolescent Development

## 5. Sexual Development — 115
Kate Mills Drury and William M. Bukowski

| | |
|---|---|
| Introduction | 115 |
| Learning Bases | 118 |
| Social Bases | 127 |
| Conclusion: Healthy Sexual Development | 137 |
| Acknowledgement | 138 |
| References | 138 |

## 6. Sexual Behavior of Prepubertal Children — 145
Christopher Campbell, Ashwini Mallappa, Amy B. Wisniewski, and Jane F. Silovsky

| | |
|---|---|
| Introduction | 145 |
| Defining Prepubertal | 145 |
| Theories of why Puberty is Occurring at Earlier Ages | 148 |
| Sexual Behavior in Prepubertal Children | 152 |
| Sexual Behavior in Children with Early Pubertal Development | 160 |
| Prepubertal Children and Gender Identity Disorder | 161 |
| Summary | 162 |
| References | 163 |

## 7. Sexual Development in Adolescents — 171
J. Dennis Fortenberry

| | |
|---|---|
| The Conceptual Organization of Adolescent Sexuality Development | 172 |
| Sexual Socialization | 173 |
| Sexual Selfhood | 177 |
| Sexual Repertoire | 178 |
| Summary | 186 |
| References | 187 |

## 8. Sexual Development in Girls: "Normative" Development and Development of Paraphilias and Sexual Offending Behaviors — 193
Lucia F. O'Sullivan and Scott T. Ronis

Introduction — 193
Understanding "Normative" Sexual Development — 193
Paraphilias and Sexual Offending in Girls — 202
Conclusions — 212
References — 212

## 9. The Sexual Health of Adolescents: When, Where, and Why Adolescents Use Contraceptives — 221
Lori A.J. Scott-Sheldon and Blair T. Johnson

Overview of Adolescent Sexual Behavior and Consequences of Unprotected Sex — 222
Contraceptives — 225
Predictors of Contraceptive Use and Non-Use — 228
Promoting Contraceptive Use — 236
Conclusions — 241
References — 243

## 10. Influence of Alcohol and Illicit Drug Use on Sexual Behavior — 253
Michael Windle, Jessica M. Sales, and Rebecca C. Windle

Descriptive Epidemiology — 254
Alcohol, Drugs, Interpersonal Violence, and Sexual Behaviors — 263
Theories and Common Mechanisms of Influence Among Alcohol, Drugs, and Sexual Behaviors — 264
Selective Findings from Prevention and Intervention Studies — 266
Conclusions and Future Directions — 269
Acknowledgement — 270
References — 271

## 11. Sexual-Minority, Gender-Nonconforming, and Transgender Youths — 275
Lisa M. Diamond

First Things First: Defining the Population — 276
Same-Sex Attractions: Not Always Early and Exclusive — 279
Mental Health of Sexual-Minority Youths — 283
Gender-Nonconforming Youths — 286
Transgender Youth — 288
Exposure to Stigmatization — 290
Conclusion — 293
References — 294

# Part Four: Children and Adolescents as Sexual Abuse Victims

### 12. Epidemiology of Child and Adolescent Sexual Abuse     303
Samantha L. Friedenberg, David J. Hansen, and Mary Fran Flood

| | |
|---|---|
| Defining Child Sexual Abuse | 304 |
| Incidence and Prevalence of Child and Adolescent Sexual Abuse | 307 |
| Victim and Abuse Characteristics | 309 |
| Disclosure and Allegations of Child Sexual Abuse | 313 |
| Outcomes of Child Sexual Abuse | 316 |
| Conclusion | 319 |
| References | 319 |

### 13. Child Sexual Abuse and Adolescent Sexuality     325
Christine Wekerle, Terry Bennett, and Karen Francis

| | |
|---|---|
| Child Sexual Abuse Statistics | 327 |
| Professional Responsibilities in CSA | 328 |
| Sexual Behavior Problems | 331 |
| Juvenile Sex Offending | 335 |
| Juvenile Sex Offending—the Role of CSA | 337 |
| Summary | 340 |
| References | 341 |

### 14. Memory and Complications to the Interviewing of Suspected Child and Adolescent Victims     347
Matthew Fanetti, Rachel Fondren-Happel, and William T. O'Donohue

| | |
|---|---|
| Introduction | 347 |
| General Memory Issues | 349 |
| General Trends in Child Memory | 358 |
| Evaluating Interviews for Potential Bias | 360 |
| Child Advocacy Centers | 363 |
| How CACs Interview | 363 |
| Other Training | 367 |
| References | 368 |

### 15. Treating Children and Adolescents in the Aftermath of Sexual Abuse     371
Elisabeth Pollio, Alissa Glickman, Leah Behl, and Esther Deblinger

| | |
|---|---|
| Introduction | 371 |
| Review of Evidence-Based Treatments for Child Sexual Abuse | 372 |
| Review of Trauma-Focused Cognitive Behavioral Therapy Research | 375 |

|   |   |   |
|---|---|---|
|   | Description of Trauma-Focused Cognitive Behavioral Therapy | 378 |
|   | A Case Study of TF-CBT for Child Sexual Abuse with Sexually Reactive Behaviors | 385 |
|   | Conclusion | 397 |
|   | References | 397 |

**16. Medical Assessment and Treatment of Suspected Child and Adolescent Victims of Sexual Abuse** — 401
Reena Isaac and Angelo P. Giardino

|   |   |
|---|---|
| Introduction | 401 |
| Overview and Approach to the Medical Evaluation | 402 |
| Timing of Physical Examination | 406 |
| Preparation of the Child for Examination | 407 |
| Examination | 409 |
| Documentation | 414 |
| Multidisciplinary Teams | 415 |
| References | 416 |

**17. Teaching Sexual Abuse Prevention Skills to Children** — 419
Raymond G. Miltenberger and Laura Hanratty

|   |   |
|---|---|
| Sexual Abuse Prevention Skills | 421 |
| Assessment of Safety Skills | 423 |
| Training Approaches | 428 |
| References | 444 |

**18. Adolescence and Commercial Sexual Exploitation: Prostituted Girls in the US** — 449
Linda M. Williams

|   |   |
|---|---|
| Introduction | 449 |
| Social Context of Commercial Sex and Adolescence | 453 |
| How Youth Get Involved in CSE | 456 |
| Research on Common Features of Commercial Sexual Exploitation | 462 |
| Community Response | 464 |
| References | 466 |

**19. Legal Responses to Adolescent Victims of Sexual Violence** — 469
Roger J.R. Levesque

|   |   |
|---|---|
| Dominant Legal Responses to the Sexual Victimization of Adolescents: Their Processes and Inherent Limitations | 471 |
| The Victim's Rights Movement | 485 |
| Conclusions | 489 |
| References | 490 |

## Part Five: Children with Sexual Behavior Problems and Adolescent Sexual Offenders

### 20. Children with Sexual Behavior Problems — 497
Jane F. Silovsky, Lisa M. Swisher, Jimmy Widdifield, Jr., and Vicky L. Turner

| | |
|---|---|
| Introduction | 497 |
| Definitions | 498 |
| Differentiating Typical Sexual Development from Problematic Sexual Behavior | 499 |
| Prevalence, Origins, and Conceptualization of Problematic Sexual Behavior | 501 |
| Clinical Assessment | 506 |
| Treatment Planning | 509 |
| Systems Barriers and Supports | 512 |
| Summary and Conclusions | 513 |
| References | 513 |

### 21. Adolescents Adjudicated for Sexual Offenses — 519
Amanda M. Fanniff and Judith V. Becker

| | |
|---|---|
| Characteristics of Adolescent Males Adjudicated for Sexual Offenses | 520 |
| Assessment of Adolescents Adjudicated for Sexual Offenses | 521 |
| Treatment for Adolescents Adjudicated for Sexual Offenses | 534 |
| Conclusions | 539 |
| References | 539 |

### 22. Legal Responses to Adolescents' Sexual Offending — 547
Roger J.R. Levesque

| | |
|---|---|
| Introduction | 547 |
| Juvenile Justice System Responses | 548 |
| Criminal Justice Responses | 557 |
| Furthering Legal Reforms | 565 |
| Conclusion | 569 |
| References | 571 |

*Index* — *575*

# LIST OF CONTRIBUTORS

**Estrellita Ballester**
University of Connecticut, Storrs, Connecticut, USA

**Judith V. Becker**
University of Arizona, Tucson, Arizona, USA

**Leah Behl**
University of Medicine and Dentistry of New Jersey, Stratford, New Jersey, USA

**Terry Bennett**
McMaster University, Hamilton, Ontario, Canada

**Daniel S. Bromberg**
Special Psychological Services, LLC, Bloomfield, New Jersey, USA

**William M. Bukowski**
Concordia University, Montréal, Québec, Canada

**Christopher Campbell**
University of Oklahoma Health Sciences Center, Oklahoma City, Oklahoma, USA

**Esther Deblinger**
University of Medicine and Dentistry of New Jersey, Stratford, New Jersey, USA

**J. Dennis Fortenberry**
Indiana University School of Medicine, Indianapolis, Indiana, USA

**Lisa M. Diamond**
University of Utah, Salt Lake City, Utah, USA

**Matthew Fanetti**
Missouri State University, Springfield, Missouri, USA

**Amanda M. Fanniff**
Palo Alto University, Palo Alto, California, USA

**Rachel Fondren-Happel**
Missouri State University, Springfield, Missouri, USA

**Karen Francis**
McMaster University, Hamilton, Ontario, Canada

**Mary Fran Flood**
University of Nebraska-Lincoln, Lincoln, Nebraska, USA

**Samantha L. Friedenberg**
University of Nebraska-Lincoln, Lincoln, Nebraska, USA

**Angelo P. Giardino**
Baylor College of Medicine and Texas Children's Hospital, Houston, Texas, USA

**Alissa Glickman**
*University of Medicine and Dentistry of New Jersey, Stratford, New Jersey, USA

**Laura Hanratty**
University of South Florida, Tampa, Florida, USA

**David J. Hansen**
University of Nebraska-Lincoln, Lincoln, Nebraska, USA

**Tania B. Huedo-Medina**
University of Connecticut, Storrs, Connecticut, USA

**Reena Isaac**
Baylor College of Medicine and Texas Children's Hospital, Houston, Texas, USA

**Blair T. Johnson**
University of Connecticut, Storrs, Connecticut, USA

**Michael Lavin**
San Antonio, Texas, USA

**Roger J.R. Levesque**
Indiana University, Bloomington, Indiana, USA

**Ashwini Mallappa**
University of Oklahoma Health Sciences Center, Oklahoma City, Oklahoma, USA

**Kate Mills Drury**
Concordia University, Montréal, Québec, Canada

**Raymond G. Miltenberger**
University of South Florida, Tampa, Florida, USA

**William T. O'Donohue**
University of Nevada, Reno, Nevada, USA

**Lucia F. O'Sullivan**
University of New Brunswick, Fredericton, New Brunswick, Canada

**Elisabeth Pollio**
University of Medicine and Dentistry of New Jersey, Stratford, New Jersey, USA

**Scott T. Ronis**
University of New Brunswick, Fredericton, New Brunswick, Canada

**Jessica M. Sales**
Emory University, Atlanta, Georgia, USA

**Lori A.J. Scott-Sheldon**
The Miriam Hospital and Brown University, Providence, Rhode Island, USA

**Stacy Shaw**
Boys Town Center for Behavioral Health, Boys Town, Nebraska, USA

**Jane F. Silovsky**
University of Oklahoma Health Sciences Center, Oklahoma City, Oklahoma, USA

**Gregory S. Snyder**
Boys Town Center for Behavioral Health, Boys Town, Nebraska, USA

**Lisa M. Swisher**
University of Oklahoma Health Sciences Center, Oklahoma City, Oklahoma, USA

**Vicky L. Turner**
University of Oklahoma Health Sciences Center, Oklahoma City, Oklahoma, USA

**Christine Wekerle**
McMaster University, Hamilton, Ontario, Canada

**Jimmy Widdifield, Jr.**
University of Oklahoma Health Sciences Center, Oklahoma City, Oklahoma, USA

**Linda M. Williams**
University of Massachusetts Lowell, Lowell, Massachusetts, USA

**Michael Windle**
Emory University, Atlanta, Georgia, USA

**Rebecca C. Windle**
Emory University, Atlanta, Georgia, USA

**Amy B. Wisniewski**
University of Oklahoma Health Sciences Center, Oklahoma City, Oklahoma, USA

# PREFACE

Sexual thoughts, feelings, and behaviors are of central importance throughout the lifespan and across cultures. Every known society, both current and ancient, has had rules regarding who may have sexual relations with whom and under what circumstances. The acceptability or proscription of autoerotic behavior has received a focus that is equally as strong. In today's world, considerable attention is being given to the management of children, adolescents, and adults whose sexual behaviors cross acceptable boundaries and infringe on the well-being of others. Because experiences throughout childhood and adolescence have a significant impact on development throughout the lifespan (Fox & Rutter, 2010), understanding the origins of sexual interests and behaviors is clearly of importance.

The scientific study of human sexuality is fraught with an assortment of ethical and practical obstacles. Such obstacles are magnified when attempting to study childhood and adolescent sexuality. Paradoxically, much more is known about the sexual thoughts, feelings, and experiences of minors who have experienced and/or perpetrated sexual abuse than about "normal" sexual development. The foregoing situation is problematic, as surprisingly little is known about what constitutes "normal" sexual development in children and adolescents. The goal of this book is to synthesize what is currently known about human sexual development early in the lifespan and about factors that derail sexual development. The Handbook should be of utility to a wide range of professionals including the following: clinical, forensic, and developmental psychologists; child psychiatrists and other mental health professionals; pediatricians and nurse practitioners; and attorneys. We expect that students in these fields will find this volume to be of utility. Professionals involved in the development and evaluation of programs for sexuality education, sexual health clinics, and public policy makers will likely find the Handbook to be a valuable resource, as well.

The first part of the book contains a chapter on ethical issues. The four parts that follow cover the following topics: research strategies; child and adolescent sexual development; children and adolescents as sexual abuse victims; and children and adolescents with sexual behavior problems.

Part Two, Research Strategies, addresses techniques commonly employed in child and adolescent sexuality research, as well as less frequently used strategies. Such strategies include meta-analytic techniques and small-n research designs. Part Three, Child and Adolescent Development, addresses sexual development, both pre-and post-puberty. We include chapters on factors influencing condom and contraceptive use in adolescents, influences of alcohol and illicit drug use on sexual behavior, and on sexual minority adolescents. Part Four, Children and Adolescents as Sexual Abuse Victims, covers epidemiology, psychological and medical assessment and treatment, prevention of sexual abuse, adolescents involved in prostitution and pornography, and legal issues pertaining to adolescent victims. In Part Five, the final section of the book, readers will find a chapter on children who display sexual behavioral problems, and another on adolescents adjudicated for having committed sexual offenses. The section concludes with an excellent chapter on legal responses to adolescent sexual offending.

It is our hope that this book will need substantive revisions and additions as more research on child and adolescent sexuality becomes available.

Daniel S. Bromberg, Ph.D., ABPP<br>
William T. O'Donohue, Ph.D.

## REFERENCE

Fox, N. A., & Rutter, M. (2010). Introduction to the special section on the effects of early experience on development. *Child Development, 81*(1), 23–27.

# ACKNOWLEDGEMENTS

I (DSB) gratefully acknowledge those who taught me: Murray and Marcia Bromberg, my parents and first teachers; Craig S. Edelbrock; Blair T. Johnson; and Seth Aldrich. My thanks to my wife, Shelley, and our two daughters, Lauren and Sarah, who waited patiently for me while I worked on this book. My deepest thanks to Bill O'Donohue for collaborating on this project.

I (WTO) thank my family, Jane, Katie, and Anna, for all their support and kindness. I thank Daniel Bromberg for his excellent scholarship, unflagging good humor, and all his hard work.

PART One

# Ethical Issues Pertaining to the Sexuality of Minors

# CHAPTER 1

# Choosing for Children

**Michael Lavin**
San Antonio, Texas[1]

## THE RUDIMENTS OF CONSENT

When clinicians treat a child because of a sexual disorder or behavior, they must manage difficulties that have to do with treating any child and also difficulties that have to do with salience of sex in American culture. Let us begin with the general difficulties.

Everybody now concedes that children are not miniature adults. Because children are not adults, two central principles that govern the treatment of adults have their importance reversed. For competent adults, their liberty interests take precedence over their welfare interests. Competent adults are at liberty to refuse standard treatments and even lifesaving treatments. An adult's refusal of a low-risk, beneficial treatment may raise clinical eyebrows and result in an assessment of that adult's competence, but the general rule is that competent adults get to decide to what they will submit. They must consent to their treatments. Young children have no such right, though the older children get, the harder it becomes to overrule their wishes, as they have the capacity to consent. Still, the importance of liberty has its day in America. Even young children do get asked to assent to treatments, but minor children lacking decisional capacity have no veto power over beneficial treatments.

Clinicians do, on standard accounts, have a duty, barring emergencies, to obtain permission before treating a child; however, the child's mother or father, the persons who, unless disqualified or absent, do consent to treatment, have grave constraints placed on their deciding. These constraints may not apply when deciding for an incompetent adult. In particular, a parent has a legal obligation to make treatment decisions for their children based on what is in the child's best interest. When a person other than the patient must decide what treatments to accept or reject, the custom is to call him a proxy. Parents are proxies for their children. Their duty

---

[1] Correspondence to: Michael Lavin PhD, 1440 South Grandview Avenue, Dubuque, IA 52003-8773. Phone 563-582-6815; email ml1952@stanfordalumni.org

is to decide what is in the child's "best interest." When a proxy decides for somebody other than a child, the proxy may sometimes have a duty or permission to ignore what is in the patient's best interests, and decide as the patient would decide if he were competent to decide. For example, a man may need a blood transfusion. If he is a Jehovah's Witness, his wife may refuse the transfusion, even if it is likely to save his life. She may rely on her reasonable beliefs of what he would wish done in this situation, rather than the best interest standard. In practice, some parents may make treatment decisions based on their understanding of what their child wants, but the ordinary understanding is that they are to rely on what is in the child's best interests to make a decision.

The Best Interest Standard is in fact misnamed. Despite the name, few parents can make decisions based on a literal reading of this standard. Often nobody knows what is in the best interest of the child. The remote consequences of a decision may be unknowable. There may be disagreements about what to include in the calculation of a child's best interest, or even what weight to assign different factors. One parent may think a child in a persistent vegetative state should receive aggressive treatment to keep him alive in that state, whilst other parents would opt for minimal care. Whatever the law says about cases of this kind, and that may vary from jurisdiction to jurisdiction, there is no definitive answer to what is in the child's best interest in many cases.

What then must proxies relying on the Best Interest Standard do? They must do what all parents do. They must agree to good enough care. A parent must consent to have a child examined after a rape, but may decline a recommendation for psychoanalysis to help the child cope with its sequelae, though they would have an obligation to agree to a briefer form of psychotherapy if the child needed it. There need be no agreement in many cases about what assessments and treatments a parent must accept, as reasonable people for any number of reasons could disagree about what the child needs. If the best interest standard were literally true, the same facts should yield the same decision in each case.

As a matter of law, parents do provide consent to the treatment of their children, and barring legally carved out circumstances—for example a daughter need not obtain permission from her father for treatment, if the father has raped her—parents do in most instances have to consent for a clinician to provide treatment to their children.

Why? Tradition is part of it. It is the done thing. Money is a part of it. In many instances where consent matters, children lack a means of paying for the services. But perhaps there are deeper reasons than either tradition or money.

Consent derives from a Latin word that means "with knowledge." When somebody consents to something, he does more than just agree to it. People consent in situations that have gravity. Consent fits best in contexts where something that matters is at stake. The moral idea is rooted in simultaneous respect of a person's liberty and welfare. When persons consent to an assessment or treatment, they are to know what is at stake for them. One might think of the consent as requiring an informed mind and a free will. What is involved? There are at least two general requirements:

1. A conveyance of information that
   1. is understood; and
   2. is complete and relevant to the choices.
2. A volitional requirement that
   1. entails an uncoerced choice;
   2. entails practical reason; and
   3. results in a public authorization of any chosen intervention for which there has been an adequate conveyance of information.

Readers should avoid literalism in regard to these requirements. Understanding information, for example, is a scalar quality. It admits of degrees. Complete information relevant to a choice is at best aspirational. Rational patients resent consent forms that omit important benefits or side effects of an intervention, as these omissions prevent their choosing wisely. They are not interested in whether their therapist is left-handed. Likewise, "uncoerced" does not mean that the patient has no compelling reasons for making his choice. Few people would agree to prolonged exposure therapy for PTSD, if they were asymptomatic. Having a condition for which one is being treated does not count as coercion; being told you will be gelded in your psychology course unless you agree to doing the assignments does count as coercion. It is sometimes difficult to tell whether choice is coerced, but it is often very clear that a choice was not coerced.

Practical reasoning guides choice. Theoretical reason seeks the truth. Practical reason seeks apt choices. To have practical reason, human beings must have the capacity to make use of what they know and believe. They must also have sane goals (viz., I want to be healthy, I want to stop stealing women's shoes, etc.), as well as an understanding of how to use what they know to help them get what they want. People differ in how well they can engage in practical reasoning. Adults with disorders that can impair practical reason, as do Alzheimer's disease or mental disorders in the psychotic spectrum, are sometimes unable to meet the volitional requirement. Some children, for example younger ones, are incapable of meeting it.

These requirements for consent illuminate what happens in an ordinary consent process. It has five elements. Each requirement rests on the conveyance of information, its comprehension, and the employment of practical reason to choose an offered intervention, and the free choice of interventions. After all, if one proposes to impose an intervention, these five features of the consent process are beside the point, even though it is indeed possible to tick through this process with a patient incapable of consent, as would happen with young children, demented, insane, or comatose patients.

1. The proposed intervention is explained.
2. The intervention's benefits are explained.
3. The intervention's risks are explained.
4. The same is done for alternatives to proposed intervention, including doing nothing.
5. The patient is invited to ask questions.

Now that the complexities of the consent process are in relief, they pose obstacles to children that will lessen as the children age. With the passage of time, children grow in their ability to understand what clinicians tell them and to use what they are told to make a free choice from alternatives. In philosophical terms, the theoretical and practical reason of children matures and improves with time. For a variety of reasons, legal systems tend to simplify the task of determining when a human being is free to make choices about their medical treatment, by providing an age of majority. So, when a person in the United States reaches particular age milestones, he is left at liberty to make certain decisions for himself, until at the age of 21 there is a presumption in favor of his decisional capacity to make the choices of a fully fledged citizen.

## HOT BUTTON CASE

Despite the emotion attaching to sexual decisions, it is difficult to discern any ground for thinking that they necessitate a novel theory of informed consent; however, there are reasons why a child may strain to acquire the capacities to make choices about sex whilst still young.

Just as children's minds evolve towards adulthood, so do their bodies. Changes in the body have an impact on what children desire. Prior to puberty, a child faces a set of "natural" and "social" pressures favoring gender conformity. Girls and boys face expectations having to do with names, etiquette, dress, choice of friends, sexual attraction, play, competition, eating, and self concept. On the list goes.

Perhaps one of the earliest sexual difficulties a child faces involves the embrace or rejection of the alleged implications of its anatomical sex, though other sexual challenges also face a child. Many people report being aware of bisexual, homosexual, or heterosexual partner preferences at an early age. Depending on a child's overt responses to these early challenges, it may face conflict with parents or other significant adults. As a result, therapists may decide to decline treatment to children whose parents have decided to pursue therapy aimed at producing a child whose sexual behavior is a closer approximation to what the proxies electing treatment desire.

Consider the plight of a transgendered child. Four general grounds for declining to treat a transgendered child are readily discernible. First, a therapist may disapprove of the proposed treatment. Second, the therapist, whether he is approving or disapproving, may believe he is incompetent to achieve the desired results. Third, a therapist may believe that the proposed treatment is something to which no proxy can consent because it is contrary to the good-enough interests of the child. A therapist might reach this conclusion for any number of reasons. If the child dissents from the proposed treatment, the therapist may believe it wrong to impose treatment against the child's dissent. Even if the child assents to proposed treatment, the therapist might decline because he believes it contrary to the child's interests. Fourth, a therapist may conclude that, no matter what the law says, a child has the decisional capacity to consent to accept or decline to accept treatment, because the child has the decisional capacity to give informed consent, implying the proxy is the wrong person from whom to accept consent or to let determine what is to be done. If so, a therapist may conclude that he has no right to overrule a competent minor's decision to decline treatment.

If the parents wish their transgendered child's treatment to aim at producing behaviors congruent with the behaviors of conventional heterosexual children, these four grounds may produce conflict with the parents. The same kind of conflict arises in the more frequently discussed case of parents wishing a gay child to receive treatment aimed at making him straight. The conflict is unavoidable, even if at first glance it appears avoidable by, for example, citing incompetence to achieve the aim as the reason for declining the treatment request. For even if, as is arguably likely, nobody possesses a reliable therapy for making a transgendered child or gay child conform to the gender and sexual behavior preferences of his parents, the therapist declining therapy has to decide what to tell the parents.

The American Psychological Association (APA) does have guidelines and resolutions regarding the treatment of gays, lesbians, and bisexuals, and also has a resolution condemning discrimination against transgendered, gender variant, or gender nonconforming persons (APA, 2011); however, neither the guidelines nor resolutions are standards that bind members, under threat of sanctions, to a particular stance towards the GBLT population. Psychologists might dissent from either the guidelines or the resolution without making themselves vulnerable to formal sanctions, as would be the case for violations of APA ethics code standards (APA, 2010).

The relevant guidelines and resolutions regarding treatment of gays, lesbians, and bisexuals do argue that any efforts aimed at changing the sexual orientation of a gay person should include a warning that no effective treatments to accomplish this goal are known to exist, despite the existence of organizations claiming otherwise. The resolution on transgendered people does call for improved treatments for gender variance, but the context of the document makes clear that the goal is not to bring a transgendered person into alignment with the regnant gender expectations for a transgendered person's anatomical sex. Instead, the treatment mentioned aims at making it easier for transgendered persons to live in the gender role of their choice. Provisions of medical, legal, and social services furthering this goal are endorsed, rather than enforcement of gender norms.

Given the stance of the APA, there is ground for asserting a duty of psychologists declining to treat, whether they approve of what the parents are proposing or not, to inform them that the "official" position of the leading psychological association is that there is no reason to believe there exists, in the present state of knowledge, treatment that will work to achieve their goal. If a therapist rejects the APA's reading of the effectiveness of efforts to change a person's sexual orientation or gender nonconformance, he has a duty to explain why he disagrees. To omit this information would constitute a deception, and limit a proxy's ability to make informed choices on behalf of the gay or transgendered child. In the language of informed consent explained in the prior section, the conveyance of information for obtaining consent is defective.

Now if a therapist disapproves of the proxy's choice for a child, that fact does not justify withholding information from a proxy, so the duty to inform the patient of the relevant information, even if a therapist disapproves of it, stands; however, aside from life-threatening emergencies, therapists have no duty to provide services that they disapprove of. Even if it were possible to "cure" a gender variant child, a therapist has no duty to do so, any more than he would have a duty to "cure" a left-handed child, if he could do so. There are many reasons for this view. In non-emergencies, a therapist is, just as is the patient or his proxy, an autonomous agent. His professional duties may constrain how he provides or does not provide elective procedures, but he has the option of deciding whether to provide them. For example, a psychologist might refuse to provide services designed to assist a gay child in coming out because, for example, her religious convictions forbid her to do so.

Serious moral difficulties emerge if a therapist believes that, for example, no proxy has a right to impose a particular treatment on a child. Treatments to realign sexual orientation or align gender to identify with sexual identity count as examples. Given the guidelines of the APA and its resolutions on transgendered human beings, a psychologist has the makings of an argument for the conclusion that it is contrary to a proxy's duty to make treatment decisions in accordance with the best interest standard to seek to "cure" a transgendered child or gay child. Underlying this argument is the notion that the therapist or the APA is the true upholder in these cases of a child's good-enough interests; the idea being that treatment in these cases of the kind desired by the parents always is contrary to the good-enough interests of the child.

A clear example of this kind of case arises when the secular perspective of what counts as being in a child's best interests, as represented by the APA, collides with parents' religiously informed perspective on what counts as being in a child's best interests. These disputes arising from assertions about what is a spiritual benefit are slippery. Few Americans would be willing to agree that it is permissible for Somali parents to infibulate their daughters on the ground that it is their time-honored custom in parts of east Africa, has religious benefits and sanctions, and is a boon to chastity, even if some of these claims turn out to be true. On the other hand, many people are willing to permit Amish parents to decline customary medical procedures and treatments, or to permit secular parents to circumcise their sons. The moral terrain in these disputes is treacherous for many reasons. A central difficulty is the weight, if any, to assign to certain kinds of interests, and who is to assign the weight, especially in the absence of a consensus. For example, as a matter of law, parents must assign the education of their children a high weight. In the United States, a parent may no longer refuse to school a daughter on the ground that, in this parent's view of a wife's duties, she has no need of education. Views like this may be latent in certain religious communities, but they occur at the periphery of American social practice. Parental views about the importance of chastity, as evidenced by numerous and fairly dubious chastity campaigns, as well as a parent's being allowed to regulate their child's sexual behavior, are less often challenged. Parents seeking to "cure" a child of homosexuality may well believe that failure to do so imperils that child's soul. A parent who sincerely believes that his child's homosexuality or gender noncomformity damns him is going to resist efforts to view that child's behavior, as does the APA (2011), as a normal, even if infrequent, variant of human sexuality.

This collision between a child's parents' view of its best interest and expert views, as embalmed in the APA guidelines and resolutions, of a child's best interest has no easy solution. The conflict of these contending views of best interest emerges from a conflict between narrower and wider views of how to interpret or understand the child's best interest, or indeed anybody's best interests.

## THE GOOD, THE BAD, AND BEST INTERESTS

As already observed, best interest literally construed is too high a standard to be plausible as a guide to how a proxy is to select treatment options for a child. Nevertheless, there is a venerable tradition in philosophy that runs at least back to Aristotle, and championed to this day by philosophers such as the late Philippa Foot (2003), that maintains that what is good for a child or, for that matter any number of organisms and artifacts in the world as we know it, is an ascertainable fact. Take a few simple instances. If you wish a guitar to function as a guitar, adequate humidification is good for it, whilst knocking holes into the guitar or warping its neck are bad for it. Flowers flourish under specifiable climatic and soil conditions, and die in others. Likewise, provided one is willing, as the APA is, to assume certain functions as "normal," then one can establish what is good or bad for a child in regard to those ends or, in psychspeak, outcomes. To keep living, a child, just as a plant, requires certain environmental conditions. To learn to speak a human language, a child must have certain kinds of exposure. To have a healthy body and mind, a child must receive a diet in a certain range, love, and an education of a particular type.

Psychological science has made contributions to identifying what is good for children just as medicine has. Medicine has shown that it is bad for children not to get certain vitamins. If they do not, they can develop pellagra, beriberi, rickets, or scurvy. Or have stunted minds. Psychologists have learnt that children learn to read better with some programs of instruction than others, and that a variety of traumata can devastate a child's mental health. In the best circumstances psychology speaks with the authority of a science when its recommendations flow from research. A scientific claim that fluoridated water prevents tooth decay without poisoning the child defeats well-intended, febrile-right parental claims that fluoride is a poison that, in the proposed dosage, will harm their child.

Even though some parental claims are wrong as a matter of science, others are not so easily dismissed. In particular, all people, including scientists, rely on an indefinitely large number of culturally available beliefs to reach conclusions about what is good for them, as well as people they care about. Although some of these culturally available beliefs lack scientific authorities, people normally allow them to enter into calculations of well-being. For example, many people believe prayer to be to a person's advantage. As a result, many parents teach their children to pray. Even if psychology fails to establish through scientific method the benefits of prayer, prayerful people believe their religious traditions make the case for prayer compelling. In fact, failure of a priest to pray or offer prayer might well count as an instance of religious malpractice, and a refusal of a Catholic priest to endorse prayer as part of what is in a Catholic child's best interest would also count as spiritual malpractice, even if contemporary psychological science were to establish that people derive no demonstrable benefit from either petitionary or contemplative prayer. To avert confusion, it is unlikely for a variety of reasons that science could ever establish this conclusion. And it is obvious why. Just as religious people may believe that living an honest life is to their advantage in the next life, even if it appears not to have produced the hoped for result in this world, a prayerful individual may believe that the answers to his deepest prayers will occur after, not before, he dies. Science cannot settle that, because it is not ordered to investigate that.

To go further, at least in some faith traditions, the authority of the priest, the rabbi, the imam, or other religious figures to teach what is and is not good for its members is definitive of what it is to be a member of that tradition. What would it mean, for example, for a Catholic to deny that the Church's sacraments and observance of Church teachings are good for him or form part of what is the good life for him? The simplest answer is that this catholic has ceased to be a Catholic. What would it mean for Catholic parents to view it as a matter of indifference whether their children lived in harmony or disharmony with Church orthodoxy?

A solely scientific account of what is good for human beings has no hope of saying what role, if any, religious goods and other goods ascertained without reliance on the sciences have. Science might establish that eating pork or beef will provide excellent protein sources for a child; it cannot establish under what circumstances, if any, Jain parents or Jewish parents must conclude that their child's best interest is to eat beef or pork.

What, though, as in the case of parents deciding whether to seek to alter the orientation of their child or to challenge a child's gender variance, are psychologists to do if parents justify their therapeutic choices with reference to culturally available beliefs that support conclusions different from the conclusions reached via reliance on secular science, as in the APA guidelines? Not all culturally available beliefs can override scientific findings about what is good or bad for a child. Parents may not refuse lifesaving treatments because, for example, their religious beliefs forbid blood transfusions. Doctors in the United States are not going to remove a girl's clitoris because the parents' culture supports doing so.

Perhaps in these two instances what stands out is the physical damage that a child will suffer if the parents' view of what furthers their child's good is honored. Unlike death and removal of non-diseased body parts, psychological harms are harder to identify or assess, making it harder to decide what needs balancing.

One obvious harm in regard to attempts to enforce gender boundaries or stop a preference for same-sex sex is that the treatment, at least if one accepts the APA guidelines' conclusions (2011), is futile. It is very difficult to know what to make of this claim. If the claim is that nothing in the treatment repertoire of psychologists could get a child with male genitals and a preference first exhibited in childhood for behaving as most female children do—playing with dolls, dressing as girls in our culture dress rather than as boys do—to desist from doing so, that is exceedingly hard to believe. After all, enforcement of these norms has been the norm in our culture, which is why the guidelines are *controversial*. One reason for APA's issuing them is to make it possible for more children to express their preferences in regard to orientation and gendered behavior without enduring what the APA views as hateful prejudice. But the idea that the therapy cannot work in regard to the expression of behavior or in terms of reducing the frequency of its occurrence is suspect at best.

An alternative goal of therapy would be for the therapist and parents to have as their goal the change of the underlying dispositions that lead to the behaviors that distress the parents, though perhaps not the child. Although one can imagine this alternative as a coherent aim, this goal still has a secondary goal as well, namely, the elimination of expressions of the underlying preferences or schemata involved in producing the observed behaviors. More importantly, however, even if this therapeutic goal is unattainable, it is not the only possible goal for therapy, as was made clear in the previous paragraph. Nor is it even unusual to admit this kind of minimalism. Many parents are more than happy to have a child behave with less aggression, to engage in less stealing, or to tell fewer lies, even if the human propensity to hit, steal, and lie remains. Of course they may also hope that once somebody begins to hit, steal, and lie less often that changes in their motivational structure will occur as well, so that it becomes easier to sustain these improvements.

How to think about what is good and what is not is more complicated than APA's facile empiricism about it would lead one to believe. A theory of value attempts to identify what is valued for its own sake versus what is valued for the sake of something else. Classical utilitarianism, in the hands of Bentham, and some earlier forms of hedonism famously identified pleasure as the sole good valued for its own sake. Whatever else was valued was, the story went, valued for being instrumental for attaining pleasure. Utilitarianism went on to say that right actions could be determined by asking what, of all possible actions available to an agent, maximized total pleasure in the universe. Moral reasoning became a calculus of pleasure. Of course there are theories at odds with classical utilitarianism. Reasons for diverging from classical utilitarianism exist if somebody believes in a plurality of goods valued for their own sake, as did the opponent of utilitarianism W.D. Ross and the renegade utilitarian G.E. Moore. Other moral theories, unlike utilitarianism, accepted the idea that determining what is the right thing to do is not merely a matter of doing accurate calculations about what maximizes total pleasure. For example, a pleasure-optimizing act might violate a right, or be at odds with a person's duty. In addition, much ordinary moral thinking attaches importance to moral traditions. It is fantastic, as well as ignorant, to suppose that the virtues of chastity, obedience, or vows of silence are valued by religious people because their practice has no costs to mental health. Once one acknowledges a potential plurality of goods valued for their own sake, as well as a plurality of what is intrinsically bad, the difficulty of the APA's style of argumentation against parents who wish their homosexual, bisexual, or transgendered children to be treated with a view to changing their orientation, as well as their therapist supporters, becomes clear. Even a definitive demonstration that these children are at graver risk of incurring a psychological defect than untreated children is irrelevant for settling disputes with anybody holding a broader view of the good and the bad. Somebody with a broader view of the good and bad might still believe it is appropriate to try to keep people from being disobedient, being unchaste, engaging in same-sex sex, or cross-dressing, even if there are psychological costs. As a scientific organization, the APA has a duty to provide accurate scientific information about homosexual, bisexual, and transgendered children, as well as the known consequences of treating these conditions; however, unless somebody is in the grip of the dubious idea that nothing else is relevant to decisions about whether to ban or allow "treatment," no immediate conclusions about proscriptions on treatment are entailed. So far as I can tell, there are no effective treatments against lying or adultery, if effective treatment means "cure," but one might still think it worthwhile to reduce their frequency. If anybody doubts the argument just given, attempt this thought experiment. Suppose it has been demonstrated that the APA concluded, after a dispassionate review of available science, that voluntary sexual activity between adult siblings or between adult children and their parents had no discernible effect, good or bad, on mental or physical health. Rationalists might well wish to claim that prohibitions on incest between adults would thereby be shown to be superstitious relics. A scientific moral system ought to dispense with what tradition has to say about the incest and permit it in the case of willing adults. If somebody disagrees, he must do so for reasons other than demonstrable harm of the kind the APA studies show to the parties. He might wish to contend that other people are hurt or offended by incestuous conduct; however, even if this is true, it falls short of the traditional view. The traditional view of the matter holds that incest is a grave wrong even if performed willingly and in secret. Anybody finding the traditional view comprehensible has recognized the appeal, whatever its ultimate coherence, of a view of what is good and bad, right and wrong, whose underpinnings extend beyond appeals to what science is positioned to demonstrate as good or bad outcomes to human beings.

Anybody willing to grant that the rightness or wrongness of what human beings do or choose to pursue does not depend solely on their empirically established consequences is free to reject what amounts to ultimate opinion testimony from the APA. If so, even if the APA's arguments established that gay, bisexual, or transgendered children suffer no psychological or physical harm from their orientations or behavior, their parents may have other reasons for wishing them to change their orientation if that is possible or, less ambitiously, to change its expression if that is possible. And this could be so even if, which is unlikely, the parents subscribed to the APA's code of ethics, because the parents may have a broader view of what is morally relevant than the APA construal of what is morally relevant.

## MORAL DISAGREEMENT

Moral disagreements can arise for a variety of reasons. Persons can disagree about relevant moral principles, disagreeing about what the principles are, their formulation, their ordering, or their weighting. They can disagree about morality being driven by principles. They can disagree, as made plain above, about what is and is not good or bad. They may disagree about the relevant facts. They can disagree about the strength of inferences made from available information from this or that moral system.

Some disagreements may well amount to disagreements about facts, or in some cases principles. Other disagreements may have a different form. Sometimes people disagree in attitude (Stevenson, 1972). You may approve of chastity. I may disapprove. One might imagine, it seems, a situation where we agree about the relevant facts concerning chastity, but disagree in attitude about it. It seems possible, for example, that two people could disagree in attitude about the importance of respecting parents' choices for their children, with no obvious way of proceeding to reach agreement. Simple non-moral cases make the point. If you like Lima beans and I hate them, we might agree on the properties of a Lima bean without ever being able to reach agreement on liking or disliking them. There is in these cases an impasse with no clear way of resolving it, other than to continue the conversation.

Moral thinking does differ from this, as the thought is that in moral reasoning an argument requires the provision of reasons (Rachels & Rachels, 2011). These may take one full-circle in the present case. A religious parent's reasons for wishing therapy for a gay, bisexual, or transgendered child may involve the teachings of that parent's church. By the nature of the case, these types of reasons are unavailable to professional scientific organizations. The APA may point out that the best science does not support what some religious parents would like to believe about the mental health consequences of being gay, bisexual, lesbian, or transgender, but their decision to seek to realign their child's sexual preference is not based solely on what the science does or does not show. To insist that only the science matters is to have reverted to a narrow rationalistic conception of the good, and there are powerful reasons to be wary of rationalism in politics (Oakeshott, 1991).

## LARGE ISSUES

If the APA or other scientific bodies lack the ability to speak with ultimate authority on topics in morality, what role do they have? It seems reasonable for scientific bodies to make sure that factual claims about gay, lesbian, bisexual, and transgendered children are indeed factual. Accurate knowledge can have, over time, an immense impact on opinion. The facts about smoking have led to a revolution in public policy. Gone are the days of people smoking in restaurants and offices. Growing evidence about the damage to the brain that playing football can cause is also likely to have an impact on decisions about what changes, if any, to make play safer. The facts influence attitudes over time. They do not have the dictatorial force that the APA guidelines imply to mandate attitudes.

Recognizing that parents may, in their role of proxies, assess the well-being of their children with a broader understanding of the good than a scientific body does means that conflicts may arise between the parents and the scientific body, or even between the parents and prevailing social customs. As previously mentioned, sometimes the divergence is extreme, as when parents oppose having their children vaccinated, transfused with blood, or given a lifesaving medical procedure. The law may at times overrule parental preferences, especially when judges conclude that the harm faced by the child is sufficiently grave to call into question the parents' right to impose a preference at variance with what most people believe is an apt one. In addition, and more importantly, difficulties may arise with older children. The closer children come to their majority, the likelier it is that they have the ability to assess their best interests. Consider the case of older gay, lesbian, bisexual, or transgendered children. If a child has the capacity to offer an informed consent to receiving or not receiving a treatment, the fact that parents perhaps have legal authority to overrule the child is, morally speaking, beside the point. To impose treatment in this instance on the child is a violation of the child's autonomy. The parents may believe that they know better than their 16-year-old child what is good for him, but that is not relevant. The justification for proxy consents is that the proxy is deciding for somebody who lacks the decisional capacity to decide for himself. But that condition is not met if the child has that capacity. To be autonomous does not require accepting a particular theory of value. After all, one reason choices may differ is that people have different values or, even if they share the same values, may weight them differently. A parent may have a legal "right" to impose, or veto, a child's consent or refusal of a particular treatment, but if the child has the capacity to provide an informed consent to treatment or non-treatment, parents are wrong to interfere, though perhaps they have a right to refuse to pay for treatment that is at odds with their own preferences.

If parents object that they do not attach any value to letting a child decide, they have moved beyond the idea of being a proxy decision-maker. Instead, they are asserting power over their child that is independent of the theory of consent that structures discussions of consent, namely, that of a proxy making decisions for the benefit of somebody lacking the capacity to provide informed consent. Once the child has that capacity, there is no need of a proxy. Proxies are needed for cases when the capacity to consent is absent. The chief threat to a competent child's making an informed consent may turn out to be the parents. They may seek to coerce the child or limit the child's access to information necessary for giving an informed consent.

The subject of this chapter may seem unduly narrow. However, it is the principles governing its resolution that ultimately matter. Again and again, therapists face situations where parents, perhaps, wish something of which their professional associations may disapprove or the therapist disapproves. The idea that parents may likely use a broader conception of the good than therapists or scientific organizations is a crucial one for clear thinking in deciding what to make of a parent's decision as a proxy. The fact that younger children have not, but older children often do have, the capacity to decide what kind of treatment they want has implications, both welcome by parents in regard to younger children and unwelcome with regard to older children. These implications may be unwelcome as well, since they imply that a therapist may have to decide whether he is willing to support morally dubious laws that might impose legal duties that collide with moral ones. For example, even if a state proscribes discussing contraceptives with a competent minor child, a therapist must decide whether to deprive a competent child of this information about how to regulate conception more efficiently. It seems likelier that there will be prudent reasons for observing the state's mandates than moral reasons. The same goes for the betrayal of confidences that have come from children old enough to make a competent and informed request that their confidentiality be respected in regard even to their parents. With relevant distinctions of this chapter in hand, readers can work out positions on these topics. But this method does not guarantee agreement at the end of inquiry. Different principles, different weightings or orderings of them, different views of what is good or bad, different understandings of the facts now known, different preferences may lead to intractable disagreements. Disagreements about facts are likelier to yield to rational inquiry. Disagreements about attitudes, especially attitudes as volatile and historically conditioned as attitudes about families, may resist resolution. There may be no solution other than to keep talking, or agree to disagree.

## REFERENCES

American Psychological Association, (2010). *Ethical principles of psychologists and code of conduct: 2010 amendments.* Washington, DC: Author.

American Psychological Association, (2011). *APA policy statements on lesbian, gay, bisexual, & transgender concerns: Public Interest Directory.* Washington, DC: Author.

Foot, P. (2003). *Natural goodness.* New York, NY: Oxford University Press.

Oakeshott, M. (1991). *Rationalism in politics and other essays—new expanded edition.* Indianapolis, IN: Liberty Fund.

Rachels, J., & Rachels, S. (2011). *The elements of moral philosophy* (7th ed.). New York, NY: McGraw Hill.

Stevenson, CL. (1972). *Ethics and language.* New Haven, CT: Yale University Press.

PART *Two*

# Research Strategies: How Do We "Know" What We "Know?"

# CHAPTER 2

# Research Methods

## Current Strategies, Obstacles to Research, and Future Directions

**Daniel S. Bromberg*  and William T. O'Donohue[†]**
*Special Psychological Services, LLC, Bloomfield, New Jersey[1], [†]University of Nevada, Reno, Nevada

Relatively little is known about the base rate and types of sexual behaviors that are "normative" in children (deGraaf & Rademakers, 2006; deGraaf & Rademakers, 2011; Elkovitch, Latzman, Hansen, & Flood, 2009) and adolescents (Bancroft, 2006, p. 19; Barbaree & Marshall, 2006, p. 5). Knowing the base rates of phenomena is important, because one cannot know how typical or uncommon a phenomenon is without first knowing its base rate in the population. The dearth of knowledge regarding base rates of normative sexual behaviors in young persons is problematic because such lack of knowledge reduces the ability of clinical scientists to understand and produce effective interventions for statistically non-normative and/or problematic sexual behaviors.

The vast majority of empirical research on sexuality in prepubescent children[2] has been conducted in Western societies (i.e., North America, Western Europe, Australia, and New Zealand) and has examined sexual issues within the context of sexual abuse. When combining the search terms child(ren) and sexual(ity) in the PsychINFO, Medline, and Social SciSearch databases, 99% of the articles treat sexual behavior in prepubescent children as a part or consequence of sexual abuse (deGraaf & Rademakers, 2011).

We will begin this chapter by discussing the assortment of reasons for the paucity of empirical studies regarding childhood sexuality. We will then discuss the research strategies that have been employed in this domain, and examine the strengths and shortcomings of these approaches.

---

[1] Correspondence to: Daniel S. Bromberg, Special Psychological Services, LLC, 315 Broad Street, Bloomfield, NJ 07003.
[2] For ease of communication, we will use the term "children" to denote individuals under the age of 18 years. We will use the phrase "prepubescent children" when referring specifically to children under 13 years of age.

Next, we will present research strategies that have been employed in other childhood domains, but have not been used in the study of childhood sexual behavior. This chapter will conclude with a discussion of other underutilized or heretofore unexplored research strategies for advancing our knowledge regarding this important domain of human development.

## WHY THE DEARTH OF RESEARCH ON CHILD AND ADOLESCENT SEXUALITY?

There are at least three factors that explain the dearth of research on child and adolescent sexuality. First, prepubescent children have been viewed as asexual beings (Borneman & Lombardi-Nash, 1994; DePalma & Atkinson, 2006) with sexual thoughts, feelings, and drives coming to the fore only at about the onset of puberty. Such a view may have part of its origin in the psychoanalytic concept of the "latency period" in childhood development. During the "latency period," sexual urges are supposedly submerged while children exert their energies in the acquisition of cultural and academic skills.

The second factor underlying the paucity of research in this domain is the difficulty inherent in studying childhood and adolescent sexuality. There are formidable obstacles to studying sexuality in minors. These obstacles include the following: generating research proposals that are acceptable to the parents/guardians of potential participants; protecting children and adolescents from potential harm as mandated by the Ethical Code of Psychologists; and obtaining institutional review board (IRB) approval to conduct such research (Mustanski, 2011; Wiederman, 2002a,b).

The third factor underlying the dearth of research on child and adolescent sexuality is the difficulty inherent in obtaining accurate self-report information from children. Some children, particularly young children, have a very limited vocabulary with which to discuss sexual phenomena. The reading skills of many young children are not sufficiently advanced to allow for independent completion of self-report scales. Similarly, many young children have not yet developed the cognitive skills to complete self-report scales with accuracy. The foregoing factors have rendered this important area of research particularly challenging to undertake.

## STRENGTHS AND SHORTCOMINGS OF RESEARCH STRATEGIES EMPLOYED

Methodologies that have been employed in the study of children's sexual behavior include the following: case studies and interviews of children and adolescents regarding their sexual behaviors; retrospective reports made by young adults (largely aged 18 to 21) of their sexual behaviors during childhood and adolescence; and non-systematic observation of young children's sexual behaviors by their teachers and mothers with data collected by way of informant reports on behavior-rating scales. The relatively small body of research on which extant knowledge is based is riddled with methodological shortcomings.

## Case Studies and Interviews with Minors

Some anecdotal information about the sexual experiences of children and adolescents has been gathered (e.g., Langfeldt, 1990; Langfeldt, 1994; Martinson, 1994). For example, Langfeldt (1990) offered some information about the sexual behaviors of boys and provided a quotation to illustrate his assertion. He said: "When children meet for the purpose of having sex, they seldom speak about it directly. They often start having sex with an initial ritual, such as playing strip poker or games where the winner can request some sexual activity. Some children simply start by reading pornography, where being turned on is the excuse for further sex. In this case pornography does not serve as a cause of sexual play but serves to legitimize the homosexual activity" (p. 190).

> Normally it's only four of us all between 12 and 14 years. We use Peter's room most of the time. That is the safest place and no one gets in there. Sometimes we go to his room for no reason, but I think all of us know that we are going to have sex. Peter will lock the door and then we will look into some magazines which are already boring us because we have seen them hundreds of times. Then we talk about how the pictures turn us on and start to check each other's cock to see if we all got a hard on, and then we pull them out, undress and start to suck and masturbate each other (p. 190).

Interviews with children can be useful in providing insight into private events (Anderson, Hawkins, & Scotti, 1997), that is, children's perspectives, on their own sexual behaviors. Such information is also useful in learning about the range of sexual behaviors in which some minors engage, ages at which these behaviors occur, psychological reactions to these events, and for generating hypotheses that can be experimentally tested. Of course, such anecdotal information provides no insight into the frequency with which such behaviors occur within the general population.

## Retrospective Recall of Young Adults

Some scientists have assessed young adults' recollections of sexual behaviors in which they engaged (or had been engaged by peers or significantly older persons) during childhood and adolescence (e.g., Larsson & Svedin, 2002; Leitenberg, Detzer, & Srebnik, 1993; Leitenberg, Greenwald, & Tarran, 1989). Recollections of previous sexual behaviors were assessed by way of questionnaires.

It has been pointed out that much extant human sexuality research is based on the assumption that participants report their sexual histories honestly and accurately (Okami, 2002). However, self-reported sexual behaviors are susceptible to several sources of error and bias (Catania, McDermott, & Pollack, 1986; Trivedi & Sabini, 1998; Wiederman, 2002a,b), even when such self-reports are made under anonymous testing conditions (Fisher, 2007; Meston, Heiman, Trapnell, & Paulhus, 1998). Although this research strategy has been advantageously employed in the study of childhood sexual behavior, it has significant shortcomings.

## Informant Reports and Rating Scales

Behavior-rating scales have historically had an important role in assessing emotional and behavioral problems in children and adolescents. Scales such as the Child Sexual Behavior Inventory (Friedrich, 1997) and the Child Behavior Checklist (Achenbach, 1991) have also been utilized to obtain information about normative and non-normative sexual behaviors displayed by children. Edelbrock (1988) described the advantages of using behavior-rating scales. These advantages include the following: standardization of what questions are asked, which reduces variability in the information obtained and ensures that relevant target behaviors will be assessed; standardization of how questions are asked, which reduces subjectivity in making judgments and increases reliability; rating scales are fast and economical, both financially and in terms of professional time expended, particularly when undertaking large-scale assessment programs; and they yield quantitative indices of child and adolescent behaviors that are useful in assessing stability of behaviors as well as changes in behaviors, especially in response to interventions. In addition, these scales can be psychometrically evaluated, and studies can be conducted regarding their reliability and, to some extent, their validity.

However, information informants provide by way of behavior-rating scales is also subject to bias and may be contaminated by an assortment of variables (Eckert, Dunn, Guiney, & Codding, 2000; Merrell, 2000; Yoder & Symons, 2010, pp. 2–3). Edelbrock (1988) and others have pointed out that information obtained by way of behavior-rating scales has at least the following limitations: it is assumed, sometimes erroneously, that raters understand the construct(s) being rated and know which behaviors are relevant to a given construct; raters must be able to form a cumulative impression of the construct being rated from the stream of behaviors that the rater has observed the target(s) emit; raters differ in the exposure that they have had to the target child(ren), and this differential exposure may affect the accuracy of their ratings; and characteristics of raters themselves (e.g., maternal depression) may effect ratings provided (Mandal, Olmi, & Wilczynski, 1999). Although behavior-rating scales have also been advantageously employed in the study of childhood sexual behavior, we have highlighted several shortcomings of this methodology.

deGraaf & Rademakers (2011) provided a useful summary of much of the research that has employed children as research participants. Their summary of extant research in this domain is displayed in Table 2.1.

# RESEARCH STRATEGIES UTILIZED IN INVESTIGATING DOMAINS OF CHILDHOOD BEHAVIOR OTHER THAN CHILDHOOD SEXUAL BEHAVIOR

## Meta-Analysis

Meta-analytic techniques are an assortment of quantitative strategies used to summarize the results of multiple studies in a given domain. The goal is to summarize the body of research about a particular phenomenon using quantitative, in contrast to qualitative, indices. The results of a meta-analysis are commonly expressed as an *effect size*. Although there are several indices of effect sizes, one frequently used metric is Cohen's $d$. In general terms, this is calculated by subtracting the mean of the control group from the mean of the treatment group and dividing by a pooled standard deviation. The resulting effect size indicates the magnitude of the difference between the groups in standard deviation units. Readers are referred to Huedo-Medina, Ballester, & Johnson (this volume) for a more detailed discussion of meta-analyses.

We are unaware of any meta-analyses that have been conducted on studies that have examined "normative" sexual development of, and behaviors displayed by, children. There is a parsimonious explanation why such meta-analyses have not been conducted. There must be a substantive quantity of constituent empirically-based studies that employ relatively similar methodologies to conduct a meta-analysis. The dearth of studies in this domain, in combination with use of different methodologies, has precluded use of such powerful statistical strategies for summarizing the body of research findings on child sexual development and behavior.

**Table 2.1** Characteristics of Studies Reviewed by deGraaf & Rademakers (2011)

| Study | Topic | Sample | Method |
|---|---|---|---|
| Ballester & Gil (2006) | Sexual behavior, attitudes, and feelings | 243 boys and 227 girls, aged 9–14 | Survey |
| Bancroft, Herbenick, & Reynolds (2003) | Masturbation and orgasm, pre- and post-pubertal | 134 men and 149 women, college students, aged 18–22 | Retrospective survey |
| Berends & Caron (1994) | Knowledge of conception and birth | 26 boys and 14 girls, aged 5–12, and their parents | Interviews, supported by drawings |
| Brilleslijper-Kater & Baartman (2000) | Knowledge of sexuality | 32 boys and 31 girls, Dutch, aged 2–6, and their parents | Interviews, supported by drawings |
| T. A. Campbell & Campbell (1986) | Questions about sexuality-related topics | High school students, aged 11–14, total number and gender distribution unknown | Categorization of 874 questions, collected in the classroom |
| Davies, Glaser, & Kossof (2000) | Sexual behavior and responses from preschool staff | 58 preschool staff for children aged 2–5, gender of children unknown | Observations by day care personnel |
| Finkelhor (1981) | Sexual experiences between siblings in childhood | 796 college students, two-thirds women, 17% older than 24 | Retrospective survey |
| Friedrich, Grambsch, Broughton, & Kuiper (1991) | Sexual behavior | 458 boys and 422 girls, aged 2–12 | Observations by mothers |
| Friedrich, Fisher, Broughton, Houston, & Shafran (1998) | Sexual behavior | 560 boys and 553 girls, aged 2–12 | Observations by mothers |
| Friedrich, Sandfort, Oostveen, & Cohen-Kettenis (2000) | Differences in sexual behavior between the Netherlands and the United States | 807 boys and 656 girls, Dutch and American, aged 2–6 | Observations by mothers |
| Galenson (1990) | Masturbation | 70 boys and girls, aged 0–2, gender distribution unknown | Observations by researcher |

| | | | |
|---|---|---|---|
| Goldman & Goldman (1982) | Knowledge of sexuality and sources of information | 419 boys and 419 girls, aged 5–15, American, English, Swedish, and Australian | Interviews |
| Goldman & Goldman (1988) | Sexual behavior during childhood and adolescence | 1,000 Australian college students, aged 18–23, gender distribution unknown | Retrospective survey |
| Gordon, Schroeder, & Abrams (1990) | Knowledge of sexuality | 74 boys and 56 girls, aged 2–7 | Interviews, supported by drawings |
| Gundersen, Melas, & Skar (1981) | Sexual behavior | 60 preschool teachers of children aged 3–7, gender of children unknown | Observations by preschool teachers |
| Halstead & Waite (2001) | Sexual values and attitudes | 35 socially disadvantaged children, aged 9–10, gender distribution unknown | Focus groups |
| Hatfield, Schmitz, Cornelius, & Rapson (1988) | Feelings of "passionate love" | 114 boys and 122 girls, aged 4–18, Hawaiian | Interviews |
| Haugaard (1996) | Sexual encounters between children and responses from professionals | 199 men and 465 women, college students, mean age 20, and 337 experts | Retrospective survey |
| Haugaard & Tilly (1988) | Sexual encounters between children before age 13 and accompanying feelings | 425 men and 664 women, college students, mean age 19.2 | Retrospective survey |
| Kaeser, DiSalvo, & Moglia (2000) | Sexual behavior | 360 boys and 343 girls, aged 5–7 | Diary observations by preschool teachers |
| Kuik (2003) | Talking about sex and romance | 19 girls and 11 boys, about 11 years old | Observations by researcher, interviews, surveys, drawings, and drama tasks |

*(Continued)*

Table 2.1 (Continued)

| Study | Topic | Sample | Method |
|---|---|---|---|
| S. Lamb (2004) | Sexual play and feelings between the ages 6 and 12 | 30 females, aged 7–18, and 92 women, aged 19–72 | Retrospective interviews |
| S. Lamb & Coakley (1993) | Childhood sexual play and accompanying feelings | 128 women, college students, mean age 20.6 | Retrospective survey, open questions |
| Larsson & Svedin (2002b) | Sexual behavior | 96 boys and 89 girls, aged 3–6 | Observations by parents and preschool teachers |
| Larsson & Svedin (2002a) | Solitary and interpersonal sexual behavior before age 13 | 127 males and 142 females, senior high school students, mean age 18.6 | Retrospective survey |
| Lindblad, Gustafsson, Larsson, & Lundin (1995) | Sexual behavior | 125 boys and 126 girls, Swedish, aged 2–6 | Observations by day care personnel |
| Lopez Sanchez, Del Campo, & Guijo (2002) | Sexual behavior and accompanying feelings before age 11 | 115 teachers and 93 parents of children aged 0–11, gender unknown, and 139 males and 308 females, aged 14–22 | Observations by teachers and parents, and retrospective survey among high school and college students |
| Nelson (1986) | Sexual experiences with family members in childhood and accompanying feelings | 100 men and women, aged 19–73, with incest experience | Retrospective survey |
| Oostveen, Meulmeester, & Cohen-Kettenis (1994) | Sexual behavior | 190 boys and 172 girls, aged 5 and 6 | Observations by parents |
| O'Sullivan & Meyer-Bahlberg (2003) | Interest in boys | 57 African American and Latin American girls, aged 10–13 | Focus groups |
| Ott & Pfeiffer (2009) | Cognitions about sexual abstinence | 6 boys and 16 girls, aged 11–14 | Interviews |
| Paikoff (1995) | Sexual behavior | 26 boys and 18 girls, aged 9–11 | Interviews |
| Phipps-Yonas, Yonas, Turner, & Kauper (1993) | Sexual behavior and sexual knowledge | 556 day care providers for children aged 1–6, gender distribution unknown | Observations by day care providers |

| | | | |
|---|---|---|---|
| Rademakers, Laan, & Straver (2000) | Body awareness and experiences with physical intimacy | 16 boys and 15 girls, aged 8–9, and their parents | Interviews, supported by drawings |
| Renold (2005) | Talking about sex and romance | 26 boys and 33 girls, about 10 years old | Observations by researcher, interviews |
| Reynolds, Herbenick, & Bancroft (2001) | Sexual behavior and sexual feelings before high school | 149 men and 154 women, aged 18–22, college students | Retrospective online survey |
| Rosenfeld, Bailey, Siegel, & Bailey (1986) | Touching of breasts and genitalia of the parents | 324 boys and 252 girls, aged 2–10 | Observations by parents |
| Sandfort & Cohen-Kettenis (2000) | Sexual behavior | 351 boys and 319 girls, Dutch, aged 0–11 | Observations by mothers |
| Sandnabba, Santtila, Wannas, & Krook (2003) | Sexual behavior | 183 boys and 181 girls in day care, aged 2–7 | Observations by day care personnel |
| Schoentjes, Deboutte, & Friedrich (1999) | Sexual behavior | 416 boys and 501 girls, Flemish, aged 2–12 | Observations by parents |
| Schuhrke (2000) | Interest in other people's genitals | 15 boys and 11 girls, observed at age 1 and at age 6 | Diary observations by parents |
| Thigpen, 2009 | Sexual behavior | 31 boys and 24 girls, African American, aged 2–12 | Observations by parents |
| Thorne & Luria (1986) | Talking about sex and romance | Fourth and fifth graders of four schools, interviews with 27 children, gender distribution unknown | Observations by researchers, interviews |
| Volbert (2000) | Knowledge of sexuality | 84 boys and 63 girls, aged 2–6 | Interviews, supported by drawings |

Reproduced, with permission, from deGraaf & Rademakers (2011).

## Single-Case Experimental Designs for Treatment Studies

Snyder & Shaw (this volume) provide a substantive discussion of the use of single-case experimental designs (also referred to as "small-n designs") to answer an assortment of questions about sexuality. Nonetheless, we believe that the use of single-case experimental methodology to answer questions regarding childhood sexuality is of sufficient importance to warrant some discussion here.

Single-case experimental designs are used by scientist-practitioners who employ strategies from the experimental analysis of behavior (Baer, Wolf, & Risley, 1968). These designs are those in which the effects of an intervention are evaluated with one, or few, subjects. There is an assortment of single-case designs including, but not limited to, reversal designs, alternating treatment designs, multiple baseline designs, and changing criterion designs. Snyder and Shaw (this volume) discuss the purpose of each design, and similarities and differences between them. However, there is a common purpose underlying all such experimental designs. Single-case designs are utilized for *experimental analysis*, that is, to demonstrate experimentally the extent to which the effects of manipulating aspects of the environment reliably result in behavioral change in one or more of the subjects. Single-case experimental designs meet "Chambless criteria" for assessing if a given treatment should be considered empirically-supported (Chambless & Ollendick, 2001).

Barlow & Hersen (1984) discussed the origins of single-case experimental designs. They noted that most psychologists probably became familiar with the work of the mathematician R.A. Fisher during their graduate studies. Fisher invented most of the sophisticated statistical procedures that are currently used for comparing *groups* of individuals. As a young mathematician during the 1930s, Fisher worked at an agricultural station and concerned himself with the yield from a given plot of land under an assortment of variables, such as variety of plant, treatment of the soil, et cetera. In agricultural work, the outcome for an individual plant is irrelevant. The outcome of interest is the yield from a *group* of plants on a particular plot. The emphasis on examining group averages permeated not just agricultural work, but psychological research, at least through the mid-1960s.

In the early 1950s, Eysenck (1952) published a now-renowned article suggesting that psychotherapy was not as effective as was commonly believed. In the mid-1960s, in an equally renowned article, Bergin (1966) examined some of the factors that might explain the findings of Eysenck (1952) and others. He found that in psychotherapy outcome studies, some patients improved, while the condition of others deteriorated. When such outcomes were averaged, beneficial and ineffective (or iatrogenic) effects of psychotherapy canceled one another and resulted in an overall finding of no effect as compared with a control group. The foregoing suggested that it was premature to conclude that psychotherapy is ineffective. Paul (1967) suggested that the question: "Is psychotherapy effective?" is too simplistic. The more appropriate question for psychotherapy outcome researchers to address is the following: "*What* treatment, by *whom*, is most effective for *this* individual with *that* specific problem, and under *which* set of circumstances?" (p. 111). Use of single-case experimental designs enables us to answer this question.

Group comparison designs have several limitations (Barlow & Hersen, 1984), two of which are particularly relevant to our discussion. One shortcoming is that group comparison results are of limited utility to clinicians. Because findings from research using group designs reflect an *average* response to treatment, a clinician cannot determine whether his/her own client is similar to patients in the sample who improved, reaped no benefit, or whose condition worsened within the context of an overall group improvement.

The second limitation is the problem of amassing sufficient numbers of subjects to study who have a particular problem. For example, the incidence of necrophilia in the general population of adolescents is unknown, but is believed to be minimal. Gathering a sufficient number of adolescents with necrophilia to be involved in a treatment study using a group design would be virtually impossible.

Given the foregoing discussion, readers might conclude that we believe single-case experimental designs to be superior to group research designs for purposes of sexuality research. Such a conclusion would be erroneous. One sort of research design is not inherently superior to another design any more so than a hammer is inherently superior to a screwdriver, or vice-versa. Skillful craftsmen, scientists, and clinicians all select the tool that is most appropriate to achieve a desired result in response to a particular problem.

## Self-Monitoring of Sexual Thoughts and Behaviors

Self-monitoring is an assessment procedure wherein individuals are taught to observe target behaviors in their repertoire and to generate an accurate record of these observations. Hence, self-monitoring is comprised of both self-observing and self-recording target behaviors (Cole & Bambara, 1992). For example, the number of times per day a 16-year-old boy experiences fantasies of having sexual contact with same-age, peri-pubertal and prepubescent girls can be recorded by that adolescent boy. One advantage of such a method is that a private event such as the specific details comprising one or more sexual fantasies can be recorded and studied. A second advantage is that this sort of data collection procedure is unobtrusive. A third advantage is that A-B-C (antecedent-behavior-consequence) sequences can be recorded and used to generate hypotheses about factors that cause or maintain specific sexual behaviors. These data can also be used to assess the frequency with which children engage in particular sexual fantasies or behaviors. For example, if, over the course of a month, self-monitoring data reflect that our hypothetical 16-year-old boy masturbates to orgasm approximately 33% of the time to fantasies involving female peers, peri-pubertal girls, and prepubescent girls, it is appropriate to tentatively conclude that the adolescent has a heterosexual orientation, but does not adequately discriminate based upon age.[3]

However, a preponderance of evidence suggests that the activity of purposefully attending to one's own behavior and self-recording of one's observations may result in a change in the behavior being targeted for change (Gardner & Cole, 1988; Shapiro & Cole, 1993). This phenomenon has been referred to as *reactivity*. Reactive effects of self-monitoring have been advantageously utilized to improve a range of social, behavioral, and academic problems in school settings (Cole & Bambara, 2000, p. 204; Shapiro & Cole, 1999; Shapiro, DuPaul, & Bradley-Klug, 1998). The potent reactive effects of self-monitoring limit its utility as an assessment strategy, but increase its utility as a treatment strategy.

## Direct, Systematic Observations of Childhood Sexual Behaviors

The highest fidelity data that can be obtained about children's sexual behavior may be obtained by way of direct, systematic observation (and measurement) of sexual behaviors. Direct, systematic observational methodology has the following attributes: target behaviors are operationally defined so as to be readily observed; they follow standardized coding procedures; they provide quantitative scores that do not vary from observer to observer; and they can be assessed for reliability and validity across

---

[3] For research, rather than for forensic, purposes.

observers, time, and settings (Volpe & McConaughy, 2005). Such methodology has significantly advanced our understanding of important aspects of childhood and adolescent functioning. For example, direct, systematic observations of behavior have been advantageously used to advance knowledge in academic (e.g., Maag, Reid, & DiGangi, 1993), social/recreational (e.g., Leff & Lakin, 2005; Pelham, Gnagy, Greiner, Waschbusch, Fabiano, & Burrows-McLean, 2010), and other realms.

Despite the many advantages that would accrue from collection of direct, systematic observations of sexual behaviors, an assortment of practical, ethical, and legal constraints have historically precluded use of this methodology in studying sexual behavior. From a pragmatic perspective, it is probable that it would be difficult to obtain informed consent from parents to conduct such research. Moreover, until the recent advent of sophisticated video surveillance and recording technology, only those behaviors displayed within an observer's sight could be captured. Many childhood behaviors, particularly those of a sexual nature, are displayed out of the view of adults. The foregoing circumstance may explain why reports of childhood sexual behaviors often decrease with age in studies that employ some form of observational methodology, but generally increase with age in studies that employ retrospective methodologies (deGraaf & Rademakers, 2011). Finally, recording sexual behaviors while avoiding reactive effects of observation has been a significant impediment to employing observational methodology. As discussed above, reactivity refers to the effects of an assessment procedure on the behavior(s) being assessed (Kazdin, 1979). Cooper, Heron, & Heward (2007) point out that it is prudent to employ assessment methods that are as unobtrusive as possible to minimize the possibility of reactivity.

Ethical constraints in childhood sexuality research have historically been significant. There are principles that are assumed to underlie ethical practice in research with humans, two of which are relevant to the present matter. These principles are respect for persons and beneficence. The principle of respect for persons dictates that all people should be treated as autonomous and should be protected from risk. Hoagwood & Cavaleri (2010) noted that "protection is especially important for persons with diminished autonomy, including children and adolescents" (p. 12). The principle of beneficence dictates that researchers are obligated to seek to minimize possible harm to research participants, and to maximize positive outcomes that might accrue from participating in research. Creating video footage of minors engaging in the most private of human behaviors would place the minors depicted at substantial risk for emotional harm if such video footage were to be lost or stolen. Readers are referred to Ringheim (1995) for a more complete discussion of ethical issues involved in childhood sexuality research.

The most significant legal barrier to the use of direct, systematic observations of sexual behaviors is the possibility that collection of such data might well run foul of statutes regarding production of child pornography. Attempting to obtain a waiver to conduct such research from the office of a state's attorney general would likely be in vain, unless or until an institutional review board (IRB) approved such an investigation. Because of the high-risk nature of such research, based upon ethical principles and possible reactions of minors' legal guardians, an IRB would be unlikely to approve such research (Mustanski, 2011).

However, there is precedent for use of direct, systematic observations of (nonsexual) behaviors in a recreational (camp) setting. Pelham et al., (2010) described how such methodology has been used in the treatment of children with Attention-Deficit/Hyperactivity Disorder in summer camp settings.

Use of direct, systematic observations of behavior in a camp setting may be said to have ecological validity. Ecological validity is "the extent to which measurement contexts resemble or take place in naturally occurring (unmanipulated) and frequently experienced contexts" (Yoder & Symons, 2010, p. 10). Behavior is a function of multiple events, and numerous events have multiple effects on behavior. Ecological approaches take into account the complex interrelationships between environments and behaviors (Cooper, Heron, & Heward, 2007; Martens & Witt, 1988). Factors that affect a given individual's sexual behavior include, but are not limited to, the following: physiological conditions (e.g., sexual arousal); physical aspects of the environment (e.g., presence or absence of peers and adults); and prior reinforcement history (e.g., having received reprimands for displaying sexual behaviors). To date, direct, systematic observation and recording of children's sexual behaviors by researchers has not been employed as a research strategy (deGraaf & Rademakers, 2011).

## DIRECTIONS FOR FUTURE RESEARCH
### Might Direct, Systematic Observational Methodology be Utilized?

Because of advances in sophisticated monitoring and recording technology, it is now technically possible to generate a "data mine" regarding normative sexual behaviors[4] in children. Bromberg (2011) devised a strategy for collecting data about the normative sexual behaviors of boys within a sleepaway camp setting. The strategy overcomes many of the ethical and technical barriers that have previously precluded such research. Nonetheless, given the increasingly conservative nature of IRBs in the United States over time, we believe it is improbable that the methodology would obtain IRB approval. Thus, Bromberg devised an intriguing strategy for obtaining data that would significantly advance our knowledge regarding the normative sexual development of boys, but a strategy that is unlikely to gain approval for use. We elected not to include this methodological proposal in this chapter, as a proposal that is unlikely to gain IRB approval is of little use to the scientific community.

## Neuroimaging Studies

Recent advances in neuroimaging technology have enabled researchers to explore an assortment of questions about the biological underpinnings of human sexuality in ways that were previously not possible. Magnetic resonance imaging (MRI) techniques involve having a participant lie on a table with his or her head inside a large magnet. Protons inside the brain's atoms line up with the magnetic field and are temporarily moved out of alignment by radio waves aimed at the head. As the protons move back into position, they emit radio waves that a computer uses to generate a brain image. Functional magnetic resonance imaging (fMRI) produces essentially a movie, rather than a still image, of the brain. fMRI technology capitalizes on the facts that blood contains iron and travels to specific brain regions as these regions are activated. Oxygenated blood travels to a brain region, and the iron affects the magnetic field, which is detected by a scanner.

Neuroimaging studies have been conducted on adults to advance our knowledge of phenomena such as brain areas activated during sexual arousal and orgasm (e.g., Salonia, Giraldi, Chivers, Geordiadis, Levin, Maravilla, & McCarthy, 2010), and to explore a possible etiology of pedophilia in men (e.g., Cantor, Kabani, Christensen, Zipursky, Barbaree, et al., 2008). Cantor et al. (2008) conducted a study in which they analyzed MRI images of men who had engaged in illegal sexual behaviors with children, admitted having pedophilic interests, and/or displayed clinically significant responses to child stimuli on phallometric testing. The MRIs of this group were compared

---

[4] In the present context, we use the term "normative" in an actuarial manner, that is, common in the general population of children.

with those of men who had committed non-sexual offenses. On average, men in the former group had decreased bilateral white matter volumes of the temporal and parietal lobes relative to men in the latter group. (The groups did not differ in grey matter or cerebrospinal fluid.) It was also found that these regions followed and were limited to two particular fiber bundles (i.e., the superior fronto-occipital fasciculus and the right arcuate fasciculus). These particular fiber bundles connect cortical regions that respond to sexual stimuli. The authors concluded that the temporal and parietal lobes function as a network for recognizing sexual stimuli, and that pedophilia may result from a partial disconnection within that network.

Although neuroimaging technology has been used with children, we are unaware of any neuroimaging studies that have been conducted to assess sexual issues in this population. It is likely that such studies would be profitable in learning about the origins of sexual thoughts, feelings, and behaviors, particularly if used within the context of genetic studies.

## Genetic Testing

It is likely that our understanding of the hereditary basis of many aspects of human functioning, including the development of sexual preferences, will be enhanced by completion of the sequencing of the human genome (Pang, Baum, & Lam, 2000, as cited in Tercyak, 2009). For certain medical conditions, predictive genetic tests are sometimes offered to individuals to assist in determining one's risk of developing a given disease later in life. When viewed in tandem with information such as family history, environmental exposures, and lifestyle behavior, risk information learned through genetic testing can guide medical decision-making, including informing decisions about prevention and treatment options that are likely to be effective for a given individual's risk profile (Beery & Williams, 2007, as cited in Tercyak, 2009). Despite the utility of such information for predicting the occurrence of certain medical conditions, the technology is not sufficiently advanced to be useful in understanding sexual development at present.

Some investigators (e.g., Langstrom, Grann, & Lichtenstein, 2002) have examined genetic and environmental influences on problematic sexual behaviors in young children. Information obtained from the Swedish Twin Registry and from parental ratings using items from the Sex Problems scale of the Child Behavior Checklist (Achenbach, 1991) was used to examine the relative contributions of genetic and environmental influences on problematic masturbatory behavior in young children. Although this methodology yielded some intriguing findings, it is our assessment that an assortment of confounds preclude use of this research strategy to draw unambiguous conclusions about the relative contributions of genetic and environmental factors to problematic sexual behaviors.

## Investigations Using Samples Drawn from Non-White US Samples and Using Children from Non-Western Nations

The range of normative sexual behaviors among African American children in the United States, aged 2 to 12, is virtually unknown. We are aware of only one empirical study on this population that has been published in a peer-reviewed journal (i.e., Thigpen, 2009). Similarly, essentially nothing is known about normative sexual development in other non-White child populations, both in the United States and in non-Western nations.

There is evidence that race and an assortment of cultural factors have an interactive effect on children's sexual development. The effects of culture and the mechanisms by which culture and race interact are essentially unknown. Bhugra, Popelyuk, & McMullen (2010) pointed out that cultures define those behaviors that are "normal" and those which are "deviant." Definitions of normalcy and deviance are affected by factors such as religious beliefs. Confounding of culture and religious beliefs, among other factors, has made it extremely difficult for scientists to collect data on sexual development in children from developing nations.

## SIGNIFICANT DILEMMAS IMPEDING ADVANCEMENT OF KNOWLEDGE IN THE FIELD

Researchers need to be creative regarding their respective choices of methodologies given the host of constraints discussed in this chapter. Some of these constraints may be permanent. It is difficult to imagine institutional review boards taking radically more permissive positions on human sexuality research, particularly with minors, or subjects being less reactive and more truthful reporters of sexual thoughts, feelings, and experiences. The foregoing has two implications: (1) We, as professionals and as a field, need to be appropriately modest about what we know. Constraints limit the amount of evidence we can generate to confirm or dismiss our hypotheses. We are in a field that requires a Socratic humility. (2) In deciding policy and the ethics of such research, we need to balance the harm that might be done to child subjects with the harm that might occur by *failing* to gather knowledge about sexual thoughts, feelings, and behaviors early in the lifespan. For example, there are reasonable arguments to be made against collecting data on adolescents' sexual behavior. However, a collective dearth of such information places sexually active adolescents at risk for an assortment of medical and emotional problems, as pathways to STDs, including HIV, are not well understood. These are difficult ethical and pragmatic issues that merit serious consideration and debate.

## REFERENCES

Achenbach, T. M. (1991). *Manual for the child behavior checklist/4–18 and 1991 profile*. Burlington, VT: University of Vermont, Department of Psychiatry.

Anderson, C. M., Hawkins, R. P., & Scotti, J. R. (1997). Private events in behavior analysis: Conceptual basis and clinical relevance. *Behavior Therapy, 28,* 157–179.

Baer, D. M., Wolf, M. M., & Risley, T. R. (1968). Some current dimensions of applied behavior analysis. *Journal of Applied Behavior Analysis, 1,* 91–97.

Bancroft, J. (2006). Normal sexual development. In H. E. Barbaree, & W. L. Marshall (Eds.), *The juvenile sex offender (pp. 19–57)* (2nd ed.). New York, NY: Guilford.

Barbaree, H. E., & Marshall, W. L. (Eds.). (2006). *The juvenile sex offender* (2nd ed.). New York, NY: Guilford.

Barlow, D. H., & Hersen, M. (1984). *Single case experimental designs: Strategies for studying behavior change* (2nd ed.). New York, NY: Pergamon.

Beery, T. A., & Williams, J. K. (2007). Risk reduction and health promotion behaviors following genetic testing for adult-onset disorders. *Genetic Testing, 11,* 111–123.

Bergin, A. E. (1966). Some implications of psychotherapy research for therapeutic practice. *Journal of Abnormal Psychology, 71,* 235–246.

Bhugra, D., Popelyuk, D., & McMullen, I. (2010). Paraphilias across cultures: Contexts and controversies. *Journal of Sex Research, 47,* 242–256.

Borneman, E., & Lombardi-Nash, M. A. (1994). *Childhood phases of maturity: Sexual developmental psychology*. Amherst, NY: Prometheus.

Bromberg, D. S. (2011). A methodological proposal for advancing knowledge regarding the range of "normative" sexual behaviors displayed by boys. Unpublished manuscript.

Cantor, J. M., Kabani, N., Christensen, B., Zipursky, R. B., Barbaree, H. E., Dickey, R., et al. (2008). Cerebral white matter deficiencies in pedophilic men. *Journal of Psychiatric Research, 42,* 167–183.

Catania, J. A., McDermott, L. J., & Pollack, L. M. (1986). Questionnaire response bias and face-to-face interview sample bias in sexuality research. *Journal of Sex Research, 22,* 52–72.

Chambless, D. L., & Ollendick, T. H. (2001). Empirically supported psychological interventions: Controversies and evidence. *Annual Review of Psychology, 52,* 685–716.

Cole, C. L., & Bambara, L. M. (1992). Issues surrounding the use of self-management interventions in the schools. *School Psychology Review, 21,* 193–201.

Cole, C. L., & Bambara, L. M. (2000). Self-monitoring: Theory and practice. In E. S. Shapiro, & T. R. Kratochwill (Eds.), *Behavioral assessment in schools: Theory, research, and clinical foundations (pp. 202–232)* (2nd ed.). New York, NY: Guilford.

Cooper, J. O., Heron, T. E., & Heward, W. L. (2007). *Applied behavior analysis* (2nd ed.). Upper Saddle River, NJ: Pearson.

deGraaf, H., & Rademakers, J. (2006). Sexual behavior of prepubertal children. *Journal of Psychology & Human Sexuality, 18,* 1–21.

deGraaf, H., & Rademakers, J. (2011). The psychological measurement of childhood sexual development in Western societies: Methodological challenges. *Journal of Sex Research, 48,* 118–129.

DePalma, R., & Atkinson, E. (2006). The sound of silence: Talking about sexual orientation and schooling. *Sex Education, 6,* 333–349.

Eckert, T. L., Dunn, E. K., Guiney, K. M., & Codding, R. S. (2000). Self reports: Theory and research in using rating scale measures. In E. S. Shapiro, & T. R. Kratochwill (Eds.), *Behavioral assessment in schools (pp. 288–322)* (2nd ed.). New York, NY: Guilford.

Edelbrock, C. (1988). Informant reports. In E. S. Shapiro, & T. R. Kratochwill (Eds.), *Behavioral assessment in schools (pp. 351–383)*. New York, NY: Guilford.

Elkovitch, N., Latzman, R. D., Hansen, D. J., & Flood, M. F. (2009). Understanding child sexual behavior problems: A developmental psychopathology framework. *Clinical Psychology Review, 29*, 586–598.

Eysenck, H. J. (1952). The effects of psychotherapy: An evaluation. *Journal of Consulting Psychology, 16*, 319–324.

Fisher, T. D. (2007). Sex of experimenter and social norm effects on reports of sexual behavior in young men and women. *Archives of Sexual Behavior, 36*, 89–100.

Friedrich, W. N. (1997). *Child sexual behavior inventory professional manual*. Odessa, FL: Psychological Assessment Resources, Inc.

Gardner, W. I., & Cole, C. L. (1988). Self-monitoring procedures. In E. S. Shapiro, & T. R. Kratochwill (Eds.), *Behavioral assessment in schools: Conceptual foundations and practical applications (pp. 206–246)*. New York, NY: Guilford.

Hoagwood, K. E., & Cavaleri, M. A. (2010). Ethical issues in child and adolescent psychosocial treatment research. In J. R. Weisz, & A. E. Kazdin (Eds.), *Evidence-based psychotherapies for children and adolescents (pp. 10–27)* (2nd ed.). New York, NY: Guilford.

Huedo-Medina, T. B., Ballester, E., & Johnson, B. T. (this volume). Research syntheses related to childhood and adolescent sexuality: A critical review. In D.S. Bromberg & W.T. O'Donohue (Eds.), *Handbook of child and adolescent sexuality: Developmental and forensic psychology (pp. 41–96)*. New York, NY: Elsevier.

Kazdin, A. E. (1979). Unobtrusive measures in behavioral assessment. *Journal of Applied Behavior Analysis, 12*, 713–724.

Langfeldt, T. (1990). Early childhood and juvenile sexuality, development and problems. In M. E. Perry (Ed.), *Handbook of sexology, Volume VII, Childhood and adolescent sexology (pp. 179–200)*. New York: Elsevier.

Langfeldt, T. (1994). Aspects concerning the development and therapy of sexual deviant patterns in children. *Nordisk Sexologi, 12*, 105–110.

Langstrom, N., Grann, M., & Lichtenstein, P. (2002). Genetic and environmental influences on problematic masturbatory behavior in children: A study of same-sex twins. *Archives of Sexual Behavior, 31*, 343–350.

Larsson, I., & Svedin, C. G. (2002). Sexual experiences in childhood: Young adults' recollections. *Archives of Sexual Behavior, 31*, 263–273.

Leff, S. S., & Lakin, R. (2005). Playground-based observational systems: A review and implications for practitioners and researchers. *School Psychology Review, 34*, 475–488.

Leitenberg, H., Detzer, M. J., & Srebnik, D. (1993). Gender differences in masturbation and the relation of masturbation experience in preadolescence and/or early adolescence to sexual behavior and sexual adjustment in young adulthood. *Archives of Sexual Behavior, 22*, 87–98.

Leitenberg, H., Greenwald, E., & Tarran, M. J. (1989). The relation between sexual activity among children during preadolescence and/or early adolescence and sexual behavior and sexual adjustment in young adulthood. *Archives of Sexual Behavior, 18*, 299–313.

Maag, J. W., Reid, R., & DiGangi, S. A. (1993). Differential effects of self-monitoring attention, accuracy, and productivity. *Journal of Applied Behavior Analysis, 26*, 329–344.

Mandal, R. L., Olmi, D. J., & Wilczynski, S. M. (1999). Behavior rating scales: Concordance between multiple informants in the diagnosis of attention-deficit/hyperactivity disorder. *Journal of Attention Disorders, 3*, 97–103.

Martens, B. K., & Witt, J. C. (1988). Ecological behavior analysis. In M. Hersen, R. M. Eisler, & P. M. Miller (Eds.), *Progress in behavior modification* (Vol. 22, pp. 115–140). Beverly Hills, CA: Sage.

Martinson, F. M. (1994). *The sexual life of children*. Westport, CT: Bergin & Garvey.

Merrell, K. W. (2000). Informant reports: Theory and research in using child behavior rating scales in school settings. In E. S. Shapiro, & T. R. Kratochwill (Eds.), *Behavioral assessment in schools (pp. 233–256)* (2nd ed.). New York, NY: Guilford.

Meston, C. M., Heiman, J. R., Trapnell, P. D., & Paulhus, D. L. (1998). Socially desirable responding and sexuality self-reports. *Journal of Sex Research, 35*, 148–157.

Mustanski, B. (2011). Ethical and regulatory issues with conducting sexuality research with LGBT adolescents: A call to action for a scientifically informed approach. *Archives of Sexual Behavior, 40*, 673–686.

O'Sullivan, L. F. (2003). Methodological issues associated with studies of child sexual behavior. In J. Bancroft (Ed.), *Sexual development in childhood (pp. 23–33)*. Bloomington, IN: Indiana University Press.

Okami, P. (2002). Dear diary: A useful but imperfect method. In M. W. Wiederman, & B. E. Whitley (Eds.), *Handbook for conducting research on human sexuality (pp. 195–207)*. Mahwah, NJ: Erlbaum.

Pang, C. P., Baum, L., & Lam, D. S. (2000). Hunting for disease genes in multi-functional diseases. *Clinical Chemistry & Laboratory Medicine, 38*, 819–825.

Paul, G. L. (1967). Strategy of outcome research in psychotherapy. *Journal of Consulting Psychology, 31*, 104–118.

Pelham, W. E., Gnagy, E. M., Greiner, A. R., Waschbusch, D. A., Fabiano, G. A., & Burrows-MacLean, L. (2010). Summer treatment programs for Attention-Deficit/Hyperactivity Disorder. In J. R. Weisz, & A. E. Kazdin (Eds.), *Evidence based psychotherapies for children and adolescents (pp. 277–292)* (2nd ed.). New York, NY: Guilford.

Ringheim, K. (1995). Ethical issues in social science research with special reference to sexual behaviour research. *Social Science & Medicine, 40*, 1691–1697.

Salonia, A., Giraldi, A., Chivers, M. L., Georgiadis, J. R., Levin, R., Maravilla, K. R., et al. (2010). Physiology of women's sexual function: Basic knowledge and new findings. *Journal of Sexual Medicine, 7*, 2637–2660.

Shapiro, E. S., & Cole, C. L. (1993). Self-monitoring. In T. H. Ollendick, & M. Hersen (Eds.), *Handbook of child and adolescent assessment (pp. 124–139)*. Boston, MA: Allyn and Bacon.

Shapiro, E. S., & Cole, C. L. (1999). Self-monitoring in assessing children's problems. *Psychological Assessment, 11*, 448–457.

Shapiro, E. S., DuPaul, G. J., & Bradley-Klug, K. L. (1998). Self-management as a strategy to improve the classroom behavior of adolescents with ADHD. *Journal of Learning Disabilities, 31*, 545–555.

Snyder, G. S., & Shaw, S. (this volume). Small-n research design. In D. S. Bromberg & W. T. O'Donohue (Eds.), *Handbook of child and adolescent sexuality: Developmental and forensic psychology (pp. 97–114)*. New York, NY: Elsevier.

Tercyak, K. P. (2009). Genetics and genetic testing. In M. C. Roberts, & R. G. Steele (Eds.), *Handbook of pediatric psychology (pp. 721–736)* (4th ed.). New York, NY: Guilford.

Thigpen, J. W. (2009). Early sexual behavior in a sample of low-income, African American children. *Journal of Sex Research, 46*, 67–79.

Trivedi, N., & Sabini, J. (1998). Volunteer bias, sexuality, and personality. *Archives of Sexual Behavior, 27*, 181–195.

Volpe, R. J., & McConaughy, S. H. (2005). Systematic direct observational assessment of student behavior: Its use and interpretation in multiple settings: An introduction to the miniseries. *School Psychology Review, 34*, 451–453.

Wiederman, M. W. (2002a). Institutional review boards and conducting sexuality research. In M. W. Wiederman, & B. E. Whitley (Eds.), *Handbook for conducting research on human sexuality (pp. 479–504)*. Mahwah, NJ: Erlbaum.

Wiederman, M. W. (2002b). Reliability and validity of measurement. In M. W. Wiederman, & B. E. Whitley (Eds.), *Handbook for conducting research on human sexuality (pp. 25–50)*. Mahwah, NJ: Erlbaum.

Yoder, P., & Symons, F. (2010). *Observational measurement of behavior*. New York, NY: Springer.

# CHAPTER 3

# Research Syntheses Related to Childhood and Adolescent Sexuality: A Critical Review

**Tania B. Huedo-Medina, Estrellita Ballester, and Blair T. Johnson**
University of Connecticut, Storrs, Connecticut[1]

## INTRODUCTION

The study of child and adolescent sexuality, like many other scientific fields, is experiencing a veritable knowledge explosion. There are thousands of published studies with many more accruing daily, not to mention the growing number of unpublished studies. A February 10, 2012 search using the electronic database PsycINFO produced 569 empirical studies focusing primarily on child and adolescent sexuality (i.e., child* and sex* and adolesc* in key words). Examining a single study in isolation is quite likely to be a biased, and potentially ineffective, way to explore child and adolescent sexuality. There is simply too much evidence related to child and adolescent sexuality to consider when researching and/or planning to conduct new studies or reviews.

In an effort to obtain the most up-to-date and accurate information regarding a specific area within child and adolescent sexuality, researchers, policy makers, and community service providers increasingly turn to systematic reviews and meta-analyses (also labeled research syntheses, quantitative reviews, or quantitative syntheses). More rigorous than narrative reviews, systematic reviews use scientific methods to synthesize information gathered from a large number of studies (Cooper & Hedges, 2009; Johnson & Boynton, 2008; Johnson, Scott-Sheldon, Snyder, Noar, & Huedo-Medina, 2008). Systematic reviews feature comprehensive searches, replicable methodologies, and, when they include meta-analysis, they add sophisticated statistical analyses. When performed with high quality, both

---

[1] Correspondence to: Tania B. Huedo-Medina, Assistant Professor, Department of Allied Health Sciences, University of Connecticut. 358 Mansfield Road, Unit 1101. Storrs, CT, 06269-1101. Phone 860-486-0105. tania.huedo-medina@uconn.edu

techniques provide comprehensive evaluations of the child and adolescent literature. Such reviews are "systematic" in the sense that they follow scientific methods to search for studies, to describe their features, grade the quality of evidence, and to gauge their results. Meta-analyses take it a step further, gauging individual results on a common metric and conducting analyses of the pooled results, identifying statistical inconsistencies, determining the generalizability of study findings, and attempting to use coded features to explain any inconsistencies in results. In effect, a meta-analysis enables an empirically justified history of research on a given topic. The results of systematic reviews, and especially of meta-analyses, can be used to guide future research and advise policy makers and community service providers in decision-making so as to improve the quality and length of human life.

Systematic reviews are in general a scientific endeavor with identifiable and replicable methods that are necessary in order to produce reliable and valid reviews (Cooper, Hedges, & Valentine, 2009). Therefore, it is more important than ever that the consumers of child and adolescent sexuality reviews understand meta-analytic procedures, and the quality of the systematic reviews and meta-analyses produced until now. Meta-analysis consumers also need to know the potentials and limitations of those reviews, as well as how best to utilize systematic reviews' conclusions and meta-analytic findings in order to advance future endeavors in research and child and adolescent health policy. With these goals in mind, this chapter aims: (1) to survey the general concept of systematic review and meta-analysis with a particular focus on child and adolescent sexuality; (2) to present basic systematic review procedures, including meta-analytic analysis; and (3) to review and discuss the quality, benefits, and limitations of the available child and adolescent sexuality reviews and meta-analyses, isolating the most needed topics for future research.

## SYSTEMATIC REVIEWS AND META-ANALYSIS: EVIDENCE-BASED RESOURCES

Despite early controversy regarding the methods used by meta-analysts, systematic reviews and meta-analysis have become quite common and well accepted, because scholars realize that careful application of these techniques often will yield the clearest conclusions about a research literature (Cooper & Hedges, 2009; Cooper et al., 2009; Hunt, 1997). Even the most casual reader of scientific journals can easily witness the widespread acceptance of meta-analysis. The recent review by Johnson, Scott-Sheldon, & Carey (2010) documented the growing application of meta-analysis to a broad range of health behavior change interventions, with adolescents and sexuality being one of the growing topics. Those interested in synthesizing child and adolescent research have asked and answered many questions through the use of systematic reviews and meta-analyses.

Child and adolescent sexuality research has focused on many different topics, but particularly on sexual risk behavior, pregnancy, juvenile sex offenders, and child sexual abuse. A recent international household survey (excluding China) found that 11% of females and 6% of males between 15 and 19 years of age have had sex before the age of 15 (UNICEF, 2011), an age range that coincides with school attendance (Kirby, 2002). School-based programs have been implemented to circumvent the increase of teenage pregnancy and sexual risk behaviors. Bennett & Assefi's (2005) review examined trials that compared school-based abstinence-only programs versus abstinence-plus programs and that measured the incidence of teenage pregnancy. They concluded that the abstinence-plus programs increased contraceptive use. Nonetheless, it is still unclear whether one program is more effective than another in reducing sexual risk behavior among teens (e.g., Bennett & Assefi, 2005). This controversy still exists about the effectiveness of abstinence-only programs in decreasing or preventing sexual behaviors (Johnson, Scott-Sheldon, Huedo-Medina, & Carey, 2011; Underhill, Operario, & Montgomery, 2007). Although school-based sexual education programs may contribute to increased sexual knowledge (Song, Pruitt, McNamara, & Colewell, 2000), the correlation between knowledge and behavior is questionable (Bennett & Assefi, 2005).

In spite of the fact that, worldwide, 5 million young people (15–24 years old) are HIV-positive, this group is often overlooked in HIV/AIDS interventions (UNICEF, 2010). Several reviews have reported on outcomes regarding HIV/AIDS-related knowledge, behavioral intentions, attitudes, beliefs, self-efficacy, and sexual risk behavior change (e.g., condom use, abstinence). Research focusing on behavioral interventions has been shown to reduce adolescents' risk for Sexually Transmitted Infections (STIs), particularly through increasing condom use, reducing or delaying frequencies of penetrative sex, and increasing communication skills to negotiate safer sex and acquire condoms (Johnson et al., 2011). Effects were large when the adolescents targeted were institutionalized, the intervention had more sessions, and the intervention focused on safer sex rather than abstinence. This research conveys appropriate preventive methods for a sample of HIV-negative adolescents (Johnson et al., 2011), yet more research needs to be done in order to assess which interventions are appropriate and most effective in different settings and populations. Future reviews should also integrate ecological theories, individual and contextual resources, and biological approaches (Johnson et al., 2011; Malow, Kershaw, Sipsma, Rosenberg, & Devieux, 2007).

The knowledge we can gain through research about the contextual and demographic characteristics of the studies will allow tailoring of the efficacy of interventions. Despite the evidence about the effect of individual resources, few studies have reported results disaggregated for structural and population factors. Differences found in young adults cannot be traced to childhood experiences if systematic studies do not exist (Johnson et al., 2010; Sherr, Mueller, & Varrall, 2009).

Another important focus in the child and adolescent sexuality area is the effectiveness of treatment programs among juvenile sex offenders, measured by the rate of sexual recidivism. A meta-analysis focusing on juvenile sex offenders and recidivism rates found that the offenders engaged in non-sexual more than sexual re-offending (Redlak, 2003). This finding is consistent with other reviews measuring sexual recidivism rates (mean of 7.08%, SD = 3.9%) and general recidivism rates (43.4%, SD = 18.9%) among adolescents (Caldwell, 2010). Thus, general recidivism rates tend to be about four times higher than sexual rates among adolescents (Caldwell, 2010). Four outcomes were found to be related to sexual recidivism: associations with delinquent peers; other crimes against persons; attitudes toward rape and sexual assault; and family normlessness (Redlak, 2003). Although neither the level of secured placement (e.g., community, secured custody) nor the use of arrest or conviction has significantly influenced sexual recidivism rates (Caldwell, 2010), disassociating from delinquent peers alone dramatically reduced the rate of sexual recidivism among juvenile sex offenders (Redlak, 2003). Other methods such as cognitive behavioral treatment also have been identified to effectively reduce rates of recidivism (Genovés, Morales, & Sánchez-Meca, 2006).

Childhood sexual abuse (CSA) is a related topic that presents an extensive scientific literature based on adults who have suffered CSA when they were children or adolescents; however, not many studies report on this topic when the sample are in fact still children or adolescents. The literature that has focused on CSA among young people has covered several different topics, such as the development of self-injurious behavior among adolescents who have experienced CSA (Klonsky & Moyer, 2008), as well as a linkage between pregnancy increase and CSA (Macdonald, Higgins, & Ramchandani, 2006). Treatments have been sought to address the immediate and long-term effects of CSA; a systematic review concluded that cognitive behavioral approaches may have a positive impact (Macdonald et al., 2006).

Scholars focusing on adolescent and child research have also contributed to discussion of issues surrounding the technique of meta-analysis itself. For instance, a commentary (McKay, Fisher, Maticka-Tyndale, & Barrett, 2001) criticized DiCenso, Guyatt, Willan, & Griffith's (2002) systematic review's finding that sex education programs do not work. The systematic review focused on outcomes related to pregnancy prevention, and did not include studies that focused on STI/HIV prevention. This exclusion criterion consequently may have eliminated studies that contained information regarding the increase of contraceptive use, which could have resulted in reducing pregnancy rates (McKay et al., 2001). It is important to understand appropriately what implications systematic reviews and meta-analyses have. Often the "ingredients" that make up such scholarly works are broadly conceived and misunderstood.

Historically, scholars used informal methods known as *narrative reviewing*—a summary of the results of individual primary studies sometimes guided by a count of the number of studies that had either produced or failed to produce statistically significant findings in the hypothesized direction. Narrative reviews have appeared in many different contexts and still serve a useful purpose in writing that does not have a comprehensive literature review as its goal (e.g., textbook summaries, introductions to journal articles reporting primary research). Nonetheless, narrative reviews can also prove to be inadequate for reaching definitive conclusions about the degree of empirical support for a phenomenon, or for a theory regarding the phenomenon.

One indication of this inadequacy is that independent narrative reviews of the same literature often have reached different conclusions. Kirby (1999), for example, found that youth development programs addressing non-sexual risk factors reduced the rates of pregnancy and childbearing. In contrast, Frost & Forrest's (1995) review found that addressing sexual risk factors (e.g., abstinence, contraceptive use, and negotiation skills) reduced pregnancy rates and were particularly more successful among younger adolescents. With the growing popularity of meta-analysis, some of this controversy diminished, at least among scholars; results have shown that educational and contraceptive interventions are *both* efficacious in lowering the rates of unintended pregnancies. Yet, this effect was inconclusive for secondary outcomes (e.g., contraceptive use, initiation of sexual intercourse, STIs, childbirth, abortion) among adolescents (Oringanje, Meremikwu, Eko, Esu, Meremikwu, & Ehiri, 2009).

Comparisons between narrative and meta-analytic or even reviews in other domains (e.g., delinquency prevention and job training) have found similar results, with narrative reviews underestimating treatment effects (Mann, 1994). The reasons for such inaccurate conclusions hinge on at least three problems that scholars have addressed in great detail (Glass, McGaw, & Smith, 1981; Rosenthal, 1991; Rosenthal & DiMatteo, 2001):

1. Narrative reviews generally gather only a convenient sample of studies; there is no systematic scientific method used to find relevant studies.
2. Narrative reviews fail to content-code the studies either for theoretically important aspects or for aspects that gauge methodological quality, with the result that the accuracy of the review's claims about the characteristics of the studies and the quality of their methods is difficult to judge.
3. Narrative reviews typically rely on statistical significance of results rather than using gauges of effect size magnitude. As a result, narrative reviewers often reach erroneous conclusions about a pattern in a series of studies, even when there are as few as 10 studies (Cooper & Rosenthal, 1980).

These problems are compounded by the increasing number of studies available to review—and, as we have noted, large literatures are more and more the norm in childhood and adolescent sexuality related topics. In contrast, systematic reviews and meta-analytic procedures used to gather, code, and analyze study outcomes provide an improved alternative method to synthesize information gathered from a large number of studies. Indeed, meta-analysis is the best available tool to conduct these empirical histories of a phenomenon, to show how researchers have addressed the phenomenon, and to show how results may have changed over time when there are enough studies to be meta-analyzed. Systematic reviews and meta-analyses have become critical in our understanding and contextualizing of new research findings. Acknowledging scholars' scientific, ethical, and financial responsibility to demonstrate how new research is related to existing knowledge, the British medical journal *The Lancet* now requires authors to reference an existing meta-analysis, conduct their own meta-analysis, or to describe the quantitative findings that have appeared since a prior meta-analysis (Young & Horton, 2005).

As much of an advance as it presents, meta-analysis in particular is not without criticism (Sharpe, 1997). Six common criticisms (Bangert-Drowns, 1997; Rosenthal & DiMatteo, 2001) are: (1) bias in sampling the findings; (2) papers included may vary in quality; (3) non-independence of effect sizes; (4) overemphasis on differences between individual effects (e.g., differences between means); (5) unpublished studies are under-represented and published studies over represented; and (6) the "apples and oranges" problem (i.e., summarizing studies with varying methodologies). Although these criticisms bear some resemblance to the criticisms of narrative reviews that we listed above, most of them have arisen out of mis-understandings of meta-analytic methodology.

The importance of comparing study findings accurately has made scholars dedicate considerable effort to making the review process as reliable and valid as possible in an effort to circumvent the criticisms listed above. These efforts highlight the fact that research synthesis is a scientific endeavor with identifiable and replicable methods that are necessary in order to produce reliable and valid reviews (Cooper et al., 2009).

## SYSTEMATIC REVIEW AND META-ANALYSIS PROCEDURES

Conducting a meta-analysis generally involves seven steps: (1) determining a research question within a particular literature with common variables under consideration; (2) defining the inclusion/exclusion criteria that will set boundaries for the final sample of studies; (3) locating relevant studies; (4) coding studies for their distinctive sample, methods, and content characteristics; (5) estimating the size of each study's effect on a standardized metric; (6) analyzing the database; and (7) interpreting and presenting the results. Systematic reviews usually accomplish steps 1 through 4, and sometimes even step 5, and they end with conclusions (in step 7) based on their systematic description of the studies. The details and success of each step heavily depend on those preceding. For example, it is easier to set boundaries for studies (step 2) and to find the studies (step 3) if the analyst has first done a good job of defining the meta-analytic question and reviewing relevant theoretical domains (step 1). In symmetric fashion, even the earlier steps should be accomplished with an eye to the steps that follow. For example, defining a problem too broadly (step 1) may result in ambiguities in the following methods (steps 2 through 6), as well as in interpretation (step 7).

## Defining the Question

The first conceptual step is to specify, with great clarity, the phenomenon under review. Ordinarily a synthesis evaluates evidence relevant to a single hypothesis, defined in terms of the variables that underlie the phenomenon. To select the variables on which to focus, the analyst studies the history of the research problem and of typical studies in the literature, or even some previous systematic reviews that may already exist. Typically, the research problem will be defined as a relation between two variables, such as the influence of an independent variable on a dependent variable.

It is essential in this conceptual analysis to take into account the history of the research problem and of typical studies in the literature. Theoretical articles, earlier reviews, and empirical articles should be examined for the interpretations they provide of the phenomenon under investigation. When scholars have debated different explanations, the synthesis should be designed to address these competing explanations, if possible.

The most common way to test competing explanations is to examine how the findings pattern across studies using possible moderators (also called effect modifiers) between the dependent, the effect size, and the independent variable, sample, study, methodological, intervention, and setting characteristics. This approach, advancing beyond the simple question of *whether* the independent variable is related to the dependent variable, addresses the question of *when*, or under what circumstances, the magnitude or sign of the association varies.

## Setting Boundaries for the Sample of Studies

Clearly, only some studies will be relevant to the conceptual relationship that is the focus of the meta-analysis, so analysts must define inclusion/exclusion criteria. This step is similar conceptually to defining the universe of content to be included in a content analysis. Decisions about the inclusion of studies are important, because the inferential power is going to be limited by the number of studies in the sample. Boundary-setting is often a lengthy process that forces reviewers to weigh conceptual and practical issues. The sample of studies is routinely defined by such criteria as the presence of the key variables and acceptable measures and quantitative information about them, the type of methodology used, and study quality that can be part of the coding in order to evaluate the influence of different designs and other methodological characteristics.

Analysts often set the boundaries of the synthesis so that the methods of included studies differ widely only on critical moderator dimensions.

The moderators are intended to delineate the literature or expand upon the theory of interest. If other, extraneous dimensions are held relatively constant across the reviewed studies by carefully defining the selection criteria, the moderator variable results ought to be more clearly and easily interpreted. An example of a situation suggesting the need for a moderator analysis is a meta-analysis of studies evaluating HIV prevention interventions for adolescents. These programs varied in the degree to which they increased condom use for adolescents in the intervention compared with the control condition (Johnson, Carey, Marsh, Levin, & Scott-Sheldon, 2003; Johnson, Scott-Sheldon, Huedo-Medina, & Carey, 2011). In such circumstances, the odds grow that different population mean effects exist within different groups of studies. Indeed, subsequent moderator analyses showed, in part, that interventions were more successful to the extent that they provided more condom skills training.

Other moderators that can be relevant are geographic setting, culture, or study population. If the phenomenon under investigation is group-specific, then including the studies covering other groups may well only obscure the phenomenon. Alternatively, an analyst may choose to treat the setting, culture, or population as a moderating variable and test for differences when the literature includes enough studies for each group. Including reports from diverse settings, cultures, and populations also increases the degree to which the results can be generalized and to detect moderator variable effects.

Developing selection criteria is often a process that continues as the researchers examine more studies, and thereby uncover the full range of research designs that have been used to investigate a particular hypothesis. If some studies meeting preliminary criteria established conditions that are judged to be extremely atypical or flawed, the selection criteria may need to be modified to exclude them.

## Locating the Literature of Studies

Because including a large number of studies generally increases the value of a synthesis—and even more so if it is meta-analytic—it is important to locate as many studies as possible that might be suitable for inclusion, the third step of a systematic review. It is conventionally the tacit goal of a systematic review to obtain *all* of the relevant studies based on the researcher's well-defined research question, or at minimum a random sample of them, in the event of a very large literature (Card, 2012).

To ensure that most, if not all, studies are located, reviewers are well advised to err in the direction of being overly inclusive in their search procedures. As described elsewhere (Cooper, 1998; Lipsey & Wilson, 2001; White, 1994), there are many ways to find relevant studies, and analysts are almost always well-advised to use them all. Because computer searches of publication databases seldom locate all of the available studies, it is important to supplement them by:

1. Examining the reference lists of existing reviews (or consulting systematic reviews in specific databases, such as *The Cochrane Library Plus* and the *Campbell Library* (The Campbell Collaboration, 2012; The Cochrane Collaboration, 2012), which regularly update available existing reviews), and of studies in the targeted literature;
2. Obtaining published sources that have cited seminal articles within the literature (e.g., Web of Knowledge and Google Scholar sites);
3. Contacting the extant network of researchers who work on a given topic to ask for new studies or unpublished studies; and
4. By manually searching important journals to find some reports that might have been overlooked by other techniques.

The last strategy is especially important for more recent papers that might not yet be included in the electronic databases. Although such a comprehensive search may seem overwhelming, it is imperative if the goal is to retrieve all studies relevant to the topic of interest. Indeed, researchers who have compared searches retrieved from several databases have found that database searching is an insufficient means of literature retrieval, and even find differences among electronic reference databases (Lemeshow, Blum, Berlin, Stoto, & Colditz, 2005). The review team should carefully record their methods of locating studies, including the names and databases that were searched, and for each database the time period covered, the keywords and combinations used, and the number of relevant citations. The details of the search procedure should be included in the methods section of the meta-analysis report, to enable readers to make adequate judgments about the adequacy of the procedures used and to permit other analysts to replicate the search (Moher, Liberati, Tetzlaff, & Altman, 2009; Shea, Grimshaw, Wells, et al., 2007; Shea, Hamel, Wells, et al., 2009).

## Coding Studies for Their Distinctive Characteristics

Once the sample of studies is retrieved, the fourth step in the process is to code them. Coding a systematically collected set of studies is very similar to coding for content analysis. A coding sheet or an electronic database worksheet and a coding manual need to be created, pre-tested, and revised. The variables to be coded and the possible values need to be operationalized precisely. Study characteristics may be either continuous variables, with values existing along ratio, interval, or ordinal scales, or categorical variables having discrete numbers of values that reflect qualitative differences between those values. A master codebook can explain the details for each category, or this information can be included in the database worksheet.

To the extent that the analyst team codes many features of the study, they should distinguish between study features that they expect on an a priori basis to account for variation among the studies' effect sizes, on the one hand, and those that provide merely descriptive information about the usual context of studies in the literature, on the other hand (Johnson & Eagly, 2000; Johnson & Eagly, in press). Only the latter will be relevant for a systematic review. A meta-analysis may be criticized for "fishing" for significant findings if it appears that too many study dimensions were tested as moderators of the magnitude of effects. Separating the study dimensions has the advantage of keeping the review as theory-driven as possible (testing a few moderator variables), while at the same time being appropriately descriptive of the literature in question (including many descriptive variables).

To increase the reliability and accuracy of the coding, coding should be carried out by two or more coders, coders should be carefully trained, the coding instructions should contain sufficient detail that a new coder could apply the scheme and obtain similar results, and disagreements between coders should be resolved through discussion or with a third coder. Good supervision is critical, including spot checks, trial runs, and having expert(s) working close to the coders, as well as comprehensive manuals to facilitate understanding and to solve problems and questions. An appropriate index of intercoder reliability (Krippendorf, 1980) should be calculated and reported in the final report.

## Estimating the Magnitude of Effect in Each Study

The fifth step is to estimate the standardized effect size for each study, which quantitatively captures the phenomenon under scrutiny. Yet, as studies almost always vary widely in terms of choice of statistic as well as sample size, rendering a comparison across the studies is complicated.

The solution is to impose the same effect size metric on all of the studies. Fortunately, nearly all inferential statistics (e.g., $t$-tests, $F$-tests) and many descriptive statistics (e.g., means and standard deviations) can be converted into an effect size (Cooper et al., 2009; Glass et al., 1981; Johnson & Eagly, 2000; Lipsey & Wilson, 2001; Rosenthal, 1991). In consulting and using such guides, it is important to make sure that the best formulae are employed. Failing to do so could result in effect size estimates that are biased in liberal or conservative directions. As an example, $t$- and $F$-values can derive from both within- and between-subjects designs, and formulae exist for both types of designs (Morris & DeShon, 2002). Applying the formulae for the between-subjects cases to the within-subjects cases overestimates their magnitude considerably (Dunlap, Cortina, Vaslow, & Burke, 1996; Morris & DeShon, 2002; Seignourel & Albarracin, 2002). Analysts must carefully consider how the designs of the studies may affect the calculated effect size. If there are enough studies, it may sometimes be fruitful to consider conducting parallel, separate meta-analyses for studies with differing designs. Nonetheless, the goal is to convert summary statistics into effect sizes that can be statistically integrated.

## Effect Sizes of Association (r, d, and OR)

Effect size indexes usually gauge the association between two variables; an exception to this rule is the arithmetic mean (see Johnson & Eagly, in press; Lipsey & Wilson, 2001). Among indices of association, the most commonly used are the standardized mean difference ($d$) and the correlation coefficient ($r$), although odds ratios ($OR$) are popular in some fields, such as medicine and public health. The standardized mean difference, which expresses the finding in standard deviation units, was first proposed by Cohen (1969). Hedges (1981) showed that Cohen's $d$, which is now often labeled $g$, overestimates population effect sizes to the extent that sample sizes are small, and he provided a correction for this bias; with the bias corrected, this effect estimate is conventionally known as $d$ (McGrath & Meyer, 2006). Other commonly used effect sizes are the correlation coefficient, $r$, which gauges the association between two variables, and the $OR$, which gauges the association between two categorical variables (Lipsey & Wilson, 2001).

Conventionally, meta-analysts select $r$ as the effect size if most of the studies that are integrated report correlations between two continuous variables. If most of the studies report ANOVAs, $t$-tests, and chi-squares for comparisons between two groups (e.g., experimental vs. control), analysts typically select *d*. If both variables are dichotomous, then they typically select the *OR* (Haddock, Rindskopf, & Shadish, 1998). The positive or negative sign of *r* or *d* is defined so that studies with opposite outcomes have opposing signs; instances with exactly 0 have exactly no association or no difference, respectively. Further, those with values less than 0 have opposite results to those with values more than 0. In the case of the *OR*, instances with exactly 1 show exactly no difference; values less than 1 are opposed from those more than 1. Analyses of the *OR* use the logged form and then transform output values for interpretation back into the *OR* form.

## Analyzing the Meta-Analytic Databases

Once the effect sizes are calculated, the sixth phase in the process is to analyze the data. In this section, we will assume that the goal is to use quantitative techniques to gauge differences between or across clusters of studies; those who wish to use artifact corrections of effect sizes, or to avoid significance testing, may be wise to pursue other techniques (Hall & Brannick, 2002; Hunter & Schmidt, 2004). An exhaustive survey of general analytic approaches to meta-analysis is beyond the scope of the current chapter, but further discussions and comparisons are available elsewhere (Field, 2001, 2005; Hall & Brannick, 2002; Huedo-Medina & Johnson, 2010; Hunter & Schmidt, 2004; Sanchez-Meca & Marin-Martinez, 1997). The general steps involved in the analysis of effect sizes usually are: (1) to aggregate effect sizes across the studies to determine the overall strength of the relation between the examined variables; (2) to analyze the consistency of the effect sizes across the studies; (3) to diagnose outliers among the effect sizes; and (4) to perform tests of whether study attributes moderate the magnitude of the effect sizes.

### *Averaging Effect Sizes*

As a first step in a quantitative synthesis, the study outcomes are combined by averaging the effect sizes with each weighted by the inverse of its variance ($v$) which typically rests heavily on sample size (Hedges & Olkin, 1985); some approaches advocate weighting each effect size by $N$ (Hunter & Schmidt, 2004). Such procedures give greater weight to the more reliably estimated study outcomes, which are in general those with the larger samples (Hedges, Cooper, & Bushman, 1992). As a test for significance of this weighted mean effect size ($T_+$), a confidence interval is typically computed around this mean, based on its standard deviation,

$T_+ \pm 1.96(v_+)^{1/2}$, where 1.96 is the unit-normal value for a 95% *CI* (assuming a non-directional hypothesis). If the confidence interval (*CI*) includes zero (0.00), the value indicating exactly no difference, it may be concluded that, aggregated across all studies, there is no significant effect or association between the group assignment and the outcome measure.

## *Determining how Inconsistent Effect Sizes Are*

The next concern is whether the studies can be adequately described by a single effect size, which is assessed by calculating the homogeneity (or heterogeneity) indexes in relation to the included effect sizes, which gauge the amount of variability in the effect sizes around the mean (Cochran, 1954; Hedges, 1981; Hunter & Schmidt, 2004; Rosenthal, 1991). If the effect sizes share a common, underlying, population effect size, then they would differ only by unsystematic sampling error. The test statistic $Q$ evaluates the hypothesis that the effect sizes are consistent, and has an approximate $\chi^2$ (Chi-square) distribution with $k-1$ degrees of freedom, where $k$ is the number of studies. If $Q$ is significant, the hypothesis of the homogeneity (or consistency) of the effect sizes is not accepted, and heterogeneity is inferred. In this event, the weighted mean effect size may not adequately describe the outcomes of the set of studies, because it is likely that quite different mean effects exist in different groups of studies. Further analysis is warranted to test potential moderating variables responsible for different mean effects. $Q$ deserves careful interpretation, in conjunction with inspecting the values of the effect sizes. Even if the homogeneity test is non-significant, significant moderators could be present, especially when $Q$ is relatively large (Johnson & Turco, 1992; Rosenthal, 1995). Also, $Q$ could be significant even though the effect sizes are very close in value, especially if the sample sizes are very large. Finally, if the number of studies is small, tests of homogeneity are known to have lowered power to detect the null hypothesis of homogeneity (Hardy & Thompson, 1998; Harwell, 1997). Higgins and Thompson (2002) introduced a homogeneity index, $I^2$, whose values range from 0 to 100, where high values indicate more variability among the effect sizes. The $I^2$ index is subject to the same conditions and qualifications as is $Q$; its benefit is to standardize comparisons between meta-analyses, while providing the same information as $Q$ (Huedo-Medina, Sanchez-Meca, Marin-Martinez, & Botella, 2006).

## Detection of Outliers

Outliers are detected by using graphical techniques or by examining residuals of meta-analytic models. Studies yielding effect sizes identified as outliers can be examined to determine if they appear to differ methodologically from other studies. In general, the diagnosis of outliers should occur prior to calculating moderator analyses; this diagnosis may locate a value or two that are so discrepant from the other effect sizes that they would dramatically alter any models fitted to effect sizes. Under such circumstances, these outliers should be removed from subsequent phases of the data analysis. More normally, outliers can be examined by analyzing potential moderators of effect sizes, as discussed in the next section. That is, effect sizes that are apparently outliers may in fact be associated with the coded features of the studies.

## Analysis of Potential Moderators of Effect Sizes

Ordinarily, analyst teams want to test a priori hypotheses about what explains variations in effect sizes across studies. To determine the relation between study characteristics and the magnitude of the effect sizes, both categorical factors and continuous factors can be tested. Instead of using such familiar primary-level statistics as $t$, $F$, or $r$ to evaluate whether study dimensions relate to the magnitude of effect sizes, it is best to use statistics that take full advantage of the information in each study's effect size (Hedges & Olkin, 1985; Johnson & Eagly, in press; Johnson & Turco, 1992). In *categorical models*, which are analogous to the analysis of variance, analyses may show that weighted mean effect sizes differ in magnitude between the subgroups established by dividing studies into classes based on study characteristics. In such cases, it is as though the meta-analysis is broken into sub-meta-analyses based on their methodological features.

Similarly, *continuous models*, which are analogous to regression models, examine whether study characteristics that are assessed on a continuous scale are related to the effect sizes. As with categorical models, some continuous models may be completely specified, in the sense that the systematic variability in the effect sizes is explained by the study characteristic that is used as a predictor. Goodness-of-fit statistics enable analysts to determine the extent to which categorical, continuous, or mixtures of these models provide correct depictions of study outcomes. Finally, multiple moderators may appear in these models, provided sufficient numbers of studies exist.

## Publication Bias

Our discussion of published vs. unpublished studies raises the issue of *publication bias*, defined as a bias by authors, reviewers, and editors against null reports, or worse, bias against reports whose data actually oppose a popular hypothesis. Although scholars commonly consider it a bias by the "establishment" against publishing null or reversed effects, in fact even study authors may exhibit a bias about reporting data that fail to support a pet theory, leaving these findings in the proverbial file drawer, probably not even written-up for publication (Greenwald, 1975). Of course, to the extent that a meta-analysis team has located and retrieved unpublished studies, it is possible to test for publication bias directly by using publication status as a moderator of effect sizes; in such cases, analyst teams should be alert to the possibility that the "unpublished" studies they have obtained are in fact those likely in the passage of time to become published. Yet, even when only published studies are included, it is still possible to test for publication bias through the use of a growing number of techniques (Card, 2012; Sutton, 2009; Thornton & Lee, 2000). The simplest method is to inspect a *funnel plot* of the distribution of effect sizes, which graphs effect sizes as a function of their sample sizes (or, more correctly, the inverse of their variance). Such plots should reveal a normal distribution if publication bias is not present. Gaps or asymmetries in the graph, therefore, reveal potential publication bias. More sophisticated techniques attempt to quantify these gaps, as in the trim-and-fill method (Duval & Tweedie, 2000), or to estimate what the mean effect size would be if theoretically missing effect sizes were included (Hedges & Vevea, 1996; Vevea & Hedges, 1995). An important caveat is that heterogeneity clouds interpretation of such graphs (Lau, Ioannidis, Terrin, Schmid, & Olkin, 2006). Another popular technique is to calculate the fail-safe *N*, which is the number of null-result studies necessary to reduce the mean effect size to non-significance (Rosenthal, 1991); an implausibly high number would suggest that publication bias is trivial. Despite the popularity of the technique, critics have noted that the index lacks a distribution theory, and therefore it is not known how likely a particular fail-safe *N* value would be to occur based on chance (Begg, 1994). Some even recommend against this statistic's use in any circumstance (Vevea & Woods, 2005).

Even when publication bias seems obvious, analysts are wise to consider alternative reasons why the pattern may have occurred: it may be that the methods of larger studies differed systematically from those of smaller studies. In particular, as we alluded, publication bias is less of an issue when effect sizes lack homogeneity and moderators can be identified. Potential publication bias should be considered in the light both of the degree of homogeneity and of how effect sizes pattern according to features of the studies. Indeed, under such circumstances, the threat of publication bias often diminishes entirely.

## Interpreting and Presenting the Results

Every systematic review should describe its sample of studies in a manner that informs interpretation of the studies' findings. Reviews' conclusions hinge on what information the original studies present. If most or all studies used retrospective rather than prospective methods, for example, the review's findings also are limited in this respect. Meta-analyses also reach statistical inferences: they can report on the trends of the studies in relation to a given phenomenon. If the mean effect is non-significant and the homogeneity statistic is small and non-significant, an analyst might conclude that there is no linkage between the variables under consideration. In such cases, it is wise to consider the amount of statistical power that was available; if the total number of research participants in the studies integrated was small, it is possible that additional data would support the existence of the effect. Even if the mean effect is significant and the homogeneity statistic is small and non-significant, concerns about the mean effect's magnitude arise. Johnson and Eagly (in press) and Card (2012) provide additional recommendations about presentations of meta-analyses.

## SURVEY OF SYSTEMATIC REVIEWS OF CHILD AND ADOLESCENT SEXUALITY

Many meta-analyses and systematic reviews focusing on adolescent and child sexuality have been published in recent years. They vary in terms of their subtopics, main procedures, and most likely in terms of their methodological quality, given that reviewing techniques in general have improved markedly over the last few decades. Another reason that published syntheses likely have varied widely in methodological quality is the simple fact that it can be difficult to review empirical research related to child and adolescent sexuality. The nuances that we have covered in this chapter bear witness to the myriad issues and cautions that analyst teams should bear in mind in accomplishing a good research synthesis. Research synthesis is simultaneously a teleological as well as a historical process, qualitative as well as quantitative. Because of their clear advantages, we anticipate that scholars who focus on child and adolescent sexuality will increasingly be expected to conduct systematic, rather than mere narrative, reviews. Editors and reviewers are well advised to consider that, although systematic reviews generally are preferable to narrative reviews, they are also much more taxing to perform.

## Method

Meta-analyses and systematic reviews were retrieved from electronic databases. A May 18, 2011 search using the terms "child AND adolescent AND sexuality" resulted in 27 citations in the PubMed database, 23 citations in the PsycINFO database, and 6 citations in Google Scholar. Forty-two additional reports were found using the archive maintained by the Synthesis of HIV & AIDS Research Project, and by examining reference lists of excluded reviews. All the reports were retrieved for more careful inspection by two raters. To be eligible for this study, reports of meta-analyses or systematic review had to satisfy four a priori inclusion criteria: (1) use only samples of children and/or adolescents; (2) address any aspect about child and adolescent sexuality; (3) conduct a systematic search; and (4) provide a description of the studies. The reviews were excluded if the sample consisted of college students only (Lau et al., 2006). Because the search was not limited in terms of time, this review also permitted inferences about temporal trends in this literature.

Several teams of scholars have developed indexes and checklists to evaluate the methodological quality of systematic reviews and meta-analyses (Moher et al., 2009; Shea et al., 2007; Shea et al., 2009; Stroup, Berlin, Morton, et al., 2000). We commenced with the PRISMA checklist and the AMSTAR questionnaire to gauge the methodological quality, because the relevance and reliability of the latter with regard to systematic reviews and specifically to meta-analyses in health has already been shown. Of the 11 AMSTAR items, all were incorporated except Item 11 ("Was the conflict of interest stated?"), which was excluded because the team deemed it not relevant enough for this literature. In addition, two new items were created and AMSTAR item 3 was divided into two items, resulting in

13 total items. Two members of the team refined these items (BTJ, TBHM), and the other critiqued and suggested improvements (EB). These scale items were then evaluated based on a trial of two studies and clarified. Finally, two coders (TBHM, EB) applied the scale to all 67 reports in the sample ($M$ Cohen's $\kappa = 0.93$). Disagreements between coders were resolved through discussion.

Table 3.1 lists the individual quality items in the scale, includes the rationale for each question, and where relevant, indicates whether the item was created for the scale. AMSTAR items 1, 6, 8 were clarified somewhat, AMSTAR items 2, 5, 7, and 9 were augmented including an ordinal scale up to 2 or 3 (AMSTAR item 9) points depending on how thoroughly the study reports performing a particular item. Finally, item 3 was divided into two items—one that focuses on the comprehensiveness of the search and the other on whether the search is replicable—because it is possible for a report to be comprehensive yet not be replicable. An item gauging whether the variables were clearly defined was added, because we noticed that many different variables can relate to outcome of interest in any particular review. Moreover, many measures can be used to indicate a particular outcome. The other added item addressed the fact that, in the case of meta-analysis, many effect size indexes can be used; some are more appropriate than others depending on the metric, type of design, and other factors. This item was included to make sure the studies justify how, in the case

**Table 3.1** AMSTAR$_{CAS}$ Items and Their Definitions Included to Assess Methodological Quality of the Meta-Analyses and Reviews in the Sample[a]

| Question | Rationale for Question (Source) |
|---|---|
| **A. A priori design** | |
| 1. Was an "a priori" design provided? (0–1) | The research question and inclusion criteria should be established before the conduct of the review. *Is it stated that these were finalized before commencing the review?* (Clarified form of AMSTAR item 1) |
| **B. Literature search and duplicate effort** | |
| 2. Were population variables defined and considered in the methods? (0–1) | *The authors should have defined the variables they will measure as indicators of the variables in the relationship or effect studied.* (Authors) |

(*Continued*)

**Table 3.1** (Continued)

| Question | Rationale for Question (Source) |
|---|---|
| 3. Was there duplicate study selection and data extraction? (0–2) | There should be independent data extractors and a consensus procedure for disagreements should be in place to *score 1. If inter-rater reliability reported, then score 2.* (Augmented from AMSTAR item 2) |
| 4. Was a comprehensive literature search performed? (0–2) | At least two electronic sources should be searched. The report must include years and databases used (e.g., Central, EMBASE, and MEDLINE) to *score 1. All searches should be supplemented by consulting current contents, reviews, textbooks, specialized registers, or experts in the particular field of study, and by reviewing the references in the studies found to score 2.* (Augmented from AMSTAR item 3) |
| 5. Is it possible to replicate the search? (0–2) | *The Method or Supplementary Materials should make it possible for a second party to replicate the search, including all databases, search terms, and operators.* Key words and/or MESH terms must be stated or available from the authors and where feasible the search strategy should be provided to *score 1. If authors report MeSH terms were used for searching, they must be stated in methods OR provided in supplementary material to be considered a "2."* A note to contact the author for complete search strategy is also acceptable. (Augmented from AMSTAR item 3) |
| 6. Did the inclusion criteria permit grey literature? (0–1) | The authors should state that they searched for reports regardless of their publication type. The authors should state whether or not they excluded any reports (from the systematic review), based on their publication status, language, etc. (AMSTAR item 4) |
| 7. Was a list of studies (included and excluded) provided? (0–2) | A list of included and excluded studies should be provided. *A descriptive summary of reasons for excluding studies should be provided such as in a QUORUM or PRISMA figure to score 1. If an actual list of excluded studies is included or available upon request then score will be 2.* (Augmented from AMSTAR item 5) |

**C. Coding of studies**

| | |
|---|---|
| 8. Were the characteristics of the included studies provided? (0–1) | In an aggregated form such as a table, data from the original studies should be provided on the participants, interventions, and outcomes. The ranges of characteristics in all the studies analyzed, e.g., age range, race, sex, relevant socioeconomic data, and type of population. *Data must be presented for each study individually in a table to receive a score of "1"; simply providing population or study description in the text is not sufficient.* (Clarified form of AMSTAR item 6) |

*(Continued)*

**Table 3.1** (Continued)

| Question | Rationale for Question (Source) |
|---|---|
| **9.** Was the scientific quality of the included studies assessed and documented? (0–2) | "A priori" methods of assessment should be provided (e.g., for effectiveness studies if the author(s) chose to include only randomized, double-blind, placebo controlled studies, or allocation concealment as inclusion criteria); for other types of studies alternative items will be relevant. *If study quality was assessed and documented with a tool and/or scale choose 2; if only discussed choose 1.* (Augmented from AMSTAR item 7) |
| **D. Analysis and interpretation** | |
| **10.** Did results depend on study quality, either overall, or interaction with moderators? (0–1) | *Studies with higher methodological rigor (e.g., with a scale such as PEDro, Jadad's scale) should yield clearer findings, other factors equal.* (Clarified from AMSTAR item 8) |
| **11.** Were the methods used to combine the findings of studies appropriate? (0–3) | For the pooled results, a test should be done to ensure the studies were combinable, to assess their homogeneity (i.e., $\chi^2$ for homogeneity or $I^2$). If heterogeneity exists, random-effects assumptions should be incorporated and/or the clinical appropriateness of combining should be taken into consideration (i.e., is it sensible to combine?). *If a test of homogeneity was conducted, the $\chi^2$ or $I^2$ value is reported along with a report of the statistical assumptions (i.e., fixed vs. random-effects), and moderator analysis was conducted, choose 3; if they report at least weighted effect size, choose 2; if they report some of the information about heterogeneity but not all, choose 1; if they do not report information about analysis, choose 0.* (Augmented from AMSTAR item 9) |
| **12.** Was the effect-size index chosen justified, statistically? (0–2) | *Comparisons of studies' results may be biased in the face of uncontrolled variables (e.g., standard deviations and sample sizes that vary widely across studies). If authors provide ES equation/explain their ES calculation and relate it to the various study designs and methods of reporting results, choose 2; if authors provide ES information but do not relate it to various study designs, choose 1; if ES is not discussed at all, choose 0.* (Authors) |
| **13.** Was the likelihood of publication bias assessed? (0–1) | Asymmetries in effect sizes are examined as evidence of potential publication bias and include a combination of graphical aids (e.g., funnel plot, other available tests) and/or statistical tests (e.g., Egger regression test). (AMSTAR item 10) |

[a] Items in italics were adapted from the original scale or added by the authors.

of meta-analytic reviews, results were represented. Because this expanded AMSTAR scale addresses quality in reviews of childhood and adolescent sexuality (CAS), we labeled it AMSTAR$_{CAS}$. Each item was completed according to whether the report fully satisfied the criterion, partially satisfied it, did not satisfy it, or whether it was not possible to answer whether the report satisfied the criterion. Some items were deemed not to apply to systematic reviews. The percentage of AMSTAR$_{CAS}$ items that each reported study satisfied completely, out of the number that were relevant, served as a *broad index* of methodological quality.

## Results

Figure 3.1 shows the progression of citations through the steps of the selection process, Table 3.2 summarizes each study qualitatively, and Table 3.3 lists the characteristics of the reviews. The 33 systematic reviews and 34 meta-analyses that qualified for this review were published between 1986 and 2011, and reviewed widely varying child and adolescent sexuality

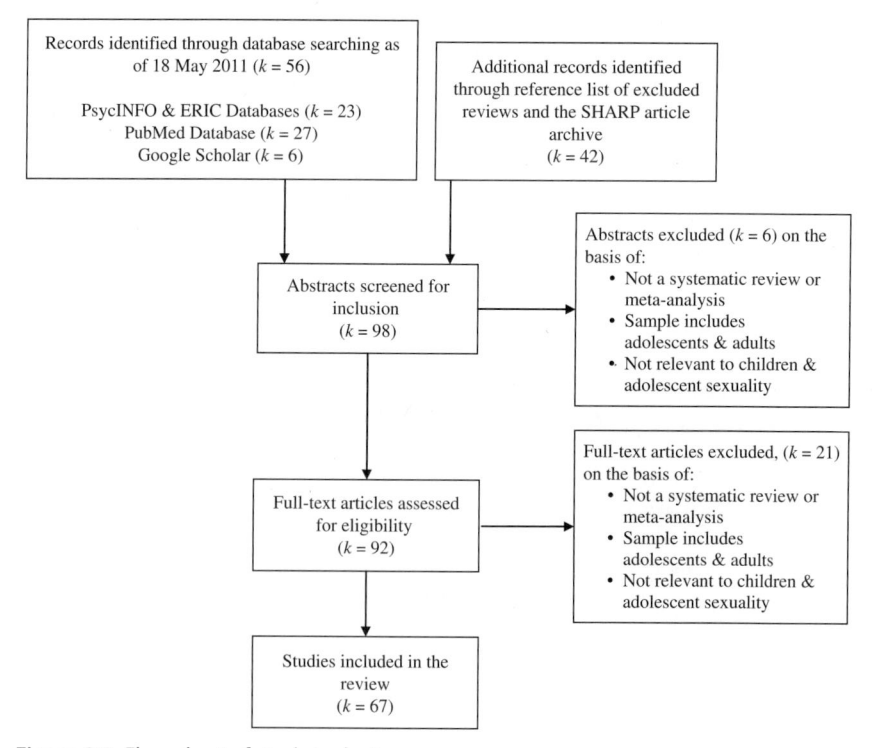

**Figure 3.1** Flow chart of study inclusion.

Table 3.2 Description of Included Reviews Addressing Child and Adolescent Sexuality*

| Citation | Focus | Outcomes |
|---|---|---|
| Afable-Munsuz et al. (2006) | To ascertain the relationship between acculturation and sexual behavior in Latinos | Sexual risk behaviors, fertility-related outcomes, beliefs and norms related to healthy outcomes |
| Applegate (1998) | Reviewed AIDS education programs | Knowledge, change in attitude, behavior, and behavioral intentions |
| Bennett et al. (2005) | School-based abstinence programs vs. contraceptive plus abstinence programs | Pregnancy rates, contraceptive use, knowledge, and abstinence |
| Bertrand et al. (2006) | To review the strength of the evidence for the effects of three types of mass media interventions (radio only, radio with supporting media, or radio and television with supporting media) on HIV/AIDS-related behavior among young people in developing countries, and to assess whether these interventions reach the threshold of evidence needed to recommend widespread implementation | Sexual risk behavior, HIV knowledge, self-efficacy, change in social norms, interpersonal communication, and increased access to the health services |
| Brener et al. (2003) | Effect of cognitive and situational factors on self-reports | Alcohol, drug, and tobacco use, behaviors on unintentional injuries and violence, dietary, sexual behavior, and physical activity |
| Caldwell (2010) | Methodological factors, and population or study characteristics in relation to sexual recidivism rates | Sexual to non-sexual recidivism |
| Chookaew (2004) | HIV/AIDS prevention interventions, program design and implementation on behavior change | Knowledge, attitudes, beliefs, self-efficacy and behaviors |
| Corcoran et al. (2007) | Examining the effect of teenage parent programs to reduce repeat pregnancy | Repeat pregnancy |

* A complete list of the citations is available from the authors.

(Continued)

Table 3.2 (Continued)

| Citation | Focus | Outcomes |
|---|---|---|
| DiCenso et al. (2002) | Effectiveness of primary prevention strategy for sexual behavior | Delay sexual intercourse, improve use of birth control, and reduce incidence of unintended pregnancy |
| DiCenso (1996) | Determining predictors and effectiveness of primary prevention strategies in improving responsible sexual behavior | Sexual intercourse, birth control use, and/or pregnancy |
| DiClemente et al. (2005) | Assessing program and methodological characteristics related to sexual risk behaviors | Reducing the risk of acquiring sexually transmitted infections |
| Downing et al. (2011) | Assess and compare parent/family-based programs in reducing poor sexual health outcomes using quality assessment and methodological critique | Reduce poor sexual health outcomes, increase communication about sex and relationships |
| Franklin et al. (1997) | Primary prevention of pregnancy | Sexual activity, contraceptive use, and pregnancy rates or childbirths |
| Gallant et al. (2004) | Evaluated school-based HIV/AIDS risk reduction programs in Sub-Saharan Africa | Knowledge, attitude, intentions, and sexual risk behavior change |
| Genoves et al. (2006) | Assess the quality and effectiveness of treatment programs decreasing the reoffense rate in secure corrections | Reduce recidivism rates |
| Guyatt et al. (2000) | Compare the results of randomized trials and observational studies of interventions to prevent adolescent pregnancy | Sexual risk behavior and pregnancy |
| Herrick et al. (2011) | Examining whether sexual minority youth report higher rates of sex while intoxicated | Frequency of sex under drug effects |

| | | |
|---|---|---|
| House, Bates, et al. (2010) | Assess the relation between competence and sexual-plus-reproductive health outcomes | Ever had sex, recent sex, early sexual debut, use of contraception, condom use, number of partners, frequency of sex, sexual risk index, STI infection, pregnancy, and intentions |
| House, Mueller, et al. (2010) | Assess the influence of character on sexual and reproductive health | Pregnancy |
| Imamura et al. (2007) | Review micro-level studies to identify possible risk or protective factors of pregnancy | Possible risk or protective factors of pregnancy |
| Jemmott et al. (2000) | Review the effects of behavioral interventions on heterosexual HIV sexual risk behavior | Condom use, abstinence, number of partners, perceived self-efficacy, behavioral intentions |
| Johnson et al. (2003) | Review studies testing the effects of HIV sexual risk reduction interventions | Improve risk reduction in same-sex groups and the effectiveness of participant features |
| Johnson et al. (2011) | Update the review on testing the efficacy of HIV sexual risk reduction interventions | Self-report of protected penetrative sexual behavior, communication with sexual partners, objective measurements and biological markers |
| Juarez et al. (1999) | Evaluate and assess the quality of school AIDS prevention programs | Knowledge, attitudes, intentions, sexual risk behavior |
| Kennedy (2006) | Sexual risk behaviors among African Americans | Sexual risk behavior |
| Kim et al. (2008) | Review and methodologically appraise peer-led sex education interventions and evaluate Harden's recommendations | Adherence to Harden et al. (1999) recommendations, sexual risk behavior, knowledge, unintended pregnancy, attitudes, intentions |
| Kim et al. (1997) | Review AIDS prevention interventions in reducing risk behaviors, and examine intervention design issues in relation to outcome measures | Sexual risk behavior, knowledge, attitudes, intentions |
| Kirby et al. (1994) | School-based programs' impact on behavior | Reduce sexual risk-taking behaviors |
| Kirby et al. (2009) | Curriculum-based sex and STD/HIV education programs, impact on behavior | Safer sex behavior change |

*(Continued)*

Table 3.2 (Continued)

| Citation | Focus | Outcomes |
|---|---|---|
| Kirby et al. (2005) | Analyze the impact programs have on sexual risk-taking behaviors | Factors that affect sexual risk behaviors, STI and pregnancy rates, knowledge, and attitudes |
| Kirby et al. (2007) | Evaluate the impact of curriculum-based sex and HIV education programs on sexual behavior | Factors that affect sexual risk behaviors, STI and pregnancy rates, knowledge, and attitudes |
| Klonsky et al. (2008) | Determine the association between childhood sexual abuse and self-injurious behavior | Sexual abuse and self-injurious behavior |
| Lazarus et al. (2010) | Examine the effectiveness of STI interventions | STIs and HIV |
| Levin (2002) | Examine the effectiveness of HIV prevention interventions | Knowledge, attitudes, subjective norms, behavioral intentions, and HIV preventive behavior |
| Macdonald et al. (2006) | Assess the efficacy of cognitive behavioral approaches on sequelae in sexually abused children | Immediate- and long-term sequelae of sexually abused children |
| Magnussen et al. (2004) | Assess the effects of interventions to prevent HIV/AIDS in less developed countries | Safer sex practices, knowledge and perception of risk (HIV/AIDS), self-efficacy of condom negotiation and refusal, uptake of VCT, and reduction in incidence of HIV/AIDS/STDs |
| Marshal et al. (2008) | Review and methodologically critique the relationship between sexual orientation and substance use | Sexual orientation and substance use |
| McCann et al. (2008) | Analyze recidivism rates, assess the role of antisociality and sexual deviancy in sex offenders | Recidivism rates, antisociality, and sexual deviancy |
| Meade et al. (2005) | Document and identify correlates of biological and behavioral outcomes, and review sexual risk reduction interventions | Rates of STD, repeat pregnancy, condom use, and contraception |
| Meyer et al. (2011) | Assess the advance of emergency contraception | Contraception |
| Michielsen et al. (2010) | Assess the effectiveness of HIV prevention interventions on sexual behavior change | Sexual risk behavior |

| | | |
|---|---|---|
| Mmari et al. (2009) | Assess the risk and protective factors in reproductive health in developing countries | Ever had premarital sex, condom use, pregnancy, early childbearing, STIs, and HIV |
| Morrison-Beedy et al. (2004) | Identify rigorous HIV prevention interventions | Sexual behavior and/or biological outcomes |
| Mullen et al. (2002) | Assess the effect of behavioral and social interventions on sexual risk, and the variation in outcomes | Unprotected sex, number of partners, and risk index |
| Nevius (2002) | Assess the efficacy of the prevention of sexual health risk behaviors | Education and parent-child communication about prevention of sexual health risk behaviors, involvement in extracurricular activities, timing of education, intervention, and communication with children |
| Noll et al. (2009) | Relationship between CSA and adolescent pregnancy | Pregnancy and CSA |
| Oringanje et al. (2009) | Assess the effects of primary prevention interventions on unintended pregnancies | Unintended pregnancy |
| Paul-Ebhohimhen et al. (2008) | Evaluate school-based sexual health interventions to prevent HIV/AIDS and STIs | Knowledge, attitudes, behavioral intentions, abstinence, and condom use |
| Pedlow et al. (2003) | Review and methodologically critique HIV risk reduction interventions measuring sexual risk behaviors | Sexual risk behaviors |
| Pedlow et al. (2004) | Clarify rationale for designing and identifying developmentally appropriate strategies and interventions, review RCTs of sexual risk reduction interventions, and provide recommendations for research | Sexual risk behaviors |

*(Continued)*

Table 3.2 (Continued)

| Citation | Focus | Outcomes |
|---|---|---|
| Reading et al. (2007) | Review the prevalence of sexual transmission of genital herpes in children | Sexual transmission |
| Redlak (2003) | Identify predictor variables of recidivism of sex offenders | Sexual recidivism |
| Reitzel et al. (2005) | Effectiveness of sexual offender treatment on recidivism rates among sexual offenders | Recidivism rates |
| Robin et al. (2004) | Factors impacting sexual risk reduction programs' effectiveness | Delay sexual intercourse, condom use, contraceptive use, and frequency of sex |
| Sales et al. (2006) | Examine the strengths of STI risk reduction interventions in a variety of venues | HIV and STI risk reduction |
| Schonbucher et al. (2011) | Prevalence of CSA in Switzerland | CSA prevalence |
| Seto et al. (2010) | Examine the comparison among sex offenders and other offenders | Criminal history, conduct problems, antisocial personality traits/attitudes/beliefs/associations, and substance use |
| Sherr et al. (2009) | Review measures and effects of HIV on neurocognitive outcomes | Neurocognitive outcomes |
| Shoveller et al. (2006) | Assess the degree to which ecological approaches were integrated into empirical research regarding intervention to prevent STIs among adolescents | Integration of an ecological approach, methodological quality, and STI risk behaviors |
| Song et al. (2000) | Analyze the effects of school-based sexuality education on knowledge | Sexual knowledge |
| Tolou-Shams et al. (2010) | Review HIV prevention interventions in juvenile justice settings | HIV attitudes, knowledge, and behaviors |
| Underhill et al. (2008) | To assess the effects of abstinence-plus programs for HIV prevention in high-income countries | HIV attitudes, knowledge, behaviors, and biological self-report |

| | | |
|---|---|---|
| Underhill et al. (2007) | To assess the effects of abstinence-only programs for HIV prevention in high-income countries | HIV behaviors and biological self-report |
| Walker et al. (2004) | Effectiveness of treatments for male adolescent sexual offenders | Recidivism, deviant sexual attitudes and behaviors, and arousal in response to deviant sexual stimuli |
| Whitley et al. (1986) | Contraceptive use in relation to the career model and the decision model | Contraceptive use |
| Wilcox et al. (1997) | Evaluation of abstinence-only programs | HIV knowledge, sexual risk behavior, attitudes, skills, communication, pregnancies, STI, and HIV reduction |
| Yamada et al. (1999) | Effectiveness of primary prevention programs in preventing STDs | Sex behavioral outcomes, diagnosed cases of STDs |

AIDS, acquired immune deficiency syndrome; HIV, human immunodeficiency virus; STD/STI, sexually transmitted disease/infection; CSA, child sexual abuse; RCT, randomized controlled trial; VCT, voluntary counseling and testing.

Table 3.3 Characteristics of the Reviews

| Citation | Review | Year Range of the Search | k (hits) | N | Search Strategy | Key Words | Coding Strategy | Type of Studies | Age | Language | Analysis |
|---|---|---|---|---|---|---|---|---|---|---|---|
| Caldwell (2010) | M | NS | 57 (NS) | 11,219 | Databases, reference list, and contact personnel | List | NS | NS | Under 18 years at the time of the offense | NS | Weighted effect size and moderator analysis |
| Chookaew (2004) | M | 1990–2002 | 28 (3,680) | 13,668 | Databases, reference list, and hand search journals | NS | Agreement 98.9% and quality assessment | RCT | 11–21 | English | Weighted effect size under fixed and random effects, Q for homogeneity, publication bias (funnel plot), and moderator analysis |
| Corcoran et al. (2007) | M | 1970–2004 | 16 (60) | NS | Databases, reference list, hand search journals, and contact personnel | List | Double coding, and quality assessment | Controlled and non-randomized comparison trials | NS | English | Weighted effect size under fixed and random effects, Q for homogeneity, publication bias (fail safe n), and moderator analysis |
| DiCenso et al. (2002) | M | 1970–2000 | 22 (NS) | NS | Databases and reference list | NS | Quality assessment | RCT | 11–18 | NS | Weighted effect size under random effects, $\chi^2$ for homogeneity and moderator analysis |

| DiCenso (1996) | M | 1970–May1993 | NS (1,034) | NS | Databases and reference list | List | κ=0.94, and quality assessment | RCT and cohort studies | NS | English or a language for which a translator was available | Weighted effect size under fixed effects, $\chi^2$ for homogeneity and moderator analysis |
| --- | --- | --- | --- | --- | --- | --- | --- | --- | --- | --- | --- |
| Franklin et al. (1997) | M | 1978–1995 | 32 (>500) | NS | Databases | NS | Double coding and quality assessment | Experimental and quasi-experimental | NS | NS | Weighted effect size, $\chi^2$ for homogeneity, publication bias (fail safe n), and moderator analysis |
| Genoves et al. (2006) | M | 1970–2003 | 30 (1,299) | 5,833 | Databases and hand search journals | List | Double coding | Experimental and quasi-experimental | NS | English, Spanish, French, Portuguese, German, and Italian | Weighted effect size under fixed and random effects, Q for homogeneity and moderator analysis |
| Guyatt et al. (2000) | M | 1970–May1993 | 30 (1,404) | NS | Databases, reference list, hand search, and contact personnel | NR | Double coding | Experimental and observational | <18 | NR | Weighted effect size under random effects, and $\chi^2$ for homogeneity |
| Herrick et al. (2011) | M | NS | 6 (2,917) | NS | Databases | Examples | $r=0.98$ | NS | ≤21 | NS | Weighted effect size under random effects, publication bias (fail-safe n, Begg and Egger's tests), and moderator analysis |

(*Continued*)

Table 3.3 (Continued)

| Citation | Review | Year Range of the Search | k (hits) | N | Search Strategy | Key Words | Coding Strategy | Type of Studies | Age | Language | Analysis |
|---|---|---|---|---|---|---|---|---|---|---|---|
| Jemmott et al. (2000) | M | NS | 36 (NS) | 30,656 | NS | NS | NS | Experimental and quasi-experimental | 11–21 | NS | Weighted effect size and moderator analysis |
| Johnson et al. (2003) | M | <Jan-2001 | 45 (NS) | 35,282 | Databases, reference list, hand search journals, conference proceedings, and contact personnel | NS | Inter-rater reliability of 0.91 | Experimental and quasi-experimental | NS | NS | Weighted effect size, under fixed effects, Q for homogeneity and moderator analysis |
| Johnson et al. (2011) | M | <Dec-2008 | 67 (NS) | 51,240 | Databases, reference list, hand search journals, and contact personnel | NS | Inter-rater reliability of 0.91 and quality assessment | RCT and quasi-experimental | NS | NS | Weighted effect size under mixed, fixed, and random effects, $\chi^2$ for homogeneity, and moderator analysis |
| Kennedy (2006) | M | 1993–2003 | 79 (671) | 3,976 | Databases, reference list, hand search journals, and contact personnel | List | $r=0.90$, $\kappa=0.75$ | NS | $\leq 21$ | English | Weighted effect size under fixed and random effects, Q for homogeneity, and moderator analysis |

| | | | | | | | | |
|---|---|---|---|---|---|---|---|---|
| Kim et al. (2008) | M | 1998–2005 | 13 (4,500) | NS | Databases, reference list, hand search journals, and contact personnel | List | Quality assessment | RCT and quasi-randomized controlled trials | 10–19 | English | Weighted effect size under random effects, $I^2$ for homogeneity, publication bias (funnel plot) |
| Kim et al. (1997) | M | Jan 1983–Nov 1995 | 40 (102) | NS | Databases, reference list, hand search journals, and published conference abstracts | List | NS | NS | 10–18 | NS | Weighted effect size, $\chi^2$ for homogeneity, and moderator analysis |
| Kirby et al. (2009) | M | 1990> | 55 (NS) | NS | NS | NS | NS | Experimental and quasi-experimental, with pretest and posttest data and matching | NS | NS | NS |
| Klonsky et al. (2008) | M | <June 2006 | 56 (156) | NS | Databases | List | NS | NS | NS | NS | Weighted effect size, under fixed and random effects, Q for homogeneity, publication bias (funnel plot and Egger's test), and moderator analysis |

(*Continued*)

Table 3.3 (Continued)

| Citation | Review | Year Range of the Search | k (hits) | N | Search Strategy | Key Words | Coding Strategy | Type of Studies | Age | Language | Analysis |
|---|---|---|---|---|---|---|---|---|---|---|---|
| Levin (2002) | M | 1989–1999 | 58 (NS) | 25,000 | Databases, reference list and tables of content in relevant journals | List | Inter-rater reliability of 0.88 | Experimental and quasi-experimental | mean age <18 | NS | Weighted effect size under fixed effects, Q for homogeneity, and moderator analysis |
| Macdonald et al. (2006) | M | June 2008 | 10 (377) | NS | Databases, reference list, and contact personnel | Boolean | Double coding and quality assessment | RCT and quasi-randomized controlled trials | <18 | NS | Weighted effect size under random effects, $I^2$ and $\chi^2$ for homogeneity, and moderator analysis |
| McCann et al. (2008) | M | NS | 18 (50) | 3,189 | Databases | List | NS | Longitudinal design | <20 | NS | Weighted effect size under fixed effects, Q for homogeneity, and moderator analysis |
| Michielsen et al. (2010) | M | May 2009 | 31 (758) | 50,990 | Databases, reference list, websites, and previous reviews | List | Double coding and quality assessment | Randomized and parallel group studies | 10–25 | NS | Weighted effect size under random effects, $I^2$ for homogeneity, publication bias (funnel plot), and moderator analysis |

Inclusion Criteria

| | | | | | | | | |
|---|---|---|---|---|---|---|---|---|
| Mullen et al. (2002) | M | 1988–1998 | 20 (24) | NS | Databases, hand search, and contact personnel | NS | Double coding | NS | 13–19 | NS | Weighted effect size under fixed and random effects, Q for homogeneity, publication bias (funnel plot, Egger's and Begg's test), and moderator analysis |
| Nevius (2002) | M | 1966–2001 | 69 (150) | 38,104 | Databases and books | NS | NS | NS | 11–24 | NS | Weighted effect size, Q for homogeneity, and moderator analysis |
| Noll et al. (2009) | M | 1980–2007 | 13 (407) | NS | Databases, reference sections of identified studies, and literature reviews | Examples | Inter-rater reliability of 0.69–1 | NS | NS | English | Weighted effect size under random effects, Q for homogeneity, and moderator analysis |
| Oringanje et al. (2009) | M | Nov 2009 | 41 (98) | 95,662 | Databases, cross-reference, hand search, and contact personnel | Boolean | Double coding and quality assessment | Individual and cluster RCTs | 10–19 | NS | Weighed effect size under fixed and random effects, $I^2$ and $\chi^2$ for homogeneity, publication bias (funnel plot), and moderator analysis |

(*Continued*)

Table 3.3 (Continued)

| Citation | Review | Year Range of the Search | k (hits) | N | Search Strategy | Key Words | Coding Strategy | Type of Studies | Age | Language | Analysis |
|---|---|---|---|---|---|---|---|---|---|---|---|
| Redlak (2003) | M | NS | 13 (NS) | 1,681 | Databases, papers, and contact personnel | List | NS | Matched longitudinal or retrospective design with FUPs | NS | NS | NS |
| Reitzel et al. (2005) | M | 1975–2003 | 33 (929) | 5,335 | Databases and reference list | List | $\kappa=0.85$, quality assessment | Random assignment or quasi-experimental | 7–20 | NS | Weighted ESs under random-effects model, Q for homogeneity, publication bias (file drawer), and moderator analysis |
| Seto et al. (2010) | M | 1975–2008 | 59 (NS) | 17,248 | Databases, reference list, conference abstracts, and contact personnel | List | Double coding | NS | 12–18 | English | Weighted effect size under random effects, Q for homogeneity, and moderator analysis |
| Song et al. (2000) | M | 1960–1997 | 67 (345) | NS | Databases, manual searches, and letters requesting unpublished reports | Examples | NS | NS | grades 5–12 | NS | Weighted effect size |

Inclusion Criteria

| | | | | | | | | | |
|---|---|---|---|---|---|---|---|---|---|
| Tolou-Shams et al. (2010) | M | NS | 16 (259) | 3,700 | Databases and reference list | Examples | NS | RCTs with pretest | 13–18 | NS | Weighted effect size |
| Walker et al. (2004) | M | NS | 10 (12) | NS | Databases, contact personnel via email and phone | List | NS | Experimental and quasi-experimental | NS | NS | Weighted effect size |
| Whitley et al. (1986) | M | NR | 134 (NS) | NS | Databases and reference list | List | NS | Experimental and quasi-experimental | NS | NS | Effect size |
| Wilcox et al. (1997) | M | NR | 31 (NS) | NS | Databases and contact personnel | NS | NS | Experimental, quasi-experimental, and single group comparison | NS | NS | Vote counting |
| Marshal et al. (2008) | M and SR | NS | 18 (289) | NS | Databases, reference list, and contact personnel | Examples | Inter-rater reliability of 0.95 | NS | mean age<18 (upper bound<21) | NS | Weighted effect size under random and mixed effects, Q for homogeneity, and publication bias (Egger's and Begg's tests), moderator analysis |
| Afable-Munsuz et al. (2006) | SR | 1985–2006 | 17 (705) | NS | Databases and reference list | List | NS | Experimental and quasi-experimental | <25 | English | NA |

(*Continued*)

**Table 3.3** (Continued)

| Citation | Review | Year Range of the Search | k (hits) | N | Search Strategy | Key Words | Coding Strategy | Type of Studies | Age | Language | Analysis |
|---|---|---|---|---|---|---|---|---|---|---|---|
| | | | | | | | | | Inclusion Criteria | | |
| Applegate (1998) | SR | 1998 | 42 (42) | NS | Databases and reference list | List | NS | RCT | <20 | NS | NA |
| Bennett et al. (2005) | SR | 1980–2002 | 16 (19) | 34,158 | Databases and reference lists | List | NS | RCT | NS | English | NA |
| Bertrand et al. (2006) | SR | 1990–2004 | 15 (NS) | NS | Databases and reference lists | NS | Quality assessment | Experimental, quasi-experimental, and single group comparison | 8–30 | NR | NA |
| Brener et al. (2003) | SR | 1980> | NS | NS | Databases and reference lists | List | NS | NS | NS | NS | NA |
| DiClemente et al. (2005) | SR | 1990> | 9 (354) | NS | Databases | List | Agreement 95% and quality assessment | RCT | NS | NS | NA |
| Downing et al. (2011) | SR | 1990–2009 | 17 (12,108) | NS | Databases | NS | Double coding and quality assessment | SR, M, RCT, NRCT, and CBA | NS | NS | NA |

| Gallant et al. (2004) | SR | 1990–2002 | 14 (32) | NS | Databases, tables of contents, and publication lists from international organizations | NS | Quality assessment | Quasi-experimental with pretest and posttest | <25 | NS | NA |
| House, Bates, et al. (2010) | SR | 1985–2007 | 27 (NS) | NS | Databases and reference list | List | NS | Longitudinal and cross sectional | ≤20 | English | NA |
| House, Mueller, et al. (2010) | SR | 1985–2007 | 131 (NS) | NS | Databases and reference list | Examples | Quality assessment | Longitudinal and cross sectional | ≤20 | English | NA |
| Imamura et al. (2007) | SR | 1995–2005 | 20 (4,444) | NS | Databases, reference lists, and contact personnel | List | Double coding and quality assessment | NS | 13–19 | NS | NA |
| Juarez et al. (1999) | SR | 1990–1995 | 29 (544) | NS | Database | List | Quality assessment | Experimental and quasi-experimental | 13–19 | English, Spanish, and French | NA |
| Kirby et al. (1994) | SR | NS | 23 (NS) | NS | Databases, journals, and contact personnel | NS | NS | Experimental and quasi-experimental | NS | NS | NS |

*(Continued)*

Table 3.3 (Continued)

| Citation | Review | Year Range of the Search | k (hits) | N | Search Strategy | Key Words | Coding Strategy | Type of Studies | Age | Language | Analysis |
|---|---|---|---|---|---|---|---|---|---|---|---|
| Kirby et al. (2005) | SR | 1990> | 83 (NS) | NS | Databases, journals, review of literature, and contact personnel | NS | Double coding | Experimental and quasi-experimental, with pretest and posttest data and matching | 9–24 | NS | NS |
| Kirby et al. (2007) | SR | 1990> | 83 (NS) | NS | Databases, journals, review of literature, and contact personnel | NS | NS | Experimental and quasi-experimental, with pretest and posttest data and matching | 9–24 | NS | NS |
| Lazarus et al. (2010) | SR | 1995–Nov 2005 | 19 (15,892) | NS | Databases | Examples | NS | NS | NS | NS | NA |
| Magnussen et al. (2004) | SR | NS | 16 (NS) | NS | Databases, reference list, hand search journals, and conference proceedings | List | NS | RCT and quasi-experimental | 11–25 | NS | NA |

Inclusion Criteria

| Meade et al. (2005) | SR | 1981–2003 | 51 (NS) | NS | Databases and reference list | List | NS | Longitudinal design | ≤19 (samples with age ≤22 if majority teen) | English | NA |
| Meyer et al. (2011) | SR | 1950–2009 | 19 (NS) | NS | Databases and reference list | List | NS | RCT | ≤24 | English | NA |
| Mmari et al. (2009) | SR | NS | 61 (11,562) | NS | Databases, reference list, and contact personnel | NS | NS | NS | 10–24 | NS | NA |
| Morrison-Beedy et al. (2004) | SR | 1990–2004 | 10 (1,042) | NS | Databases, NIH and CRISP project databases | List | Double coding | RCT | ≤19 | English | NA |
| Paul-Ebhohimhen et al. (2008) | SR | 1986–2006 | 10 (1,020) | NS | Databases, Google, and literature references | Boolean | Double coding and quality assessment | Repeated measures design with control group | <19 | NS | NA |
| Pedlow et al. (2003) | SR | Sep 2000 | 22 (97) | NS | Databases, and reference sections from articles and reviews | List | NS | RCT | 13–19 | NS | NA |
| Pedlow et al. (2004) | SR | <Feb 2003 | 24 (NS) | NS | Databases | NS | NS | RCT | 11–18 | NS | NA |

(*Continued*)

Table 3.3 (Continued)

| Citation | Review | Year Range of the Search | k (hits) | N | Search Strategy | Key Words | Coding Strategy | Type of Studies | Age | Language | Analysis |
|---|---|---|---|---|---|---|---|---|---|---|---|
| Reading et al. (2007) | SR | 2005 | 13 (265) | NS | Databases and additional referenced papers | List | Quality assessment | NS | NS | NS | NA |
| Robin et al. (2004) | SR | 1990–2000 | 24 (101) | NS | Databases, registry, and hand search journals | NS | Double coding | RCT and quasi-experimental | NS | English | NA |
| Sales et al. (2006) | SR | 1994–2004 | 39 (910) | NS | Databases and reviews | Boolean | NS | NS | NS | NS | NA |
| Schonbucher et al. (2011) | SR | Feb 2010 | 15 (352) | NS | Databases and reference list | List | Double coding, and quality assessment | NS | <18 | NR | NA |
| Sherr et al. (2009) | SR | 1988–2007 | 54 (111) | NS | Databases, and hand search coverage of grey literature | Examples | Double coding | NS | Infant–19 | NS | NA |
| Shoveller et al. (2006) | SR | 1995–June 2000 | 35 (584) | NS | Databases, reference list, and hand search | List | Double coding | Experimental and quasi-experimental | 12–18 | English | NA |

Inclusion Criteria

| Underhill et al. (2008) | SR | Feb 2012 | 37 (235) | 37,724 | Databases, cross-reference, hand search, and contact personnel | Boolean | Double coding and quality assessment | RCTs and quasi-RCTs | 11.3–19.3 | NR | NA |
| Underhill et al. (2007) | SR | Feb 2012 | 13 (326) | 15,940 | Databases, cross-reference, hand search, and contact personnel | Boolean | Double coding and quality assessment | RCTs and quasi-RCTs | 9–19.25 | NR | NA |

M, meta-analysis; SR, systematic review; $k$, number of primary studies; (hits), number of relevant citations; N, sample size; RCT, randomized controlled trial; NRCT, non-randomized controlled trial; NA, not applicable; NS, not specified; NR, no restriction; FUPs, follow-ups; CSA, child sexual abuse; $\kappa$, kappa; $r$, intraclass correlation coefficient; $I^2$, homogeneity index (Higgins & Thompson, 2002); $\chi^2$, chi-square test; $\leq$, less than or equal to; $\geq$, greater than or equal to; $<$, less than; $>$, greater than; Boolean, Cochrane search (inclusion of all the terms and combinations); List, provided a list of key words; Example, provided examples of keywords used; CBA, studies controlled before and after.

topics (Table 3.2). The most common focus of the reviews is HIV/AIDS interventions (27.3% of the systematic reviews and 26.5% of the meta-analyses), followed by sexual risk reduction interventions in general or in relation to situational factors (27.3% of the systematic reviews and 14.7% of the meta-analyses), and pregnancy outcome related to other variables or pregnancy prevention interventions (12.1% of the systematic reviews and 17.7% of the meta-analyses). Some systematic reviews focused on HIV and/or STI interventions (6.1%), but none of the meta-analyses had STI interventions as a main focus. A large number of the meta-analyses (20.6%) focused on sex offenders and sexual recidivism, and only 5.9% on sex and substance use, but none of the systematic reviews did. A focus that was not very frequent for either systematic reviews or meta-analyses is sexual abuse in relation to sexual health of children and/or adolescents (3% and 5.9%, respectively). The age of the sample was defined in the inclusion/exclusion criteria for 76.7% of the included reviews, but only 20.9% of the reports followed the World Health Organization (WHO, 2012) range for adolescents (10 to 19 years). None of the reviews included only adolescents. Of the systematic reviews, 6.1% and 17.6% of the meta-analyses included children and adolescents, and the latter were older than the WHO (2012) definition for adolescents. Eighteen percent of the meta-analyses and 6% of the systematic reviews reported ages in the WHO (2012) range and above, and 14.7% of the meta-analyses and 33.3% of the systematic reviews included that age range and below. The age range was not reported in about the same percentage of systematic reviews and meta-analyses, 30.3% vs. 35.3%.

The number of studies included in the reviews varied from 6 to 134 ($M = 34.85 \pm 26.55$), with a similar range for systematic reviews (9 to 131; $M = 30.75 \pm 25.22$) and for meta-analyses (6 to 134; $M = 38.82 \pm 25.58$); one systematic review and one meta-analysis did not report the number of studies included. Most of the studies included in these reviews were randomized controlled trials (RCTs), or followed a quasi-experimental design (51.5% and 47.1% for systematic reviews and meta-analyses, respectively). More systematic reviews than meta-analyses had as an inclusion criterion exclusively including RCTs (21.2% and 11.8%, respectively). Three of the meta-analyses and five of the systematic reviews included only studies with quasi-experimental designs. Only three (9.1%) systematic reviews reported their total number of participants ($M = 2,661 \pm 9,031$), and only 16 (47.1%) of the meta-analyses provided a total sample size ($M = 11,552 \pm 21,188$).

As Table 3.4 shows, total methodological quality ranged from 14.29% to 90.48% of the total points possible ($M = 54.7 \pm 16.8\%$), with significantly

**Table 3.4** Item-by-item Methodological Quality of Meta-Analyses and Systematic Reviews Related to Adolescents and Child Sexuality as Judged by the AMSTAR$_{CAS}$[a]

| | Individual Items | | | | | | | | | | | | | | Percent |
|---|---|---|---|---|---|---|---|---|---|---|---|---|---|---|---|
| Review | 1 | 2 | 3 | 4 | 5 | 6 | 7 | 8 | 9 | 10 | 11 | 12 | 13 | Total | Satisfactory |
| **Meta-analyses** | | | | | | | | | | | | | | | |
| Caldwell (2010) | 1 | 1 | 0 | 2 | 1 | 1 | 0 | 1 | 0 | 0 | 2 | 0 | 0 | 9 | 42.9 |
| Chookaew (2004) | 1 | 1 | 2 | 2b | 0 | 1 | 2 | 1 | 1 | 0 | 3 | 2 | 1 | 17 | 81.0 |
| Corcoran et al. (2007) | 1 | 1 | 1 | 2 | 1 | 1 | 0 | 1 | 2 | 0 | 3 | 1 | 1 | 15 | 71.4 |
| DiCenso (1996) | 1 | 1 | 2 | 2 | 1 | 1 | 1 | 1 | 1 | 0 | 3 | 1 | 0 | 15 | 73.3 |
| DiCenso et al. (2002) | 1 | 1 | 0 | 2 | 0 | 1 | 0 | 1 | 1 | 0 | 3 | 0 | 0 | 11 | 71.4 |
| Franklin et al. (1997) | 1 | 1 | 1 | 1 | 0 | 0 | 0 | 1 | 2 | 0 | 3 | 2 | 1 | 13 | 61.9 |
| Genoves et al. (2006) | 1 | 1 | 1 | 2 | 1 | 1 | 0 | 1 | 2 | 0 | 3 | 2 | 0 | 13 | 86.7 |
| Guyatt et al. (2000) | 1 | 1 | 1 | 2 | 0 | 1 | 0 | 0 | 0 | 0 | 2 | 1 | 0 | 9 | 42.9 |
| Herrick et al. (2011) | 1 | 1 | 2 | 1 | 1 | 0 | 0 | 1 | 0 | 0 | 2 | 0 | 1 | 10 | 47.6 |
| Jemmott et al. (2000) | 1 | 1 | 0 | 0 | 0 | 0 | 0 | 1 | 0 | 0 | 2 | 2 | 0 | 7 | 33.3 |
| Johnson et al. (2003) | 1 | 1 | 2 | 2 | 0 | 1 | 0 | 1 | 0 | 0 | 3 | 2 | 0 | 13 | 61.9 |
| Johnson et al. (2011) | 1 | 1 | 2 | 2 | 0 | 1 | 1 | 1 | 2 | 1 | 3 | 2 | 0 | 17 | 81.0 |
| Kennedy (2006) | 1 | 1 | 2 | 2 | 1 | 1 | 1 | 1 | 0 | 0 | 3 | 1 | 0 | 14 | 66.7 |
| Kim et al. (2008) | 1 | 1 | 0 | 2 | 1 | 1 | 0 | 1 | 2 | 0 | 2 | 0 | 1 | 12 | 52.4 |
| Kim et al. (1997) | 1 | 1 | 0 | 2 | 1 | 1 | 0 | 1 | 0 | 0 | 3 | 1 | 0 | 11 | 57.1 |
| Kirby et al. (2009) | 1 | 1 | 0 | 0 | 0 | 0 | 0 | 1 | 0 | 0 | 0 | 0 | 0 | 3 | 46.7 |
| Klonsky et al. (2008) | 1 | 0 | 0 | 1 | 1 | 1 | 1 | 1 | 0 | 0 | 3 | 1 | 1 | 10 | 47.6 |
| Levin (2002) | 1 | 1 | 2 | 2 | 1 | 1 | 0 | 1 | 0 | 0 | 3 | 1 | 0 | 13 | 61.9 |
| Macdonald et al. (2006) | 1 | 1 | 1 | 2 | 2 | 1 | 1 | 1 | 2 | 1 | 3 | 2 | 0 | 18 | 85.7 |
| Marshal et al. (2008) | 1 | 1 | 2 | 2 | 1 | 1 | 0 | 1 | 0 | 0 | 3 | 1 | 1 | 14 | 66.7 |
| McCann et al. (2008) | 1 | 1 | 0 | 1 | 1 | 1 | 0 | 1 | 0 | 0 | 3 | 2 | 0 | 11 | 52.4 |
| Michielsen et al. (2010) | 1 | 1 | 1 | 2 | 1 | 1 | 1 | 1 | 1 | 1 | 3 | 1 | 1 | 16 | 76.2 |

(*Continued*)

Table 3.4 Continued

| Review | \multicolumn{13}{c}{Individual Items} | Total | Percent Satisfactory |
|---|---|---|---|---|---|---|---|---|---|---|---|---|---|---|---|
| | 1 | 2 | 3 | 4 | 5 | 6 | 7 | 8 | 9 | 10 | 11 | 12 | 13 | | |
| Mullen et al. (2002) | 1 | 1 | 1 | 2 | 0 | 1 | 2 | 1 | 0 | 0 | 3 | 2 | 1 | 15 | 71.4 |
| Nevius (2002) | 1 | 1 | 0 | 1 | 0 | 1 | 0 | 0 | 0 | 0 | 3 | 2 | 0 | 10 | 47.6 |
| Noll et al. (2009) | 1 | 1 | 2 | 2 | 1 | 0 | 0 | 1 | 0 | 0 | 3 | 1 | 0 | 12 | 57.1 |
| Oringanje et al. (2009) | 1 | 1 | 1 | 2 | 2 | 1 | 2 | 1 | 1 | 1 | 3 | 2 | 1 | 19 | 90.5 |
| Redlak (2003) | 1 | 1 | 0 | 2 | 1 | 1 | 0 | 1 | 0 | 0 | 0 | 0 | 0 | 7 | 33.3 |
| Reitzel et al. 2005 | 1 | 1 | 2 | 2 | 1 | 1 | 0 | 1 | 1 | 0 | 3 | 2 | 1 | 16 | 76.2 |
| Seto et al. (2010) | 1 | 1 | 1 | 2 | 1 | 1 | 0 | 1 | 0 | 0 | 3 | 2 | 0 | 13 | 61.9 |
| Song et al. (2000) | 1 | 1 | 0 | 2 | 1 | 1 | 0 | 1 | 0 | 0 | 3 | 0 | 0 | 10 | 47.6 |
| Tolou-Shams et al. (2010) | 1 | 1 | 0 | 2 | 1 | 1 | 0 | 1 | 0 | 0 | 1 | 2 | 0 | 10 | 66.7 |
| Walker et al. (2004) | 1 | 1 | 0 | 2 | 1 | 1 | 0 | 1 | 0 | 0 | 1 | 2 | 0 | 10 | 47.6 |
| Whitley et al. (1986) | 1 | 1 | 0 | 2 | 1 | 1 | 0 | 0 | 0 | 0 | 0 | 0 | 0 | 6 | 28.6 |
| Wilcox et al. (1997) | 1 | 1 | 0 | 2 | 0 | 1 | 0 | 1 | 0 | 0 | 0 | 1 | 0 | 7 | 33.3 |

**Systematic reviews**

| | | | | | | | | | | | | | | | |
|---|---|---|---|---|---|---|---|---|---|---|---|---|---|---|---|
| Afable-Munsuz et al. (2006) | 1 | 1 | 0 | 2 | 1 | 1 | 0 | 1 | 0 | | | | | 7 | 46.7 |
| Applegate (1998) | 1 | 1 | 0 | 2 | 1 | 1 | 0 | 1 | 0 | | | | | 7 | 46.7 |
| Bennett et al. (2005) | 1 | 1 | 0 | 2 | 1 | 1 | 0 | 1 | 0 | | | | | 7 | 46.7 |
| Bertrand et al. (2006) | 1 | 1 | 0 | 2 | 0 | 1 | 0 | 1 | 1 | | | | | 7 | 46.7 |
| Brener et al. (2003) | 1 | 0 | 0 | 2 | 1 | 1 | 0 | 1 | 0 | | | | | 6 | 40.0 |
| DiClemente et al. (2005) | 1 | 1 | 2 | 1 | 1 | 0 | 0 | 1 | 2 | | | | | 10 | 66.7 |
| Downing et al. (2011) | 1 | 1 | 1 | 1 | 0 | 0 | 1 | 1 | 2 | | | | | 8 | 53.3 |
| Gallant et al. (2004) | 1 | 1 | 0 | 2 | 0 | 1 | 0 | 1 | 1 | | | | | 7 | 46.7 |
| House, Bates et al. (2010) | 1 | 1 | 0 | 2 | 1 | 1 | 0 | 1 | 0 | | | | | 7 | 46.7 |
| House, Mueller et al. (2010) | 1 | 0 | 0 | 2 | 1 | 1 | 0 | 1 | 1 | | | | | 7 | 46.7 |

| | | | | | | | | | |
|---|---|---|---|---|---|---|---|---|---|
| Juarez et al. (1999) | 1 | 1 | 0 | 0 | 0 | 0 | 1 | 8 | 53.3 |
| Kirby et al. (1994) | 1 | 1 | 0 | 2 | 1 | 0 | 0 | 5 | 33.3 |
| Kirby et al. (2005) | 1 | 1 | 1 | 2 | 0 | 1 | 1 | 7 | 40.0 |
| Kirby et al. (2007) | 1 | 1 | 0 | 2 | 0 | 1 | 1 | 6 | 14.3 |
| Lazarus et al. (2010) | 1 | 1 | 0 | 1 | 1 | 0 | 1 | 5 | 33.3 |
| Magnussen et al. (2004) | 1 | 1 | 0 | 2 | 1 | 1 | 1 | 7 | 46.7 |
| Meade et al. (2005) | 1 | 1 | 0 | 2 | 1 | 1 | 1 | 7 | 46.7 |
| Meyer et al. (2011) | 1 | 1 | 0 | 2 | 1 | 1 | 1 | 7 | 46.7 |
| Mmari et al. (2009) | 1 | 1 | 0 | 2 | 0 | 1 | 1 | 6 | 40.0 |
| Morrison-Beedy et al. (2004) | 1 | 1 | 1 | 2 | 1 | 1 | 1 | 8 | 53.3 |
| Paul-Ebhohimhen et al. (2008) | 1 | 1 | 1 | 2 | 2 | 1 | 1 | 11 | 73.3 |
| Pedlow et al. (2003) | 1 | 1 | 0 | 2 | 1 | 1 | 1 | 7 | 46.7 |
| Pedlow et al. (2004) | 1 | 1 | 0 | 0 | 0 | 0 | 1 | 3 | 20.0 |
| Reading et al. (2007) | 1 | 1 | 0 | 2 | 1 | 1 | 1 | 8 | 53.3 |
| Robin et al. (2004) | 1 | 1 | 1 | 2 | 0 | 1 | 1 | 7 | 46.7 |
| Sales et al. (2006) | 1 | 1 | 0 | 2 | 2 | 1 | 1 | 8 | 53.3 |
| Schonbucher et al. (2011) | 1 | 1 | 1 | 2 | 1 | 1 | 1 | 10 | 66.7 |
| Sherr et al. (2009) | 1 | 1 | 1 | 2 | 1 | 1 | 1 | 8 | 53.3 |
| Shoveller et al. (2006) | 1 | 0 | 1 | 2 | 0 | 0 | 0 | 4 | 26.7 |
| Underhill et al. (2008) | 1 | 1 | 1 | 2 | 2 | 1 | 1 | 12 | 80.0 |
| Underhill et al. (2007) | 1 | 1 | 1 | 2 | 2 | 1 | 1 | 12 | 80.0 |
| Yamada et al. (1999) | 1 | 1 | 1 | 2 | 2 | 1 | 2 | 12 | 80.0 |

[a]See Table 3.1 for scoring.

($p = 0.043$) higher quality for meta-analyses ($M = 58.8 \pm 18.3\%$) than for systematic reviews ($M = 50.5 \pm 14.1\%$). More recent meta-analyses have marginally better scores than earlier meta-analyses ($r = 0.32, p = 0.064$), but this pattern was not present among systematic reviews ($r = 0.12, p = 0.50$).

All reviews (100%) satisfactorily followed a priori designs, but almost half did not satisfy quality criteria items related to study selection (52.2%) and literature search and duplicate effort (31.3%); more than three-quarters of the reviews provided no lists of included and excluded studies (77.6%); over half did not evaluate the scientific quality of the included studies (64.2%). Of the items applicable only to meta-analyses (items from 10 to 13), almost none of the meta-analyses (88.2%) interpreted their results in relation to the study quality; yet most did meet assumptions about heterogeneity and moderator analyses (88.3%); a large percentage of the meta-analyses discussed and/or described in detail the type of effect size metric they used (79.4%); finally, only 32.3% assessed the likelihood of publication bias (see Table 3.5).

## Discussion

Child and adolescent sexuality (CAS) research has been synthesized as early as 1986 (Whitley & Schofield, 1986), but the evidence we have gathered suggests that more and better reviews are needed. It was rare that any of the 67 meta-analyses and systematic reviews that we quality coded satisfied even 75% of the quality criteria on the AMSTAR$_{CAS}$, although it should be noted reviews conducted before the AMSTAR was developed had no particular quality guidelines to follow. Qualitatively, as well, many CAS topics remain of contemporary interest (e.g., child sexual abuse, sex and substance use). Our findings (Table 3.2) indicate that a majority of the reviews focused on HIV/AIDS interventions, although this finding may seem to contradict UNICEF's statements (2010). Nonetheless, it is true that interventions have focused primarily on particular groups (e.g., HIV-negative adolescents), therefore enforcing the concept that specific interventions are appropriate for some populations but not all. With the growing use of technology, greater access to different populations, settings, and valid health information (Malow et al., 2007), we may see an increase of literature in this area of research.

The fact that many reviews have been conducted in the same areas of investigation suggests that scholars are not viewing the existence of a systematic review or meta-analysis as a dead end for a literature, a point beyond which nothing more needs to be known. Alternatively, it

Table 3.5 Items Assessing Methodological Quality of the 67 Reviews, Observed Interjudge Agreement, and Tallies of the Reviews for which the Item was not Applicable (NA), Unknown, Addressed, and Completely Satisfactory[a]

| Question | Percent Agreement | Unknown | Addressed | Completely Satisfactory |
|---|---|---|---|---|
| **A. A priori design** | | | | |
| 1. Was an "a priori" design provided? | 100 | 0% | 100% | NA |
| **B. Literature search and duplicate effort** | | | | |
| 2. Were population variables defined and considered in the methods? | 91 | 6% | 94% | NA |
| 3. Was there duplicate study selection and data extraction? | 100 | 52.2% | 31.3% | 16.4% |
| 4. Was a comprehensive literature search performed? | 98 | 6% | 11.9% | 82.1% |
| 5. Is it possible to replicate the search? | 87 | 31.3% | 58.2% | 10.4% |
| 6. Did the inclusion criteria permit grey literature? | 85 | 19.4% | 80.6% | NA |
| 7. Was a list of studies (included and excluded) provided? | 92 | 77.6% | 13.4% | 9% |
| **C. Coding of studies** | | | | |
| 8. Were the characteristics of the included studies provided? | 99 | 6% | 94% | NA |
| 9. Was the scientific quality of the included studies assessed and documented? | 87 | 64.2% | 35.8% | NA |
| **D. Analysis and interpretation (applicable to the 34 meta-analyses)** | | | | |
| 10. Did results depend on study quality, either overall or in interaction with moderators? | 93 | 88.3% | 11.8% | NA |
| 11. Were the methods used to combine the findings of studies appropriate? | 94 | 11.8% | 23.6% | 64.6% |
| 12. Was the effect size index chosen justified, statistically? | 98 | 20.5% | 32.3% | 47.1% |
| 13. Was the likelihood of publication bias assessed? | 96 | 67.6% | 32.34% | NA |

[a] See Table 3.1 for the rationale to each question.

is plausible that some reviews were conducted with no knowledge of a competing review, because not all reviews appear in all common research literature databases. Comparisons of the results of such reviews would seem valuable for future scholarship. Contradictions between reviews deserve attention, especially when they result from strong methods (such as those that fulfill more of the AMSTAR$_{CAS}$ items). Indeed, speaking more generally, carefully conducted reviews can often be the best medicine for a literature, by documenting the robustness with which certain associations are attained, resulting in a sturdier foundation on which future theories may rest. A carefully conducted systematic review or meta-analysis of primary-level studies can be designed with the complete literature in mind and therefore have a better chance of contributing new knowledge. In this fashion, scientific resources can be directed most efficiently toward gains in knowledge.

As time passes and new studies continue to accrue rapidly, it seems unavoidable that social scientists must rely more on quantitative syntheses to inform them about the knowledge that has accumulated in their research. Although it is possible that systematic reviews and, particularly, meta-analyses will become the purview of an elite class of researchers who specialize in research integration, as Johnson & Eagly (2000) concluded, it seems more likely that meta-analysis is becoming a routine part

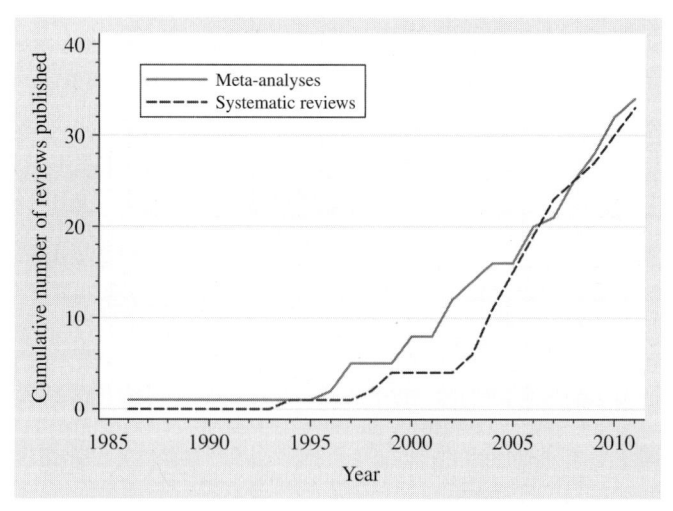

**Figure 3.2** Temporal trends in the numbers of meta-analytic and systematic reviews published, relevant to childhood and adolescent sexuality.

of graduate training in many fields, developing the skills necessary to plying the art and science of meta-analysis to integrate findings across studies as part of their research activities. Indeed, Figure 3.2 shows that reviews related to childhood and adolescent sexuality, whether meta-analytic or systematic, have been published with increasing frequency in the last decade. We are confident that future reviewers will continue to offer such contributions, and will do so with increasingly good methods such as we have advocated in this chapter.

## ACKNOWLEDGEMENT

The preparation of this chapter was facilitated by US Public Health Service grant R01 MH58563-14 to Blair T. Johnson.

## REFERENCES

Bangert-Drowns, R. L. (1997). Some limiting factors in meta-analysis. In W. J. (1997). Bukoski (Ed.), *Meta-analysis of drug abuse prevention programs (National Institute on Drug Abuse Research Monograph)* (Vol. 170). Rockville, MD: U.S. Department of Health and Human Services.

Begg, C. B. (1994). Publication bias. In H. Cooper, & L.V. Hedges (Eds.), *The handbook of research synthesis*. New York, NY: Russell Sage Foundation.

Bennett, S. E., & Assefi, N. P. (2005). School-based teenage pregnancy prevention programs: A systematic review of randomized controlled trials. *Journal of Adolescent Health, 36*(1), 72–81. doi:10.1016/j.jadohealth.2003.11.097.

Caldwell, M. F. (2010). Study characteristics and recidivism base rates in juvenile sex offender recidivism. *International Journal of Offender Therapy and Comparative Criminology, 54*(2), 197–212. doi:10.1177/0306624X08330016.

Card, N. A. (2012). *Applied meta-analysis for social science research*. New York, NY: Guilford Press.

Cochran, W. G. (1954). The combination of estimates from different experiments. *Biometrics, 10*, 101–129.

Cohen, J. (1969). *Statistical power analysis for the behavioral sciences*. New York, NY: Academic Press.

Cooper, H. (1998). *Integrative research: A guide for literature reviews* (3rd ed.). Newbury Park, CA: Sage.

Cooper, H., & Hedges, L.V. (2009). Research synthesis as a scientific process. In H. Cooper, & L.V. Hedges (Eds.), *The handbook of research synthesis and meta-analysis*. New York, NY: Russell Sage.

Cooper, H., Hedges, L.V., & Valentine, J. C. (2009). *The handbook of research synthesis and meta-analysis*. New York: Russell Sage.

Cooper, H., & Rosenthal, R. (1980). Statistical versus traditional procedures for summarizing research findings. *Psychological Bulletin, 87*, 442–449.

DiCenso, A., Guyatt, G., Willan, A., & Griffith, L. (2002). Interventions to reduce unintended pregnancies among adolescents: Systematic review of randomised controlled trials. *British Medical Journal, 324*(7351), 1426–1430. doi:10.1136/bmj.324.7351.1426.

Dunlap, W. P., Cortina, J. M., Vaslow, J. B., & Burke, M. J. (1996). Meta-analysis of experiments with matched groups or repeated measures designs. *Psychological Methods, 1*, 170–177.

Duval, S., & Tweedie, R. (2000). Trim and fill: A simple funnel-plot-based method of testing and adjusting for publication bias in meta-analysis. *Biometrics, 56*(2), 455–463.

Field, A. P. (2001). Meta-analysis of correlation coefficients: A Monte Carlo comparison of fixed- and random-effects methods. *Psychological Methods, 6,* 161–180.

Field, A. P. (2005). Is the meta-analysis of correlation coefficients accurate when population correlations vary? *Psychological Methods, 10,* 444–467.

Frost, J. J., & Forrest, J. D. (1995). Understanding the impact of effective teenage pregnancy prevention programs. *Family Planning Perspectives, 27,* 188–195.

Genovés, V. G., Morales, L. A., & Sánchez-Meca, J. (2006). What works for serious juvenile offenders? A systematic review. *Psicothema, 18*(3), 611–619.

Glass, G. V., McGaw, B., & Smith, M. L. (1981). *Meta-analysis in social research.* Beverly Hills, CA: Sage.

Greenwald, A. G. (1975). Consequences of prejudice against the null hypothesis. *Psychological Bulletin, 82,* 1–20.

Haddock, C. K., Rindskopf, D., & Shadish, W. R. (1998). Using odds ratio as effect sizes for meta-analysis of dichotomous data: A primer on methods and issues. *Psychological Methods, 3,* 339–353.

Hall, S. M., & Brannick, M. T. (2002). Comparison of two random-effects methods of meta-analysis. *Journal of Applied Psychology, 87,* 377–389.

Harden, A., Weston, R., & Oakley, A. (1999). *A review of the effectiveness and appropriateness of peer-delivered health promotion interventions for young people.* London, UK: Social Science Research Unit, Institute of Education, University of London.

Hardy, R. J., & Thompson, S. G. (1998). Detecting and describing heterogeneity in meta-analysis. *Statistics in Medicine, 17,* 841–856.

Harwell, M. (1997). An empirical study of Hedge's homogeneity test. *Psychological Methods, 2,* 219–231.

Hedges, L. V. (1981). Distribution theory for Glass' estimator of effect size and related estimators. *Journal of Educational Statistics, 6,* 107–128.

Hedges, L. V., Cooper, H., & Bushman, B. J. (1992). Testing the null hypothesis in meta-analysis: A comparison of combined probability and confidence interval procedures. *Psychological Bulletin, 111,* 188–194.

Hedges, L. V., & Olkin, I. (1985). *Statistical methods for meta-analysis.* Orlando, FL: Academic Press.

Hedges, L. V., & Vevea, J. L. (1996). Estimating effect size under publication bias: Small sample properties and robustness of a random effects selection model. *Journal of Educational and Behavioral Statistics, 21,* 299–333.

Higgins, J. P. T., & Thompson, S. G. (2002). Quantifying heterogeneity in a meta-analysis. *Statistics in Medicine, 21,* 1539–1558.

Huedo-Medina, T. B., & Johnson, B. T. (2010). *Modelos estadísticos en meta-análisis [Statistical models in meta-analysis].* A Coruña, Spain: Netbiblio.

Huedo-Medina, T. B., Sánchez-Meca, J., Marín-Martínez, F., & Botella, J. (2006). Assesing heterogeneity in meta-analysis: Q statistics or $I^2$ index? *Psychological Methods, 11,* 193–206.

Hunt, M. (1997). *How science takes stock: The story of meta-analysis.* New York, NY: Russell Sage.

Hunter, J. E., & Schmidt, F. L. (2004). *Methods of meta-analysis: Correcting error and bias in research findings* (2nd ed.). Newbury Park, CA: Sage.

Johnson, B. T., & Boynton, M. H. (2008). Cumulating evidence about the social animal: Meta-analysis in social-personality psychology. *Soc Personal Psychol Compass, 2,* 817–841.

Johnson, B. T., Carey, M. P., Marsh, K. L., Levin, K. D., & Scott-Sheldon, L. A. J. (2003). Inteventions to reduce sexual risk for human immunodeficiency virus in adolescents, 1985–2000: A research synthesis. *Archives of Pediatrics & Adolescent Medicine, 157,* 381–388.

Johnson, B. T., & Eagly, A. H. (2000). Quatitative synthesis of social psychological research. In H. T. Reis, & C. M. Judd (Eds.), *Handbook of research methods in social and personality psychology*. London, UK: Cambridge University Press.

Johnson, B. T., & Eagly, A. H. (in press). Meta-analysis of research in social and personality psychology. In H. T. Reis, & C. M. Judd, (Eds.), *Handbook of research methods in social and personality psychology*. London, UK: Cambridge University Press.

Johnson, B. T., Scott-Sheldon, L. A. J., & Carey, M. P. (2010). Meta-synthesis of health behavior change meta-analyses. *American Journal of Public Health*, 100, 2193–2198. doi:10.2105/AJPH.2008.155200.

Johnson, B. T., Scott-Sheldon, L. A. J., Huedo-Medina, T. B., & Carey, M. P. (2011). Interventions to reduce sexual risk for human immunodeficiency virus in adolescents: A meta-analysis of trials, 1985-2008. *Arch Pediatr Adolesc Med*, 165(1), 77–84.

Johnson, B. T., Scott-Sheldon, L. A. J., Snyder, L. B., Noar, S. M., & Huedo-Medina, T. B. (2008). Contemporary approaches to meta-analysis of communication research. In M. D. Slater, A. Hayes, & L. B. Snyder (Eds.), *The Sage guide to advanced data analysis methods for communication research*. Thousand Oaks, CA: Sage.

Johnson, B. T., & Turco, R. (1992). The value of goodness-of-fit indices in meta-analysis: A comment on Hall and Rosenthal. *Communication Monographs*, 59, 388–396.

Kirby, D. (1999). Reflections on two decades of research on teen sexual behavior and pregnancy. *Journal of School Health*, 69(3), 89–94.

Kirby, D. (2002). The impact of schools and school programs upon adolescent sexual behavior. *The Journal of Sex Research*, 39(1), 27–33.

Klonsky, E. D., & Moyer, A. (2008). Childhood sexual abuse and non-suicidal self-injury: Meta-analysis. *Br J Psychiatry*, 192(3), 166–170.

Krippendorf, K. (1980). *Content analysis*. Beverly Hills, CA: Sage.

Lau, J., Ioannidis, J. P. A., Terrin, N., Schmid, C. H., & Olkin, I. (2006). The case of the misleading funnel plot. *BMJ*, 333, 597–600.

Lemeshow, A. R., Blum, R. E., Berlin, J. A., Stoto, M. A., & Colditz, G. A. (2005). Searching one or two databases was insufficient for meta-analysis of observational studies. *Journal of Clinical Epidemiology*, 58, 867–873.

Lipsey, M. W., & Wilson, D. B. (2001). *Practical Meta-analysis*. Thousand Oaks, CA: Sage.

Macdonald, G. M., Higgins, J. P. T., & Ramchandani, P. (2006). Cognitive-behavioural interventions for children who have been sexually abused. *Cochrane Database Syst Rev*, 2012 May 16;5:CD001930.

Malow, R. M., Kershaw, T., Sipsma, H., Rosenberg, R., & Devieux, J. G. (2007). HIV preventive interventions for adolescents: A look back and ahead. *Current HIV/AIDS Reports*, 4, 173–180.

Mann, C. (1994). Can meta-analysis make policy? *Science*, 266, 960–962.

McGrath, R. E., & Meyer, G. J. (2006). When effect sizes disagree: The case of r and d. *Psychological Methods*, 11, 386–401.

McKay, A., Fisher, W., Maticka-Tyndale, E., & Barrett, M. (2001). Adolescent sexual health education: Does it work? Can it work better? An analysis of recent research and media reports. *Canadian Journal of Human Sexuality*, 10(3-4), 127–135.

Moher, D., Liberati, A., Tetzlaff, J., & Altman, D. G. (2009). Preferred reporting items for systematic reviews and meta-analyses: The PRISMA statement. *PLoS Med*, 6(7) doi:10.1371/journal.pmed.1000097.

Morris, S. B., & DeShon, R. P. (2002). Combining effect size estimates in meta-analysis with repeated measures and independent-group designs. *Psychological Methods*, 7, 105–125.

Oringanje, C., Meremikwu, M. M., Eko, H., Esu, E., Meremikwu, A., & Ehiri, J. E. (2009). Interventions for preventing unintended pregnancies among adolescents. *Cochrane Database Syst Rev*(4): CD005215.

Redlak, A. S. (2003). *An exploratory meta-analysis of the predictor variables of juvenile sex offenders who sexually recidivate.* California School of Professional Psychology (Doctoral dissertation). Available from Dissertations and Theses database. (UMI No. 3092415).

Rosenthal, R. (1991). *Meta-analytic procedures for social research (rev. ed.).* Beverly Hills, CA: Sage.

Rosenthal, R. (1995). Writting meta-analytic reviews. *Psychological Bulletin, 118,* 183–192.

Rosenthal, R., & DiMatteo, M. R. (2001). Meta-analysis: Recent developments in quantitative methods for literature reviews. *Annual Review of Psychology, 52,* 59–82.

Sánchez-Meca, J., & Marín-Martínez, F. (1997). Homogeneity tests in meta-analysis: A Monte-Carlo comparison of statistical power and Type I error. *Quality & Quantity, 31,* 385–399.

Seignourel, P., & Albarracín, D. (2002). Calculating effect sizes for designs with between-subjects and within-subjects factors: Methods for partially reported statistics in meta-analysis. *Metodologia de las Ciencias del Comportamiento, 4,* 273–289.

Sharpe, D. (1997). Of apples and oranges, file drawers and garbage: Why validity issues in meta-analysis will not go away. *Clinical Psychology Review, 17,* 881–901.

Shea, B. J., Grimshaw, J. M., Wells, G. A., et al. (2007). Development of AMSTAR: A measurement tool to assess the methodological quality of systematic reviews. *BMC Medical Research Methodology, 7,* 10–17.

Shea, B. J., Hamel, C., Wells, G. A., et al. (2009). AMSTAR is a reliable and valid measurement tool to assess the methodological quality of systematic reviews. *J Clin Epidemiol, 62*(10), 1013–1020.

Sherr, L., Mueller, J., & Varrall, R. (2009). Evidence-based gender findings for children affected by HIV and AIDS—A systematic overview. *AIDS Care, 21*(Suppl. 1), 83–97. doi:10.1080/09540120902923105.

Song, E. Y., Pruitt, B. E., McNamara, J., & Colewell, B. (2000). A meta-analysis examining effects of school sexuality education programs on adolescents' sexual knowledge, 1960–1997. *Journal of School Health, 70*(10), 413–416.

Stroup, D. F., Berlin, J. A., Morton, S. C., et al. (2000). Meta-analysis of observational studies in epidemiology: A proposal for reporting meta-analysis of observational studies in epidemiology (MOOSE) group. *JAMA, 283*(15), 2008–2012.

Sutton, A. J. (2009). Publication bias. In H. Cooper, L. V. Hedges, & J. C. Valentine (Eds.), *The handbook of research synthesis and meta-analysis (pp. 435–452)* (2nd ed.). New York, NY US: Russell Sage Foundation.

The Campbell Collaboration. (2012), from <http://www.campbellcollaboration.org/>.

The Cochrane Collaboration. (2012), from <http://www.cochrane.org/>.

Thompson, R., & Web of Knowledge Web site. Retrieved May 18, 2011, from <apps.isiknowledge.com/>. Updated 2012.

Thornton, A., & Lee, P. (2000). Publication bias in meta-analysis: Its causes and consequences. *Journal of Clinical Epidemiology, 53,* 207–216.

Underhill, K., Operario, D., & Montgomery, P. (2007). Abstinence-only programs for HIV infection prevention in high-income countries. *Cochrane Database of Systematic Reviews*(4): CD005421.

UNICEF. (2010). Annual report.

UNICEF. (2011). The State of the World's Children 2011: Adolescence - An age of opportunity, from <http://www.unicef.org/publications/index_57468.html>

Vevea, J. L., & Hedges, L. V. (1995). A general linear model for estimating effect size in the presence of publication bias. *Psychometrika, 60,* 419–435.

Vevea, J. L., & Woods, C. M. (2005). Publication bias in research synthesis: Sensitivity analysis using a priori weight functions. *Psychological Methods, 10,* 428–443.

White, H. D. (1994). Scientific communication and literature retrieval. In H. Cooper, & L. V. Hedges (Eds.), *The handbook of research synthesis.* New York, NY: Russell Sage.

Whitley, B. E., Jr., & Schofield, J. W. (1986). A meta-analysis of research on adolescent contraceptive use. *Population and Environment*, *8*(3 & 4), 173–203.
World Health Organization. (2012). *Adolescent Health*.
Young, C., & Horton, R. (2005). Putting clinical trials into context. *The Lancet*, *366*, 107–108.

# CHAPTER 4

# Applications of Small-n Research Design in Child and Adolescent Sexuality

**Gregory S. Snyder and Stacy Shaw**
Boys Town Center for Behavioral Health, Boys Town, Nebraska[1]

## INTRODUCTION

The scope of behavior analysis is broad, and the methods developed within this field are generic and readily applicable to any potential subject matter and observable phenomena where individual variability and change are at issue. Indeed, adoption of small-n research designs in medicine, occupational therapy, and psychopharmacology reflects appreciation and respect for improved clinical decision-making and knowledge of individual responding. For example, over 20 years ago, in an examination of 57 published small-n clinical trials in medicine, Guyatt, Keller, Jaeschke, Rosenbloom, Adachi, & Newhouse (1990) observed that nearly 39% of trials prompted immediate changes to treatment, as a result of observed effects, with an additional 18% of physicians ceasing interventions that were planned to continue indefinitely. Overall, the authors concluded that nearly 50 of the total 57 small-n clinical trials studied in their center resulted in observable change in the course of patient care by producing clear clinical and/or statistical distinctions among competing treatments. Human sexuality, sexual development, and remediation of problematic sexual behaviors are equally accessible to small-n methods. We will provide readers with an introduction to the use of small-n methods, and will include examples and considerations for normative and problematic sexualized behavior of children and adolescents, though we have included some examples of adult populations because of the paucity of existing research with children and adolescents. Although we are ardent supporters of small-n designs ourselves, we acknowledge that they are not a panacea.

[1] Correspondence to: Gregory Snyder, Director of Behavioral Health Research, Boys Town Center for Behavioral Health, 13603 Flanagan Blvd., Boys Town, NE 68010. Phone 402-498-3251; email Gregory.Snyder@boystown.org

Large-group experimental designs, such as the Randomized Controlled Trial (RCT), are the analytic tools most frequently used by clinical scientists. Conventional group designs employ random assignment, statistical probability, and sample size to establish causality between measured variables. Indeed, large-scale group methodology continues to be useful in extending our knowledge and evaluating the efficacy of novel treatments. However helpful this is when evaluating and comparing treatment effectiveness in large populations, having a working knowledge of only a single empirical method to the exclusion of other equally valid options is folly. The inherent strengths of group-based designs which rely on statistical analyses of aggregate data are also their greatest weaknesses when explaining individual behavior. Data from individual participants are averaged within groups, and it is the *group* data that are subjected to statistical analyses. Completing the analyses inevitably obscures individual differences. Therefore, applying results from large-group designs to particular individuals is fraught with potential problems. Skinner (1953) criticized conventional methods, believing them to be inferior because knowledge of any "average" individual is useless when clinicians are faced with any particular individual. Examining Skinner's criticism using a contrived example, let's suppose that authors of a published RCT observe that participation in a reinforcement-based skill-training curriculum compared with a wait-list control produced a statistically significant decline in recidivism among a group of adolescent sex offenders. General conclusions about the effect are warranted, though expecting any particular adolescent sex offender who enters your office to respond similarly will likely result in disappointment. Results only outline trends of "average" differences between groups, and result in comparison of two treatment groups. In addition, conventional group methods rely upon statistical power that is dependent upon both sample and effect size (Cohen, 2003). Obtaining sufficient numbers of subjects, creating adequate control groups, and maintaining homogeneity among participants within conditions often conflicts with practical limitations in money, time, and physical resources. These constraints are only heightened when exotic or low base rate behaviors are the phenomena of interest.

As to conventional group aggregation of individuals within "cells," small-n methodology attends to differences through frequent measurement of subject-level data throughout all phases of experimentation. Data remain disaggregated, and analysis is often visual, using logic to deduce causal relationships. Experiment-wise error is reduced as the subject serves both in the "control" and "experimental" phases, with the express purpose of identifying the effects of a variable (e.g., treatment X) on a particular individual. Because data are separate and analyzed individually, statistical analysis is unnecessary, thus further eliminating the need for large sample sizes and constructing adequate control groups.

Small-n designs also lend themselves quite well to component analyses. Specific treatment modules can be systematically introduced and withdrawn to identify whether an individual component is the "active ingredient," or whether synergistic/additive effects of separate components within a larger treatment package exist. Therefore, results obtained through small-n research have rich clinical applicability. Finally, as one does not need to have a working knowledge of multivariate statistics or structural equation modeling, accessibility of results by those in clinical practice increases (Allen, Friman, & Sanger, 1992).

## MEASUREMENT

Problem description and response to intervention is at the heart of useful clinical science. The capacity to describe and modify behavior depends wholly on our ability to accurately measure the phenomenon of interest. In the absence of reliable and valid measurement, our knowledge is meager and limited. Because prediction of, and influence over, behavior is the goal of behavioral science, accurate, valid, and reliable measurement of behavior is essential (Kazdin, 2011). Simply stated, behavior targeted for change must be capable of being measured in such a way as to distinguish when it is present and when it is not (Barlow & Hersen, 1973; Hersen, 2009; Kazdin, 2011). Friman (2009) highlighted a variety of considerations that affect the measurement validity in small-n designs. First, behavior targeted for change should have social validity (Wolf, 1978). First introduced as "social importance" by Montrose Wolf (1978), social validity refers to the subjective value of any particular goals, social appropriateness of the procedures, and lastly the social importance of the effects produced by the methods employed. While seemingly pedestrian, this issue is often overlooked or ill-planned by even the most seasoned clinicians and academicians. Thus, social validity of any measurement is paramount to the success of any methodologically rigorous experiment (Friman, 2009; Kazdin, 1982). For example, Rekers & Lovaas (1974) conducted a methodologically sound intervention targeting feminine (cross-gendered) play and verbal behavior exhibited by a 5-year-old boy. Feminine and masculine play behavior and verbalizations were recorded during clinic sessions and by parents at home, yielding total percentages of gender-consistent (masculine) and gender-inconsistent (feminine) behaviors that were assessed throughout the baseline, treatment, generalization, and reversal elements of the study. Despite the success in obtaining remarkably high inter-observer reliability during home observations (median 94%), selecting gender-based verbal and play behavior as a variable would not be acceptable in today's society, even receiving criticism at the time of publication in 1974 (Davidson, 1976; Winkler, 1977).

According to Friman (2009), to achieve clinical significance, the behaviors assessed must deviate from the normative range, exhibit chronicity across both time and setting, and result in functional impairment in the individual. For instance, while penile tumescence, measured via penile plethysmograph, is often used as a dependent variable for studying male arousal to fetishized objects, reduced arousal may not correspond to reductions in fetishized object use. Thus, while an intervention such as covert sensitization may result in decreased tumescence, and the individual might report appetitive declines, our knowledge of the specific target behavior outside the treatment milieu is limited. While capturing behavior discretely in controlled settings is desirable, measurement of the phenomena in the natural environment should be of paramount importance.

Variables selected for repeated measurement in a small-n design fall into two domains: measures involving time and/or measures involving "countability" (Friman, 2009). Falling under the general rubric of time, response latency and response duration represent the most commonly employed target variables in small-n designs. Response latency refers to the time elapsed between a specific event and the onset of a response, and response duration refers to the time elapsed between onset and cessation of the target behavior. For instance, Abel, Blanchard, Barlow, & Mavissakalian (1975) employed physiological measures of penile tumescence, though specifically measuring the latency between recitation of an erotic story and erection. In many other studies, penile tumescence, as measured by penile plesthymograph, is often paired with repeatedly measured self-reported thoughts and emotions of approach toward relevant stimuli. Duration measurements are often helpful with episodic data that is of extended duration. For instance, duration of masturbation could potentially be a target for measurement because the behavior occurs at high enough rates to make frequency counting an impractical task. As noted previously, small-n designs are frequently used to measure behaviors that have a discrete beginning and end point, and can readily be observed and counted by the subject or by others. Frequency simply refers to the degree by which units or episodes of the behavior are discrete and objectively "countable." While counting the behaviors themselves, frequency measurement can also be employed to track latency between specific behaviors during discrete intervals of time.

## Baseline Measurement

Given the emphasis of behavioral research on observable behavior, behaviors should be able to be measured simultaneously by multiple observers. Similar to conventional group designs, repeated measurements should avoid introducing any extraneous variability by maintaining standardized procedures for measurement such that the time, place, methods, persons, and conditions are constant. Once measurement of a behavior has begun, most small-n designs begin with establishing a baseline. Establishing a baseline means measuring a behavior in the absence of treatment. Because response to intervention or manipulation of an independent variable is of foremost importance, obtaining a well established steady-state in behavior, or baseline, prior to any experimental manipulation is important. Baseline observations provide a description of the behavior as it exists without intervention and allow for the prediction of future behavior, also in the absence of intervention (Kazdin, 1982). The latter function is a subtlety that is frequently overlooked. When shifting from baseline to treatment, the fundamental objective is to determine if a clinically significant discrepancy between baseline and treatment conditions can be established. In order to predict behavior, a valid and reliable measurement is needed.

## WITHDRAWAL AND REVERSAL DESIGNS (AB, ABAB)

The roots of reversal and withdrawal designs lie within the uncontrolled case studies that characterize most of the early case descriptions in clinical psychiatry, medicine, and psychology. Case history methods certainly fostered our understanding of co-occurring symptoms (i.e., syndromes), and aided the development and dissemination of clinical interventions. Simple pre-intervention (baseline) behavior is recorded (A), with the subject subsequently exposed to intervention (B). Given that there may be competing explanations for any observed effect in this scenario, more conservative reversal/withdrawal designs have been developed. The ABAB reversal design is one of the simplest, yet most powerful, devices in single-subject research. As with virtually all other small-n methods, the subject's behavior is measured in the absence of intervention, thereby establishing a baseline.

The experimental variable (B) is introduced while the target behavior continues to be measured. Once stability in the measurement has been established the independent, or experimental, variable is removed, and original baseline conditions are re-established. After experimental/clinical control of the behavior has been demonstrated, subjects then experience a second exposure to the independent variable (B). Changes in target behavior during the first B phase, compared with baseline, are open to explanations of their causality other than the effect of B. However, if the changes are replicated in an iteration of a baseline and treatment sequence, extraneous environmental events and uncontrolled variables pose a lesser threat to the internal validity of the experiment. Single-withdrawal (AB) designs are used but are quite limited in establishing causality, even with replication across multiple subjects. Many other non-measured variables may have co-occurred along with the treatment conditions, that, without a return to baseline and repeated intervention (B phase), remain plausible explanations for any observed effect.

For example, ter Kuile, Bulté, Weijenborg, Beekman, Melles, & Onghena (2009) evaluated the efficacy of an exposure-based treatment for vaginismus using a replicated AB design. Ten women with vaginismus, a fear-based condition in which women avoid any kind of vaginal penetration despite a desire for penetration, participated in treatment consisting of graduated exposure to vaginal penetration. The primary outcome measure was presence or absence of successful intercourse attempts (i.e., sexual intercourse with vaginal penetration), as recorded in a daily diary. Diary ratings revealed a significant increase in successful intercourse attempts from baseline (A) to treatment (B) for 9 of the 10 participants (Figure 4.1). Despite the multiple replications of the AB design reported in the study, the lack of a return to baseline and additional exposure to the independent variable (i.e., treatment) allows for many competing explanations of the effects observed, and limits the conclusions that can be made by the authors. While changes in vaginal penetration may have resulted from the graduated exposure treatment, the normal course of the target behavior is unknown and could have increased simply as the women involved in the study began attending to it. In this example, it is impossible to "unlearn" the intervention, which would be required in a return to baseline condition, as one cannot take away the experience of exposure. Therefore, return to baseline was impossible, precluding a second exposure to the treatment variable.

Without additional environmental controls (as in Multiple Baseline, discussed below), we are unaware of the normal course of behavior in

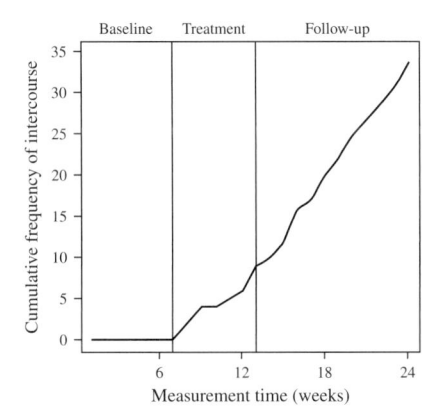

Applications of Small-n Research Design in Child and Adolescent Sexuality 103

**Figure 4.1** Frequency of penetrative vaginal intercourse in women with vaginismus treated by graduated exposure to vaginal penetration. *Source: ter Kuile et al. (2009).*

the absence of the intervention; the observed effects could be due to placebo, or other unassessed and co-occurring environmental variables could systematically be affecting behavior as well (Risley & Wolf, 1973). Thus, without further application of the intervention with the subject in the controlled setting, it is quite possible that an unassessed intervening variable serendipitously occurred during treatment to produce the change in the observed behavior targeted for intervention. It is also reasonable to suspect that a change in the dependent variable or target behavior could have been documented without any treatment having been introduced.

The additional baseline (A) and experimental (B) phase in the reversal/withdrawal design provides increased confidence when drawing conclusions about the causal influence of the independent variable. The incremental value, when establishing causal relationships between behavior and environment, of additional consecutive baseline (A) and experimental (B) conditions is exemplified by Sanger & Friman (1990), who investigated the effect of underwear fit on sperm production using an ABAB design. Each of two adult male subjects wore either tight or loose-fitting underwear for three months (A) before alternating to the other condition for three months (B). Two more alternations (AB) were made to complete the ABAB design. Weekly sperm specimens were gathered to assess sperm production, and results indicated that sperm production increased gradually in the loose-fitting condition, and decreased gradually in the tight-fitting condition (Figure 4.2). As with the previous example, delineating baseline responding in the absence of intervention was critical, though Sanger & Friman (1990) enhanced explanatory power by replicating the results

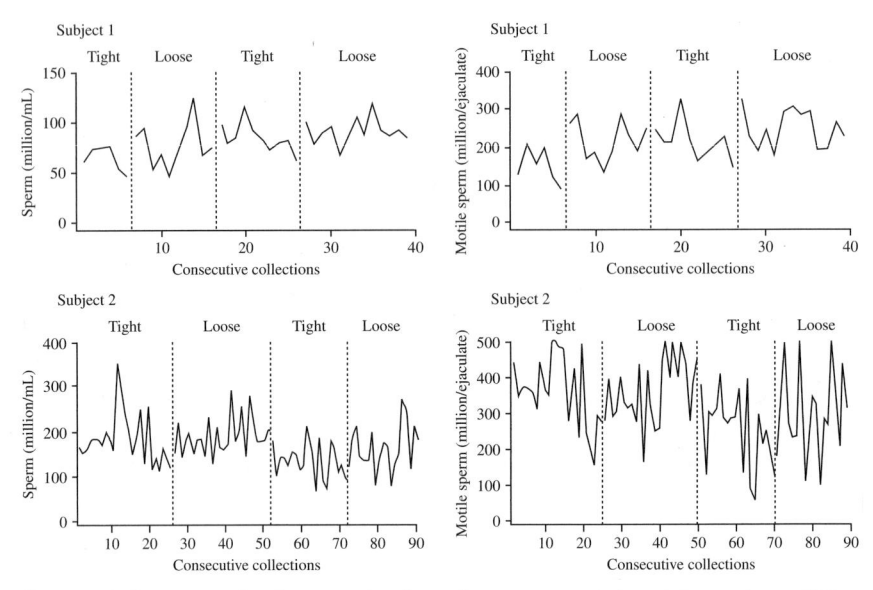

**Figure 4.2** Sperm production per ejaculate of two men wearing tight- or loose-fitting underwear, measured in an ABAB experimental design. *Source: Sanger and Friman (1990).*

through an additional application (and withdrawal) of the independent variable. In this way, each subject served as his own control, and other potential explanations for the differences in observed motile sperm counts were reduced. Further confounding variables such as season were also eliminated, as subjects 1 and 2 were separated by four months, leaving underwear fit as the sole explanatory variable which could account for the observed differences in both total number of sperm and total motile sperm.

## MULTIPLE-BASELINE DESIGNS

There are many times when "un-learning" or "un-experiencing" the experimental variable or treatment condition, necessary for successful application of the ABAB reversal design, is not possible. There are still many other times when withdrawal of a treatment is ill-advised or unethical, as the target of measurement ought not, for sake of the individual or society, to return to baseline frequency. The ethical challenges with returning to baseline conditions are easy to imagine, especially within the domain of deviant sexual behaviors occurring in children and adolescents. For example, consider the assessment of an intensive treatment/intervention protocol for adolescents who have engaged in familial sexualized behavior;

once treatment is initiated, allowing the behavior to potentially recur if baseline conditions are recreated would likely result in harm to others in the community. Use of the multiple-baseline technique addresses these problems of irreversibility. Since its introduction by Baer, Wolf, & Risley (1968), many alternate forms have been developed, though the current chapter will only cover the three most basic and widely used variants: multiple baseline (MBL) across subjects; MBL across behaviors; and MBL across settings. As the nomenclature for all three MBL variants implies, similarities far surpass their differences, and all address the irreversibility dilemma (Cooper, Heron, & Heward, 2007; Barlow, Nock, & Hersen, 2009).

Multiple-baseline designs establish baseline rates of the measured behavior across multiple subjects, functionally independent behaviors, or settings/conditions. Exposure to the treatment, or independent variable, is staggered, with baseline measurement and conditions present with all remaining untreated subjects, behaviors, or settings. The independent variable is sequentially introduced after stability is demonstrated in the previously exposed subject, behavior, or setting. All MBL designs assume independence of the behavior, individual, or setting, such that interventions or variables introduced will have a specific effect on a selected behavior exhibited by an identified individual within a specific context. Introduction of the independent variable sequentially across persons, settings, or behaviors allows conclusions about causality to be drawn. A change in behavior that occurs only when the intervention is introduced suggests that the intervention itself caused the change; however, to rule out potentially confounding variables, sequencing of the change elements, or independent variable of interest, is critical. This time-lagged, controlled application of the intervention allows one to derive causal explanations for behavior (Cooper, Heron, & Heward, 2007). Theoretically, only two baselines are absolutely necessary to draw any conclusion about causality. Nonetheless, current standards among journal editors and academicians dictate that at least three to five baselines be employed.

## Multiple Baseline Across Subjects

In the MBL-across-subjects design, a single target behavior is selected for repeated measurement in at least two (ideally three to five) subjects. Settings and environmental conditions among all involved subjects should remain constant to eliminate any added source of uncontrolled variability. Once steady-state responding has been achieved, an independent variable is applied to one subject, while maintaining baseline conditions

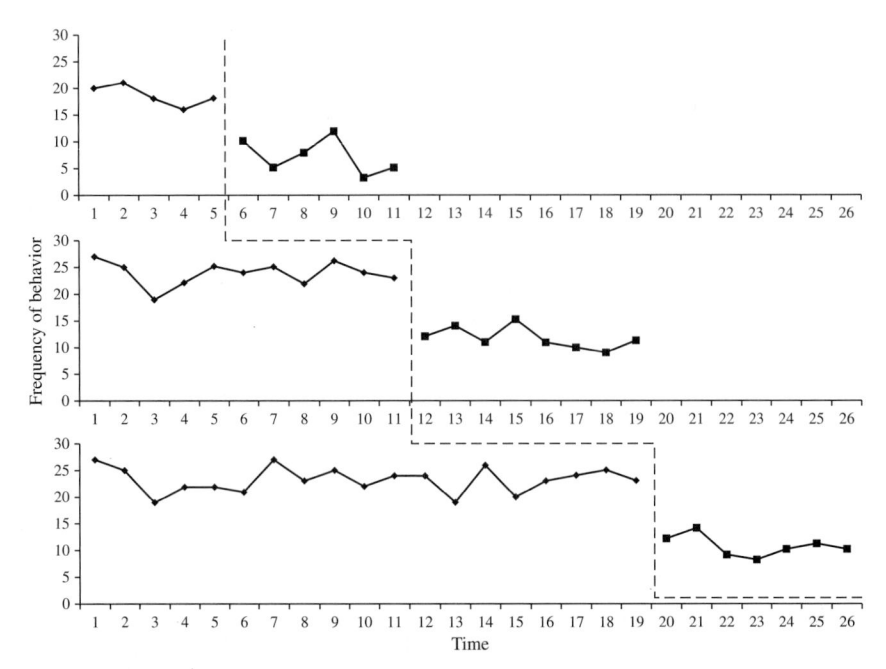

**Figure 4.3** Contrived data to illustrate a MBL-across-subjects study. The three subjects are introduced to the treatment in a staggered fashion.

in the remaining subjects. This is replicated for the second, third, and fourth subjects, respectively, all while maintaining baseline conditions for remaining participants. In Figure 4.3, we present contrived data for a MBL-across-subjects study. Baseline frequency of the target behavior, let us say genital rubbing, is assessed for all three participants. Once steady-state responding, or baseline, is established, Subject 1 (top) experiences the independent variable, say a token-based reward procedure for incompatible behavior exhibited with hands. Subjects 2 and 3 during this time remain in baseline conditions, with measurements continuing in all three subjects at the same rate and under the same conditions. Following steady-state responding in Subject 1, Subject 2 experiences the experimental variable, while Subject 3 remains in baseline. This process continues with the third and any other remaining subjects in the study. Unlike simple replication, exemplified by ter Kulie (2009), MBL procedures establish baseline simultaneously in all subjects to avoid introducing extraneous variability, and to allow conclusions about causality to be made.

Dukes & McGuire (2009) investigated the effects of a training protocol to improve sexual decision-making in mentally retarded adults;

their design combined a MBL across subjects and behaviors (see below). Knowledge and decision-making was measured via questionnaire once per week in all four young adults with moderate retardation. Participants then began a sexual education program tailored for individuals with intellectual disabilities, with starting dates staggered by one week. Assessment continued weekly so that baseline measurements continued for the participants who had not yet begun the treatment. As shown in Figure 4.4, scores increased significantly following the start of treatment for all participants.

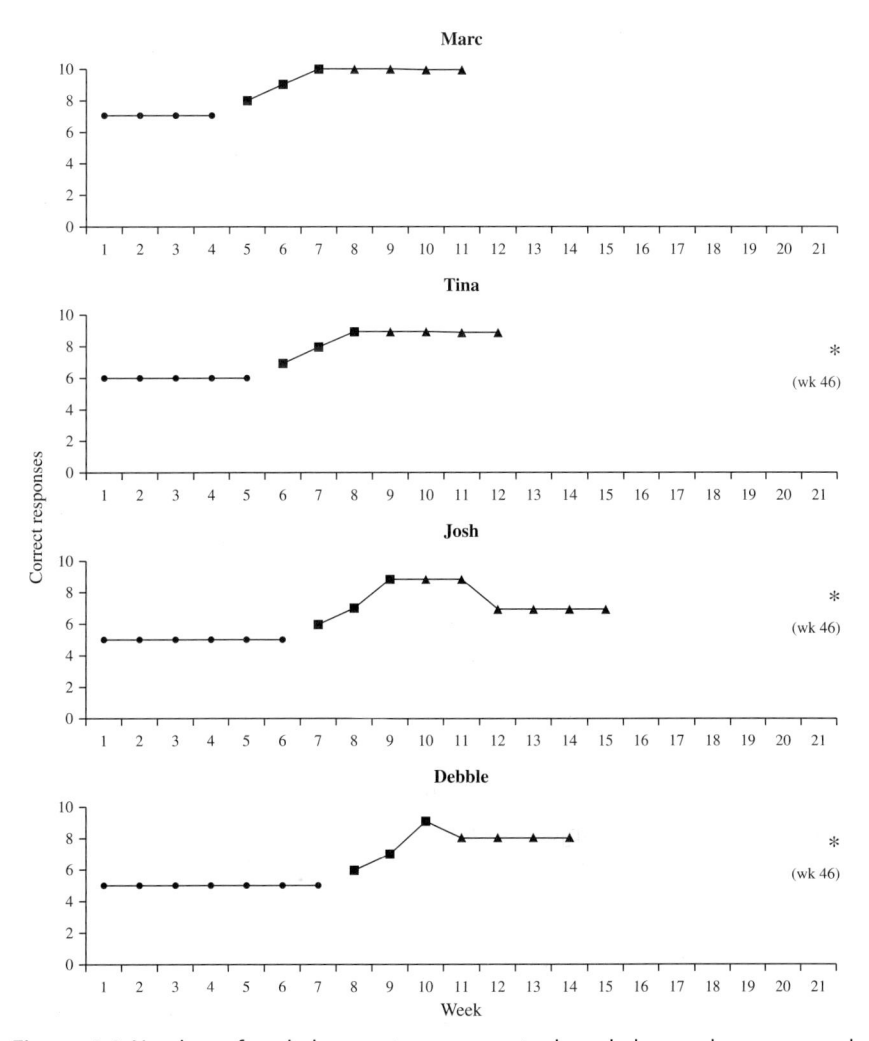

**Figure 4.4** Number of coded correct responses to knowledge probes on sexual decision-making. *Source: Dukes and McGuire (2009).*

The significant difference between baseline (A) and treatment (B) for all four participants despite the staggered start of treatment allows one to have confidence that the change in behavior was a result of the treatment, and not some other variable.

## Multiple Baseline Across Behaviors

MBL across behaviors begins with concurrent measurement of two or more behaviors of a single participant. Once a steady-state in the target behaviors of interest has been achieved, the investigator systematically applies an independent variable to one of the behaviors, while maintaining baseline conditions for the remaining behavior or behaviors. This is continued until either a steady-state of the dependent variable is achieved, or until the behavior of interest reaches a certain threshold criterion. Alford, Webster, & Sanders (1980) used a MBL-across-behaviors design to evaluate the efficacy of a covert sensitization intervention on sexually deviant behavior of a 21-year-old man. The man was receiving inpatient treatment for obscene phone calling and exhibitionism. Treatment consisted of repetitive pairing of deviant sexual scenarios delivered via audiotape and covert aversive imagery, including imagining suffocation, nausea, and arrest. The man's penile tumescence was measured during baseline, 13 treatments session, and at 1-, 2-, and 10-month follow-up. Obscene phone calling was targeted first, followed by exhibitionism. Penile response to non-deviant sexual scenarios was also recorded for comparison. Results indicated that penile response to both deviant sexual scenarios decreased significantly following intervention, whereas penile response to the non-deviant stimuli remained unchanged (Figure 4.5). Although obscene phone calling and exhibitionism were addressed sequentially and in that order, penile response to exhibitionism decreased substantially following the intervention for obscene phone calling. This is likely because the two deviant sexual behaviors were not independent, and/or because researchers instructed the participant to use aversive imagery to all deviant sexual stimuli outside of sessions, beginning at the first treatment session.

## Multiple Baseline Across Settings

In MBL across settings, one measurement is targeted in the same subject across two or more settings or conditions. Similar to the criteria for introducing the independent variable in the across-behaviors design,

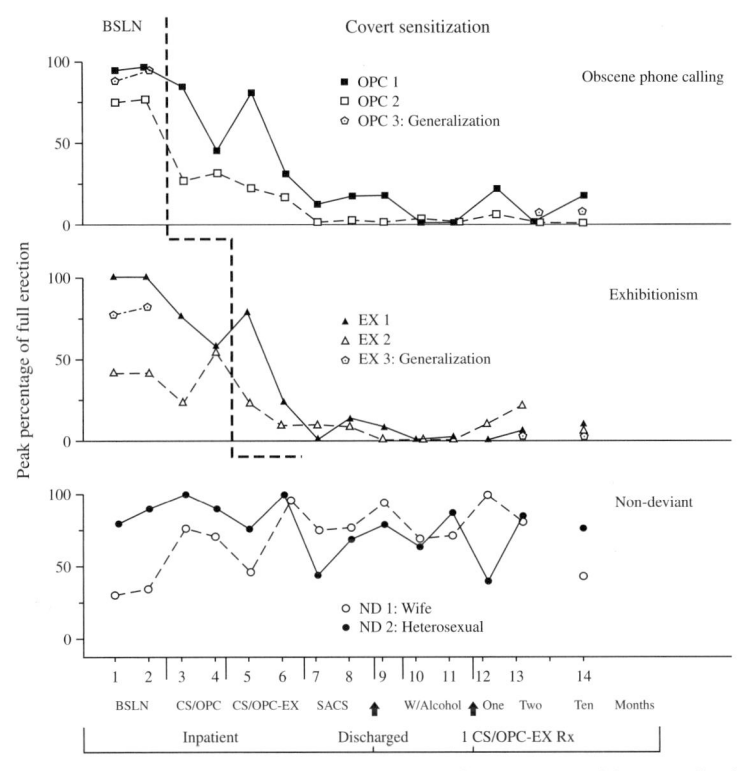

**Figure 4.5** Results of a MBL-across-behaviors study of a man treated for sexually deviant behaviors: obscene phone calling and exhibitionism. *Source: Alford et al. (1980).*

once either criterion level performance has been achieved or steady-state responding in the dependent variable is observed, the independent variable is then introduced into the remaining setting or environment. Richman, Ponticas, Page, & Epps (1986) provide a clear example of a combined MBL across conditions and subjects design in their evaluation of a skills-training program on independent menstrual care among four different intellectually disabled adolescent females. Training and assessment of proper sanitary napkin use occurred sequentially in three conditions: presence of a stained sanitary napkin; stained underwear; and stained napkin with leakage. Clearly visible in Figure 4.6, for each participant, correct responding for each scenario increased significantly only after training was initiated for that particular scenario (MBL across settings). Results indicated that when collapsed across target scenarios, correct responding to probes increased significantly in response to the skills training for all participants (MBL across subjects).

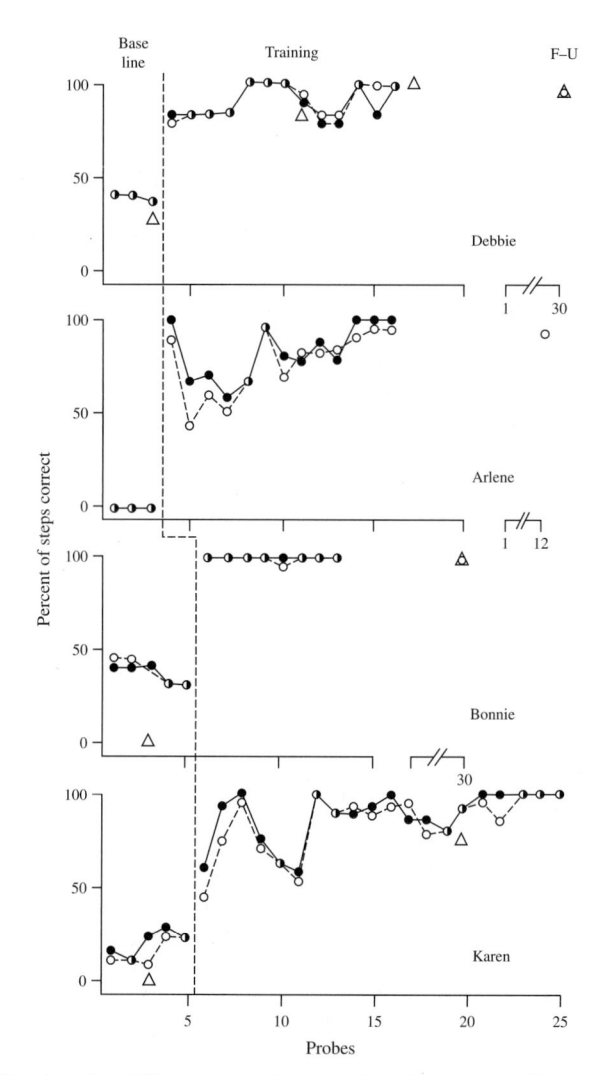

**Figure 4.6** Results of a MBL-across-settings study of four mentally retarded women in a skills-training program on independent menstrual care. open symbols show follow-up data. *Source: Richman et al. (1986).*

## CONCLUSIONS

Reversal/withdrawal (ABAB) and the three basic MBL variants—across subjects, settings, and behaviors—provide a unique view into individual responses to treatment. Beyond the rudimentary reversal/withdrawal designs and the MBL procedures detailed above, behavioral scientists have devised many other complex small-n designs that maintain a high degree of internal consistency and provide for logical extensions of causation to any observed effect. Across all permutations of elements among small-n designs, similarities far surpass any technical differences that exist among various strategies. However, behavioral science, as with all branches of natural science, seeks parsimony in demonstrating and explaining causal relationships among variables. Emphasizing subject-level data, change (or lack of change) in response to intervention over time, ease of use, and sheer elegance in demonstrating causal relationships among variables should place these strategies high on the list of methodologies. Similar to their conventional group-design counterpart, small-n methodologies are particularly useful in addressing some questions, while being inappropriate in addressing others. Clinical scientists and practicing clinicians should have a working knowledge of both group and small-n design methods when attempting to either explain relationships among phenomena or target those phenomena for change.

## ACKNOWLEDGEMENT

We would like to extend our sincerest appreciation to Patrick Friman, Ph.D., ABPP, in providing insightful feedback in the preparation of this chapter. He provided wonderful guidance and many helpful suggestions that were readily incorporated throughout this manuscript. We are grateful for his thoughtfulness and expertise.

## REFERENCES

Abel, G. G., Blanchard, E. B., Barlow, D. H., & Mavissakalian, M. (1975). Identifying specific erotic cues in sexual deviations by audiotaped descriptions. *Journal of Applied Behavior Analysis, 8*, 247–260.

Alford, G. S., Webster, J. S., & Sanders, S. H. (1980). Covert aversion of two interrelated deviant sexual practices: Obscene phone calling and exhibitionism: A single case analysis. *Behavior Therapy, 11*, 15–25.

Allen, K. D., Friman, P. C., & Sanger, W. G. (1992). Small n research designs in reproductive toxicology. *Reproductive Toxicology, 6*, 115–121.

Baer, D. M., Wolf, M. M., & Risley, T. R. (1968). Some current dimensions of applied behavior analysis. *Journal of Applied Behavior Analysis, 1*, 91–97.

Barlow, D. H., & Hersen, M. (1973). Single-case experimental designs: Uses in applied clinical research. *Archives of General Psychiatry, 29*, 319–325.

Barlow, D. H., Nock, M., & Hersen, M. (2009). *Single case experimental designs: Strategies for studying behavior for change*. Boston, MA: Pearson/Allyn and Bacon.

Cohen, J. (2003). *Applied multiple regression: Correlation analysis for the behavioral sciences*. Mahwah, New Jersey; London: Lawrence Erlbaum Associates.

Cooper, H., Heron, T. E., & Heward, W. L. (2007). *Applied behavior analysis*. Upper Saddle River, NJ: Pearson/Merrill-Prentice Hall.

Davidson, G. C. (1976). Homosexuality: The ethical challenge. *Journal of Consulting and Clinical Psychology, 44,* 157–162.

Dukes, E., & McGuire, B. E. (2009). Enhancing capacity to make sexuality-related decisions in people with an intellectual disability. *Journal of Intellectual Disability Research, 53,* 727–734.

Friman, P. C. (2009). Behavior assessment. In D. Barlow, M. Nock, & M. Hersen (Eds.), *Single case experimental designs: Strategies for studying behavior for change (pp. 99–134)* (3rd ed.). Boston, MA: Allyn & Bacon.

Guyatt, G. H., Keller, J. L., Jaeschke, R., Rosenbloom, D., Adachi, J. D., & Newhouse, M. T. (1990). The n-of-1 randomized controlled trial: Clinical usefulness. Our three-year experience. *Annals of Internal Medicine, 112,* 293–299.

Hersen, B. N. (2009). *Single case experimental designs: Strategies for studying behavior change* (3rd ed.). Boston, MA: Allyn and Bacon.

Kazdin, A. E. (1982). *Single-case research designs: Methods for clinical and applied settings.* New York, NY: Oxford University Press.

Kazdin, A. E. (2011). *Single-case research designs: Methods for clinical and applied settings* (2nd ed.). New York, NY: Oxford University Press.

Rekers, G. A., & Lovaas, O. I. (1974). Behavioral treatment of deviant sex-role behaviors in a male child. *Journal of Applied Behavior Analysis, 7,* 173–190.

Richman, G. S., Ponticas, Y., Page, T. J., & Epps, S. (1986). Simulation procedures for teaching independent menstrual care to mentally retarded persons. *Applied Research in Mental Retardation, 7,* 21–35.

Risley, T. R., & Wolf, M. M. (1973). Strategies for analyzing behavioral change over time. In J. R. Nesselroade, & H. W. Reese (Eds.), *Life-span developmental psychology: Methodological issues.* Oxford, UK: Academic Press.

Sanger, W. G., & Friman, P. C. (1990). Fit of underwear and male spermatogenesis: A pilot investigation. *Reproductive Toxicology, 4,* 229–232.

Skinner, B. F. (1953). *Science and human behavior.* New York, NY: Macmillan.

ter Kuile, M. M., Bulté, I., Weijenborg, P. T. M., Beekman, A., Melles, R., & Onghena, P. (2009). Therapist-aided exposure for women with lifelong vaginismus: A replicated single-case design. *Journal of Consulting and Clinical Psychology, 77,* 149–159.

Winkler, R. C. (1977). What types of sex-role behavior should behavior modifiers promote? *Journal of Applied Behavior Analysis, 10,* 549–552.

Wolf, M. M. (1978). Social validity: The case for subjective measurement or how applied behavior analysis is finding its heart. *Journal of Applied Behavior Analysis, 11,* 203–214.

# PART Three

# Child and Adolescent Development

# CHAPTER 5

# Sexual Development

### Kate Mills Drury and William M. Bukowski
Concordia University, Montréal, Québec, Canada[1]

## INTRODUCTION

At any age and at any point in history, coming up with a definition of what sex is and its origins is not easy. When one of the authors of this chapter wondered during his preadolescent years about what "sex" meant, he decided to look in the pages of a dictionary to find the one true definition. To his simultaneous bewilderment and relief, he discovered that his suspicions that a multitude of meanings were ascribed to sex were correct. The number of definitions for "sex" was large and the meanings were varied. As he had suspected, sex was not just one aspect of human functioning and experience, but instead had to do with many domains including some that, at least on the surface, had little to do with each other in a direct way. Sex was implicated with everything, from the political to the molecular. There was no doubt that sex was a complicated aspect of human nature.

Is there anyone who would deny this remarkable complexity? It is hard to imagine that any thinking and feeling person would not recognize sex as a gloriously complicated domain of human experience that can bring individuals both pleasure and pain across multiple aspects of their functioning. Yet, in contradiction to what a pubescent boy might learn from a dictionary, research on the development of sexuality has been rather sterile. Instead of recognizing and exploring the large number of ways that sex enters into our lives, and the multiple processes that underlie sexual development, the modal approach to the development of sexuality tends to be steeped in biology and behavior. Certainly, these aspects of functioning experience deserve attention but, from our point of view, they are only a part of the grander story.

The definition that one gives to "sex" is dependent, in part, on one's theoretical orientation. A central challenge to defining sex is to recognize that it involves a multitude of difficult-to-define intrapersonal

---

[1] Correspondence to either author at Psychology/CRDH, Concordia University, 7141 rue Sherbrooke Ouest, Montréal, Québec, Canada H4A 2H3.

processes and a broad set of interpersonal behaviors, some of which are overt physical events (i.e., genital stimulation) that can be measured and recorded in direct empirical ways. These overt behaviors can be seen, at least in part, as an expression of our atavistic heritage. The intra- and interpersonal aspects of sex have temporally *proximate* antecedents (e.g., fantasies, biological processes of sexual arousal) that derive from an extraordinarily complex interaction of temporally *remote* antecedents (i.e., biological factors) that come from physiological (e.g., hormonal) factors rooted in our genetic inheritance that can be modified by experience (see Pfaus, Kippin, Coria-Avila, Gelez, Afonso, & Ismail, et al., 2012). Ultimately, sexual behaviors and one's intrapersonal experience of being a sexual being are, in part, the result of social influences to which a child is exposed (e.g., sexually permissive vs. restrictive society, religious beliefs within any particular society).

The point of departure for our chapter is the claim that these questions about what sex is need to form the ground for a discussion of this larger story of sexual development. Our goal in this chapter is to try to describe what this larger account of sexual development would look like. Our approach is based on four basic premises. The first premise has been alluded to already. It is that sexuality is not a single thing, but is instead linked to and implicated in multiple forms of functioning. These domains include feelings, urges and motivation, forms of attention, emotions, aspects of the self, biological processes, moral precepts, modes of self-presentation, relationships and interactions, and one's perceptions of others. The second premise follows from the first. It is that sexuality is an integrative form of development, perhaps the most integrative aspect of human development. By integrative we mean that a central process of sexuality concerns the intersection and coordination of its many intrapersonal and interpersonal components. Examples include the integration of: (1) one's urges and the self-concept; (2) one's feelings, moral orientation, and interpersonal expectations; and (3) relationship experiences and goals.

The third premise is that sexuality is a form of development that varies across age, and that sexuality at one age is in part determined by experiences at a younger age. The implication of this premise is that sexuality needs to be understood according to the developmental context in which it is embedded. Moreover, it needs to be studied from both a "lifespan" and a "life history" perspective (Bukowski, Li, Dirks, & Bouffard, in press). Whereas the lifespan approach is focused on developmental processes from within a particular moment of the life course (e.g., adolescence), the life history approach is concerned with understanding stability and change in a form of functioning from one time of the life course to another (e.g., early adolescence to adulthood). The final premise is that coming up with a definition of what would comprise normal sexuality would be as or more difficult than defining sex. Any definition of normal sexuality would need to be highly abstracted rather than reliant on concrete descriptions, and it would need to emphasize the synthesis between the multiple aspects of functioning that we have mentioned already. On nearly every aspect of sexuality, the variability between people and across the lifespan is simply too large for the creation of a meaningful "norm."

The chapter is divided into two sections. We begin with a discussion of how sex is learned, focusing on motivational processes and on research grounded in social learning theory and gender schema theory. Then we turn our attention to how sex is essentially an interpersonal experience. The central theme of each section is the claim that sexuality is deeply rooted in social and interpersonal processes. We acknowledge that the chapter is set on a heteronormative stage, which unquestionably leads to an incomplete representation of human sexual development. For reasons of space, scope, and expertise we have focused exclusively on the development of heterosexuality, though we agree with exhortations from researchers to combine research on sexual minority and heterosexual youth (Diamond, 2003). For an excellent overview of the sexual development of sexual minority youth see Diamond, Savin-Williams, & Dubé (1999).

It may be useful to first say a few words about the processes underlying sexual differentiation by which the undifferentiated zygote (i.e., the fertilized egg) becomes either a male or a female. This process is regulated by a complex interaction between genetic and hormonal factors. The very young fetus has no anatomical or hormonal sex; only its karyotype distinguishes the male fetus from the female. Specific genes in the karyotype of the male and female fetus lead to gonadal differences which lead to hormonal differences, and then to anatomic differences. The male Y chromosome carries a critical gene that determines the formation of the testes. This gene, known as *SRY*, appears to work with other genes to direct the production of a protein that induces the differentiation of cells that become the testes. Early evidence of the gonads can be seen by 6–8 weeks of gestation. By this age the fetus has both mesonephric (wolffian) and paramesonephric (müllerian) ducts. The subsequent development of one set and degeneration of the other depends on the presence or absence of two testicular hormones: testosterone and AMH.

Testosterone causes each wolffian duct to develop into the epididymis, vas deferens, and seminal vesicles. Without male testosterone levels, wolffian ducts degenerate and disappear. Müllerian ducts develop into a uterus, fallopian tubes, and upper vagina unless AMH induces degeneration. The presence of a uterus is stronger evidence of absence of testes than the state of the external genitalia. By 7 weeks, one can see the genital tubercle, urogenital groove and sinus, and labioscrotal folds. In females, without excess androgens, these become the clitoris, urethra and vagina, and labia. By 8 to 12 weeks males develop signs of external genitalia as androgens stimulate the tissue that will become the penis and the scrotum. Androgens (e.g., dihydrotestosterone (DHT)) lead to external masculinization. These processes are activated again at puberty, when androgen levels again become disparate. Male levels of testosterone directly induce growth of the penis, and indirectly (via DHT) the prostate. The formation of this physical apparatus is just one part of the broader processes of sexual development.

## LEARNING BASES

An essential part of growing up is the task of navigating how to become a healthy sexual adult; the question at hand is how do we *learn* how to do this? How do we gather information, assign meaning, and enact our sexualities? What motivates and influences these processes? We have seen that biology plays a central role in human sexual development; however, it is our contention that sexuality is derived from the functions of the physical body but gains *meaning* through an interplay with the individual's surroundings, thus giving the individual the opportunity to determine his or her own identity, and his or her own sexuality (Larsson, 2002). Some sex researchers conceptualize sexual learning within a Skinnerian and Pavlovian framework of operant and classical conditioning. This body of research is extensive and is well represented in the literature. We have chosen a different framework within which to discuss sexual learning; our approach embeds the growing individual within a social context and draws on motivation theory, social learning theory, and gender schema theory.

### Motivation

Motivation is commonly defined as an intervening process or internal state of an organism that impels or drives it to action. In this sense, motivation is an energizer of behavior that plays a fundamental role in learning. As human beings we are naturally motivated to satisfy our drives and needs (Maslow, 1943) and, in the process, we learn the optimal ways of doing so. We are also motivated to increase our experiences of pleasure (incentive theory) and decrease those of pain (drive theory). The multifaceted nature of sexual behavior allows for its use in the satisfaction of many needs (physiological, safety, love/belonging, self-esteem, and self-actualization). Logically, sexual behavior would satisfy different drives or needs depending on the individual's development. While in childhood sexuality might satisfy a drive rather than a need and be motivated by curiosity and incentivized by pleasure, in adolescence and adulthood sexual behavior may satisfy several needs (e.g., physiological, self-esteem, love/belonging). In line with this view, we see a progression in sexual behaviors from birth to age 12; however, the behaviors vary from child to child, and all children do not naturally take part in all the behaviors in the respective age group (Gil, 1993).

Evidence from several researchers has pointed to the critical role of physical touch in early development. Studies by Field (2002) and Stack (2007) have shown that physical touch is a necessary component of healthy development. Body-to-body contact has been shown to regulate arousal levels, to promote the communication of emotions, and to facilitate the formation of interpersonal bonds. According to theory on personality development, physical contact forms the foundation of the self-concept via a process of internalization. Sullivan (1953) proposed that, during childhood, children use experiential information derived directly from their interactions with others to create the self-concept. He proposed that during early childhood the self-concept was essentially composed of two basic components that he called the "good me" and the "bad me." Sullivan proposed that each of them was created via an integrative process that brought together the physical feelings derived from interpersonal experiences with caregivers. The "good me" was the result of feelings of satisfaction and tenderness from interactions with parents, and the "bad me" was the result of feelings of anxiety and rejection experienced in these interactions. Sullivan took a very sensory approach to the origins of the self. His emphasis on the importance of body-to-body contact points to an implicit sexuality. For him the experience of warmth was literal in the sense that feelings of "warmth" would derive from the experience of being held warmly by a caregiver, whereas feelings of anxiety, on the other hand, would be taken from the experience of being held in rigid or cold manners.

Further empirical studies on childhood sexual behavior carried out in recent years lend support to the notion that early sexual behavior is normal, developmentally distinct, and motivated by pleasure and curiosity. This body of work can be divided into three methodologies: studying children who have been admitted for treatment due to concern about their sexual behavior; retrospective reports from young adults on their experiences of sexuality; and reports from parents or child care staff on their observations of children's sexual activities. Taken together these studies confirm that: (1) children are naturally curious about their own bodies and those of others, and can take part in sexual investigations of their, own body and in games with other children; (2) behaviors that imitate adult sexuality are very uncommon in observations of normal groups of children; and (3) children can vary in their interest in sexuality (Larsson, 2002).

The research seems to be conclusive that children are naturally curious about their bodies and about sex, that they explore their bodies—including touching and sometimes masturbating their genitals—from birth, that they ask questions about sex as they begin to ask questions about other aspects of society, and that they play sex games like doctors and nurses with other children from an early age (for review see McKee, Albury, Dunne, Grieshaber, Hartley, & Lumby, et al., 2010). Similarly, in adolescence, Moore & Rosenthal (2006), found that the most common motive, for both boys and girls, preceding first intercourse was curiosity. These studies indicate that *curiosity* is an important avenue through which children are *motivated to learn* about their bodies in general and about their sexual feelings, like pleasure, in particular. Learning about sexuality, like all learning, transpires within a social and cultural space, meaning that cultural beliefs and expectations about sexuality provide the parameters within which an individual learns. Put simply, children learn the rules of sexuality in the same way as they learn everything else, by being attentive to their surroundings. Each society constructs and shapes a suitable and rewarding sexuality for its own society. The sexuality of girls and boys develops on this basis, in an interplay with their surroundings and in accordance with society's expectations and assumptions. Children grow up in a particular social context, and over time internalize its norms and values concerning sexual behaviors (Larsson, 2002).

Childhood sexuality receives more or less research attention depending on the political climate of the day. The current zeitgeist upholds a belief in childhood sexual innocence; as a result, with a few notable exceptions (Constantine & Martinson, 1981; Goldman & Goldman, 1982; Sandfort & Rademakers, 2000), little scientific research has been carried out on the sexual development and behavior of children under the age of 12. According to Bancroft (2003) we are currently in a cycle of moral panic about childhood sexual abuse, and one consequence of this is that rational debate and scientific inquiry into normal childhood sexual development is currently very difficult. Since Freud, a century ago, we have to a certain extent accepted that children are sexual beings from birth, but we continue to find ourselves surrounded by a lack of theory, lack of methodological knowledge, and lack of empirical data in the area of normal childhood sexuality. Not surprisingly, sexuality is as infrequently discussed in other social spheres (schools, families) as it is in research circles. Consequently, unlike the rest of the child's life where it has ample opportunities to learn, the child is deprived of the chance to understand his or her own development, due to sexuality being made invisible (Plummer, 1991). As children undertake the task of learning about sexuality they apply lessons learned from other areas of development, such as the unparalleled importance of gender as a tool for understanding themselves and the world.

## Cognitive Social Learning Theory (Bandura, 1977, 1986)

The theory suggests that humans learn behaviors by observing others and choosing which behaviors to imitate. Behaviors that are rewarded are more likely to be repeated, whereas behaviors that are punished are less likely to be repeated. According to cognitive social learning theory, gender differences in behavior are created because boys and girls observe different behaviors in same-gender models, and are reinforced and punished for different behaviors. In particular, boys and girls learn gender-appropriate behaviors because they are reinforced for gender role-consistent behaviors and punished for gender role-inconsistent behaviors (Mischel, 1966). In addition, boys and girls prefer to imitate same-gender models, which further increases their attention to gender role-consistent behaviors. Cognitive social learning theory suggests that boys and girls do not need to be directly rewarded or punished in order to learn which behaviors are appropriate to imitate. Instead, they may learn appropriate gender role behaviors simply by observing the rewards and punishments directed toward other same-gender models. Finally, boys and girls internalize these standards for gender appropriate behavior and regulate their own behavior in accordance with gender norms.

## Gender Schema Theory (Bem, 1981; Martin & Halverson, 1981)

Research evidence suggests that infants have knowledge of gender categories and use this information to parse the world into meaningful parts (Martin & Ruble, 2004; Poulin-Dubois, Serbin, Kenyon, & Derbyshire, 1994). From a very young age, children identify their own gender and gender group, and develop a belief system regarding the behaviors that are consistent with being a girl or boy or woman or man (Ruble & Martin, 1998). It has been argued that gender cognitions play a significant role as organizers of gender development (Martin & Fabes, 2001). The emergence of gender identity and growing understanding of the stability of social group membership affects children's motivation to learn about gender, to gather information about their gender group, and to act like other group members (Ruble & Martin, 1998). This motivation involves the child's "deliberate efforts to learn about a social category that he or she is actively constructing as part of a process of finding meaning in the social world" (Martin & Ruble, 2004, p. 68). In other words, children's recognition of the social significance of gender motivates them to learn about and comply with gender norms.

"What we term healthy and natural sexuality is formed from the society we live in and depends on our gender" (Larsson, 2002, p. 11). As the quote indicates, it has been argued before (e.g., Ehrhardt, 2000; Larsson, 2002; Tolman, 1999; Zosuls, Miller, Ruble, Martin, & Fabes, 2011) and it is our contention now that children learn about sexuality through a gendered lens. As mentioned above, gender is an extremely salient characteristic of our social environment and has been characterized as "the most visible and dramatic subdivision within our species" (Weisgram, Bigler, & Liben, 2010). Children, in a rather rigidly categorical way, use this social grouping to ascribe meaning to their reality. Just as children learn that social behavior is gendered, so they learn that sexual behavior is gendered.

For example, parents often express appreciation when a boy displays his penis at the ages of 2 or 3, which gives the boy the sense that he has a valuable body part. In contrast, when girls are seen to touch their sexual organs, reactions are more negative. This gender-based value system is thus passed on to the child right from birth. Gender is one of the first and the probably most obvious characteristic children learn in categorizing other people. Therefore, gender is also crucial to self-development, including sexual identity.

There is empirical evidence of this phenomenon. For example, in an Irish study of children between the ages of 2 and 7 years, most children had some name for their own sexual organs; however, 51% of the boys did not have a word for the girls' sexual organs and 12% of the girls did not have any name for the boys' genitals, as far as their mothers were aware (Fitzpatrick, Deehan, & Jennings, 1995). Concordantly, another study of Swedish children of a similar age group evidenced that it was less common to name the sexual organs of girls than boys.

No time is wasted when it comes to starting the process of gender-related socialization. Starting at birth there is a curiosity about the gender-related category to which a newborn belongs (Intons-Peterson & Reddel, 1984). Infants themselves have been observed to recognize a difference between pictures of the faces of boys and girls by the time they are 4 months old (Quinn, Yahr, Kuhn, Slater, & Pascalis, 2002). These perceptual discriminations appear to be due to differences in facial features alone. By the time they are 22-months-old, infants can correctly use words such as "girl" and "boy." Although the modal 2-year-old child knows that these sex-related categories exist, they do not reliably place themselves in one of them until at least age 3, and they do not recognize that this categorization is a stable feature of the self until age 4 or 5 (Ruble, Martin, & Berenbaum, 2006). These changes have been largely traced to changes in cognitive-related processes linked to the perception of self and other.

One repercussion of these aspects of the self-concept is the preference for associating with same-sex peers (Rubin, Bukowski, & Parker, 2006). Throughout childhood, children show a strong preference for interacting with members of their own gender (Bukowski, Gauze, Hoza, & Newcomb, 1993). Although this preference has been observed to peak during preadolescence (Sippola, Bukowski, & Noll, 1997), it is feature of social relations across the lifespan.

### *Learning from Each Other*
Children's peer contexts are segregated by gender, meaning that children tend to group themselves according to sex, or into boys' groups and girls' groups. Gender segregation is one of the most powerful and pervasive social phenomena to exist in early childhood (Leaper 1994; Maccoby, 1990). Gender segregation starts around 3 years and becomes progressively stronger throughout middle childhood (Maccoby & Jacklin, 1987). As such, same-gender peer interactions provide a primary socialization context for young children (Fabes, Martin, & Hanish, 2007). In fact, Maccoby (1998) argues that these established patterns of interactive styles among girls and boys may have a strong influence on gender-specific differences in sexual behavior throughout the life cycle (e.g., women's greater need for intimacy and men's emphasis on sexual performance).

According to Anke Ehrhardt:

> *Girls and boys begin to have increased contact in adolescence under new parameters of physical attraction. They must adapt to cross-gender interactions with very little experience and very little guidance by adults, especially in our society where*

*sex and gender education is at best sporadic. Boys and girls also come to these cross-gender interactions with expectations that they will encounter the same patterns of behavior they have experienced in their same-gender peer groups. Young women expect more reciprocal agreement; instead they are confronted with masculine patterns that are focused to a greater degree on performance, dominance, and competition.*

**(Ehrhardt, 2000, p. 11)**

It is our contention that this social dimorphism along the heterosexual dimensions of male/female, masculine/feminine creates the social context within which sexual identities emerge. In other words, what we learn about what it means to be a boy or a girl eventually cascades into the realm of sexual behavior, and consequently the knowledge we have acquired regarding gender is applied to sexuality. We believe that this process is occurring throughout childhood, as we have seen there is ample evidence for gender socialization (Bigler & Liben, 2007; Maccoby, 1998) and for sexual behavior in childhood (McKee et al., 2010).

In line with our hypothesis, research has in fact supported the theory that children learn about sex through a gendered lens. In an effort to identify sexually abused from non-abused children, Friedrich and colleagues developed the Child Sexual Behavior Inventory. Their large normative sample consisted of 880 2- to 12-year-old children living in the United States. Research with three versions of the scale "clearly indicated that sexual behavior was ubiquitous in preteen children" (Friedrich, 2003, p. 111). Developmentally related sexual behaviors were defined as behaviors endorsed by at least 20% of mothers for a specific age-gender group. Of note, the items overlapped considerably across gender and demonstrated a developmental pattern with clear age differences in behavior between 2–6-year-olds and 7–12-year-olds. The five items endorsed by more than 20% of mothers were the same for 2–5-year-old boys and girls (e.g., stands too close to people; touches or tries to touch their mother's or other women's breasts), as well as the three items endorsed by more than 20% of mothers for 7–12-year-old girls and boys (e.g., touches sex parts at home; tries to look at people when they are nude or undressing). In a similar effort in Sweden, Lindblad and colleagues studied the sexual behavior of 251 children, aged 2–6 years, at day-care centers. The results from these two unique normative samples suggest that sexual behavior is: (1) very common in childhood; and (2) ranges from highly frequent general behavior (e.g., observing the genitalia of other children) to infrequent more-specific behavior (e.g., masturbating with an object) (Lindblad, Gustafsson, Larsson, & Lundin, 1995).

Another source of illumination is the Kinsey data (Kinsey, Pomeroy, & Martin, 1948; Kinsey, Pomeroy, Martin, & Gebhard, 1953). Ehrhardt (2000) summarized the data from interviews with prepubertal children and retrospective accounts from adolescents, and found about half of the girls and more than half of the boys talked about socio-sexual behaviors. Additionally, 33% of girls and 44% of boys reported same-sex sexual behavior. In a study comparing a sample from 1998–1999 (Study A) with the original Kinsey sample from 1953 (Study B) on childhood sexual experiences with peers found the following overall percentages for males (A: 87.2%; B: 68%) and females (A: 84.4%; B: 42%) (Reynolds, Herbenick, & Bancroft, 2003). The gender difference is apparent in Study B but not Study A, which was evident in a number of areas of this cross-sectional study, and according to the authors "reflects a more widespread reduction in gender differences in sexual behavior over the past 50 years" (p. 151).

## *Developmental Implications*

Ehrhardt (2000) believes that gender is of critical importance in the unfolding of sexuality between men and women. Eleanor Maccoby (1998) argues that gender differences in childhood in interactional styles are of critical importance for the sexual interaction between adolescent girls and boys and, subsequently, between women and men. Research in this area has shown that, beginning at a very young age (33 months), girls find it difficult to influence boys (Jacklin & Maccoby, 1978; Serbin, Sprafkin, Elman, & Doyle, 1982). Jacklin and Maccoby (1978) found that, in a mixed-gender group, if one child acted in an undesirable way toward another child, such as taking a toy away, a girl would respond to a boy's verbal request to stop, whereas the opposite interaction, a girl's vocal prohibition, would have no effect on the boy's behavior. Similarly, Serbin and colleagues (1982) found that the influence technique typically adopted by girls (polite suggestions) was instrumental in influencing other girls, teachers, and other adults, but increasingly ineffective with boys. Furthermore, girls have been found to increase their use of typically male power-assertive strategies during disagreements with boys, whereas boys have not been found to increase their use of typically female conflict-mitigation strategies in their disagreements with girls (Miller, Danaher, & Forbes, 1986). Thus, children hold beliefs about what it means to act like a boy or a girl, and these gendered behaviors reflect social hierarchies and power imbalances which privilege masculine characteristics over feminine characteristics. This could help shed light on the finding that the link between adolescent sexual behaviors and adjustment varies by gender.

Adolescent females evaluate first intercourse significantly more negatively than do males (Woody, Russel, D'Souza, & Woody, 2000), and depressed affect is more strongly related to early intercourse for girls than for boys (Whitbeck, Yoder, Hoyt, & Conger, 1999). Furthermore, research on self-esteem found similar gender differences, with sexually active adolescent males reporting higher self-esteem than sexually active adolescent females or virgin males (Welsh, Grello, & Harper, 2003). However, in the context of romantic relationships, researchers found no gender differences in the associations between sexual behavior and either relationship satisfaction or commitment, suggesting that the meaning of sex may differ for adolescent girls when it occurs within the context of a romantic relationship.

## Sexual Double Standard

In terms of gender differences in sexuality, the sexual double standard plays a role in determining which sexual behaviors men and women are likely to imitate. According to the sexual double standard, norms about gender-appropriate sexual behaviors developed based on evolutionary explanations; today, the double standard holds that casual sex and multiple sex partners are acceptable for men, but not for women (Milhausen & Herold, 1999). This sexual double standard is regulated by punishing women for sexually permissive behaviors, such as having multiple sexual partners and engaging in casual sex, but not punishing men for the same behaviors (Crawford & Popp, 2003; Kreager & Staff, 2009). The punishment may be as simple as disapproval from one's peers. Although some research suggests that many individuals do not personally endorse a sexual double standard, they still perceive that the sexual double standard exists in the media and among their peers (Milhausen & Herold, 1999). Cognitive social learning theory would suggest that men and women internalize these standards for gendered sexual expression, and regulate their behaviors and attitudes in accordance with the sexual double standard. Therefore, this theory would predict a measureable gender difference in sexual behaviors and attitudes such that men are more likely than women to engage in sexual behavior with more partners and hold more permissive attitudes toward behaviors such as casual sex and multiple sex partners (Petersen & Hyde, 2011). The sexual double standard would help explain why intercourse might represent an expression of status or power in younger adolescent boys (O'Sullivan, Meyer-Bahlburg, & Watkins, 2000; Savin-Williams & Diamond, 2004), or why younger adolescent girls attempt to use sex as a means of treating depressive feelings (Welsh, Grello, & Harper, 2003). These issues will be explored in greater depth in the following section.

## SOCIAL BASES
### Culture

Sexual behavior varies across cultures, time, and social groups, and is shaped on the basis of the prevailing conditions in the child's environment. Because of this, cultural comparisons provide an especially illuminated view of the social processes underlying the development of sexuality. The work of Herdt (1984) is particularly illustrative. He identified 53 distinct societies in the Pacific and Papua New Guinea that have what he termed "age structured homosexual practice." In a longitudinal study of the Sambia of Highland Papua New Guinea, Herdt described an elaborate pattern of sexual identity development, marked by what Westerners would deem dramatic and perhaps even unnatural discontinuity. Same-sex sexual contact between young boys is socially enforced; youth are forbidden to engage in male-female interactions until they are married. Furthermore, married men are permitted homosexual activities until their wives give birth, after which all such activity must cease. This pattern is drastically different from the Western construction of sexual orientation and the meaning of sexual preference. Herdt concludes that "the Sambia pattern of coercive and obligatory homosexual activity is simply a more extreme form of the many social influences that regulate sexuality across all societies, ours included" (p. 9).

Not only do we see differences *between* Western and non-Western cultures, but numerous studies have documented different cultural patterns of sexual development *within* Western cultures. In a cross-cultural comparison between North American and Swedish children aged 3 to 6, more sexual behavior was reported among the Swedish children (Larsson, Svedin, & Friedrich, 2000). This cultural difference is attributable to parental reports of their child's behavior as well as how children are sexualized in a particular sexual context. A study comparing American and Dutch children proffered similar results, Dutch children also showed more sexual behavior than American children. Previous studies indicate that American children grow up in a stricter and more guarded environment concerning sexual issues (Frayser, 1994; Schmidt, 1993). Taken together, these behavioral differences may indicate a cultural difference in attitudes to child sexuality in the United States and Scandinavia. Cross-cultural work investigating attitudes towards child sexuality compared responses from the United States, Ireland, Sweden, and the Netherlands, and found that the first two countries have the lowest figures for young people who considered sexual activity among children to be normal. Figures for Sweden and the Netherlands were at comparable levels (Cavanagh Johnson & Feldmeth, 1993).

According to Schwartz and Rutter (1998), certain cultures, such as in Sweden, are "sex positive" meaning that, for example, premarital sex is accepted and people are expected to be sexually knowledgeable and experienced. By comparison, in Ireland, citizens are expected to adhere to the Catholic Church's strict prohibitions against extramarital sex, birth control, and the expression of lust. It goes without saying that experiences of sexual development will differ depending on which cultural context one finds oneself in. One way in which the texture or fabric of culture is conveyed is through norms and values, another is through what have been termed social scripts. We will turn to this shortly, but first the interpersonal nature of sexual development is discussed.

## Interpersonal Context

Although sexual development is typically treated as a form of individual development, sexuality and sexual behavior have strong links to interpersonal experiences. Sexual behavior is largely interpersonal. Even when one experiences sexual pleasure alone, it is often accompanied by an image or fantasy of a real or imagined other. Given this fundamental interpersonal component, any attempt to understand sexuality needs to recognize it as an interpersonal experience. Moreover, because interpersonal relationships have been a part of a person's developmental history, sexual development consists of introducing a new and powerful set of personal and interpersonal dynamics into their interactions and relationships. This need to bring together two formidable aspects of function must be one of the most challenging aspects of successful development.

Even without the inclusion of a sexual component, adolescent friendship relationships pose their own risks and challenges. During this developmental period, friendships take on new characteristics that place extra stress on one's ability to negotiate the balance between the self and the other (Sippola & Bukowski, 1999; Bukowski, Buhrmester, & Underwood, 2011). In adolescent friendships the features of intimacy and security are added to the presence of friendship features, especially common activity preferences and help. The task for adolescents is to transform their friendship relationships from activity- and interaction-based experiences to relationship experiences that include high levels of interpersonal closeness that involve one's internal states (Bukowski, Simard, DuBois, & Lopez, 2011). As friendships take on these more complicated features, there are new opportunities and risks. They provide opportunities for the psychological benefits (e.g., a sense of strong validation of the self), but they also provide demands and risks. The demands include the need to develop skills that will promote and manage closeness and intimacy with another, presumably co-equal partner. The most important new risk is the heightened opportunity for rejection. Adding sex into these new forms of relationships adds to the demands and the risks of this experience.

For the modal heterosexual adolescent a particular challenge is learning how to interact with the other sex. Given that peer experiences throughout childhood are largely restricted to experiences with same-sex peers, establishing relationships with other-sex peers means having to function in new ways with the "other" with whom one has had a limited amount of prior experience. In this regard, sexual minority adolescents who wish to develop sexually intimate relationships with same-sex peers might have a slight advantage. This advantage, however, is likely to be very small relative to the challenges of engaging in relations that are not given universal approval. These relations pose opportunities for rejection far beyond that which is experienced by heterosexual adolescents.

## Social Scripts

Social scripts are culturally supported ways of being in a given situation, for example in a restaurant or on a bus. In an attempt to address the gendered nature of sexuality and preserve the inherently social and interpersonal nature of these processes, researchers have applied social script theory to sexuality. *Social Scripting Theory* (Abelson, 1981) provides an interesting social-cognitive lens through which to explore the ways in which gender and sexual development interact. The theory rests on the assumption that people follow internalized scripts when constructing meaning out of behavior, responses, and emotions. Abelson, (1976) described a script as "a coherent sequence of events expected by the individual, involving him either as a participant or an observer" (p. 33). Scripts are cognitive models that people employ to guide and evaluate social and sexual behavior; they guide behavior both interpersonally and intrapersonally. The production and maintenance of social scripts is described as follows:

> Social scripts are communicated through the examples displayed by members of the culture who have already adopted the scripts as well as through mass media depictions of how people act and react in particular situations. Also, the very structure and the institutions of a society contribute to the formation of scripts, such as in the case of marriage laws and vows and laws against sexual behaviors or certain types of partners. Societal scripts specify the appropriate objects, aims, and desirable qualities of [social] interactions. They also provide individual actors with instruction as to the appropriate times, places, sequences, and so forth with regard to [social] activity.
>
> Wiederman (2005, p. 496)

Having established a general understanding of the content, structure, and function of social scripts, we would like to apply social scripting theory to our discussion of the development of sexuality. Keeping our developmental perspective, we will draw on research from childhood (playground scripts), young adulthood (dating scripts), and adulthood (sexual scripts).

### *Playground Scripts*

As has been said previously, but deserves repeating, "in our culture, gender and sexuality are deeply intertwined; 'woman/man,' and especially, 'femininity/masculinity' are categories loaded with heterosexual meanings" (Thorne & Luria, 1986, p. 176). Through observation, Thorne & Luria (1986) explore the segregated gender arrangements of middle childhood as contexts for learning adolescent and adult sexual scripts. Their focus is "on how the gender-specific contexts of middle childhood may help shape the sexual scripts—the social relations and meanings associated with desire—of adolescent girls and boys" (p. 180). Their findings were in line with what Gagnon & Simon (1973) had originally suggested: that two strands of sexuality are differently emphasized among adolescent boys and girls. According to their observations, girls emphasize and learn about the emotional and romantic aspects of sexual development before the explicitly sexual. The sequence for boys is the reverse, commitment to sexual acts precedes commitment to emotion-laden, intimate relationships and the rhetoric of romantic love. These differences are not always easily resolved, and are thought to underlie the tension that persists between the scripts of men and women.

In elementary school life, sexual idioms function to construct and maintain gender segregation: "gender-marked rituals of teasing, chasing, and pollution heighten the boundaries between boys and girls" (p. 187). According to Thorne & Luria (1986), these rituals also convey assumptions which get integrated into later sexual scripts: "(1) that girls and boys are members of distinctive, opposing, and sometimes antagonistic groups; (2) that cross-gender contact is potentially sexual and contaminating, fraught with both pleasure and danger; (3) that girls are more sexually defined (and polluting) than boys" (p. 188).

Thorne & Luria (1986) argue that because children's sexual knowledge is fragmentary and distinctly different from that of adults, scripting in same-gender peer groups may be more about gender than sexual orientation. In this sense, at this age, children are learning about masculinity and femininity rather than sexuality per se, although heterosexuality is embedded within these concepts. Boys are learning from boys about pornography, rule transgression, and homophobia, and girls are learning from girls about romance, intimate relationships, popularity, and appearance: "girls remark on their own and others' appearance long before they talk about issues of attractiveness to boys. The concern with appearance, and the pattern of performing and being watched, may be integrated into sexual expression later" (p. 185). Thus, girls and boys transition to adolescent sexual intimacy from different and asymmetrical gender subcultures, which promote different sexual meanings. As such, they bring somewhat different needs, capacities, and types of knowledge to their burgeoning heterosexual relationships, making these spaces of "coming together" difficult to negotiate. Thorne & Luria (1986) conclude their paper with two questions: How, in the shift away from these less sexual definitions of gender in childhood does sexuality become seen and experienced as an intrinsic "personal characteristic? And, how are different sexualities constructed?" (p. 189). Let us turn to the sexual scripts of young adulthood, with attention to changes over the life course, in an attempt to provide answers to these questions.

### *Dating Scripts*

Rose & Frieze (1993) examined whether traditional gender roles continue to define courtship interactions. Their research is based on the premise that the fundamentals of sexual scripts, particularly gender roles, are acquired during childhood and adolescence (Simon & Gagnon, 1986). The research on playground sexual scripts provides support for this assumption. Stereotyped gender roles designate the male as possessing the object of desire and the female as embodying the object of desire. These roles are expressed by men assuming the proactive role in initiating sexual behavior and women adopting the reactive role in setting the boundaries of sexual behavior. Earlier research by Rose & Frieze (1993) found that young adults' descriptions of a first date were highly scripted, particularly along gender lines. In their comparison of hypothetical versus actual dating scenarios (Rose & Frieze, 1993): "hypothetical scripts appeared to form a core action sequence that was embellished during actual dates … a major emphasis of both hypothetical and actual scripts was a strong degree of gender typing" (p. 507). Their findings showed that:

> Men's proactive role encompassed initiating the date (asking for and planning it), controlling the public domain (driving and opening doors), and starting sexual interaction (initiating physical contact, making out, kissing goodnight). Women's reactive role focused on the private domain (concern about appearance, enjoying the date), participating in the structure of the date provided by the man (being picked up, having doors opened), and responding to his sexual overtures. Such gender differences serve to give men more power in the initial stages of the relationship.
>
> *Rose & Frieze (1993, p. 507)*

They go on to say that their results suggest that "changing social norms have not had much effect on female and male roles early in relationship development" (p. 508). Though their findings cannot shed light on later stages of relationship development, they do provide evidence that gender differences learned in childhood and adolescence may inform later heterosexual dating interactions and sexual behaviors. As a final example of gendered sexual scripts, let us turn to research addressing the role of gendered scripts in explicitly sexual behavior.

## *Sexual Scripts*

Sexual scripts—defining who does what, with whom, when, and what it means—are determined by a culture's view of gender (Miller & Simon, 1981) and, we would add, heteronormativity. In heterosexual relationships, "issues of control, initiation and dominance continue to play a crucial role in women's and men's gender scripts of sexual behavior" (Ehrhardt, 2000, p. 12). Ehrhardt and colleagues have conducted a series of qualitative studies with several hundred women and men in order to explore contemporary gender scripts between them. Through their research they have "become keenly aware of gender differences between women and men in their expectations, behaviors, and styles of interaction" (p. 12) (Seal & Ehrhardt, 2003; Seal, Wagner-Raphael, & Ehrhardt, 2000). According to this group of researchers, men still play the dominant role by controlling sexual interactions, and both women and men expect men to initiate sexual activity most of the time. There is some suggestion that social changes have led to a softening of gendered sexual scripts (men initiate and women set boundaries). Ehrhardt and colleagues found that many men acknowledge the existence of traditional gender scripts and understand their role as initiators; however, while men are aware of the norm, many feel burdened by the expectation. When asked how they would feel if a woman took the initiative in romance or sexual encounters, they felt positive about women initiating romance, though they had trouble generating examples of this from their own experiences, and were more ambivalent about women taking the initiative in sexual encounters. In comparison, the interviews with women revealed that some women now believe that initiation should be shared. While the norm of male initiation prevails, subgroups of both women and men wish for more equal participation. However, more research is needed to determine whether women are equal partners and can feel free and comfortable as men to initiate sexual interaction.

In spite of social change and movement toward a more egalitarian sexual script, sexual behavior continues to pose a much greater threat for women than for men. From childhood sexual abuse, to dating violence, to rape, to prostitution, to pornography, the threat and reality of violence becomes deeply embedded in the phenomenology of female sexuality. This experience and specter of violence undoubtedly affects the behavior of girls and women in sexual encounters. For example, in a study done in the 1970s, the top fantasy for both men and women was "having sex with someone you love." The second highest "having sex with strangers," was appealing to twice as many men as women (Hunt, 1974). This difference might not be reflecting desire for recreational sex, but rather a different relationship to the idea of a stranger. Women who wish to engage in sex with a stranger *must* evaluate the possibility of coercion and violence; if the fear and potential for violence were removed, women might be equally desiring of recreational sex.

Unarguably, a central channel through which sexual scripts, (expectations, behaviors, and outcomes) are communicated is the media—movies, television, news, and the Internet. Moore & Rosenthal (2006) interviewed adolescents about gender, sexuality, and romance. The internalization of media ideals can be seen in the following response to the question "What do the words 'romantic love' mean to you?"

> From movies and things, I see it everywhere. When you think you have the right person, and you have someone forever, and you don't want to break up. You love them and they love you, and you think there is nothing wrong and you are perfect for each other.
>
> Rosenthal & Moore (2006, p. 135)

## Media

Unlike the rest of the child's life, where development is instructed and nurtured, when it comes to sexuality children are faced with the task of discovering and deciphering sexuality on their own. Neither information nor guidance is provided from most parents, and the prevailing cultural value (at least in the United States) is that sexual behavior is unconditionally unhealthy outside of marriage (Welsh, Haugen, Widman, Darling, & Grello, 2005). We have seen that children turn to friends in order to circumvent these cultural proscriptions and lacunae surrounding sex. They also rely heavily on the mass media for information about sexual norms, values, and behaviors.

Research on media as sexual socializer is plagued by the same problems as all media impact research—the question of directionality. Are adolescents who watch sexual media more "sexual" to begin with, or are they curious and/or unintentionally exposed, and thus imposed upon by it? (Brown, Steele, & Walsh-Childers, 2002). In a media-saturated culture this distinction becomes near impossible to disentangle. Despite this methodological limitation, one consistent finding in the field is the moderating effect of parental presence in associations between viewing sexual media and sexual attitudes and to some extent behavior; however, as children age they become increasingly less likely to consume media with their parents (Schooler, Kim, & Sorsoli, 2006).

The media has long been considered a primary source of sexuality information for young people, and has now most likely superseded parental supremacy in its influence. Within the developmental context of increasing differentiation and distance from parental influence, Brown (Brown et al., 2002) conceptualizes sexual media consumption as part of a larger media "identity toolkit" that adolescents utilize as a means of exploring the self and identity; in this way she suggests that media can serve as a kind of sexual super peer. Research supports this notion: in a national survey on sexual health, youth aged 10 to 15 years most frequently name the mass media, including movies, TV, magazines, and music, as their source of information about sex and intimacy. Smaller percentages name parents, peers, sexuality education programs, and professionals as sources (Kaiser Family Foundation, 1997). What children and adolescents see, hear, and read in the media is assumed to influence their social development and behavior. Buhi & Goodson (2007) argued that there is a strong theoretical basis for assuming that sexual content in the media shapes adolescents' beliefs, attitudes, norms, and intentions to have sex. In support of their assumption, empirical evidence suggests exposure to sexual content on television (e.g., sexually oriented genres and programs with high sex content) is associated with expectations about sex, perceptions of peer sexual behavior, sexually permissive attitudes, and sexual initiation (Brown et al., 2002; Tolman, Kim, Schooler, & Sorsoli, 2007; Ward, 2003; Ward & Friedman, 2006), but that these associations are moderated by both gender and race (Hennessy, Bleakley, Fishbein, & Jordan, 2009).

Media and sexual socialization research has become increasingly complex and nuanced in recent years, conducting analyses that incorporate gender, race, and class (Ward, 2003; Ward, Hansborough, & Walker, 2005). Research on gendered processes has found that media that convey traditional gender roles are associated with endorsement of more traditional perspectives regarding male and female sexuality (Kim, Sorsoli, Collins, Zylbergold, Schooler, & Tolman, 2007; Rivadeneyra & Lebo, 2008; Ward et al., 2005). Additionally, the research has revealed associations between non-behavioral negative sexual outcomes (e.g., endorsement of coercion in heterosexual relationships and negative attitudes about sex) and media images enacting traditional gendered relational practices and scripts.

It is important to bear in mind that media is not a monolithic evil. Media researchers in the past decade have also examined how media can support young people's sexual development (Bay-Cheng, Robinson, & Zucker, 2009; Ward & Friedman, 2006). For example, online environments function as spaces in which adolescents can search out peers, ask questions about sexual topics, and construct sexual identities (Suzuki & Calzo, 2004). Research has also shown that teen chat rooms can provide safe environments in which teenagers can learn to exchange information with peers and explore their emerging sexuality in healthy, positive ways (Subrahmanyam, Greenfield, & Tynes, 2004).

## Pornography, Coercion, and Sexual Violence

With the increasing availability of pornography on the Internet, the question of how these representations of sexual behavior, sexuality, and gender roles is affecting sexual development has been of interest to researchers. In one study of adolescents aged 14–19, sexual violence, unwanted sex, and pornography were all correlated (Bonino, Ciairano, Rabaglietti, & Cattelino, 2006). In a study on sexual behavior (Bonino, Cattelino, & Ciairano, 2005), researchers investigated gender differences in pornography and sexual violence: they found that exposure to pornography, whether in the form of magazines or videos, was more frequent for boys, a finding that has support in other work (e.g., Larsson, 2002). In addition, boys were significantly more often the perpetrators of sexual violence, whereas girls were more often the victims. In an initial exploratory descriptive study comparing Italy and The Netherlands, researchers found that in both countries: girls were more often the victims of sexual harassment; pornography and sexual violence were correlated; and sexual harassment was correlated with other types of antisocial behavior, such as aggression, theft, and vandalism (Bijstra, Ciairano, & Jackson, 2001).

As for pornography's role in the increased acceptance of sexually abusive attitudes, some studies have shown that, at least under certain conditions, if societal norms condone or tolerate unwanted sex, then sexual harassment becomes more acceptable and sometimes even more prevalent (Fitzgerald, Drasgow, Hulin, Gelfand, & Magley, 1997; Malamuth & Check, 1985). With regard to approval of sexual harassment and rape, Goodchilds & Zellman (1984) found that a high percentage of adolescents of both sexes felt that it was acceptable to force a girl to have sex. They examined explicitly the adolescents' beliefs about why one might force another into sexual intercourse; two-thirds of the sample felt that rape was acceptable if the girl had sexually excited the boy, meaning that adolescents impute responsibility and blame to the victim of sexual violence rather than to the perpetrator. In a study by Thompson & Holland (1998), adolescents considered insistence and pressure a legitimate component, or even a requirement, of the male sexual role. Therefore, it appears that in Western society, sexual attitudes are linked to social stereotypes and to different socialization processes, which are more likely to portray girls as passive receptors and boys as active agents, and which lead us to enact and evaluate sexual behavior differently based on gender (Ciairano, Bonino, Kliewer, Miceli, & Jackson, 2006; Graber, Brooks-Gunn, & Galen, 1998; Moore & Rosenthal, 2006). As we have seen, enactment of cultural constructions of male and female sexuality can have profoundly adverse outcomes, for both genders.

## Sexual Double Standard

A review of 30 studies, most conducted with adolescents, published since 1980 found evidence of the continued existence of different standards of permissiveness for girls and boys (Crawford & Popp, 2003). In a three-year ethnographic study of middle-school peer culture, Eder, Evans, & Parker (1995) showed that girls, but never boys, could be derogated for showing interest in sex or sexual assertiveness. Making the first move was not tolerated for girls, with sanctions against female sexual agency including negative comments about dressing attractively. In other research with young adolescents, girls describe their fear of the epithet slut (Orenstein, 1994), and the dilemma of negotiating the narrow space between prude and slut (Tolman, 2002; Drury, Raufelder, & Bukowski, 2012). Whereas a tarnished reputation is a major issue for girls, the fear of which results in sexual desire being expressed mainly in the context of romantic love and commitment, boys are encouraged to be sexually active, and their reputations are enhanced by more sexual activity (Moore & Rosenthal, 2006). The sexual double standard is encoded within heterosexuality, which has been defined as a set of norms and behaviors which, by the power of masculine culture (and supported by both sexes), allows sexual freedom for young men but not young women as part of their identity development (Holland, Ramazanoglu, Sharpe, & Thompson, 1998).

The social processes that underlie sexual behavior, such as the double standard, were recently uncovered in a series of brilliant experiments. Conley, Moors, Matsick, Ziegler, & Valentine (2011) debunked several widely held to be true gender differences in sexual behavior, and showed that these differences could in fact be explained by stigma against women for expressing sexual desires; women's socialization to attend to other's needs rather than their own; and, more broadly, a double standard that dictates (different sets of) appropriate sexual behaviors for men and women. For example, a belief that one will be stigmatized harshly partially explains gender differences in casual sex, such that when women feel that they can avoid being stigmatized for their behavior, gender differences are diminished. This research clearly illustrates: (1) the gendered nature of sexual behavior; and (2) the social bases of sexual development and behavior. Research with adolescents supports the work being done by Conley and colleagues.

## CONCLUSION: HEALTHY SEXUAL DEVELOPMENT

Considering the complexity of sexual development, a lifelong process spanning myriad domains of experience including feelings, urges and motivation, forms of attention, emotions, aspects of the self, biological processes, moral precepts, modes of self-presentation, relationships and interactions, and one's perceptions of others, we believe that the guidance that we provide as parents, teachers, entertainers, and politicians to help elucidate this incredibly enigmatic process should be equally comprehensive and complex. In an effort to provide some of this guidance, a group of multidisciplinary researchers studying children's sexual development developed a framework for researching healthy sexual development (McKee et al., 2010). The 15 identified domains of sexual development were: freedom from unwanted activity; an understanding of consent; education about biological aspects; understanding of safety; relationship skills; agency; lifelong learning; resilience; open communication; sexual development should not be "aggressive, coercive, or joyless;" self-acceptance; awareness and acceptance that sex is pleasurable; understanding of parental and societal values; awareness of public/private boundaries; and being competent in mediated sexuality. The social policy implications of these guidelines are obvious, as is the stark discrepancy between where we are and where we need to be. We feel that these domains provide an excellent framework within which to provide guidance and to enact change.

## ACKNOWLEDGEMENT

Work on this paper was supported by grants to both authors from the Social Sciences and Humanities Research Council of Canada and by a University Research Chair to the second author.

## REFERENCES

Abelson, R. P. (1981). Psychological status of the script concept. *American Psychologist*, *36*, 715–729.
Bancroft, J. (Ed.). (2003). *Sexual development in childhood*. Bloomington, IN: Indiana University Press.
Bandura, A. (1977). *Social learning theory*. Englewood Cliffs, NJ: Prentice Hall, Inc.
Bandura, A. (1986). *Social foundations of thought and action: A social cognitive theory*. Englewood Cliffs, NJ: Prentice-Hall, Inc.
Bay-Cheng, L. Y., Robinson, A. D., & Zucker, A. N. (2009). Behavioral and relational contexts of adolescent desire, wanting, and pleasure: Undergraduate women's retrospective accounts. *Journal of Sex Research*, *46*(6), 511–524.
Bem, S. (1981). Gender schema theory: A cognitive account of sex typing. *Psychological Review*, *88*, 354–364.
Bigler, R. S., & Liben, L. S. (2007). Developmental intergroup theory: Explaining and reducing children's social stereotyping and prejudice. *Current Directions in Psychological Science*, *16*(3), 162–166. doi:10.1111/j.1467-8721.2007.00496.x.
Bijstra, J., Ciairano, S., & Jackson, S. (2001, August). Sexual harassment among Italian and Dutch adolescents: Relations with psychological and psychosocial factors and implications for health prevention. Paper presented at the Xth European Conference on Developmental Psychology, Uppsala, Sweden.

Bonino, S., Cattelino, E., & Ciairano, S. (2005). *Adolescents and risk: Behaviors, functions and protective factors*. New York, NY: Springer Verlag.

Bonino, S., Ciairano, S., Rabaglietti, E., & Cattelino, E. (2006). Use of pornography and self-reported engagement in sexual violence among adolescents. *European Journal of Developmental Psychology, 3*(3), 265–288. doi:10.1080/1.

Brown, J., Steele, J., & Walsh-Childers, K. (2002). *Sexual teens, sexual media: Investigating media's influences on adolescent sexuality*. Mahwah, NJ: Erlbaum.

Buhi, E. R., & Goodson, P. (2007). Predictors of adolescent sexual behavior and intention: A theory-guided systematic review. *Journal of Adolescent Health, 40*, 4–21. doi:10.1016/j.jadohealth.2006.09.027.

Bukowski, W. M., Buhrmester, D., & Underwood, M. K. (2011). Peer relations as a developmental context. In M. K. Underwood, & L. H. Rosen (Eds.), *Social development: Relationships in infancy, childhood, and adolescence (pp. 153–179)*. New York, NY: Guilford Press.

Bukowski, W. M., Gauze, C., Hoza, B., & Newcomb, A. F. (1993). Differences and consistency in relations with same-sex and other-sex peers during early adolescence. *Developmental Psychology, 29*, 255–263.

Bukowski, W. M., Li, K. Z., Dirks, M., & Bouffard, T. (in press). Developmental science and the study of successful development. *International Journal of Developmental Science*.

Bukowski, W. M., Simard, M., Dubois, M., & Lopez, L. (2011). Representations, process, and development: A new look at friendship in early adolescence. In E. Amsel, & J. G. Smetana (Eds.), *Adolescent vulnerabilities and opportunities: Developmental and constructivist perspectives (pp. 159–181)*. New York, NY: Cambridge University Press. 10.1017/CBO9781139042819.010.

Cavanagh Johnson, T., & Feldmeth, J. R. (1993). Sexual behaviors – a continuum. In I. E. Gil, & T. Cavanagh Johnson (Eds.), *Sexualized children (pp. 39–52)*.

Ciairano, S., Bonino, S., Kliewer, W., Miceli, R., & Jackson, S. (2006). Dating, sexual activity, and well-being in Italian adolescents. *Journal of Clinical Child and Adolescent Psychology, 35*, 275–282. doi:10.1207/s15374424jccp3502_11.

Conley, T. D., Moors, A. C., Matsick, J. L., Ziegler, A., & Valentine, B. A. (2011). Women, men and the bedroom: Methodological and conceptual insights that narrow, reframe, and eliminate gender differences in sexuality. *Current Directions in Psychological Science*, 296–300.

Constantine, L., & Martinson, F. (1981). *Children and sex*. Boston, MA: Little, Brown and Company.

Crawford, M., & Popp, D. (2003). Sexual double standards: A review and methodological critique of two decades of research. *Journal of Sex Research, 40*, 13–26. doi:10.1080/00224490309552163.

Diamond, L. M. (2003). New paradigms for research on heterosexual and sexual-minority development. *Journal of Clinical Child and Adolescent Psychology, 32*, 490–498. doi:10.1207/S15374424JCCP3204_1.

Diamond, L. M., Savin-Williams, R. C., & Dubé, E. M. (1999). Sex, dating, passionate friendships, and romance: Intimate peer relations among lesbian, gay, and bisexual adolescents. In W. Furman, B. Brown, & C. Feiring (Eds.), *The development of romantic relationships in adolescence (pp. 175–210)*. New York, NY: Cambridge University Press.

Drury, K., Raufelder, D., & Bukowski, B. (2012). Sex and gender: Themes from interviews with adolescents. Poster presented at the Gender Development Research Conference. San Francisco, USA.

Eder, D., Evans, C., & Parker, S. (1995). *School talk: Gender and adolescent culture*. New Brunswick, NJ: Rutgers University Press.

Ehrhardt, A. A. (2000). Gender, sexuality, and human development. In J. Bancroft (Ed.), *The role of theory in sex research (pp. 3–16)*. Bloomington, IN: Indiana University Press.

Fabes, R. A., Martin, C. L., & Hanish, L. D. (2007). The next 50 years: Considering gender as a context for understanding young children's peer relationships. In G. W. Ladd (Ed.),

*Appraising the human developmental sciences: Essays in honor of Merrill-Palmer Quarterly (pp. 186–199)*. Detroit, MI: Wayne State University Press.

Field, T. (2002). Infants' need for touch. *Human Development*, 45, 100–103. doi:10.1159/000048156.

Fitzgerald, L. F., Drasgow, F., Hulin, C. L., Gelfand, M. J., & Magley, V. J. (1997). Antecedents and consequences of sexual harassment in organizations: A test of an integrated model. *Journal of Applied Psychology*, 82, 578–589. doi:10.1037/0021-9010.82.4.578.

Fitzpatrick, C., Deehan, A., & Jennings, S. (1995). Children's sexual behaviour and knowledge: A community study. *Irish Journal of Psychological Medicine*, 12, 87–91.

Frayser, S. (1994). Defining normal childhood sexuality: An anthropological approach. *Annual Review of Sex Research, Society for the Scientific Study of Sex*, 173–217.

Friedrich, W. N. (2003). Studies of sexuality of nonabused children. In J. Bancroft (Ed.), *Sexual development in childhood (pp. 107–120)*. Bloomington, IN: Indiana University Press.

Gagnon, J. H., & Simon, W. (1973). *Sexual Conduct*. Chicago, IL: Aldine.

Gil, E. (1993). *Age-appropriate sex play versus problematic sexual behaviors: Sexualized children: Assessment and treatment of sexualized children and children who molest (pp. 21–40)*. Rockville: MD: Launch Press.

Goldman, R., & Goldman, J. (1982). *Children's sexual thinking: A comparative study of children aged 5 to 15 years in Australia, North America, Britain, and Sweden*. Boston, MA: Routledge & Kegan Paul.

Goodchilds, J. D., & Zellman., G. L. (1984). Sexual signaling and sexual aggression in adolescent relationships. In N. M. Malamuth, & E. Donnerstein (Eds.), *Pornography and sexual aggression*. San Diego, CA: Academic Press.

Graber, J. A., Brooks-Gunn, J., & Galen, B. R. (1998). Betwixt and between: Sexuality in the context of adolescent transitions. In R. Jessor, & R. Jessor (Eds.), *New perspectives on adolescent risk behavior (pp. 270–316)*. New York, NY: Cambridge University Press.

Hennessy, M., Bleakley, A., Fishbein, M., & Jordan, A. (2009). Estimating the longitudinal association between adolescent sexual behavior and exposure to sexual media content. *Journal of Sex Research*, 46, 586–596. doi:10.1080/00224490902898736.

Herdt, G. H. (1984). *Ritualized homosexuality in Melanesia*. Berkeley & Los Angeles, CA: University of California Press.

Holland, J., Ramazanoglu, C., Sharpe, S., & Thompson, R. (1998). *The male in the head: Young people, heterosexuality and power*. London, UK: The Tufnell Press.

Hunt, M. (1974). *Sexual behavior in the 1970s*. Oxford, UK: Playboy Press.

Intons-Peterson, M. J., & Reddel, M. (1984). What do people ask about a neonate? *Developmental Psychology*, 20, 358–359. doi:10.1037/0012-1649.20.3.358.

Jacklin, C. N., & Maccoby, E. E. (1978). Social behavior at thirty-three months in same-sex and mixed-sex dyads. *Child Development*, 49(3), 557–569. doi:10.2307/1128222.

Kaiser Family Foundation, (1997). *Talking with kids about tough issues*. Menlo Park, CA: Author.

Kim, J. L., Sorsoli, C., Collins, K., Zylbergold, B. A., Schooler, D., & Tolman, D. L. (2007). From sex to sexuality: Exposing the heterosexual script on primetime network television. *Journal of Sex Research*, 44, 145–157.

Kinsey, A. C., Pomeroy, W. B., & Martin, C. E. (1948). *Sexual behavior in the human male*. Philadelphia, PA: W.B. Saunders.

Kinsey, A. C., Pomeroy, W. B., Martin, C. E., & Gebhard, P. H. (1953). *Sexual behavior in the human female*. Philadelphia, PA: W.B. Saunders.

Kreager, D. A., & Staff, J. (2009). The sexual double standard and adolescent peer acceptance. *Social Psychology Quarterly*, 72(2), 143–164. doi:10.1177/019027250907200205.

Larsson, I. (2002). Sexual abuse of children: Child sexuality and sexual behavior. Report written for the Swedish National Board of Health and Welfare.

Larsson, I., Svedin, C. -G., & Friedrich, W. N. (2000). Difference and similarities in sexual behavior among pre-schoolers in Sweden and USA. *Nordic Journal of Psychiatry, 54*, 251–257. doi:10.1080/080394800448110.

Leaper, C. (1994). Exploring the consequences of gender segregation on social relationships. In C. Leaper (Ed.), *Childhood gender segregation: Causes and consequences (pp. 67–86)*. San Francisco, CA: Jossey-Bass.

Lindblad, F., Gustafsson, P. A., Larsson, I., & Lundin, B. (1995). Preschoolers' sexual behavior at daycare centers: An epidemiological study. *Child Abuse & Neglect, 19*, 569–577. doi:10.1016/0145-2134(95)00016-2.

Maccoby, E. (1990). Gender and relationships: A developmental account. *American Psychologist, 45*, 513–520.

Maccoby, E. E. (1998). *The two sexes: Growing up apart, coming together*. Cambridge, MA: Belknap Press/Harvard University Press.

Maccoby, E. E., & Jacklin, C. (1987). Gender segregation in childhood. In H. W. Reese & H. W. Reese (Eds.), *Advances in child development and behavior* (Vol. 20, pp. 239–287). San Diego, CA: Academic Press.

Malamuth, N. M., & Check, J. V. (1985). The effects of aggressive pornography on beliefs in rape myths: Individual differences. *Journal of Research in Personality, 19*, 299–320. doi:10.1016/0092-6566(85)90021-2.

Martin, C., & Halverson, C. (1981). A schematic processing model of sex typing and stereotyping in children. *Child Development, 52*, 1119–1134.

Martin, C. L., & Fabes, R. A. (2001). The stability and consequences of young children's same-sex peer interactions. *Developmental Psychology, 37*, 431–446.

Martin, C. L., & Ruble, D. (2004). Children's search for gender cues: Cognitive perspectives on gender development. *Current Directions in Psychological Science, 13*, 67–70.

Maslow, A. H. (1943). Preface to motivation theory. *Psychosomatic Medicine*, 585–592.

McKee, A., Albury, K., Dunne, M., Grieshaber, S., Hartley, J., Lumby, C., et al. (2010). Healthy sexual development: A multidisciplinary framework for research. *International Journal of Sexual Health, 22*, 14–19. doi:10.1080/19317610903393043.

Milhausen, R. R., & Herold, E. S. (1999). Does the sexual double standard still exist? Perceptions of university women. *Journal of Sex Research, 36*, 361–368. doi:10.1080/00224499909552008.

Miller, P. Y., & Simon, W. (1981). The development of sexuality in adolescence. Joseph Adelson (Ed.), *Handbook of adolescent psychology*. New York, NY: Wiley.

Miller, P., Danaher, D., & Forbes, D. (1986). Sex-related strategies for coping with interpersonal conflict in children aged five and seven. *Developmental Psychology, 22*, 543–548.

Mischel, Walter (1966). A social-learning view of sex differences in behavior. In Eleanor E. Maccoby (Ed.), *The development of sex differences (pp. 56–81)*. Stanford, CA: Stanford University Press.

Moore, S., & Rosenthal, D. (2006). *Sexuality in adolescence: Current trends*. New York, NY: Routledge.

Orenstein, P. (1994). *Schoolgirls: Young women, self-esteem and the confidence gap*. New York, NY: Anchor Books.

O'Sullivan, L. F., Meyer-Bahlburg, H. L., & Watkins, B. X. (2000). Social cognitions associated with pubertal development in a sample of urban, low-income, African-American and Latina girls and mothers. *Journal of Adolescent Health, 27*(4), 227–235. doi:10.1016/S1054-139X(99)00111-1.

Petersen, J. L., & Hyde, J. (2011). Gender differences in sexual attitudes and behaviors: A review of meta-analytic results and large datasets. *Journal of Sex Research, 48*(2–3), 149–165. doi:10.1080/00224499.2011.551851.

Pfaus, J. G., Kippin, T. E., Coria-Avila, G. A., Gelez, H., Afonso, V. M., Ismail, N., et al. (2012). Who, what, where, when (and maybe even why)? How the experience of sexual reward

connects sexual desire, preference, and performance. *Archives of Sexual Behavior, 41*, 31–62. doi:10.1007/s10508-012-9935-5.
Plummer, K. (1991). Understanding childhood sexualities. In T. Sandfort, E. Brongersma, & A. van Naerssen (Eds.), *Male intergenerational intimacy: Historical, socio-psychological, and legal perspectives*. New York, NY: Harrington Park Press.
Poulin-Dubois, D., Serbin, L. A., Kenyon, B., & Derbyshire, A. (1994). Infants' intermodal knowledge about gender. *Developmental Psychology, 30*, 436–442.
Quinn, P. C., Yahr, J., Kuhn, A., Slater, A. M., & Pascalis, O. (2002). Representation of the gender of human faces by infants: A preference for female. *Perception, 31*, 1109–1121. doi:10.1068/p3331.
Reynolds, M. A., Herbenick, D. L., & Bancroft, J. (2003). The nature of childhood sexual experiences: Two studies 50 years apart. In J. Bancroft (Ed.), *Sexual development in childhood*. Bloomington, IN: Indiana University Press.
Rivadeneyra, R., & Lebo, M. J. (2008). The association between television-viewing behaviors and adolescent dating role attitudes and behaviors. *Journal of Adolescence, 31*, 291–305. doi:10.1016/j.adolescence.2007.06.001.
Rose, S., & Frieze, I. H. (1993). Young singles' contemporary dating scripts. *Sex Roles, 28*, 499–509.
Rubin, K. H., Bukowski, W. M., & Parker, J. G. (2006). Peer interactions, relationships, and groups. In N. Eisenberg, W. Damon, R. M. Lerner, N. Eisenberg, W. Damon, & R. M. Lerner (Eds.), *Handbook of child psychology: Vol. 3, Social, emotional, and personality development (pp. 571–645)* (6th ed.). Hoboken, NJ: John Wiley & Sons Inc.
Ruble, D. N., & Martin, C. L. (1998). Gender development. In W. Damon (Ed.), *Handbook of child psychology (pp. 933–1016)*. New York, NY: John Wiley & Sons Inc.
Ruble, D. N., Martin, C., & Berenbaum, S. A. (2006). Gender development. In N. Eisenberg, W. Damon, R. M. Lerner, N. Eisenberg, W. Damon, & R. M. Lerner (Eds.), *Handbook of child psychology: Vol. 3, Social, emotional, and personality development (pp. 858–932)* (6th ed.). Hoboken, NJ: John Wiley & Sons Inc.
Sandfort, Th. G. M., & Rademakers, J. (Eds.). (2000). *Childhood sexuality: Normal sexual behavior and development*. New York, NY: Haworth Press.
Savin-Williams, R. C., & Diamond, L. M. (2004). Sex. In R. M. Lerner, L. Steinberg, R. M. Lerner, & L. Steinberg (Eds.), *Handbook of adolescent psychology (pp. 189–231)* (2nd ed.). Hoboken, NJ: John Wiley & Sons Inc.
Schmidt, W. E. (1993). Sweden redefines sexual revolution. In C. S. Wren, & W. T. Ethridge (Eds.), *Themes of times: Human sexuality*. New York, NY: Prentice Hall and the New York Times.
Schooler, D., Kim, J. L., & Sorsoli, L. (2006). Setting rules or sitting down: Parental mediation of television consumption and adolescent self-esteem, body image, and sexuality. *Sexuality Research & Social Policy: A Journal of the NSRC, 3*, 49–62. doi:10.1525/srsp.2006.3.4.49.
Schwartz, P., & Rutter, V. (1998). *The gender of sexuality*. Thousand Oaks, CA: Pine Forge Press.
Seal, D., & Ehrhardt, A. A. (2003). Masculinity and urban men: Perceived scripts for courtship, romantic, and sexual interactions with women. *Culture, Health & Sexuality, 5*(4), 295–319. doi:10.1080/136910501171698.
Seal, D., Wagner-Raphael, L. I., & Ehrhardt, A. A. (2000). Sex, intimacy, and HIV: An ethnographic study of a Puerto Rican social group in New York City. *Journal of Psychology & Human Sexuality, 11*(4), 51–92. doi:10.1300/J056v11n04_03.
Serbin, L., Sprafkin, C., Elman, M., & Doyle, A. (1982). The early development of sex-differentiated patterns of social influence. *Canadian Journal of Behavioural Science/Revue Canadienne des Sciences du Comportement, 14*, 350–363.
Simon, W., & Gagnon, J. H. (1986). Sexual scripts: Permanence and change. *Archives of Sexual Behavior, 15*, 97–120.

Sippola, L. K., & Bukowski, W. M. (1999). Self, other and loneliness from a developmental perspective. In K. Rotenberg, & S. Hymel (Eds.), *Loneliness during childhood and adolescence (pp. 280–295)*. New York, NY: Cambridge University Press.

Sippola, L., Bukowski, W. M., & Noll, R. B. (1997). Age differences in children's and early adolescents' liking for same-sex and other-sex peers. *Merrill-Palmer Quarterly, 43*, 547–561.

Stack, D. M. (2007). The salience of touch and physical contact during infancy: Unraveling some of the mysteries of the somesthetic sense. In G. Bremner, & A. Fogel (Eds.), *Blackwell handbook of infant development*. Oxford, UK: Blackwell Publishing Ltd. 10.1002/9780470996348.ch13.

Subrahmanyam, K., Greenfield, P. M., & Tynes, B. (2004). Constructing sexuality and identity in an online teen chat room. *Journal of Applied Developmental Psychology, 25*, 651–666. doi:10.1016/j.appdev.2004.09.007.

Sullivan, H. (1953). *The interpersonal theory of psychiatry*. New York, NY: W W Norton & Co.

Suzuki, L. K., & Calzo, J. P. (2004). The search for peer advice in cyberspace: An examination of online teen bulletin boards about health and sexuality. *Journal of Applied Developmental Psychology, 25*, 685–698. doi:10.1016/j.appdev.2004.09.002.

Thompson, R., & Holland, J. (1998). Sexual relationships, negotiation and decision making. In J. Coleman, & D. Roker (Eds.), *Teenage sexuality: Health, risk and education*. Amsterdam, The Netherlands: Harwood Academic Publisher.

Thorne, B., & Luria, Z. (1986). Sexuality and gender in children's daily worlds. *Social Problems, 33*, 176–190.

Tolman, D. L. (1999). Femininity as a barrier to positive sexual health for adolescent girls. *Journal of American Medical Women's Association, 54*, 133–138.

Tolman, D. L. (2002). Femininity as a barrier to positive sexual health for adolescent girls. In A. E. Hunter, C. Forden, A. E. Hunter, & C. Forden (Eds.), *Readings in the psychology of gender: Exploring our differences and commonalities (pp. 196–206)*. Needham Heights, MA: Allyn & Bacon.

Tolman, D. L., Kim, J. L., Schooler, D., & Sorsoli, C. L. (2007). Rethinking the associations between television viewing and adolescent sexuality development: Bringing gender into focus. *Journal of Adolescent Health*, 84.e9–84.e16.

Ward, L. M. (2003). Understanding the role of entertainment media in the sexual socialization of American youth: A review of empirical research. *Developmental Review, 23*, 347–388. doi:10.1016/S0273-2297(03)00013-3.

Ward, L. M., & Friedman, K. (2006). Using TV as a guide: Associations between television viewing and adolescents' sexual attitudes and behavior. *Journal of Research on Adolescence, 16*, 133–156. doi:10.1111/j.1532-7795.2006.00125.x.

Ward, L., Hansbrough, E., & Walker, E. (2005). Contributions of music video exposure to black adolescents' gender and sexual schemas. *Journal of Adolescent Research, 20*, 143–166. doi:10.1177/0743558404271135.

Wiederman, M. W. (2005). The gendered nature of sexual scripts. *The Family Journal, 13*, 496–502. doi:10.1177/1066480705278729.

Weisgram, E. S., Bigler, R. S., & Liben, L. S. (2010). Gender, values, and occupational interests among children, adolescents, and adults. *Child Development, 81*(3), 778–796. doi:10.1111/j.1467-8624.2010.01433.x.

Welsh, D. P., Grello, C. M., & Harper, M. S. (2003). When love hurts: Depression and adolescent romantic relationships. In P. Florsheim (Ed.), *Adolescent romantic relations and sexual behavior: Theory, research, and practical implications (pp. 185–211)*. Mahwah, NJ: Lawrence Erlbaum Associates Publishers.

Welsh, D. P., Haugen, P. T., Widman, L., Darling, N., & Grello, C. M. (2005). Kissing is good: A developmental investigation of sexuality in adolescent romantic couples. *Sexuality Research & Social Policy*, 32–41. doi:10.1080/00224490902867871.

Whitbeck, L. B., Yoder, K. A., Hoyt, D. R., & Conger, R. D. (1999). Early adolescent sexual activity: A developmental study. *Journal of Marriage & The Family, 61,* 934–946. doi:10.2307/354014.

Woody, J. D., Russel, R., D'Souza, H. J., & Woody, J. K. (2000). Adolescent non-coital sexual activity: Comparisons of virgins and non-virgins. *Journal of Sex Education & Therapy, 25*(4), 261–268.

Zosuls, K. M., Miller, C., Ruble, D. N., Martin, C., & Fabes, R. A. (2011). Gender development research in sex roles: Historical trends and future directions. *Sex Roles, 64,* 826–842. doi:10.1007/s11199-010-9902-3.

# CHAPTER 6

# Sexual Behavior of Prepubertal Children

Christopher Campbell, Ashwini Mallappa, Amy B. Wisniewski, and Jane F. Silovsky
University of Oklahoma Health Sciences Center, Oklahoma City, Oklahoma[1]

## INTRODUCTION

Despite many parents' wishes, sexual development begins at an early age (in utero in fact) and progresses throughout childhood into adolescence. Puberty is an important marker as a critical time of physical growth and psychosocial development, changing forever how youth perceive themselves and relationships, as they advance into adulthood. This chapter will review typical sexual behavior in prepubertal children. We will begin by defining puberty and review the physical changes of puberty. The recent trends of earlier onset of puberty will be described in the context of current theories. Typical sexual knowledge and behaviors are described beginning in infancy and through school-age years, including distinguishing typical sex play from more problematic behaviors. Typical sexual knowledge and behaviors are influenced by social environment, culture, and media, and these factors are discussed. The impact of early-onset puberty or precocious puberty on sexual behavior in children is provided, though current research is limited. The chapter ends with a brief discussion of gender identity disorder.

## DEFINING PREPUBERTAL

The term *puberty* is used to define the developmental process of physical changes as the body matures from childhood to adulthood. Normal pubertal progression results from the sustained activation of the hypothalamic–pituitary–gonadal (HPG) hormone axis. This sustained activation starts

---

[1] Correspondence to: Jane Silovsky, Center on Child Abuse and Neglect, U. Oklahoma Health Sciences Center, 940 NE 13th Street, 3B3406, Oklahoma City, OK 73104. Phone: 405-271-8858; email Jane-Silovsky@ouhsc.edu

with the pulsatile release of the hormone gonadotropin-releasing hormone (GnRH) from the hypothalamus that then signals the release of two other hormones from the anterior pituitary gland: luteinizing hormone and follicle-stimulating hormone. Secretion of luteinizing hormone (LH) and follicle-stimulating hormone (FSH) is needed to stimulate the gonads (i.e., testes, ovaries) to produce the sex hormones testosterone and estrogen. These sex hormones are necessary to initiate and sustain the development of secondary sexual characteristics, such as breast development and pubic hair growth. The HPG axis maintains homeostasis via negative feedback mechanisms, a control mechanism commonly employed by the endocrine system, as well as other physiologic systems (see Figure 6.1).

Progression through puberty is measured by observing the timing and sequence of changes of secondary sexual characteristics in boys and girls. The staging system used to describe these changes is Tanner Staging (or Sexual Maturity Ratings), and different Tanner Staging criteria are used for breast (females), genital (males), and pubic hair (in both sexes) development (Tanner, 1986). Tanner Stage 1 is used to define prepubertal status, while Tanner Stage 2 indicates the initial production of gonadal hormones and the onset of puberty. Pubertal progression continues as more sex hormones are produced, and Tanner Stage ratings of 3 and 4 are used to describe the further development of secondary sex characteristics over

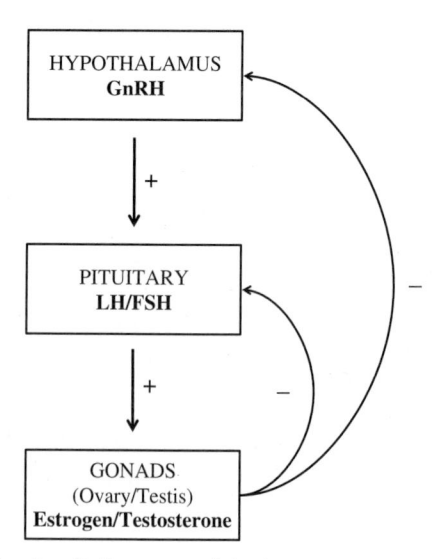

**Figure 6.1** Hypothalamic–pituitary–gonadal axis.

time. Finally, Tanner Stage 5 indicates that the pubertal maturation process is complete.

*Adrenarche* is the maturation of the adrenal gland, which leads to the development of pubic hair, axillary hair, adult body odor, and changes in the pilosebaceous gland in both sexes. Adrenarche (which usually starts between 6 and 8 years of age in boys and girls alike) is not a sign of true puberty and refers to the biochemical ability of the adrenal glands to synthesize adrenal androgens (Del Giudice, Angeleri, & Manera, 2009). The two major adrenal androgens are dehydroepiandrosterone (DHEA) and dehydroepiandrosterone sulfate (DHEAS). Adrenal gland maturation occurs independently of the HPG axis activation that is needed to initiate and sustain pubertal development (Oberfield, Sopher, & Gerken, 2011). Premature adrenarche (usually a benign and normal variant of development) is defined as development of pubic hair before 8 years of age in girls and 9 years of age in boys (Williams, Ward, & Hughes, 2011).

Pubertal progression in both boys and girls is also accompanied by observable physical changes. The first physical sign of puberty in boys is testicular enlargement, occurring at approximately 11.5 years of age. *Spermarche*, or the ability to produce sperm, typically occurs around 13.5 years of age (Rosenfield, Lipton, & Drum, 2009). Accompanying the onset of sperm production is facial hair growth and deepening of the voice, which is attained by approximately 15 years of age (Rosen, 2004). *Thelarche* (or breast budding) is normally the first physical sign of puberty in females, and is caused by the action of estrogen on breast tissue. The mean age of thelarche is 10.2 years (range: 8.2–12.1 years; Rosenfield et al., 2009). *Menarche* is the onset of menstruation in girls and occurs approximately 2.5 years after thelarche (mean age of onset is 12.6 years), with some variation depending on ethnicity (Susman & Rogol, 2004).

Pubertal development is also accompanied by a growth spurt that typically occurs when pubertal development progresses to Tanner Stage 3 for girls and Tanner Stage 4 for boys. In girls, the duration of puberty is typically 3.5 years, but may range from 2 years to 6 years (Zacharias, Wurtman, & Shatzoff, 1970). The process often lasts longer in boys, with pubertal maturation not ending until 17 years of age (Rosen, 2004). There is considerable debate about the typical age of pubertal onset for girls, with earlier onset noted as described in the next section (for additional information on puberty, please see Rosen, 2004; Susman & Rogol, 2004).

## THEORIES OF WHY PUBERTY IS OCCURRING AT EARLIER AGES

The average age at menarche has decreased from 17 to 13 years of age from the early 19th to the mid-20th century, presumably as a result of improved nutrition and living standards among children (Aksglaede, Olsen, Sorensen, & Juul, 2008; Garn, 1987; Parent et al., 2003). However, during the past several decades the initiation of pubertal maturation is occurring at even earlier ages, particularly thelarche in girls (Burt Solorzano & McCartney, 2010; Jasik & Lustig, 2008; Walvoord, 2010).

While debate exists regarding the definition of "normal" pubertal timing in children, two observations are largely accepted by physicians and researchers. First, if the timing of pubertal onset in humans is in fact influenced by environmental factors (e.g., obesity, endocrine-disrupting compounds), then the result is earlier onset of pubertal maturation. Second, the vast majority of observations of changes in pubertal onset are in females, not males (Fowler et al., 2011). In fact, earlier onset of thelarche is the most common observation in studies that attempt to define changing ranges for pubertal onset. Thus, theories that consider causes of earlier pubertal development in females are described below.

### Obesity

Childhood obesity is a growing public health concern, and a variety of factors (e.g., environmental, lifestyle choices, culture) are playing critical roles in the rising prevalence of childhood obesity across the globe (Dehghan, Akhtar-Danesh, & Merchant, 2005). Between 1980 and 2003, the prevalence of obesity in children increased from 5.0% to 13.9% for children aged 2–5, from 6.5% to 18.8% for 6–11-year-old children, and from 5.0% to 17.4% for youth 12–19 years of age (Centers for Disease Control National Center for Health Statistics, 2004). Nutritional risk factors that have been linked to childhood obesity include excessive sugar intake in soft drinks, lower consumption of fruits and vegetables, and increased portion size (Dehghan et al., 2005).

The increasing incidence of childhood obesity is a concerning aspect of child health that has mirrored the rise in earlier puberty. Evidence supporting a causative role for obesity in early puberty includes observations of increasing body mass index (BMI) prior to pubertal onset in children studied over time (Kaplowitz, 2008). Interestingly, rapid weight gain as early as infancy and toddler years predicts early onset of puberty. Girls who are born small for gestational age but who rapidly gain weight postnatally are most at risk for early menarche, illustrating the interaction of pre- and postnatal factors in the timing of pubertal onset (Sloboda, Hickey, & Hart, 2011). Therefore, the *timing* of weight gain and the *amount* of weight gained are important when considering the impact of obesity on early puberty. Additionally, there are both sex and race differences in childhood obesity (Wisniewski & Chernausek, 2009) and early puberty (Golub et al., 2008). Thus, associations between obesity and pubertal onset may be best understood when considered in the context of sex and race.

Several mechanisms have been proposed to explain how childhood obesity might contribute to early puberty in girls (Jasik & Lustig, 2008). The first proposal advocates that leptin (a hormone secreted by fat cells) signals the GnRH pulse generator to initiate and maintain pubertal maturation once a sufficient amount of energy store has been established. Presumably, an overweight girl would attain this energy store, and thus enter puberty, earlier than normal and underweight girls of similar age (Matkovic et al., 1997). A second proposal suggests that estrogen secreted from fat cells results in early thelarche (Davidson, Susman, & Birch, 2003). Finally, a third proposal takes the timing of weight gain into consideration when explaining early pubertal maturation in overweight children. This theory addresses elevated adrenal androgens observed in children with low birth weight followed by rapid weight gain during infancy (Ong & Dunger, 2004) triggering early puberty (Jasik & Lustig, 2008). These proposed mechanisms are not mutually exclusive, and it is likely that multiple mechanisms are at work to result in early puberty among overweight girls.

## Endocrine-Disrupting Compounds

Endocrine-disrupting compounds (EDCs) are synthetic or naturally occurring compounds that can mimic or block the physiologic effects of steroids in animals. EDCs are ubiquitous, and people are exposed to these agents via water and food intake, breathing contaminated air, or absorption through the skin (Colón, Caro, Bourdony, & Rosario, 2000; Daxenberger, Ibarreta, & Meyer, 2001; Ganmaa & Sato, 2005; Schell & Gallo, 2010). Examples of EDCs include bisphenol A (BPA), chemicals in some pesticides (e.g., methoxychlor, chlorpyrifos, dichlorodiphenyltrichloroethane or DDT), as well as natural chemicals in human and animal food (e.g., phytoestrogens; Diamanti-Kandarakis et al., 2009). Prevalence and rates of exposure in the general population, as well as impact of low doses on later development, are difficult to measure given the multiple methods of contact to a variety of EDCs with potential delayed and interactive effects; however, evidence has accumulated to recommend public policy and regulation changes (Diamanti-Kandarakis et al., 2009; Endocrine Society, 2009).

In the context of altered pubertal timing, EDCs have been shown to act as estrogen agonists or androgen antagonists (Bourguignon et al., 2010). Exposure to EDCs is thought to contribute to early thelarche and menarche observed in girls from the United States, Europe, and China (Buck Louis et al., 2008; Toppari & Juul, 2010). It is also possible that exposure to EDCs is a cause of the increased incidence of true precocious puberty recently documented among girls (Mouritsen et al., 2010; Toppari & Juul, 2010). Importantly, EDC exposure is suspected in cases of early puberty in affected children who are neither overweight nor obese (Aksglaede, Sorensen, Petersen, Skakkebaek, & Juul, 2009; Teilmann, Juul, Skakkebaek, Toppari, 2002).

EDCs affect the onset of puberty through multiple mechanisms of action (Mouritsen et al., 2010). For example, early exposure to EDCs results in enhanced pulsatile secretions of GnRH from the hypothalamus (Raiser et al., 2008). Fetuses exposed to EDCs exhibit altered numbers of kisspeptin neurons in the hypothalamus and pituitary (Bellingham et al., 2009). These neurons are necessary to initiate function of the GnRH pulse generator that drives pubertal maturation. Additionally, EDCs can stimulate and block estrogen and androgen receptors, respectively, as well as inhibit their steroidogenesis (Dickerson & Gore, 2007). For more information on EDCs, see Diamanti-Kandarakis et al. (2009) and the Endocrine Society (2009).

## Social Environment

While it is generally accepted that pubertal development is influenced by a wide variety of genetic, hormonal, nutritional, and environmental factors, the onset of puberty has also been linked to several familial psychosocial factors (Arim, Tamonte, Shapka, Dahinten, & Willms, 2011). For instance, increased stressful conditions within the family (Tremblay & Frigon, 2005), parent–child conflict (Graber, Brooks-Gunn, & Warren, 1995), and caregiver dynamics and mental health (e.g., maternal psychopathology, absence of a father, presence of a stepfather or maternal boyfriend, dysfunctional family relationships; Ellis & Garber, 2000) have all predicted earlier pubertal maturation in girls. For boys, marital conflict, absence of a father, and emotional distance from the mother are factors that have been associated with earlier pubertal onset (Kim & Smith, 1998,

1999). Conversely, times of extreme stress which are accompanied by poor nutrition (e.g., during a period of war) are linked to pubertal delay (Tahirovic, 1998; van Noord & Kaaks, 1991).

As research in this area has expanded, several theories and hypotheses have emerged to describe and potentially explain the timing of pubertal maturation (for reviews, see Belsky, Steinberg, & Draper, 1991; Ellis, 2004; Ge & Natsuaki, 2009). For instance, paternal investment theory (Draper & Harpending, 1982; Ellis 2004) stresses the unique influence of fathers on pubertal development, such that daughters reared without a father in the home are predicted to mature and initiate sexual relationships at earlier ages. More recently, James and colleagues developed an integrated evolutionary–developmental model that incorporates sex-specific pathways linking father presence–absence and stressors in and around the family to pubertal maturation, self-perceived mate value, timing of sexual debut, and sexual risk-taking (James, Ellis, Schlomer, & Garber, 2012). It is important to note that studies examining racial and ethnic differences in pubertal timing have produced conflicting results. Likewise, research findings related to socioeconomic status (SES) have produced mixed results, with some findings suggesting that higher SES is associated with earlier pubertal onset (e.g., Qamra, Mehta, & Deodhar, 1991), and other studies indicating that higher SES is linked to later pubertal development (e.g., Ellis & Essex, 2007).

Popular writings and media researchers have theorized that *media* may be contributing to onset of puberty, with perhaps the link being via childhood obesity impacted in a variety of ways (e.g., sedentary media usage conflicts with time spent in physical activities, unhealthy advertisements may lead to poor food choices, excessive snacking while using media; Kaiser Family Foundation, 2004). Between the late 1970s and 2000, the percentage of American children 6 to 11 years of age who were overweight more than doubled (6.5% to 18.8%; Ogden et al., 2006). During that same period, there was also an explosion in media usage by children (e.g., television, video games, computers), with the average child now spending 5½ hours per day using various forms of media (Roberts & Foehr, 2004). Interestingly, the timing of reduced ages of pubertal onset fits the timing of increased exposure to media. However, correlation does not prove causation, and current research findings have not linked media use to physical changes. It is possible that the utilization of sedentary media mediates the relationship between obesity and pubertal onset. That is, increased sedentary media usage by children may increase their BMI and result in earlier puberty. Next steps include examining whether increased "exergaming" (e.g., utilization of Nintendo's Wii, Microsoft Kinect), which increases energy expenditure, is associated with weight reductions and later pubertal onset (Graf, Pratt, Hester, & Short, 2009).

## SEXUAL BEHAVIOR IN PREPUBERTAL CHILDREN

Over the past three decades, clinical and research efforts have increasingly focused on sexual behaviors in childhood. Prior to the early 1980s, the sexual behavior of children was rarely discussed in clinical or research realms (Friedrich, 2005). In the 1980s, overt sexual behaviors by a child were at times interpreted as an indicator of sexual abuse. In fact, of all publications in the PsychINFO, Medline, and Social SciSearch databases that combine child(ren) and sexual(ity) in their titles, only 1% do *not* treat child sexual behaviors as a consequence (or part of) of sexual abuse (De Graaf & Rademakers, 2011). However, research supports that a range of sexual behaviors are common in children, and origins of even problematic and harmful sexual behaviors are diverse, and not singularly a reflection of sexual abuse (Friedrich, 2005). The following sections are designed to provide an overview of the range of typical sexual knowledge and sexual behaviors exhibited in prepubertal children.

### Early Childhood: Infants, Toddlers, and Preschoolers (0 to 6 Years)

*Sexual Knowledge*

Children tend to actively learn about the world through listening, looking, touching, and imitating (Silovsky & Swisher, 2008), and both toddlers and preschool children are increasingly curious, often asking "why?" or "what's that?" Unsurprisingly, children are curious about a wide range of subjects within their environment, including topics related to sexual development and sexual behaviors. Increased curiosity about bodies, body parts, and sexual behaviors can stem from a variety of experiences, including many that typically occur during early childhood, such as children changing or bathing together.

Research on childhood sexual knowledge of toddlers and preschoolers has examined understanding of genital differences, pregnancy, birth, procreation, sexual activities, and sexual abuse. For instance, children as young as 3 years of age can identify their own sex, and children 3 to 4 years of age are often aware of genital differences between boys and girls (Gordon,

Schroeder, & Abrams, 1990; Volbert, 2000). Both boys and girls are more likely to know and label male (rather than female) genitalia (Bem, 1989; Fraley, Nelson, Wolf, & Lozoff, 1991; Moore & Kendall, 1971). Typically, preschool children have a vague understanding of pregnancy and childbirth until approximately 6 years of age. According to research by Volbert (2000), approximately one-third of 6-year-old children knew about the concept of fertilization, and most children were able to report some knowledge of intrauterine growth and birth (either by Cesarean or vaginal delivery). Preschool-aged children also reported a limited knowledge of adult sexual behavior, and most often reported behaviors that are frequently exhibited in public places (e.g., kissing, cuddling). In fact, only 9% of 3-year-old children mentioned explicit sexual behaviors, which increased to 21% for children 6 years of age; 8% of 6-year-old children were able to provide detailed descriptions of sexual acts (Volbert, 2000).

## Sexual Behavior

Research findings indicate that sexual arousal begins to emerge prior to birth, with ultrasound images demonstrating that a male fetus can experience a penile erection even before birth, and erections have also been directly observed immediately after birth (Kelly, 2008; Martinson, 1981; Masters, Johnson, & Kolodny, 1982; Rutter, 1971). There is also evidence of vaginal lubrication (occurring in regular cycles) from the time a female is born (DeLamater & Friedrich, 2002; Singer, 2002). Previously mentioned curiosity of preschool children may include questions related to sexual topics and exploratory self-touch behaviors (Gordon & Schroeder, 1995). Findings also suggest that self-exploration (i.e., children touching and playing with their own genitalia) begins as early as 7 months of age, and self-touch behaviors are more commonly found in boys than girls (Rutter, 1971; Thigpen, 2009). Research indicates that genital activity may increase between 15 and 19 months of age and include alternative strategies to stimulate genitals (e.g., pressing the thighs together, rubbing genitals against an object; Galenson, 1990). Self-touch and/or self-rubbing behaviors may be pleasurable for children, and some males appear to exhibit pelvic thrusting coupled with physiological responses that are consistent with orgasms (e.g., sequences of tension-building, rhythmic muscular contractions; Kelly, 2008). However, it is important to note that the self-touch and self-rubbing behaviors are often soothing for a child (much like rubbing a soft blanket or sucking their thumb), and there is no evidence of sexual fantasy or other factors related to adult masturbatory behaviors.

Common sexual behaviors for children aged 2 to 5 years (i.e., found in at least a quarter of normative samples) include: (1) looking at others when they are nude; (2) intruding on others' physical boundaries (e.g., stand too close to others); (3) touching adults' breasts; and (4) touching their own genitalia, even in public (Friedrich, 1997; Friedrich et al., 2001). However, while some degree of genital self-stimulation for children under 5 years of age may be apparent to caregivers, overt self-touch often diminishes after 5 years of age, presumably because the child learns that it is a behavior that must be concealed and done in private (Bancroft, Herbenick, & Reynolds, 2003; Friedrich, Grambsch, Broughton, Kuiper, & Beilke, 1991).

## Sexual Play

Sexual play is commonly defined as showing one's own body parts and looking at and/or briefly touching another child's body parts (e.g., "playing doctor;" Silovsky, 2009). Sexual play is common for preschool-aged children who are often curious about their own body as well as the bodies of others (Gordon & Schroeder, 1995). Distinguished from problematic sexual behaviors, childhood sex play behaviors: (1) occur spontaneously and intermittently; (2) are mutual and non-coercive; and (3) are not associated with strong negative emotions or reactions in the children (Chaffin et al., 2006; Silovsky & Bonner, 2003). Sex play typically occurs among children who know and play with each other regularly (rather than between strangers), and children who are of similar age and abilities (Silovsky & Swisher, 2008). Because it occurs among children who play together, children may engage in both same-gender and cross-gender interpersonal sexual play, and the sexual play may include siblings (Lamb & Coakley, 1993; Rutter, 1971).

Experiencing sexual play at least once during childhood appears prevalent (over 66–80% of adults in retrospective research) and can occur in children as young as 2 or 3 years (Lamb & Coakley, 1993; Larsson & Svedin, 2001; Reynolds, Herbenick, & Bancroft, 2003). For instance, 9% of caregivers of preschool children reported that their child engaged in non-intrusive sexual play (e.g., showing sex parts to other children), while 4.5% of these caregivers reported that their child had touched another child's sex parts (Friedrich, 1997).

With research on the development and revisions of the Child Sexual Behavior Inventory, Friedrich and colleagues have also been able to identify sexual behaviors that are rare in early childhood. For instance, intrusive sexual play (e.g., putting finger or objects in another child's vagina or rectum), as well as sexual acts that were planned or aggressive, were not reported by anyone in a normative sample of mothers of preschool children (Friedrich, 2002). Other rare behaviors in early childhood include: (1) putting objects in vagina/rectum; (2) putting mouth on sex parts; and (3) pretending toys are having sex (Davies, Glaser, & Kossoff, 2000; Friedrich, 1997; Larsson & Svedin, 2001).

## School-Age Children (7 to 12 years)
### Sexual Knowledge
As children grow, so does their knowledge of sexual topics (e.g., pregnancy, birth, adult sexual activity), particularly within the school-age period. For example, by 10 years of age most youths have basic understanding of puberty, reproductive processes, and childbirth (Gordon & Schroeder, 1995). School-aged youth who are curious about sexual development and behaviors often obtain their sex information from same-sex peers, independent reading, and/or the Internet (Kelly, 2008). However, findings from a study of more than 7,000 children and adolescents indicated that the majority of girls (72%) and boys (54%) preferred to first consult with their mother about sex-related questions (Ackard & Neumark-Stainer, 2001). Obviously, the accuracy of a child's sexual knowledge depends in part on the youth's exposure to correct informal and formal educational information/materials.

### Sexual Behavior
While the amount of *observed* sexual behavior steadily declines during the childhood years, research suggests that sexual behaviors continue through the school-age period (Friedrich, Fisher, Dittner, Broughton, & Houston, 1998). Retrospective research suggests that adults in the children's lives were not aware of childhood sex play (Lamb & Coakley, 1993). School-age children are typically guided by societal rules, which could restrict the types of sexual behavior demonstrated in public (Silovsky & Swisher, 2008). Further, modesty emerges during the school-age period, particularly true for girls who become increasingly shy and private with undressing and hygiene activities (Gordon, 2003). As sexual behaviors are more concealed, caregivers may not directly observe or be aware of sexual behaviors (Friedrich et al., 1998).

Not surprisingly, types of sexual behaviors in school-aged children are different from those in younger children. For instance, school-age children are much less likely to touch their private parts in public or touch adult females' breasts than preschool children (Friedrich, 1997). Also, masturbatory behaviors occur during the school-age period, and retrospective research from a sample of American college students indicated that 40% of women and 38% of men reported masturbating before puberty; mean age of initial masturbation was 8.3 for women and 10.1 for men (Bancroft et al., 2003). Boys typically exhibit a significant increase in masturbatory behaviors during the school-age period (Rutter, 1971), and the first ejaculation typically occurs between 11 and 15 years of age; most often during masturbation but occasionally through a nocturnal emission (i.e., "wet dream;" Kelly, 2008). A more recent study by Reynolds and colleagues (2003) suggested earlier average ages at first orgasm (girls = 8.5 years; boys = 9.6 years). Overall, masturbatory and orgasmic behaviors are difficult to assess, as most of the current research is based on retrospective studies (De Graaf & Rademakers, 2006).

During the early school-age years, friendship choices and social interactions are most typically with same-sex children. However, romantic interests in the opposite or same sex increase near the end of this developmental period with the onset of puberty. As puberty approaches, it is common for school-aged youth to: (1) focus on sexual body parts; (2) be curious about sexual behavior; and (3) have increased interest in sexual stimulation. Exploratory sexual play of this nature (i.e., periodic and without coercion/force that occurs between children of similar age/abilities) has not been found to negatively impact long-term adjustment, nor has it been related to later sexual orientation (Friedrich, Whiteside, & Talley, 2004; Greenwald & Leitenberg, 1989; Lamb & Coakley, 1993; Okami, Olmstead, & Abramson, 1997). One area of inconsistent results relates to sexual play among siblings, with some research suggesting greater distress when this occurs during the school-age years (Finkelhor, 1980). Greater distress when childhood sexual play occurs with siblings may be related to the social taboo nature of the behavior, as well as subtle coercive behaviors or greater frequency of the sexual behavior.

Typical sexual play and exploration in school-aged youth is not associated with a preoccupation with sex, nor does it typically involve advanced sexual behaviors (e.g., oral sex, intercourse). Some sexual behaviors are rare for school-aged youth. A small but substantial portion of school-age children are involved in more explicit sexual activity (e.g., sexual intercourse) at the end of this period (Center for Disease Control and Prevention, 2002). For example, in an urban low socioeconomic sample of youth, a third reported having sexual intercourse (median age 11 years; Stanton et al., 1994). Sexual acts that are intrusive, planned, coerced, and aggressive are not typical for school-aged children, and are perceived as problematic and needing professional attention (Friedrich, 2002).

### *Impact of Media/Technology on Sexual Behavior*
With the infusion of media and technology into nearly every aspect of Western society, it is not surprising that implicit and explicit messages about sexual behavior are provided to youth not only through family, friends, neighbors, the community, but also via a variety of media (e.g., television, movies, music videos, music lyrics, video games, magazines, Internet, cell phones). For instance, in the United States, women and girls are often depicted in a sexualized manner in nearly every medium, such as television programs (e.g., Grauerholz & King, 1997; Ward, 1995), television commercials (e.g., Lin, 1997), music videos (e.g., Gow, 1996), magazines (e.g., Krassas, Blauwkamp, & Wesselink, 2003), and, more recently, in video games and the Internet.

A detailed discussion about the impact of sexual media messages on the social, emotional, and behavioral functioning of youth is beyond the scope of this chapter (for more information, see the Report of the APA Task Force on the Sexualization of Girls, 2007). Briefly stated, sexual media messages have been associated with diminished sexual health and increased sexual risk-taking (e.g., decreased condom use, diminished sexual assertiveness; Impett, Schooler, & Tolman, 2006; Schooler, Ward, Merriwether, & Caruthers, 2005), stronger acceptance of sexual harassment (Strouse, Goodwin, & Roscoe, 1994), increased rates of plastic surgery (American Society of Plastic Surgeons, 2011), and negative self-images which could lead to sexual problems in adulthood (e.g., Graham, Sanders, Milhausen, & McBride, 2004; Wiederman, 2000).

More recently, a significant amount of attention has been devoted to "sexting." *Sexting* refers to sending and receiving sexually explicit images, videos, or text via cell phone (Weisskirch & Delevi, 2011). The prevalence rates of youth sexting vary considerably, but recent data suggests that between 9.6% and 20% of youth have created or received nude (or nearly nude) images of themselves or others via text messaging (Mitchell, Finkelhor, Jones, & Wolak, 2011; Smith, 2010). Notably, the percentage of youth who created sexually explicit images that potentially violate child pornography laws is low (1.0%; Mitchell et al., 2011). However, in many states there are currently legal consequences for sexting, with several teenagers penalized for sending and receiving photographs of their peers (Weiss & Samenow, 2010). Given that showing genitals to another individual (e.g., "show me yours and I'll show you mine") and looking at pornographic pictures in older childhood is relatively common (Larsson & Svedin, 2002), the use of contemporary strategies to accomplish traditional sexual behaviors is likely to result in substantial controversy. Thus, researchers, clinicians, and policy makers would benefit from future studies examining the short- and long-term impact of sexual behaviors and technology.

## *Sexual Behavior Problems*

Although consensus as to what constitutes typical and healthy relationships does not exist (Heiman, Leiblum, Esquilin, & Pallitto, 1998), guidelines are available to assist caregivers with determining if their child's sexual behaviors are problematic. Briefly stated, caregivers should be concerned when their child's sexual behaviors are characterized by one (or more) of the following: (1) occur frequently; (2) do not respond to typical parental interventions or strategies; (3) cause physical or emotional harm to any child; (4) involve children of widely differing ages or abilities, such as a 10-year-old child who has sexual behaviors with a 4-year-old child; (5) were initiated with strong, negative feelings (e.g., anger, anxiety); and/or (6) involve any type of coercion, force, or aggression (Silovsky, 2009). Sexual behavior problems for children and adolescents are discussed in Chapters 20 and 21.

## Cultural Factors Impacting Sexual Development and Behavior

It is important to note that culture and social context impacts the rates of "typical" behaviors, as the frequencies of the behaviors described above can differ by the population and situation studied (e.g., Davies, Glaser, & Kossoff, 2000; Friedrich, Sandfort, Oostveen, & Cohen-Kettenis, 2000; Larsson & Svedin, 2001; Larsson, Svedin, & Friedrich, 2000). Children's sexual behavior (both private and public), modesty, intimacy, and relationships are impacted by their family's and communities' cultural values, beliefs, practices, and norms (Silovsky & Swisher, 2008; Silovsky, Swisher, Widdifield, & Burris, 2011). Further, sexual behaviors are also influenced by familial interactions and interpersonal experiences (Friedrich et al., 1991; Martinson, 1981), as well as a wide range of current and historical factors such as religion, spirituality, and socioeconomic status. To provide a general framework, societies can be classified into three general categories (i.e., restrictive, semirestrictive, and permissive) to describe their sexual attitudes, beliefs, and practices (Ford & Beach, 1951).

Most Western societies are classified as "restrictive," and intentionally impede or limit sexual knowledge and experiences during childhood (Goldman & Goldman, 1982). Alternatively, higher frequencies of sexual behaviors in children have been found in more permissive social environments where nudity is acceptable, privacy is not reinforced, and exposure to sexualized material is common (as opposed to social environments that reinforce modesty and privacy; Friedrich et al., 2001). Similarly, caregivers' attitudes towards children's sexuality have been found to impact children's sexual knowledge and behavior (Gordon et al., 1990). For example, caregivers who report a more liberal or relaxed approach to parenting (e.g., family nudity, co-bathing, witnessing intercourse, and co-sleeping) also report higher levels of general sexual behaviors (e.g., self-touch, touching of parental genitals) for their children (Gagnon, 1985; Rosenfeld, Bailey, Siegel, & Bailey, 1986); and these differences remain after controlling for several other family variables (Friedrich et al., 1998). More recently, Thigpen & Fortenberry (2009) interviewed 227 African American caregivers and found that: (1) caregiver high school level education; (2) familial beliefs (sexual feelings/curiosity are normal; co-sleeping is permissible); and (3) unmarried/single family structure were related to greater reports of child sexual behavior.

Limited research exists on the impact of socioeconomic status or the influence of race or ethnicity on sexual behaviors in children. One study by Thigpen, Pinkston, & Mayefsky (2003) found that African American caregivers reported: (1) less self-touch behaviors (both at home and in public; (2) fewer instances of rubbing their body against people/furniture; (3) fewer incidents of showing their sex parts to adults; (4) fewer attempts to look at others while they are undressing; and (5) less interest in the opposite sex when compared with larger normative samples (i.e., Friedrich, 1997; Friedrich et al., 2001). In interpreting these results, the authors acknowledge that restrictive sexual beliefs and attitudes (either culturally or religiously based) could impact a caregiver's parenting and perceptions of behaviors (e.g., greater modesty within a family may lead to fewer overt sexual behaviors by children). In a related manner, while sexual behavioral differences have been reported between Western and non-Western countries, these studies rely primarily on adult reports, and thus may reflect differences in the perceptions of the population sample, child behavior differences, or both (De Graaf & Rademakers, 2006).

# SEXUAL BEHAVIOR IN CHILDREN WITH EARLY PUBERTAL DEVELOPMENT

## Premature Adrenarche

Premature adrenarche is usually a benign and normal variant of sexual development that is characterized by the development of pubic hair before 8 years of age in girls and 9 years of age in boys (Williams et al., 2011). A review of studies assessing self-reported "first love" indicated that many respondents experienced romantic feelings toward same- or opposite-sex individuals prior to puberty (Janssen, 2008). Interestingly, first romantic feelings, or "crushes" often coincide with the timing of adrenarche (Herdt & McClintock, 2000). Thus, observations of children with premature adrenarche are of interest to determine if romantic or sexual behavior is precocious or otherwise atypical in this group.

Two investigations have identified behavioral differences between girls and boys (ages 6–9 years) with premature adrenarche and unaffected, age-matched children. Findings from both self- and parent-reporting suggested that girls with premature adrenarche were more likely to exhibit oppositional defiant disorder, anxiety, depression, and disruptive behaviors than the comparison group (Dorn, Hitt, & Rotenstein, 1999; Dorn et al., 2008). However, questions pertaining to sexual behavior are absent in the limited number of investigations that have been conducted.

## Precocious Puberty

Precocious puberty in girls is defined as the onset of thelarche prior to 8 years of age, or menarche before 9 years of age. For boys, precocious puberty refers to genital development before 9 years of age. A brain imaging study of boys with familial precocious puberty revealed that these children responded faster to emotional stimuli and also exhibited different patterns of hippocampal activity during emotional processing compared with controls. However, sexual behavior was not measured.

Early maturing girls are more likely to report problems with body image and also increased sexual activity compared with later maturing girls. Perhaps related to dissatisfaction with their body image, early maturing girls (but not boys) are also more likely to report social anxiety than are children who experience typical timing of pubertal onset (Blumenthal et al., 2011). On the other hand, early maturing boys are more likely to report increased sexual activity and illicit substance use (Ehrhardt & Meyer-Bahlburg, 1994; Michaud, Suris, & Deppen, 2006).

More recently, two follow-up studies were conducted to investigate if behavioral correlates of early reproductive development in girls (e.g., mental distress, increased sexual activity) persist into adolescence and early adulthood. In the first study, girls with early menarche initially reported elevated mental distress and increased number of sexual partners. However, an elevated level of mental distress and increased number of sexual partners did not persist over the 3-year follow-up period (Lien, Haavet, & Dalgard, 2010). Similar results were found in a second study, where young girls with early breast development and/or menarche exhibited increased use of illicit substances, earlier age at first intercourse, and poorer psychiatric functioning initially, but these behaviors reportedly ameliorated by 19–21 years of age (Copeland et al., 2010). Thus, while precocious or early puberty are related to earlier timing of first intercourse and greater number of sex partners, these differences appear to dissipate by the late teenage years.

## PREPUBERTAL CHILDREN AND GENDER IDENTITY DISORDER

Historically, *gender role* refers to the behaviors, attitudes, and dispositions that are typically associated with either the male or female social role (Money, Hampson, & Hampson, 1955), whereas *gender identity* refers to the psychological sense of maleness or femaleness (Stoller, 1964). The learning of gender roles typically begins in early childhood, and children learn to label themselves in various ways and are able to recognize the attributes, attitudes, and behaviors that are considered socially appropriate for each sex (Kelly, 2008). At home, in school, and during play activities children often grow up in two distinct subcultures, each characterized by different expectations and behaviors (Maccoby, 1998). Traditionally, boy playgroups have been characterized as rough-and-tumble hierarchies, whereas girl groups tend to emphasize the maintenance of relationships and mutuality. These group expectations establish a foundation of gender identity and role (Kelly, 2008). Although gender role behavior is seen as early as one year of age, it is important to note that cross-gender behaviors frequently occur in early childhood. For instance, dressing like the opposite sex has been found in 14% of boys and 10% of girls (Friedrich, 1997; Friedrich et al., 2001).

However, even in early childhood, some boys and girls abandon expected gender roles, and the nonconformity with traditional male and female identities may create some level of discomfort (Kelly, 2008). According to the *Diagnostic and Statistical Manual of Mental Disorders, Fourth*

*Edition, Text Revision (DSM-IV-TR)*, Gender Identity Disorder (GID) is characterized by a strong and persistent identification with the opposite sex, and also great distress with one's own sex, resulting in impairments in important areas of functioning (American Psychiatric Association, 2000). The estimated worldwide prevalence of GID is rare compared with many other psychiatric disorders (Hoshiai et al., 2010), and GID has not been formally studied using epidemiological methods for children (Zucker & Cohen-Kettenis, 2008). Informal child estimates range from 0.003% to 3% for boys, and 0.001% to 1.5% for girls (American Psychiatric Association, 1994).

Since the diagnosis of GID was first introduced in the third edition of the DSM (American Psychiatric Association, 1980), the pathologization and treatment of cross-gender behaviors and identity (particularly in children) has been a source of debate within the literature (e.g., Bem, 1993; Fagot, 1992; Neisen, 1992; Nordyke, Baer, Etzel, & LeBlanc, 1977; Zucker 1999). Current concerns of a diagnosis of GID in children include, but are not limited to, the following: (1) the validity of the diagnostic criteria in the DSM-IV-TR; (2) limited research and methodological problems—reliance of caregiver-reports and controversial inclusion criteria for research participants; and (3) controversial therapies associated with GID, including reparative or conversion therapies—both of which have been opposed by the American Psychological Association (for reviews, see Bartlett, Vasey, & Bukowski, 2000; Kamens, 2011). For more information on the latest research with GID, see the special issue of *Child and Adolescent Psychiatric Clinics of North America* (2011, Volume 20, Issue 4).

## SUMMARY

Sexual knowledge and behavior is established in the preschool years and continues to progress throughout early childhood into puberty. Expectations for sexual behavior are best understood in the context of the child's psychosocial development. For example, preschool children are naturally curious about the world, and this includes being curious about their and others' bodies and physical differences. Sex play occurs during preschool and school age years, although it becomes more concealed with awareness of social mores. Onset of puberty, particularly thelarche in girls, is occurring at an earlier age, with current theories focused on obesity and endocrine-disrupting compounds. In addition to physical development, typical sexual knowledge and behaviors are influenced by social environment, culture, and media. Challenges to measuring and researching sexual knowledge, behavior, and other areas of sexual development in young children are notable, and limit current findings and our ability to tease out the multifaceted impacts on sexual development.

## REFERENCES

Ackard, D. M., & Neumark-Stainer, D. (2001). Health care information sources for adolescents: Age and gender differences on use, concerns, and needs. *Journal of Adolescent Health, 29*, 170–176.

Aksglaede, L., Olsen, L. W., Sorensen, T. I., & Juul, A. (2008). Forty years trends in timing of pubertal growth spurt in 157,000 Danish school children. *PLoS One, 3*, e2728.

Aksglaede, L., Sorensen, K., Petersen, J. H., Skakkebaek, N. E., & Juul, A. (2009). Recent decline in age at breast development: The Copenhagen Puberty Study. *Pediatrics, 123*, e932–e939.

APA Task Force on the Sexualization of Girls, (2007). *Report of the APA Task Force on the Sexualization of Girls*. Washington, DC: American Psychological Association. Retrieved from <www.apa.org/pi/wpo/sexualization.html>.

American Psychiatric Association, (1980). *Diagnostic and statistical manual of mental disorders* (3rd ed.). Washington, DC: Author. [text rev.].

American Psychiatric Association, (1994). *Diagnostic and statistical manual of mental disorders* (4th ed.). Washington, DC: Author.

American Psychiatric Association, (2000). *Diagnostic and statistical manual of mental disorders* (4th ed.). Washington, DC: Author. [text rev.].

American Society of Plastic Surgeons. (2011). *2000/2010/2011 cosmetic surgery procedures*. Retrieved from <www.plasticsurgery.org/News-and-Resources/2011-Statistics-.html>.

Arim, R. G., Tramonte, L., Shapka, J. D., Dahinten, V. S., & Willms, J. D. (2011). The family antecedents and the subsequent outcomes of early puberty. *Journal of Youth and Adolescence, 40*, 1423–1435.

Bancroft, J., Herbenick, D., & Reynolds, M. (2003). Masturbation as a marker of sexual development: Two studies 50 years apart. In J. Bancroft (Ed.), *Sexual development in childhood (pp. 156–185)*. Bloomington, IN: Indiana University Press.

Bartlett, N. H., Vasey, P. L., & Bukowski, W. M. (2000). Is gender identity disorder in children a mental disorder. *Sex Roles, 43*, 753–785.

Bellingham, M., Fowler, P. A., Amezaga, M. R., Rhind, S. M., Cotinot, C., Mandon-Pepin, B., et al. (2009). Exposure to a complex cocktail of environmental endocrine-disrupting compounds disturbs the kisspeptin/GPR54 system in ovine hypothalamus and pituitary gland. *Environmental Health Perspectives, 117*, 1556–1562.

Belsky, J., Steinberg, L., & Draper, P. (1991). Childhood experience, interpersonal development, and reproductive strategy: An evolutionary theory of socialization. *Child Development, 62*, 647–670.

Bem, S. L. (1989). Genital knowledge and gender constancy in preschool children. *Child Development, 60*, 649–662.

Bem, S. L. (1993). *The lenses of gender: Transforming the debate on sexual inequality*. New Haven, CT: Yale University Press.

Blumenthal, H., Leen-Feldner, E. W., Babson, K. A., Gahr, J. L., Trainor, C. D., & Frala, J. L. (2011). Elevated social anxiety among early maturing girls. *Developmental Psychology, 47*, 1113–1140.

Bourguignon, J. P., Rasier, G., Lebrethon, M. C., Gérard, A., Naveau, E., & Parent, A. S. (2010). Neuroendocrine disruption of pubertal timing and interactions between homeostasis of reproduction and energy balance. *Molecular and Cellular Endocrinology, 324*, 110–120.

Buck Louis, G. M., Gray, L. E., Marcus, M., Ojeda, S. R., Pescovitz, O. H., Witchel, S. F., et al. (2008). Environmental factors and puberty timing: Expert panel research needs. *Pediatrics, 121*, S192–S207.

Burt Solorzano, C. M., & McCartney, C. R. (2010). Obesity and the pubertal transition in girls and boys. *Reproduction, 140*, 399–410.

Center for Disease Control and Prevention, (2002). Trends in sexual risk behaviors among high school students – United States: 1991–2001. *Morbidity and Mortality Weekly Report, 51*, 856–861.

Centers for Disease Control National Center for Health Statistics, (2004). *NHANES data on the prevalence of overweight among children and adolescents: United States, 2003–2004*. Hyattsville, MD: Author.

Chaffin, M., Berliner, L., Block, R., Johnson, T. C., Friedrich, W., Louis, D., et al. (2006). *Report of the ATSA Task Force on Children with Sexual Behavior Problems*. Beaverton, OR: Association for the Treatment of Sexual Abusers.

Colón, I., Caro, D., Bourdony, C. J., & Rosario, O. (2000). Identification of phthalate esters in the serum of young Puerto Rican girls with premature breast development. *Environmental Health Perspective, 108*, 895–900.

Copeland, W., Shanahan, L., Miller, S., Costello, E. J., Angold, A., & Maughan, B. (2010). Outcomes of early pubertal timing in young women: A prospective population based study. *The American Journal of Psychiatry, 167*, 1218–1225.

Davidson, K. K., Susman, E., & Birch, L. (2003). Percent body fat at age 5 predicts earlier pubertal development among girls at age 9. *Pediatrics, 111*, 815–821.

Davies, S. L., Glaser, D., & Kossoff, R. (2000). Children's sexual play and behavior in pre-school settings: Staff's perceptions, reports, and response. *Child Abuse and Neglect, 24*, 1329–1343.

Daxenberger, A., Ibarreta, D., & Meyer, H. H. D. (2001). Possible health impact of animal oestrogens in food. *Human Reproduction Update, 7*, 340–355.

De Graaf, H., & Rademakers, J. (2006). Sexual development of prepubertal children. *Journal of Psychology & Human Sexuality, 18*, 1–21.

De Graaf, H., & Rademakers, J. (2011). The psychological measurement of childhood sexual development in Western societies: Methodological challenges. *Journal of Sex Research, 48*, 118–129.

Dehghan, M., Akhtar-Danesh, N., & Merchant, A. T. (2005). Childhood obesity, prevalence and prevention. *Nutrition Journal, 4*, 24.

DeLamater, J., & Friedrich, W. N. (2002). Human sexual development. *The Journal of Sex Research, 39*, 10–14.

Del Giudice, M., Angeleri, R., & Manera, V. (2009). The juvenile transition: A developmental switch point in human life history. *Developmental Review, 29*, 1–31.

Diamanti-Kandarakis, E., Bourguignon, J., Giudice, L. C., Hauser, R., Prins, G. S., Soto, A. M., et al. (2009). Endocrine-disrupting chemicals: An Endocrine Society Scientific Statement. *Endocrine Reviews, 30*, 293–342.

Dickerson, S. M., & Gore, A. C. (2007). Estrogenic environmental endocrine-disrupting chemical effects on reproductive neuroendocrine function and dysfunction across the life cycle. *Reviews in Endocrine & Metabolic Disorders, 8*, 143–159.

Dorn, L. D., Hitt, S. F., & Rotenstein, D. (1999). Biopsychological and cognitive differences in children with premature vs on-time adrenarche. *Archives of Pediatrics Adolescent Medicine, 153*, 137–146.

Dorn, L. D., Rose, S. R., Rotenstein, D., Susman, E. J., Huang, B., Loucks, T. L., et al. (2008). Differences in endocrine parameters and psychopathology in girls with premature adrenarche versus on-time adrenarche. *Journal of Pediatric Endocrinology & Metabolism, 21*, 439–448.

Draper, P., & Harpending, H. (1982). Father absence and reproductive strategy: An evolutionary perspective. *Journal of Anthropological Research, 38*, 255–273.

Ehrhardt, A. A., & Meyer-Bahlburg, H. F. (1994). Psychosocial aspects of precocious puberty. *Hormone Research, 41*, 30–35.

Ellis, B. J. (2004). Timing of pubertal maturation in girls: An integrated life history approach. *Psychological Bulletin, 130*, 920–958.

Ellis, B. J., & Essex, M. J. (2007). Family environments, adrenarche, and sexual maturation: A longitudinal test of a life history model. *Child Development, 78*, 1799–1817.

Ellis, B. J., & Garber, J. (2000). Psychosocial antecedents of variation in girls' pubertal timing: Maternal depression, stepfather presence, and marital and family stress. *Child Development, 71*, 485–501.

Endocrine Society, (2009). *Position statement: Endocrine-disrupting chemicals*. Chevy Chase, MD: Authors.

Fagot, B. (1992). Review of the "sissy boy syndrome" and the development of homosexuality. *Archives of Sexual Behavior, 21*, 327–332.

Finkelhor, D. (1980). Sex among siblings: A survey of prevalence, variety, and effects. *Archives of Sexual Behavior, 9*, 171–194.

Ford, C. S., & Beach, F. A. (1951). *Patterns of sexual behavior*. New York, NY: Harper.

Fowler, P. A., Bellingham, M., Sinclair, K. D., Evans, N. P., Pocar, P., Fischer, B., et al. (2012). Impact of endocrine-disrupting compounds on female reproductive health. *Molecular and Cellular Endocrinology 355*(2), 231–239. [Epub ahead of print].

Fraley, M. C., Nelson, E. C., Wolf, A. W., & Lozoff, B. (1991). Early genital naming. *Journal of Developmental and Behavioral Pediatrics, 12*, 301–305.

Friedrich, W. N. (1997). *Child sexual behavior inventory: Professional manual*. Odessa, FL: Psychological Assessment Resources.

Friedrich, W. N. (2002). *Psychological assessment of sexually abused children and their families*. Thousand Oaks, CA: Sage.

Friedrich, W. N. (2005). Correlates of sexual behavior in young children. *Journal of Child Custody, 2*, 41–55.

Friedrich, W. N., Fisher, J., Dittner, C., Broughton, D., & Houston, M. (1998). Normative sexual behavior in children: A contemporary sample. *Pediatrics, 101*, e9.

Friedrich, W. N., Fisher, J., Dittner, C., Acton, R., Berliner, L., Butler, J., et al. (2001). Child sexual behavior inventory: Normative, psychiatric, and sexual abuse comparisons. *Child Maltreatment, 6*, 37–49.

Friedrich, W. N., Grambsch, P., Broughton, D., Kuiper, J., & Beilke, R. (1991). Normative sexual behavior in children. *Pediatrics, 88*, 456–464.

Friedrich, W. N., Sandfort, T. G., Oostveen, M., & Cohen-Kettenis, J. (2000). Cultural differences in sexual behavior: 2–6 year old Dutch and American Children. *Journal of Psychology and Human Sexuality, 12*, 117–129.

Friedrich, W. N., Whiteside, S. P., & Talley, N. J. (2004). Noncoercive sexual contact with similarly aged individuals: What is the impact? *Journal of Interpersonal Violence, 19*, 1075–1084.

Gagnon, J. H. (1985). Attitudes and responses of parents to pre-adolescent masturbation. *Archives of Sexual Behavior, 14*, 451–466.

Galenson, E. (1990). Observation of early infantile sexual and erotic development. In M. E. Perry (Ed.), *Handbook of sexology: Vol. 7. Childhood and adolescent sexology (pp. 169–179)*. Amsterdam, The Netherlands: Elsevier.

Ganmaa, D., & Sato, A. (2005). The possible role of female sex hormones in milk from pregnant cows in the development of breast, ovarian and corpus uteri cancers. *Medical Hypotheses, 65*, 1028–1037.

Garn, S. M. (1987). The secular trend in size and maturational timing and its implications for nutritional assessment. *The Journal of Nutrition, 117*, 817–823.

Ge, X., & Natsuaki, M. N. (2009). In search of explanations for early pubertal timing effects on developmental psychopathology. *Current Directions in Psychological Science, 18*, 327–331.

Goldman, R., & Goldman, J. (1982). *Children's sexual thinking: A comparative study of children aged 5 to 15 years in Australia, North America, Britain and Sweden*. Boston, MA: Routledge and Kegan Paul.

Golub, M. S., Collman, G. W., Foster, P. M., Kimmel, C. A., Raipert-De Meyts, E., Reiter, E. O., et al. (2008). Public health implications of altered puberty timing. *Pediatrics, 121*, 218–230.

Gordon, B. N. (2003). Sexual development. In T. H. Ollendick, & C. S. Schroeder (Eds.), *Encyclopedia of clinical child and pediatric psychology (pp. 591–593)*. New York, NY: Kluwer Academic/Plenum Publishers.

Gordon, B. N., & Schroeder, C. S. (1995). *Sexuality: A developmental approach to problems*. New York, NY: Plenum Publishing Corp.

Gordon, B. N., Schroeder, C. S., & Abrams, J. M. (1990). Age and social-class differences in children's knowledge of sexuality. *Journal of Clinical Child Psychology, 19*, 33–43.

Gow, J. (1996). Reconsidering gender roles on MTV: Depictions in the most popular music videos of the early 1990s. *Communication Reports, 9*, 151–161.

Graf, D. L., Pratt, L. V., Hester, C. N., & Short, K. R. (2009). Playing active video games increases energy expenditure in children. *Pediatrics, 124*, 534–540.

Graber, J. A., Brooks-Gunn, J., & Warren, M. P. (1995). The antecedents of menarcheal age: Heredity, family environment and stressful life events. *Child Development, 66*, 346–359.

Graham, C. A., Sanders, S. A., Milhausen, R., & McBride, K. (2004). Turning on and turning off: A focus group study of the factors that affect women's sexual arousal. *Archives of Sexual Behavior, 33*, 537–548.

Grauerholz, E., & King, A. (1997). Primetime sexual harassment. *Violence Against Women, 3*, 129–148.

Greenwald, E., & Leitenberg, H. (1989). Long-term effects of sexual experiences with siblings and non-siblings during childhood. *Archives of Sexual Behavior, 18*, 389–399.

Heiman, M. L., Leiblum, S., Esquilin, S. C., & Pallitto, L. M. (1998). A comparative survey of beliefs about "normal" childhood sexual behavior. *Child Abuse & Neglect, 22*, 289–304.

Herdt, G., & McClintock, M. (2000). The magical age of 10. *Archives of Sexual Behavior, 29*, 587–606.

Hoshiai, M., Matsumoto, Y., Sato, T., Ohnishi, M., Okabe, N., Kishimoto, Y., et al. (2010). Psychiatric comorbidity among patients with gender identity disorder. *Psychiatry and Clinical Neurosciences, 64*, 514–519.

Impett, E. A., Schooler, D., & Tolman, D. L. (2006). To be seen and not heard: Femininity ideology and adolescent girls' sexual health. *Archives of Sexual Behavior, 21*, 628–646.

James, J., Ellis, B. J., Schlomer, G. L., & Garber, J. (2012). Sex-specific pathways to early puberty, sexual debut, and sexual risk taking: Tests of an integrated evolutionary–developmental model. *Developmental Psychology 48*(3), 687–702. [Advance online publication].

Janssen, D. F. (2008). First love: A case study in quantitative appropriation of social concepts. *The Quantitative Report, 13*, 178–203.

Jasik, C. B., & Lustig, R. H. (2008). Adolescent obesity and puberty: The "perfect storm". *Annals of the New York Academy of Sciences, 1135*, 265–279.

Kaiser Family Foundation (2004, February). *The role of media in childhood obesity*. Retrieved from <http://www.kff.org/entmedia/upload/the-role-of-media-in-childhood-obesity.pdf>.

Kamens, S. R. (2011). On the proposed sexual and gender identity diagnoses for DSM-5: History and controversies. *The Humanistic Psychologist, 39*, 37–59.

Kaplowitz, P. B. (2008). The link between body fat and the timing of puberty. *Pediatrics, 121*, 208–217.

Kelly, G. F. (2008). *Sexuality today* (9th ed.). Boston, MA: McGraw-Hill Higher Education.

Kim, K., & Smith, P. K. (1998). Retrospective survey of parental marital relations and child reproductive development. *International Journal of Behavioral Development, 22*, 729–751.

Kim, K., & Smith, P. K. (1999). Family relations in early childhood and reproductive development. *Journal of Reproductive Infant Psychology, 17*, 133–148.
Krassas, N. R., Blauwkamp, J. M., & Wesselink, P. (2003). "Master your Johnson:" Sexual rhetoric in *Maxim* and *Stuff* magazines. *Sexuality & Culture, 7*, 98–119.
Lamb, S., & Coakley, M. (1993). "Normal" childhood sexual play and games: Differentiating play from abuse. *Child Abuse and Neglect, 17*, 515–526.
Larsson, I., & Svedin, C. G. (2001). Sexual behaviour in Swedish preschool children, as observed by their parents. *Acta Paediatrica, 90*, 436–444.
Larsson, I., & Svedin, C. G. (2002). Sexual experiences in childhood: Young adults' recollections. *Archives of Sexual Behavior, 31*, 263–273.
Larsson, I., Svedin, C. G., & Friedrich, W. N. (2000). Differences and similarities in sexual behaviour among pre-schoolers in Sweden and USA. *Nordic Journal of Psychiatry, 54*, 251–257.
Lien, L., Haavet, O. R., & Dalgard, F. (2010). Do mental health and behavioural problems of early menarche persist into late adolescence? A three year follow-up study among adolescent girls in Oslo, Norway. *Social Science & Medicine, 71*, 529–533.
Lin, C. (1997). Beefcake versus cheesecake in the 1990s: Sexist portrayals of both genders in television commercials. *Howard Journal of Communications, 8*, 237–249.
Maccoby, E. E. (1998). *The two sexes: Growing up apart, coming together*. Cambridge, MA: Harvard University Press.
Martinson, F. M. (1981). Eroticism in infancy and childhood. In L. L. Constantine, & F. M. Martinson (Eds.), *Children and sex: New findings, new perspectives (pp. 23–35)*. Boston, MA: Little, Brown and Company.
Masters, W. H., Johnson, V. E., & Kolodny, R. C. (1982). *Human sexuality*. Boston, MA: Little, Brown and Company.
Matkovic, V., Ilich, J. Z., Skugor, M., Badenhop, N. E., Goel, P., Clairmont, A., et al. (1997). Leptin is inversely related to age at menarche in human females. *Journal of Clinical Endocrinology and Metabolism, 82*, 3239–3245.
Michaud, P. A., Suris, J. C., & Deppen, A. (2006). Gender-related psychological and behavioural correlates of pubertal timing in a national sample of Swiss adolescents. *Molecular and Cellular Endocrinology, 255*, 172–178.
Mitchell, K. J., Finkelhor, D., Jones, L. M., & Wolak, J. (2011). Prevalence and characteristics of youth sexting: A national study. *Pediatrics, 129*, 1–8.
Money, J., Hampson, J. G., & Hampson, J. L. (1955). An examination of some basic sexual concepts: The evidence of human hermaphroditism. *Bulletin of the Johns Hopkins Hospital, 97*, 301–319.
Moore, J. E., & Kendall, D. G. (1971). Children's concepts of reproduction. *Journal of Sex Research, 7*, 42–61.
Mouritsen, A., Aksglaede, L., Sorensen, K., Mogensen, S. S., Leffers, H., Main, K. M., et al. (2010). Hypothesis: Exposure to endocrine-disrupting chemicals may interfere with timing of puberty. *International Journal of Andrology, 33*, 346–359.
Neisen, J. (1992). Gender identity disorder of childhood: By whose standard and for what purpose? A response to Rekers and Morey. *Journal of Psychology and Human Sexuality, 5*, 65–67.
Nordyke, N. S., Baer, D. M., Etzel, B. C., & LeBlanc, J. M. (1977). Implications of the stereotyping and modification of sex role. *Journal of Applied Behavior Analysis, 10*, 553–557.
Oberfield, S. E., Sopher, A. B., & Gerken, A. T. (2011). Approach to the girl with early onset of pubic hair. *The Journal of Clinical Endocrinology and Metabolism, 96*, 1610–1622.
Ogden, C. L., Carroll, M. D., Curtin, L. R., McDowell, M. A., Tabak, C. J., & Flegal, K. M. (2006). Prevalence of overweight and obesity in the United States, 1999–2004. *The Journal of the American Medical Association, 295*, 1549–1555.

Okami, P., Olmstead, R., & Abramson, P. R. (1997). Sexual experiences in early childhood: 18-year longitudinal data from the UCLA Family Lifestyles Project. *Journal of Sex Research, 34,* 339–347.

Ong, K. K., & Dunger, D. B. (2004). Birth weight, infant growth and insulin resistance. *European Journal of Endocrinology, 151,* 131–139.

Parent, A. S., Teilmann, G., Juul, A., Skakkebaek, N. E., Toppari, J., & Bourguignon, J. P. (2003). The timing of normal puberty and the age limits of sexual precocity: Variations around the world, secular trends, and changes after migration. *Endocrine Reviews, 24,* 668–693.

Qamra, S. R., Mehta, S., & Deodhar, S. D. (1991). A mixed-longitudinal study on the pattern of pubertal growth: Relationship to socioeconomic status and caloric-intake-IV. *Indian Pediatrics, 28,* 147–156.

Rasier, G., Parent, A. S., Gérard, A., Denooz, R., Lebrethon, M. C., Charlier, C., et al. (2008). Mechanisms of interaction of endocrine-disrupting chemicals with glutamate-evoked secretion of gonadotropin-releasing hormone. *Toxicological Sciences, 102,* 33–41.

Reynolds, M. A., Herbenick, D. L., & Bancroft, J. (2003). The nature of childhood sexual experiences: Two studies 50 years apart. In J. Bancroft (Ed.), *Sexual development in childhood (pp. 134–155).* Bloomington, IN: Indiana University Press.

Roberts, D., & Foehr, U. (2004). *Kids and media in America.* Cambridge, MA: Cambridge University Press.

Rosen, D. S. (2004). Physiologic growth and development during adolescence. *Pediatrics in Review, 25,* 194–200.

Rosenfeld, A., Bailey, R., Siegel, B., & Bailey, G. (1986). Determining incestuous contact between parent and child: Frequency of children touching parents' genitals in a nonclinical population. *Journal of the American Academy of Child & Adolescent Psychiatry, 25,* 481–484.

Rosenfield, R. L., Lipton, R. B., & Drum, M. L. (2009). Thelarche, pubarche, and menarche attainment in children with normal and elevated body mass index. *Pediatrics, 123,* 84–88.

Rutter, M. (1971). Normal psychosexual development. *The Journal of Child Psychology and Psychiatry, 11,* 259–283.

Schell, L. M., & Gallo, M. V. (2010). Relationships of putative endocrine disruptors to human sexual maturation and thyroid activity in youth. *Physiology & Behavior, 99,* 246–253.

Schooler, D., Ward, L. M., Merriwether, A., & Caruthers, A. (2005). Cycles of shame: Menstrual shame, body shame, and sexual decision-making. *Journal of Sex Research, 42,* 324–334.

Silovsky, J. F. (2009). *Taking action: Support for families of children with sexual behavior problems.* Brandon, VT: Safer Society Press.

Silovsky, J. F., & Bonner, B. L. (2003). Sexual behavior problems. In T. H. Ollendick, & C. S. Schroeder (Eds.), *Encyclopedia of clinical child and pediatric psychology (pp. 589–591).* New York, NY: Kluwer Press.

Silovsky, J. F., & Swisher, L. (2008). Sexual development and sexual behavior problems. In M. L. Wolraich, P. Dworkin, D. Drotar, & E. Perrin (Eds.), *Developmental and behavioral pediatrics: Evidence and practice (pp. 805–824).* Philadelphia, PA: Elsevier.

Silovsky, J., Swisher, L., Widdifield, J., & Burris, L. (2011). Children with sexual behavior problems. In P. Goodyear-Brown (Ed.), *The handbook of child sexual abuse: Prevention, assessment and treatment.* Hoboken, NJ: John Wiley & Sons.

Singer, M. (2002). Childhood sexuality: An interpersonal-intrapsychic integration. *Contemporary Sexuality, 36,* i–viii.

Sloboda, D. M., Hickey, M., & Hart, R. (2011). Reproduction in females: The role of the early life environment. *Human Reproduction Update, 17,* 210–227.

Smith, T. (2010, March). Study: 20 percent of teens engage in sexting. *TimesDaily.com.* Retrieved from <http://www.timesdaily.com/article/20100316/ARTICLES/3165039?Title=Study-20-percent-of-teens-engage-in-sexting>.

Stanton, B., Li, X., Black, M., Ricardo, I., Galbraith, J., Kaliee, L., et al. (1994). Sexual practices and intentions among low-income urban African-Americans. *Pediatrics, 93,* 966–973.
Stoller, R. J. (1964). A contribution to the study of gender identity. *The International Journal of Psychoanalysis, 45,* 220–226.
Strouse, J. S., Goodwin, M. P., & Roscoe, B. (1994). Correlates of attitudes toward sexual harassment among early adolescents. *Sex Roles, 31,* 559–577.
Susman, E. J., & Rogol, A. D. (2004). Puberty and psychological development. In R. M. Lerner, & L. Steinberg (Eds.), *Handbook of Adolescent Psychology (pp. 15–44).* New York, NY: John Wiley & Sons.
Tahirovic, H. F. (1998). Menarchal age and the stress of war: An example from Bosnia. *European Journal of Pediatrics, 157,* 978–980.
Tanner, J. M. (1986). Normal growth and techniques of growth assessment. *Clinics in Endocrinology and Metabolism, 15,* 411–451.
Teilmann, G., Juul, A., Skakkebaek, N. E., & Toppari, J. (2002). Putative effects of endocrine disrupters on pubertal development in the human. *Best Practice & Research Clinical Endocrinology & Metabolism, 16,* 105–121.
Thigpen, J. W. (2009). Early sexual behavior in a sample of low-income, African American children. *Journal of Sex Research, 46,* 67–79.
Thigpen, J. W., & Fortenberry, J. D. (2009). Understanding variation in normative childhood sexual behavior: The significance of family context. *Social Service Review, 83,* 611–631.
Thigpen, J. W., Pinkston, E. M., & Mayefsky, J. H. (2003). Normative sexual behavior of African American children. In J. Bancroft (Ed.), *Sexual development in childhood (pp. 241–254).* Bloomington, IN: Indiana University Press.
Toppari, J., & Juul, A. (2010). Trends in puberty timing in humans and environmental modifiers. *Molecular and Cellular Endocrinology, 324,* 39–44.
Tremblay, L., & Frigon, J. Y. (2005). Precocious puberty in adolescent girls: A biomarker of later psychosocial adjustment problems. *Child Psychiatry and Human Development, 36,* 73–94.
van Noord, P. A., & Kaaks, R. (1991). The effect of wartime conditions and the 1944-45 "Dutch famine" on recalled menarcheal age in participants of the DOM breast cancer screening project. *Annals of Human Biology, 18,* 57–70.
Volbert, R. (2000). Sexual knowledge of preschool children. *Journal of Psychology and Human Sexuality, 12,* 5–26.
Walvoord, E. C. (2010). The timing of puberty: Is it changing? Does it matter? *The Journal of Adolescent Health, 47,* 433–439.
Ward, L. M. (1995). Talking about sex: Common themes about sexuality in the prime-time television programs children and adolescents view most. *Journal of Youth & Adolescence, 24,* 595–615.
Weiss, R., & Samenow, C. P. (2010). Smart phones, social networking, sexting and problematic sexual behaviors – A call for research. *Sexual Addiction and Compulsion, 17,* 241–246.
Weisskirch, R. S., & Delevi, R. (2011). "Sexting" and adult romantic attachment. *Computers in Human Behavior, 27,* 1697–1701.
Wiederman, M. (2000). Women's body image self-consciousness during physical intimacy with a partner. *Journal of Sex Research, 37,* 60–68.
Williams, R. M., Ward, C. E., & Hughes, I. A. (2011). Premature adrenarche. *Archives of Disease in Childhood, 97,* 250–254.
Wisniewski, A. B., & Chernausek, S. D. (2009). Gender in childhood obesity: Family environment, hormones, and genes. *Gender Medicine, 6,* 76–85.
Zacharias, L., Wurtman, R. J., & Shatzoff, M. (1970). Sexual maturation in contemporary American girls. *American Journal of Obstetrics Gynecology, 108,* 833–846.

Zucker, K. J. (1999). Commentary of Richardson's (1996) "Setting limits on gender health." *Harvard Review of Psychiatry, 7*, 37–42.

Zucker, K. J., & Cohen-Kettenis, P. (2008). Gender identity disorder in children and adolescents. In D. L. Rowland, & L. Incrocci (Eds.), *Handbook of sexual and gender identity disorders (pp. 376–422)*. Hoboken, NJ: John Wiley & Sons.

## FURTHER READING

Lawrence, A. (2010). Proposed revisions to gender identity disorder diagnoses in the DSM-5. *Archives of Sexual Behavior, 39*, 1253–1260.

# CHAPTER 7
# Sexual Development in Adolescents

**J. Dennis Fortenberry**
Indiana University School of Medicine, Indianapolis, Indiana[1]

This chapter examines adolescent sexuality development framed by three key aspects of sexual behavior: abstinence; masturbation; and partnered sexual activities. This framing resonates with recent trends in theory and research that emphasize the roles of sexuality in healthy adolescent development (Fortenberry, 2003; Halpern, 2010; Welsh & Kawaguchi, 2000). In contrast, many perspectives on adolescent sexuality development are limited by focus on problematized aspects of adolescent sexual development: the timing and context of first heterosexual penile-vaginal intercourse; association of sexual activity with substance use and other health-harming behaviors; contraceptive use; sexually transmitted infections (STI), including those due to human immunodeficiency viruses (HIV); and pregnancy. Less predominant but still frequently addressed themes in adolescent sexuality research include sexual coercion, non-coital sexual behaviors, exposure to and use of sexually explicit media, and same-sex sexual experiences (Brown & Brown, 2006; Kirby, 2001; Kotchick, Shaffer, Forehand, & Miller, 2001; Wood, Maforah, & Jewkes, 1998). Data related to these problematized aspects of sexuality development are often used to justify policy, public health, and clinical interventions intended (typically) to restrain adolescent sexual behaviors. The focus on problematic outcomes and emphasis on social, familial, and individual restraint of sexual expression obscures the more nuanced influences of sexuality within adolescent development, and incompletely traces the trajectories of healthy adolescent sexuality and subsequent adult sexual health.

Thus, the chapter approaches adolescents' sexual development by acknowledging positive aspects of adolescents' sexuality and sexual

---

[1] Correspondence to: Dennis Fortenberry, Indiana University School of Medicine, Department of Pediatrics, 410 West 10th Street, HITS 100, Indianapolis, IN 46202-5225. Phone 317-274-8812; email jfortenb@iupui.edu

behaviors, as well as the social risks of stigma, and the health risks of unplanned pregnancy and sexually transmitted infections. This approach is based in a sexual health perspective that includes the recognition of sexual rights, choice, and consent as the foundation of sexual health.

## THE CONCEPTUAL ORGANIZATION OF ADOLESCENT SEXUALITY DEVELOPMENT

Elements of sexuality and sexual interest are observable in children, but reorganization of the hormonal, anatomic, and neuropsychological substrates of sex during early adolescence profoundly alters the individual, and the interpersonal, familial, and social significance of these changes. Adolescence brings into play detailed social rules governing sexual display, sexual interaction, mating, and reproduction. The emergence of sexual cognitions, sexual interests, and a variety of sexual behaviors is a hallmark of adolescence, but—at any given point in adolescence—many adolescents express their sexuality without any sexual behavior at all. A scientifically informed perspective on adolescent sexuality and sexual health should address abstinence, unpartnered sexual behavior, and partnered sexual behaviors each as developmentally appropriate elements of adolescent sexuality development.

The phrase "adolescent sexuality development" is used here to echo the contemporary perspective that sexuality is an expected element of adolescent development rooted in sexual socialization, the emergence of sexual selfhood, and sexual repertoire (Tolman & McClelland, 2011). *Sexual socialization* refers to the social contexts in which adolescents develop sexual knowledge and experiences. Family, peers, and partners are sources of knowledge and experience and provide reference points for interpretation and meaning. Schools and religious organizations channel cultural values and knowledge, as well as giving infrastructure for sexual learning and experiences. A large range of media provide visual, auditory, and textual frames for learning and evaluating sexual information and standards of sexual behavior. *Sexual selfhood* refers to sexual subjectivity, identity, and gender, as well as the development of a self who imagines (in the present or the future) sexual relationships and the experience of sexual pleasure. Sexual selfhood also incorporates the awareness of sexual desire by others, and of one's capacity to desire others. *Sexual repertoire* refers to the behaviors (both unpartnered and partnered) about which adolescents develop knowledge, accrue experience, and choose. In other words, sexual repertoire is the set of sexual behaviors that summarize the content of an adolescent's sexual experience at any given point (Hensel, Fortenberry, & Orr, 2008). The three classes of behaviors that comprise adolescents' sexual repertoire—abstinence, unpartnered sex (masturbation), and partnered sexual behaviors—are seen as recurring microsocial events organized in specific spatial contexts, each event with situationally specific subjective experiences, interpretations, and outcomes.

This theoretical perspective has several advantages. Adolescent sexual development is seen as a product of many influences, with different trajectories of timing, pace, and accrual of sexual experience. Adolescence is also a period of constrained sexual autonomy in traditional and legal views, with various ages between age 12 and 18 years set as arbitrary thresholds for specific expressions of sexuality, such as partnered sexual intercourse (Donovan, 1997). Even research on adolescent sexuality is restricted by cultural and regulatory boundaries that identify adolescents as "vulnerable," and therefore excluded from certain classes of research (Dixon-Mueller, 2008).

A theoretical perspective that incorporates abstinence as well as masturbation and partnered sex permits a developmental perspective that does not value one set of behaviors over another. Likewise, sexual identity distinctions such as heterosexuality and homosexuality have no priority within this perspective on normal development. Socio-religious statuses such a virgin/non-virgin, without sexual experience/sexually experienced, not sexually active/sexually active, and unmarried/married are also unrecognized. These statuses are seen (at best) as irrelevant to understanding of adolescent sexual development. At worst, these statuses create stigma that restricts sexual rights and impairs sexual justice.

Perhaps the most important advantage of this theoretical perspective is the decomposition of sexual development into a series of events occurring within specific contexts and relationships, each contributing to an accrual of sexual learning, sexual self-awareness, and sexual competence. This allows us to consider sexual development as an aggregate of learning and experience rather than a set of arbitrary transitions or a single fixed trajectory of normality.

## **SEXUAL SOCIALIZATION**

### **Family Sexual Culture and Parents' Influence**

Parents and families play a central role in the ways young people become sexual. By the time of the transition from late childhood to early adolescence, parents already have contributed years of sexual socialization to their children. Gender attitudes (Crouter, Whiteman, McHale, & Osgood, 2007), words for genitals and linkage of genitals to reproduction (Fraley, Nelson, Wolf, & Lozoff, 1991), exposure to adult nudity (Friedrich, Grambsch, Broughton, Kuiper, & Beilke, 1991; Schoentjes, Deboutte, & Friedrich, 1999), parents' dating behaviors (Barber & Demo, 2006), viewing of adults' sexual behaviors (Okami, Olmstead, Abramson, & Pendleton, 1998), participation in conversations about sex and reproduction with adults (Pontecorvo, Fasulo, & Sterponi, 2001; Raffaelli & Duckett, 1989), and norms for dyadic relationships (Bos & Sandfort, 2010) are but a few of the components of family sexual culture. Family sexual culture refers to adolescents' values, attitudes, and behaviors influenced by parents and siblings (Thigpen & Fortenberry, 2009). In short, family sexual culture represents a specific means of sexual socialization, by which specific social and religious sexual values and attitudes are reinforced (Fingerson, 2005).

Family sexual culture provides a useful context from which to examine *direct* parental influences on adolescent sexuality and sexual behavior. Parents' communication about sexuality and sexual behavior is a particular aspect of family sexual culture. In general, parents act as controllers and restrainers of adolescent sexuality and expressions of sexual behavior. Examples of direct influences of family sexual culture include family nudity, parental communication about sexuality and sex, supervision of sexual exposure opportunities (e.g., access to sexually explicit media; dating). Nudity within families is associated with relatively few short-term (Friedrich et al., 1991; Schoentjes et al., 1999; Thigpen, 2009) or long-term (Okami et al., 1998) effects on adolescents' sexuality and sexual behavior. Family sexual culture even influences the language learned by children to refer to genitals (Fraley et al., 1991).

Adolescents who perceive their parents to be more sexually liberal may have more sex partners (Fingerson, 2005). Findings suggest that the more sexually liberal teens think their mothers are, the more likely the teens are to have higher numbers of sex partners. Talking about sex and having a strong connection between mothers and teens contribute to sexual norm transmission. The more talk about sex there is within the dyad, the more likely the teen is to have had sex. The stronger the connection between mothers and teens, the less likely the teen is to have had sex. Finally, for boys, verbal communication with their mothers is more important in sexual norm transmission; and for girls, having a good connection in the dyad is more important. It is also important to note that sexual socialization occurs through interaction of parents with adolescents, rather than through a unidirectional transmission from parents (de Graaf, Vanwesenbeeck, Woertman, & Meeus, 2011). A substantial body of research demonstrates that aspects of family sexual culture influence adolescent sexual behaviors. Most of this research focuses on ways in which parenting behaviors are associated with older age at first penile-vaginal intercourse, fewer intercourse partners, and greater use of condoms and contraceptives (de Graaf et al., 2011). Family sexual culture may even influence the space in which adolescents' sexual activities occur. For example, Dutch parents have a greater willingness than American parents to acknowledge and encourage adolescents' sexual relations at home (Schalet, 2011).

Research emphasis on families' influence on the timing and expression of specific sexual and contraceptive behaviors has obscured the potential importance of family sexual culture and aspects of sexual health: sexual assertiveness; control; esteem; and satisfaction. For example, among Dutch adolescents, greater parental support was associated with greater sexual assertiveness and satisfaction, controlling for effects of parental knowledge. Parental knowledge, however, was associated with assertiveness, control, esteem, and satisfaction, even while controlling for mediation effects of parental support (de Graaf et al., 2010). Parents may also influence sexuality development indirectly through more general parenting approaches to provision of support, control, and monitoring. Most research appears to be based in a quasi-theoretical perspective that increased levels of support, control, and monitoring are associated with fewer sexual partners and less unprotected sex during transition from high school to college. Perceived parental awareness and caring also moderates the relationship with liberal sexual values (Wetherill, Neal, & Fromme, 2010).

## Peers and Friends in Sexual Socialization

If parents are influences that typically restrain adolescent sexuality (especially sexual behavior), peers and friends are thought to have the opposite effect (Bleakley, Hennessy, Fishbein, & Jordan, 2009). These are complex influences, however, and a more considered perspective suggests at least five areas in which peers and friends directly and indirectly influence sexuality and sexual behaviors: providing more general models for lifestyles that are relatively more conventional (and less deviant) or more deviant (and less conventional); providing models for sexual attitudes and behaviors, serving as sources of information; serving as sources of social approval and disapproval for specific attitudes and behaviors; and serving as sources of sexual partners and potential partners.

Covariation of sexual behaviors with other unconventional or deviant behaviors is a robust finding from samples of adolescents from all over the world. Earlier onset of sexual behavior, alcohol and other drug use, cigarette use, and delinquent behaviors form a constellation of behaviors associated with greater psychosocial unconventionality and friendships with likewise unconventional peers (Costa, Jessor, Donovan, & Fortenberry, 1995). Peers and friends also provide models for sexual attitudes and behaviors. The magnitude of this influence is substantial: a 10% increase in the proportion of friends that initiate sexual intercourse is associated with a 5% increase in an adolescent's likelihood of initiation (Ali & Dwyer, 2011). Note that this is a perception of friends' behaviors that seem to be important, since most adolescents do not have direct knowledge of friends' sexual behaviors. For better or for worse, peers and friends are important sources of information about sexuality and sexual behavior: even parents believe that adolescents get most of their information from friends (Lagus, Bernat, Bearinger, Resnick, & Eisenberg, 2011). Interchanges with friends about sexuality may match the unstructured and informal approaches to information gathering used by young people to explore new topics and validate information obtained from other sources (Powell, 2008).

## Sexually Explicit Media and Adolescent Sex

Contemporary adolescents have access to a variety of sexually explicit media (e.g., television, internet, chat lines, books, magazines) with exposures often beginning at age 14 or earlier (Štulhofer, Buško, & Landripet, 2010; Ybarra & Mitchell, 2005). Onset of puberty is associated with an increase in the use of sexually explicit media among boys (Lofgren-Mårtenson & Månsson, 2010; Skoog, Stattin, & Kerr, 2009), likely in relation to masturbation rather than in association with partnered sexual behaviors (Hald, 2006). Exposure to sexually explicit media may be unintentional, but is often intentionally chosen for sexual content (Bleakley, Hennessy, & Fishbein, 2011). Exposure to sexually explicit materials during early adolescence (i.e., by age 14) is associated with several subsequent effects on sexual socialization: more restrictive gender role attitudes; more permissive norms for sexual behavior; and sexual harassment (among adolescent men). Earlier initiation of oral and vaginal sex, as well as number of sexual partners, is also linked to early exposure to sexually explicit media (Braun-Courville & Rojas, 2009).

One form of contemporary sexually explicit media—"sexting"—has received substantial popular attention but relatively little research (Weiss & Samenow, 2010). Sexting involves the transmission of sexual text or nude or sexual photographs via cellular smart phones. Up to 20% of adolescents report sending or receiving sexual visual images (cited in O'Keefe & Clarke-Pearson, 2011). No data describe the integration of such texts/images into adolescents' sexual lives. However, some jurisdictions interpret sexting in the context of child pornography laws, prosecution of which certainly has important long-term consequences (Ostrager, 2010).

## SEXUAL SELFHOOD

Increasingly evolved cognitive assessments of one's sexual self are part of the more general process of adolescents' developing self-concept (Harter, 1990). Some aspects of sexual self-concept are apparent in early adolescence, well before onset of partnered sexual behaviors (Butler, Miller, Holtgrave, Forehand, & Long, 2006; Ott, Pfeiffer, & Fortenberry, 2006). Exposure to new experiences additionally shapes generalizations about the sexual self, which may in turn influence the timing and choice of future sexual behaviors (Andersen & Cyranowski, 1994; Buzwell & Rosenthal, 1996; Cyranowski & Andersen, 1998; O'Sullivan & Brooks-Gunn, 2005). Three general domains of self-concept are associated with the ways sexuality and sexual behaviors develop in adolescence.

### Sexual Openness

Sexual openness refers to a willingness to experience and express sexual desire, a sense of entitlement to one's chosen sexual experiences, and an engagement with the pleasure associated with sex (Horne & Zimmer-Gembeck, 2005, 2006). In general, greater sexual openness is associated with later onset of intercourse, consent for intercourse, with condom use, and with decreased pregnancy rates (Welsh & Kawaguchi, 2000). Higher rates of sexual arousability and attention to arousal were associated with an increased likelihood of a young woman's reporting being in a loving relationship, and with positive reports of different sexual activities (O'Sullivan, Meyer-Bahlburg, & McKeague, 2006). Adolescents—at least adolescent women—of the same age vary in sexual openness, but the general developmental trajectory of sexual openness is one of increase from middle through late adolescence (Hensel, O'Sullivan, & Fortenberry, 2011).

### Sexual Self-Esteem

Sexual self-esteem includes one's affective appraisals of sexual thoughts, feelings, and behaviors as well as perceptions of body in the sexual context

(Horne & Zimmer-Gembeck, 2006). Partnered sex often involves revealing of the body, especially the genitals, to others. A general sense of comfort with one's body and genitals is associated with higher levels of sexual comfort, greater satisfaction with sexual interactions, and decreased levels of risky behavior (Schick, Calabrese, Rima, & Zucker, 2010). Genital self-image may be associated with recent trends in pubic hair removal, especially among younger women (Herbenick, Schick, Reece, Sanders, & Fortenberry, 2010). A more general sense of sexual self-esteem is also associated with a more positive view of sexual activity, more assurance in sexual situations, decreased risk-taking with casual partners, and greater sexual satisfaction (Impett & Tolman, 2006). It may be that adolescents with higher sexual self-esteem place higher value on their sexual being and experiences, and by extension are willing to engage a sexual partner in discussing issues related to sexual encounters, such as satisfaction, emotions, and willingness to participate in risk (Rostosky, Dekhtyar, Cupp, & Anderman, 2008). As with sexual openness, sexual self-esteem generally increases during middle and late adolescence, even among those with relatively low self-esteem during middle adolescence (Hensel et al., 2011).

## Sexual Anxiety

Negative reactions to sexuality—such as anxiety, shame, and guilt—may be related to social or familial attempts to control adolescents' sexuality and sexual behaviors (Higgins, Trussell, Moore, & Davidson, 2010; Woo, Brotto, & Gorzalka, 2011). Sexual anxiety among adolescents is associated with greater endorsement of abstinence beliefs, lower perceived sexual readiness or likelihood of intercourse in the near future, as well as with fewer reports of having a boyfriend, having been in love, or having engaged in kissing, fondling, or coitus (O'Sullivan et al., 2006). Sexual anxiety appears to decrease during adolescence, perhaps as a consequence of accruing experience (Hensel et al., 2011; O'Sullivan & Brooks-Gunn, 2005).

## SEXUAL REPERTOIRE

## Abstinence

Abstinence is widely used in discussions about sex education, in debates about the role of public health in adolescent sexuality, and in research about sexually transmitted infections and unplanned pregnancy (Ott & Santelli, 2007). Abstinence is defined here as refraining from oral, vaginal, and anal partnered sexual behaviors, although no single definition

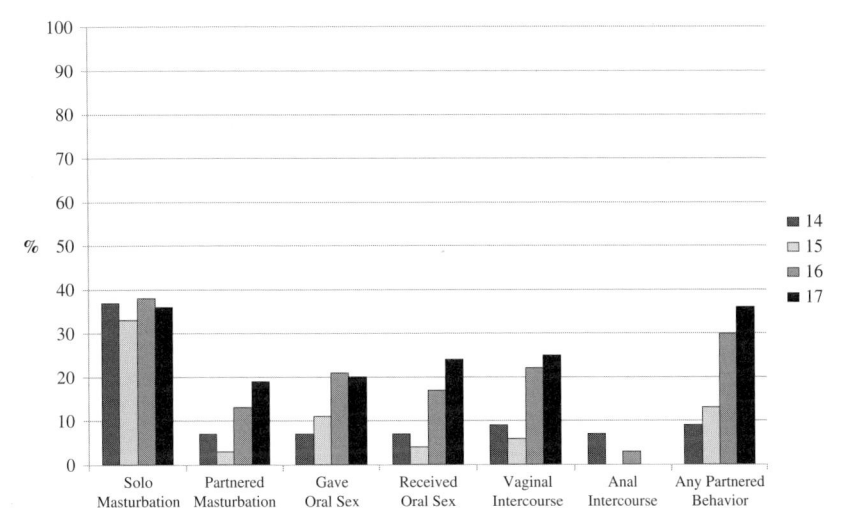

**Figure 7.1** Sexual behaviors in past 90 days, US adolescent women ages 14–17. *Data obtained from Herbenick et al. (2010).*

perfectly captures the range of sexual interactions included in many young people's definitions of abstinence (Bersamin, Fisher, Walker, Hill, & Grube, 2007). Some definitions of abstinence include masturbation and sexual thoughts (Byers, Henderson, & Hobson, 2009), and abstinence as a behavioral descriptor is often conflated with cultural concepts such as virginity and chastity (Fahs, 2010). If abstinence is defined as refraining from masturbation as well as partnered sexual behaviors, most American adolescents are abstinent at any given time (see Figures 7.1 and 7.2).

Abstinence is often discussed as if an adolescent either "is" or "is not" abstinent, allowing little insight into the ways adolescents incorporate the developing experience of sexuality into sociocultural expectations for abstinence. Many adolescents hold clear views about abstinence which distinguishes adolescents' sexual abstinence from the sexual abstinence of younger children (De Graaf & Rademakers, 2011; Rademakers, Rademakers, & Straver, 2003). Such views about abstinence coincide with emergence of conscious sexual identities, motivations, and desires during early and middle adolescence (Reynolds & Herbenick, 2003). Emergence of sexual cognitions is likely hormonally mediated in association with adrenarche and pubarche (Ellis & Essex, 2007; Graber, Nichols, & Brooks-Gunn, 2010; Herdt & McClintock, 2000; Oberfield & White, 2009). Self-relevant sexual thoughts are seen even among 9-11-year-old boys and

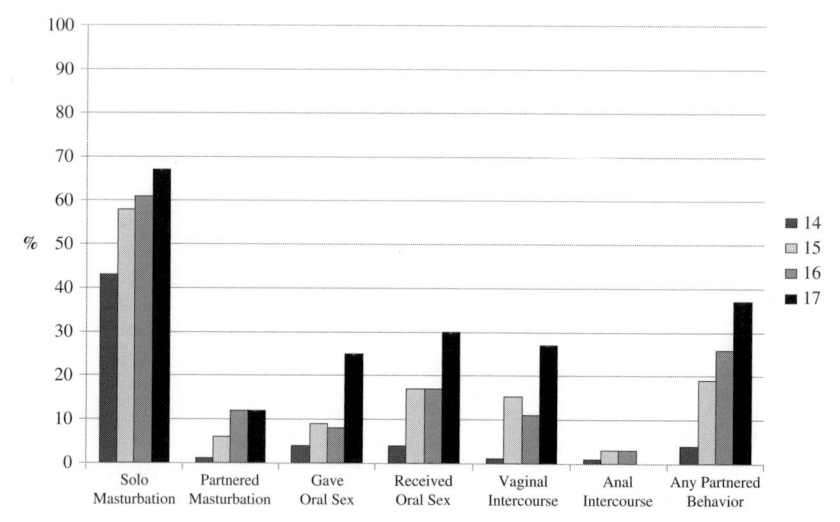

Figure 7.2 Sexual behaviors in past 90 days, US adolescent men ages 14–17. *Data obtained from Herbenick et al. (2010).*

girls (Butler et al., 2006). Of those reporting sexual thoughts, about 10% reported initiation of partnered sexual touching. Prospective studies suggest that sexual cognitions become evident over a short period of time, perhaps as little as three months (Ott & Pfeiffer, 2009).

Framing abstinence as a behavior chosen within the context of sexual motivations and desires creates a developmentally appropriate framework for considering abstinence as a developmentally appropriate sexual behavior that is separated from social, cultural, and religious issues of chastity, virginity, and non-virginity. Young adolescents describe abstinence as a normal aspect of a continuum that uses "developmental readiness" as a standard for motivated decisions about shifting from sexually abstinent behavior to sexual activity (Ott et al., 2006). Stronger attitudes about abstinence and intentions to be abstinent are associated with increased likelihood of abstinence six months later (Masters, Beadnell, Morrison, Hoppe, & Gillmore, 2008). Interactions of abstinence and sex cognitions were important, in that adolescents with high levels of abstinence intentions and high levels of sex intentions were less likely to be abstinent six months later (Masters et al., 2008). Satisfaction with abstinence (identified by items such as "being sexually abstinent makes me feel good") is correlated with abstinence intentions, beliefs, and norms (Buhi, Goodson, Neilands, & Blunt, 2011).

## Masturbation

Masturbation is the second most common adolescent sexual behavior—after abstinence (Fortenberry et al., 2010) (Figures 7.1 and 7.2). Masturbation remains subject to substantial social and religious disapproval although contemporary medical views hold masturbation developmentally normal, and health-neutral if not health-enhancing (Coleman, 2002; Leitenberg, Detzer, & Srebnik, 1993). However, it seems oddly contradictory that a purportedly "normal" (and even "healthy") behavior is so little addressed in sexuality education curricula, in discussions between adolescents and parents, and between adolescents and physicians (Robbins et al., 2011).

The age of onset of masturbation is not well-defined. Retrospective studies suggest average ages of 13 and 15 years for men and women, respectively (Pinkerton, Bogart, Cecil, & Abramson, 2002). The prevalence of recent masturbation increases with age among adolescent men: about 43% of 14-year-olds report masturbation in the past 90 days compared with 67% of 17-year-olds (Robbins et al., 2011). In contrast, the percentage of 14–17-year-old women reporting recent masturbation is about 36% (Robbins et al., 2011). Rates of masturbation remain high over the lifespan, especially among men (Herbenick et al., 2010; Kontula & Haavio-Mannila, 2002). This suggests that masturbation serves important functions to sexual development, and that these functions are not fully supplanted by partnered sexual behavior in adolescence, or at any point in the lifespan (Das, 2007; Das, Parish, & Laumann, 2009; Gerressu, Mercer, Graham, Wellings, & Johnson, 2008; Kontula & Haavio-Mannila, 2002; Robinson, Bockting, & Harrell, 2002).

Masturbation is associated with other adolescent sexual behaviors. Among American 14-17-year-olds, those reporting masturbation in the past year report higher levels of several forms of partnered sex, including given/received oral sex, penile-vaginal intercourse, and penile-anal intercourse (Robbins et al., 2011). Gender differences are evident in that women's masturbation prevalence increased from 34% among those reporting penile-vaginal sex occurring less frequently than four times in the last four weeks to 72% among those women reporting at least 16 occasions. In contrast, the prevalence of masturbation was most frequent among men reporting fewer than four occasions of sex in the last four weeks (Gerressu et al., 2008).

Masturbation may provide a means of gaining familiarity and comfort with one's sexual responses and genitals (Hogarth & Ingham, 2009).

Masturbation and non-coital orgasm among young women is associated with higher levels of sexual self-awareness, greater efficacy achieving pleasure, and more resistance to gendered double standards (Horne & Zimmer-Gembeck, 2005). Young men—but not young women—who report masturbation in the past year are substantially more likely to report condom use with penile-vaginal intercourse than young men who do not report masturbating (Robbins et al., 2011).

## Partnered Sex

Partnered sexual behaviors become prominent during mid- and late adolescence (Herbenick et al., 2010). These behaviors include sexual kissing, breast and genital touching, partnered masturbation, fellatio, cunnilingus, penile-vaginal intercourse, and penile-anal intercourse. Other partnered behaviors such as sexual exchange via electronic media (e.g., phone sex, "sexting"), and shared viewing of sexually explicit media also emerge during this time. The essential element of this aspect of adolescent sexuality is the sexual dyad. The nature and content of the dyadic relationship defines a substantial perspective on social attitudes, motivations, and outcomes (e.g., STI, pregnancy) of adolescents' sexual relations.

### *Sexual Partnering and Sexual Relationships*

Much of adolescent sexuality development is tied to the centrality of sexual dyads in human sexuality, and the importance placed on two biological sexes (female and male) as essential elements of dyads. Sex plays a complex role in the formation and maintenance of many dyadic relationships, and serves different functions in relationships with different partners (Giordano, Manning, & Longmore, 2010). Even within partnerships, the relational, recreational, and reproductive functions of sex vary in relevance and salience at different times. Sexual factors predominate in some relationships: exchange of sex for money, drugs or rent, or single encounters with poorly known partners are examples. Up to half of adolescents report having sex outside of a dating context, but many choose partners who are friends or ex-girlfriends/boyfriends (Manning, Giordano, & Longmore, 2006). The sexual behavior content of these typically short-term relationships is highly varied, with a substantial proportion not involving penile-vaginal or penile-anal intercourse (Epstein, Calzo, Smiler, & Ward, 2009).

For many adolescents, sexual activity occurs within the context of an established relationship characterized by terms indicating relative commitment and exclusivity (e.g., friend, boyfriend/girlfriend, or fiancée)

(Manning, Flanigan, Giordano, & Longmore, 2009). In the past, many sexual relationships occurred in dating relationships with a subsequent marriage partner, and dating relationships remain important contexts for adolescents' sexual activity (Giordano et al., 2010; Manning, Giordano, Longmore, & Hocevar, 2011). Serial romantic and sexual relationships—serial monogamy—represent a temporal sequence of sexual relationships characterized by commitment and sexual exclusivity, not necessarily leading to marriage or cohabitation. Many young adults—but relatively few adolescents—establish cohabiting relations with a partner, often prior to marriage (Cohen & Manning, 2010).

## *Partnered Sexual Behaviors*

Partnered, non-coital sexual behaviors such as kissing, non-genital sexual touching, genital touching, and oral-genital intercourse may comprise the majority of a given sexual encounter or may form sets of behaviors that accompany coital sexual behaviors. For many adolescents, non-coital behaviors provide an experiential scaffold for first coitus (O'Sullivan, Cheng, Harris, & Brooks-Gunn, 2007; Schuster, Bell, & Kanouse, 1996; Smith & Udry, 1985) or allow partnered sexual interaction with reduced risk of pregnancy or sexually transmitted infection (Uecker, Angotti, & Regnerus, 2008).

Kissing likely serves multiple roles in human mating, including provision of olfactory clues about health of a mate, promotion of bonding, and initiation of sexual arousal (Hughes, Harrison, & Gallup, 2007). Kissing is perhaps the sexual behavior most directly observed by adolescents through visual media (Callister, Stern, Coyne, Robinson, & Bennion, 2011; Pardun, L'Engle, & Brown, 2005) and the first sexual experience with both same-sex and different-sex partners (Owen, Rhoades, Stanley, & Fincham, 2010; Smiler, Frankel, & Savin-Williams, 2011). Kissing is especially characteristic of the partnered sexual interactions of younger (e.g., 12–13-year-old) adolescents (Williams, Connolly, & Cribbie, 2008), but is also associated with stability and satisfaction in adolescent romantic relationships (Welsh, Haugen, Widman, Darling, & Grello, 2005). Kissing may also be important as part of the context of parent–adolescent communication about sex and sexuality (Beckett et al., 2010).

The prevalence of other partnered sexual behaviors among American 14-17-year-olds is depicted in Figure 7.1 (females) and Figure 7.2 (males) (Herbenick et al., 2010). The prevalence of given and received oral-genital sex is of particular interest in adolescent sexuality development, as these distinct sexual behaviors may have markedly different patterns of organization and associations with gender, with sexual self-concept, and with sexual partnerships (McKay, 2004). The prevalence of oral-genital sex appears to have increased in recent years, perhaps in response to greater emphasis on the value of virginity and media popularized "risks" associated with coitus (Cornell & Halpern-Felsher, 2006; Grunseit, Richters, Crawford, Song, & Kippax, 2005; Halpern-Felsher, Cornell, Kropp, & Tschann, 2005). Oral-genital sexual behaviors may also represent sexual learning that emphasizes exchange, physical intimacy, and pleasure as well as "safer" sexual behaviors (Ehrhardt, 1996). To the extent that non-coital sexual behaviors provide opportunity to experience partnered arousal, sexual agency, and sexual control, oral-genital sexual behaviors could be an important part of the development of healthy sexuality during adolescence and young adulthood (Horne & Zimmer-Gembeck, 2005).

Oral-genital sexual behaviors may occur in isolation, or in combination with other sexual behaviors (Hensel et al., 2008), reflecting the context of behaviors on a particular day. For example, partner support and sexual interest are both lower on days when young women report giving oral sex only to male partner, but higher on days when both coitus and given oral-genital sex are reported (Fortenberry & Hensel, 2011). A similar pattern is reported for received oral-genital sex. Situational factors such as menses also increase the likelihood of young women giving oral-genital sex to a male partner, if sexual contact happens at all (Hensel, Fortenberry, & Orr, 2007).

Vaginal-penile sex is often viewed in both popular and professional dialogue as the *sine qua non* of sexual development. Many societies develop separate language and social status for adolescents before and after an initial vaginal sexual experience. However, the range and meanings of sexual behaviors available to adolescents suggest the need for a more nuanced perspective. For example, a recent daily diary study showed no difference in daily mood on days before and after first coitus (Tanner, Hensel, & Fortenberry, 2010).

Data from the National Survey of Sexual Health and Behavior (NSSHB) provided age-specific rates of a range of sexual behaviors of adolescents aged 14–19 years (Fortenberry et al., 2010; Herbenick, et al., 2010). Vaginal intercourse was a rare event for the majority of 14–15-year-olds, with 90% of males and 88% of females never having engaged in such sex. Among 16–17-year-olds, vaginal sex occurred more frequently.

However, only approximately one-third of males and females in this age group reported ever having vaginal sex. Among 18–19-year-olds, 63% of males and 64% of females reported experiencing vaginal sex at least once during their lifetime.

Anal-penile sex, and especially receptive anal sex, was a low occurring behavior among most adolescents. For instance, among 18–19-year-old males, lifetime prevalence rates of receptive and insertive anal sex were 4% and 10%, respectively. Among adolescent women, anal sex was also a very low occurring event and was endorsed at a rate of 4% among 14–15-year-olds and 7% among 16–17-year-olds. Higher rates of anal sex were reported among 18–19-year-old adolescent females, with over 20% having experienced anal sex at least once during their lifetimes (Herbenick et al., 2010).

## *Subjective Sexual Experiences*

Subjective aspects of sex acts are clearly important elements of adults' sex (Meston & Buss, 2007), but are virtually unaddressed in the research literature about adolescent sexuality, sexual behavior, and sexual consequences. Sexual arousal summarizes the complex psychological and physiologic activation associated with sexual stimuli (Levin, 2002). Many models of adult sexual response assume that sexual desire precedes and generates sexual arousal, but these models have been especially criticized as less accurate for women (Graham, Sanders, Milhausen, & McBride, 2004). Our cultural mythology (exemplified in the phrase "raging hormones") suggests that adolescence is a time of innate, hormonally-mediated sexual arousal. This view has been supplemented by contemporary neuropsychological data suggesting a developmental imbalance in dual brain systems associated with sensation-seeking and behavioral control (Steinberg et al., 2008). Surprisingly little is known about the role played by arousal and sexual interest, although diary-based studies of a single cohort of adolescent women showed that greater sexual interest on a given day was associated with sexual activity on that day, whether the behavior was first lifetime coitus, coitus, fellatio, cunnilingus, anal intercourse, or coitus during menses (Fortenberry & Hensel, 2011).

Adolescents do identify pleasure as an important motivation for sex, although young women place less emphasis on pleasure than young men (Latka, Kapadia, & Fortin, 2008; Suvivuo, Tossavainen, & Kontula, 2010). Research on sexual pleasure among adolescents largely addresses perceptions of the effects of condom (or contraceptive) use on pleasure (Higgins, Hoffman, Graham, & Sanders, 2008). Even young adolescent men without coital experience mention interference with pleasure as a negative aspect of condom use (Rosenberger, Bell, McBride, Fortenberry, & Ott, 2010). Sexual pleasure has also emerged—because of the potential lubricating qualities of vaginal microbicides—as an important element of microbicide acceptability, even for young women (Tanner et al., 2009).

We know almost nothing about physiologic or psychological correlates of orgasm in adolescents. The average age of retrospectively reported first orgasm is 13 years and 17 years of age for men and women, respectively (Reynolds & Herbenick, 2003). These data refer in part to orgasm from masturbation, but demonstrate that the capacity for orgasm is present in adolescence. About 10% of adolescent women report orgasm with first heterosexual coitus (Raboch & Bartak, 1983). Among 18–24-year-old Swedish women, 26% reported that first orgasm occurred in association with penile-vaginal intercourse, and an additional 25% from cunnilingus or partner masturbation (Fugl-Meyer, Oberg, Lundberg, Lewin, & Fugl-Meyer, 2006). In a national Australian survey, 84% of 16–19-year-old men and 52% of women reported an orgasm at their most recent sexual encounter (Richters, Visser, Rissel, & Smith, 2006).

## SUMMARY

The approach to normal sexuality development proposed in this chapter reflects a perspective that sexuality is built from multiple influences, that specific sexual statuses are not relevant to a consideration of normality, and that abstinence, masturbation, and partnered sexual behaviors are equally important elements of adolescent sexuality development. Taken together, this perspective demonstrates a connection of adolescent to adult sexuality, and the place of these sexualities in sexual health through the lifespan. Healthy adolescent sexual development implies a broad social commitment to adolescents' sexual rights and to accurate sexuality education that recognizes abstinence, masturbation, and partnered sexual behaviors as developmentally appropriate sexual choices. This developmental perspective supports the importance of a broad range of contraceptive and STI/HIV prevention services, recognizing that these will be needed eventually for most adolescents. Finally, this perspective on sexual development implies that healthy long-term relationships will unfold in the context of sexually healthy partners.

# REFERENCES

Ali, M. M., & Dwyer, D. S. (2011). Estimating peer effects in sexual behavior among adolescents. *Journal of Adolescence, 34*, 183–190.
Andersen, B. L., & Cyranowski, J. M. (1994). Women's sexual self-schema. *Journal of Personality & Social Psychology, 67*, 1079–1100.
Barber, B. L., & Demo, D. H. (2006). The kids are alright (at least, most of them): Links between divorce and dissolution and child well-being. In M. A. Fine, & J. H. Harvey (Eds.), *Handbook of divorce and relationship dissolution (pp. 289-231ll)*. Mahwah, NJ: Lawrence Erlbaum Associates.
Beckett, M. K., Elliott, M. N., Martino, S., Kanouse, D. E., Corona, R., Klein, D. J., et al. (2010). Timing of parent and child communication about sexuality relative to children's sexual behaviors. *Pediatrics, 125*, 34–42.
Bersamin, M. M., Fisher, D. A., Walker, S., Hill, D. L., & Grube, J. W. (2007). Defining virginity and abstinence: Adolescents' interpretations of sexual behaviors. *Journal of Adolescent Health, 41*, 182–188.
Bleakley, A., Hennessy, M., & Fishbein, M. (2011). A model of adolescents' seeking of sexual content in their media choices. *Journal of Sex Research, 48*, 309–315.
Bleakley, A., Hennessy, M., Fishbein, M., & Jordan, A. (2009). How sources of sexual information relate to adolescents' beliefs about sex. *American Journal of Health Behavior, 33*, 37–48.
Bos, H., & Sandfort, T. G. M. (2010). Children's gender identity in lesbian and heterosexual two-parent families. *Sex Roles, 62*, 114–126.
Braun-Courville, D. K., & Rojas, M. (2009). Exposure to sexually explicit Web sites and adolescent sexual attitudes and behaviors. *Journal of Adolescent Health, 45*, 156–162.
Brown, R. T., & Brown, J. D. (2006). Adolescent sexuality. *Primary Care; Clinics in Office Practice, 33*, 373–390.
Buhi, E. R., Goodson, P., Neilands, T. B., & Blunt, H. (2011). Adolescent sexual abstinence: A test of an integrative theoretical framework. *Health Education & Behavior, 38*, 63–79.
Butler, T. H., Miller, K. S., Holtgrave, D. R., Forehand, R., & Long, N. (2006). Stages of sexual readiness and six-month stage progression among African-American pre-teens. *Journal of Sex Research, 43*, 378–386.
Buzwell, S., & Rosenthal, D. (1996). Constructing a sexual self: Adolescents' sexual self-perceptions and sexual risk-taking. *Journal of Research on Adolescence, 6*, 489–513.
Byers, E. S., Henderson, J., & Hobson, K. M. (2009). University students' definitions of sexual abstinence and having sex. *Archives of Sexual Behavior, 38*, 665–674.
Callister, M., Stern, L. A., Coyne, S. M., Robinson, T., & Bennion, E. (2011). Evaluation of sexual content in teen-centered films from 1980 to 2007. *Mass Communication & Society, 14*, 454–474.
Cohen, J., & Manning, W. (2010). The relationship context of premarital serial cohabitation. *Social Science Research, 39*, 766–776.
Coleman, E. (2002). Masturbation as a means of achieving sexual health. In W. O. Bockting, & E. Coleman (Eds.), *Masturbation as a means of achieving sexual health (pp. 5–16)*. New York, NY: The Haworth Press.
Cornell, J. L., & Halpern-Felsher, B. L. (2006). Adolescents tell us why teens have oral sex. *Journal of Adolescent Health, 38*, 299–301.
Costa, F. M., Jessor, R., Donovan, J. E., & Fortenberry, J. D. (1995). Early initiation of sexual intercourse: The influence of psychosocial unconventionality. *Journal of Research on Adolescence, 5*, 93–121.
Crouter, A. C., Whiteman, S. D., McHale, S. M., & Osgood, D. W. (2007). Development of gender attitude traditionality across middle childhood and adolescence. *Child Development, 78*, 911–926.

Cyranowski, J. M., & Andersen, B. L. (1998). Schemas, sexuality, and romantic attachment. *Journal of Personality & Social Psychology, 74*, 1364–1379.

Das, A. (2007). Masturbation in the United States. *Journal of Sex & Marital Therapy, 33*(4), 301–317.

Das, A., Parish, W. L., & Laumann, E. O. (2009). Masturbation in urban China. *Archives of Sexual Behavior, 38*, 108–120.

De Graaf, H., & Rademakers, J. (2011). The psychological measurement of childhood sexual development in Western societies: Methodological challenges. *Journal of Sex Research, 48*, 118–129.

de Graaf, H., Vanwesenbeeck, I., Woertman, L., & Meeus, W. (2011). Parenting and adolescents' sexual development in western societies: A literature review. *European Psychologist, 16*, 21–31.

de Graaf, H., Vanwesenbeeck, I., Woertman, L., Keijsers, L., Meijer, S., & Meeus, W. (2010). Parental support and knowledge and adolescents' sexual health: Testing two mediational models in a national Dutch sample. *Journal of Youth and Adolescence, 39*, 189–198.

Dixon-Mueller, R. (2008). How young is "too young"? Comparative perspectives on adolescent sexual, marital, and reproductive transitions. *Studies in Family Planning, 39*, 247–262.

Donovan, P. (1997). Can statutory rape laws be effective in preventing adolescent pregnancy? *Family Planning Perspectives, 29*, 30–34.

Ehrhardt, A. A. (1996). Our view of adolescent sexuality: A focus on risk behavior without the developmental context. *American Journal of Public Health, 86*, 1523–1525.

Ellis, B. J., & Essex, M. J. (2007). Family environments, adrenarche, and sexual maturation: A longitudinal test of a life history model. *Child Development, 78*, 1799–1817.

Epstein, M., Calzo, J. P., Smiler, A. P., & Ward, L. M. (2009). "Anything from making out to having sex": Men's negotiations of hooking up and friends with benefits scripts. *Journal of Sex Research, 46*, 414–424.

Fahs, B. (2010). Daddy's little girls: On the perils of chastity clubs, purity balls, and ritualized abstinence. *Frontiers - A Journal of Women Studies, 31*, 116–142.

Fingerson, L. (2005). Do mothers' opinions matter in teens' sexual activity? *Journal of Family Issues, 26*, 947–974.

Fortenberry, J. D. (2003). Adolescent sex and the rhetoric of risk. In D. Romer (Ed.), *Reducing adolescent risk: Toward an integrated approach (pp. 293–300).* Thousand Oaks, CA: Sage Publications, Inc.

Fortenberry, J. D., & Hensel, D. J. (2011). The association of sexual interest and sexual behaviors among adolescent women: A daily diary perspective. *Hormones & Behavior, 59*, 739–744.

Fortenberry, J. D., Schick, V., Herbenick, D., Sanders, S. A., Dodge, B., & Reece, M. (2010). Sexual behaviors and condom use at last vaginal intercourse: A national sample of adolescents ages 14 to 17 years. *Journal of Sexual Medicine, 7*(Suppl. 5), 305–314.

Fraley, M. C., Nelson, E. C., Wolf, A. W., & Lozoff, B. (1991). Early genital naming. *Journal of Developmental & Behavioral Pediatrics, 12*, 301–304.

Friedrich, W. N., Grambsch, P., Broughton, D., Kuiper, J., & Beilke, R. L. (1991). Normative sexual behavior in children. *Pediatrics, 88*, 456–464.

Fugl-Meyer, K. S., Oberg, K., Lundberg, P. O., Lewin, B., & Fugl-Meyer, A. (2006). On orgasm, sexual techniques, and erotic perceptions in 18- to 74-year-old Swedish women. *Journal of Sexual Medicine, 3*, 56–68.

Gerressu, M., Mercer, C. H., Graham, C. A., Wellings, K., & Johnson, A. M. (2008). Prevalence of masturbation and associated factors in a British national probability survey. *Archives of Sexual Behavior, 37*, 266–278.

Giordano, P. C., Manning, W. D., & Longmore, M. A. (2010). Affairs of the heart: Qualities of adolescent romantic relationships and sexual behavior. *Journal of Research on Adolescence, 20*, 983–1013.

Graber, J. A., Nichols, T. R., & Brooks-Gunn, J. (2010). Putting pubertal timing in developmental context: Implications for prevention. *Developmental Psychobiology, 52*, 254–262.

Graham, C. A., Sanders, S. A., Milhausen, R. R., & McBride, K. R. (2004). Turning on and turning off: A focus group study of the factors that affect women's sexual arousal. *Archives of Sexual Behavior, 33*, 527–538.

Grunseit, A., Richters, J., Crawford, J., Song, A., & Kippax, S. (2005). Stability and change in sexual practices among first-year Australian university students (1990–1999). *Archives of Sexual Behavior, 34*, 569–582.

Hald, G. M. (2006). Gender differences in pornography consumption among young heterosexual Danish adults. *Archives of Sexual Behavior, 35*, 577–585.

Halpern, C. T. (2010). Reframing research on adolescent sexuality: Healthy sexual development as part of the life course. *Perspectives on Sexual & Reproductive Health, 42*, 6–7.

Halpern-Felsher, B. L., Cornell, J. L., Kropp, R. Y., & Tschann, J. M. (2005). Oral versus vaginal sex among adolescents: Perceptions, attitudes, and behavior. *Pediatrics, 115*, 845–851.

Harter, S. (1990). Self and identity development. In S. S. Feldman, & G. R. Elliott (Eds.), *At the threshold: The developing adolescent* (pp. 352–387). Cambridge, MA: Harvard University Press.

Hensel, D. J., Fortenberry, J. D., & Orr, D. P. (2007). Situational and relational factors associated with coitus during vaginal bleeding among adolescent women. *Journal of Sex Research, 44*, 269–277.

Hensel, D. J., Fortenberry, J. D., & Orr, D. P. (2008). Variations in coital and noncoital sexual repertoire among adolescent women. *Journal of Adolescent Health, 42*, 170–176.

Hensel, D. J., O'Sullivan, L. F., & Fortenberry, J. D. (2011). The developmental association of sexual self-concept with oral-genital sex and coitus among adolescent women. *Journal of Adolescence, 34*, 675–684.

Herbenick, D., Reece, M., Schick, V., Sanders, S. A., Dodge, B., & Fortenberry, J. D. (2010). Sexual behavior in the United States: Results from a national probability sample of men and women ages 14–94. *Journal of Sexual Medicine, 7*(Suppl. 5), 255–265.

Herbenick, D., Schick, V., Reece, M., Sanders, S., & Fortenberry, J. D. (2010). Pubic hair removal among women in the United States: Prevalence, methods, and characteristics. *Journal of Sexual Medicine, 7*, 3322–3330.

Herdt, G., & McClintock, M. (2000). The magical age of 10. *Archives of Sexual Behavior, 29*, 587–606.

Higgins, J. A., Hoffman, S., Graham, C. A., & Sanders, S. A. (2008). Relationships between condoms, hormonal methods, and sexual pleasure and satisfaction: An exploratory analysis from the Women's Well-Being and Sexuality Study. *Sexual Health, 5*, 321–330.

Higgins, J. A., Trussell, J., Moore, N. B., & Davidson, J. K. (2010). Virginity lost, satisfaction gained? Physiological and psychological sexual satisfaction at heterosexual debut. *Journal of Sex Research, 47*, 384–394.

Hogarth, H., & Ingham, R. (2009). Masturbation among young women and associations with sexual health: An exploratory study. *Journal of Sex Research, 46*, 558–567.

Horne, S., & Zimmer-Gembeck, M. J. (2005). Female sexual subjectivity and well-being: Comparing late adolescents with different sexual experiences. *Sexual Research and Social Policy, 2*, 25–40.

Horne, S., & Zimmer-Gembeck, M. J. (2006). The female sexual subjectivity inventory: Development and validation of a multidimensional inventory for late adolescents and emerging adults. *Psychology of Women Quarterly, 30*, 125–138.

Hughes, S. M., Harrison, M. A., & Gallup, G. G., Jr. (2007). Sex differences in romantic kissing among college students: An evolutionary perspective. *Evolutionary Psychology, 5*(3), 612–631.

Impett, E. A., & Tolman, D. L. (2006). Late adolescent girls' sexual experiences and sexual satisfaction. *Journal of Adolescent Research, 21*, 628–646.

Kirby, B. D. (2001). Understanding what works and what doesn't in reducing adolescent sexual risk-taking. *Family Planning Perspectives, 33*, 276–281.

Kontula, O., & Haavio-Mannila, E. (2002). Masturbation in a generational perspective. *Journal of Psychology & Human Sexuality, 14,* 49–83.

Kotchick, B. A., Shaffer, A., Forehand, R., & Miller, K. S. (2001). Adolescent sexual risk behavior: A multi-system perspective. *Clinical Psychology Review, 21,* 493–519.

Lagus, K. A., Bernat, D. H., Bearinger, L. H., Resnick, M. D., & Eisenberg, M. E. (2011). Parental perspectives on sources of sex information for young people. *Journal of Adolescent Health, 49,* 87–89.

Latka, M. H., Kapadia, F., & Fortin, P. (2008). The female condom: Effectiveness and convenience, not "female control," valued by U.S. urban adolescents. *AIDS Education & Prevention, 20,* 160–170.

Leitenberg, H., Detzer, M. J., & Srebnik, D. (1993). Gender differences in masturbation and the relation of masturbation experience in preadolescence and/or early adolescence to sexual behavior and sexual adjustment in young adulthood. *Archives of Sexual Behavior, 22,* 87–98.

Levin, R. J. (2002). The physiology of sexual arousal in the human female: A recreational and procreational synthesis. *Archives of Sexual Behavior, 31,* 405–411.

Lofgren-Mårtenson, L., & Månsson, S. -A. (2010). Lust, love, and life: A qualitative study of Swedish adolescents' perceptions and experiences with pornography. *Journal of Sex Research, 47,* 568–579.

Manning, W. D., Flanigan, C. M., Giordano, P. C., & Longmore, M. A. (2009). Relationship dynamics and consistency of condom use among adolescents. *Perspectives on Sexual & Reproductive Health, 41,* 181–190.

Manning, W. D., Giordano, P. C., & Longmore, M. A. (2006). Hooking up: The relationship contexts of "nonrelationship" sex. *Journal of Adolescent Research, 21,* 459–483.

Manning, W. D., Giordano, P. C., Longmore, M. A., & Hocevar, A. (2011). Romantic relationships and academic/career trajectories in emerging adulthood. In F. D. Fincham, & M. Cui (Eds.), *Romantic relationships in emerging adulthood (pp. 317–333).* New York, NY: Cambridge University Press.

Masters, N. T., Beadnell, B. A., Morrison, D. M., Hoppe, M. J., & Gillmore, M. R. (2008). The opposite of sex? Adolescents' thoughts about abstinence and sex, and their sexual behavior. *Perspectives on Sexual & Reproductive Health, 40,* 87–93.

McKay, A. (2004). Oral sex among teenagers: Research, discourse, and education. *Canadian Journal of Human Sexuality, 13,* 201–203.

Meston, C. M., & Buss, D. M. (2007). Why humans have sex. *Archives of Sexual Behavior, 36,* 477–507.

Oberfield, S. E., & White, P. C. (2009). Adrenarche. *Reviews in Endocrine & Metabolic Disorders, 10,* 1–2.

Okami, P., Olmstead, R., Abramson, P. R., & Pendleton, L. (1998). Early childhood exposure to parental nudity and scenes of parental sexuality ("primal scenes"): An 18-year longitudinal study of outcome. *Archives of Sexual Behavior, 27,* 361–384.

O'Keeffe, G. S., & Clarke-Pearson, K. (2011). The impact of social media on children, adolescents, and families. *Pediatrics, 127,* 800–804.

Ostrager, B. (2010). SMS. OMG! LOL! TTYL: Translating the law to accommodate today's teens and the evolution from texting to sexting. *Family Court Review, 48,* 712–726.

O'Sullivan, L. F., & Brooks-Gunn, J. (2005). The timing of changes in girls' sexual cognitions and behaviors in early adolescence: A prospective, cohort study. *Journal of Adolescent Health, 37,* 211–219.

O'Sullivan, L. F., Cheng, M. M., Harris, K. M., & Brooks-Gunn, J. (2007). I wanna hold your hand: The progression of social, romantic and sexual events in adolescent relationships. *Perspectives on Sexual & Reproductive Health, 39,* 100–107.

O'Sullivan, L. F., Meyer-Bahlburg, H. F. L., & McKeague, I. W. (2006). The development of the sexual self-concept inventory for early adolescent girls. *Psychology of Women Quarterly, 30,* 139–149.

Ott, M. A., & Pfeiffer, E. J. (2009). "That's nasty" to curiosity: Early adolescent cognitions about sexual abstinence. *Journal of Adolescent Health, 44*, 575–581.

Ott, M. A., & Santelli, J. S. (2007). Abstinence and abstinence-only education. *Current Opinion in Obstetrics & Gynecology, 19*, 446–452.

Ott, M. A., Pfeiffer, E. J., & Fortenberry, J. D. (2006). Perceptions of sexual abstinence among high-risk early and middle adolescents. *Journal of Adolescent Health, 39*, 192–198.

Owen, J. J., Rhoades, G. K., Stanley, S. M., & Fincham, F. D. (2010). "Hooking up" among college students: Demographic and psychosocial correlates. *Archives of Sexual Behavior, 39*, 653–663.

Pardun, C. J., L'Engle, K. L., & Brown, J. D. (2005). Linking exposure to outcomes: Early adolescents' consumption of sexual content in six media. *Mass Communication & Society, 8*, 75–91.

Pinkerton, S. D., Bogart, L. M., Cecil, H., & Abramson, P. R. (2002). Factors associated with masturbation in collegiate sample. *Journal of Psychology & Human Sexuality, 14*, 103–121.

Pontecorvo, C., Fasulo, A., & Sterponi, L. (2001). Mutual apprentices: The making of parenthood and childhood in family dinner conversations. *Human Development, 44*, 340–361.

Powell, E. (2008). Young people's use of friends and family for sex and relationships information and advice. *Sex Education, 8*, 289–302.

Raboch, J., & Bartak, V. (1983). Coitarche and orgastic capacity. *Archives of Sexual Behavior, 12*, 409–413.

Rademakers, J., Rademakers, M. J. C., & Straver, C. J. (2003). Body awareness and physical intimacy: An exploratory study. In J. Bancroft (Ed.), *Sexual development in childhood* (Vol. 1, pp. 121–126). Bloomington, IN: Indiana University Press.

Raffaelli, M., & Duckett, E. (1989). "We were just talking…": Conversations in early adolescence. *Journal of Youth and Adolescence, 18*, 567–582.

Reynolds, M. A., & Herbenick, D. L. (2003). Using computer-assisted self-interview (CASI) for recall of childhood sexual experiences. In J. Bancroft (Ed.), *Sexual development in childhood* (pp. 77–81). Bloomington IN: Indiana University Press.

Richters, J., Visser, R., Rissel, C., & Smith, A. (2006). Sexual practices at last heterosexual encounter and occurrence of orgasm in a national survey. *Journal of Sex Research, 43*, 217–226.

Robbins, C. L., Schick, V., Reece, M., Herbenick, D., Sanders, S. A., Dodge, B., et al. (2011). Prevalence, frequency, and associations of masturbation with partnered sexual behaviors among US adolescents. *Archives of Pediatrics & Adolescent Medicine, 165*, 1087–1093.

Robinson, B. B. E., Bockting, W. O., & Harrell, T. (2002). Masturbation and sexual health: An exploratory study of low income African American women. *Journal of Psychology & Human Sexuality, 14*, 85–102.

Rosenberger, J. G., Bell, D. L., McBride, K. R., Fortenberry, J. D., & Ott, M. A. (2010). Condoms and developmental contexts in younger adolescent boys. *Sexually Transmitted Infections, 86*, 400–403.

Rostosky, S. S., Dekhtyar, O., Cupp, P. K., & Anderman, E. M. (2008). Sexual self-concept and sexual self-efficacy in adolescents: A possible clue to promoting sexual health? *Journal of Sex Research, 45*(3), 277–286.

Schalet, A. T. (2011). *Not under my roof: Parents, teens, and the culture of sex*. Chicago IL: University of Chicago Press.

Schick, V. R., Calabrese, S. K., Rima, B. N., & Zucker, A. N. (2010). Genital appearance dissatisfaction: Implications for women's genital image self-consciousness, sexual esteem, sexual satisfaction, and sexual risk. *Psychology of Women Quarterly, 34*, 394–404.

Schoentjes, E., Deboutte, D., & Friedrich, W. (1999). Child sexual behavior inventory: A Dutch-speaking normative sample. *Pediatrics, 104*, 885–893.

Schuster, M. A., Bell, R. M., & Kanouse, D. E. (1996). The sexual practices of adolescent virgins: Genital sexual activities of high school students who have never had vaginal intercourse. *American Journal of Public Health, 86*, 1570–1576.

Skoog, T., Stattin, H., & Kerr, M. (2009). The role of pubertal timing in what adolescent boys do online. *Journal of Research on Adolescence, 19*, 1–7.
Smiler, A. P., Frankel, L. B. W., & Savin-Williams, R. C. (2011). From kissing to coitus? Sex-of-partner differences in the sexual milestone achievement of young men. *Journal of Adolescence, 34*, 727–735.
Smith, E. A., & Udry, J. R. (1985). Coital and non-coital sexual behaviors of white and black adolescents. *American Journal of Public Health, 75*, 1200–1203.
Steinberg, L., Albert, D., Cauffman, E., Banich, M., Graham, S., & Woolard, J. (2008). Age differences in sensation seeking and impulsivity as indexed by behavior and self-report: Evidence for a dual systems model. *Developmental Psychology, 44*, 1764–1778.
Štulhofer, A., Buško, V., & Landripet, I. (2010). Pornography, sexual socialization, and satisfaction among young men. *Archives of Sexual Behavior, 39*, 168–178.
Suvivuo, P., Tossavainen, K., & Kontula, O. (2010). "Can there be such a delightful feeling as this?" Variations of sexual scripts in Finnish girls' narratives. *Journal of Adolescent Research, 25*, 669–689.
Tanner, A. E., Hensel, D. J., & Fortenberry, J. D. (2010). A prospective study of the sexual, emotional, and behavioral correlates associated with young women's first and usual coital events. *Journal of Adolescent Health, 47*, 20–25.
Tanner, A. E., Zimet, G., Fortenberry, J. D., Reece, M., Graham, C., & Murray, M. (2009). Young women's use of a vaginal microbicide surrogate: The role of individual and contextual factors in acceptability and sexual pleasure. *Journal of Sex Research, 46*, 15–23.
Thigpen, J. W. (2009). Early sexual behavior in a sample of low-income, African American children. *Journal of Sex Research, 46*, 67–79.
Thigpen, J. W., & Fortenberry, J. D. (2009). Understanding variation in normative childhood sexual behavior: The significance of family context. *Social Service Review, 83*, 611–631.
Tolman, D. L., & McClelland, S. I. (2011). Normative sexuality development in adolescence: A decade in review, 2000–2009. *Journal of Research on Adolescence, 21*, 242–255.
Uecker, J. E., Angotti, N., & Regnerus, M. D. (2008). Going most of the way: "Technical virginity" among American adolescents. *Social Science Research, 37*, 1200–1215.
Weiss, R., & Samenow, C. P. (2010). Smart phones, social networking, sexting and problematic sexual behaviors—A call for research. *Sexual Addiction & Compulsivity, 17*, 241–246.
Welsh, D. P., & Kawaguchi, M. C. (2000). A normative perspective of adolescent girls' developing sexuality. In C. B. Travis, & J. W. White (Eds.), *Sexuality, society, and feminism (pp. 111–140)*. Washington, DC: American Psychological Association.
Welsh, D. P., Haugen, P. T., Widman, L., Darling, N., & Grello, C. M. (2005). Kissing is good: A developmental investigation of sexuality in adolescent romantic couples. *Sexuality Research & Social Policy: A Journal of the NSR, 2*, 32–41.
Wetherill, R. R., Neal, D. J., & Fromme, K. (2010). Parents, peers, and sexual values influence sexual behavior during the transition to college. *Archives of Sexual Behavior, 39*, 682–694.
Williams, T., Connolly, J., & Cribbie, R. (2008). Light and heavy heterosexual activities of young Canadian adolescents: Normative patterns and differential predictors. *Journal of Research on Adolescence, 18*, 145–172.
Woo, J. S. T., Brotto, L. A., & Gorzalka, B. B. (2011). The role of sex guilt in the relationship between culture and women's sexual desire. *Archives of Sexual Behavior, 40*, 385–394.
Wood, K., Maforah, F., & Jewkes, R. (1998). "He forced me to love him": Putting violence on adolescent sexual health agendas. *Social Science & Medicine, 47*, 233–242.
Ybarra, M. L., & Mitchell, K. J. (2005). Exposure to Internet pornography among children and adolescents: A national survey. *CyberPsychology & Behavior, 8*, 473–486.

CHAPTER 8

# Sexual Development in Girls

## "Normative" Development and Development of Paraphilias and Sexual Offending Behaviors

**Lucia F. O'Sullivan and Scott T. Ronis**
University of New Brunswick, Fredericton, New Brunswick, Canada[1]

## INTRODUCTION

In a culture that has actively denied childhood sexuality in the past, then discouraged or hampered research on this topic, it should come as no surprise that there is relatively little sound information available to us regarding what constitutes normative sexuality among youth—especially compared with the wealth of work generated in other areas of child development. A result of this near-blackout of inquiry and discovery is that sexual thoughts, interests, behaviors, and responses in childhood have been viewed as largely pathological (Ryan, 2000). Our lack of familiarity with patterns of normative sexual development heightens the chances of over-reacting to a child's expression of typical behaviors or overlooking possibly problematic sexual behaviors, such as paraphilias and sexual offenses against others (Sandnabba, Santtila, Wannäs, & Krook, 2003). Thus, it behooves us to approach this topic objectively and rationally, as much as we are able, to identify significant gaps in our working body of knowledge, and formulate a way forward.

## UNDERSTANDING "NORMATIVE" SEXUAL DEVELOPMENT

The wealth of research dedicated to addressing problematic sexual outcomes among youth, particularly girls, dramatically outweighs the literature devoted to the study of positive forms of "normative" sexual development.

---

[1] Correspondence to: Lucia F. O'Sullivan, PhD, Department of Psychology, University of New Brunswick, P.O. Box 4400, Fredericton, New Brunswick, Canada, E3B 5A3; Phone 1-506-458-7698; fax 1-506-447-3063; email osulliv@unb.ca

These problem areas include predictors of early first intercourse (Boislard & Poulin, 2011; Cubbin, Brindis, Jain, Santelli, & Braveman, 2010; Lammers, Ireland, Resnick, & Blum, 2000; Longmore, Manning, & Giordano, 2001; Miller et al., 1997), adolescent pregnancy (Casares, Lahiff, Eskenazi, & Halpern-Felsher, 2010; Upadhya & Ellen, 2011), and sexual risk behaviors (Walton et al., 2011). From the literature, one would easily conclude that "normative" is synonymous with "problematic." Granted, it is difficult to define non-problematic, developmentally appropriate events. We use the term "normative" sexual development to include the range of sexual experiences from birth through adolescence. Of course, sexual development extends through old age, but our focus here is on childhood sexual development. Moreover, we use the term "normative" to refer to typical, common, age-appropriate, or developmentally expected, not pathological, trajectories alone in the progression toward sexual maturation.

It is important to note that atypical behaviors are not necessarily problematic, so indices of prevalence alone do not suffice (De Graaf & Rademakers, 2011). For example, Friedrich and colleagues (Friedrich, Grambsch, Broughton, Kuiper, & Beilke, 1991) screened 880 children (2–12 years) for absence of abuse and found that, among these children, each of 36 sexual behaviors that are common among adults were reported at some level of frequency, even those behaviors that the researchers expected to be unlikely (e.g., mouth on sex parts). The occurrence of specific behaviors does, however, tend to vary fairly predictably with age (Sandfort & Cohen-Kettenis, 2000). Where possible, we have taken this into account in summarizing normative development.

The dearth of sound research on normative sexual development can be attributed to a number of factors. First, and most notably, are sociocultural factors associated with great discomfort surrounding the issue of childhood sexuality, and a "deep suspicion" of research that addresses sexuality from a positive, or non-pathological, perspective. Many have speculated on our need to preserve a view of children as "innocent," "pure," and untainted by sexual thoughts, feelings, or experiences (Jackson, 1990). Second, given the range of experiences characterizing childhood sexual development, it is extremely difficult to define which behaviors constitute "normative" experiences, even using a statistical definition of what is common or typical. Unwanted sexual contact, for instance, consistently appears to be a common occurrence in childhood (Moore et al., 2010), yet most would exclude it from definitions of sexual development that capture growth and maturation. Indeed, there is considerable disagreement across disciplines regarding how best to define healthy sexual development (Haugaard, 1996). Third, studies of sexual development depend primarily on retrospective reports (Larsson & Svedin, 2002; Ryan, 2000), which are subject to a range of recall and reporting biases (O'Sullivan, 2008). Other common sources of data are secondary sources, such as parents or teachers, who may not be reliable in their interpretations or reporting of children's sexual events, or else have selective opportunities to witness sexual behaviors (Friedrich & Trane, 2002). Children learn very early that sexual behaviors should be hidden, that their bodies are shameful or dirty, and that showing or touching their genitals is forbidden (Kaestle & Allen, 2011). Relatively rare in the literature are studies capturing children's self-reports, in large part because children lack the insight or skills required to verbalize their experiences in ways that are meaningful to adults or are reluctant to describe their sexual lives to adults, as in the cases of adolescents. They have learned to keep such matters private, especially from strangers, and access to children is controlled by caregivers, who often believe that such inquires are ultimately harmful or exploitive (Ryan, 2000; Thigpen & Fortenberry, 2009) (see De Graaf & Rademakers, 2011 for a review of methods in this field). Finally, research on childhood experiences has been hindered or prevented altogether at the institutional level, including ethical review boards, courts, and even political bodies, who cite their commitment to protecting public interests (Okami, Olmstead, & Abramson, 1997; Rind, 2008).

Fortunately, there are some invaluable studies that overcame these obstacles, to which we can turn to summarize what is known about childhood sexual development. Using a biopsychosocial perspective, we review here research on physiological changes from prenatal life to adolescence, development of sexual attitudes and cognitions, sexual milestones, and sociocultural factors that influence sexual trajectories. We also describe gender differences in sexual development for each of these areas, controversial and unexplained findings, and notable gaps in the literature.

## Physiological Responses and Sexual Maturation

Much of the research on childhood sexuality prior to the 1990s documented the capacity for sexual response before birth and in infants (Calderone, 1983; Ford & Beach, 1963; Galenson & Riophe, 1974). Ultrasound studies revealed that male fetuses experience erections and female fetuses are able to experience orgasm (Siccardi, 1996). Young infants often touch or fondle their genitals, but it is unclear to what extent it is purposeful. Even though these behaviors may appear to be used for sexual self-stimulation, there has been debate as to whether infants in the first year of life are capable of volitional behavior required for masturbation (Martinson, 1973). The rhythmic manipulation that we associate with masturbation is noted around 2.5 years of age (Martinson, 1994), and orgasms are possible from such stimulation at these early ages (Conn & Kanner, 1940; Ford & Beach, 1951; Kinsey, Pomeroy, Martin, & Gebhard, 1953; Levine, 1957). From adult reports, 40% of women and 38% of men reported masturbating prepubertally, the remainder began to masturbate postpubertally (43% and 61% of women and men, respectively) or not at all (Bancroft, Herbenick, & Reynolds, 2003). Genital manipulation and masturbatory behavior in general are more common among boys than girls (Thigpen & Fortenberry, 2009).

Touching or fondling the genitals of others is occasionally a component of sex play (e.g., playing doctor) with same-aged peers, which is frequently noted among children around the ages of 4 or 5. Friedrich and colleagues found rates of the following behaviors in their sample of 880 normal children (2–12 years old): touches others sex parts (6.0%); touches breasts (30.7%); kisses nonfamily children (33.9%); and rubs body against people (6.7%) (Friedrich et al., 1992). Related behaviors and those indicating possible sexual interest include: shows sex parts to children (8.1%); touches sex parts in public (19.7%); tries to look at people undressing (28.5%); and talks about sexual acts (5.7%). It is unclear why, but sex play may be more common among girls than among boys (Sandnabba et al., 2003). More often, children simply look at the genitals of their peers rather than touch or stimulate them in some way, although touching and stimulating is certainly not uncommon (Sandnabba et al., 2003). Haugaard (1996) found that 59% of American college students recalled one or more childhood sexual experiences with another child, whereas 88% responded affirmatively in a Swedish sample of college students (Larsson & Svedin, 2002). Relatively few adults indicate that an adult knew of their childhood sexual games (Larsson & Svedin, 2002; Ryan, 2000). Despite concerns about the corruptive influence of early sexual experiences, there appears to be no impact of childhood sexual play on long-term sexual behaviors or development in general (Leitenberg, Greenwald, & Tarran, 1989; Okami et al., 1997).

Although orgasms are possible at young ages, generally only girls can experience a sexual response cycle that resembles that of their adult counterparts. Boys are not capable of ejaculation until they reach puberty, as it is dependent on hormone production and maturation of internal structures. Research on masturbation is scant, despite the ubiquity of the behavior, but retrospective reports and reports from secondary sources indicate that rates of masturbation increase steadily over the childhood years (Nechay, 2010).

Puberty heralds a range of rapid and conspicuous changes in physical appearance, most notably in height and the development of secondary sex characteristics, and the maturation of internal reproductive structures. Although defined in biological terms, puberty has been of interest to many social scientists because of the associations between pubertal development and behavior changes, particularly with regard to sexual behaviors. Among girls, the majority of studies of pubertal development have focused on changes associated with menarche, a late-occurring stage in the pubertal process. There has been considerable concern in recent years about the possibility of accelerated sexual development resulting from the decreasing age of menarche, although there is little indication that menarche promotes the onset of partnered sexual activities (James, Ellis, Schlomer, & Garber, 2012). Even so, menarche represents for many an indisputable sign of a girl's altered sexual capacity, one that signals reproductive maturity and adult female status (O'Sullivan, Meyer-Bahlburg, & Watkins, 2000). The male equivalent, spermarche (i.e., first ejaculation), is also associated with sociocultural referents of desire, but seems to have far less emotional connotations for adults. For example, more than half (54%) of parents of sons aged 10–13 years indicated that they had "never thought about it" in reference to their sons' first ejaculation (Frankel, 2002), whereas the majority of parents of daughters aged 10–13 years reported that they had initiated discussions about sexual propriety when they learned that their daughters had reached menarche (O'Sullivan, Meyer-Bahlburg, & Watkins, 2000).

## Sexual Cognitions in the Developing Child

Curiosity about sexuality, particularly the activities comprising partnered sexual interactions, typically increases steadily throughout childhood despite a growing awareness of sociocultural taboos regarding sexuality and sexual behaviors, and of adult restrictions on talking about sex and exploring one's body (Ryan, 2000). Children begin to show greater inhibitions, shyness, and physical modesty around 5 years of age (Sandnabba et al., 2003). Their physical explorations with peers are replaced by or augmented with stories or jokes about sexual matters or bodily functions. Children's peers become an audience for such humor and a significant source of information about sex (Larsson & Svedin, 2002). Sexuality is a common theme in their conversations (Kuik, 2003), a preoccupation in their thinking (Miller & Benson, 1999), and the basis of many "chase and kiss" games (Paikoff, 1995).

Young children develop sexual cognitions that guide their understanding of sexuality. This family of cognitions includes attitudes, sexual norms, stereotypes, and scripts—all of which represent meaningful representations in thought of sexuality and one's sexual self in relation to others. Research on girls 12–15-years-old showed that changes in sexual cognitions, such as sexual self-esteem, sexual agency, and sexual arousability, actually preceded corresponding changes in sexual experiences (O'Sullivan & Brooks-Gunn, 2005). These findings suggest that girls adapt their sexual self-concepts, that is, their views of themselves as sexual people, before they gain new sexual experiences rather than (solely) in response to these experiences. More longitudinal research is needed, however, to clarify the trajectories further.

Children develop complex meanings about sexual experiences, including gendered interactions, often long before their own partnered sexual experiences begin. They are exposed to an extraordinary amount of sexual information, often inadvertently, through sexualized media (Orenstein, 2011) and interactions with older peers. Common experiences among children 6–12 years of age include sexualized interactions with peers (e.g., spying in bathrooms, lifting skirts, sexual teasing), and looking at sexually explicit media and images, such as pornography (Larsson & Svedin, 2002).

Many young people learn about sex from watching others engage in sex—either their peers or via media. Although these activities may appear voyeuristic or exhibitionistic, they likely reflect the lack of private spaces available to young people for sex, given that private spaces for such activities tend to be controlled by adults. Thus, adolescents' sexual lives frequently take place in semi-private or public spaces. Inner-city youth, for instance, have such limited opportunities for privacy that they report that sexual activities often take place in fairly public spaces, including designated areas in parks, rooftops, stairwells, and at "hooky parties," which are impromptu parties held during school hours while parents are absent (O'Sullivan & Meyer-Bahlburg, 2003). Because adolescent dating norms have shifted so that dating generally occurs in mixed-peer groups rather than in solitary pairings (at first) (Connolly, Craig, Goldberg, & Pepler, 2004), sexual norms have evolved whereby young people split off from the group to engage in sexual activity nearby (Paikoff, 1995). As such, young people often purposely or inadvertently witness the sexual experiences of others, and appear to develop and elaborate sexual norms from what they learn.

Indeed, peer involvement in the sexual socialization process of children and adolescents should not be minimized. Not only are peers a significant source of sex information, they partly regulate the sexual behavior and experiences of others. Researchers have found that young girls in particular are castigated or bullied by other girls, or sexually harassed by male peers for (presumed) sexual permissiveness (Shute, Owens, & Slee, 2008). Those who have little or no sexual experience risk being viewed as immature, prudish, or withholding, and are mocked or pressured by peers to catch up. Even so, there continues to be strong social castigation of girls who engage in sexual experience for pleasure or recreational interests rather than for love or affection reasons alone (O'Sullivan & Meyer-Bahlburg, 2003). Girls learn the importance of sexual attractiveness to boys and men (Tolman, 2002; Welles, 2005), whereas boys learn the value of pursuing sexual opportunities with girls, while eschewing romantic attachments. These beliefs comprise what researchers term the "traditional sexual script" (Byers, 1995), and they continue to be endorsed consistently by adolescents today (Joshi, Peter, & Valkenburg, 2011; Krahé, Bieneck, & Scheinberger-Olwig, 2007; Stephens & Phillips, 2003).

## Sexual Milestones in Behaviors and Partnerships

The onset of puberty frequently corresponds with an increase in sexual exploration and, for some youth, the initiation of a range of partnered sexual activities. Long before first intercourse occurs, however, a range of "pre-coital" sexual experiences take place in a fairly predictable manner. In studies analyzing the progression of social, romantic, and sexual events among adolescents, kissing and holding hands typically precedes breast fondling, then manual genital contact, touching partner under/without clothes, then touching partner's genitals, oral sex, and sexual intercourse (O'Sullivan & Brooks-Gunn, 2005; O'Sullivan, Mantsun, Harris, & Brooks-Gunn, 2007). First oral sex tends to occur within six months of vaginal intercourse (Lindberg, Jones, & Santelli, 2008; Ronis & O'Sullivan, 2011). Generally, low intimacy sexual activities precede highly intimate, genitally focused activities, likely in part reflecting increased confidence and comfort over time. For sexual minority youth, gender tends to trump orientation in terms of predicting sexual behavior (Savin-Williams & Diamond, 2000). Attractions precede contact, which precedes labeling and disclosure.

Far less is known about children's experiences of sexual desire and arousal. Most research in this area addresses adults' desire for or arousal to girls and boys (Lykins et al., 2010) rather than the experience of sexual desire, arousal, or interest among children themselves. The majority of adults recall experiencing sexual arousal prior to puberty (Ryan, 2000). Researchers report considerable difficulty eliciting discussions of these feelings among girls (Knoth, Boyd, & Singer, 1988). They appear reluctant or unable to identify feelings of arousal, corresponding to what Fine (1988) has referred to as the "missing discourse of desire." Girls appear far more willing to acknowledge interest in boys or curiosity about sex than to admit feeling strong emotional or physiological needs or drives. Compared with boys, girls tend to report a later age of first sexual fantasies, greater attention to relationship cues, and less emphasis on visual sexual cues (Gold & Gold, 1991). They also report more sexual guilt and shame than do boys, corresponding to a socialization that reinforces sexual reserve to a large extent (Larsson & Svedin, 2002).

But do these expectations and emotions reflect girls' actual experiences? One study found that girls (12–14 years) expected to experience primarily strong negative emotions with their first sexual encounters, but later recalled primarily strong positive emotions for both first intercourse and most recent occasions of sex (O'Sullivan & Hearn, 2008). In another study using interviews with children aged 8 and 9 years, the majority of children reported strong positive attitudes toward physical intimacy, and one-third were actively interested in being in love and experiencing physical intimacy with peers, especially cuddling (Rademakers, Laan, & Straver, 2000). Thus, positive experiences appear to override some of the negative socialization that children encounter. Certainly, the mass media (television, Internet, movies, music, and magazines) play a large role in enhancing the appeal of sexual interactions for youth (L'Engle, Brown, & Kenneavy, 2006).

Research on children's sexual interest, desire, fantasy, and arousal is so sparse that it is necessary to draw upon the adult literature to generate insights into potential dynamics among children. For example, Chivers' (2010) review of research on gender differences in specificity of arousal makes clear that women's sexual response is largely non-specific, whereas men's sexual response is quite specific. That is, women tend to be aroused to a wide range of stimuli, not just stimuli that they report preferring. Men's sexual arousal is far more discriminatory—restricted, for the most part, to the stimuli that they report preferring. Although comparable research with adolescents or children has yet to be conducted, it is possible that girls, too, experience arousal to a far wider range of sexual stimuli than do boys and men. Another parallel to adult sexuality research that may also apply to youth is that there is generally low agreement between genital measures of sexual arousal in women (e.g., vasocongestion) and subjective reports of sexual arousal (Chivers, Seto, Lalumière, Laan, & Grimbos, 2010). Women's bodies reveal rapid sexuality-related physiological changes in response to sexual stimuli, but these physiological changes do not correspond to women's psychological experiences of sexual interest, desire, or arousal. Men, and possibly boys, typically show high concordance in these indices. When their bodies respond sexually, they tend also to experience the corresponding psychological dimensions of arousal. Another parallel in this realm relates to the notable fluidity found in adolescent women's sexual identities and behaviors over time (Diamond, 2000). Longitudinal research with girls has yet to be conducted, but research with women reveals that female sexual desire and response is exceptionally flexible, especially relative to male sexual desire and response.

Yet another area of adult sexuality research that may be relevant to youth is research on sexual dysfunctions. Women, in particular, experience high rates of sexual dysfunction. For example, a national probability survey of adults (18–59 years) in the United States found that 32% of women reported low sexual interest, 26% reported anorgasmia, and 27% reported experiencing no sexual pleasure at all (Laumann, Paik, & Rosen, 1999). One of the first studies of sexual dysfunction among adolescents found high levels of desire, pleasure, and satisfaction from their sexual lives and few gender differences in this regard (O'Sullivan & Majerovich, 2008). Yet reports of lifetime problems among adolescents revealed high percentages of female participants having trouble reaching orgasm (86.7%) and feeling little or no sexual interest or desire in their sexual interactions (81.2%). Research with even younger teens is underway. This line of research could generate useful insights into normative trajectories in sexual development.

In short, this review makes clear that children display a range of sexual behaviors, including self-stimulation, sexual touching, curiosity about sexuality, and even forms of exhibitionism and voyeurism. There is a growing body of literature that indicates that it is normal for children and adolescents to engage in a variety of sexual behaviors as they mature, and experience sexual problems or difficulties in sexual expression along the way.

## PARAPHILIAS AND SEXUAL OFFENDING IN GIRLS

Given the variability in defining girls' normative sexual development, it is not surprising that we also know little about girls' atypical sexual interests and behaviors. Furthermore, the literature on paraphilias and sexual offending is almost nonexistent for girls and very limited for women (Fedoroff, Fishell, & Fedoroff, 1999; Moser, Kleinplatz, Zuccarini, & Reiner, 2004), with the exception of some descriptive, single-case studies (e.g., Messerschmidt, 2011; Richards, 1990; Sass, 1975; Zaviačič, 1994). There are likely several reasons for this paucity of research. First, society tends to view women as maternal and caring (Hetherton, 1999) or sexually passive and innocent (Denov, 2003; Oliver, 2007). Consistent with this pattern, there seems to be a taboo in studying girls' paraphilias and sexually abusive behavior (Christiansen & Thyer, 2002). Second, the prevalence of paraphilias and sexually abusive behavior among girls appears to be very low relative to the rate for boys (Roe-Sepowitz & Krysik, 2008), and, as such, studying this population is very difficult. Third, atypical sexual behavior by girls is often considered relatively harmless compared with sexual abuse by males (Oliver, 2007), which contributes to limited access and interest in studying this population. Finally, the definitions of paraphilias and sexually abusive behavior, especially among girls, are imprecise. In particular, sexual offenses are defined by legal statutes, which vary by jurisdiction (Moser et al., 2004). Moreover, as we will soon discuss, definitions of abnormal sexual interests and behaviors are based on evolving societal values (Bhugra, Popelyuk, & McMullen, 2010). As a result, it is difficult to include and examine standard samples of girls with histories of paraphilias and sexually abusive behavior. Clearly, we are at the beginning stages of trying to understand paraphilic disorders and sexual offending among girls.

### Defining Abnormal Sexuality

Normal and "abnormal" sexual interests and behaviors are defined and differentiated by the broader society and individual cultures in which individuals are embedded (Bhugra et al., 2010; Moser & Kleinplatz, 2005; Thornton, 2010). Although paraphilias have been generally defined as "any powerful and persistent sexual interest other than sexual interest in copulatory or precopulatory behavior with phenotypically normal, consenting adult human partners" (Blanchard, 2010, p. 367), distinctions between normative and abnormal interests are not always clear. What may be unusual in one circumstance may be considered typical in others

(Moser et al., 2004). Furthermore, as noted earlier, there are often different societal standards for boys and girls. Although the scientific literature covers sexual development and developmental milestones, very little focus is given to abnormal, or atypical sexual cognitions, urges, fantasies, or behaviors among girls.

In an attempt to provide some objectivity to normal and abnormal sexual development, the Diagnostic and Statistical Manual of Mental Disorders describes a number of paraphilias. The paraphilic disorders have been listed under the *Sexual and Gender Identity Disorders* section in DSM-IV, and will likely be presented in a separate section in DSM-V. There are a few key points worth mentioning in general about previous and proposed descriptions of paraphilic disorders in regard to girls. First, although there is no explicit age criterion for any of the disorders, it is presumed that individuals should be old enough to be aware of their manifest fantasies, urges, or behaviors. Second, there are no symptomatic differences described between girls and boys for any of the paraphilic disorders. However, it seems likely, even in the absence of epidemiological data, that some disorders (e.g., frotteuristic disorder) are predominately unique to boys. Moreover, masculine pronouns have been used to describe two diagnostic categories (i.e., frotteurism, exhibitionism), which reinforces the notion that girls do not exhibit these disorders (Fedoroff et al., 1999). Finally, although there is some movement toward classifying people on continua of severity or functional impairment rather than in diagnostic categories, it is unlikely that the resulting profiles will be compared against normed age or sex criteria. Overall, some have suggested that the proposed diagnoses for paraphilias in DSM-V will actually reverse some of the improvements since the publication of the first and second editions of the DSM (Singy, 2010).

One interesting development of late has been the sensationalized stories of youth employing technologies for sexual expression. For example, there is widespread concern that both boys and girls are sending and receiving nude pictures of themselves or others whom they know (known commonly as "sexting") (Lenhart, 2009; Mitchell, Finkelhor, Jones, & Wolak, 2012)—which by some accounts may appear to involve exhibitionistic behaviors. Unfortunately, there is conflicting research on the prevalence of such behavior. Although a few studies with adolescent samples have found between 15% to 66% of youth report sending a nude or semi-nude photo of themselves to others (Ferguson, 2011; Henderson, 2011), a large, cross-sectional national study using individual interviews (Mitchell et al., 2012) found that only 2.5% of youth report appearing in nude or semi-nude pictures or videos (61% were girls). It is likely that such disparate results reflect the assessments used (e.g., anonymous self-report measures, interviews) included in these studies. Other examples of the interaction of technology and sexuality, such as the impact of viewing pornography or sex-based multiplayer video games (Sabina, Wolak, & Finkelhor, 2008), have been sensationalized in the media. Perhaps these behaviors are deviant and sexually motivated, but it seems more likely that they reflect a normal developmental process of engaging in exploratory or attention-seeking behavior, albeit with occasional unintended consequences. However, it seems important for researchers to examine the interactions of ever-evolving technology and sexual attitudes and behaviors.

## Prevalence of Paraphilias and Sexual Offending

Given the limited focus on atypical sexual interests and behavior among girls (Moser et al., 2004), it is difficult to identify the prevalence of various paraphilic disorders. However, studies with adult samples have demonstrated that men significantly outnumber women. Langström and colleagues (Langström & Hanson, 2006; Langström & Zucker, 2005) found that 4.1% of men and 2.1% of women reported at least one exhibitionistic behavior, 11.5% of men and 3.9% of women reported at least one voyeuristic episode, and 2.8% of men and 0.4% of women reported at least one episode of transvestic fetishism. Thus, although similar research has not been conducted on child or adolescent samples, it is possible that the ratios of boys to girls for these behaviors are consistent with those of adults.

It is also possible to speculate about the prevalence of paraphilias in girls based on research on female juvenile sexual offending, which includes some paraphilic disorders (e.g., sadism, exhibitionism, frotteurism, voyeurism), as well as other sexual behaviors for which individuals have been caught. Based on research on clinical or juvenile justice samples, girls constitute 5–10% of the juvenile sexual offender population (Roe-Sepowitz & Krysik, 2008; Vick, McRoy, & Matthews, 2002). However, this may represent an underestimate that is unique to girls, because of the notion that girls cannot perpetrate sexual abuses (Oliver, 2007) and because offenses are often hidden behind caretaking behavior (e.g., hugging or fondling a child while in the role as caretaker) (Tsopelas, Spyridoula, & Athanasios, 2011), or else are especially stigmatized among girls (Deering & Mellor, 2010). In some community-based samples of high school students (Borowsky, Hogan, Ireland, 1997; Kjellgren, Priebe,

Svedin, Mossige, & Langström, 2009; Lodico, Gruber, & DiClemente, 1996), the reported prevalence of sexually abusive behavior perpetrated by girls is even lower, with approximately 1% of girls reporting sexually coercive behaviors (i.e., talking someone into sex, using pressure, or forcing someone to have sex).

## Characteristics of Paraphilias and Sexually Abusive Behavior

If one assumes that specific sexual interests and behaviors are abnormal, and that they are consistently abnormal for both males and females, then it is worth examining the etiology of atypical sexual development. However, given that research on girls' paraphilias is generally nonexistent, there is no consensus on biological or genetic markers, psychosocial factors, or means by which sexual interests and behaviors evolve or wane over the life course (Moser et al., 2004). As such, we are limited to research on the correlates of female juvenile sexual offending, and on retrospective data from women who report paraphilias.

Some unique demographic and situational characteristics have been noted as distinguishing girls who sexually offend from boys who sexually offend. Female juvenile sexual offenders are more likely to be white, commit their offenses with an accomplice, be significantly younger in age at their first arrest, have younger victims, victimize both boys and girls, and are less likely to commit rape than are male juvenile sexual offenders (Araji, 1997; Vandiver, 2010; Vandiver & Teske, 2006). Overall, girls are more likely to have known the victim as an acquaintance, possibly in a caretaking situation (Vandiver & Walker, 2002). There may be critical periods or situations in which sexually abusive behavior is more likely for girls, such as after the arrival of a new spouse or new children in a family, upon the approach of puberty, and when given the responsibility of babysitting for another child (Tardiff, Auclair, Jacob, & Carpentier, 2005).

Technological advances, such as the development of brain scanning, neuroimaging techniques, and gene sequencing, have led the way for researchers to study biological explanations for atypical sexual behavior (Stinson, Sales, & Becker, 2008). However, nearly all of the research has focused on adult males' sexually deviant behavior, or on the biological differences between men and women as potential characteristics that are linked to atypical sexual expressions. Nevertheless, it seems important to consider this research to suggest possible links in atypical sexual interests and behaviors in girls. For example, there is some evidence indicating that individuals who are sexually attracted to young children often have left temporal lobe abnormalities, which are also associated with difficulties in speech and verbal understanding (Lang, 1993; Langevin, Wortzman, Wright, & Handy, 1989). On the other hand, right temporal lobe abnormalities are most often found in individuals who have committed violent sexual offenses (Lang, 1993). Other research suggests that abnormalities in the frontal lobe, which is responsible for reasoning, impulse control, and problem solving, are linked to atypical sexual interests and behavior (Cummings, 1999). Elevated levels of several hormones (e.g., testosterone, cortisol) and abnormalities in neurotransmitter activity (e.g., lower levels of serotonin, increased levels of dopamine and norepinephrine) also may play a facilitative role in sexual aggression and atypical sexual arousal (Bain et al., 1988; Coccaro & Kavoussi, 1996). Despite focusing on biological explanations, researchers have not studied girls, and theories that link atypical sexual interests or behaviors to biological processes are still in their infancy.

Girls who are involved in sexually abusive behavior typically have a range of difficulties in their individual adjustment, family and peer relations, and academic performance. They often have high rates of depression, anxiety, and post-traumatic stress disorder (Vick et al., 2002), and score low on measures of self-esteem and high on neuroticism (Hendriks & Bijleveld, 2006). Other common comorbid diagnoses include conduct disorder, attention deficit hyperactivity disorder, and oppositional defiant disorder. In one of the few studies to compare sexually offending girls to an age-matched group of nonsexual offending girls, Kubik, Hecker, & Righthand (2002) found that sexual offenders actually had significantly fewer antisocial behavior problems, including violence and substance misuse. Female juvenile sexual offenders generally come from chaotic and disorganized families, with poor parental supervision and higher prevalence of parental alcohol and drug use (Bumby & Bumby, 1997; Righthand & Welch, 2005; Roe-Sepowitz & Krysik, 2008; Vick et al., 2002). Moreover, these girls often exhibit difficulty in same-age peer relations (Righthand & Welch, 2005). Some researchers have found that female juvenile sexual offenders generally have average IQs, but are more likely to have academic difficulties and school behavior problems, such as truancy, than do nondelinquent samples (Bumby & Bumby, 1997; Roe-Sepowitz & Krysik, 2008). Other researchers note an increased prevalence of learning disabilities and difficulties relative to nonsexual offenders (McCartan, Law, Murphy, & Bailey, 2011).

A number of studies have examined the victimization histories and exposure to sexual material during childhood of female juvenile sexual offenders. Overall, female juvenile sexual offenders are often victims of some combination of physical, sexual, and emotional abuse and neglect during childhood (Hendriks & Bijleveld, 2006; Righthand & Welch, 2005; Vick et al., 2002). In addition, female juvenile sexual offenders are significantly more likely to have been victims themselves relative to nonsexual offenders (McCartan et al., 2011). The prevalence of sexual victimization ranges from 50% to 100%, and the rate of physical abuse, which is found less consistently in studies, ranges from 21% to 80% (Bumby & Bumby, 1997; Fehrenbach & Monastersky, 1988; Hunter, Lexier, Goodwin, Browne, & Dennis, 1993; Mathews, Hunter, & Vuz, 1997). Female juvenile sexual offenders are more likely than boys with similar offense histories to have been sexually abused, and to have witnessed domestic violence and sexual abuse at home (Kubik, Hecker, & Righthand, 2002; Schwartz, Cavanaugh, Pimental, & Prentky, 2006). Furthermore, frequent and early exposure to pornography may increase the likelihood of deviant sexual urges, fantasies, or behaviors by creating and maintaining unhealthy notions of sex and intimate relationships (Flood, 2009). Because pornography exposure, at least after the age of 13, is highly typical for girls as well as boys (Sabina et al., 2008), it is unlikely that exposure itself directly influences unhealthy sexual expression unless exposure is extreme in form (Johansson & Hammarén, 2007).

We should make clear that female juvenile sexual offenders are unlikely to represent a homogeneous group (Mathews et al., 1997; McCartan et al., 2011). Mathews and colleagues (1997) have suggested that there may be three subgroups of female sexual offenders, each with distinct characteristics. The first may be a small, yet distinct, subgroup of girls who engage in a single or a few incidents of offending of a non-related child, usually within the context of babysitting. Offenders in this group are thought to have little evidence of individual psychopathology, previous maltreatment, or significant family difficulties, and their behavior may be motivated by sexual experimentation. Youth in the second subgroup, representing approximately half of female juvenile sexual offenders, engage in their sexual offending as part of a broader pattern of antisocial and delinquent behavior, and they are likely to have individual and interpersonal difficulties similar to those of nonsexual offenders. Finally, a smaller but significant subgroup of female juvenile sexual offenders report moderate levels of psychopathology, family maladaptive functioning, and previous maltreatment, and their sexual offending may be triggered and modeled after their own victimization experiences. Thus, these youth may not be looking for sexual satisfaction per se, but instead may be trying to decrease feelings of anger, confusion, anxiety, shame, and loneliness resulting from their own victimization (Higgs, Canavan, & Meyer, 1992; Vick et al., 2002). Overall, it is likely that girls' sexually abusive behavior is multidetermined by difficulties in their individual and interpersonal adjustment.

## Theoretical Perspectives

Given the limited empirical research on paraphilias and atypical sexual behavior among girls, there are no theories explaining its etiology and maintenance. However, some theories that have been posited for boys and men may be pertinent. For example, from a developmental perspective, boys develop differently than do girls, as they typically learn genital pleasure more readily and perhaps earlier (Galenson & Riophe, 1974). In addition, parents typically socialize their sons and daughters differently, applying double standards to encourage boys to express their sexuality while discouraging similar expressions by girls (Bhugra et al., 2010). Although this perspective only explains why there are differences found between boys and girls, it is reasonable to assume that many girls who express atypical sexual behavior may share developmental characteristics in common with boys in general.

A number of theories have suggested that individual and interpersonal factors uniquely contribute to atypical sexual expressions. For example, attachment theory (Marshall, 2010) has been used to suggest that poor parental attachment can lead to a child not learning appropriate role expectations and ways to behave. In turn, the individual may be more likely to sexually offend as a way to derive satisfaction and intimate closeness, albeit in socially inappropriate ways. Behavioral (classical and operant conditioning) and social learning theories have been used to suggest that atypical sexual expressions are learned through reinforcement or modeling. It is possible, for example, that a girl who begins to engage in sexual experimentation with atypical sexual objects may learn that she could use these stimuli to gain sexual satisfaction (Abel, Osborn, Anthony, & Gardos, 1992). Moreover, a girl who is exposed to pornography or to being sexually victimized may view her experience as normative and not harmful, and may be more likely to initiate similar behavior patterns (Burton, Miller, & Shill, 2002; Ryan, 2002). This abused–abuser hypothesis is consistent with the higher rates of sexual victimization among girls with histories of sexual offenses compared with girls from the general population.

However, the mechanism involved in the link between victimization and offending is not well understood.

Evolutionary theories are prominent in the literature (see Stinson et al., 2008) in describing processes of normal and atypical sexual behaviors. In general, evolutionary researchers have posited that sexual behavior is motivated by a drive to maximize reproductive success and survival of offspring, and that there are gender-specific reproductive capabilities and mate selection needs. Accordingly, males, in an attempt to pass on their genetic traits, are thought to be more sexually driven and aggressive than are females. Furthermore, greater reproductive costs (e.g., pregnancy, childbirth, nursing of offspring) presumably lead females to be much more selective about mate selection than are males. Sexual coercion and rape have been suggested as evolving from limitations or barriers to successful mating. With regard to girls, it is possible that girls who are sexually aggressive may have some impairments that may otherwise predispose them not to be chosen as mates. However, the view that girls might overcome possible mating deficits by engaging in atypical sexual behavior is purely speculative.

Some explanations for aggressive sexual behavior suggest that it represents a drive to obtain power, control, or dominance rather than a product of any sexual motivation. Largely attributed to the feminist movement (e.g., Saunders & Kashubeck-West, 2006), this view has emphasized that people in positions of societal power (e.g., men) act to assert their dominance. This view may help to explain why some girls in roles of authority (e.g., babysitter, older sibling) commit sexual offenses against younger children. Like the evolutionary perspective, this view has limited explanatory capacity for understanding girls' paraphilias and offending. To offset a focus exclusively on control or on any other single domain, some theories (e.g., precondition model; Finkelhor, 1984; confluence model; Malamuth, Linz, Heavey, Barnes, & Acker, 1995) have integrated various perspectives to explain sexual aggression and other atypical sexual expressions. Although most of the theoretical research has focused on men and boys, there may be implications for explaining why girls have atypical sexual interests and behaviors.

## Treatment Approaches

Given the limited understanding of girls' atypical sexual cognitions, fantasies, urges, and behaviors, there is no model treatment approach targeted specifically at girls. However, based on theoretical research on children's sexuality and on current treatment approaches for boys identified as exhibiting atypical sexual interests or behaviors, there are likely important implications for interventions with girls. As a first line of intervention, sexual education should be targeted toward parents, teachers, and healthcare professionals to increase awareness and understanding about sexual development (Ryan, 2000). Although sometimes considered controversial, comprehensive sexual education for children can reduce the risk of children developing sexually aberrant patterns of behavior.

Young children who seem to exhibit sexualized fantasies and behaviors are often assessed and treated for possible physical or sexual victimization, or indirect exposure to sexual experiences (e.g., at home, on television or via the Internet). In these cases, clinicians provide information at a developmentally appropriate level regarding the differences between appropriate and inappropriate sexual expression (Moser et al., 2004). In addition, they typically explore and address feelings of being defective, as well as guilt and shame. Treatment often targets interventions with the caregivers to alleviate their anxieties about the potentially inappropriate sexual expression, identify and prevent possible exposure to direct or indirect physical or sexual abuse, and address any family concerns or conflicts.

Current treatment practices with female juvenile sexual offenders frequently incorporate approaches designed for adult offenders and used with male juvenile sexual offenders (Vick et al., 2002). These treatment approaches typically emphasize group psychotherapy from a cognitive-behavioral perspective and tend to be offense-specific (Fanniff & Becker, 2006). Major components of treatment emphasize the youth's open disclosure of the offense, empathy for victims, and making plans for relapse prevention (Walker & McCormick, 2004). Other components incorporated to varying degrees include sexual education, emphasizing the consequences of the offending behavior, increasing impulse control, developing social skills, identifying and modifying maladaptive cognitions, and teaching about the sexual assault cycle.

Multisystemic therapy (MST), which addresses the known correlates of juvenile sexual offending through home and community-based services (see Ronis & Borduin, 2007), has demonstrated some success working with youth with problem sexual behaviors. According to studies with long-term follow-up data (Borduin, Schaeffer, & Heiblum, 2009; Letourneau et al., 2009), youth receiving MST have been shown to be significantly less likely to commit sexual crimes and nonsexual crimes than youth receiving usual services (e.g., group therapy, cognitive therapy). Furthermore, youth receiving MST experienced relatively improved mental health functioning and reduced out-of-home placements. Although studies have predominately included boys and have not directly addressed potential differences between female juvenile sexual offenders and male juvenile sexual offenders, MST appears to hold some promise for girls as well as boys.

## Gaps in the Literature

Even compared to what is known about patterns of normative sexuality among children, we are at the very earliest stages of understanding paraphilias and sexually abusive behaviors among girls. There are a number of gaps and unexplained findings in the literature, largely reflecting handicaps from methodological limitations. Small sample sizes and inadequate statistical approaches have limited our ability to identify prototypical sexual expressions among girls (Johansson-Love & Fremouw, 2006; Slotboom, Hendriks, & Verbruggen, 2011). Moreover, most of the available research has included unstandardized measures of psychosocial adjustment or chart reviews, which has called into question the reliability of findings and our ability to generalize to girls with atypical sexual expressions. Few studies have included longitudinal data or appropriate comparison groups (e.g., female juvenile nonsexual offenders, community sample of female youth), and without these methodological features it is difficult to determine whether observed results are linked with paraphilias or sexual offending among girls, or with normative sexual development.

A critical examination of the definitions of paraphilias and sexually abusive behaviors, as well as key factors associated with such expressions, is needed to advance our understanding. For example, although there is ample support for a link between early childhood victimization and atypical sexual behaviors (Roe-Sepowitz & Krysik, 2008), researchers have had difficulty reliably identifying such experiences and the mediating factors that link the two experiences (Johansson-Love & Fremouw, 2006).

Of particular note, our knowledge about differences between girls and boys is speculative at this point. Although their expression may at times seem similar, there are likely unique etiological and contextual explanations. For example, both girls and boys may engage in sexual exhibitionism, but their motivations behind this behavior probably differ, given the dramatically different sexual socialization they encounter through childhood and adolescence and possibly essential differences between male and female sexual drives. For example, exhibitionism in boys may be driven by sexual motives, whereas for girls these behaviors may be driven by more social motives. Nevertheless, the unique and common qualities of this and other behaviors are vastly understudied. Qualitative and experimental research may provide some key answers to contextual questions.

## CONCLUSIONS

There is no possibility of advancing our understanding of the development of paraphilias and sexual offending behaviors until we have a meaningful comparative standard of normative, or typical, sexual development. Research using various methodological approaches (Bancroft, 2003), such as anonymous, online methodology, or prospective research on children, should be incorporated. In the absence of such an understanding, health, welfare, and justice systems will continue to rely on arbitrary, inconsistent, subjective, and occasionally contradictory criteria for making these distinctions. In addition, researchers need to expand beyond *a priori* classifications that are based on a template of adult paraphilias or male sexual offending. The case for paraphilias among girls is far murkier than that for sexual offenses: we simply do not know the prevalence of paraphilias among girls because the definitions we use and how they apply to girls is not clear. In terms of sexual offending, girls have been found to account for approximately 10% of the juvenile population. This behavior is likely determined by multiple characteristics, and there may be subtypes of girls who commit sexual offenses. Interventions, at least based on our current knowledge, should focus primarily on sexual education for youth as well as for parents, teachers, and medical professionals. More intensive intervention may be required based on a broader set of problems (e.g., history of victimization, behavior problems in general) presented by the youth.

## REFERENCES

Abel, G. G., Osborn, C. A., Anthony, D., & Gardos, P. (1992). Current treatments of paraphiliacs. *Annual Review of Sex Research*, *3*, 255–290.

Araji, S. (1997). *Sexually aggressive children: Coming to understand them*. Thousand Oaks, CA: Sage Publications.

Bain, J., Langevin, R., Hucker, S., Dickey, R., Wright, P., & Schonberg, C. (1988). Sex hormones in pedophiles: I. Baseline values of six hormones; II. The gonadotropin releasing hormone test. *Annals of Sex Research*, *1*, 443–454. doi:10.1007/BF00878108.

Bancroft, J. (2003). Conclusions from a theoretical perspective. In J. Bancroft (Ed.), *Sexual development in childhood (pp. 449–454)*. Bloomington, IN: Indiana University Press.

Bancroft, J., Herbenick, D. L., & Reynolds, M. A. (2003). Masturbation as a marker of sexual development. In J. Bancroft (Ed.), *Sexual development in childhood (pp. 156–185)*. Bloomington, IN: Indiana University Press.

Bhugra, D., Popelyuk, D., & McMullen, I. (2010). Paraphilias across cultures: Contexts and controversies. *Journal of Sex Research, 47,* 242–256. doi:10.1080/00224491003699833.

Blanchard, R. (2010). The DSM diagnostic criteria for transvestic fetishism. *Archives of Sexual Behavior, 39,* 363–372. doi:10.1007/s10508-009-9541-3.

Boislard, P., & Poulin, M. (2011). Individual, familial, friends-related and contextual predictors of early sexual intercourse. *Journal of Adolescence, 34,* 289–300. doi:10.1016/j.adolescence.2010.05.002.

Borduin, C. M., Schaeffer, C. M., & Heiblum, N. (2009). A randomized clinical trial of multisystemic therapy with juvenile sexual offenders: Effects on youth social ecology and criminal activity. *Journal of Consulting and Clinical Psychology, 77,* 26–37. doi:10.1037/a0013035.

Borowsky, I. W., Hogan, M., & Ireland, M. (1997). Adolescent sexual aggression: Risk and protective factors. *Pediatrics, 100,* 1–8. doi:10.1542/peds.100.6.e7.

Bumby, K. M., & Bumby, N. H. (1997). Adolescent female sexual offenders. In B. K. Schwartz, & H. R. Cellini (Eds.), *The sex offender: Volume II: New insights, treatment innovations, and legal developments (pp. 10–16).* Kingston, NJ: Civic Research Institute.

Burton, D. L., Miller, D. L., & Schill, C. T. (2002). A social learning theory comparison of the sexual victimization of adolescent sexual offenders and nonsexual male delinquents. *Child Abuse and Neglect, 26,* 893–907. doi:10.1016/S0145-2134(02)00360-5.

Byers, E. S. (1995). How well does the traditional sexual script explain sexual coercion? Review of a program of research. *Journal of Psychology & Human Sexuality, 8,* 7–25. doi:10.1300/J056v08n01_02.

Calderone, M. (1983). Fetal erection and its message to us. *Sex Information and Education Council of the United States, 11,* 9–10.

Casares, W. N., Lahiff, M., Eskenazi, B., & Halpern-Felsher, B. L. (2010). Unpredicted trajectories: The relationship between race/ethnicity, pregnancy during adolescence, and young women's outcomes. *Journal of Adolescent Health, 47,* 143–150. doi:10.1016/j.jadohealth.2010.01.013.

Chivers, M. L. (2010). A brief update on the specificity of sexual arousal. *Sexual and Relationship Therapy, 25,* 407–414.

Chivers, M. L., Seto, M. C., Lalumière, M. L., Laan, E., & Grimbos, T. (2010). Agreement of self-reported and genital measures of sexual arousal in men and women: A meta-analysis. *Archives of Sexual Behavior, 39,* 5–56. doi:10.1007/s10508-009-9556-9.

Christiansen, A. R., & Thyer, B. A. (2002). Female sexual offenders: A review of empirical research. *Journal of Human Behavior in the Social Environment, 6,* 1–16. doi:10.1300/J137v06n03_01.

Coccaro, E. F., & Kavoussi, R. J. (1996). Neurotransmitter correlates of impulsive aggression. In D. M. Stoff, & R. B. Cairns (Eds.), *Aggression and violence: Genetic, neurobiological, and biosocial perspectives (pp. 67–85).* Mahwah, NJ: Erlbaum.

Conn, J. H., & Kanner, L. (1940). Spontaneous erections in early childhood. *Journal of Pediatrics, 16,* 337–340. doi:10.1016/S0022-3476(40)80153-4.

Connolly, J., Craig, W., Goldberg, A., & Pepler, D. (2004). Mixed-gender groups, dating, and romantic relationships in early adolescence. *Journal of Research on Adolescence, 14,* 185–207. doi:10.1111/j.1532-7795.2004.01402003.x.

Cubbin, C., Brindis, C. D., Jain, S., Santelli, J., & Bravman, P. (2010). Neighborhood poverty, aspirations and expectations, and initiation of sex. *Journal of Adolescent Health, 47,* 399–406. doi:10.1016/j.jadohealth.2010.02.010.

Cummings, J. L. (1999). Neuropsychiatry of sexual deviations. In R. Osview (Ed.), *Neuropsychiatry and mental health services (pp. 363–384).* Washington, DC: American Psychiatric Press.

De Graaf, H., & Rademakers, J. (2011). The psychological measurement of childhood sexual development in Western societies: Methodological challenges. *Journal of Sex Research, 48,* 118–129. doi:10.1080/00224499.2011.555929.

Deering, R., & Mellor, D. (2010). What is the prevalence of female-perpetrated child sexual abuse? A review of the literature. *American Journal of Forensic Psychology, 28,* 25–53.

Denov, M. S. (2003). The myth of innocence: Sexual scripts and the recognition of child sexual abuse by female perpetrators. *The Journal of Sex Research, 40,* 303–314. doi:10.1080/00224490309552195.

Diamond, L. M. (2000). Sexual identity, attractions, and behavior among young sexual-minority women over a 2-year period. *Developmental Psychology, 36,* 241–250. doi:10.1037/0012-1649.36.2.241.

Fanniff, A. M., & Becker, J. V. (2006). Specialized assessment and treatment of adolescent sex offenders. *Aggression and Violent Behavior, 11,* 265–282. doi:10.1016/j.avb.2005.08.003.

Fedoroff, J. P., Fishell, A., & Fedoroff, B. (1999). A case series of women evaluated for paraphilic sexual disorders. *The Canadian Journal of Human Sexuality, 8,* 127–140.

Fehrenbach, P. A., & Monastersky, C. (1988). Characteristics of female adolescent sex offenders. *American Journal of Orthopsychiatry, 58,* 148–151. doi:10.1111/j.1939-0025.1988.tb01575.x.

Ferguson, C. J. (2011). Sexting behaviors among young Hispanic women: Incidence and association with other high-risk sexual behaviors. *Psychiatric Quarterly, 82,* 239–243. doi:10.1007/s11126-010-9165-8.

Fine, M. (1988). Sexuality, schooling and adolescent females: The missing discourse of desire. *Harvard Educational Review, 58,* 29–53.

Finkelhor, D. (1984). *Child sexual abuse: New theory and research.* New York, NY: Free Press.

Flood, M. (2009). The harms of pornography exposure among children and young people. *Child Abuse Review, 18,* 384–400. doi:10.1002/car.1092.

Ford, C. S., & Beach, F. A. (1951). *Patterns of sexual behavior.* Oxford, UK: Harper & Hoeber.

Ford, C. S., & Beach, F. A. (1963). Development of sexual behavior in human beings. In R. Grinder (Ed.), *Studies in adolescence (pp. 433–445).* New York, NY: MacMillan.

Frankel, L. (2002). "I've never thought about it:" Contradictions and taboos surrounding American males' experiences of first ejaculation (semenarche). *The Journal of Men's Studies, 11,* 37–54. doi:10.3149/jms.1101.37.

Friedrich, W. N., & Trane, S. T. (2002). Sexual behavior in children across multiple settings. *Child Abuse & Neglect, 26,* 243–245. doi:10.1016/S0145-2134(01)00322-2.

Friedrich, W. N., Grambsch, P., Broughton, D., Kuiper, J., & Beilke, R. L. (1991). Normative sexual behavior in children. *Pediatrics, 88,* 456–464.

Friedrich, W. N., Grambsch, P., Damon, L., Hewitt, S. K., Koverola, C., Lang, R. A., et al. (1992). Child sexual behavior inventory: Normative and clinical comparison. *Psychological Assessment, 4,* 303–311. doi:10.1037/1040-3590.4.3.303.

Galenson, E., & Riophe, H. (1974). The emergence of genital awareness during the second year of life. In R. C. Friedman, R. M. Richart, & R. L. Van de Wiele (Eds.), *Sex differences in behavior (pp. 32–38).* New York, NY: John Wiley & Sons.

Gold, S. R., & Gold, R. G. (1991). Gender differences in first sexual fantasies. *Journal of Sex Education & Therapy, 17,* 207–216.

Haugaard, J. J. (1996). Sexual behaviors between children: Professionals' opinions and undergraduates' recollections. *Families in Society: Journal of Contemporary Human Services, 77,* 81–89.

Henderson, L. (2011). Sexting and sexual relationships among teens and young adults. *McNair Scholars Research Journal, 7,* 31–39.

Hendriks, J., & Bijleveld, C. C. (2006). Female adolescent sex offenders—An exploratory study. *Journal of Sexual Aggression, 12,* 31–41. doi:10.1080/13552600600568937.

Hetherton, J. (1999). The idealization of women: Its role in the minimization of child sexual abuse by females. *Child Abuse and Neglect, 23,* 161–174. doi:10.1016/S0145-2134(98)00119-7.

Higgs, D. C., Canavan, M. M., & Meyer, W. J. (1992). Moving from defense to offense: The development of an adolescent female sex offender. *The Journal of Sex Research, 29,* 131–139.

Hunter, J. A., Lexier, L. J., Goodwin, D. W., Browne, P. A., & Dennis, C. (1993). Psychosexual, attitudinal, and developmental characteristics of juvenile female sexual perpetrators in a residential treatment setting. *Journal of Child and Family Studies, 2*, 317–326. doi:10.1007/BF01321228.

Jackson, S. (1990). Demons and innocents: Western ideas on children's sexuality in historical perspective. In M. E. Perry (Ed.), *Childhood and adolescent sexology (pp. 23–49)*. New York, NY: Elsevier.

James, J., Ellis, B. J., Schlomer, G. L., & Garber, J. (2012). Sex-specific pathways to early puberty, sexual debut, and sexual risk taking: Tests of an integrated evolutionary-developmental model. *Developmental Psychology, 48(3), 687–702*. doi:10.1037/a0026427.

Johansson, T., & Hammarén, N. (2007). Hegemonic masculinity and pornography: Young people's attitudes toward and relations to pornography. *Journal of Men's Studies, 15*, 57–70. doi:10.3149/jms.1501.57.

Johansson-Love, J., & Fremouw, W. (2006). A critique of the female sexual perpetrator research. *Aggressive and Violent Behavior, 11*, 12–26. doi:10.1016/j.avb.2005.05.001.

Joshi, S. P., Peter, J., & Valkenburg, P. M. (2011). Scripts of sexual desire and danger in US and Dutch teen girls magazines: A cross-national content analysis. *Sex Roles, 64*, 463–474. doi:10.1007/s11199-011-9941-4.

Kaestle, C. E., & Allen, K. R. (2011). The role of masturbation in healthy sexual development: Perceptions of young adults. *Archives of Sexual Behavior, 11*, 983–994. doi:10.1007/s10508-010-9722-0.

Kinsey, A. C., Pomeroy, W. B., Martin, C. E., & Gebhard, P. H. (1953). *Sexual behavior in the human female*. Philadelphia, PA: Saunders.

Kjellgren, C., Priebe, G., Svedin, C. G., Mossige, S., & Langström, N. (2009). Female youth who sexually coerce: Prevalence, risk, and protective factors in two national high school surveys. *Journal of Sexual Medicine, X*, 1–9. doi:10.1111/j.1743-6109.2009.01495.x.

Knoth, R., Boyd, K., & Singer, B. (1988). Empirical tests of sexual selection theory: Predictions of sex differences in onset, intensity, and time course of sexual arousal. *Journal of Sex Research, 24*, 73–89. doi:10.1080/00224498809551399.

Krahé, B., Bieneck, S., & Scheinberger-Olwig, R. (2007). Adolescents' sexual scripts: Schematic representations of consensual and non-consensual heterosexual interactions. *Journal of Sex Research, 44*, 316–327.

Kubik, E. K., Hecker, J. E., & Righthand, S. (2002). Adolescent females who have sexually offended: Comparisons with delinquent adolescent female offenders and adolescent males who sexually offend. *Journal of Child Sexual Abuse, 11*, 63–83. doi:10.1300J070v11n03_04.

Kuik, S. (2003). Leaving childhood: Sexuality and how children become adolescents. *Netherlands' Journal of Social Sciences, 39*, 11–22.

L'Engle, K. L., Brown, J. D., & Kenneavy, K. (2006). The mass media are an important context for adolescents' sexual behavior. *Journal of Adolescent Health, 38*, 186–192. doi:10.1016/j.jadohealth.2005.03.020.

Lammers, C., Ireland, M., Resnick, M., & Blum, R. (2000). Influences on adolescents' decision to postpone onset of sexual intercourse: A survival analysis of virginity among youths aged 13 to 18 years. *Journal of Adolescent Health, 26*, 42–48. doi:10.1016/S1054-139X(99)00041-5.

Lang, R. A. (1993). Neuropsychological deficits in sexual offenders: Implications for treatment. *Sexual and Marital Therapy, 8*, 181–200. doi:10.1080/02674659308408193.

Langevin, R., Wortzman, G., Wright, P., & Handy, L. (1989). Studies of brain damage and dysfunction in sex offenders. *Annals of Sex Research, 1*, 401–415. doi:10.1007/BF00851321.

Langström, N., & Hanson, R. K. (2006). High rates of sexual behavior in the general population: Correlates and risk factors. *Archives of Sexual Behavior, 35*, 37–52. doi:10.1007/s10508-006-8993-4.

Langström, N., & Zucker, K. J. (2005). Transvestic festishism in the general population: Prevalence and correlates. *Journal of Sex and Marital Therapy, 31*, 87–95. doi:10.1080/00926230590477934.

Larsson, I., & Svedin, C. (2002). Sexual experiences in childhood: Young adults' recollections. *Archives of Sexual Behavior, 31*, 263–273. doi:10.1023/A:1015252903931.

Laumann, E. O., Paik, A., & Rosen, R. C. (1999). Sexual dysfunction in the United States: Prevalence and predictors. *JAMA, 281*, 537–544. doi:10.1001/jama.281.6.537.

Leitenberg, H., Greenwald, E., & Tarran, M. J. (1989). The relation between sexual activity among children during preadolescence and/or early adolescence and sexual behavior and sexual adjustment in young adulthood. *Archives of Sexual Behavior, 18*, 299–313. doi:10.1007/BF01541950.

Lenhart, A. (2009). *Teens and sexting: How and why minor teens are sending sexually suggestive nude or nearly nude images via text messaging*. Washington, DC: Pew Research Center. Retrieved from http://pewresearch.org/assets/pdf/teens-and-sexting.pdf.

Letourneau, E. J., Henggeler, S. W., Borduin, C. M., Schewe, P. A., McCart, M. R., Chapman, J. E., et al. (2009). Multisystemic therapy for juvenile sexual offenders: 1-year results from a randomized effectiveness trial. *Journal of Family Psychology, 23*, 89–102. doi:10.1037/a0014352.

Levine, M. L. (1957). Pediatric observations on masturbation in children. *Psychoanalytic Study of the Child, 6*, 117–124.

Lindberg, L. D., Jones, R., & Santelli, J. S. (2008). Noncoital sexual activities among adolescents. *Journal of Adolescent Health, 43*, 231–238. doi:10.1016/j.jadohealth.2007.12.010.

Lodico, M., Gruber, E., & DiClemente, R. (1996). Childhood sexual abuse and coercive sex among school-based adolescents in a Midwestern state. *Journal of Adolescent Health, 18*, 211–217. doi:10.1016/1054-139X(95)00167-Q.

Longmore, M. A., Manning, W. D., & Giordano, P. C. (2001). Preadolescent parenting strategies and teens' dating and sexual initiation: A longitudinal analysis. *Journal of Marriage and the Family, 63*, 332–335. doi:10.1111/j.1741-3737.2001.00322.x.

Lykins, A. D., Cantor, J. M., Kuban, M. E., Blak, T., Dickey, R., Klassen, P. E., et al. (2010). Sexual arousal to female children in gynephilic men. *Sexual Abuse: Journal of Research and Treatment, 22*, 279–289. doi:10.1177/1079063210372141.

Malamuth, N. M., Linz, D., Heavey, C. L., Barnes, G., & Acker, M. (1995). Using the confluence model of sexual aggression to predict men's conflict with women: A 10-year follow-up. *Journal of Personality and Social Psychology, 69*, 353–369. doi:10.1037/0022-3514.69.2.353.

Marshall, W. L. (2010). The role of attachments, intimacy, and loneliness in the etiology and maintenance of sexual offending. *Sexual and Relationship Therapy, 25*, 73–85. doi:10.1080/14681990903550191.

Martinson, F. M. (1973). *Infant and child sexuality: A sociological perspective*. St. Peter, MN: Book Mark.

Martinson, F. M. (1994). The sexual life of children. In the M. E. Perry (Ed.), *Handbook of sexology: VII childhood and adolescent sexology*. Amsterdam, The Netherlands: Elsevier.

Mathews, R., Hunter, J. A., & Vuz, J. (1997). Juvenile female sex offenders: Clinical characteristics and treatment issues. *Sexual Abuse: A Journal of Research and Treatment, 9*, 187–199. doi:10.1007/BF02675064.

McCartan, F. M., Law, H., Murphy, M., & Bailey, S. (2011). Child and adolescent females who present with sexually abusive behaviors: A 10-year UK prevalence study. *Journal of Sexual Aggression, 17*, 4–14. doi:10.1080/12552600.2010.488302.

Messerschmidt, J. W. (2011). The struggle for heterofeminine recognition: Bullying, embodiment, and reactive sexual offending by adolescent girls. *Feminist Criminology, 6*, 203–233. doi:10.1177/1557085111408062.

Miller, B. C., & Benson, B. (1999). Romantic and sexual relationship development during adolescence. In W. Furman, B. B. Brown, & C. Feiring (Eds.), *The development of romantic relationships in adolescence (pp. 99–124)*. Cambridge, UK: Cambridge University Press.

Miller, B. C., Norton, M. C., Curtis, T., Hill, E. J., Schvaneveldt, P., & Young, M. H. (1997). The timing of sexual intercourse among adolescents: Family, peer and other antecedents. *Youth and Society, 29*, 54–83. doi:10.1177/0044118X97029001003.

Mitchell, K. J., Finkelhor, D., Jones, L. M., & Wolak, J. (2012). Prevalence and characteristics of youth sexting: A national study. *Pediatrics, 129*, 1–8. doi:10.1542/peds.2011-1730.

Moore, E. E., Romaniuk, H., Olsson, C. A., Jayasinghe, Y., Carlin, J. B., & Patton, G. C. (2010). The prevalence of childhood sexual abuse and adolescent unwanted sexual contact among boys and girls living in Victoria, Australia. *Child Abuse & Neglect, 34*, 379–385. doi:10.1016/j.chiabu.2010.01.004.

Moser, C., & Kleinplatz, P. J. (2005). Does heterosexuality belong in the DSM? *Lesbian and Gay Psychology Review, 6*, 261–267.

Moser, C., Kleinplatz, P. J., Zuccarini, D., & Reiner, W. G. (2004). Situating unusual child and adolescent sexual behavior in context. *Child and Adolescent Psychiatry Clinics of North America, 13*, 569–589. doi:10.1016/j.chc.2004.02.007.

Nechay, A. (2010). Infantile masturbation/gratification. *Journal of Pediatric Neurology, 8*, 31.

O'Sullivan, L. F. (2008). Challenging assumptions regarding the validity of self-report measures: The special case of sexual behavior. *Journal of Adolescent Health, 42*, 207–208. doi:10.1016/j.jadohealth.2008.01.002.

O'Sullivan, L. F., & Brooks-Gunn, J. (2005). The timing of changes in girls' sexual cognitions and behaviors in early adolescence: A prospective, cohort study. *Journal of Adolescent Health, 37*, 211–219. doi:10.1016/j.jadohealth.2004.08.019.

O'Sullivan, L. F., & Majerovich, J. (2008). Difficulties with sexual functioning in a sample of male and female late adolescents and young adult university students. *Canadian Journal of Human Sexuality, 17*, 109–121.

O'Sullivan, L. F., & Meyer-Bahlburg, H. F. L. (2003). African American and Latina inner-city girls' reports of romantic and sexual development. *Journal of Social and Personal Relationships, 20*, 221–238. doi:10.1177/0265407503020002006.

O'Sullivan, L. F., Mantsun, M., Harris, K. M., & Brooks-Gunn, J. (2007). I wanna hold your hand: The progression of social, romantic and sexual events in adolescent relationships. *Perspectives on Sexual and Reproductive Health, 39*, 100–107. doi:10.1363/3910007.

O'Sullivan, L. F., Meyer-Bahlburg, H. F. L., & Watkins, B. X. (2000). Social cognitions associated with pubertal development in a sample of urban, low-income, African-American and Latina girls and mothers. *Journal of Adolescent Health, 27*, 227–235. doi:10.1016/S1054-139X(99)00111-1.

O'Sullivan, L. F., & Hearn, H. D. (2008). Predicting first intercourse among urban early adolescent girls: The role of emotions. *Cognition and Emotion, 22*, 168–179. doi:10.1080/02699930701298465.

Okami, P., Olmstead, R., & Abramson, P. R. (1997). Sexual experiences in early childhood: 18-year longitudinal data from the UCLA Family Lifestyles Project. *Journal of Sex Research, 34*, 339–347. doi:10.1080/00224499709551902.

Oliver, B. E. (2007). Preventing female-perpetrated sexual abuse. *Trauma, Violence, and Abuse, 8*, 19–32. doi:10.1177/1524838006296747.

Orenstein, P. (2011). *Cinderella ate my daughter: Dispatches from the front lines of the new girlie-girl culture*. New York, NY: HarperCollins.

Paikoff, R. (1995). Early heterosexual debut: Situations of sexual possibility during transition to adolescence. *American Journal of Orthopsychiatry, 65*, 389–401. doi:10.1037/h0079652.

Rademakers, J., Laan, M., & Straver, C. J. (2000). Studying children's sexuality from the child's perspective. *Journal of Psychology & Human Sexuality, 12*, 49–60. doi:10.1300/J056v12n01_04.

Richards, A. K. (1990). Female fetishes and female perversions: Hermine Hug-Hellmuth's "a case of female foot or more properly boot fetishism" reconsidered. *Psychoanalytic Review, 77*, 11–23.

Righthand, S., & Welch, C. (2005). Characteristics of youth who sexually offend. *Journal of Child Sexual Abuse, 13*, 15–32. doi:10.1300/J070v13n03_02.

Rind, B. (2008). The Bailey affair: Political correctness and attacks on sex research. *Archives of Sexual Behavior, 37*, 481–484. doi:10.1007/s10508-008-9334-0.

Roe-Sepowitz, D., & Krysik, J. (2008). Examining the sexual offenses of female juveniles: The relevance of childhood maltreatment. *American Journal of Orthopsychiatry, 78*, 405–412. doi:10.1037/a0014310.

Ronis, S. T., & Borduin, C. M. (2007). Individual, family, peer, and academic characteristics of male juvenile sexual offenders. *Journal of Abnormal Child Psychology, 35*, 153–163. doi:10.1007/s10802-006-9058-3.

Ronis, S. T., & O'Sullivan, L. F. (2011). A longitudinal analysis of predictors of male and female adolescents' transitions to intimate sexual behavior. *Journal of Adolescent Health, 49*, 321–323. doi:10.1016/j.jadohealth.2010.12.010.

Ryan, G. (2000). Childhood sexuality: A decade of study. Part I—Research and curriculum development. *Child Abuse and Neglect, 24*, 33–48. doi:10.1016/S0145-2134(99)00118-0.

Ryan, G. (2002). Victims who go on to victimize others: No simple explanations. *Child Abuse and Neglect, 26*, 891–892. doi:10.1016/S0145-2134(02)00359-9.

Sabina, C., Wolak, J., & Finkelhor, D. (2008). The nature and dynamics of Internet pornography exposure for youth. *Cyberpsychology and Behavior, 11*, 691–693. doi:10.1089/cpb.2007.0179.

Sandfort, T. G. M., & Cohen-Kettenis, P. T. (2000). Sexual behavior in Dutch and Belgian children as observed by their mothers. *Journal of Psychology & Human Sexuality, 12*, 105–115.

Sandnabba, N. K., Santtila, P., Wannäs, M., & Krook, K. (2003). Age and gender specific sexual behaviors in children. *Child Abuse & Neglect, 27*, 579–605. doi:10.1016/S0145-2134(03)00102-9.

Sass, F. A. (1975). Sexual asphyxia in the female. *Journal of Forensic Sciences, 20*, 181–185.

Saunders, K. J., & Kashubeck-West, S. (2006). The relations among feminist identity development, gender-role orientation, and psychological well-being in women. *Psychology of Women Quarterly, 30*, 199–211. doi:10.1111/j.1471-6402.2006.00282.x.

Savin-Williams, R. C., & Diamond, L. M. (2000). Sexual identity trajectories among sexual-minority youths: Gender comparisons. *Archives of Sexual Behavior, 29*, 607–627. doi:10.1023/A:1002058505138.

Schwartz, B. K., Cavanaugh, D., Pimental, A., & Prentky, R. (2006). Descriptive study of precursors to sex offending among 813 boys and girls: Antecedent life experiences. *Victims and Offenders, 1*, 61–77. doi:10.1080/15564880500498986.

Shute, R., Owens, L., & Slee, P. (2008). Everyday victimization of adolescent girls and boys: Sexual harassment, bullying or aggression? *Sex Roles, 58*, 477–489. doi:10.1007/s11199-007-9363-5.

Siccardi, G. G. (1996). Ultrasonographic observation of a female fetus' sexual behavior in utero. *American Journal of Obstetric Gynecology, 175*, 753.

Singy, P. (2010). What's wrong with sex? *Archives of Sexual Behavior, 39*, 1231–1233. doi:10.1007/s10508-010-9650-z.

Slotboom, A.-M., Hendriks, J., & Verbruggen, J. (2011). Contrasting adolescent female and male sexual aggression: A self-report study on prevalence and predictors of sexual aggression. *Journal of Sexual Aggression, 17*, 15–33. doi:10.1080/13552600.2010.544413.

Stephens, D. P., & Phillips, L. D. (2003). Freaks, gold diggers, divas, and dykes: The sociohistorical development of adolescent African American women's sexual script. *Sexuality & Culture, 7*, 3–49. doi:10.1007/BF03159848.

Stinson, J. D., Sales, B. D., & Becker, J. V. (2008). *Sex offending: Causal theories to inform research, prevention, and treatment*. Washington, DC: American Psychological Association.

Tardiff, M., Auclair, N., Jacob, M., & Carpentier, J. (2005). Sexual abuse perpetrated by adult and juvenile females: An ultimate attempt to resolve a conflict associated with maternal identity. *Child Abuse and Neglect, 29,* 153–167. doi:10.1016/j.chiabu.2004.05.006.

Thigpen, J. W., & Fortenberry, J. D. (2009). Understanding variation in normative childhood sexual behavior: The significance of family context. *Social Service Review, 83,* 611–632. doi:10.1086/650401.

Thornton, D. (2010). Evidence regarding the need for a diagnostic category for a coercive paraphilia. *Archives of Sexual Behavior, 39,* 411–418. doi:10.1007/s10508-009-9583-6.

Tolman, D. L. (2002). *Dilemmas of desire: Teenage girls talk about sexuality.* Cambridge, MA: Harvard University Press.

Tsopelas, C., Spyridoula, T., & Athanasios, S. (2011). Review on female sexual offenders: Findings about profile and personality. *International Journal of Law and Psychiatry, 34,* 122–126. doi:10.1016/j.ijlp.2011.02.006.

Upadhya, K. K., & Ellen, J. M. (2011). Social disadvantage as a risk for first pregnancy among adolescent females in the United States. *Journal of Adolescent Health, 49,* 538–541. doi:10.1016/j.jadohealth.2011.04.011.

Vandiver, D. M. (2010). Assessing gender differences and co-offending patterns of a predominately "male-oriented" crime: A comparison of a cross-national sample of juvenile boys and girls arrested for a sexual offense. *Violence and Victims, 25,* 243–264. doi:10.1891/0886-6708.25.2.243.

Vandiver, D. M., & Teske, R., Jr. (2006). Juvenile female and male sex offenders: A comparison of offender, victim, and judicial processing characteristics. *International Journal of Offender Therapy and Comparative Criminology, 50,* 148–165. doi:10.1177/030662 4X05277941.

Vandiver, D., & Walker, J. (2002). Female sex offenders: An overview and analysis of 40 cases. *Criminal Justice Review, 27,* 284–300. doi:10.1177/073401680202700205.

Vick, J., McRoy, R., & Matthews, B. (2002). Young female sex offenders: Assessment and treatment issues. *Journal of Child Sexual Abuse, 11,* 1–23. doi:10.1300/J070v11n02_01.

Walker, C. E., & McCormick, D. (2004). Current practices in residential treatment for adolescent sex offenders: A survey. *Journal of Child Sexual Abuse, 13,* 245–255. doi:10.1300/J070v13n03_12.

Walton, M. A., Resko, S., Whiteside, L., Chermack, S. T., Zimmerman, M., & Cunningham, R. M. (2011). Sexual risk behaviors among teens at an urban emergency department: Relationship with violent behaviors and substance use. *Journal of Adolescent Health, 48,* 303–305. doi:10.1016/j.jadohealth.2010.07.005.

Welles, C. E. (2005). Breaking the silence surrounding female adolescent sexual desire. *Women & Therapy, 28,* 31–45. doi:10.1300/J015v28n02_03.

Zaviačič, M. (1994). Sexual asphyxiophilia (Koczwarism) in women and the biological phenomenon of female ejaculation. *Medical Hypotheses, 42,* 318–322. doi:10.1016/0306-9877(94)90006-X.

# CHAPTER 9

# The Sexual Health of Adolescents

## When, Where, and Why Adolescents Use Contraceptives

### Lori A.J. Scott-Sheldon* and Blair T. Johnson[†]

*The Miriam Hospital and Brown University, Providence, Rhode Island[1], [†]University of Connecticut, Storrs, Connecticut

Adolescence, the period of transition from childhood to adulthood, is marked by significant physical, emotional, and cognitive changes. One of the most profound developmental changes occurring during early adolescence is puberty, followed by sexual identity formation (Kroger, 2007; Susman & Rogol, 2009). This process begins when adolescents become aware of their sexual desires, occurs prior to and after the onset of sexual intercourse, and may continue well into adulthood (Graber, Brooks-Gunn, & Galen, 1998). Adolescent sexuality is an integral feature of adolescent development.

Sexuality is essential for human life, often expressed through individual thoughts, feelings, and desires, and experienced through sexual behaviors and interpersonal relationships (World Health Organization, 2006). Adolescents' expressions and experiences of sexuality are profoundly shaped by the social and cultural context in which they live (Tolman & McClelland, 2011). In the United States, adolescents are often faced with conflicting messages vis-à-vis sexuality. Expressions of sexuality are often limited and/or disavowed by families, teachers, and religious leaders, but are readily displayed in the media, creating confusion among adolescents seeking guidance regarding their emerging sexuality (R.T. Brown & Brown, 2006). To achieve reproductive and sexual health and prevent sexual ill-health, adolescents' emerging sexuality must be recognized as a normative aspect of adolescent development.

A responsible, safe, and fulfilling sexual life experience requires a positive approach to sexuality and sexual relationships, as well as an understanding of

---

[1] Correspondence to: Lori A.J. Scott-Sheldon, PhD, Centers for Behavioral and Preventive Medicine, The Miriam Hospital, Coro building, suite 309, One Hoppin Street, Providence, RI 02903. Phone 401-793-8714; fax 401-793-8059; email lori_scott-sheldon@brown.edu

the interpersonal, social, and culture factors (e.g., gender violence, discrimination) that may lead to sexual ill-health (World Health Organization, 2006). Sexual health involves positive sexual expression, coupled with the possibility of satisfying and safe sexual experiences. As adolescents begin to explore their sexuality, including the initiation of sexual activity, they may be at risk for sexual ill-health. Sexually active adolescents may experience a number of short- and long-term consequences. Potential short-term consequences include early pregnancy and/or unsafe abortion, sexually transmitted infections (STIs), and sexual coercion and/or violence (Kaiser Family Foundation, 2011). Acquiring an STI during adolescence may lead to long-term consequences. For example, the human papillomavirus (HPV), the most common STI, is associated with the development of cervical, anal, vulvar, vaginal, penile, and oropharyngeal cancers many years after its acquisition and initial diagnosis (Datta, Dunne, Saraiya, & Markowitz, 2012). Clearly, achieving sexual health among adolescents is a public health priority.

To promote sexual health, public policy experts, health educators, physicians, and clinicians benefit from extensive knowledge and understanding of adolescents' sexual behavior, including when, where, and why contraceptives are used. This chapter begins with an overview of adolescents' sexual behavior and negative consequences associated with risky sexual behavior, followed by information on the effectiveness and use of contraceptives, as well as predictors of adolescents' contraceptive use and non-use. Although much of the research is focused on condoms, we also present general information across a broad range of contraceptives. Behavioral interventions to promote condom use among adolescents are reviewed. We also address the importance of providing adolescents with access to healthcare services and effective contraceptives. Finally, we conclude by offering suggestions for improving sexual health among adolescents.

## OVERVIEW OF ADOLESCENT SEXUAL BEHAVIOR AND CONSEQUENCES OF UNPROTECTED SEX

### Adolescent Sexual Behavior

Sexual exploration, including the initiation of sexual activity, increases as part of the normative development of adolescents' sexual identity (Graber et al., 1998). During this period, adolescents experience a range of feelings and initiate behaviors that may put them at risk for unwanted pregnancy, sexually transmitted infections, or sexual coercion. Sexual identity development often begins with non-coital behaviors, including fantasy and masturbation, followed by the initiation of sexual intercourse (Feldmann & Middleman, 2002).

Most contemporary adolescents experience sexual intercourse before their 19th birthday (Abma, Martinez, & Copen, 2010). Although the proportion of sexually experienced adolescents has declined since the mid-1980s, first sexual experience, defined as heterosexual vaginal-penile sex, generally occurs at about age 17 (Abma et al., 2010; Martinez, Copen, & Abma, 2011). Adolescents' first sexual experience is most often with a steady relationship partner, but approximately one-quarter of adolescents have sex for the first time with a new or casual partner (Martinez et al., 2011). Two-thirds of never-married adolescents report having two or more sexual partners, including one-fifth with six or more partners since their sexual debut (Martinez et al., 2011).

Adolescents' first sexual experience most often occurs long before marriage. In the United States, most people marry in their mid- to late-twenties (Kreider & Ellis, 2011). Nearly 90% of young adults aged 18 to 27, participating in a national longitudinal survey, had had premarital sex (Halpern, Waller, Spriggs, & Hallfors, 2006). The discrepancy between age at first sex and age at first marriage results in a span of approximately 10 years between sexual initiation and marriage. During this interval, adolescents and young adults are at increased risk for unintended pregnancy, sexually transmitted infections, and sexual coercion. Adolescents who initiate sexual intercourse before the age of 15 are at even greater risk for negative health consequences. Early age at first sexual intercourse is associated with having more sexual partners, first sex with a new or casual partner, inconsistent contraceptive use, sex under the influence of alcohol and/or drugs, and substance use (Dillon et al., 2010; Magnusson, Masho, & Lapane, 2012; Martinez et al., 2011). These findings highlight the need for greater understanding of adolescent sexual decision-making.

## Unintended Pregnancy, Sexually Transmitted Infections, and Sexual Coercion

### Unintended Pregnancy

Pregnancy and birth rates among teenagers in the United States are the highest of all developed countries (Bearinger, Sieving, Ferguson, & Sharma, 2007; Santelli & Melnikas, 2010). Teenage pregnancy is associated with adverse health, social, and economic consequences for children, parents, and society at large (Hoffman, 2006). The estimated total annual cost associated with teenage childbearing in the United States is $10.9 billion

(The National Campaign to Prevent Teen and Unplanned Pregnancy, 2011). While these costs are staggering, pregnancy and birth rates have declined in the United States since the 1950s, saving billions of dollars (Hoffman, 2006; Santelli & Melnikas, 2010). After a brief rise in the United States, birth rates for teenage females, aged 15 to 19, fell 8% from 2007 to 2009—reaching a historic low of 39 births per 1,000 in this age group (Ventura & Hamilton, 2011). Birth rates have fallen for all ethnic groups, but rates among African American, Hispanic, and Native American adolescents remain significantly higher than those for white and Asian adolescents (Ventura & Hamilton, 2011). Reductions in sexual activity and increased condom and contraceptive use have contributed to the recent declines in teenage pregnancy (for a review, see Santelli & Melnikas, 2010).

### *Sexually Transmitted Infections*

Adolescents continue to be at considerable risk for HIV and other STIs in the United States. Over 50,000 young people between the ages of 13 and 24 are estimated to be living with HIV/AIDS (Centers for Disease Control and Prevention, 2011a). Although the incidence of HIV has remained steady since 2006, new diagnoses of HIV have increased 21% among adolescents and young adults (Prejean et al., 2011). Further, approximately half of all new STIs occur among adolescents between the ages of 15 and 24 (Centers for Disease Control and Prevention, 2011c). Adolescents are at increased risk of acquiring STIs due to a variety of biological, behavioral, and cultural factors. Factors that place adolescents at greater risk for STIs include an early age of sexual debut, inconsistent or incorrect use of condoms, and experimentation with alcohol and other substances (Centers for Disease Control and Prevention, 2008). In the most recent *National Survey of Family Growth*, 43% of adolescents were sexually active, and 20% had four or more sexual partners (Centers for Disease Control and Prevention, 2011c). Frequent and concurrent partners are associated with STI incidence in adolescents (Kelley, Borawski, Flocke, & Keen, 2003). Reducing sexual risk behaviors as a means to avert new STIs, especially HIV, among adolescents is a public health priority (US Department of Health and Human Services).

### *Sexual Coercion*

Many adolescents fall victim to sexual violence from dating partners or acquaintances. Data from national samples of high school students find high rates of sexual coercion and/or violence: 10% have experienced dating violence and 8% experienced forced sexual intercourse (Gavin et al., 2009). Compared with high school boys, more than twice as many high school girls have been forced to have sex (Eaton et al., 2010). Adolescents, especially girls, are at increased risk for STIs, including HIV, as a result of coercive and violent sex. Sexual coercion is associated with having multiple sexual partners, unprotected sex, alcohol and/or drug use before sex, substance use, and STIs (Soomar, Fisher, & Mathews, 2009; Teitelman, Dichter, Cederbaum, & Campbell, 2007). Male perpetrators of relationship violence reported non-use of condoms within steady, often abusive, relationships (Raj et al., 2007). Unwanted sexual activity also increases adolescent girls' risk of pregnancy (Blythe, Fortenberry, Temkit, Tu, & Orr, 2006). Furthermore, adolescents who report forced sexual intercourse are more likely to experience negative psychological outcomes and increased suicide attempts (Howard & Wang, 2005). Sexual coercion prevents adolescents from achieving sexual health.

## CONTRACEPTIVES

Adolescents continue to report high rates of contraceptive use. Seventy-eight percent of women and 85% of men report using a contraceptive method at first sex; rates at most recent sexual intercourse were slightly higher, with 86% of women and 93% of men reporting any method of contraceptive use at last sex (Martinez et al., 2011). Among adolescents, condoms are used more frequently than any other method of contraception, followed by oral contraceptive pills. The most recent *National Survey of Family Growth* found that sexually active adolescents, between the ages of 15 and 17, reported using condoms 68% of the time and oral contraceptives 16% of the time at first sexual intercourse. Nonetheless, 22% of adolescents used no method of contraception during their first sexual intercourse. Adolescents who fail to use contraceptives are 90% more likely to become pregnant within a year (Guttmacher Institute, 2010). Correct and consistent contraceptive use, defined as using a method as it is designed to be used, can be highly effective at preventing pregnancy and/or STIs (Trussell, 2011).

### Effectiveness of Hormonal and Barrier Contraceptives Methods

To ensure the sexual health of adolescents, the American Academy of Pediatrics recommends comprehensive adolescent healthcare that includes a detailed sexual health history, a discussion on abstinence and/or appropriate contraceptive use, and prevention of STIs, including HIV (Blythe & Diaz, 2007). Abstinence is the most effective method to avoid unintended pregnancy and STIs, including HIV. In addition to continued abstinence, several types of contraceptive methods are available and appropriate for adolescents who intend to become sexually active, or adolescents who are already sexually active. These include hormonal methods, barrier methods, and other methods such as natural family planning (see Trussell, 2011). Although hormonal methods are highly effective in preventing pregnancy, they do not prevent STIs, which as we have noted can have serious repercussions not just for sexual health, but for health more generally. To avert STIs, including HIV, sexually active adolescents should be encouraged to use latex condoms correctly and consistently during each sexual event (Blythe & Diaz, 2007). Dual contraceptive methods (hormonal contraceptives and condoms) provide the best protection against pregnancy *and* STIs, but adolescents' use of dual methods is less common than their use of oral contraceptive pills (OCPs) or condoms alone (Martinez et al., 2011).

### *Hormonal Methods*

Hormonal methods, such as OCPs, interfere with ovulation, fertilization, or implantation of a fertilized egg. OCPs are the most common hormonal method used to prevent pregnancy among adolescent women (Gupta, Corrado, & Goldstein, 2008; Trussell, 2011). In addition to preventing pregnancy, OCPs have been shown to be helpful in treating acne, polycystic ovary syndrome, and dysmenorrhea (for a review, see Gupta et al., 2008). Among the 2.9 million adolescent women who use contraceptives, more than half use OCPs (Guttmacher Institute, 2010; Martinez et al., 2011). Although OCPs prevent pregnancy 99.7% of the time if used perfectly, typical use failure rates are much higher, especially among adolescents (Burke & Blumenthal, 2001; Gupta et al., 2008). Furthermore, some medications, such as antibiotics, may reduce the effectiveness of OCPs. Among adolescents, OCPs may also be less effective because of non-adherence (Kost, Singh, Vaughan, Trussell, & Bankole, 2008). Concerns about the potential side effects (e.g., weight gain) of OCPs may reduce adherence. To increase adherence, healthcare providers are advised to provide adolescents with ongoing education for the initiation and continuation of OCPs.

Other hormonal methods available include progestin implants, injections, the patch, and vaginal ring. Implanon®, the only progestin implant now available in the United States, is a simple and highly effective contraceptive tool to prevent pregnancy for up to three years duration (Tolaymat & Kaunitz,

2007). The annual failure rate of Implanon® is less than 1% (Trussell, 2011), but it may not be used in cases of extreme menstrual irregularities. In a clinical sample of adolescent women between the ages of 12 and 24, extreme menstrual irregularities, mostly often occurring during the first year, led to its removal among 22% of the women (Deokar, Jackson, & Omar, 2011).

Injections (Depo-Provera®), transdermal patch (Ortho Evra®), and the vaginal ring (NuvaRing®) are also highly effective for preventing pregnancy, with annual failure rates consistent with those of OCPs and progestin implants (Trussell, 2011). Few adverse side effects have been experienced among adolescents using the transdermal patch or vaginal ring (Bodner, Bodner-Adler, & Grunberger, 2011; Brache & Faundes, 2010). Aversive side effects associated with hormonal injections include acne, weight gain, and menstrual irregularities (Gupta et al., 2008). Most importantly, hormone injections may significantly decrease bone density in adolescent women (Cromer, Blair, Mahan, Zibners, & Naumovski, 1996; Kass-Wolff, 2001). Nonetheless, a recent longitudinal study showed that weight gain associated with the use of Depo-Provera® may reduce the loss of bone density among adolescents (Bonny, Secic, & Cromer, 2011).

## *Barrier Methods*

Barrier methods, such as condoms, sponges, and cervical caps, are used to prevent sperm from reaching the egg. The effectiveness of each barrier method to prevent unintended pregnancy, if used correctly and consistently, varies (Trussell, 2011), but condoms are often used incorrectly or inconsistently (Seidman & Rieder, 1994; Sznitman, Horner, et al., 2009; Sznitman, Romer, et al., 2009). To date, condoms are the only barrier method that is effective in reducing both unintended pregnancy and STIs, including HIV. Although correct and consistent condom use provides an effective method of disease prevention (Pinkerton & Abramson, 1997), at least 34% of adolescents report that they did not use a condom the last time they had sex (Eaton et al., 2010). Research shows that adolescents who use a condom at their first sexual experience are more likely to use condoms for subsequent sexual events, and report fewer STIs than adolescents who do not use a condom at their first sexual experience (Shafii, Stovel, & Holmes, 2007). Thus, encouraging condom use during adolescents' first sexual experience should be a priority. Indeed, the use of condoms at first sexual experience has increased. A recent national survey of adolescents, 15 to 19 years of age, found that 68% of women and 80% of men reported using condoms during their first sexual intercourse (Martinez et al., 2011).

## PREDICTORS OF CONTRACEPTIVE USE AND NON-USE

Correct and consistent use of contraceptives is critical in preventing unintended pregnancy and avoiding STIs, including HIV (Centers for Disease Control and Prevention, 2011b; Paz-Bailey et al., 2005; Santelli, Morrow, Anderson, & Lindberg, 2006). Despite this knowledge, adolescents use contraceptives inconsistently. In a nationally representative sample of sexually active adolescents, less than half of the women and two-thirds of men reported consistent condom use in the month prior to the survey (Martinez et al., 2011). Recent national survey data also indicates that adolescent men's condom use increased from 55% in 1991 to 70% in 2005, but has remained at similar levels since 2005 (Eaton et al., 2011). Furthermore, adolescent women fail to adhere to their oral contraceptive pill prescriptions more than twice as often as older women (Kost et al., 2008). Young people are also less likely to use condoms as they intend than older people (Albarracín, Kumkale, & Johnson, 2004). One reason why adolescents may fail to use contraceptives consistently is lowered autonomy and heightened sensitivity to social demands (Johnson & Boynton, 2010). Understanding adolescents' failure to use contraceptive methods consistently is critical to reducing the health, economic, and social burden of unintended pregnancy and STIs.

Over the past two decades, researchers have recommended adopting an ecological framework to better understand health behaviors. An ecological perspective posits that there are multiple influences on health behaviors, including intrapersonal, interpersonal, and environmental factors (see Johnson, Redding, et al., 2010; Sallis, Owen, & Fisher, 2008). Recognizing the multiple influences on adolescents' contraceptive use, we used an ecological framework to organize the research on contraceptive use and non-use among adolescents. Numerous studies have examined factors associated with contraceptive use. Among adolescents, intrapersonal (e.g., biological, psychological, and behavioral), interpersonal (e.g., social and cultural), and environmental factors have been associated with the use and non-use of condoms and other contraceptives (for reviews, see DiClemente et al., 2008; Sheeran, Abraham, & Orbell, 1999; Williams & Fortenberry, 2011).

### Intrapersonal Factors
*Biological and Developmental Factors*
Studies have shown that a number of biological and developmental characteristics influence contraceptive use. Early menarche is associated with

an earlier onset of sexual activity (Posner, 2006). For women, initiating sexual activity at a younger age is associated with lower contraceptive use (Martinez et al., 2011). Similarly, younger men report lower rates of condom use at first sex than older men (Martinez et al., 2011). Adolescent women's failure to use contraception at first sex may be due to their sexual partners' age, as both younger age and having an older male partner is associated with reduced contraceptive use (Manlove, Ikramullah, Mincieli, Holcombe, & Danish, 2009; Martinez et al., 2011). Condom use during the first sexual experience is important, because adolescents who used condoms at first sex are more likely to use condoms at their most recent sexual event (Shafii et al., 2007).

Adolescents' contraception and condom use is also associated with ethnicity. Contraception use among women varies by ethnicity: non-Hispanic white women are more likely to use contraception, specifically the oral contraceptive pill, at first sex compared with non-Hispanic black women (Martinez et al., 2011). Compared with non-Hispanic white men, non-Hispanic black men are more likely to use condoms at first sex and report consistent condom use in the past month (Manlove et al., 2009; Manlove, Ikramullah, & Terry-Humen, 2008; Martinez et al., 2011), whereas Hispanic adolescent men were less likely to use condoms than non-Hispanic white men (Manlove et al., 2008). Although research has shown significant gender and ethnic differences with respect to contraceptive use, other psychosocial factors (e.g., socioeconomic status, education) may account for those differences.

## *Psychological and Behavioral Factors*

An extensive literature has examined individual-level variables in relation to adolescents' risk behavior. Albarracín et al. (2004) carried out a meta-analysis of studies examining the variables in the theories of reasoned action (TRA; Fishbein, 1980) and planned behavior (TPB; Ajzen, 1991) in relation to condom use (viz., attitude, subjective norm, intention, and, for the TPB, perceived behavioral control as well), including 125 studies generally examining sexually active adolescents and adults. Age was a large moderator of the association between the variables specified by the TRA and TPB. That is, the association (1) between perceived behavioral control and behavior; (2) between control and intention was markedly larger for younger than older samples; and (3) importantly, the association between intention and future behavior was larger for older rather than younger samples. The implication is that as adolescents develop control over a behavior, and as they acquire the necessary cognitive and other resources, they can enact safer behavior (Johnson, Redding, et al., 2010).

Consistent with this conclusion is the Albarracín et al. (2004) finding that intention–behavior relations increased substantially in samples that had completed high school. Evidence gathered in meta-analyses of other domains corroborate these findings (e.g., exercise; Hagger, Chatzisarantis, & Biddle, 2002). A range of other evidence on adolescents also supports the conclusion that increasing competency (e.g., academic, cognitive, and social competencies) is associated with increased use of contraception (House, Bates, Markham, & Lesesne, 2010), and that failures of contraception can result from ambivalence (Stevens-Simon, Kelly, Singer, & Cox, 1996). Similarly, variables such as alcohol consumption interfere with contraception use and decrease condom use (Woodrome, Zimet, Orr, & Fortenberry, 2006). To be sure, adolescents are still often behaving in unhealthy ways, but it is likely that factors other than simple intentions are causally implicated.

### *Personality Characteristics*

Adolescent risk-taking behaviors may be explained by personality characteristics such as impulsivity and sensation-seeking, which have been consistently associated with sexual risk-taking, including unprotected sexual intercourse (Hoyle, Fejfar, & Miller, 2000). Impulsivity, defined as "the tendency to act without attending to the consequences of one's actions" (Hoyle et al., 2000, p. 1210) is associated with non-use of contraception and condoms at last sex (Kahn, Kaplowitz, Goodman, & Emans, 2002). A distinct but similar personality characteristic, sensation-seeking, has been linked to a wide range of risky behaviors (Zuckerman, 2007). Among African American adolescent women, sensation-seeking is associated with lower condom use at last sexual intercourse with a steady or non-steady partner (Spitalnick et al., 2007). Sensation-seeking also predicts future behaviors: higher impulsive sensation-seeking scores at baseline predicted lower condom use at last sex measured six months later in a sample of criminally involved youth (Bryan, Ray, & Cooper, 2007). Recent research suggests that the association between sensation-seeking and risky behaviors among adolescents is mediated by judgments of the costs and benefits. That is, the association between sensation-seeking and engaging in risky behaviors, including unprotected sex, were mediated by weighing the benefits of the behavior higher than its costs (Maslowsky, Buvinger, Keating, Steinberg, & Cauffman, 2011).

### New Research on Intrapersonal Factors

Adolescents take more risks than children or adults, but this risk-taking should be considered normative adolescent developmental behavior that is biologically driven. Recent advances in developmental neuroscience suggest that risk-taking is heightened during adolescence because of the temporal gap between the activation of the socio-emotional system (increased reward-seeking), occurring around the time of puberty, and the slow maturation of the cognitive control system (increased self-regulation and impulse control) (Steinberg, 2007, 2008, 2010). Other research suggests that variations in genes that regulate neurotransmitter functioning (and hence, impulsivity) are associated with lower contraceptive use among adolescents (Daw & Guo, 2011). This research highlights the importance of focusing on structural changes to improve adolescents' sexual health (e.g., increased access to reproductive and contraceptive healthcare) rather than attempts to increase risk-awareness.

## Interpersonal Factors

### Family

Parents and caregivers play an important role in the sexual health of adolescents. Parental style and communication are associated with adolescents' sexual activity and contraceptive use (for a review, see Commendador, 2010). Parental processes (being supportive, increased behavioral monitoring) are associated with increased condom use among sexually active adolescents (Parkes, Henderson, Wight, & Nixon, 2011). Moreover, Frisco (2005) found that parental monitoring is also associated with the use of specific birth control methods. In extreme cases of low parental monitoring, extreme risk behaviors may emerge: in 1999, a cluster of syphilis cases emerged in teens living in a prosperous Georgia town. Investigators learned that parental oversight of the teens was lax, permitting them to gather unsupervised and model sexual acts that they simultaneously viewed on cable television programs; consonant with the present analysis, the teens were motivated to engage in these acts to gain favor with each other (e.g., Luthar, 2003).

Prior research also shows that frequent communication with parents is associated with adolescents' increased use of contraceptives and/or condoms (DiClemente et al., 2001). Despite these findings, a recent telephone survey of parents of adolescents living in the Midwest United States found that less than half of the parents discussed where to obtain condoms or oral contraceptive pills with their child (Eisenberg, Sieving, Bearinger, Swain, & Resnick, 2006). Furthermore, parents tended to wait until their child entered a romantic relationship before communicating about prevention methods. Parents may be missing an important opportunity to assist their child develop healthy sexual attitudes and behaviors (see also Krauss & Miller, 2012). This factor is particularly important given that adolescents, especially young men, 14 to 16 years old, reported that family members, especially males (e.g., fathers, brothers), are the most important source for condom information and obtaining condoms (Rosenberger, Bell, McBride, Fortenberry, & Ott, 2010).

## Peers

Seventy-six percent of adolescents report that peers are an important source of sexual health information (The Henry J. Kaiser Family Foundation, 2003). Although parents play an important role in adolescents' sexual decision-making, peer norms influence adolescents' contraceptive use. Using longitudinal data, Ali, Amialchuk, & Dwyer (2011) examined the role of peer social networks in contraceptive behavior, and found a 10% increase in the proportion of classmates who used contraception increased individual contraceptive use by 5%. In another longitudinal study of adolescents' health, friends' sexual behavior (i.e., whether they had engaged in unprotected or protected vaginal sex) increased adolescents' risk of unprotected sexual intercourse (C. Kim, Gebremariam, Iwashyna, Dalton, & Lee, 2011). Furthermore, parental attitudes about sex and/or contraception were not associated with adolescents' contraceptive use after controlling for adolescents' baseline attitudes and behavior.

## Relationships and Partner Characteristics

Relationship and partner characteristics are important predictors of contraceptive and condom use. Research generally shows that condom use occurs in the context of casual or new partner relationships, but decreases over time such that condom use is less frequent in established relationships. Among adolescent women, consistent contraception use in most recent relationship is associated with shorter relationships (Manlove, Ryan, & Franzetta, 2004). Research shows that condom use within relationships decreases over time as a function of increase in sexual intercourse frequency (Sayegh, Fortenberry, Shew, & Orr, 2006); decreasing use of condoms typically occurs within three weeks of the first sexual intercourse (Fortenberry, Tu, Harezlak, Katz, & Orr, 2002). As relationships intensify, the use of hormonal contraceptive methods increases (Kenyon, Sieving, Jerstad, Pettingell, & Skay, 2010; Ott, Adler, Millstein, Tschann, & Ellen, 2002). Lack of condom use in more established relationships increases adolescents' risk of STIs, including HIV. This pattern is especially concerning, given that adolescents tend to engage in serially monogamous relationships (Kelley et al., 2003).

Partner communication about contraceptive and condom use prior to first sexual intercourse also predicts the use of protection. Prior research with adolescent women shows that consistent contraception use is associated with condom communications with a partner before sexual intercourse (Kenyon et al., 2010; Manlove et al., 2004). In contrast, poor partner communication about condoms predicts condom non-use (L. K. Brown et al., 2008). Non-use of condoms was also associated with the perception that condoms reduce sexual pleasure, and the perception that partners will not approve of condom use (L. K. Brown et al., 2008). Furthermore, perceived partner support of hormonal birth control methods at baseline is associated with hormonal contraceptive use 12 months later (Kenyon et al., 2010).

## Cultural and Contextual Factors
### Community
Communities in which adolescents live are instrumental in shaping their perceptions of what is socially acceptable, appropriate, and allowed (i.e., social norms), which strongly influence adolescents' sexual and contraceptive behavior. For example, Browning, Burrington, Leventhal, & Brooks-Gunn (2008) found that neighborhood structural disadvantage, operationalized as neighborhoods with elevated levels of poverty, residential instability, and ethnic heterogeneity, among adolescents, between the ages of 11 and 16, residing in Chicago, affected adolescents' high-risk sexual activity (i.e., having two or more sexual partners). Neighborhood structural disadvantages are also associated with condom use among adolescents: condom use was lower if adolescents' perceived their neighborhood to be less socially cohesive (Kerrigan, Witt, Glass, Chung, & Ellen, 2006). Furthermore, neighborhood structural disadvantage is also associated with adolescents' STI acquisition (J. L. Ford & Browning, 2011). Stressful life circumstances often eclipse HIV as a health concern, with survival needs forcing people into riskier practices and transactional relationships (Gibbons et al., 2004; Lane et al., 2004).

### Religious Beliefs
Religious activity and beliefs are often implicated as a protective factor for risky sexual behavior. Prior research shows that religiosity is associated with reduced sexual behavior (Rostosky, Regnerus, & Wright, 2003; Rostosky, Wilcox, Wright, & Randall, 2004; Sinha, Cnaan, & Gelles, 2007).

The association between religiosity and condom use is less clear. In contrast to Sheeran et al.'s (1999) meta-analysis, which found no association between religiosity and condom use, Zaleski & Schiaffino (2000) found a negative association between religiosity and condom use among sexually active adolescents. Other research shows that the association between religion and condom use is more complex. Religious commitments to remain abstinent until marriage (i.e., virginity pledges) delay the onset of sexual intercourse, but may not impact subsequent condom use (Martino, Elliott, Collins, Kanouse, & Berry, 2008). Research has shown that virginity pledges *decrease* the likelihood of condom use at first sex (Bearman & Bruckner, 2001), but condom use at most recent sex did not differ between those who had or had not made virginity pledges (Bruckner & Bearman, 2005).

Religiosity may also be a protective factor among ethnic minorities. Among African American adolescent women, a negative association between religion and risky sexual behavior was found such that religious adolescents were more likely to delay sexual intercourse and use condoms when sexual intercourse was initiated (McCree, Wingood, DiClemente, Davies, & Harrington, 2003). Similarly, Landor, Simons, Simons, Brody, & Gibbons (2011) found that religion was negatively associated with a number of sexual risk behaviors, including unprotected sex, among African American adolescents. Research has also shown that religiosity is a protective factor for Latinos. Villarruel, Jemmott, Jemmott, & Ronis (2007) found religiosity was the only significant predictor of condom use.

## Media

Contemporary adolescents interact with a media environment that is ever-more saturated with messages about sex, and that often appears to condone risky behaviors ranging from unsafe sex to smoking to casual drug use. Furthermore, less than 1% of media content provides information or depictions of healthy sexual behavior (Hust, Brown, & L'Engle, 2008). Policymakers face a daunting task when they endeavor to lower adolescents' risk behavior. Indeed, a recent survey of meta-analyses examining health promotion interventions suggests that adolescents exhibit less change than older individuals, often exhibiting no behavior change compared with control groups (Johnson, Scott-Sheldon, & Carey, 2010). Yet the impact of health promotion campaigns with adolescents also varies widely, and appears to depend reliably on many factors. To the extent that one can generalize and extend these findings, hopes may rise that media campaigns can better reduce adolescent risk behaviors.

A broad picture of media influences on adolescents emerges from many literatures and from many cumulative efforts to promote adolescent sexual health. Two recent meta-analyses relate well to pure media effects. First, Noar, Benac, & Harris (2007) reviewed the literature on tailoring of health communication messages, which took the form of letters, manuals/booklets, pamphlets/leaflets, newsletters/magazines, or calendars. Overall, tailoring meant a small improvement to message success across the 57 reviewed studies, and no age effects emerged, but the studies predominantly focused on adults rather than adolescents. Our meta-analysis of trials of computer-delivered messages across multiple health domains, including physical activity, overweight and obesity, tobacco use, substance use, safer sexual behavior, eating disorders, and more general health maintenance, showed that the computer-delivered interventions were successful for most of these behaviors (Portnoy, Scott-Sheldon, Johnson, & Carey, 2008). The studies sampled a wide range of ages; age often did relate to the magnitude of effects, although not in the domain of sexual health. In particular, the strategies worked significantly better for younger samples with regard to tobacco use, although it was a relatively small sample of studies. These results suggest that pure media effects can be larger than in-person interpersonal interventions and align with our findings that, across health promotion meta-analyses, brief interventions have proven more successful than long, intensive interventions (Johnson, Scott-Sheldon, & Carey, 2010).

In sum, much evidence across multiple health behaviors suggests that change is generally more difficult to achieve in adolescents than in adults. Unfortunately, extant meta-analyses have focused little on stages of adolescence, which limits the generalizability of the results. Yet, it is known that some methods of influence are more relevant (e.g., computer-based strategies), perhaps because of tailoring, and that these combine to increase impact. These encouraging findings are suggestive that adolescents will dedicate significant thought to voluntary media such as they find on the Internet. The findings also suggest that adolescents may well often use their defenses against interpersonal influence attempts from organized campaigns, and perhaps especially sexual behaviors. These campaigns appear only to succeed to any large extent when they satisfy an important need, such as to improve condom use skills or to increase motivation to act in a safe fashion.

## PROMOTING CONTRACEPTIVE USE
### Behavioral Change Theories

The most commonly used theories and models to change health behavior are cognitive and individual in orientation (Conner & Norman, 2005; de Wit & Stroebe, 2004; Lopez, Tolley, Grimes, & Chen-Mok, 2009). Among the most popular are Social Cognitive Theory (SCT; Bandura, 1986), the TRA (Fishbein, 1980), and the TPB (Ajzen, 1991). The TRA and TPB each include individual's attitudes and social norms about particular behaviors, which are in turn based on beliefs about the behavior and about others, respectively. The TRA and TPB both assume that attitudes and normative influences are theorized to affect behavior through intentions about the behavior in question. The TPB adds a variable, perceived behavioral control—the extent to which an individual perceives control over the specific behavior—that may relate either to intentions or to behavior (or both). The SCT presumes that self-efficacy, or confidence to undertake a specific behavior, underlies action tendencies: the more one has self-efficacy to do it, the more one will do it. The TRA, TPB, and SCT thus predict that adolescents will enact particular contraceptive behaviors to the extent that they have positive attitudes toward a particular contraceptive action, perceive supportive social norms, perceive control over the behavior (or high self-efficacy regarding it), and intend to do it. These perspectives are also congenial to the perspective that changing these elements will result in changes to behavior.

Thus, at their hearts, cognitive perspectives embrace the relatively rational principle that individuals can autonomously guide or change their behavior. Unfortunately, as we have seen, adolescents are less likely to exhibit rational behavior than young adults. Their intentions appear more facile and subject to rapidly emerging social-environmental factors (e.g., peer pressure). Indeed, as Johnson (2010) concluded, neither theories of change nor experimental tests of such theories have often directly incorporated this developmental stage. In essence, then, the cognitive theories are treating adolescents as though they are already young adults, despite strong evidence regarding neurological differences that take place during this period of life (Steinberg, 2008). Indeed, Johnson (2010) concluded that the factors that predict change in response to an appeal should vary from pre-adolescent stages through young adulthood. Younger targets should be more subject to emotional appeals, have weak attitudes, and rarely be skeptical (relative to young adults). Unfortunately, to date, no research has yet thoroughly investigated these predictions, and especially not with regard to contraceptive behavior. Finally, as much as the evidence appears to support an ecological perspective of adolescent behavior, to date models of change have not richly incorporated such aspects. One that shows some promise is the Network-Individual-Resource (NIR) theory (Johnson, Redding, et al., 2010), which posits that individuals function within one or more networks to fulfill their needs. These networks continually or intermittently interact with individuals to affect levels of resources that both the individual and network possess and wield: (1) mental resources, including efficacy, control, intentions, skills, and attitudes; and (2) tangible resources, including money, condoms, and physical health. The goal of the individual is to use the network to fulfill the deficit in resources. The implication is that network, resource, and power factors converge to put adolescents at risk for STIs, HIV, and pregnancy. Deficits in mental (e.g., coping skills) and tangible (e.g., housing) resources on the part of either an individual adolescent or his or her networks (families, peers) can lead to risky sexual interactions.

## Behavioral Interventions to Increase Contraceptive Use

Behavioral interventions are often implemented to reduce adolescents' risky sexual behavior by addressing deficits in adolescents' sexual and reproductive knowledge, increasing motivation to reduce risky sexual behaviors, and providing skills training to improve adolescents' ability to enact risk prevention behaviors. A number of meta-analytic and narrative reviews have examined the impact of behavioral interventions to improve condom or contraceptive use among adolescents (DiCenso, Guyatt, Willan, & Griffith, 2002; Franklin, Grant, Corcoran, Miller, & Bultman, 1997; Johnson, Carey, Marsh, Levin, & Scott-Sheldon, 2003; Johnson, Scott-Sheldon, Huedo-Medina, & Carey, 2011; C. R. Kim & Free, 2008; N. Kim, Stanton, Li, Dickersin, & Galbraith, 1997; Meade & Ickovics, 2005; Mullen, Ramirez, Strouse, Hedges, & Sogolow, 2002; Robin et al., 2004; Underhill, Operario, & Montgomery, 2007). Our meta-analyses (Johnson et al., 2003; Johnson et al., 2011) reviewed relatively intensive behavioral interventions to reduce risk of sexually transmitted HIV in adolescents, who were usually non-institutionalized and predominately sexually active. These programs varied from 1 to 50 sessions; they were as brief as 5 minutes total and as long as 42 hours; they often used elicitation research to generate the content of the interventions. Content also varied widely, with some trials incorporating school-based sex education, some with condom-skills training, and some with other predominant content.

Table 9.1 Meta-Analyses Focused on Health Promotion Trials

| Behavior | k of Studies | M Age of Sample in Years | M $d_+$ | Homogeneity ($I^2$) |
|---|---|---|---|---|
| Abstinence (Silva, 2002) | 12 | 14 | 0.044† | 81.64† |
| Pregnancy rates (Kirby, 2007) | 30 | 15 | 0.050† | 46.40† |
| Pregnancy rates, sexual behavior, birth control use (Guyatt, DiCenso, Farewell, Willan, & Griffith, 2000) | 30 | 15 | −0.027 | 63.99† |
| Averaged behavioral sexual risk index (Mullen et al., 2002) | 2 | 15 | 0.25† | 0 |
| Condom use (Johnson et al., 2003) | 42 | 15 | 0.073† | 47.33† |
| Frequency of sexual encounters (Johnson et al., 2003) | 38 | 15 | 0.049† | 1.76 |
| Unprotected intercourse (Mullen et al., 2002) | 13 | 15 | 0.19† | 70.66† |
| Number of sexual partners (Mullen et al., 2002) | 8 | 16 | 0.29† | 49.53 |
| Sexually transmitted diseases (Mullen et al., 2002) | 2 | 16 | −0.11 | 53.19 |

*Source:* Johnson, Scott-Sheldon, & Carey (2010).
Mean effect sizes ($d_+$) are positive for differences that favor health promotion in the treatment group (usually relative to a control group) and are expressed as the standardized mean difference effect size. Homogeneity ($I^2$) values may range between 0 (no more than sampling error observed, i.e., homogeneous) and 100 (heterogeneity).
†$p<0.05$.

Some trials provided condoms. They generally took measures of condom use or sexual frequencies at some distance from the intervention, about 14 weeks after the intervention ended. Overall, interventions had a very small (but significant) impact, increasing condom use ($d_+ = 0.07$) and decreasing the frequencies with which adolescents had sex ($d_+ = 0.05$).

These mean effect sizes lie in the middle of a range of effects shown for adolescents more generally; health promotion meta-analyses focusing on adolescents have yielded smaller effect sizes (ranging from −0.11 to 0.29) than those focusing on adults, even within the same content area (Johnson, Redding, et al., 2010). Table 9.1 lists sexual health promotion meta-analyses' results focused on adolescents, which Johnson, Redding, et al. (2010) reviewed. These reviews consistently find that behavioral intervention targeting *HIV risk reduction* increases condom use and decreases unprotected sex. Interventions targeting *pregnancy prevention* do not improve contraceptive use. Future research should examine how behavioral interventions might increase both contraceptive and condom use (i.e., dual protection methods) to reduce unintended pregnancy and STI/HIV acquisition among adolescents. Other more recent meta-analyses have isolated adolescents from adults and found similar results. Our meta-analysis focusing on HIV prevention for African Americans found similar impact on condom use across the ages studied; yet, adolescents reduced the number of partners they reported whereas adults did not, especially at relatively long intervals after the interventions ended (Johnson et al., 2009). Importantly, behavioral interventions can have much larger, positive impacts on adolescents' sexual behavior.

## Access to Reproductive Health and Contraceptive Services

Access to comprehensive and confidential reproductive health and contraceptive services is critical to ensuring the sexual health of adolescents (Feldmann & Middleman, 2002). Nearly 40% of women between the ages of 15 and 19 used sexual or reproductive healthcare services in 2002 (Frost, 2008). Confidentiality concerns drastically impact adolescents' willingness to seek healthcare services (C. A. Ford, Millstein, Halpern-Felsher, & Irwin, 1997). If parental notification of prescription contraceptives from federally funded family-planning clinics was mandated, only 30% of adolescent women seeking services without their parents' knowledge would return to the family planning clinic (Jones, Purcell, Singh, & Finer, 2005). Despite these findings, state laws limit the ability of healthcare providers to offer contraceptive services to minors without parental consent. Only 21 states and the District of Columbia permit all minors under the age of 17 to consent to contraceptive services; 25 states restrict consent to contraceptive services; and 4 states have no specific consent policy (Guttmacher Institute, 2011). Perceived access to contraceptives is associated with the use of contraception and the consistency of contraceptive use (Ryan, Franzetta, & Manlove, 2007). Policies limiting adolescents' access to contraceptive services do not reduce sexual activity; instead, they increase their risk of unintended pregnancy and STIs (Santelli, Ott, Lyon, Rogers, & Summers, et al., 2006).

Unlike hormonal contraceptives, most barrier methods are available over-the-counter, without a prescription. The male condom is the most commonly used barrier method due to its widespread availability, low cost (as compared with hormonal methods), and portability. Adolescents report purchasing condoms through retail establishments (e.g., pharmacies), rather than obtaining free condoms from healthcare settings or friends (Klein et al., 2001). To prevent unintended pregnancy after unprotected sexual intercourse, emergency contraceptives are available, without a prescription, for adolescents 17 years of age and older (Duffy & Gold, 2011). A recent decision by the US Department of Health and Human Services to deny over-the-counter access, without age restriction, of the emergency contraceptive, Plan B One-Step®, was denounced by the American Academy of Pediatrics, the American College of Obstetricians and Gynecologists, and the Society of Adolescent Health and Medicine, as it continues to place restrictions on adolescent women's ability to manage their reproductive health (American Academy of Pediatrics, 2011).

## Continuing Debate on Promoting Contraceptives among US Adolescents

The promotion and provision of contraceptives to American adolescents remains controversial. Some argue that programs to promote and/or provide contraceptives (e.g., as part of comprehensive sexual education) encourage sexual activity and increase the risk of unwanted pregnancy and STIs, whereas proponents argue that these programs increase adolescents' contraceptive use when sex is initiated and reduce the risks of an unwanted pregnancy and/or STIs. Public policy reflects this ongoing debate: despite evidence showing that abstinence-only education is ineffective, the President's fiscal year 2013 budget allocated $50 million to fund abstinence-only programs (mandatory Title V funding) (Sexuality Information and Education Council of the United States, 2012). A recent analysis of sexual education policies found that states emphasizing abstinence-only education had higher rates of teenage pregnancy and birth (Stanger-Hall & Hall, 2011). In contrast, accumulating evidence shows that comprehensive programs that emphasize abstinence but also promote contraceptive use do not increase sexual activity among sexually inexperienced teens, but are effective in reducing unwanted pregnancy and STIs when teens become sexually active (Chin et al., 2012; Kirby, 2007, 2008; Kohler, Manhart, & Lafferty, 2008; Underhill et al., 2007). Despite recent declines, the 2010 United States teen birth rate ranks higher than that of any other developed country, with approximately 368,000 births among adolescents 15 to 19 years old (Centers for Disease Control and Prevention, 2012). Moreover, nearly half of all new STIs occur among adolescents and young adults aged 15 to 24 (Weinstock, Berman, &

Cates, 2004). The economic impact of adolescent pregnancy and STIs in the United States is substantial; teen births cost the taxpayer approximately $10.9 billion annually, (The National Campaign to Prevent Teen and Unplanned Pregnancy, 2011), and the medical costs associated with treating adolescents for STIs are approximately $6.5 billion (Chesson, Blandford, Gift, Tao, & Irwin, 2004). Because most adolescents initiate sexual activity long before they are married (Halpern et al., 2006), preventing unwanted pregnancy and STIs benefits not only the health and well-being of the adolescent, but also society as a whole.

Promoting contraceptives among adolescents is *not* associated with an earlier age at sexual debut, increased sexual activity, or a higher risk of pregnancy and/or STIs (Kirby, 2007; Kohler et al., 2008). In fact, research shows that improved contraceptive use accounted for 77% of the decline in adolescent pregnancy risk from 1995 to 2002 (Santelli, Lindberg, Finer, & Singh, 2007). Providing adolescents with accurate, clear, and comprehensive information is imperative for adolescents' sexual health. The public debate about the most appropriate method for educating adolescents may be slowly waning; public support for a comprehensive approach to educating adolescents about sex has risen to 82% of American adults (Bleakley, Hennessy, & Fishbein, 2006). Consistent with the position of the Society of Adolescent Medicine (Santelli, Ott, Lyon, Rogers, & Summers, 2006), we affirm that withholding information on contraceptives or presenting inaccurate information is unethical. Providing adolescents with access to comprehensive and confidential reproductive health and contraceptive services is critical (Feldmann & Middleman, 2002). Moreover, health educators, clinicians, and medical providers have an ethical obligation to provide accurate information to their students or patients (Santelli, Ott, Lyon, Rogers, & Summers, 2006). To this point, the American Academy of Pediatrics also recommends using a comprehensive approach to sexual education and services for adolescent patients, while ensuring confidentiality (Blythe & Diaz, 2007). Reducing unintended pregnancy or STIs will require comprehensive reproductive and sexual health information and services for all adolescents.

## CONCLUSIONS

Sexuality is a normative aspect of adolescent development. Achieving sexual and reproductive health requires an understanding of adolescents' developing self, including sexual identity formation, and the contexts in which these developments occur (Tolman & McClelland, 2011).

Achieving sexual health also requires the knowledge and skills to prevent potential negative consequences of sexual behavior. A number of behavioral interventions to prevent pregnancy and reduce sexually transmitted diseases among adolescents have been developed, implemented, and evaluated (Johnson et al., 2003; Johnson et al., 2011). Overall, these interventions have been successful in reducing unprotected sex, sexual initiation, and the frequency of sex. Based on these findings, several strategies to prevent unintended pregnancy and sexually transmitted infections, including HIV, are recommended: (1) tailor and target interventions to the specific needs of adolescents, recognizing that adolescents are not a homogeneous group of individuals, but rather, that adolescents come from a variety of influential socioeconomic, ethnic, and cultural backgrounds. (2) Promote condom use prior to sexual debut. Research has shown that adolescents who use a condom at their sexual debut are more likely to use condoms on future sexual occasions. (3) Include family members in intervention efforts. Family members, especially parents, play an important role in the delay of sexual activity and the increase in contraceptive use. (4) Promote the dual use of condoms and oral contraceptives. Use of dual protection decreases the chance that an unintended pregnancy or sexually transmitted infection will occur. Despite the benefits of dual-protection methods, less than one-third of physicians prescribed or provided condoms to their adolescent patients during routine preventive care (Henry-Reid et al., 2010). Reducing unintended consequences of adolescent sexual behavior will not only require individual-level strategies, but also strategies that consider structural factors (e.g., economic, social, and cultural) that impact adolescent sexual behavior.

The sexual health of adolescents is a public health priority. The promotion of adolescents' sexual health will require a multifaceted approach that considers the intrapersonal, interpersonal, and contextual influences on sexuality and sexual behavior. Doing so will require more research to increase our understanding of adolescents' sexuality, including sexual decision-making. That is, we need to better understand the psychological, physical, and cognitive factors associated with the initiation or delay of sexual activity, across time. Adolescents must also be protected from sexual coercion and violence. Individual, community, and governmental action is required to change cultural norms associated with non-consensual sex, increasing the possibility of satisfying and safe sexual experiences. Finally, age-appropriate sexual and reproductive health information, contraceptives, and services should be made available at low- or no-costs to adolescents. Services that target the specific needs of adolescents should be made available in locations which adolescents frequent, such as schools and community centers.

Promoting the sexual health and well-being of adolescents is of utmost priority. As adolescents begin to explore their sexuality, including the initiation of sexual activity, they often may be at risk for sexual ill-health. Consequences of sexual behavior include unintended pregnancy and sexually transmitted infections. A number of interpersonal, intrapersonal, and environmental factors contribute to adolescents' sexual behavior. Behavioral interventions to reduce sexual risk have been effective among adolescents. To achieve sexual and reproductive health, adolescents' emerging sexuality must be recognized as a normative aspect of adolescent development.

## REFERENCES

Abma, J. C., Martinez, G. M., & Copen, C. E. (2010). Teenagers in the United States: Sexual activity, contraceptive use, and childbearing, national survey of family growth 2006–2008. *Vital and Health Statistics, 23*(30), 1–47.

Ajzen, I. (1991). The theory of planned behavior. *Organizational Behavior and Human Decision Processes, 50*, 179–211.

Albarracín, D., Kumkale, G. T., & Johnson, B. T. (2004). Influences of social power and normative support on condom use decisions: A research synthesis. *AIDS Care, 16*(6), 700–723.

Ali, M. M., Amialchuk, A., & Dwyer, D. S. (2011). Social network effects in contraceptive behavior among adolescents. *Journal of Developmental and Behavioral Pediatrics, 32*(8), 563–571.

American Academy of Pediatrics. (2011). Medical groups denounce HHS decision on access to emergency contraception [Press Release]. Retrieved December 7, 2011, from <http://www.aap.org/advocacy/washing/emergencycontraception12711.pdf>.

Bandura, A. (1986). *Social foundations of thought and action: A social cognitive theory*. Englewood Cliffs, NJ: Prentice-Hall.

Bearinger, L. H., Sieving, R. E., Ferguson, J., & Sharma, V. (2007). Global perspectives on the sexual and reproductive health of adolescents: Patterns, prevention, and potential. *Lancet, 369*(9568), 1220–1231.

Bearman, P., & Bruckner, H. (2001). Promising the future: Virginity pledges and first intercourse. *American Journal of Sociology, 106*, 859–912.

Bleakley, A., Hennessy, M., & Fishbein, M. (2006). Public opinion on sex education in US schools. *Archives of Pediatrics & Adolescent Medicine, 160*(11), 1151–1156.

Blythe, M. J., & Diaz, A. (2007). Contraception and adolescents. *Pediatrics, 120*(5), 1135–1148.

Blythe, M. J., Fortenberry, J. D., Temkit, M., Tu, W., & Orr, D. P. (2006). Incidence and correlates of unwanted sex in relationships of middle and late adolescent women. *Archives of Pediatrics & Adolescent Medicine, 160*(6), 591–595.

Bodner, K., Bodner-Adler, B., & Grunberger, W. (2011). Evaluation of the contraceptive efficacy, compliance, and satisfaction with the transdermal contraceptive patch system Evra: A comparison between adolescent and adult users. *Archives of Gynecology and Obstetrics, 283*(3), 525–530.

Bonny, A. E., Secic, M., & Cromer, B. A. (2011). Relationship between weight and bone mineral density in adolescents on hormonal contraception. *Journal of Pediatric and Adolescent Gynecology, 24*(1), 35–38.

Brache, V., & Faundes, A. (2010). Contraceptive vaginal rings: A review. *Contraception, 82*(5), 418–427.

Brown, L. K., DiClemente, R., Crosby, R., Fernandez, M. I., Pugatch, D., Cohn, S., et al. (2008). Condom use among high-risk adolescents: Anticipation of partner disapproval and less pleasure associated with not using condoms. *Public Health Reports, 123*(5), 601–607.

Brown, R. T., & Brown, J. D. (2006). Adolescent sexuality. *Primary Care, 33*(2), 373–390.

Browning, C. R., Burrington, L. A., Leventhal, T., & Brooks-Gunn, J. (2008). Neighborhood structural inequality, collective efficacy, and sexual risk behavior among urban youth. *Journal of Health and Social Behavior, 49*(3), 269–285.

Bruckner, H., & Bearman, P. (2005). After the promise: The STD consequences of adolescent virginity pledges. *Journal of Adolescent Health, 36*(4), 271–278.

Bryan, A., Ray, L. A., & Cooper, M. L. (2007). Alcohol use and protective sexual behaviors among high-risk adolescents. *Journal of Studies on Alcohol and Drugs, 68*(3), 327–335.

Burke, A. E., & Blumenthal, P. D. (2001). Successful use of oral contraceptives. *Seminars in Reproductive Medicine, 19*(4), 313–321.

Centers for Disease Control and Prevention, (2008). *HIV/AIDS among youth*. Atlanta, GA.

Centers for Disease Control and Prevention, (2011a). *HIV surveillance report, 2009*. Retrieved November 30, 2011, from <http://www.cdc.gov/hiv/topics/surveillance/resources/reports/index.htm>.

Centers for Disease Control and Prevention, (2011b). Male latex condoms and sexually transmitted dieseases. Retrieved December 12, 2011, from <http://www.cdc.gov/condomeffectiveness/latex.htm>.

Centers for Disease Control and Prevention, (2011c). *Sexually transmitted disease surveillance 2010*. Atlanta, GA: Department of Health and Human Services.

Centers for Disease Control and Prevention, (2012). Sexual experience and contraceptive use among female teens–United States, 1995, 2002, and 2006–2010. *Morbidity and Mortality Weekly Report, 4*(61), 297–301.

Chesson, H. W., Blandford, J. M., Gift, T. L., Tao, G., & Irwin, K. L. (2004). The estimated direct medical cost of sexually transmitted diseases among American youth, 2000. *Perspectives on Sexual and Reproductive Health, 36*(1), 11–19.

Chin, H. B., Sipe, T. A., Elder, R., Mercer, S. L., Chattopadhyay, S. K., Jacob, V., et al. (2012). The effectiveness of group-based comprehensive risk-reduction and abstinence education interventions to prevent or reduce the risk of adolescent pregnancy, human immunodeficiency virus, and sexually transmitted infections: Two systematic reviews for the Guide to Community Preventive Services. *American Journal of Preventive Medicine, 42*(3), 272–294.

Commendador, K. A. (2010). Parental influences on adolescent decision making and contraceptive use. *Pediatric Nursing, 36*(3), 147–156.

Conner, M., & Norman, P. (2005). Predicting health behaviour: A social cognitition approach. In M. Conner, & P. Norman (Eds.), *Predicting health behaviour (pp. 1–27)*. New York, NY: Open University Press.

Cromer, B. A., Blair, J. M., Mahan, J. D., Zibners, L., & Naumovski, Z. (1996). A prospective comparison of bone density in adolescent girls receiving depot medroxyprogesterone acetate (Depo-Provera), levonorgestrel (Norplant), or oral contraceptives. *Journal of Pediatrics, 129*(5), 671–676.

Datta, D., Dunne, E. F., Saraiya, M., & Markowitz, L. (2012). Human papillomaviruses. In J. M. Zenilman, & M. Shahmanesh (Eds.), *Sexually transmitted infections: Diagnosis, management, and treatment (pp. 43–55)*. Sudbury, MA: Jones & Bartlett Learning.

Daw, J., & Guo, G. (2011). The influence of three genes on whether adolescents use contraception, USA 1994–2002. *Population Studies (Camb), 65*(3), 253–271.

de Wit, J., & Stroebe, W. (2004). Social cognition models of health behaviour. In A. Kaptein, & J. Weinman (Eds.), *Health psychology (pp. 52–83)*. Oxford, UK: Blackwell Publishing.

Deokar, A. M., Jackson, W., & Omar, H. A. (2011). Menstrual bleeding patterns in adolescents using etonogestrel (ENG) implant. *International Journal of Adolescent Medicine and Health, 23*(1), 75–77.

DiCenso, A., Guyatt, G., Willan, A., & Griffith, L. (2002). Interventions to reduce unintended pregnancies among adolescents: Systematic review of randomised controlled trials. *BMJ, 324*(7351), 1426.

DiClemente, R. J., Crittenden, C. P., Rose, E., Sales, J. M., Wingood, G. M., Crosby, R. A., et al. (2008). Psychosocial predictors of HIV-associated sexual behaviors and the efficacy of prevention interventions in adolescents at-risk for HIV infection: What works and what doesn't work? *Psychosomatic Medicine, 70*(5), 598–605.

DiClemente, R. J., Wingood, G. M., Crosby, R., Cobb, B. K., Harrington, K., & Davies, S. L. (2001). Parent-adolescent communication and sexual risk behaviors among African American adolescent females. *Journal of Pediatric, 139*(3), 407–412.

Dillon, F. R., De La Rosa, M., Schwartz, S. J., Rojas, P., Duan, R., & Malow, R. M. (2010). US Latina age of sexual debut: Long-term associations and implications for HIV and drug abuse prevention. *AIDS Care, 22*(4), 431–440.

Duffy, K., & Gold, M. A. (2011). Adolescents and emergency contraception: Update 2011. *Current Opinion in Obstetrics & Gynecology, 23*(5), 328–333.

Eaton, D. K., Kann, L., Kinchen, S., Shanklin, S., Ross, J., Hawkins, J., et al. (2010). Youth risk behavior surveillance–United States, 2009. *MMWR Surveillance Summaries, 59*(5), 1–142.

Eaton, D. K., Lowry, R., Brener, N. D., Kann, L., Romero, L., & Wechsler, H. (2011). Trends in human immunodeficiency virus- and sexually transmitted disease-related risk behaviors among U.S. high school students, 1991–2009. *American Journal of Preventive Medicine, 40*(4), 427–433.

Eisenberg, M. E., Sieving, R. E., Bearinger, L. H., Swain, C., & Resnick, M. D. (2006). Parents' communication with adolescents about sexual behavior: A missed opportunity for prevention? *Journal of Youth Adolescence, 35*, 893–902.

Feldmann, J., & Middleman, A. B. (2002). Adolescent sexuality and sexual behavior. *Current Opinion in Obstetrics & Gynecology, 14*(5), 489–493.

Fishbein, M. (1980). A theory of reasoned action: Some applications and implications. *Nebraska Symposium on Motivation, 27*, 65–116.

Ford, C. A., Millstein, S. G., Halpern-Felsher, B. L., & Irwin, C. E., Jr. (1997). Influence of physician confidentiality assurances on adolescents' willingness to disclose information and seek future health care. A randomized controlled trial. *JAMA, 278*(12), 1029–1034.

Ford, J. L., & Browning, C. R. (2011). Neighborhood social disorganization and the acquisition of trichomoniasis among young adults in the United States. *American Journal of Public Health, 101*(9), 1696–1703.

Fortenberry, J. D., Tu, W., Harezlak, J., Katz, B. P., & Orr, D. P. (2002). Condom use as a function of time in new and established adolescent sexual relationships. *American Journal of Public Health, 92*(2), 211–213.

Franklin, C., Grant, D., Corcoran, J., Miller, P., & Bultman, L. (1997). Effectiveness of prevention programs for adolescent pregnancy: A meta-analysis. *Journal of Marriage and Family, 59*, 551–567.

Frisco, M. L. (2005). Parental involvement and young women's contraceptive use. *Journal of Marriage and Family, 67*, 110–121.

Frost, J. J. (2008). Trends in US women's use of sexual and reproductive health care services, 1995–2002. *American Journal of Public Health, 98*(10), 1814–1817.

Gavin, L., MacKay, A. P., Brown, K., Harrier, S., Ventura, S. J., Kann, L., et al. (2009). Sexual and reproductive health of persons aged 10–24 years – United States, 2002–2007. *MMWR Surveillance Summaries, 58*(6), 1–58.

Gibbons, F. X., Gerrard, M., Vande Lune, L. S., Wills, T. A., Brody, G., & Conger, R. D. (2004). Context and cognition: Environmental risk, social influence, and adolescent substance use. *Personality and Social Psychology Bulletin, 30*, 1048–1061.

Graber, J. A., Brooks-Gunn, J., & Galen, B. R. (1998). Betwixt and between: Sexuality in the context of adolescent transitions. In R. Jessor (Ed.), *New perspectives of adolescent risk behavior (pp. 270–316).* Cambridge, MA: Cambridge University Press.

Gupta, N., Corrado, S., & Goldstein, M. (2008). Hormonal contraception for the adolescent. *Pediatrics in Review, 29*(11), 386–396. [quiz 397].

Guttmacher Institute. (2010). *In brief: Facts on contraceptive use in the United States.* Retrieved December 5, 2011, from http://www.guttmacher.org/pubs/fb_contr_use.html.

Guttmacher Institute. (2011, December 1). State policies in brief: Minors' access to contraceptive services. Retrieved December 7, 2011, from <http://www.guttmacher.org/statecenter/spibs/spib_MACS.pdf>.

Guyatt, G. H., DiCenso, A., Farewell, V., Willan, A., & Griffith, L. (2000). Randomized trials versus observational studies in adolescent pregnancy prevention. *Journal of Clinical Epidemiology, 53*(2), 167–174.

Hagger, M. S., Chatzisarantis, N. L., & Biddle, S. J. (2002). The influence of autonomous and controlling motives on physical activity intentions within the Theory of Planned Behaviour. *British Journal of Health Psychology, 7*(Part 3), 283–297.

Halpern, C. T., Waller, M. W., Spriggs, A., & Hallfors, D. D. (2006). Adolescent predictors of emerging adult sexual patterns. *Journal of Adolescent Health, 39*(6) 926, e921-910.

Henry-Reid, L. M., O'Connor, K. G., Klein, J. D., Cooper, E., Flynn, P., & Futterman, D. C. (2010). Current pediatrician practices in identifying high-risk behaviors of adolescents. *Pediatrics, 125*(4), e741–e747.

Hoffman, S. (2006). *By the numbers: The public costs of teen childbearing.* Washington, DC: National Campaign to Prevent Teen Pregnancy.

House, L. D., Bates, J., Markham, C. M., & Lesesne, C. (2010). Competence as a predictor of sexual and reproductive health outcomes for youth: A systematic review. *Journal of Adolescent Health, 46*(3 Suppl), S7–S22.

Howard, D. E., & Wang, M. Q. (2005). Psychosocial correlates of U.S. adolescents who report a history of forced sexual intercourse. *Journal of Adolescent Health, 36*(5), 372–379.

Hoyle, R. H., Fejfar, M. C., & Miller, J. D. (2000). Personality and sexual risk taking: A quantitative review. *Journal of Personality, 68*(6), 1203–1231.

Hust, S. J. T., Brown, J. D., & L'Engle, K. L. (2008). Boys will be boys and girls better be prepared: An analysis of the rare sexual health messages in young adolescents' media. *Mass Communication & Society, 11,* 3–23.

Johnson, B.T. (2010). *Contextual influences on adolescent risk behavior: Mass media.* Technical report commissioned by the National Research Council's and Institute of Medicine Board on Children, Youth, and Families Committee on the Science of Adolescence, for the Workshop on *Understanding and Preventing Adolescent Risk Behavior: Integrating Findings across Domains of Influence.*

Johnson, B. T., & Boynton, M. B. (2010). Putting attitudes in their place: Behavioral prediction in the face of competing variables. In J. P. Forgas, J. Cooper, & W. Crano (Eds.), *The psychology of attitudes: The Sydney symposium of social psychology (pp. 19–38).* London, UK: Cambridge University Press.

Johnson, B. T., Carey, M. P., Marsh, K. L., Levin, K. D., & Scott-Sheldon, L. A. (2003). Interventions to reduce sexual risk for the human immunodeficiency virus in adolescents, 1985–2000: A research synthesis. *Archives of Pediatrics & Adolescent Medicine, 157*(4), 381–388.

Johnson, B. T., Redding, C. A., DiClemente, R. J., Mustanski, B. S., Dodge, B., Sheeran, P., et al. (2010). A network-individual-resource model for HIV prevention. *AIDS Behavioral, 14*(Suppl 2), 204–221.

Johnson, B.T., Scott-Sheldon, L. A., & Carey, M. P. (2010). Meta-synthesis of health behavior change meta-analyses. *American Journal of Public Health, 100*(11), 2193–2198.

Johnson, B. T., Scott-Sheldon, L. A., Huedo-Medina, T. B., & Carey, M. P. (2011). Interventions to reduce sexual risk for human immunodeficiency virus in adolescents: A meta-analysis of trials, 1985–2008. *Archives of Pediatrics & Adolescent Medicine, 165*(1), 77–84.

Johnson, B. T., Scott-Sheldon, L. A., Smoak, N. D., Lacroix, J. M., Anderson, J. R., & Carey, M. P. (2009). Behavioral interventions for African Americans to reduce sexual risk of HIV: A meta-analysis of randomized controlled trials. *Journal of Acquired Immune Deficiency Syndromes, 51*(4), 492–501.

Jones, R. K., Purcell, A., Singh, S., & Finer, L. B. (2005). Adolescents' reports of parental knowledge of adolescents' use of sexual health services and their reactions to mandated parental notification for prescription contraception. *JAMA, 293*(3), 340–348.

Kahn, J. A., Kaplowitz, R. A., Goodman, E., & Emans, S. J. (2002). The association between impulsiveness and sexual risk behaviors in adolescent and young adult women. *Journal of Adolescent Health, 30*(4), 229–232.

Kaiser Family Foundation. (2011). *Sexual Health of Adolescents and Young Adults in the United States*. Menlo Park, CA. Retrieved from <http://www.kff.org/womenshealth/upload/3040-05.pdf>.

Kass-Wolff, J. H. (2001). Bone loss in adolescents using Depo-Provera. *Journal of the Society of Pediatric Nurses, 6*(1), 21–31.

Kelley, S. S., Borawski, E. A., Flocke, S. A., & Keen, K. J. (2003). The role of sequential and concurrent sexual relationships in the risk of sexually transmitted diseases among adolescents. *Journal of Adolescent Health, 32*(4), 296–305.

Kenyon, D. B., Sieving, R. E., Jerstad, S. J., Pettingell, S. L., & Skay, C. L. (2010). Individual, interpersonal, and relationship factors predicting hormonal and condom use consistency among adolescent girls. *Journal of Pediatric Health Care, 24*(4), 241–249.

Kerrigan, D., Witt, S., Glass, B., Chung, S. E., & Ellen, J. (2006). Perceived neighborhood social cohesion and condom use among adolescents vulnerable to HIV/STI. *AIDS Behavioral, 10*(6), 723–729.

Kim, C. R., & Free, C. (2008). Recent evaluations of the peer-led approach in adolescent sexual health education: A systematic review. *Perspectives on Sexual and Reproductive Health, 40*(3), 144–151.

Kim, C., Gebremariam, A., Iwashyna, T. J., Dalton, V. K., & Lee, J. M. (2011). Longitudinal influences of friends and parents upon unprotected vaginal intercourse in adolescents. *Contraception, 83*(2), 138–144.

Kim, N., Stanton, B., Li, X., Dickersin, K., & Galbraith, J. (1997). Effectiveness of the 40 adolescent AIDS-risk reduction interventions: A quantitative review. *Journal of Adolescent Health, 20*(3), 204–215.

Kirby, D. B. (2007). Emerging answers, research findings on programs to reduce teen pregnancy and sexually transmitted disease. Retrieved from <http://www.thenationalcampaign.org/EA2007/EA2007_full.pdf>.

Kirby, D. B. (2008). The impact of abstinence and comprehensive sex and STD/HIV education programs on adolescent sexual behavior. *Sexuality Research & Social Policy, 5*, 18–27.

Klein, J., Rossbach, C., Nijher, H., Geist, M., Wilson, K., Cohn, S., et al. (2001). Where do adolescents get their condoms? *Journal of Adolescent Health, 29*(3), 186–193.

Kohler, P. K., Manhart, L. E., & Lafferty, W. E. (2008). Abstinence-only and comprehensive sex education and the initiation of sexual activity and teen pregnancy. *Journal of Adolescent Health, 42*(4), 344–351.

Kost, K., Singh, S., Vaughan, B., Trussell, J., & Bankole, A. (2008). Estimates of contraceptive failure from the 2002 National Survey of Family Growth. *Contraception, 77*(1), 10–21.

Krauss, B. J., & Miller, K. S. (2012). Parents as HIV/AIDS educators. In W. Pequegnat, C. C. Bell, B. J. Krauss, & K. S. Miller (Eds.), *Family and HIV/AIDS* (pp. 97–120). New York, NY: Springer.

Kreider, R. M., & Ellis, R. (2011). Number, timing, and duration of marriages and divorces: 2009: *Current population reports.* Washington, DC: U.S. Census Bureau. P70-125.

Kroger, J. (2007). *Identity development: Adolescence through adulthood.* Thousand Oaks, CA: Sage.

Landor, A., Simons, L. G., Simons, R. L., Brody, G. H., & Gibbons, F. X. (2011). The role of religiosity in the relationship between parents, peers, and adolescent risky sexual behavior. *Journal of Youth Adolescent, 40*(3), 296–309.

Lane, S. D., Rubinstein, R. A., Keefe, R. H., Webster, N., Cibula, D. A., Rosenthal, A., et al. (2004). Structural violence and racial disparity in HIV transmission. *Journal of Health Care for the Poor and Underserved, 15*(3), 319–335.

Lopez, L. M., Tolley, E. E., Grimes, D. A., & Chen-Mok, M. (2009). Theory-based strategies for improving contraceptive use: A systematic review. *Contraception, 79*(6), 411–417.

Luthar, S. S. (2003). The culture of affluence: Psychological costs of material wealth. *Child Development, 74*(6), 1581–1593.

Magnusson, B. M., Masho, S. W., & Lapane, K. L. (2012). Early age at first intercourse and subsequent gaps in contraceptive use. *Journal of Women's Health (Larchmt), 21*(1), 73–79.

Manlove, J., Ikramullah, E., & Terry-Humen, E. (2008). Condom use and consistency among male adolescents in the United States. *Journal of Adolescent Health, 43*(4), 325–333.

Manlove, J., Ikramullah, E., Mincieli, L., Holcombe, E., & Danish, S. (2009). Trends in sexual experience, contraceptive use, and teenage childbearing: 1992–2002. *Journal of Adolescent Health, 44*(5), 413–423.

Manlove, J., Ryan, S., & Franzetta, K. (2004). Contraceptive use and consistency in U.S. teenagers' most recent sexual relationships. *Perspectives on Sexual and Reproductive Health, 36*(6), 265–275.

Martinez, G., Copen, C. E., & Abma, J. C. (2011). Teenagers in the United States: Sexual activity, contraceptive use, and childbearing, 2006–2010 National Survey of Family Growth. National Center for Health Statistics. *Vital and Health Statistics, 23*, 31.

Martino, S. C., Elliott, M. N., Collins, R. L., Kanouse, D. E., & Berry, S. H. (2008). Virginity pledges among the willing: Delays in first intercourse and consistency of condom use. *Journal of Adolescent Health, 43*(4), 341–348.

Maslowsky, J., Buvinger, E., Keating, D. P., Steinberg, L., & Cauffman, E. (2011). Cost-benefit analysis mediation of the relationship between sensation seeking and risk behavior. *Personality and Individual Differences, 51*(7), 802–806.

McCree, D. H., Wingood, G. M., DiClemente, R., Davies, S., & Harrington, K. F. (2003). Religiosity and risky sexual behavior in African-American adolescent females. *Journal of Adolescent Health, 33*(1), 2–8.

Meade, C. S., & Ickovics, J. R. (2005). Systematic review of sexual risk among pregnant and mothering teens in the USA: Pregnancy as an opportunity for integrated prevention of STD and repeat pregnancy. *Social Science & Medicine, 60*(4), 661–678.

Mullen, P. D., Ramirez, G., Strouse, D., Hedges, L. V., & Sogolow, E. (2002). Meta-analysis of the effects of behavioral HIV prevention interventions on the sexual risk behavior of sexually experienced adolescents in controlled studies in the United States. *Journal of Acquired Immune Deficiency Syndromes, 30*(Suppl 1), S94–S105.

Noar, S. M., Benac, C. N., & Harris, M. S. (2007). Does tailoring matter? Meta-analytic review of tailored print health behavior change interventions. *Psychological Bulletin, 133*(4), 673–693.

Ott, M. A., Adler, N. E., Millstein, S. G., Tschann, J. M., & Ellen, J. M. (2002). The trade-off between hormonal contraceptives and condoms among adolescents. *Perspectives on Sexual and Reproductive Health, 34*(1), 6–14.

Parkes, A., Henderson, M., Wight, D., & Nixon, C. (2011). Is parenting associated with teenagers' early sexual risk-taking, autonomy and relationship with sexual partners? *Perspectives on Sexual and Reproductive Health, 43*, 30–40.

Paz-Bailey, G., Koumans, E. H., Sternberg, M., Pierce, A., Papp, J., Unger, E. R., et al. (2005). The effect of correct and consistent condom use on chlamydial and gonococcal infection among urban adolescents. *Archives of Pediatrics & Adolescent Medicine, 159*(6), 536–542.

Pinkerton, S. D., & Abramson, P. R. (1997). Effectiveness of condoms in preventing HIV transmission. *Social Science & Medicine, 44*(9), 1303–1312.

Portnoy, D. B., Scott-Sheldon, L. A., Johnson, B. T., & Carey, M. P. (2008). Computer-delivered interventions for health promotion and behavioral risk reduction: A meta-analysis of 75 randomized controlled trials, 1988–2007. *Preventive Medicine, 47*(1), 3–16.

Posner, R. B. (2006). Early menarche: A review of research on trends in timing, racial differences, etiology and psychosocial consequences. *Sex Roles, 54*, 315–322.

Prejean, J., Song, R., Hernandez, A., Ziebell, R., Green, T., Walker, F., et al. (2011). Estimated HIV incidence in the United States, 2006–2009. *PLoS One, 6* e17502–e17502.

Raj, A., Reed, E., Miller, E., Decker, M. R., Rothman, E. F., & Silverman, J. G. (2007). Contexts of condom use and non-condom use among young adolescent male perpetrators of dating violence. *AIDS Care, 19*(8), 970–973.

Robin, L., Dittus, P., Whitaker, D., Crosby, R., Ethier, K., Mezoff, J., et al. (2004). Behavioral interventions to reduce incidence of HIV, STD, and pregnancy among adolescents: A decade in review. *Journal of Adolescent Health, 34*(1), 3–26.

Rosenberger, J. G., Bell, D. L., McBride, K. R., Fortenberry, J. D., & Ott, M. A. (2010). Condoms and developmental contexts in younger adolescent boys. *Sexually Transmitted Infections, 86*(5), 400–403.

Rostosky, S. S., Regnerus, M. D., & Wright, M. L. (2003). Coital debut: The role of religiosity and sex attitudes in the Add Health Survey. *Journal of Sex Research, 40*(4), 358–367.

Rostosky, S. S., Wilcox, B. L., Wright, M. L. C., & Randall, B. A. (2004). The impact of religiosity on adolescent sexual behavior: A review of the evidence. *Journal of Adolescent Research, 19*, 677–697.

Ryan, S., Franzetta, K., & Manlove, J. (2007). Knowledge, perceptions, and motivations for contraception: Influence on teens' contraceptive consistency. *Youth & Society, 39*, 182–208.

Sallis, J. F., Owen, N., & Fisher, E. B. (2008). Ecological models of health behavior. In K. Glanz, B. K. Rimer, & K. Viswanath (Eds.), *Health behavior and health education: Theory, research, and practice (pp. 465–485)* (4th ed.). San Francisco, CA: Jossy-Bass.

Santelli, J. S., & Melnikas, A. J. (2010). Teen fertility in transition: Recent and historic trends in the United States. *Annual Review of Public Health, 31*, 371–383. [374 p following 383].

Santelli, J. S., Lindberg, L. D., Finer, L. B., & Singh, S. (2007). Explaining recent declines in adolescent pregnancy in the United States: The contribution of abstinence and improved contraceptive use. *American Journal of Public Health, 97*(1), 150–156.

Santelli, J. S., Morrow, B., Anderson, J. E., & Lindberg, L. D. (2006). Contraceptive use and pregnancy risk among U.S. high school students, 1991–2003. *Perspectives on Sexual and Reproductive Health, 38*(2), 106–111.

Santelli, J. S., Ott, M. A., Lyon, M., Rogers, J., & Summers, D. (2006). Abstinence-only education policies and programs: A position paper of the Society for Adolescent Medicine. *Journal of Adolescent Health, 38*(1), 83–87.

Santelli, J. S., Ott, M. A., Lyon, M., Rogers, J., Summers, D., & Schleifer, R. (2006). Abstinence and abstinence-only education: A review of U.S. policies and programs. *Journal of Adolescent Health, 38*(1), 72–81.

Sayegh, M. A., Fortenberry, J. D., Shew, M., & Orr, D. P. (2006). The developmental association of relationship quality, hormonal contraceptive choice and condom non-use among adolescent women. *Journal of Adolescent Health, 39*(3), 388–395.

Seidman, S. N., & Rieder, R. O. (1994). A review of sexual behavior in the United States. *The American Journal of Psychiatry, 151*(3), 330–341.

Sexuality Information and Education Council of the United States. (2012). President's fiscal year 2013 budget proves continued commitment to sex education. Retrieved May 15, 2012, from <http://www.siecus.org/index.cfm?fuseaction=Feature.showFeature&FeatureID = 2122>.

Shafii, T., Stovel, K., & Holmes, K. (2007). Association between condom use at sexual debut and subsequent sexual trajectories: A longitudinal study using biomarkers. *American Journal of Public Health, 97*(6), 1090–1095.

Sheeran, P., Abraham, C., & Orbell, S. (1999). Psychosocial correlates of heterosexual condom use: A meta-analysis. *Psychological Bulletin, 125*(1), 90–132.

Silva, M. (2002). The effectiveness of school-based sex education programs in the promotion of abstinent behavior: A meta-analysis. *Health Education Research, 17*(4), 471–481.

Sinha, J. W., Cnaan, R. A., & Gelles, R. J. (2007). Adolescent risk behaviors and religion: Findings from a national study. *The Journal of Adolescent, 30*(2), 231–249.

Soomar, J. N., Fisher, A. J., & Mathews, C. (2009). Sexual coercion and adolescent risk behaviour: A systematic literature review. *Journal of Child and Adolescent Mental Health, 21*(2), 103–126.

Spitalnick, J. S., DiClemente, R. J., Wingood, G. M., Crosby, R. A., Milhausen, R. R., Sales, J. M., et al. (2007). Brief report: Sexual sensation seeking and its relationship to risky sexual behaviour among African-American adolescent females. *The Journal of Adolescent, 30*(1), 165–173.

Stanger-Hall, K. F., & Hall, D. W. (2011). Abstinence-only education and teen pregnancy rates: Why we need comprehensive sex education in the U.S. *PLoS One, 6*(10), e24658.

Steinberg, L. (2007). Risk-taking in adolescence: New perspectives from brain and behavioral sciences. *Current Directions in Psychological Science, 16*, 55–59.

Steinberg, L. (2008). A social neuroscience perspective on adolescent risk-taking. *Developmental Review, 28*(1), 78–106.

Steinberg, L. (2010). A dual systems model of adolescent risk-taking. *Developmental Psychobiology, 52*(3), 216–224.

Stevens-Simon, C., Kelly, L., Singer, D., & Cox, A. (1996). Why pregnant adolescents say they did not use contraceptives prior to conception. *Journal of Adolescent Health, 19*(1), 48–53. [discussion 54–45].

Susman, E. J., & Rogol, A. (2009). Puberty and psychological development (3rd ed.). In R. M. Lerner & L. Steinberg (Eds.), *Handbook of adolescent psychology* (Vol. 1). Hoboken, NJ: Wiley & Sons.

Sznitman, S. R., Horner, J., Salazar, L. F., Romer, D., Vanable, P. A., Carey, M. P., et al. (2009). Condom failure: Examining the objective and cultural meanings expressed in interviews with African American adolescents. *Journal of Sex Research, 46*(4), 309–318.

Sznitman, S. R., Romer, D., Brown, L. K., DiClemente, R. J., Valois, R. F., Vanable, P. A., et al. (2009). Prevalence, correlates, and sexually transmitted infection risk related to coitus interruptus among African-American adolescents. *Sexually Transmitted Diseases, 36*(4), 218–220.

Teitelman, A. M., Dichter, M. E., Cederbaum, J. A., & Campbell, J. C. (2007). Intimate partner violence, condom use and HIV risk for adolescent girls: Gaps in the literature and future directions for research and intervention. *Journal of HIV/AIDS Prevention in Children & Youth, 8*(2), 65–93.

The Henry J. Kaiser Family Foundation. (2003). National Survey of Adolescents and Young Adults: Sexual health knowledge, attitudes, and experiences. Retrieved December 12, 2011, from <http://www.kff.org/youthhivstds/upload/National-Survey-of-Adolescents-and-Young-Adults.pdf>.

The National Campaign to Prevent Teen and Unplanned Pregnancy. (2011). Counting it up: The public costs of teen childbearing. Retrieved May 15, 2012, from <http://www.thenationalcampaign.org/costs/pdf/counting-it-up/key-data.pdf>.

Tolaymat, L. L., & Kaunitz, A. M. (2007). Long-acting contraceptives in adolescents. *Current Opinion in Obstetrics & Gynecology, 19*(5), 453–460.

Tolman, D. L., & McClelland, S. I. (2011). Normative sexuality development in adolescence: A decade in review, 2000–2009. *Journal of Research on Adolescence, 21,* 242–255.

Trussell, J. (2011). Contraceptive failure in the United States. *Contraception, 83*(5), 397–404.

Underhill, K., Operario, D., & Montgomery, P. (2007). Systematic review of abstinence-plus HIV prevention programs in high-income countries. *PLoS Medicine, 4*(9), e275.

US Department of Health and Human Services. *Health People 2020.* Retrieved December 5, 2011, from <http://www.healthypeople.gov/2020/default.aspx>.

Ventura, S. J., & Hamilton, B. E. (2011). U.S. teenage birth rate resumes decline. *NCHS Data Briefs, 58,* 1–8.

Villarruel, A. M., Jemmott, J. B., III, Jemmott, L. S., & Ronis, D. L. (2007). Predicting condom use among sexually experienced Latino adolescents. *Western Journal of Nursing Research, 29*(6), 724–738.

Weinstock, H., Berman, S., & Cates, W., Jr. (2004). Sexually transmitted diseases among American youth: Incidence and prevalence estimates, 2000. *Perspectives on Sexual and Reproductive Health, 36*(1), 6–10.

Williams, R. L., & Fortenberry, J. D. (2011). Update on adolescent condom use. *Current Opinion in Obstetrics & Gynecology, 23*(5), 350–354.

Woodrome, S. E., Zimet, G. D., Orr, D. P., & Fortenberry, J. D. (2006). Dyadic alcohol use and relationship quality as predictors of condom non-use among adolescent females. *Journal of Adolescent Health, 38*(3), 305–306.

World Health Organization. (2006). Defining sexual health: Report of a technical consultation on sexual health. Geneva, Switzerland.

Zaleski, E. H., & Schiaffino, K. M. (2000). Religiosity and sexual risk-taking behavior during the transition to college. *Journal of Adolescent, 23*(2), 223–227.

Zuckerman, M. (2007). *Sensation seeking and risky behavior.* Washington, DC: American Psychological Association.

# CHAPTER 10

# Influence of Alcohol and Illicit Drug Use on Sexual Behavior

Michael Windle, Jessica M. Sales, and Rebecca C. Windle
Emory University, Atlanta, Georgia[1]

Adolescence is a phase in the lifespan characterized by numerous changes in biological (e.g., puberty), psychological (e.g., self-identity), and social (e.g., romantic relationships) levels of organization, as well as the initiation and expression of behaviors related to substance use and sexual behavior (Windle et al., 2008). The intersection among age normative (e.g., puberty) and non-normative (e.g., sexual abuse) events, developmental changes in biopsychosocial systems, and substance use and sexual behavior is critical both to understanding adolescent development and to devising prevention programs and social policies that serve to promote positive health and deter immediate and long-term adverse outcomes. National survey data have clearly indicated that adolescents engage in high rates of both substance use and sexual behavior (Eaton et al., 2010; Johnston, O'Malley, Bachman, & Schulenberg, 2011), and that the combination of these behaviors lead to deleterious short- and long-term health outcomes. As such, the focus of this chapter is on the intersection of these discrete behaviors among teens, and on recent prevention and treatment efforts aimed at ameliorating their adverse health effects.

In pursuing this objective, the chapter is divided into five components. First, descriptive epidemiologic findings are provided on national studies of the intersection between substance use and sexual behaviors during adolescence. Second, the interrelationships among substance use, violence, and sexual behaviors are presented, with specific reference to childhood physical and sexual abuse and subsequent substance use and sexual behavior, and substance use and dating violence/sexual assault. Third, some common theories and proposed mechanisms that account for the interrelations between substance use and sexual behavior are provided. These are not intended to be exhaustive, but rather representative of ways of viewing these relationships

---

[1] Correspondence to: Michael Windle, PhD, Emory University, Department of Behavioral Science and Health Education, 1518 Clifton Road NE, Room 564, Atlanta, GA 30322. Phone 404-727-9868; email mwindle@emory.edu

and possible explanatory mechanisms. Fourth, selective findings from prevention and intervention studies are presented to provide insight into the ways that substance use is being incorporated into prevention or intervention trials, and how it may be impacting outcomes. Fifth, conclusions and future directions are provided to further illuminate extant knowledge and new pathways to be pursued in future research to foster more impactful interventions and promote healthy adolescent behaviors and outcomes.

## DESCRIPTIVE EPIDEMIOLOGY
## Alcohol and Other Substance Use and Sexual Intercourse Patterns

The Centers for Disease Control and Prevention (CDC) collects annual health behavior statistics on nationally representative samples of 9th through 12th graders in their school settings. Known as the Youth Risk Behavior Survey (YRBS), the CDC publishes findings on a range of health-related behaviors, including substance use and sexual activity. Data from the YRBS are referred to frequently in this chapter, and substance use and sexual behavior data from the 2009 YRBS are presented in Tables 10.1 and 10.2 (Eaton et al., 2010).

Current alcohol and marijuana use, current sexual intercourse, and the high-risk behavior of binge drinking are all highly prevalent among teenagers, and this is especially evident among older adolescents (see Tables 10.1 and 10.2). Along with these high percentages is the consistent finding that substance use is strongly related to adolescents' engagement in risky sexual behaviors, and that there is a dose–response relationship in that the association with risky sexual behaviors becomes stronger with higher levels of substance use (Connell, Gilreath, & Hansen, 2009; Nkansah-Amankra, Diedhiou, Agbanu, Harrod, & Dhawan, 2011; Seth, DiClemente, Wingood, Rose, & Patel, 2011). For example, Connell et al. (2009) reported that among adolescents who participated in the 2005 YRBS, escalating levels of substance use were strongly associated with riskier sexual behavior. This was especially the case for females who evidenced greater sexual risk when their substance use behaviors were more intensive (i.e., frequent poly-substance use) relative to their male counterparts. Similarly, using data from the 2005 Colorado YRBS, Nkansah-Amankra et al. (2011) found that illegal drug use substantially increased the odds of reporting an earlier onset of sexual intercourse and of having multiple sex partners. Using data from a sample of adolescent African American females, Seth et al. (2011) analyzed longitudinal data to assess cross-temporal relationships between heavy alcohol use (i.e., ≥3 drinks in one sitting across the past 60 days) and high-risk

**Table 10.1** Prevalence of Alcohol And Marijuana Use Among Adolescents by Sex, Race/Ethnicity, and Grade—United States, 2009

| Race/ethnicity and grade level | Early onset alcohol use (<13 years)[a] Female (%) | Male (%) | Total (%) | Current alcohol use[b] Female (%) | Male (%) | Total (%) | Binge drinking[c] Female (%) | Male (%) | Total (%) |
|---|---|---|---|---|---|---|---|---|---|
| Non-Hispanic white | 15.5 | 20.3 | 18.1 | 45.9 | 43.6 | 44.7 | 27.5 | 28.0 | 27.8 |
| Non-Hispanic black | 21.9 | 27.6 | 24.9 | 35.6 | 31.2 | 33.4 | 12.1 | 15.3 | 13.7 |
| Hispanic | 23.2 | 31.0 | 27.1 | 43.5 | 42.4 | 42.9 | 23.3 | 25.1 | 24.1 |
| Grade 9 | 26.6 | 29.5 | 28.1 | 35.3 | 28.4 | 31.5 | 17.2 | 13.6 | 15.3 |
| Grade 10 | 18.5 | 25.4 | 22.2 | 41.2 | 40.1 | 40.6 | 21.1 | 23.3 | 22.3 |
| Grade 11 | 14.9 | 20.7 | 17.9 | 45.6 | 45.7 | 45.7 | 26.4 | 30.0 | 28.3 |
| Grade 12 | 10.9 | 17.3 | 14.2 | 50.7 | 52.6 | 51.7 | 30.4 | 36.6 | 33.5 |

| Race/ethnicity and grade level | Ever used marijuana[d] Female (%) | Male (%) | Total (%) | Early onset marijuana use (<13 years) Female (%) | Male (%) | Total (%) | Current marijuana use[e] Female (%) | Male (%) | Total (%) |
|---|---|---|---|---|---|---|---|---|---|
| Non-Hispanic white | 33.7 | 37.4 | 35.7 | 4.0 | 7.1 | 5.7 | 17.9 | 23.0 | 20.7 |
| Non-Hispanic black | 38.0 | 44.3 | 41.2 | 4.1 | 16.1 | 10.2 | 18.7 | 25.6 | 22.2 |
| Hispanic | 35.6 | 44.2 | 39.9 | 7.8 | 12.9 | 10.3 | 18.2 | 25.0 | 21.6 |
| Grade 9 | 25.7 | 26.9 | 26.4 | 6.8 | 11.1 | 9.1 | 15.5 | 15.5 | 15.5 |
| Grade 10 | 33.0 | 37.7 | 35.5 | 5.6 | 10.6 | 8.3 | 17.9 | 23.9 | 21.1 |
| Grade 11 | 39.5 | 44.3 | 42.0 | 4.3 | 8.6 | 6.5 | 19.5 | 26.7 | 23.2 |
| Grade 12 | 40.2 | 50.9 | 45.6 | 2.6 | 7.8 | 5.2 | 19.1 | 29.9 | 24.6 |

[a] Other than a few sips.
[b] Had at least one drink of alcohol on at least 1 day during the 30 days before the survey.
[c] Had five or more drinks in a row within a couple of hours on at least 1 day during the 30 days before the survey.
[d] Used marijuana one or more times during their life.
[e] Used marijuana one or more times during the 30 days before the survey.
Data are from the Youth Risk Behavior Surveillance Survey—United States, 2009 (Eaton et al., 2010).

sexual behaviors. Controlling for outcome measures at baseline, they found that heavy alcohol use prospectively predicted a range of unsafe sexual practices, including having sex with multiple partners during the past 60 days, and having sex while high on alcohol or drugs.

Empirical findings suggest that earlier onsets of substance use and sexual intercourse represent risk factors for unsafe sexual behaviors in later

Table 10.2 Prevalence of Sexual Behaviors Among Adolescents by Sex, Race/Ethnicity, and Grade—United States, 2009

| Race/ethnicity and grade level | Ever had sexual intercourse Female (%) | Male (%) | Total (%) | Currently sexually active[a] Female (%) | Male (%) | Total (%) | Early onset sexual intercourse (<13 years) Female (%) | Male (%) | Total (%) |
|---|---|---|---|---|---|---|---|---|---|
| Non-Hispanic white | 44.7 | 39.6 | 42.0 | 35.4 | 28.9 | 32.0 | 2.2 | 4.4 | 3.4 |
| Non-Hispanic black | 58.3 | 72.1 | 65.2 | 45.0 | 50.3 | 47.7 | 5.6 | 24.9 | 15.2 |
| Hispanic | 45.4 | 52.8 | 49.1 | 34.1 | 35.0 | 34.6 | 3.7 | 9.8 | 6.7 |
| Grade 9 | 29.3 | 33.6 | 31.6 | 21.6 | 21.2 | 21.4 | 3.6 | 11.3 | 7.7 |
| Grade 10 | 39.6 | 41.9 | 40.9 | 29.3 | 28.8 | 29.1 | 3.6 | 9.0 | 6.5 |
| Grade 11 | 52.5 | 53.4 | 53.0 | 41.5 | 39.1 | 40.3 | 2.7 | 5.9 | 4.3 |
| Grade 12 | 65.0 | 59.6 | 62.3 | 53.1 | 45.1 | 49.1 | 2.2 | 6.4 | 4.4 |

| Race/ethnicity and grade level | Had sexual intercourse with ≥4 persons during their life Female (%) | Male (%) | Total (%) | Used a condom during last sexual intercourse[b] Female (%) | Male (%) | Total (%) | Drank alcohol or used drugs before last sexual intercourse[b] Female (%) | Male (%) | Total (%) |
|---|---|---|---|---|---|---|---|---|---|
| Non-Hispanic white | 10.0 | 11.0 | 10.5 | 56.1 | 71.0 | 63.3 | 18.2 | 28.0 | 22.9 |
| Non-Hispanic black | 18.0 | 39.4 | 28.6 | 51.8 | 72.5 | 62.4 | 15.2 | 20.8 | 18.2 |
| Hispanic | 10.4 | 18.0 | 14.2 | 48.0 | 61.7 | 54.9 | 15.0 | 22.6 | 18.9 |
| Grade 9 | 6.3 | 11.1 | 8.8 | 57.7 | 69.9 | 64.0 | 23.5 | 25.9 | 24.7 |
| Grade 10 | 7.6 | 15.3 | 11.7 | 63.5 | 71.9 | 67.8 | 18.1 | 26.5 | 22.4 |
| Grade 11 | 12.9 | 17.5 | 15.2 | 54.0 | 68.9 | 61.4 | 14.7 | 25.9 | 20.3 |
| Grade 12 | 19.1 | 22.7 | 20.9 | 46.3 | 65.0 | 55.0 | 15.2 | 25.8 | 20.2 |

[a]Had sexual intercourse with at least one person during the three months before the survey.
[b]Among the 34.2% of students nationwide who were currently sexually active.
Data are from the Youth Risk Behavior Surveillance Survey—United States, 2009 (Eaton et al., 2010).

adolescence and young adulthood (Hingson, Heeren, Winter, & Wechsler, 2003; Strachman, Impett, Henson, & Pentz, 2009; Tubman, Windle, & Windle, 1996). Percentages of adolescents who reported earlier initiation of alcohol and marijuana use and of sexual intercourse are provided in Tables 10.1 and 10.2. As illustrated in these figures, the percentage of adolescents who reported drinking alcohol prior to age 13 was substantial, and this was especially true for younger teens and Non-Hispanic black and Hispanic teens. The percentages of youth who reported an earlier onset of marijuana use and sexual intercourse were lower, although a fair percentage of Non-Hispanic black males reported early onset of marijuana use (16.1%) and sexual intercourse (24.9%) relative to the other groups.

Strachman et al. (2009) reported data from a sample of young adolescents participating in a drug abuse prevention trial. They found that young adolescents' (6th and 7th graders) reports of alcohol consumption predicted earlier sexual intercourse debut which, in turn, predicted a higher number of lifetime sexual partners 10 years later. These results continued to be significant after controlling for a number of potentially confounding variables (e.g., race/ethnicity, sensation seeking, peer norms about alcohol use). Among a sample of college students, Hingson et al. (2003) found that a younger age of first drinking to intoxication was significantly related to students' reports that alcohol consumption caused unplanned sex and unprotected sex. For example, among those who reported their first intoxication to have occurred between 13 and 15 years of age, 31.4% indicated that drinking caused them to have unplanned sex in the past year. Comparable figures for those who reported first drinking to intoxication at ages 17, 18, and 19+ were, respectively, 23.0%, 17.6%, and 12.5% who reported unplanned sex due to alcohol consumption. In logistic regression models that controlled for a number of potentially confounding variables, these relationships continued to be significant, although including variables reflecting frequency of binge drinking and alcohol dependence decreased the strength of the relationship for early age of alcohol intoxication. In our own research with a school-based sample of adolescents, we found that an earlier onset of alcohol use (i.e., first getting drunk and/or first becoming a regular drinker at or before age 14 years) was significantly related to an earlier onset and more persistent pattern of sexual intercourse across a two-year period (Tubman et al., 1996).

In addition to the more general finding of the relationship between substance use and risky sexual behaviors is the finding that substance use proximal to sexual activity increases the probability that teens will engage in unsafe sexual practices, such as having intercourse with multiple partners (Cooper, Peirce, & Huselid, 1994; Morrison-Beedy, Carey, Crean, & Jones, 2011; Santelli, Robin, Brener, & Lowry, 2001). In this regard, according to the 2009 YRBS data (Table 10.2), a fair percentage of adolescents reported using substances proximal to sexual intercourse, and this was especially the case for males and younger females. Furthermore, the percentage of adolescents reporting sexual intercourse with four or more people in their lifetime was substantial, especially among Non-Hispanic black males and females, and older adolescents.

Using data from a community sample of African American and white adolescents, Cooper et al. (1994) investigated the prevalence of alcohol use at: (1) first lifetime intercourse; and (2) first intercourse with most recent partner. Rates of alcohol use concurrent with first sexual intercourse were 10%, and these rates increased to 17.5% for alcohol use at first intercourse with most recent partner. Cooper et al. suggested that the increase in alcohol use across the two sexual intercourse time points was probably due, in part, to increased age of respondents, given that the average time between these occasions was three years. Furthermore, at both intercourse occasions, adolescents who drank alcohol proximal to intercourse were more likely to engage in sexual risk behaviors (e.g., sex with a more casual vs. steady partner, failure to discuss risk-related topics such as sexual, drug, and STD history prior to intercourse) relative to those who did not drink. Morrison-Beedy et al. (2011) investigated the link between substance use and sexual behaviors in an urban sample of female adolescents (15–19 years) participating in a human immunodeficiency virus (HIV) prevention trial. The sample was predominantly African American (69%) and living in poverty (69% had participated in free school lunch programs). They found that girls who reported alcohol and/or drug use before sexual intercourse were more likely to report having multiple partners versus single partners. Also, girls who reported that their partners used alcohol and/or drugs before sexual intercourse were more likely to report having multiple partners versus single partners.

Data presented thus far have focused on the intersection of substance use and sexual behavior among heterosexual adolescents. However, it is important to investigate the substance use and sexual behaviors of sexual minority (defined in this chapter as gay, lesbian, and bisexual) adolescents who may be at greater risk to engage in unhealthy behaviors relative to their heterosexual counterparts (Brown & Melchiono, 2006; Corliss et al., 2010; Marshal et al., 2008). This minority group may be at greater risk for engagement in unhealthy behaviors, in part, due to the social stigma, prejudice, and discrimination, referred to as gay-related stress or minority stress (e.g., Haas et al., 2010), still attached to homosexuality and bisexuality and the attendant mental, physical, and emotional victimization that may occur against sexual minority adolescents (Brown & Melchiono, 2006; Haas et al., 2010).

Between 2001 and 2009, the CDC collected data (as part of the YRBS) from public high school students on sexual identity and sex of sexual contacts (Kann et al., 2011). The CDC data we present in Table 10.3 relates to the sex of sexual contacts (i.e., opposite sex only, same sex only, both sexes) rather than to sexual identity (i.e., heterosexual, gay or lesbian, bisexual).

We are presenting the former data in the event that it may be somewhat more representative of actual risk than, say, that of a young man who reports that he is heterosexual but has sex with both men and women. Based on current research findings, a somewhat greater risk would be attached to his answer that he has sex with both males and females rather than to his answer that he is heterosexual.

**Table 10.3** Alcohol, Substance Use, and Sexual Behaviors Among Sexual Minority Adolescents—United States, 2001-2009

| Variable | Opposite sex only [median (range)] | Same sex only [median (range)] | Both sexes [median (range)] |
|---|---|---|---|
| Early onset of alcohol use (<13 years) | 27.2% (21.4–35.3) | 34.5% (25.2–37.4) | 42.9% (30.4–58.4) |
| Binge drinking | 34.6% (15.9–44.4) | 32.7% (17.3–44.4) | 47.5% (33.0–63.3) |
| Early onset of marijuana use (<13 years) | 13.2% (8.7–21.0) | 18.5% (13.7–22.1) | 25.2% (18.8–44.9) |
| Current marijuana use | 33.5% (19.1–45.3) | 37.1% (25.5–44.3) | 49.1% (33.6–68.0) |
| Current cocaine use | 2.9% (0.5–8.1) | 9.2% (0.0–17.6) | 16.4% (2.4–39.2) |
| Ever used ecstasy | 7.3% (3.8–14.5) | 18.3% (8.7–23.3) | 25.2% (16.9–37.6) |
| Ever used heroin | 2.9% (1.3–5.3) | 11.2% (7.5–18.8) | 17.7% (9.9–35.8) |
| Ever used methamphetamine | 4.3% (2.2–14.1) | 15.7% (9.6–22.0) | 21.6% (12.3–44.2) |
| Ever injected illegal drugs | 2.6% (1.1–3.9) | 8.9% (3.7–16.5) | 14.1% (5.9–30.6) |
| Early onset sexual intercourse (<13 years) | 12.4% (5.3–17.8) | 15.8% (10.1–33.5) | 22.9% (13.5–42.6) |
| Ever had sexual intercourse with ≥4 persons during life | 25.8% (15.7–35.6) | 26.8% (11.4–37.3) | 44.1% (32.6–68.0) |
| Currently sexually active | 59.0% (50.8–74.9) | 52.4% (46.7–68.0) | 64.9% (58.1–87.4) |
| Used a condom during last sexual intercourse | 64.2% (58.9–73.5) | 59.6%[a] (42.5–62.6) | 44.1% (34.4–53.8) |
| Drank alcohol or used drugs before last sexual intercourse | 20.7% (14.0–24.8) | 27.2% (18.1–39.4) | 35.0% (24.1–57.6) |

[a]Male students only. Data are from the Youth Risk Behavior Surveillance Surveys—Selected Sites, United States, 2001–2009 (Kann et al., 2011).

Congruent with findings reported elsewhere (Brown & Melchiono, 2006; Corliss et al., 2010; Marshal et al., 2008), the data from the YRBS in Table 10.3 indicated that adolescents who reported having sex with same-sex partners only or with both male and female partners, relative to opposite-sex partners only, were more likely to report engagement in problematic alcohol and drug use behaviors and in risky sexual behaviors. This was especially true for adolescents who had sex with both males and females. These data suggest that sexual minority adolescents are more likely to engage in high-risk substance use and sexual behaviors, and are therefore at greater risk for adverse short- and long-term health consequences associated with these behaviors.

## Alcohol and Other Substance Use and Sexual Risk Outcomes

The risk of acquiring a sexually transmitted disease (STD), including HIV, is one of the most significant and immediate risks to the health and well-being of adolescents. This risk is substantially amplified for adolescent females because they are disproportionately impacted by STDs. Specifically, a recent CDC study estimated that approximately one in four teenage girls in the United States has a STD, and nearly half (48%) of the African American girls studied had at least one of the most common STDs (Forhan et al., 2008). Among youth, adolescent girls and minorities have been particularly affected. In 2009, females accounted for an estimated 23% of adolescents aged 13 to 19 years diagnosed with HIV infection, and 65% were black/African American, 18% were Hispanic/Latino, and 15% were white (CDC, 2011a).

A significant risk factor for acquiring an STD or HIV during adolescence is alcohol and substance use (Leigh & Stall, 1993). Alcohol or drug use may impair sexual decision-making, leading to unwanted or unprotected sexual intercourse (Castilla, Barrio, Belza, & Fuente, 1999; MacDonald, Fong, Zanna, & Martineau 2000). Prior research across multiple populations, including adolescents, suggests a link between alcohol consumption and high-risk sexual behaviors (Malow, Rosenberg, & Dévieux, 2005; Morrison et al., 2003; Thompson, Kao, & Thomas, 2005). The association between adolescent substance abuse and HIV risk has been well documented, with numerous studies indicating that adolescent substance abusers are at high risk of acquiring or transmitting HIV (e.g., Jemmott & Jemmott, 2001; Malow, Dévieux, Jennings, Lucenko, & Kalichman, 2001). This co-occurrence of substance use (e.g., alcohol, marijuana, cocaine, or other illicit drugs) and risky sexual behavior has been consistently identified across diverse samples of adolescents, ranging from normative school-aged populations to subsamples of adolescents typically identified as high-risk, such as homeless and runaway youth, those with mental illness, inner-city ethnic minorities, homosexual and bisexual adolescents, and teens in drug treatment programs or in the juvenile justice system (Donovan & McEwan, 1995).

For example, in a national survey conducted by the CDC, approximately 22% of high-school students in the United States reported using substances prior to sex (Eaton et al., 2010). Interestingly, similar rates were observed in a high-risk sample, where 25% of incarcerated adolescent males reported substance use prior to engaging in sexual activity, with 46% reporting that alcohol was readily available at the majority of social gatherings (Rolf, Nanda, Baldwin, Chandra, & Thompson, 1990). Substance-abusing adolescents are likely to report more sexual risk-taking than other high-risk adolescent sub-samples (i.e., inner-city minority youth, incarcerated youth, and homeless youth), placing them at heightened risk of acquiring or transmitting STDs or HIV (St. Lawrence, Crosby, Brasfield, & O'Bannon, 2002). For instance, adolescent substance abusers use condoms less frequently during sex, have more sexual partners, show lower self-efficacy regarding safer sexual behavior, have more permissive attitudes toward sex, lower perceived peer norms supporting safer sexual behavior, less HIV-related knowledge, and are more likely to engage in prostitution for money, drugs, food, or shelter, as well as more likely to have contracted an STD (Deas-Nesmith, Brady, White, & Campbell, 1999; Jemmott & Jemmott, 2001; Liau et al., 2002; Tapert, Aarons, Sedlar, & Brown, 2001). Furthermore, alcohol use is commonly cited as a reason for lack of condom use among high-risk adolescents (Bryan, Ray, & Cooper, 2007; Rosengard et al., 2006). These risky sexual practices are likely to persist into adulthood if the adolescent continues to abuse alcohol or illicit drugs (Tapert et al., 2001).

Alcohol use and illicit drug use have also been associated with testing positive for an STD in adolescent and young adult samples. Specifically, Cook et al. (2006) conducted a study with 448 men and women, aged 15–24, attending an urban STD clinic. Overall, 42.9% had an alcohol or marijuana disorder, and 30.6% had a confirmed STD. Participants with an alcohol or substance use disorder were significantly more likely to have multiple sexual partners, to be inconsistent condom users, and to have an STD. With a younger sample, Cook, Pollock, Rao, & Clark (2002) examined the relationship between alcohol use disorders and herpes simplex virus type 2, hepatitis B virus, and HIV among a sample of sexually active adolescents ($N = 240$, mean age 17.5) recruited from clinical and community settings, and found 55% had a lifetime history of alcohol use disorder. Among adolescent females, the seroprevalence of HSV-2 infections was significantly higher in those with an alcohol use disorder (19%), compared with those without an alcohol use disorder (10.5%). Further, Seth et al. (2011) explored alcohol use as a longitudinal predictor of sexual risk taking and STDs among African American adolescent females, a group disproportionately impacted by STDs/HIV. The results indicated that high quantity of alcohol use predicted a positive STD test for *Trichomonas vaginalis* over a 12-month follow-up period.

In addition to STDs and HIV, unintended pregnancy is a common occurrence among adolescents. While United States teens' pregnancy and birth rates have declined since 1990 (Ventura, Abma, Mosher, & Henshaw, 2009), they still remain high, and this is especially true for young women of color (CDC, 2011b). For example, in 2009, birth rates among adolescents aged 15–19 years were highest among Hispanics (70.1 per 1,000 females), followed by Non-Hispanic blacks (59.0 per 1,000 females), and then Non-Hispanic whites (25.6 per 1,000 females) (CDC, 2011b). The majority of pregnancies among teens (82%) are unplanned (Finer & Henshaw, 2006), and teen mothers are less likely to complete high school (CDC, 2011b). Further, the children of teen mothers are at risk for both short- and long-term adverse outcomes, including premature birth, low birth weight, cognitive deficits, lower educational achievement, incarceration, unemployment, and early parenthood (Cavazos-Rehg et al., 2011; CDC, 2011b).

As is the case with STDs and HIV, substance use has been found to be significantly associated with teen pregnancy. For example, Cavazos-Rehg et al. (2011) found that more-frequent marijuana use was significantly related to adolescents' reporting a history of pregnancy, as was daily cigarette use among teens who reported smoking initiation at or before 12 years of age. Likewise, Zapata, Hillis, Marchbanks, Curtis, & Lowry (2008) found that more-frequent methamphetamine use increased the odds of ever being pregnant or getting someone pregnant. Finally, Deardorff, Gonzales, Christopher, Roosa, & Millsap (2005), using path analysis with data from a sample of adolescent/young adult females, reported that earlier pubertal development was significantly related to earlier initiation of alcohol use and intercourse, that earlier initiation of alcohol use was related to earlier intercourse, and finally that earlier intercourse was related to an earlier age at first pregnancy. These findings suggest one path by which earlier alcohol use and sex may lead to earlier pregnancy among a subset (i.e., earlier pubertal development) of young women.

## ALCOHOL, DRUGS, INTERPERSONAL VIOLENCE, AND SEXUAL BEHAVIORS

Another major factor to consider when studying the intersection between adolescent substance use and sexual behaviors is interpersonal violence (IPV). Two areas of particular importance are the roles of childhood physical and sexual abuse on subsequent (adolescent and young adulthood) substance abuse and risky sexual behavior outcomes, and the roles of adolescent substance use and abuse in relation to dating violence and sexual assault. Research findings relevant to these issues are briefly summarized below.

### Childhood Sexual Abuse (CSA) and Alcohol and Drug Use

Both population-based and clinical treatment studies have supported consistent and strong associations between childhood sexual and physical abuse and a range of alcohol behaviors, including earlier age of initiation, earlier onset of alcohol disorder symptoms, more alcohol-related adverse consequences, heavier episodic (or binge) drinking, and a higher prevalence of the subsequent development of alcohol dependence (Lown, Nayak, Korcha, & Greenfield, 2011; Sartor, Agrawal, McCutcheon, Duncan, & Lynskey, 2008). For example, Lown et al. reported that individuals who reported CSA (versus no abuse) were seven times more likely to develop alcohol dependence and over 3.5 times more likely to report adverse alcohol-related consequences. Similarly, with a separate sample, Jonas et al. (2011) reported that individuals who reported CSA were 3.5 times more likely to develop alcohol dependence and over five times more likely to develop drug dependence. The findings of Jonas et al. also indicated that CSA was associated with a significant increase in the probability of sexual revictimization in adulthood. CSA has also been associated with more lifetime sexual partners and number of prior STD diagnoses (Senn, Carey, Vanable, Coury-Doniger, & Urban, 2007). Hence, CSA appears to be a critical factor in understanding the unfolding relationship between sexual behaviors, and serious levels of substance use and abuse from adolescence into young adulthood and beyond.

### Dating Violence and Alcohol and Drug Use

Estimates of dating violence among adolescents range from 15% to 40% contingent on the definitions used (e.g., verbal or physical violence versus violence resulting in a serious injury) and populations sampled (e.g., general population versus clinic samples). Despite variations in definitions and populations, most cross-sectional and more recent longitudinal studies support a significant association between alcohol or drug use and dating violence, some of which relates to more serious behaviors such as sexual assault (Rickert, Vaughan, & Wiemann, 2002). For example, Eaton, Davis, Barrios, Brener, & Noonan (2007) reported that dating violence victimization among a national sample of adolescents was 9%, and that the dating victimization was significantly associated with early alcohol initiation. In a longitudinal study of dating violence among an African American female sample, Raiford, Wingood, & DiClemente (2007) reported that using drugs at Time 1 was associated with a two-fold increase in prospective prediction of dating violence at Time 2 (1 year later) after controlling for Time 1 dating violence and other important predictors (e.g., socioeconomic status). Other studies (Wingood, DiClemente, McCree, Harrington, & Davies, 2001) have indicated that adolescent dating violence among African American females is associated with higher rates of STDs (2.8 times higher than those adolescents with no dating violence) and a 50% reduction in condom use.

Alcohol and other drug use are also frequently associated with IPV and sexual coercion among adolescents and young adults. Current estimates in the United States suggest that approximately 50% of sexual assault cases involving adolescents and young adults involve alcohol consumption (Abbey, Zawacki, Buck, Clinton, & McAuslan, 2001). Extending beyond the borders of the United States, Zablotska et al. (2009) reported on alcohol use, IPV, and sexual coercion and HIV among 3,422 Ugandan women in adolescence and early young adulthood. The findings indicated that alcohol use before sex was associated with a higher rate of physical violence and sexual coercion, as well as a higher prevalence of HIV. It was proposed that alcohol use may be used in conjunction with IPV as part of a sexual control process to obtain sex against a woman's consent. These findings, and those reported previously regarding dating violence and victimization, suggest the critical role that alcohol and other drugs may assume in ongoing negative cycles of IPV, unwanted sexual behavior, and adverse outcomes (e.g., STDs).

## THEORIES AND COMMON MECHANISMS OF INFLUENCE AMONG ALCOHOL, DRUGS, AND SEXUAL BEHAVIORS

There have been a large number of theories of adolescent sexual behavior that include either a more general problem behavior focus (e.g., sexual behavior co-occurring with delinquency, alcohol, and other drug use) or a specific focus on sexual behavior. In addition, there have been a number of mechanisms and models promulgated to facilitate inquiry into how alcohol or other drugs may directly or indirectly influence adolescent sexual behavior. Selective examples from these diverse approaches are now provided.

Problem behavior theory (PBT; Jessor, Donovan, & Costa, 1991) views adolescent sexual activity as part of a syndrome of behaviors that, in addition to sexual activity, include alcohol and other drug use, tobacco use, delinquency, and poor school performance. These behaviors tend to co-occur or co-vary during adolescence, and to be influenced by a common set of social background and contextual variables (e.g., parents' income, occupational status) and social-psychological variables (e.g., motivational and personal belief structures; parental and peer influences). PBT offers a parsimonious account of the co-occurrence of multiple problem behaviors and the roles of personal, social, and contextual factors that may be targeted in prevention programs. In addition to PBT, several theories of delinquency, including social control theory, have posited that adolescents who engage in, and foster social bonds with, social units such as the family, school, church, and community organizations are less likely to transgress societal norms and engage in delinquent behavior, including early sexual onset and multiple sexual partners (Krohn & Massey, 1980). Strong institutional linkages and emotional attachments to these entities limit non-socially sanctioned and unconventional behaviors, and promote more age normative, legal, and cultural expectations for age-appropriate prosocial behaviors, better decision-making, and delayed gratification in immediate reward situations.

Similarly, the Social Development Model (SDM) posits that multilevel developmental influences, including salient developmental contexts (e.g., neighborhood, classroom, school, and home setting characteristics), the child's social and emotional skills (e.g., communication, decision-making, conflict resolution), and parenting skills (behavior management skills, skills to train children to reduce risk for drugs) jointly influence social development in children and adolescents (Lonczak, Abbott, Hawkins, Kosterman, & Catalano, 2002). These joint influences provide opportunities for engagement in social, emotional, and cognitive growth of children in critical contexts that bode well for healthy development and may act to deter engagement in substance use and other problem behaviors, including early sexual debut and non-condom use (Lonczak et al., 2002). The SDM, like social control theory, provides an example of a social-ecological model that highlights the importance of influential social units and contexts in understanding the individual developmental course and expression of problem behaviors, including sexual behavior, and seeks to understand time-changing behaviors within a multi-level matrix of biopsychosocial factors that may serve as targets for preventive intervention studies (Kotchick, Shaffer, Forehand, & Miller, 2001).

The theories and models mentioned above incorporate adolescent sexual behavior within multilevel frameworks that include principally common predictors of diverse problem behavior outcomes (e.g., sexual activity, alcohol use, delinquency). Other adolescent sexual behavior-specific theories focus on more proximal cognitive and perceived environmental processes that influence precursors of sexual behavior, such as intentions, expectancies, perceived social norms, sex-risk negotiating skills, and self-efficacy (Buhi & Goodson, 2007; Guilamo-Ramos, Jaccard, Dittus, Gonzalez, & Bouris, 2008). These theories and models have not typically focused on the interconnection between sexual behavior and alcohol or drug use, though these concepts (intentions, expectancies, social norms) have been used to study proximal determinants of alcohol and other drug use.

In addition to general and specific theories and models of adolescent sexual behavior and alcohol and other drug use, several proposed causal mechanisms have been suggested to describe the ways in which substances promote risky sexual behavior, such as early sexual debut, having multiple sex partners, and non-condom use (Cooper, 2002; Santelli et al., 2001). For example, alcohol and other substances may function to disinhibit normal protective sexual behaviors (e.g., condom use) via its pharmacologic effect on cognitive processes (e.g., impulsive decision-making), and on emotional and behavioral self-regulation. Likewise, alcohol expectancy models would predict that individuals who believe that alcohol has a positive effect on sexual behaviors (e.g., alcohol would make me a better lover; alcohol would make me enjoy sex more) would be more likely to engage in high-risk sexual behaviors while under the influence of alcohol than those who do not hold such beliefs. The use of alcohol in relation to sexual activity in adolescence has also been proposed to serve an excuse function for engaging in sexual behavior that is subsequently regretted (e.g., I had unprotected sex because of the alcohol); thus, alcohol use may serve to excuse behaviors that otherwise would be unacceptable and violate personal and social norms.

## SELECTIVE FINDINGS FROM PREVENTION AND INTERVENTION STUDIES

Given the association between alcohol and substance use and sexual risk-taking, behavior change interventions to promote safer sexual behavior that also address the role of alcohol use on risky sexual behavior may be particularly effective. There exist many examples of HIV/STD prevention interventions for adolescents (Sales, Milhausen, & DiClemente, 2006).

Moreover, there are examples of HIV/STD prevention interventions that are conducted with individuals who have substance abuse disorders (for reviews, see Prendergast, Urada, & Podus, 2001; van Empelen et al., 2003). However, there are few interventions for teens that specifically target both substance use and sexual risk reduction in groups who are not in treatment for, or selected because of, substance use. Below we provide an overview of findings from intervention studies conducted with individuals who have substance abuse disorders (and are in treatment), followed by findings from the few studies targeting both substance use and sexual risk-taking among groups not in treatment for substance use problems.

## STD/HIV Prevention Among Youth in Treatment for Substance Use Problems

Residential drug treatment centers provide the opportunity to implement STD/HIV interventions to those seeking treatment for addiction, as treatment of the substance-abuse problem, while necessary, may not be sufficient, in and of itself, to reduce sexual risk behaviors or sustain reduction in risk behaviors over protracted periods of time (Jainchill, Yagelka, Hawke, & De Leon, 1999). Three efficacy trials of behavioral interventions for substance-abusing teens are described in the empirical literature (St. Lawrence et al., 1994; St. Lawrence, Jefferson, Alleyne, & Brasfield, 1995; St. Lawrence et al., 2002). One pilot study ($N = 17$) indicated that the behavioral skills training reduced the short-term sexual risk behaviors of substance-dependent adolescents (St. Lawrence et al., 1994). A second pilot program ($N = 34$) was conducted by this research group (St. Lawrence et al., 1995), indicating that substance-abusing adolescents randomized into a skills-training condition were more likely than the control group to report short-term reductions in risky sexual behaviors, such as reducing number of partners and increasing the rate of condom-protected sex.

The largest efficacy trial to date incorporating an adolescent substance-abusing population, all residing in a drug treatment center, was conducted by St. Lawrence and colleagues (2002). Participants ($N = 161$) were randomly assigned to receive 12 sessions of either a health education, information-only intervention (I only), information plus behavioral skills training intervention (I + B), or an information, behavioral skills training, plus a risk-sensitization motivation component intervention (I + B+M). Follow-up assessments occurred at 6 and 12 months after their discharge from the drug treatment facility. In contrast to participants in the I-only condition, participants in either the I + B or I + B+M showed more favorable attitudes towards condoms, reduced frequency of unprotected vaginal sex, better performance on behavioral skills, and substantial increases in sexual abstinence. The only noticeable difference between the I + B and the I + B+M conditions was that for those in the I + B+M condition the effects of the intervention were less resistant to decay.

There are several strengths to this program that may have contributed to its success. First, the design of the intervention was guided by a well-established and articulated theoretical framework—i.e., Fisher & Fisher's (1992) information-motivation-behavioral skills model (IMB) of AIDS-prevention behavior—which has been utilized for guiding interventions to reduce risky sexual behavior in university students and adolescents. Second, the 12-session STD/HIV risk reduction intervention was integrated into the services already provided during residential drug treatment. Additionally, the intervention was implemented by trained research staff and not treatment facility staff. Finally, as illustrated by the difference observed between conditions, the inclusion of a broad content area which was delivered across a variety of modalities (i.e., information provision, role-playing, skills training, direct feedback) resulted in a significant reduction in multiple sexual risk behaviors.

## Substance Use and STD/HIV Prevention Programs for Youth not in Treatment Programs

In addition to STD/HIV prevention interventions for youth in treatment for substance abuse issues, a few interventions have shown promising effects for reducing both substance use and sexual risk-taking. Bryan, Schmiege, & Broaddus (2009) implemented and evaluated a randomized, controlled trial of a theory-based sexual and alcohol risk-reduction intervention to reduce sexual risk-taking, frequency of intercourse while drinking, and alcohol-related problems among 484 detained adolescents. Adolescents were randomized at the group-level to one of three arms: an HIV/STD information-only control arm; a sexual risk reduction arm; or a sexual risk reduction arm that included an alcohol risk reduction component. Over the 12-month follow-up period, both the sexual risk reduction condition and the combined sexual and alcohol risk reduction condition were significantly more effective than the HIV/STD information only session in increasing condom use during sex. However, there was no statistically significant difference between the condom use behaviors reported by participants in the sexual risk reduction condition and the combined sexual and alcohol risk reduction condition. Additionally, there was limited impact on alcohol-use as a function of intervention participation. Although promising, the findings of this program have limited generalizability to non-adjudicated youth.

A pilot study of a school-based HIV risk reduction program which integrated components of substance abuse into the HIV prevention messaging was conducted by Lazebnik, Grey, & Ferguson (2001). This program, which included training on decision-making, HIV/AIDS knowledge, risky behaviors (sexual and substance related), and abstinence, was conducted over the course of four weeks (1 hour sessions once a week) with 125 Hispanic, middle-school-aged children. Overall, the intervention improved the HIV/AIDS knowledge, beliefs, and risk perceptions of the participants; however, no improvements were demonstrated for intention to change or actual behavior change among Hispanic youth who participated. Additionally, the program had no impact on the substance use variables assessed. There are several limitations to this study that should be considered. Specifically, it included a very small sample of youth from a single middle school, and the vast majority of youth in the program reported no risk-taking behaviors.

In contrast to the aforementioned studies, The Life Skills Training (LST) prevention intervention (Botvin & Griffin, 2004) teaches alcohol and drug resistance skills, and includes materials to aid the development of general personal and social competence (includes no explicit information on sexual-risk reduction). Participants in the intervention received a 30-session intervention delivered from 7th through 9th grades. This intensive intervention, implemented over several years, significantly reduced alcohol and marijuana intoxication over the course of adolescence, and among participants who received 60% or more of the intervention content, this reduction in substance use was also associated with decreased sexual risk-taking in early adulthood (Griffin, Botvin, & Nichols, 2006). Thus, enhancing personal and social skills competence and skills needed to effectively resist social pressures to use substances may carry over to resisting other risk behaviors, such as sexual risk-taking.

## CONCLUSIONS AND FUTURE DIRECTIONS

Epidemiologic findings clearly indicate high rates both of alcohol and other substance use and sexual behaviors among adolescents, and significant intersections between these two domains of risky behavior. The causal nature of this intersection and specific mechanisms remain to be determined, though several theories and mechanisms have been proposed, including general theories that suggest co-occurring syndrome behaviors with common antecedents (e.g., problem behavior theory), and mechanisms such as alcohol-induced disinhibition that increases risky sexual behavior. Evidence also supports strong interrelationships between IPV, substance use, and sexual behaviors among adolescents, with long-term consequences into adulthood.

While not exhaustive, we now highlight four areas of high priority for subsequent research on substance use and risky sexual behaviors and adverse outcomes. First, within alcohol and drug use studies there has been an increase in early, and very early, onset substance use behaviors (Zucker, Donovan, Masten, Mattson, & Moss, 2008). Further, early onset of alcohol and drug use is associated with earlier sexual debut, risky adolescent sexual behavior, and adverse outcomes (e.g., STDs). It will be important in future research to determine how these early-onset substance use and sexually risky behaviors impact, and are impacted by, the range of other ongoing biological, psychological, and social changes occurring during adolescence (Windle et al. 2008). For example, how might early-onset substance use impact ongoing maturational brain processes that are critical to inhibitory responses and decision-making that may influence sexual risk-taking? Second, it would be beneficial to expand the range of etiologic and preventive intervention studies to include both peer influences (e.g., social network analysis; peer group dynamics) and dating behavior/romantic relationships to separate sexual risk behaviors from more constructive, health-promoting behaviors surrounding romantic relationships.

Third, both etiologic and preventive intervention studies would benefit from a greater focus on critical individual difference variables such as participant's biological sex, ethnicity, personality variables, and sexual identity, and to broaden studies to the global scale by including international studies. Understanding sources of variation among these individual difference variables may facilitate more tailored preventive interventions. And fourth, preventive intervention and treatment studies need to focus more on common and unique components of comprehensive, multi-component interventions that may simultaneously address both reductions in alcohol and other substance use and risky sexual behaviors. Such multi-targeted interventions may prove to be both more efficacious and cost-effective to deter adolescent substance use and risky sexual behavior, and better able to promote positive health outcomes in adolescence and beyond.

## ACKNOWLEDGEMENT

This contribution was supported by National Institute on Alcoholism and Alcohol Abuse Grant No. K05-AA021143 and National Institute on Drug Abuse Grant No. P3ODA027827.

## REFERENCES

Abbey, A., Zawacki, T., Buck, P. O., Clinton, A. M., & McAuslan, P. (2001). Alcohol and sexual assault. *Alcohol Research & Health, 25*, 43–51.

Botvin, G. J., & Griffin, K. W. (2004). Life skills training: Empirical findings and future directions. *Journal of Primary Prevention, 25*, 211–232.

Brown, J. D., & Melchiono, M. W. (2006). Health concerns of sexual minority adolescent girls. *Current Opinion in Pediatrics, 18*, 359–364.

Bryan, A., Ray, L., & Cooper, M. L. (2007). Alcohol use and protective sexual behaviors among high-risk adolescents. *Journal of Studies on Alcohol and Drugs, 68*, 327–335.

Bryan, A. D., Schmiege, S. J., & Broaddus, M. R. (2009). HIV risk reduction among detained adolescents: A randomized, controlled trial. *Pediatrics, 124*, e1180–e1188.

Buhi, E. R., & Goodson, P. (2007). Predictors of adolescent sexual behavior and intention: A theory-guided systematic review. *Journal of Adolescent Health, 40*, 4–21.

Castilla, J., Barrio, G., Belza, M. J., & Fuente, L. (1999). Drug and alcohol consumption and sexual risk behaviour among young adults: Results from a national survey. *Drug and Alcohol Dependence, 56*, 47–53.

Cavazos-Rehg, P. A., Krauss, M. J., Spitznagel, E. L., Schootman, M., Cottler, L. B., & Bierut, L. J. (2011). Substance use and the risk for sexual intercourse with and without a history of teenage pregnancy among adolescent females. *Journal of Studies on Alcohol and Drugs, 72*, 194–198.

Centers for Disease Control and Prevention, (2011a). *2009 HIV surveillance report, 21.* <http://www.cdc.gov/hiv/topics/surveillance/resources/reports/>. Published February 2011. Accessed 6.12.11.

Centers for Disease Control and Prevention, (2011b). Vital signs: Teen pregnancy—United States, 1991-2009. *MMWR, 60*, 414–420.

Connell, C. M., Gilreath, T. D., & Hansen, N. B. (2009). A multiprocess latent class analysis of the co-occurrence of substance use and sexual risk behavior among adolescents. *Journal of Studies on Alcohol and Drugs, 70*, 943–951.

Cook, R. L., Pollock, N. K., Rao, A. K., & Clark, D. B. (2002). Increased prevalence of herpes simplex virus type 2 among adolescent women with alcohol use disorders. *Journal of Adolescent Health, 30*, 169–174.

Cook, R. L., Comer, D. M., Wiesenfeld, H. C., Chang, C. C., Tarter, R., Lave, J. R., et al. (2006). Alcohol and drug use and related disorders: An underrecognized health issue among adolescents and young adults attending sexually transmitted disease clinics. *Sexaully Transmitted Diseases, 33*, 565–570.

Cooper, M. L. (2002). Alcohol use and risky sexual behavior among college students and youth: Evaluating the evidence. *Journal of Studies on Alcohol,* (Suppl. 14), 101–117.

Cooper, M. L., Peirce, R. S., & Huselid, R. F. (1994). Substance use and sexual risk taking among Black adolescents and White adolescents. *Health Psychology, 13*, 251–262.

Corliss, H. L., Rosario, M., Wypij, D., Wylie, S. A., Frazier, A. L., & Austin, S. B. (2010). Sexual orientation and drug use in a longitudinal cohort study of U.S. adolescents. *Addictive Behaviors, 35*, 517–521.

Deardorff, J., Gonzales, N. A., Christopher, S., Roosa, M. W., & Millsap, R. E. (2005). Early puberty and adolescent pregnancy: The influence of alcohol use. *Pediatrics, 116*, 1451–1456.

Deas-Nesmith, D., Brady, K. T., White, R., & Campbell, S. (1999). HIV-risk behaviors in adolescent substance abusers. *Journal of Substance Abuse Treatment, 16*, 169–172.

Donovan, C., & McEwan, R. (1995). A review of the literature examining the relationship between alcohol use and HIV-related sexual risk-taking in young people. *Addiction, 90*, 319–328.

Eaton, D. K., Davis, K. S., Barrios, L., Brener, N., & Noonan, R. K. (2007). Associations of dating violence victimization with lifetime participation, co-occurrence, and early initiation of risk behaviors among U.S. high school students. *Journal of Interpersonal Violence, 22*, 585–602.

Eaton, D. K., Kann, L., Kinchen, S., Shanklin, S., Ross, J., Hawkins, J., et al. (2010). Youth risk behavior surveillance—United States, 2009. *Surveillance Summaries, MMWR, 59*(SS-5), 1–142.

Finer, L. B., & Henshaw, S. K. (2006). Disparities in rates of unintended pregnancy in the United States, 1994 and 2001. *Perspectives on Sexual and Reproductive Health, 38*, 90–96.

Fisher, J. D., & Fisher, W. A. (1992). Changing AIDS-risk behavior. *Psychological Bulletin, 111*, 455–474.

Forhan, S., Gottlieb, S. L., Sternberg, M. R., Xu, F., Datta, S. D., & Berman, S. (2008). *Prevalence of sexually transmitted infections and bacterial vaginosis among female adolescents in the United States: Data from the national health and nutritional examination survey (NHANES), 2003-2004.* Paper presented at the National STD Prevention Conference, Chicago, IL.

Griffin, K. W., Botvin, G. J., & Nichols, T. R. (2006). Effects of a school-based drug abuse prevention program for adolescents on HIV risk behavior in young adulthood. *Prevention Science, 7*, 103–112.

Guilamo-Ramos, V., Jaccard, J., Dittus, P., Gonzalez, B., & Bouris, A. (2008). A conceptual framework for the analysis of risk and problem behaviors: The case of adolescent sexual behavior. *Social Work Research, 32*, 29–45.

Haas, A. P., Eliason, M., Mays, V. M., Mathy, R. M., Cochran, S. D., D'Augelli, A. R., et al. (2010). Suicide and suicide risk in lesbian, gay, bisexual, and transgender populations: Review and recommendations. *Journal of Homosexuality, 58*, 10–51.

Hingson, R., Heeren, T., Winter, M. R., & Wechsler, H. (2003). Early age of first drunkenness as a factor in college students' unplanned and unprotected sex attributable to drinking. *Pediatrics, 111*, 34–41.

Jainchill, N., Yagelka, J., Hawke, J., & De Leon, G. (1999). Adolescent admissions to residential drug-treatment HIV risk behaviors pre- and posttreatment. *Psychology of Addictive Behaviors, 13*, 163–173.

Jemmott, J. B., & Jemmott, L. S. (2001). HIV behavioral interventions for adolescents in community settings. In J. L. Peterson, & R. J. DiClemente (Eds.), *Handbook of HIV prevention (pp. 103–124)*. New York, NY: Kluwer Academic/Plenum Press.

Jessor, R., Donovan, J. E., & Costa, F. M. (1991). *Beyond adolescence: Problem behavior and young adult development.* New York, NY: Cambridge University Press.

Johnston, L. D., O'Malley, P. M., Bachman, J. G., & Schulenberg, J. E. (2011). *Monitoring the future national survey results on drug use: Overview of key findings, 2010.* Ann Arbor, MI: Institute for Social Research, University of Michigan.

Jonas, S., Bebbington, P., McManus, S., Meltzer, H., Jenkins, R., Kuipers, E., et al. (2011). Sexual abuse and psychiatric disorders in England: Results from the 2007 adult psychiatric morbidity survey. *Psychological Medicine, 41*, 709–719.

Kann, L., Olsen, E. O., McManus, T., Kinchen, S., Chyen, D., Harris, W. A., et al. (2011). Sexual identity, sex of sexual contacts, and health-risk behaviors among students in grades 9-12—Youth risk behavior surveillance, selected sites, United States, 2001–2009. *Surveillance Summaries, MMWR, 60*(SS-07), 1–133.

Kotchick, B. A., Shaffer, A., Forehand, R., & Miller, K. S. (2001). Adolescent sexual risk behavior: A multi-system perspective. *Clinical Psychological Review, 21*, 493–519.

Krohn, M. D., & Massey, J. L. (1980). Social control and delinquent behavior: An examination of the elements of the social bond. *Sociological Quarterly, 21*, 529–543.

Lazebnik, R., Grey, S. F., & Ferguson, C. (2001). Integrating substance abuse content into an HIV risk-reduction intervention: A pilot study with middle school-aged Hispanic students. *Substance Abuse, 22*, 105–117.

Leigh, B. C., & Stall, R. (1993). Substance use and risky sexual behavior for exposure to HIV: Issues in methodology, interpretation, and prevention. *American Psychologist, 48*, 1035–1045.

Liau, A., DiClemente, R. J., Wingood, G. M., Crosby, R. A., Williams, K. M., Harrington, K., et al. (2002). Associations between biologically confirmed marijuana use and laboratory-confirmed sexually transmitted diseases among African American adolescent females. *Sexually Transmitted Diseases, 29*, 387.

Lonczak, H. S., Abbott, R. D., Hawkins, D., Kosterman, R., & Catalano, R. F. (2002). Effects of the Seattle development project on sexual behavior, pregnancy, birth, and sexually transmitted disease outcomes by age 21 years. *Archives of Pediatrics and Adolescent Medicine, 156*, 438–447.

Lown, E. A., Nayak, M. B., Korcha, R. A., & Greenfield, T. K. (2011). Child physical and sexual abuse: A comprehensive look at alcohol consumption patterns, consequences, and dependence from the National Alcohol Survey. *Alcoholism: Clinical and Experimental Research, 35*, 317–325.

MacDonald, T. K., Fong, G. T., Zanna, M. P., & Martineau, A. M. (2000). Alcohol myopia and condom use: Can alcohol intoxication be associated with more prudent behavior? *Journal of Personality and Social Psychology, 78*, 605–619.

Malow, R. M., Rosenberg, R., & Dévieux, J. (2005). Prevention of infection with human immunodeficiency virus in adolescent substance abusers. In H. A. Liddle, & C. L. Rowe (Eds.), *Adolescent substance abuse: Research and clinical advances (pp. 284–309)*. New York, NY: Cambridge University Press.

Malow, R. M., Dévieux, J. G., Jennings, T., Lucenko, B., & Kalichman, S. C. (2001). Substance-abusing adolescents at varying levels of HIV risk: Psychosocial characteristics, drug use, and sexual behavior. *Journal of Substance Abuse, 13*, 103–117.

Marshal, M. P., Friedman, M. S., Stall, R., King, K. M., Miles, J., Gold, M. A., et al. (2008). Sexual orientation and adolescent substance use: A meta-analysis and methodological review. *Addiction, 103*, 546–556.

Morrison, D. M., Gillmore, M. R., Hoppe, M. J., Gaylord, J., Leigh, B. C., & Rainey, D. (2003). Adolescent drinking and sex: Findings from a daily diary study. *Perspectives on Sexual and Reproductive Health, 35*, 162–168.

Morrison-Beedy, D., Carey, M. P., Crean, H. F., & Jones, S. H. (2011). Risk behaviors among adolescent girls in an HIV prevention trial. *Western Journal of Nursing Research, 33*, 690–711.

Nkansah-Amankra, S., Diedhiou, A., Agbanu, H. L. K., Harrod, C., & Dhawan, A. (2011). Correlates of sexual risk behaviors among high school students in Colorado: Analysis and implications for school-based HIV/AIDS programs. *Maternal and Child Health Journal, 15*, 730–741.

Prendergast, M. L., Urada, D., & Podus, D. (2001). Meta-analysis of HIV risk-reduction interventions within drug abuse treatment programs. *Journal of Consulting and Clinical Psychology, 69*, 389–405.

Raiford, J. L., Wingood, G. M., & DiClemente, R. J. (2007). Prevalence, incidence, and predictors of dating violence: A longitudinal study of African American female adolescents. *Journal of Women's Health, 16*, 822–832.

Rickert, V. I., Vaughan, R. D., & Wiemann, C. M. (2002). Adolescent dating violence and date rape. *Current Opinions in Obstetrics and Gynecology, 14*, 495–500.

Rolf, J., Nanda, J., Baldwin, J., Chandra, A., & Thompson, L. (1990). Substance misuse and HIV/AIDS risks among delinquents: A prevention challenge. *Substance Use and Misuse, 25*, 533–559.

Rosengard, C., Stein, L. A. R., Barnett, N. P., Monti, P. M., Golembeske, C., & Lebeau-Craven, R. (2006). Co-occurring sexual risk and substance use behaviors among incarcerated adolescents. *Journal of Correctional Health Care, 12*, 279–287.

Sales, J. M., Milhausen, R. R., & DiClemente, R. J. (2006). A decade in review: Building on the experiences of past adolescent STI/HIV interventions to optimize future prevention efforts. *Sexually Transmitted Infection, 82*, 431–436.

Santelli, J. S., Robin, L., Brener, N. D., & Lowry, R. (2001). Timing of alcohol and other drug use and sexual risk behaviors among unmarried adolescents and young adults. *Family Planning Perspectives, 33,* 200–205.

Sartor, C. E., Agrawal, A., McCutcheon, V. V., Duncan, A. E., & Lynskey, M. L. (2008). Disentangling the complex association between childhood sexual abuse and alcohol-related problems: A review of methodological issues and approaches. *Journal of Studies on Alcohol and Drugs, 69,* 718–727.

Senn, T. E., Carey, M. P., Vanable, P. A., Coury-Doniger, P., & Urban, M. (2007). Characteristics of sexual abuse in childhood and adolescence influence sexual risk behavior in adulthood. *Archives of Sexual Behavior, 36,* 637–645.

Seth, P., Sales, J. M., DiClemente, R. J., Wingood, G. M., Rose, E., & Patel, S. (2011). Longitudinal examination of alcohol use: A predictor of risky sexual behavior and *Trichomonas vaginalis* among African-American adolescents. *Sexually Transmitted Diseases, 38,* 96–101.

St. Lawrence, J. S., Crosby, R. A., Brasfield, T. L., & O'Bannon, R. E., III (2002). Reducing STD and HIV risk behavior of substance-dependent adolescents: A randomized controlled trial. *Journal of Consulting and Clinical Psychology, 70,* 1010–1021.

St. Lawrence, J. S., Jefferson, K. W., Banks, P. G., Cline, T. R., Alleyne, E., & Brasfield, T. L. (1994). Cognitive behavioral group intervention to assist substance-dependent adolescents in lowering HIV infection risk. *AIDS Education and Prevention, 6,* 425–435.

St. Lawrence, J. S., Jefferson, K. W., Alleyne, E., & Brasfield, T. L. (1995). Comparison of education versus behavioral skills training interventions in lowering sexual HIV-risk behavior of substance-dependent adolescents. *Journal of Consulting and Clinical Psychology, 63,* 154–157.

Strachman, A., Impett, E. A., Henson, J. M., & Pentz, M. A. (2009). Early adolescent alcohol use and sexual experience by emerging adulthood: A 10-year longitudinal investigation. *Journal of Adolescent Health, 45,* 478–482.

Tapert, S. F., Aarons, G. A., Sedlar, G. R., & Brown, S. A. (2001). Adolescent substance use and sexual risk-taking behavior. *Journal of Adolescent Health, 28,* 181.

Thompson, J. C., Kao, T. C., & Thomas, R. J. (2005). The relationship between alcohol use and risk-taking sexual behaviors in a large behavioral study. *Prevention Medicine, 41,* 247–252.

Tubman, J. G., Windle, M., & Windle, R. C. (1996). The onset and cross-temporal patterning of sexual intercourse in middle adolescence: Prospective relations with behavioral and emotional problems. *Child Development, 67,* 327–343.

van Empelen, P., Kok, G., van Kesteren, N. M. C., van den Borne, B., Bos, A. E. R., & Schaalma, H. P. (2003). Effective methods to change sex-risk among drug users: A review of psychosocial interventions. *Social Science and Medicine, 57,* 1593–1608.

Ventura, S. J., Abma, J. C., Mosher, W. D., & Henshaw, S. K. (2009). Estimated pregnancy rates for the United States, 1990–2005: An update. *National Vital Statistics Reports, 58,* 1–16.

Windle, M., Spear, L. P., Fuligni, A. J., Angold, A., Brown, J. D., Pine, D., et al. (2008). Transitions into underage and problem drinking: Developmental processes and mechanisms between ages 10–15. *Pediatrics*(Suppl. 4), S273–S289.

Wingood, G. M., DiClemente, R. J., McCree, D. H., Harrington, K., & Davies, S. L. (2001). Dating violence and the sexual health of black adolescent females. *Pediatrics, 107,* e72.

Zablotska, I. B., Gray, R. H., Koenig, M. A., Serwadda, D., Nalugoda, F., Kigozi, G., et al. (2009). Alcohol use, intimate partner violence, sexual coercion and HIV among women aged 15–24 in Rakai, Uganda. *AIDS Behavior, 13,* 225–233.

Zapata, L. B., Hillis, S. D., Marchbanks, P. A., Curtis, K. M., & Lowry, R. (2008). Methamphetamine use is independently associated with recent risky sexual behaviors and adolescent pregnancy. *Journal of School Health, 78,* 641–648.

Zucker, R. A., Donovan, J. E., Masten, A. S., Mattson, M. E., & Moss, H. B. (2008). Early developmental processes and the continuity of risk for underage drinking and problem drinking. *Pediatrics, 121,* S252–S272.

# CHAPTER 11

# Sexual-Minority, Gender-Nonconforming, and Transgender Youths

**Lisa M. Diamond**
University of Utah, Salt Lake City, Utah[1]

One of the most notable developments in clinical-developmental psychology over the past 20 years has been the explosion of attention to the lives of sexual-minority, gender-nonconforming, and transgender youths. Historically, adolescents who deviated from sexual and/or gender norms were considered misguided, maladjusted, or immoral, and therapeutic approaches sought to bring them back into the mainstream, whether through psychotherapy, medical treatment, or straightforward behavioral edicts. Things have undoubtedly changed. It is now widely recognized that a substantial number of adolescents deviate from conventional sexual and gender norms, and that although they are not intrinsically "disordered," they nonetheless face unique developmental challenges. Efforts to promote their healthy development no longer focus on channeling youths toward conformity with mainstream expectations, but on removing external threats to their healthy development and bolstering their internal capacities for coping with the hurdles posed by the fact that their feelings and experiences deviate from conventional norms

Toward that end, the present chapter provides an overview of the key developmental and adjustment issues faced by *sexual-minority* youths (i.e., those with same-sex attractions, fantasies, or behaviors), *gender-nonconforming* youths (i.e., those whose appearance, behavior, or interests violate traditional norms for masculinity or femininity), and *transgender* youths (i.e., those who adopt a gender identity that does not rigidly conform to their biological sex). Importantly, although these two populations are frequently confused with one another (and although there is

---

[1] Correspondence to: Lisa M. Diamond, Department of Psychology, University of Utah, 380 South 1530 East, Room 502, Salt Lake City, UT 84112. Phone 801-585-7491; email diamond@psych.uta

some overlap between them), they are nonetheless distinct. They are considered together in this chapter because of what they have in common: a set of complex psychosocial challenges deriving from the fact that their very existence challenges many of our culture's most deeply held beliefs about "normal" sexual and gender development. It would be impossible in a single chapter to comprehensively review everything that is currently known about sexual-minority and gender-variant adolescents, and hence I focus on aspects of their experiences that are most relevant for efforts to promote their positive development, seeking to correct widespread myths that have proliferated in both the scientific and popular literature. I highlight the diversity of sexual-minority populations, especially regarding the prevalence of non-exclusive rather than exclusive same-sex attractions and the diversity of youths' identity labels and self-concepts, noting the mental health implications of youths' exposure to stigma and social marginalization. I then discuss the unique experiences and needs of youths whose gender presentation deviates from traditional norms, ranging from youths who display mild to moderate forms of *gender nonconformity* to those who identify as *transgender*. Throughout this review, the goal is to replace stereotyped portrayals of "youth at risk" with more accurate and nuanced scientific information that will be of greater use to those seeking to foster positive development in these populations.

## FIRST THINGS FIRST: DEFINING THE POPULATION

Perhaps the single most important recent change in our understanding of these populations concerns their size and composition. Historically, youths with same-sex attractions or relationships have been denoted "lesbian/gay" youths, and gender variant youths have been denoted "transsexual" or "transgender" youths. However, over time, psychologists have come to appreciate the startling diversity of sexual-minority and gender-variant populations, based on clinical experience, as well as the results of large-scale representative studies.

Consider the following cases: a 15-year-old boy who has considered himself gay since he first started fantasizing about males at the age of 11; a teenage girl who falls in love with her female best friend but does not experience same-sex attractions for anyone else; an adolescent boy who engages in sexual experimentation with a male peer, but only falls in love with women; a young woman who experiences her first same-sex attractions at age 21. Do all of these individuals "count" as lesbian, gay, or bisexual? Currently, there is no reliable answer to this question, because there is no scientific consensus on the exact constellation of experiences that definitively "qualify" an individual as lesbian, gay, or bisexual. Sexual orientation is typically considered multidimensional, incorporating sexual attractions, romantic feelings, sexual behavior, and sexual fantasies. However, studies have reliably documented notable discrepancies between these domains among both adolescents and adults, as well as notable discrepancies between these domains and individuals' social and personal *identification* as a lesbian, gay, or bisexual individual.

An additional problem when it comes to adolescents is that same-sex sexuality which occurs during the adolescent years is often discounted as experimental, transitional, or otherwise insignificant. Although it is certainly true that adolescent same-sex contact is not a deterministic predictor of future same-sex sexuality, it is also the case that there is no definitive way to differentiate between youths whose same-sex interests and activities will persist into adulthood, and those who will not. For example, longitudinal research on adolescent and young adult sexual-minority women (Diamond, 2000, 2003, 2005) has found that factors such as age of first same-sex attractions, age at first sexual questioning, and age of first same-sex contact failed to distinguish women who ended up, by their mid-30s, maintaining lesbian-bisexual versus heterosexual identities. Further complicating matters is the fact that the vast majority of adolescents who report same-sex attractions or behavior also report other-sex attractions and behavior. Such mixed patterns of same-sex and other-sex attraction have been interpreted in vastly different ways—by adolescents themselves, as well as their friends and family members—over the years. Some youths with mixed patterns of attraction consider themselves bisexual or "queer," whereas others might (mistakenly) presume that the existence of other-sex attractions means, ipso facto, that they are not "really" gay and that they are undergoing a temporary phase.

In light of such complexity and diversity, *all* same-sex sexuality during the adolescent years should be treated with respect and given careful attention. Even for youth who end up identifying as heterosexual, adolescent expressions of same-sex sexuality might prove to be developmentally significant, and hence have implications for their adjustment and well-being (both positive and negative). It is to account for the diversity of adolescents' experiences with same-sex sexuality that I refer to youths with these experiences as *sexual minorities* rather than lesbian/gay/bisexual individuals. Despite the diversity of these individuals' experiences, one thing they undeniably share is that their same-sex attractions and/or experiences place them squarely outside conventional norms prescribing uniform and universal heterosexuality. The foregoing potentially exposes them to multiple personal and social ramifications such as self-stigmatization, denigration by others, harassment or victimization, lack of social support, and lack of public acknowledgement of their relationships.

Just how common *is* adolescent same-sex sexuality? The National Longitudinal Study of Adolescent Health found that 13% of American girls and 6% of American boys reported same-sex attractions, a same-sex relationship, or a nonheterosexual identity (Savin-Williams, 2005). More recent representative research (using the National Survey of Family Growth, with a national sample of nearly 14,000 individuals) found that 5.2% of male teenagers and 12.5% of female teenagers reported same-sex sexual contact (Chandra, Mosher, Copen, & Sionean, 2011). Importantly, longitudinal research indicates that same-sex behavior in adolescence is not necessarily a precursor to a sexual-minority identity. Savin-Williams & Ream (2007) found that among the adolescents in the National Longitudinal Study of Adolescent Health who reported same-sex behavior at Wave 1 (at a mean age of 16), very few (1 in 5 females and 1 in 25 males) identified as a sexual minority by Wave 3 (at a mean age of 22), and the overall percentage reporting sexual-minority identification was low (2.4% of males and 3.8% of females identified as bisexual, mostly homosexual, or homosexual). Similarly, in the National Survey of Family Growth, 2.8% of 18–19-year-old males and 7.7% of 18–19-year-old females identified as gay, lesbian, or bisexual (Chandra et al., 2011). These findings are consistent with other research conducted with large samples of adolescents, indicating that the vast majority of youth reporting same-sex attractions or same-sex behavior identify as heterosexual (Garofalo, Wolf, Wissow, Woods, & Goodman, 1999; Mosher, Chandra, & Jones, 2005; Remafedi, Resnick, Blum, & Harris, 1992).

These findings have important implications for interpreting the findings of previous research on sexual-minority youths. The majority of extant published research on the developmental and clinical issues facing sexual-minority youths is based on relatively narrow samples of youths who openly identify as lesbian/gay/bisexual/transgender (often recruited from social service organizations that serve these populations). Although these studies have provided critically important insights into the unique needs of this population, they underrepresent youths who are less open about their sexual and/or gender identity, and who may therefore be facing altogether different social-developmental concerns. Also, researchers have argued that samples of sexual-minority youths recruited from social service organizations might actually overrepresent the most troubled youths, given that these agencies tend to draw youths who *need* their services (Savin-Williams & Ream, 2003). Studies have also tended to underrepresent bisexual, ethnic-minority, rural, and working-class youths, hampering the generalizability of research findings.

## SAME-SEX ATTRACTIONS: NOT ALWAYS EARLY AND EXCLUSIVE

Two of the most common assumptions about same-sex sexuality are that: (1) nearly all individuals "discover" their same-sex orientation in early childhood; and (2) nearly all individuals are either exclusively attracted to the same sex or exclusively attracted to the other sex. In fact, both of these assumptions are starkly incorrect. Although available evidence suggests that individuals' overall predisposition to experience sexual desires for the same sex, the other sex, or both sexes is a relatively stable trait that is not amenable to forcible change, its *expression* shows considerable variability, both in its initial emergence and in its manifestation in sexual attraction, fantasy, and behavior over time.

For example, although many youths recall having experienced their first same-sex attractions around 8–12 years of age, others have no memory of same-sex attractions until late adolescence or even mid- to late adulthood (Golden, 1996; Savin-Williams, 1998, 2011), and research has documented considerable variability in sexual-minority youths' developmental trajectories (Diamond, 2008a; Rosario, Schrimshaw, & Hunter, 2008; Savin-Williams, 2005). Given the many sociocultural factors that intervene in individuals' subjective experiences and assessments of their own sexual desires (Tolman & Diamond, 2001), this should not be surprising. The important thing to remember, and to communicate to youths and the clinicians and advocates who work with them, is that the timing of an individual's first awareness of same-sex attractions is not systematically related to the intensity, exclusivity, stability, or "authenticity" of these attractions. Although an individual with late-developing attractions might wonder whether this means that he/she is not "really" gay, or whether he/she is bisexual versus gay/lesbian, there is no evidence that later-developing same-sex attractions are less exclusive or stable than earlier-developing same-sex attractions

In addition, although bisexual patterns of attraction have long been considered the exception rather than the norm, or have been considered to be indicators that individuals are "in denial" about their same-sex orientation, a number of random, representative studies conducted in numerous countries have consistently shown that the *majority* of adolescents and adults who report any same-sex attractions also report experiencing other-sex attractions (Chandra et al., 2011; Dickson, Paul, & Herbison, 2003; Laumann, Gagnon, Michael, & Michaels, 1994; Mosher et al., 2005). For example, Laumann's research team (1994) found that approximately 4% of American men and 4% of American women described themselves as attracted to both men and women, whereas only 2.4% of men and 0.3% of women described themselves as exclusively attracted to the same sex. Another large-scale representative study of American adults (Mosher et al., 2005), conducted more than a decade later, found that 5.6% of American men and nearly 13% of American women were attracted to both sexes, whereas only 1.5% of men and 0.8% of women were exclusively attracted to the same sex. Similar results have been found internationally. Analyses of the self-reported sexual attractions of 3,000 twins in the Australian Twin Registry (Bailey, Dunne, & Martin, 2000) found that 8% of men and women reported same-sex attractions and, of these individuals, 75% of men and over 90% of women *also* reported experiencing other-sex attractions. A random representative sample of New Zealanders (Dickson et al., 2003) found that approximately 6.8% of men and 18% of women reported some degree of attraction to the same sex, but only 1.2% of men and 0.8% of women were exclusively attracted to the same sex.

Research on adolescents has found the same pattern. For example, the National Survey of Family Growth found that 16% of 18–19-year-old females and 7.5% of 18–19-year-old males reported some degree of same-sex attraction, but the vast majority of these youths reported a *combination* of same-sex and other-sex attractions. Only 1.1% of males and 1.3% of females reported that they were *only* attracted to the same sex. In the Add Health study, the percentages of males reporting attractions to both sexes at Waves 1, 2, and 3 were (respectively) 6.3, 3.1, and 4.3, whereas the percentages reporting exclusive same-sex attractions were 0.9, 1.4, and 1.0. Among females, 3.9, 3.5, and 12.3% reported attractions to both sexes at Waves 1, 2, and 3, whereas 1.4, 1.0, and 0.6% reported exclusive attractions to the same sex. The consistency of these findings across surveys conducted in different cultures and among individuals of different ages suggests that the greater prevalence of nonexclusive (i.e., bisexual) attractions is a general feature of human sexuality, and is not simply attributable to a subset of gay/lesbian individuals who are "hiding" or "denying" their exclusive same-sex orientation (for a broader discussion of the historical inattention and denigration of *bisexual* patterns of attraction, see Rust, 2000b). Therefore, youths with bisexual patterns of attraction and/or behavior represent the norm, and exclusively same-sex attracted youths represent the exceptions. Yet historically, bisexual patterns of attraction or behavior, especially among adolescents, have been dismissed as indicating confusion or experimentation, and hence adolescents with such attractions are likely to experience considerable confusion about the meaning and authenticity of their experiences. Consider the following: between 1975 and 1985, only 3% of journal articles published in academic psychology journals on same-sex sexuality specifically included the word "bisexual" or "bisexuality" in the title, abstract, or subject headings. Between 1985 and 1995, this figure increased to 16%, reflecting the emerging acknowledgment of bisexuality as a legitimate sexual identity. In the past 10 years, however, that percentage has climbed only three more percentage points, demonstrating that the empirical underrepresentation of bisexuality persists (with some notable exceptions, such as Firestein, 1996, 2007; Paul, 1985, 1996; Rust, 1992, 1993, 2000a).

This omission is also reflected in the culture at large, which continues to debate the existence of bisexuality (Carey, 2005). As a result, adolescents with bisexual patterns of attraction may have trouble matching their subjective experiences of desire and infatuation with models portrayed in television, movies, and books, and may conclude that their experiences are atypical, abnormal, or inauthentic. This may be compounded if the trusted adults in their lives have the same misconceptions. Whereas all youths who undergo a period of sexual questioning must wrestle with uncomfortable questions about the ways in which their sexuality might deviate from cultural norms, this process can be especially challenging for youths whose desires directly contradict the homosexual–heterosexual dichotomy that they see portrayed in their surrounding culture. Perhaps for this reason, evidence indicates that individuals with nonexclusive attractions frequently revisit the sexual questioning process multiple times in adolescence and young adulthood, and reconsider their sexual identity labels as different attractions and relationships become differentially salient over time (Diamond, 2008b; Rust, 1992, 2000c; Savin-Williams, 2005; Weinberg, Williams, & Pryor, 1994). Some end up adopting alternative identity labels, given the inadequacy of "lesbian" and "gay" labels to adequately represent their experiences. Whereas some youths with bisexual patterns of attraction identify as "bisexual," others identify as "queer," "mostly heterosexual," or reject all identity labels (Diamond, 2008b; Weinberg et al., 1994).

Also worthy of attention is the fact that nonexclusive patterns of attraction are more common among females than among males. Every single one of the aforementioned large-scale surveys of same-sex sexuality has found that women are more likely to report attractions to both sexes than men (Bailey, Dunne, & Martin, 2000; Chandra et al., 2011; Dickson, Paul, & Herbison, 2003; Laumann, Gagnon, Michael, & Michaels, 1994; Mosher et al., 2005). Combined with the fact that nonexclusive patterns of attraction are more prevalent than exclusive same-sex attractions, this means that the total number of adolescent and adult women reporting same-sex attractions is greater than the number of adolescent and adult men reporting same-sex attractions. The reasons for this robust gender difference are unknown. One possibility is that women are simply more intrinsically bisexual than men. Supporting this possibility, a series of experimental studies has found that independent of their sexual self-identification, women appear more likely than men to show nonexclusive patterns of sexual arousal (Chivers & Bailey, 2005; Chivers, Rieger, Latty, & Bailey, 2004; Chivers, Seto, & Blanchard, 2007). Specifically, lesbian-identified and heterosexually-identified women tended to show genital arousal in response to *both* sexual images of women and sexual images of men, whereas gay-identified and heterosexually-identified men tended to show genital arousal in response to *only* women (among heterosexual men) or *only* men (among gay men). Hence, women's greater capacity for bisexual attractions might reflect an essential gender difference. Along these lines, it is interesting that Goy and Goldfoot noted over 30 years ago (1975) that in many different mammalian species, bisexuality is an intrinsically dimorphic trait which develops (through prenatal hormonal pathways) in *either* the male or the female of a species, but never both. This suggests the intriguing possibility that in humans, women are "the bisexual sex" (or at least the *more* bisexual sex), whereas males are more likely to be exclusively heterosexual or homosexual (see also Bailey, 2009; Rieger, Bailey, & Chivers, 2005). This is also consistent with an emerging body of research suggesting a basic capacity for women's sexuality to be more "fluid" or "plastic" than men's (Baumeister, 2000; Diamond, 2008b).

It is critically important for these issues—including the aforementioned gender differences—to be addressed by programs and services geared toward sexual-minority youths, so that youths wrestling with sexual identity questioning understand that late-developing and/or nonexclusive attractions are actually fairly common, and that fluctuations over time in desires for, and participation in, same-sex relationships also change. Numerous studies have found that sexual-minority youths often alternate between bisexual and gay/lesbian identities, as they reconsider their relative interest in same-sex and other-sex partners (reviewed in Savin-Williams, 2011). Similarly, studies reliably find notable discrepancies between the domains of sexual attraction, behavior, and identity, both within the same moment in time and also across time (Chandra et al., 2011; Dickson et al., 2003; Laumann et al., 1994; Savin-Williams & Ream, 2007). Hence, it is actually more common for youths to report "mismatches" between their patterns of sexual attraction, sexual behavior, and sexual identification (for example, same-sex attractions without same-sex behavior, bisexual attractions, and a heterosexual identity) than to report perfect consistency among these domains. Given that similar discrepancies have been observed among adults, there is no evidence that such "mismatches" are evidence of developmental immaturity. Rather, they are better interpreted as an inevitable consequence of the greater prevalence of nonexclusive over exclusive attractions: nonexclusive attractions obviously lend themselves to a broader range of behaviors and identifications over time, as individuals experience and express differing degrees of interest in both same-sex and other-sex partners. To account for the diversity of youths' experiences, it is exceedingly important to communicate to youths that their acceptance, support, and protection is not predicated on their conforming to a "gay archetype" requiring exclusive, unmistakable, early-appearing same-sex attractions. As noted earlier, any youth whose thoughts or behaviors stray from heterosexual norms may face confusion, self-hatred, and stigmatization, and all of these youths deserve support, attention, and advocacy.

## MENTAL HEALTH OF SEXUAL-MINORITY YOUTHS

Do youth with same-sex attractions, behaviors, or identities show greater mental health problems than their heterosexual counterparts? The answer is perhaps—it depends on which populations are being sampled. Numerous studies have found that sexual-minority youth, lumped together as a unitary unit, often report heightened feelings of stress, loneliness, anxiety, depression, and heightened use of drugs and alcohol (Consolacion, Russell,

& Sue, 2004; French, Story, Remafedi, Resnick, & Blum, 1996; Garofalo et al., 1999; Remafedi, 1999; Remafedi, French, Story, Resnick, & Blum, 1998; Rosario, Schrimshaw, & Hunter, 2004, 2006; Russell & Consolacion, 2003; Russell, Franz, & Driscoll, 2001; Russell & Seif, 2002; Savin-Williams, 2001). As with adults, stigmatization and victimization play a critical role in these problems (Balsam, Rothblum, & Beauchaine, 2005; Bontempo & D'Augelli, 2002; D'Augelli, Grossman, & Starks, 2006; D'Augelli, Pilkington, & Hershberger, 2002; Horn & Nucci, 2006; Mallon, 2001; Rivers & D'Augelli, 2001; Safe Schools Coalition of Washington, 1999; Williams, Connolly, Pepler, & Craig, 2003, 2005).

These findings have been attributed to *minority stress*, defined as the unique strain experienced as a result of occupying a socially marginalized category (Meyer, 2003). The fundamental tenet underlying the conceptualization of minority stress is that individuals learn about themselves and develop their self-concepts partly on the basis of how they are treated and perceived by others (Allport, 1954; Crocker, Major, & Steele, 1998; Goffman, 1963; Pettigrew, 1967). Hence, chronic negative evaluations, at the level of both concrete interpersonal interactions and broad-based cultural norms, have detrimental effects on sexual minorities' self-evaluations and, accordingly, their mental well-being. Given that adolescence is a period during which youths show heightened concerns about how they are viewed and treated by others, and during which their self-concepts undergo rapid and frequent revision, experiences of sexual-minority stress may be particularly acute. The notion that minority stress may account for the link between same-sex sexuality and adolescent mental health is supported by the fact that sexual-minority youth with the highest mental health risks are those who have been exposed to the greatest levels of stigmatization and victimization (Balsam et al., 2005; Bontempo & D'Augelli, 2002; D'Augelli et al., 2006; Russell & Joyner, 2001).

Yet such findings highlight a critical point: stigma, discrimination, and minority stress are *not* uniform experiences. Not only do sexual-minority adolescents face vastly different exposure to minority stress—depending on their individual family background, social class, geographic environment, religious community, level of education, and access to accurate information and supportive resources—but they are also equipped with vastly different coping resources, due to personality characteristics, familial characteristics, and institutional protections from harassment and discrimination. This helps to explain why some studies have not found significantly greater mental health problems among sexual-minority individuals than among their heterosexual counterparts. Because different studies capture different subgroups of sexual-minority youth, with different psychosocial risk factors, different degrees of exposure to prejudice and discrimination, different sets of family issues, and different coping mechanisms, such variability in the findings is to be expected (Anderson, 1998; Fitzpatrick, Euton, Jones, & Schmidt, 2005; Konik & Stewart, 2004; Meyer, 2003; Rutter & Soucar, 2002; Savin-Williams, 2001). Furthermore, social attitudes toward same-sex sexuality have been gradually changing over the years (reviewed in Loftus, 2001; Savin-Williams, 2005; Walters, 2001), reducing some sexual-minority individuals' exposure to minority stress. Hence, while some sexual-minority youths continue to face unrelenting stigma in their local communities as a result of their same-sex sexuality, others are able to live lives that are relatively free of harassment, shame, and denigration, and may enjoy full support, validation, and acceptance from friends, family members, and co-workers.

Yet one point bears emphasis: among the diverse forms of stigmatization that sexual-minority youths may experience, the single most pernicious is familial rejection. One influential study of a diverse sample of sexual-minority adults aged 21–25 (Ryan, Huebner, Diaz, & Sanchez, 2009) found that family rejection was reliably related to poorer physical and mental health outcomes, including an eight-fold increase in the risk of suicide attempts, a six-fold increase in the risk of depression, and more than a three-fold increase in the risk of substance use and unprotected sexual intercourse. Notably, males were more likely to report familial rejection than females, and Latino males reported the highest rates of family rejection overall, suggesting that cultural variations in notions of gender and sexuality must be taken into account when considering youths' differential exposure to minority stress. Perhaps even more striking, this study found that increased risks for mental and physical health problems and suicide attempts were also found for youths reporting familial disapproval rather than outright rejection: they measured youths' reports of their families' negative reactions to their sexuality, and found a linear relationship between the negativity of families' responses and their children's health outcomes. This is a particularly important finding given that many youths report that although they have disclosed their sexuality to their parents, their parents refuse to discuss it openly, and often make their disapproval known in numerous subtle ways (L. Brown, 1989; D'Augelli, Grossman, & Starks, 2005; Herdt & Beeler, 1998). Clearly, sexual-minority youths appear to be highly sensitive to familial responses to their sexuality, and even mildly negative responses have potentially negative implications for youths' adjustment and development. Future research is clearly needed on the long-term processes through which families—and particularly parents—gradually progress from initial disapproval of a family member's same-sex sexuality to increasing acceptance and tolerance.

## GENDER-NONCONFORMING YOUTHS

Much of the stigmatization that sexual-minority youths face from their immediate peers, as well as the culture at large, is inextricably tied with an explicit or implicit condemnation of gender nonconformity (reviewed in Toomey, Ryan, Diaz, Card, & Russell, 2010). Adolescence is a developmental period during which gender norms take on increased salience and significance (Hill & Lynch, 1983), and a youth's peers can be unforgiving policers of gender-appropriate behavior. In this scenario, gender nonconformity and same-sex sexuality come to be conceptualized as proxies for one another. A girl who appears too "mannish" is taunted as a lesbian, and a gay boy is considered "not a real man." Gender-nonconforming adolescents often face the same stigmatization and condemnation that are typically heaped upon openly-identified lesbian/gay/bisexual adolescents, regardless of whether they experience same-sex attractions or not. Similarly, youths with same-sex attractions who also happen to be gender-nonconforming are disproportionately likely to be suspected of homosexuality, and hence targeted for harassment and victimization (Grossman, D'Augelli, Howell, & Hubbard, 2005). Thus, it becomes critically important to take account of the range of gender-linked traits and behaviors comprising a youth's personal and externally perceived gender identity in order to make sense of his or her particular psychosocial developmental trajectory.

With this in mind, certain clarifications are in order. Gender identity refers to an individual's internalized psychological experience of being male or female, whereas gender nonconformity refers to the degree to which an individual's appearance, behavior, interests, and subjective self-concept deviate from conventional norms for masculinity/femininity. This distinction is critically important. Although research has found that some lesbian/gay/bisexual individuals are more gender-nonconforming than heterosexuals on certain traits, this does not typically extend to their core sense of internalized maleness or femaleness (Bailey, 1996; Bailey, Gaulin, Agyei, & Gladue, 1994; Bailey, Nothnagel, & Wolfe, 1995; Bailey & Zucker, 1995; Lippa, 2000; Phillips & Over, 1992, 1995; Zuger, 1988). Thus, although it has long been common to view gay men and lesbians as "reversed" in their gender identity because they possess "reversed" sexual desires, this is not generally the case. Furthermore, research has found notable diversity regarding the sexual orientations of transsexual individuals (i.e., individuals whose gender identities are discordant with their biological sex). For example, there are biological males with female gender identities who are sexually attracted to women, biological males with female gender identities who are sexually attracted to men, and so on (Chivers & Bailey, 2000; Cole, Denny, Eyler, & Samons, 2000; Denny & Green, 1996; Devor, 1993).

Research on gender-nonconforming youths lags far behind research on sexual-minority youths, and many basic questions such as "how many adolescents are gender-nonconforming" remain unanswered. One large-scale study of children 6–10 years of age (Sandberg, Meyer Bahlburg, Ehrhardt, & Yager, 1993) found that approximately 23% of boys and 39% of girls showed 10 or more different gender nonconforming behaviors. It is difficult to make inferences about the prevalence of adolescent gender nonconformity from these data, because there is evidence that, as children grow older and begin to perceive the social implications of gender nonconformity, they consciously modify their own behavior, sometimes becoming extremely gender-stereotyped in order to avoid and compensate for prior stigmatization (Hunter, 1993). At the same time, some youths who were relatively gender-typical in childhood may go through a gender-nonconforming "phase" during adolescence, as they work through changes in their internalized sense of masculinity/femininity brought about by the biological and social transitions of sexual maturation (Bancroft, 1990).

One of the most salient factors differentiating adolescents' experiences of gender nonconformity is gender itself. Mild forms of gender nonconformity are more common among women, less stigmatized, less likely to be treated as an indicator of psychiatric disturbance, and less strongly perceived to be associated with same-sex sexual orientation (Corbett, 1998, 1999; D'Augelli et al., 2006; Kosciw, Greytak, & Diaz, 2009). For example, young "tomboys" are often extremely popular with both peers and teachers (Martin, 1990), and their behavior does not typically trigger extreme parental concern unless it persists in marked form well into adolescence (reviewed in McGann, 1999). In contrast, "sissies" face more outright condemnation and social rejection (Corbett, 1999; Halderman, 2000; Rofes, 1995), and their behavior is more likely to be considered potentially pathological by parents, teachers, and physicians (Corbett, 1999; Weisz & Weiss, 1991; Zucker & Bradley, 1995).

In addition to the obvious issues of stigmatization, social ostracization, and harassment, it is important to consider the internal psychological sequelae of gender nonconformity during the adolescent years, particularly youths' concerns about the nature of their sexual identity. As noted above, as a result of cultural associations between gender nonconformity and homosexuality, gender-nonconforming youths are not only frequently suspected of being lesbian/gay/bisexual, but often wonder themselves whether this is the case, even in the absence of same-sex attractions (Hunter, 1993; McGann, 1999). This reflects the fact that there is more cultural "space" for a notion of gender-typical sexual minorities than for gender-nonconforming heterosexuals (Hunter, 1993). In other words, although people may no longer unilaterally presume that all gay men are hyper-feminine, it is still commonly presumed that any man who is hyper-feminine is likely to be gay. Thus, in addition to confronting the same risks for stigmatization, isolation, and harassment that are confronted by sexual-minority youths, gender-nonconforming youths also face the problem of having their sexual identity defined for them, often before they have even had a chance to reflect upon it themselves.

On this point, it bears noting that the association between gender nonconformity and sexual orientation is not altogether fallacious. Sexual-minority adolescents and adults recall significantly more gender-nonconforming ideation and/or behavior in childhood than do heterosexuals (Bailey et al., 1995; Bailey & Zucker, 1995; Phillips & Over, 1992, 1995), as well as reporting significantly more contemporaneous gender nonconformity (Lippa, 2000). The perennial question, of course, is why. One possibility (consistent with most folk wisdom on the issue) is that gender nonconformity and same-sex sexual orientations have a common biological etiology, whereas another possibility is that the widespread cultural conflation of these two phenomena creates a socially-induced self-fulfilling prophecy, such that sexual-minority individuals end up recalling and adopting the very gender-nonconforming behaviors that everybody expects them to recall and adopt (see Bailey, 1996). Both possibilities may be operative. The most important point is not to *assume* direct correspondence between a youths' gender nonconformity and his/her sexual identity.

## TRANSGENDER YOUTH

Whereas gender-nonconforming youth deviate from gender norms and stereotypes while maintaining a clear-cut sense of their personal identity as male or female, transgender youth are those whose gender-related *identification* does not conform to conventional standards presuming a coherent, singular, and unambiguous self-concept as male or female. Historically, most research on transgender individuals focused exclusively on *transsexuals*, who typically report feeling that there is a fundamental mismatch between their psychological sense of gender and their biological sex, and who seek to resolve this misalignment through a combination of physical transformation (via clothes, make-up, demeanor, hormones, or surgery) and a formal change in legal status (Henton, 2006; Lawrence, 2003, 2007; Sperber, Landers, & Lawrence, 2005). Although transsexualism might be the most widely known form of transgender experience (among both psychologists and laypeople alike), it is certainly not the only one. In fact, the word and concept "transgender" came into use because many individuals with more complex and ambiguous experiences of gender identity felt that they were poorly described by models of transsexualism.

One of the most important developments over the past several decades of research on gender identity and expression has been the increasing appreciation of the diversity of the transgender population (Devor, 2004; Ekins & King, 1999; Gagné, Tewksbury, & McGaughey, 1997; Halberstam, 2005; Roen, 2002). Contrary to the widespread assumption that most transgender individuals are distressed by, and hence seek to resolve and eliminate, discrepancies or ambiguities in their psychological experience and physical expression of gender, research has revealed that many transgender children, adolescents, and adults *embrace* their fluid, shifting, and ambiguous gender identifications, and do not seek unambiguous identification as male or female. For example, Gagné, Tewksbury, & McGaughey (1997) charted multiple forms of gender identity in their diverse sample of transgender participants. Although some sought a complete and clear-cut switch from one gender category to the other, others maintained various mixtures of male and female attributes, sometimes aided by the selective use of surgery and hormones, and sometimes not. The diversity of contemporary transgender experience is reflected by the wide array of identity terms adopted by transgender youths and adults, including gender blender, gender bender, gender outlaw, gender queer, drag king/queen, trans, transgender(ist), and queer (Carroll, Gilroy, & Ryan, 2002; Ekins & King, 1999; Rosser, Oakes, Bockting, & Miner, 2007).

In embracing the complexity and fluidity of their gender identities, transgender youths pose an inherent challenge to traditional assumptions that the normative and healthy endpoint of transgender identity development must involve the adoption of a stable, integrated, unambiguous identification as 100% male or 100% female (for reviews and critiques see Bornstein, 1994; Roen, 2002). After all, as recently as 1987, the Diagnostic and Statistical Manual of Mental Disorders (DSM-III) recognized a lack of coherent identity as a risk factor for poor mental health outcomes (American Psychiatric Association, 1987, as cited in Poston, 1990), and children who fail to develop a stable, psychological sense of gender (and who appear to be distressed as a result) may be diagnosed with gender identity disorder (GID) (American Psychiatric Association, 2000; Carroll et al., 2002; Levine et al., 1999). Yet there have been important conceptual and theoretical advances to gender and transgender identity development. For example, Denny, Leli, and Drescher's model (Denny, 2004) de-emphasizes the rigid gender binary that characterizes conventional models of gender identity development, and instead presumes the existence of parallel gender continuums inclusive of male and female dimensions.

Despite these changes, psychologists tend to express ambivalence about whether it is healthy for youths to embrace a permanently liminal, flexible sense of gender, instead of moving progressively toward the goal of consistently identifying as male or female (reviewed in Mallon & DeCrescenzo, 2006). Yet there are no empirical data directly speaking to this question. In contrast to the extensive body of research on conventional gender identity development (Kohlberg et al., 1974; Martin & Ruble, 2004; Ruble, Martin, & Berenbaum, 2006; Ruble et al., 2007), little research has focused on the basic developmental processes of transgender identity development in nonclinical populations (Gagné et al., 1997; Mason-Schrock, 1996), or has explored normative and resilient outcomes in this population. This is clearly an important topic for future research.

## EXPOSURE TO STIGMATIZATION

One finding regarding the mental health of transgender adolescents is unambiguously clear: social stigmatization, including physical victimization, poses the pre-eminent threat to transgender youths' mental and physical health. These findings concord with the *minority stress* model of sexual-minority health (Meyer, 2003), which specifies that sexual minorities' acute exposure to environmental stressors such as verbal or physical abuse, institutional discrimination, interpersonal harassment, and general social marginalization confers cumulative psychological stress. This stress, in turn, negatively affects both mental and physical well-being. Research documents that transgender and gender-variant individuals are subjected to widespread psychological and physical abuse (M. Brown & Rounsely, 2003; Feinberg, 1996, 2006). A recurring survey conducted by the National Coalition of Anti-Violence Programs (NCAVP) of bias-motivated violence against gender and sexual minorities has found that hate crimes against gender-nonconforming adolescents and adults accounted for one-fifth of all documented murders (National Coalition of Anti-Violence Programs 1999; 2007). A recent survey of 515 trans-identified people (392 male-to-female, 123 female-to-male) (Clements-Nolle, Marx, & Katz, 2006), reported that 28% of the respondents had been in an alcohol or drug treatment program, 62% had experienced gender discrimination, 83% had experienced gender-related verbal discrimination, 59% had experienced sexual assault (rape), and 32% had reported attempted suicide. Among the sample's youth (<25 years of age), nearly half had attempted suicide as a result of gender-based victimization.

Transgender and gender-variant *adolescents* are particularly vulnerable to environmental stressors. Such youths routinely face verbal and physical harassment at the hands of peers (D'Augelli et al., 2002; Sausa, 2005), sometimes several times a day, leaving them feeling fundamentally unsafe at school. Even youths who escape victimization in school must contend with heightened psychosocial stress in their daily lives. In addition to the normative stressors associated with adolescent social and psychological development, gender nonconforming adolescents often struggle with an inability to articulate to others *why* they feel different, and hence frequently report feeling isolated, depressed, hopeless, or utterly invisible to friends and family (Swann & Herbert, 1999). To cope with feelings of shame and isolation, transgender and gender variant youths may display a range of externalizing problems, including running away from home, dropping out of school, abusing substances, or self-harm (Burgess & Cottrell, 1936; D'Augelli, Hershberger, & Pilkington, 2001; Sausa, 2005).

In the context of these risks and stressors, what conclusions might we draw about different trajectories of transgender identity development? One likely possibility is that during the adolescent years, it may be difficult—or impossible—to tell whether a particular youth is "headed" for one trajectory or another. Although some adolescents may self-identify as transsexual at fairly early ages, expressing clear desires to permanently change their gender, it is important to remember that such youths may perceive that this is the *only* outcome of gender questioning.

The possibility of adopting a more fluid, liminal sense of gender may have never occurred to many youths; in addition, they are unlikely to have any visible models of such forms of gender fluidity. Hence, their ability to craft a meaningful autobiographical narrative which contains—and makes sense of—their conflicting and changing experiences of masculinity and femininity is impaired. Given this limitation, the healthiest identity trajectory for transgender adolescents may be one which makes no presumptions about desirable outcomes, and sets no timetables for resolution, but instead remains open to multiple possibilities over potentially long periods of time. Youths need time, support, information, and autonomy as they grapple with their own sense of gendered selfhood, and seek a comfortable and personally authentic constellation of female-typed, male-typed, and gender-neutral traits. *Changes* in this constellation—at the level of cognition as well as appearance, and occurring during adolescence as well as adulthood—may be part and parcel of the identity development process.

One thing, however, is abundantly clear: neither transgender youths nor adults can embark on this process without a basic sense of safety. As long as transgender individuals are forced to navigate their school and family worlds with an ever-present, debilitating fear of stigmatization, ostracization, humiliation, and physical violence, they cannot be expected to achieve a healthy sense of self-determination, whether such self-determination involves switching their gender identity or making peace with a lasting sense of gender fluidity.

With respect to transgender youth, it is evident that supportive adults play a key role in facilitating resilience and positive development (Garofalo, Deleon, Osmer, Doll, & Harper, 2006; Grossman & D'Augelli, 2006; Mallon & DeCrescenzo, 2006; Mallon & Woronoff, 2006; Smith, 2005). Decades of research on resilience, conducted with mainstream as well as at-risk populations, has shown that adults can strengthen youth by teaching them how to respond positively to adversity (Bernard, 2006). With respect to transgender youth in particular, adults may require special education and awareness. For example, learning the preferred name and pronoun usage of a transgender youth is critical to gaining their trust and supporting their own developmental pathway. Similarly, ensuring and maintaining confidentiality is critical for demonstrating to transgender youth that their safety will not be compromised, given the risks that these youths typically face for discrimination and violence. Finally, research on resilience (Bernard, 2006) also indicates that young people flourish when they know that adults believe and nurture their capacity to succeed.

Accordingly, it is important to encourage transgender and gender nonconforming youth to be visible and proud leaders and role models for others just like them.

## CONCLUSION

Although this review has necessarily emphasized many of the psychosocial challenges faced by sexual-minority, gender-nonconforming, and transgender youths, it is important to acknowledge that an increasing body of research has focused on the *positive* attributes, strengths, and skills of these youths (for example Savin-Williams, 2005). For example, evidence suggests that for some youths, actively wrestling with questions about their gender and sexuality can help them to foster a healthier sense of sexual agency, to become better able "to know their sexuality as feelings as well as actions, feelings to which they are entitled" (Tolman, 1994, p. 268). Even individuals who experiment with same-sex sexuality, but end up identifying as heterosexual, might benefit from temporarily broadening their definitions and conceptualizations of sexuality. In particular, participation in same-sex activity necessarily disrupts widespread cultural assumptions about the "naturalness" of heterosexuality, as well as the "naturalness" of female and male gender roles. Participation in same-sex relationships and consideration of same-sex attractions might prompt all individuals to ask themselves important, useful questions about how they conceive of their sexuality, and what types of relationships they desire in the future. This has the potential to create altogether new and healthy trajectories of sexual and gender development.

Perhaps the most important recommendation for clinicians serving sexual-minority, gender-nonconforming, and transgender youths is to take seriously the incredible diversity of these individuals' sexual profiles. This entails acknowledging and communicating to youths that the categories "heterosexual," "gay/lesbian," "bisexual," and even "female" and "male" do not represent the full range of feelings, fantasies, and relationships they may find themselves experiencing throughout the lifespan. Clinicians can play a critically important role for youths by simply providing them with a safe and supportive context within which they can consider the personal meaning of same-sex sexuality and gender expression for their current and future relationships and identity. Our current task is to chart the multiple, interacting factors producing *diversity* in their developmental pathways. A fuller understanding of such diversity will clearly advance our capacity to foster *all* youths' positive sexual and gender development over the lifespan.

# REFERENCES

Allport, G. W. (1954). *The nature of prejudice.* Reading, MA: Addison-Wesley.
American Psychiatric Association, (2000). *Diagnostic and statistical manual of mental disorders* (4th ed.). Washington, DC: American Psychiatric Association.
Anderson, A. L. (1998). Strengths of gay male youth: An untold story. *Child and Adolescent Social Work Journal, 15,* 55–71.
Bailey, J. M. (1996). Gender identity. In R. C. Savin-Williams, & K. M. Cohen (Eds.), *The lives of lesbians, gays, and bisexuals: Children to adults* (pp. 71–93). Fort Worth, TX: Harcourt Brace.
Bailey, J. M. (2009). What is sexual orientation and do women have one? In D. A. Hope (Ed.), *Nebraska symposium on motivation: Contemporary perspectives on lesbian, gay, and bisexual identities* (Vol. 54, pp. 43–63). Lincoln, NE: University of Nebraska Press.
Bailey, J. M., & Zucker, K. J. (1995). Childhood sex-typed behavior and sexual orientation: A conceptual analysis and quantitative review. *Developmental Psychology, 31,* 43–55.
Bailey, J. M., Dunne, M. P., & Martin, N. G. (2000). Genetic and environmental influences on sexual orientation and its correlates in an Australian twin sample. *Journal of Personality and Social Psychology, 78,* 524–536.
Bailey, J. M., Gaulin, S., Agyei, Y., & Gladue, B. (1994). Effects of gender and sexual orientation on evolutionarily relevant aspects of human mating psychology. *Journal of Personality and Social Psychology, 66,* 1081–1093.
Bailey, J. M., Nothnagel, J., & Wolfe, B. A. (1995). Retrospectively measured individual differences in childhood sex-typed behavior among gay men: A correspondence between self and maternal reports. *Archives of Sexual Behavior, 24,* 613–622.
Balsam, K. F., Rothblum, E. D., & Beauchaine, T. P. (2005). Victimization over the life span: A comparison of lesbian, gay, bisexual, and heterosexual siblings. *Journal of Consulting and Clinical Psychology, 73,* 477–487.
Bancroft, J. H. (1990). The impact of sociocultural influences on adolescent sexual development: Further considerations. In J. H. Bancroft, & J. M. Reinisch (Eds.), *Adolescence and puberty* (pp. 207–216). New York, NY: Oxford University Press.
Baumeister, R. F. (2000). Gender differences in erotic plasticity: The female sex drive as socially flexible and responsive. *Psychological Bulletin, 126,* 247–374.
Bernard, B. (2006). The foundations of the resiliency paradigm. In N. Henderson (Ed.), *Resiliency in action: Practical ideas for overcoming risks and building strengths in youth, families, and communities* (pp. 3–7). Ojai, CA: Resiliency in Action.
Bontempo, D. E., & D'Augelli, A. R. (2002). Effects of at-school victimization and sexual orientation on lesbian, gay, or bisexual youths' health risk behavior. *Journal of Adolescent Health, 30,* 364–374.
Bornstein, K. (1994). *Gender outlaw: Men, women, and the rest of us.* New York, NY: Routledge.
Brown, L. (1989). Lesbians, gay men, and their families: Common clinical issues. *Journal of Gay and Lesbian Psychotherapy, 1,* 65–77.
Brown, M., & Rounsely, C. (2003). *True selves: Understanding transsexualism – For families, friends, coworkers, and helping professionals.* San Francisco, CA: Jossey-Bass.
Burgess, E. W., & Cottrell, L. S. (1936). The prediction of adjustment in marriage. *American Sociological Review, 1,* 737–751.
Carey, B. (July 5, 2005). Straight, gay or lying? Bisexuality revisited. *New York Times,* 1.
Carroll, L., Gilroy, P. J., & Ryan, J. (2002). Counseling trangendered, transsexual, and gender-variant clients. *Journal of Counseling & Development, 80,* 131–138.
Chandra, A., Mosher, W. D., Copen, C., & Sionean, C. (2011). Sexual behavior, sexual attraction, and sexual identity in the United States: Data from the 2006–2008 National Survey of Family Growth. *National Health Statistics Reports, March, 3,* 1–36.

Chivers, M. L., & Bailey, J. M. (2000). Sexual orientation of female-to-male transsexuals: A comparison of homosexual and nonhomosexual types. *Archives of Sexual Behavior, 29*, 259–278.

Chivers, M. L., & Bailey, J. M. (2005). A sex difference in features that elicit genital response. *Biological Psychology, 70*, 115–120.

Chivers, M. L., Rieger, G., Latty, E., & Bailey, J. M. (2004). A sex difference in the specificity of sexual arousal. *Psychological Science, 15*, 736–744.

Chivers, M. L., Seto, M. C., & Blanchard, R. (2007). Gender and sexual orientation differences in sexual response to sexual activities versus gender of actors in sexual films. *Journal of Personality and Social Psychology, 93*, 1108–1121.

Clements-Nolle, K., Marx, R., & Katz, M. (2006). Attempted suicide among transgender persons: The influence of gender-based discrimination and victimization. *Journal of Homosexuality, 51*, 53–69.

Cole, S. S., Denny, D., Eyler, A. E., & Samons, S. L. (2000). Issues of transgender. In L. T. Szuchman, & F. Muscarella (Eds.), *Psychological perspectives on human sexuality (pp. 149–195)*. New York, NY: John Wiley & Sons.

Consolacion, T. B., Russell, S. T., & Sue, S. (2004). Sex, race/ethnicity, and romantic attractions: Multiple minority status adolescents and mental health. *Cultural Diversity & Ethnic Minority Psychology, 10*, 200–214.

Corbett, K. (1998). Cross-gendered identifications and homosexual boyhood: Toward a more complex theory of gender. *American Journal of Orthopsychiatry, 68*, 352–360.

Corbett, K. (1999). Homosexual boyhood: Notes on girlyboys. In M. Rottnek (Ed.), *Sissies and tomboys: Gender nonconformity and homosexual childhood (pp. 107–139)*. New York, NY: New York University Press.

Crocker, J., Major, B., & Steele, C. (1998). Social stigma (4th ed.). In D. T. Gilbert, S. T. Fiske, & G. Lindzey (Eds.), *The handbook of social psychology (Vols. 1 and 2, pp. 504–553)*. New York, NY: McGraw-Hill.

D'Augelli, A. R., Grossman, A. H., & Starks, M. T. (2005). Parents' awareness of lesbian, gay, and bisexual youths' sexual orientation. *Journal of Marriage & Family, 67*, 474–482.

D'Augelli, A. R., Grossman, A. H., & Starks, M. T. (2006). Childhood gender atypicality, victimization, and PTSD among lesbian, gay, and bisexual youth. *Journal of Interpersonal Violence, 21*, 1462–1482.

D'Augelli, A. R., Hershberger, S. L., & Pilkington, N. W. (2001). Suicidality patterns and sexual orientation-related factors among lesbian, gay, and bisexual youths. *Suicide and Life-Threatening Behavior, 31*, 250–264.

D'Augelli, A. R., Pilkington, N. W., & Hershberger, S. L. (2002). Incidence and mental health impact of sexual orientation victimization of lesbian, gay, and bisexual youths in high school. *School Psychology Quarterly, 17*, 148–167.

Denny, D. (2004). Changing models of transsexualism. In U. Leli, & J. Drescher (Eds.), *Transgender subjectivities: A clinician's guide (pp. 25–40)*. New York, NY: Haworth Press.

Denny, D., & Green, J. (1996). Gender identity and bisexuality. In Beth A. Firestein (Ed.), *Bisexuality: The psychology and politics of an invisible minority (102, p. 84)*. Thousand Oaks, CA: Sage Publications, Inc., [xxvii, 329 pp].

Devor, A. H. (1993). Toward a taxonomy of gendered sexuality. *Journal of Psychology and Human Sexuality, 6*, 23–54.

Devor, A. H. (2004). Witnessing and mirroring: A fourteen stage model of transsexual identity formation. *Journal of Gay & Lesbian Psychotherapy, 8*, 41–67.

Diamond, L. M. (2000). Sexual identity, attractions, and behavior among young sexual-minority women over a two-year period. *Developmental Psychology, 36*, 241–250.

Diamond, L. M. (2003). Was it a phase? Young women's relinquishment of lesbian/bisexual identities over a 5-year period. *Journal of Personality and Social Psychology, 84*, 352–364.

Diamond, L. M. (2005). A new view of lesbian subtypes: Stable vs. fluid identity trajectories over an 8-year period. *Psychology of Women Quarterly, 29*, 119–128.

Diamond, L. M. (2008a). Female bisexuality from adolescence to adulthood: Results from a 10 year longitudinal study. *Developmental Psychology, 44*, 5–14.

Diamond, L. M. (2008b). *Sexual fluidity: Understanding women's love and desire.* Cambridge, MA: Harvard University Press.

Dickson, N., Paul, C., & Herbison, P. (2003). Same-sex attraction in a birth cohort: Prevalence and persistence in early adulthood. *Social Science & Medicine, 56*, 1607–1615.

Ekins, R., & King, D. (1999). Towards a sociology of transgendered bodies. *The Sociological Review, 47*, 580–602.

Feinberg, L. (1996). *Transgender warriors: Making history from Joan of Arc to Dennis Rodman.* Boston, MA: Beacon Press.

Feinberg, L. (2006). *Drag king dreams.* New York, NY: Carroll & Graff.

Firestein, B. A. (Ed.). (1996). *Bisexuality: The psychology and politics of an invisible minority.* Thousand Oaks, CA: Sage Publications, Inc.

Firestein, B. A. (Ed.). (2007). *Becoming visible: Counseling bisexuals across the lifespan.* New York, NY: Columbia University Press.

Fitzpatrick, K. K., Euton, S. J., Jones, J. N., & Schmidt, N. B. (2005). Gender role, sexual orientation and suicide risk. *Journal of Affective Disorders, 87*, 35–42.

French, S. A., Story, M., Remafedi, G., Resnick, M. D., & Blum, R. W. (1996). Sexual orientation and prevalence of body dissatisfaction and eating disordered behaviors: A population-based study of adolescents. *International Journal of Eating Disorders, 19*, 119–126.

Gagné, P., Tewksbury, R., & McGaughey, D. (1997). Coming out and crossing over: Identity formation and proclamation in a transgender community. *Gender & Society, 11*, 478–508.

Garofalo, R., Deleon, J., Osmer, E., Doll, M., & Harper, G. W. (2006). Overlooked, misunderstood and at-risk: Exploring the lives and HIV risk of ethnic minority male-to-female transgender youth. *Journal of Adolescent Health, 38*, 230–236.

Garofalo, R., Wolf, R. C., Wissow, L. S., Woods, E. R., & Goodman, E. (1999). Sexual orientation and risk of suicide attempts among a representative sample of youth. *Archives of Pediatrics and Adolescent Medicine, 153*, 487–493.

Goffman, I. (1963). *Stigma.* Englewood Cliffs, NJ: Prentice-Hall.

Golden, C. (1996). What's in a name? Sexual self-identification among women. In R. C. Savin-Williams, & K. M. Cohen (Eds.), *The lives of lesbians, gays, and bisexuals: Children to adults (pp. 229–249).* Fort Worth, TX: Harcourt Brace.

Goy, R. W., & Goldfoot, D. A. (1975). Neuroendocrinology: Animal models and problems of human sexuality. *Archives of Sexual Behavior, 4*, 405–420.

Grossman, A. H., & D'Augelli, A. R. (2006). Transgender youth: Invisible and vulnerable. *Journal of Homosexuality, 51*, 111–128.

Grossman, A. H., D'Augelli, A. R., Howell, T. J., & Hubbard, S. (2005). Parents' reactions to transgender youths' gender nonconforming expression and identity. *Journal of Gay & Lesbian Social Services, 18*, 3–16.

Halberstam, J. (2005). *In a queer time and place: Transgender bodies, subcultural lives.* New York, NY: NYU Press.

Halderman, D. C. (2000). Gender atypical youth: Clinical and social issues. *School Psychology Review, 29*, 192–200.

Henton, D. (2006). Young, transgender, and out in east Los Angeles. In L. Messinger, & D. F. Morrow (Eds.), *Case studies on sexual orientation & gender expression in social work practice (pp. 16–18).* New York, NY: Columbia University Press.

Herdt, G., & Beeler, J. (1998). Older gay men and lesbians in families. In C. Patterson, & A. R. D' Augelli (Eds.), *Lesbian, gay, and bisexual identities in families: Psychological Perspectives (pp. 177–196).* New York, NY: Oxford University Press.

Hill, J., & Lynch, M. (1983). The intensification of gender-related role expectations during early adolescence. In J. Brooks-Gunn, & A. Peterson (Eds.), *Female puberty (pp. 201–228)*. New York, NY: Plenum.

Horn, S. S., & Nucci, L. (2006). Harassment of gay and lesbian youth and school violence in America: An analysis and directions for intervention. In C. Daiute, Z. Beykont, C. Higson-Smith, & L. Nucci (Eds.), *International perspectives on youth conflict and development (pp. 139–155)*. New York, NY: Oxford University Press.

Hunter, A. (1993). Same door, different closet: A heterosexual sissy's coming-out party. In S. Wilkinson, & C. Kitzinger (Eds.), *Heterosexuality: A feminism and psychology reader (pp. 150–168)*. London, UK: Sage.

Kohlberg, L., Ullian, D. Z., Friedman, R. C., Richart, R. M., Vande Wiele, R. L., & Stern, L. O. (1974). Stages in the development of psychosexual concepts and attitudes: *Sex differences in behavior*. Oxford, UK: John Wiley & Sons.

Konik, J., & Stewart, A. (2004). Sexual identity development in the context of compulsory heterosexuality. *Journal of Personality, 72*, 815–844.

Kosciw, J. G., Greytak, E. A., & Diaz, E. M. (2009). Who, what, where, when, and why: Demographic and ecological factors contributing to hostile school climate for lesbian, gay, bisexual, and transgender youth. *Journal of Youth and Adolescence, 38*, 976–988.

Laumann, E. O., Gagnon, J. H., Michael, R. T., & Michaels, F. (1994). *The social organization of sexuality: Sexual practices in the United States*. Chicago, IL: University of Chicago Press.

Lawrence, A. A. (2003). Factors associated with satisfaction or regret following male-to-female sex reassignment surgery. *Archives of Sexual Behavior, 32*, 299–315.

Lawrence, A. A. (2007). Transgender health concerns. In I. H. Meyer, & M. E. Northridge (Eds.), *The health of sexual minorities: Public health perspectives on lesbian, gay, bisexual, and transgender populations (pp. 473–505)*. New York, NY: Springer Science + Business Media.

Levine, S. B., Brown, G. R., Coleman, E., Cohen-Kettenis, P. T., Hage, J. J., Van Maasdam, J., et al. (1999). The standards of care for gender identity disorders. *Journal of Psychology & Human Sexuality, 11*, 1–34.

Lippa, R. A. (2000). Gender-related traits in gay men, lesbian women, and heterosexual men and women: The virtual identity of homosexual-heterosexual diagnosticity and gender diagnosticity. *Journal of Personality, 68*, 899–926.

Loftus, J. (2001). America's liberalization in attitudes toward homosexuality. *American Sociological Review, 66*, 762–782.

Mallon, G. P. (2001). Sticks and stones can break your bones: Verbal harassment and physical violence in the lives of gay and lesbian youths in child welfare settings. *Journal of Gay & Lesbian Social Services: Issues in Practice, Policy & Research, 13*, 63–81.

Mallon, G. P., & DeCrescenzo, T. (2006). Transgender children and youth: A child welfare practice perspective. *Child Welfare Journal, 85*, 215–241.

Mallon, G. P., & Woronoff, R. (2006). Busting out of the child welfare closet: Lesbian, gay, bisexual, and transgender-affirming approaches to child welfare. *Child Welfare Journal, 85*, 115–122.

Martin, C. L. (1990). Attitudes and expectations about children with nontraditional and traditional gender roles. *Sex Roles, 22*, 151–165.

Martin, C. L., & Ruble, D. (2004). Children's search for gender cues: Cognitive perspectives on gender development. *Current Directions in Psychological Science, 13*, 67–70.

Mason-Schrock, D. (1996). Transsexuals' narrative construction of the "true self." *Social Psychology Quarterly, 59*, 176–192.

McGann, P. J. (1999). Skirting the gender normal divide: A tomboy life story. In M. Romero, & A. J. Stewart (Eds.), *Women's untold stories: Breaking silence, talking back, voicing complexity (pp. 105–124)*. New York, NY: Routledge.

Meyer, I. H. (2003). Prejudice, social stress, and mental health in lesbian, gay, and bisexual populations: Conceptual issues and research evidence. *Psychological Bulletin, 129*, 674–697.

Mosher, W. D., Chandra, A., & Jones, J. (2005). *Sexual behavior and selected health measures: Men and women 15–44 years of age, United States, 2002.* Hyattsville, MD: National Center for Health Statistics. [Advance data from vital and health statistics, no. 362].

National Coalition of Anti-Violence Programs. (1999). Anti-lesbian, gay, transgender, and bisexual violence in 1999: A report of the National Coalition of Anti-Violence Programs. Retrieved June 1, 2008, from <www.ncavp.org/publications/NationalPubs.aspx>.

National Coalition of Anti-Violence Programs. (2007). Anti-lesbian, gay, transgender, and bisexual violence in 2007: A report of the National Coalition of Anti-Violence Programs. Retrieved June 1, 2008, from <www.ncavp.org/publications/NationalPubs.aspx>.

Paul, J. P. (1985). Bisexuality: Reassessing our paradigms of sexuality. In F. Klein, & T. Wolf (Eds.), *Two lives to lead: Bisexuality in men and women (pp. 21–34).* New York, NY: Harrington Park Press.

Paul, J. P. (1996). Bisexuality: Exploring/exploding the boundaries. In R. C. Savin-Williams, & K. M. Cohen (Eds.), *The lives of lesbians, gays, and bisexuals: Children to adults (pp. 436–461).* Orlando, FL: Harcourt Brace College Publishers.

Pettigrew, T. F. (1967). Social evaluation theory: Convergences and applications. *Nebraska Symposium on Motivation, 15,* 241–311.

Phillips, G., & Over, R. (1992). Adult sexual orientation in relation to memories of childhood gender conforming and gender nonconforming behaviors. *Archives of Sexual Behavior, 21,* 543–558.

Phillips, G., & Over, R. (1995). Differences between heterosexual, bisexual, and lesbian women in recalled childhood experiences. *Archives of Sexual Behavior, 24,* 1–20.

Poston, W. C. (1990). The biracial identity development model: A needed addition. *Journal of Counseling & Development, 69,* 152–155.

Remafedi, G. (1999). Sexual orientation and youth suicide. *Journal of the American Medical Association, 282,* 1291–1292.

Remafedi, G., French, S., Story, M., Resnick, M. D., & Blum, R. (1998). The relationship between suicide risk and sexual orientation: Results of a population-based study. *American Journal of Public Health, 88,* 57–60.

Remafedi, G., Resnick, M., Blum, R., & Harris, L. (1992). Demography of sexual orientation in adolescents. *Pediatrics, 89,* 714–721.

Rieger, G., Bailey, J. M., & Chivers, M. L. (2005). Sexual arousal patterns of bisexual men. *Psychological Science, 16,* 579–584.

Rivers, I., & D'Augelli, A. R. (2001). The victimization of lesbians, gay, and bisexual youths. In A. R. D'Augelli, & C. J. Patterson (Eds.), *Lesbian, gay, and bisexual identities and youth: Psychological perspectives (pp. 199–223).* New York, NY: Oxford University Press.

Roen, K. (2002). "Either/or" and "both/neither:" Discursive tensions in transgender politics. *Signs, 27,* 501–522.

Rofes, E. (1995). Making our schools safe for sissies. In G. Unks (Ed.), *The gay teen: Educational practice and theory for lesbian, gay, and bisexual adolescents (pp. 79–84).* New York, NY: Routledge.

Rosario, M., Schrimshaw, E. W., & Hunter, J. (2004). Predictors of substance use over time among gay, lesbian, and bisexual youths: An examination of three hypotheses. *Addictive Behaviors, 29,* 1623–1631.

Rosario, M., Schrimshaw, E. W., & Hunter, J. (2006). A model of sexual risk behaviors among young gay and bisexual men: Longitudinal associations of mental health, substance abuse, sexual abuse, and the coming-out process. *AIDS Education and Prevention, 18,* 444–460.

Rosario, M., Schrimshaw, E. W., & Hunter, J. (2008). Predicting different patterns of sexual identity development over time among lesbian, gay, and bisexual youths: A cluster analytic approach. *American Journal of Community Psychology, 42,* 266–282.

Rosser, B. R. S., Oakes, J. M., Bockting, W. O., & Miner, M. (2007). Capturing the social demographics of hidden sexual minorities: An internet study of the transgender population in the United States. *Sexuality Research & Social Policy: A Journal of the NSRC, 4,* 50–64.

Ruble, D. N., Martin, C. L., & Berenbaum, S. A. (2006). Gender development. In N. Eisenberg, W. Damon, & R. M. Lerner (Eds.), *Handbook of child psychology, 6th ed.: Vol 3. Social, emotional, and personality development (pp. 858–932)* Hoboken, NJ: John Wiley & Sons Inc..

Ruble, D. N., Taylor, L. J., Cyphers, L., Greulich, F. K., Lurye, L. E., & Shrout, P. E. (2007). The role of gender constancy in early gender development. *Child Development, 78,* 1121–1136.

Russell, S. T., & Consolacion, T. B. (2003). Adolescent romance and emotional health in the U.S.: Beyond binaries. *Journal of Clinical Child and Adolescent Psychology, 32,* 499–508.

Russell, S. T., & Joyner, K. (2001). Adolescent sexual orientation and suicide risk: Evidence from a national study. *American Journal of Public Health, 91,* 1276–1281.

Russell, S. T., & Seif, H. (2002). Bisexual female adolescents: A critical analysis of past research, and results from a national survey. *Journal of Bisexuality, 2,* 73–94.

Russell, S. T., Franz, B. T., & Driscoll, A. K. (2001). Same-sex romantic attraction and experiences of violence in adolescence. *American Journal of Public Health, 91,* 903–906.

Rust, P. C. R. (1992). The politics of sexual identity: Sexual attraction and behavior among lesbian and bisexual women. *Social Problems, 39,* 366–386.

Rust, P. C. R. (1993). Coming out in the age of social constructionism: Sexual identity formation among lesbians and bisexual women. *Gender and Society, 7,* 50–77.

Rust, P. C. R. (2000a). *Bisexuality in the United States: A reader and guide to the literature.* New York, NY: Columbia University Press.

Rust, P. C. R. (2000b). Criticisms of the scholarly literature on sexuality for its neglect of bisexuality. In P. C. R. Rust (Ed.), *Bisexuality in the United States: A reader and guide to the literature (pp. 5–10).* New York, NY: Columbia University Press.

Rust, P. C. R. (2000c). Heterosexual gays, heterosexual lesbians, and homosexual straights. In P. C. R. Rust (Ed.), *Bisexuality in the United States: A reader and guide to the literature (pp. 279–306).* New York, NY: Columbia University Press.

Rutter, P. A., & Soucar, E. (2002). Youth suicide risk and sexual orientation. *Adolescence, 37,* 289–299.

Ryan, C., Huebner, D., Diaz, R. M., & Sanchez, J. (2009). Family rejection as a predictor of negative health outcomes in white and latino lesbian, gay, and bisexual young adults. *Pediatrics, 123,* 346–352.

Safe Schools Coalition of Washington. (1999). Selected findings of eight population-based studies as they pertain to anti-gay harassment and the safety and well-being of sexual minority students. Retrieved May 15, 2006, 2006, from <http://www.safeschoolscoalition.org/83000youth.pdf>.

Sandberg, D. E., Meyer Bahlburg, H. F., Ehrhardt, A. A., & Yager, T. J. (1993). The prevalence of gender-atypical behavior in elementary school children. *Journal of the American Academy of Child and Adolescent Psychiatry, 32,* 306–314.

Sausa, L. A. (2005). Translating research into practice: Trans youth recommendations for improving school systems. *Gay and Lesbian Issues in Education, 3,* 15–28.

Savin-Williams, R. C. (1998). *"... And then I became gay:" Young men's stories.* New York, NY: Routledge.

Savin-Williams, R. C. (2001). Suicide attempts among sexual-minority youths: Population and measurement issues. *Journal of Consulting & Clinical Psychology, 69,* 983–991.

Savin-Williams, R. C. (2005). *The new gay teenager.* Cambridge, MA: Harvard University Press.

Savin-Williams, R. C. (2011). Identity development among sexual-minority youth. In S. Schwartz, K. Luyckx, & V. Vignoles (Eds.), *Handbook of identity theory and research (pp. 671–689).* New York, NY: Springer.

Savin-Williams, R. C., & Ream, G. L. (2003). Suicide attempts among sexual-minority male youth. *Journal of Clinical Child & Adolescent Psychology, 32,* 509–522.

Savin-Williams, R. C., & Ream, G. L. (2007). Prevalence and stability of sexual orientation components during adolescence and young adulthood. *Archives of Sexual Behavior, 36*, 385–394.

Smith, S. D. (2005). Sexually underrepresented youth: Understanding gay, lesbian, bisexual, transgender, and questioning (GLBT-Q) youth. In J. L. Chin (Ed.), *The psychology of prejudice and discrimination: Bias based on gender and sexual orientation (Vol. 3, pp. 151–199)*. Westport, CT: Praeger Publishers / Greenwood Publishing Group.

Sperber, J., Landers, S., & Lawrence, S. (2005). Access to health care for transgendered persons: Results of a needs assessment in Boston. *International Journal of Transgenderism, 8*, 75–91.

Swann, S., & Herbert, S. E. (1999). Ethical issues in the mental health treatment of gender dysphoric adolescents. *Journal of Gay & Lesbian Social Services: Issues in Practice, Policy & Research, 10*, 19–34.

Tolman, D. L. (1994). Daring to desire: Culture and the bodies of adolescent girls. In J. Irvine (Ed.), *Sexual cultures: Adolescents, communities and the construction of identity (pp. 250–284)*. Philadelphia, PA: Temple University Press.

Tolman, D. L., & Diamond, L. M. (2001). Desegregating sexuality research: Combining cultural and biological perspectives on gender and desire. *Annual Review of Sex Research, 12*, 33–74.

Toomey, R. B., Ryan, C., Diaz, R. M., Card, N. A., & Russell, S. T. (2010). Gender-nonconforming lesbian, gay, bisexual, and transgender youth: School victimization and young adult psychosocial adjustment. *Developmental Psychology, 46*, 1580–1589.

Walters, S. D. (2001). *All the rage: The story of gay visibility in America*. Chicago, IL: University of Chicago Press.

Weinberg, M. S., Williams, C. J., & Pryor, D. W. (1994). *Dual attraction: Understanding bisexuality*. New York, NY: Oxford University Press.

Weisz, J., & Weiss, B. (1991). Studying the referability of child clinical problems. *Journal of Consulting and Clinical Psychology, 59*, 266–273.

Williams, T., Connolly, J., Pepler, D., & Craig, W. (2003). Questioning and sexual minority adolescents: High school experiences of bullying, sexual harassment and physical abuse. *Canadian Journal of Community Mental Health, 22*, 47–58.

Williams, T., Connolly, J., Pepler, D., & Craig, W. (2005). Peer victimization, social support, and psychosocial adjustment of sexual minority adolescents. *Journal of Youth and Adolescence, 34*, 471–482.

Zucker, K. J., & Bradley, S. J. (1995). *Gender identity disorder and psychosexual problems in children and adolescents*. New York, NY: Guilford Press.

Zuger, B. (1988). Is early effeminate behavior in boys early homosexuality? *Comprehensive Psychiatry, 29*, 509–519.

PART *Four*

# Children and Adolescents as Sexual Abuse Victims

# CHAPTER 12

# Epidemiology of Child and Adolescent Sexual Abuse

Samantha L. Friedenberg, David J. Hansen, and Mary Fran Flood
University of Nebraska-Lincoln, Lincoln, Nebraska[1]

Child sexual abuse (CSA) is a prevalent and often stressful life event that happens to far too many young people. Clearly not a part of normal sexual and relationship development, it has the potential for significant impact on its victims and their families. Epidemiology addresses the incidence, distribution, and possible control of diseases and other factors related to health, and thus provides critical information about the scope of CSA. Even though it is not a "disease" that lends itself comfortably to epidemiological analysis, CSA constitutes a serious risk to healthy development, and epidemiological information can provide insight into conditions that place children and adolescents at risk for sexual victimization.

In this chapter, we explore the incidence and distribution of sexual abuse, and consider the challenges to a complete and accurate understanding of the epidemiology of CSA. We look first at definitions of CSA and note how discrepancies among them influence our ability to address epidemiological questions. We then explore the best estimates of the incidence, the number of new cases in a given time period, and prevalence, the total number of cases in a given population, of CSA and consider what we know, and what we do not know, about the characteristics of survivors and the outcomes of victimization. Epidemiological information comes from a variety of sources, which often rely on victim report. As the reader will see, the evidence is quite persuasive that a large proportion of victims do not disclose their abuse, and for those who eventually reveal their experiences, there is frequently a prolonged delay between the event(s) and the disclosure. While a portion of CSA cases may be discovered by third parties and therefore not require disclosure by a victim, delayed and avoided disclosure have a great impact on incidence and prevalence

---

[1] Correspondence to: David J. Hansen, University of Nebraska-Lincoln, 238 Burnett Hall, Lincoln, NE 68588-0308. Phone 402-472-2619; fax 402-472-4637; email dhansen1@unl.edu

estimates, and affect our understanding of victim and incident characteristics and abuse sequelae.

The current chapter provides information relating to prevalence, distribution, health, and psychological correlates of CSA. More in-depth discussions of issues associated with control of CSA, such as treatment and prevention, are provided in subsequent chapters of this volume (see Chapters 15, 16, and 17).

## DEFINING CHILD SEXUAL ABUSE

An accurate epidemiology relies on a clear definition of the health factor of interest. Without such precision, it is difficult to determine what meets the threshold for inclusion in studies of incidence, prevalence, or characteristics of the phenomenon. CSA presents significant challenges in this regard. It is not a medical or psychiatric diagnosis, and therefore it lacks a set of specified criteria to use in identifying cases. It affects children and adolescents of all ages, ethnicities, cultures, socioeconomic circumstances, and individual characteristics, and is not characterized by a single prognosis. Descriptions of CSA typically balance definitional requirements for specificity and precision with efforts to respect the substantial variation among victims, perpetrators, situations, abuse characteristics, and the frequency and severity of abusive acts. As a result, CSA definitions differ significantly and are especially influenced by the entity using the definition. The dictates of the legal system, research efforts, and clinical practice result in CSA definitions that are more or less specific or inclusive.

Legal definitions of CSA are necessarily more stringent than either research or clinical approaches. Precise definitions are needed in determining whether an allegation is substantiated, and are intended to ensure fair treatment for victims, their families, *and* alleged perpetrators. Substantiation decisions, which rely on legal definitions, provide the basis for investigation and may lead to court action, provision of services for affected parties, or lawful removal of children from parental care (King, Trocmé, & Thatte, 2003; Slep & Heyman, 2006).

Statutory definitions of CSA can be found at both the federal and state levels. Federal legislation provides the minimum standards for maltreatment criteria, and United States states and territories construct statutes using these guidelines and reflecting the political and social issues in each state. The Federal Child Abuse Prevention and Treatment Act (CAPTA, 1974) as amended by the CAPTA Reauthorization Act of 2010, defines child abuse and neglect as:

*Any recent act or failure to act on the part of a parent or caretaker which results in death, serious physical or emotional harm, sexual abuse or exploitation; or an act or failure to act which presents an imminent risk of serious harm.*

According to CAPTA, the term "sexual abuse" includes:

*A. The employment, use, persuasion, inducement, enticement, or coercion of any child to engage in, or assist any other person to engage in, any sexually explicit conduct or simulation of such conduct for the purpose of producing a visual depiction of such conduct; or B. the rape, and in cases of caretaker or inter-familial relationships, statutory rape, molestation, prostitution, or other form of sexual exploitation of children, or incest with children.*

Building upon these standards set by the federal government, state legislatures may include additional criteria, such as an explicit statement regarding sexual acts considered abusive, perpetrator–victim age discrepancy requirements, or minimum age to be considered a perpetrator of sexual abuse (Child Welfare Information Gateway, 2011).

Although the primary purpose of statutory definitions of CSA is to establish standards for child protection and fairness in juvenile and criminal justice proceedings, statutory definitions have clear secondary effects for knowledge about the incidence and prevalence of CSA. Reports to authorities and substantiated cases are used in determining the most credible counts of CSA. Because legal definitions guide substantiation, estimates are likely to underrepresent instances that fall outside a particular state's legal parameters. In relying on cases that have been reported to legal authorities or those that have been substantiated, descriptions of victims and abusive incidents may not be representative of the entire abused population. Recognizing that varying state statutes may decrease the reliability of nationwide surveillance of child maltreatment, the Centers for Disease Control (CDC) has proposed that CSA be defined universally as an "act of commission," in which a parent or other individual in a caregiving role deliberately attempts or completes penetration of the child's anus or genital opening, touches the child's genital area, buttocks, groin, inner thigh, breasts, or anus, or engages in a noncontact sexually abusive act (child pornography, exposing a child to sexual acts, child prostitution, etc.) (Leeb, Poulozzi, Melanson, Simon, & Arias, 2008).

A second legal distinction that is frequently blurred in research and clinical practice is that between a perpetrating caregiver (e.g., parent, step-parent) and a perpetrator who is not in a caregiving role (e.g., family acquaintances, strangers). Although a clinician will focus on children's responses to trauma regardless of their relationships with perpetrators, the legal system distinguishes between sexual abuse (with caregiver as perpetrator) and sexual assault (non-familial perpetrator, including strangers). Investigations of allegations involving non-caregiving perpetrators may be conducted exclusively by law enforcement rather than child protective systems, and the offender may be charged with sexual assault of a minor rather than CSA. When incidence or prevalence reports rely on data from health and human services departments, sexual assaults may not be included even though they involve a child or adolescent victim.

In research, definitions of CSA are guided by the specific aims of a particular study (Haugaard, 2000), with factors such as researcher preferences, convenience samples, and research questions leading to more variation in maltreatment criteria and sample characteristics across studies than among legal definitions. For example, specific inclusion criteria for research studies may set the upper limit anywhere from 15 to 18 years of age, or may limit abusive acts to those involving physical contact or penetration, to reduce variability in the sample. Further, researchers often have a preference for quantitative measures that enable studies to answer questions about degree of effects, level of severity, and interactions among variables. Sexual abuse researchers have attempted to quantify some data by developing higher-level classification systems of maltreatment. For example, numerous studies use typologies that place sexually abusive experiences on a severity continuum (Maynes & Feinauer, 1994; Russell, 1986), with non-contact abuse or fondling typically placed at the lower end of severity continua and anal or vaginal penetration at the higher end. Gold, Swingle, Hill, & Elfant (1998) devised a typology based on survivor report of the psychological impact of sexual abuse that includes the three dimensions of Coercion (sexual abuse acts requiring compliant participation), Subjugation (forced acts without necessary compliance), and Objectification (dehumanizing the victim). Due to variability between studies, it is critical to review sample characteristics and abuse definitions before using research reports to generate epidemiological estimates.

In clinical practice, precision in defining sexual abuse is sacrificed in favor of inclusiveness. Clinicians tend to provide services to individuals who perceive themselves as having experienced sexual abuse regardless of whether or not their case was officially substantiated. Adopting more lenient definitions enables mental health professionals to serve a wide range of children and families seeking services (Haugaard, 2000). For example, a clinician may provide treatment for youth who believe they were victims of sexual abuse in cases that were never substantiated by authorities. Although vague and overly inclusive definitions may increase access to services for youth in distress, such definitions are rarely used to answer epidemiological questions, because of their variation and lack of specificity.

## INCIDENCE AND PREVALENCE OF CHILD AND ADOLESCENT SEXUAL ABUSE

Variations in definitions and legal distinctions between assault and abuse make for uncertainty when attempting to accurately estimate the prevalence of CSA. Further, statistical information about CSA relies heavily on victim reports; however, it is well supported that victims do not disclose abuse immediately, and a large proportion never disclose (London, Bruck, Wright, & Ceci, 2007). This underreporting by victims, in addition to issues with research methodology, contributes to error in epidemiological estimates (Pereda, Guilera, Forns, & Gumez-Benito, 2009). Despite these limitations, national and international data are available to examine the magnitude of CSA.

Incidence data are typically gathered through government records, the criminal justice system, and self-report surveys—all of which may be utilizing different samples and definitions of CSA. For example, incidence rates from the National Child Abuse and Neglect Data System (NCANDS) yield a lower estimate of CSA than do data from the Fourth National Incidence Study of Child Abuse and Neglect (NIS-4; Sedlak et al., 2010). Current incidence rates based on Child Protective Services (CPS) data as collected through NCANDS show that, of the maltreatment cases investigated or assessed in 2010, 9.2% involved sexual abuse, indicating that a total of 63,527 American children were affected by CSA that year (US Department of Health and Human Services [US DHHS], 2011). However, CPS data include only cases where the perpetrator was an individual in a caregiving position (Barnett, Miller-Perrin, & Perrin, 2011), and rely on prompt disclosure of abuse, reporting to authorities, and substantiation of the report. Understanding that not all cases of sexual abuse are reported to or investigated by CPS, data collected for NIS-4 include reports from sentinels in the public (i.e., law enforcement agencies, hospitals, schools, mental health agencies, etc.) in addition to CPS counts (Sedlak et al., 2010). NIS-4 divides cases by Harm and Endangerment Standards, considering those cases in which physical harm to the child was observed and those who were placed at significant risk to be physically harmed, respectively. Based on NIS-4 data, approximately 135,000 (Harm Standard) to 180,500 (Endangerment Standard) children were victims of sexual abuse in 2005–2006, comprising about 24% of the national maltreated sample (Sedlak et al., 2010). In sum, national estimates of CSA incidence range from 0.85 to 2.4 per 1,000 children, according to CPS reports and NIS-4 Endangerment Standard, respectively.

Although also impacted by differences in definitions used and sample included, prevalence data typically rely on retrospective self-report surveys of adults, which help to resolve the issue of delayed disclosure. According to data from the Adverse Childhood Experiences (ACE) Survey conducted within the United States, 24.7% of women and 16% of men endorse having experienced CSA, defined as fondling, attempted intercourse (anal, oral, or vaginal), or completed intercourse by an individual at least five years older than oneself (CDC, 2010). Similarly, international surveys reveal that about 20% of women and 5–10% of men have experienced CSA (Finkelhor, 1994; Pereda et al., 2009).

Since CSA became a highly publicized issue in the 1980s, there has been a consistent decline in both reports of abuse and number of substantiated cases (Finkelhor & Jones, 2004). According to Sedlak and colleagues (2010), there was a 44% decrease in the incidence of sexual abuse between the NIS-3 in 1993 and the NIS-4 in 2005–2006. Additionally, yearly CPS reports show a 40% drop in the number of substantiated sexual abuse cases from 1992 to 2000 (Finkelhor & Jones, 2004). Administrators within CPS have suggested that changes in procedures (e.g., more conservative standards for substantiation, exclusion of cases with non-caregiving perpetrators) and less reporting by health professionals may be creating the illusion of a decline in sexual abuse cases (Jones, Finkelhor, & Kopiec, 2001); however, supporting evidence suggests at least a portion of this trend is attributable to a true decline (for a review, see Finkelhor & Jones, 2006). For example, correlates of sexual abuse such as teenage pregnancy (Moore et al., 2001) and incidences of child runaways (Hammer, Finkelhor, & Sedlak, 2002) decreased during the same period as the decline in sexual abuse cases. Increases in the incarceration of sexual abuse perpetrators (Conklin, 2003; Levitt, 2004; Rosenfeld, 2004) may also have contributed to a true decline. While emerging evidence suggests the incidence of sexual abuse is decreasing in the United States, it remains a highly prevalent issue that affects children across the world (Pereda et al., 2009).

## VICTIM AND ABUSE CHARACTERISTICS

Gaining an epidemiological understanding of CSA involves exploring the distribution of abuse, in addition to its prevalence. Whereas prevalence data allow estimation of the magnitude of CSA, knowledge of who is most affected provides a jumping-off point for preventing abuse and designing efficacious treatments. The current section provides a review of information regarding characteristics of CSA victims and their abuse experiences. Although limitations such as those spurred by differences in methodology, underreporting by victims, and variability in sample characteristics and abuse definitions may prevent a current and complete epidemiological understanding of victim and abuse characteristics, a growing body of literature provides insight into who experiences sexual abuse and the circumstances surrounding their experiences. While additional study is needed to provide a thorough understanding of victim and abuse characteristics, and therefore adequate guidance for prevention and intervention, current literature provides a starting point for developing this understanding.

### Characteristics of Sexual Abuse Victims

Children who experience sexual abuse cannot be neatly described either by demographic characteristics, abuse characteristics, or outcomes (Yancey, Hansen, & Naufel, 2011). Victims are male and female, range in age from infancy through adolescence, and represent a multitude of ethnicities and socioeconomic backgrounds. Despite this heterogeneity, youth with certain demographic characteristics have been identified as experiencing sexual abuse more often than other groups, indicating increased risk and suggesting targets for surveillance and prevention efforts.

Perhaps the most striking risk factor for experiencing CSA is gender. Data from the NIS-4 reveal that female youth are nearly 3.8 times more likely to be sexually abused than males (Sedlak et al., 2010). Research studies using retrospective self-report surveys also reflect this gender difference, with rates of victimization for females 2 to 8 times higher than those for males (Briere & Elliot, 2003; Putnam, 2003). Recent national data reported in the ACE Survey indicate that females are 1.5 times more likely to experience sexual abuse than males (CDC, 2010). It is clear that a gender difference exists for the experience of sexual abuse, although heterogeneous forms of information (i.e., CPS data, retrospective adult self-reports, or smaller-scale research studies) may be responsible for the varying magnitude of this difference. It is also uncertain whether other characteristics such as socioeconomic status (SES) and family factors contribute to the magnitude of the gender difference.

NIS-4 data do not show a significant difference in rates of CSA for varying age groups (Sedlak et al., 2010); however, other epidemiological reports indicate some variance in risk for CSA due to age. Late childhood and early adolescence have been associated with elevated risk for CSA in several studies. Examining CSA at the international level, Finkelhor (1994) reported that children are most at risk for experiencing CSA between the ages of 7 and 13 years, consistent with Briere & Elliott's (2003) sample indicating a mean age of 9.7 years at onset and 12.1 years at last abuse occurrence. Examining CPS reports, Putnam (2003) asserted that risk increases with age, noting that 10% of CSA victims are 0–3 years old, 28.4% 4–7 years, 25% 8–11 years, and 35.9% 12–17 years. Results of a recent, large-scale survey of over 7,000 English adults suggest that unwanted sexual touch is a more common sexual abuse experience for children aged 9–12 years, whereas unwanted sexual talk and non-consensual intercourse tend to peak in adolescence (Bebbington et al., 2011). Interestingly, rates of sexual abuse for youth aged 12–14 years did not decline between 1993 and 2006, whereas significant declines have been reported for those aged 3–11 years and 15–17 years (Sedlak et al., 2010). Although there seems to be some association between age and CSA risk, the nature of the relationship remains uncertain. Some of the uncertainty about the age–CSA association may be due to the common practice of overlooking age of abuse onset in research (Pereda et al., 2009).

Although some research has shown significant differences in CSA prevalence by racial group, these findings are also inconsistent (Kalof, 2000; Ullman & Filipas, 2005). While NIS-4 data (Sedlak et al., 2010) report the rate of sexual abuse per 1,000 African American children to be nearly twice the rate for European American children, that difference was not statistically significant in the large sample, consistent with other studies exploring CSA rates in different ethnic groups (Elliott & Briere, 1992; Hall & Flannery, 1984; Wyatt, 1985). On the contrary, in a survey with a smaller sample of 461 female college students (Ullman & Filipas, 2005), differences in rates of sexual abuse were significant, with African American women reporting the highest prevalence, followed by Hispanic, European American, and Asian women. However, also utilizing an undergraduate sample of women, Kalof (2000) reported highest CSA rates for Hispanic women, followed by African American, Asian, and European American women. Although racial differences appear marginal or inconsistent, it is important to note that cultural factors such as the importance of virginity and discretion about sexuality may hinder reporting of sexual abuse and, therefore, limit understanding of the distribution of abuse (Kenny & McEachern, 2000).

According to NIS-4 data, a myriad of other demographic variables are implicated in increasing a child's risk for becoming a victim of sexual abuse (Sedlak et al., 2010). Contrary to research in other forms of child maltreatment, those *without* a physical disability are 1.7 times more likely to experience sexual abuse than children with disabilities. School-aged children (3–17 years) who are not enrolled in school are 1.6 times more likely to be abused than those enrolled. Parental factors, such as employment and relationship status, are also related to rates of sexual abuse based on the NIS-4 report. Those children with parents not in the workforce are most at risk for sexual abuse compared with children whose parents are employed and those who are in the workforce but currently unemployed. Considering family structure and living arrangement, the number of children per 1,000 who experience sexual abuse are as follows: 0.5 living with two biological married parents; 4.3 living with married legal guardians (one may be a biological parent); 2.4 living with unmarried biological parents; 9.9 living with one biological parent and their unmarried partner; 2.4 living with single parents; and 5.3 living with no parent. However, the differences in rates of sexual abuse become statistically significant only when comparing children living with two married biological parents to all other categories except those living with unmarried biological parents. Children in low-SES homes—defined as those with a household income below $15,000/year, parental education level less than high school, or at least one household member participating in a poverty-related program—were three times more likely to experience sexual abuse than children not in low SES homes in the NIS-4 sample. Geographical location also impacts rates of abuse, with children in rural areas 1.6 and 2 times more likely to become sexually abused in comparison with urban centers and urban counties, respectively. In addition to these characteristics, youth in families with maternal illness, maternal alcoholism, extended maternal absences, severe marital conflict, and parental substance abuse may also be at a heightened risk for experiencing CSA (Putnam, 2003).

## Characteristics of Sexual Abuse Experiences

Sexual abuse experiences are as heterogeneous as the individuals who endure them, varying in severity, duration, frequency, and perpetrator–victim relationships. Abusive acts range from Internet solicitations or exposure to pornography, to vaginal or anal penetration. Whereas information such as gender of victims may be well documented in national surveys, specific abuse experiences are not typically reported; however, some independent research gives insight into the experiences of sexual abuse victims. For example, a recent study including 4,339 Swedish high school seniors explored gender differences in sexual abuse experiences (Priebe & Svedin, 2008). The authors reported that of female disclosers of sexual abuse, 10% experienced another exposing him/herself indecently to the victim (non-contact abuse), 69.2% experienced indecent sexual touching (contact abuse without penetration), and 20.8% experienced attempted or completed vaginal, oral, or anal intercourse. Of males disclosing, 18.4% experienced non-contact abuse, 57.3% experienced contact without penetration, and 24.3% experienced attempted or completed penetration. Similar to these rates, Bulik, Prescott, & Kendler (2001) reported 28% of their sample of 412 women experienced attempted or completed intercourse. Considering both male and female victims of sexual abuse, rates of penetration (by penis or other object) as high as 52% have been reported (Briere & Elliott, 2003). A fairly large proportion of victims report only one abusive experience; however, evidence suggests the modal number of abusive occurrences per victim is 2–5, and an astounding 11% of victims report experiencing more than 100 instances of sexual abuse (Briere & Elliott, 2003; Steel, Sanna, Hammond, Whipple, & Cross, 2004). Further, a recent survey of over 7,000 English adults suggests that sexual touching often precedes non-consensual intercourse (Bebbington et al., 2011). Taking into account the repeated nature and posited progression of abuse from non-contact or fondling to attempted or completed penetration, one could expect that a larger proportion of victims would experience non-penetrative contact abuse.

While no criteria exist for identifying perpetrators of sexual abuse, it is clear that most perpetrators are male and known to the child. The majority of CSA victims report male perpetrators, while only about 11–20% report experiencing abuse by female offenders (Sedlak et al., 2010; Steel et al., 2004). The majority of perpetrators are also known to their victim, with 46–53% of research samples reporting familial relation to their perpetrator (i.e., parent, sibling, or other relative), and as little as 5% reporting abuse by a stranger (Briere & Elliott, 2003; Bulik et al., 2001; Steel et al., 2004).

Approximately one-third of CSA victims report experiencing force or threat by the offender (Bulik et al., 2001), indicating that perpetrators employ other tactics to elicit participation in abusive acts. Developing and maintaining a relationship in which abuse continues and disclosure is controlled tends to occur through sexual grooming. During this process, the perpetrator manipulates their child victim, significant adults in the child's life, and the child's environment in order to gain access to the child, encourage compliance, and maintain secrecy for the purpose of strengthening the abusive pattern (Craven, Brown, & Gilchrist, 2006). A survey of incarcerated perpetrators revealed that 45% used a sexual grooming process, and this number may be higher when considering non-incarcerated samples (Canter, Hughes, & Kirby, 1998). Evidence of sexual grooming is often seen in cases of sexual abuse sensationalized by the media that commonly include "professional" perpetrators, or those who use their work as a means to gain access to, and conceal their sexual abuse of, children (e.g., members of the clergy, those in childcare positions, schools, athletic programs, and other child-focused programs) (Sullivan & Beech, 2002).

Unfortunately, sexual grooming is advancing along with technology and widespread access to the Internet. Potential perpetrators have direct access to youth via Internet chat rooms, email, blogs, and social networking sites, and may utilize these resources to approach youth for pornographic images or to begin a grooming process with the goal of eventually meeting in person (Kierkegaard, 2008). According to the 2006 Internet Filter Review (Ropelato, 2007), one in seven youth on the Internet received sexual solicitation, and 89% of these solicitations were made in chat rooms. With the growing popularity of social networking sites, one may expect to see an increase in perpetrator use of these sites to gain access to youth; however, research indicates that youth are more likely to receive sexual solicitations in chat rooms or via instant messaging (Ybarra & Mitchell, 2008). Risk for sexual victimization via the Internet appears to be more associated with active online interactions, rather than passive online presence such as posting a profile on Facebook© (Wolak, Finkelhor, Mitchell, & Ybarra, 2008).

## DISCLOSURE AND ALLEGATIONS OF CHILD SEXUAL ABUSE

One of the main issues impacting an accurate epidemiological understanding of sexual abuse is the small number of victims who report abuse to an adult (Hanson et al., 2003). According to a study of over 3,000 women, about 47% of victims did not reveal their experience of sexual abuse for at least five years (Smith et al., 2000). Estimates of incidence and prevalence are based on reported cases, and therefore neglect those cases that are never disclosed. In addition to the effects on incidence and prevalence estimates, delayed and non-disclosure issues have implications for understanding and treating the sequelae of sexual abuse. Specifically, in contrast to victims who report in a timely manner and receive services, children and adolescents who do not disclose are prevented from receiving mental health services, and continue to be at risk for ongoing abuse (Collings, Griffiths, & Kumalo, 2005).

Demographic characteristics such as age, ethnicity, and gender have been associated with the timing and method of disclosure, although the evidence remains inconsistent regarding the nature and direction of these relationships (Collings et al., 2005). Younger age at onset of abuse has been shown to predict delayed disclosure (Jonzon & Lindblad, 2004; Smith et al., 2000), and numerous studies show that younger children are less likely to make explicit disclosures (Collings et al., 2005). While Bybee & Mowbray (1993) suggest that children under the age of 5 years are more likely to make an explicit disclosure than children over age 5, other research indicates that preschool-age children tend to disclose in accidental manners, whereas older children may have a more purposeful and active approach to disclosure (Paine & Hansen, 2002). Few ethnic differences have been reported in regard to disclosure; however, cultural factors may influence a victim's willingness to disclose (Ullman & Filipas, 2005). In their survey of a community sample of adult Latina women, Romero, Wyatt, Loeb, Carmona, & Solis (1999) found that the majority of sexual abuse experiences occurring in childhood (60%) were not disclosed to anyone. Delaying or withholding disclosure may be more common with male victims of sexual abuse (Paine & Hansen, 2002), although there is also evidence indicating that gender differences in the disclosure process do not exist (Bybee & Mowbray, 1993; DiPietro, Runyan, & Fredrickson, 1997).

The delay between abuse and disclosure may be influenced by factors such as relationship to the perpetrator(s), age at onset of abuse, and abuse severity (Jonzon & Lindblad, 2004). Relationship to perpetrator is consistently shown to be a strong predictor of delayed disclosure (Arata, 1998; Goodman-Brown, Edelstein, Goodman, Jones, & Gordon, 2003; Kogan, 2004; Sjöberg & Lindblad, 2002). Children who have been abused by a family member tend to report the longest delays in disclosure, citing the fear of negative consequences following disclosure and a desire to be loyal to their family as reasons for delaying report (Goodman-Brown et al., 2003). Regarding incestuous relationships, disclosure is especially rare among victims of sibling sexual abuse (Carlson, Maciol, & Schneider, 2006). Smith et al. (2000) found that having a familiar perpetrator was an independent predictor of delayed disclosure in their sample of 288 women who reported rape prior to their 18th birthday. Children who are groomed by the perpetrator may also delay disclosure (Sas & Cunningham, 1995). In addition to specific characteristics associated with the abuse and potentially related to the grooming process, delays in disclosure may be due to a lack of the child's awareness that they are being sexually abused (Sas & Cunningham, 1995). In the process of grooming children, perpetrators of sexual abuse may normalize their behaviors and lead children to believe they are engaging in a typical adult–child relationship, or participating in a special game (Collings et al, 2005). For this reason, children may not recognize the need to disclose these events to other individuals.

Conflicting evidence exists regarding the relationship between abuse severity and delay of disclosure. Gomes-Schwartz, Horowitz, & Cardarelli (1990) found that individuals experiencing abuse at both ends of the spectrum (non-contact abuse and intercourse) were less likely to report, whereas Arata (1998) indicated those experiencing contact abuse were significantly less likely to report than individuals experiencing non-contact abuse. In addition, physical abuse and use of violence during sexual abuse may predict active disclosure in childhood (Jonzon & Lindblad, 2004).

Steps taken after a child discloses have a large impact on whether or not the abuse is reported. If the child's disclosure is not considered sexual abuse, is minimized in regard to its severity, or is not believed by the individual to whom the child is disclosing, the incident is not likely to be reported (Collings et al., 2005). In cases where children and families are directed to appropriate agencies, the experience of repeated interviewing may lead to inaccurate reporting of details, or recantation of abuse allegations (Cronch, Viljoen, & Hansen, 2006). Striving to minimize issues related to repeated interviewing, the National Children's Alliance (NCA) includes guidelines for forensic interviewing in their standards for accreditation as a Child Advocacy Center (CAC) (NCA, 2011). These guidelines require initial and ongoing training in the use of child-focused and legally sound procedures that aim to gather accurate information, while also minimizing the need for additional interviews. Recent evidence indicates that these efforts may have a positive impact not only for CACs, but also across the child protective system. Cross, Jones, Walsh, Simone, & Kolko (2007) reported that the total number of interviews per child is small, not only for children interviewed in CAC settings, but also for those interviewed in non-CAC settings (i.e., police or CPS custody). Forensic interviewing guidelines employed by CACs have also been shown to increase caregiver satisfaction, specifically due to perceptions of support from investigators and feelings of safety and comfort (Jones, Cross, Walsh, & Simone, 2007).

Some children, after overcoming barriers to disclosure, recant their allegations of sexual abuse. Recanting of abuse allegations has been shown to occur in 4–33% of sexual abuse cases, although lower rates have been associated with the most certain abuse cases (London, Bruck, Ceci, & Shuman, 2005). A more recent investigation indicates that about 23.1% of children whose abuse has been substantiated by CPS recant their allegations and that younger children, those abused by a parental figure, and those with an unsupportive non-offending caregiver are more likely to recant (Malloy, Lyon, & Quas, 2007). Malloy and colleagues note that the exclusion of unsubstantiated cases of sexual abuse shows that it is likely that children's recantations of abuse allegations are not associated with fabrication. Related to, but qualitatively different from recantation, an estimated 72% of children deny that abuse occurred at least once during the investigation process, mainly when initially questioned by a parent or other adult (Sorensen & Snow, 1990). Of the children who deny experiencing abuse during investigations, up to 92% reaffirm their allegation.

Despite being sensationalized in the 1980s and 1990s, false allegations of CSA appear to be quite rare. The 2010 CPS data show only 0.1% of all child maltreatment reports are intentionally falsely made (US DHHS, 2011). False reports of sexual abuse tend to be more common in ongoing divorce or custody proceedings (Piper, 2008), and it appears that false accusations may be the result of suggestibility or misperception of a nonsexual event rather than intentional manipulation of facts (Hershkowitz, Orbach, Lamb, Sternberg, & Horowitz, 2001; Jones & McGraw, 1987). Research on suggestibility indicates that children may be socially motivated to comply with interviewers, providing false reports during suggestive interviews (Bruck & Ceci, 1999). The guidelines developed by the NCA described above (NCA, 2011) are designed to guard against such suggestive interviews and assure that authorities interview children in an unbiased manner.

## OUTCOMES OF CHILD SEXUAL ABUSE

As discussed previously in this chapter, victims of sexual abuse are a heterogeneous group, comprising boys and girls of various ages and ethnic and socioeconomic backgrounds. The interactions between these child, family, and environmental factors seem to influence individual outcomes following sexual abuse, leading to equally heterogeneous abuse sequelae. While

CSA is associated with problematic sexualized behaviors, neurobiological/health outcomes, and a myriad of clinical problems (Putnam, 2003; Saywitz, Mannarino, Berliner, & Cohen, 2000), there is also a portion of victims who do not develop negative outcomes or who return to pre-abuse functioning relatively quickly following disclosure (Yancey, Hansen, & Naufel, 2011).

Post-traumatic Stress Disorder (PTSD) and problematic sexual behaviors are among the most prevalent sequelae exhibited by victims of CSA (Putnam, 2003). In addition to its own debilitating effects, PTSD also places children at risk for developing other psychiatric and medical conditions (Cohen, Berliner, & Mannarino, 2010). While sexual exploration and play are a normal part of childhood, victims of CSA are more likely to continue engaging in sexual behaviors after adult requests to stop, and they may exhibit behaviors that are considered age-inappropriate (Sapp & Vandeven, 2005). Beyond childhood, survivors of sexual abuse may continue to exhibit problematic sexual behaviors. Studying female survivors of sexual abuse, Arriola, Louden, Doldren, & Fortenberry (2005) found they were more likely to engage in unprotected sex, have more sexual partners, and engage in sex trading (e.g., engaging in sex in return for money, housing, or drugs) than non-abused women. This increased engagement in unprotected intercourse and other risky sexual behaviors increases risk for sexually transmitted infections (STI's) or unintended pregnancy (Brown, Lourie, Zlotnick, & Cohn, 2000; Parillo, Freeman, Collier, & Young, 2001).

Although early research regarding the outcomes of sexual abuse focused on psychiatric diagnoses, more recent investigations have begun exploring the health effects of childhood adversity. This new field has begun to show that adverse childhood events involving abuse or neglect tend to have the largest associations with poorer health-related quality of life (Cuijpers et al., 2011). Specific negative health outcomes such as eating disorders, chronic pelvic pain in adult women, and non-epileptic seizures in children have also been identified as occurring more often in victims of sexual abuse than in the general population (Maniglio, 2009). Further, some literature suggests that the hypothalamic–pituitary–adrenal (HPA) axis may become dysregulated in response to the experience of CSA, altering the individual's biological stress response to overproduce cortisol (De Bellis et al., 1999; Putnam, 2003). Emerging research with children has shown that cortisol levels, along with symptoms of PTSD, predict detrimental effects to the growing brain (Carrion, Weems, & Reiss, 2007). Although further research is necessary, understanding effects of abuse and trauma on brain development is likely to inform both assessment and treatment for victims of CSA.

Reported incidence of psychiatric diagnoses in the general population is quite high, but is even more elevated for victims of sexual abuse, with reported incidence is as high as 56–78% for women and 47–82% for men (Martin, Bergen, Richardson, Roeger, & Allison, 2004; Molnar, Buka, & Kessler, 2001). For those who develop psychiatric issues, the strongest associations seem to be with CSA and post-traumatic stress disorder (PTSD), drug abuse and dependence, and mania (Molnar et al., 2001). Further, there is evidence of an effect of abuse severity in the development of psychopathology. A prospective study showed that children who experienced exposure or fondling were 4.8 times more likely to develop depression, while victims of CSA involving intercourse were 8.1 times more likely to develop major depressive disorder, and 11.8 times more likely to attempt suicide, compared with non-victims (Fergusson, Horwood, & Lynskey, 1996). Twin studies controlling for the effects of family environment show an increased prevalence of substance dependence, bulimia nervosa, conduct disorder, social anxiety, and panic disorder in the abused population (Dinwiddie et al., 2000; Kendler et al., 2000; Nelson et al., 2002). Beyond correlational associations, preliminary evidence also shows that a history of CSA may predict symptoms of borderline personality disorder, depression, dissociation, and symptoms of PTSD (Wingenfeld et al., 2011).

In addition to psychological, behavioral, and neurobiological correlates, victims of CSA are at a heightened risk for subsequent sexual victimization throughout the lifespan. About one-third of victims of CSA report experiencing revictimization, and review of the research indicates that they are 2–3 times more likely to experience sexual victimization in adulthood compared with individuals without a sexual abuse history (Arata, 2002). The numerous negative outcomes of CSA are well documented, and evidence suggests that revictimization may exacerbate these effects. Adult women reporting revictimization also report experiencing heightened levels of depression, PTSD, and other anxiety disorders, as well as dissociation and substance use (Fortier et al., 2009).

While there is strong evidence that a significant portion of victims develop psychological, behavioral, or neurobiological sequelae, it is also evident that some experience limited negative effects. Between 21% and 49% of sexually abused youth present with no symptoms of clinically significant severity, and the majority of them appear to remain symptom free (Bal, Crombez, Van Oost, & Debourdeaudhuij, 2003; Kendall-Tackett, Williams, & Finkelhor, 1993). In addition, Kendall-Tackett and colleagues found that CSA victims who initially demonstrated negative outcomes tended to return to pre-abuse functioning within 18 months of disclosure. Protective factors such as child resilience, attribution of blame to the perpetrator, strong social and parental support, and receipt of immediate treatment may help prevent the development of negative outcomes (Yancey et al., 2011). Despite the absence of clinically significant problems, research suggests that treatment may still benefit these individuals by further reducing symptoms and providing education to prevent revictimization (Tavkar & Hansen, 2011).

## CONCLUSION

A wealth of knowledge regarding CSA has been accumulated since the emergence of research in this field during the latter portion of the 20th century. Attention has been focused on understanding who is affected by sexual abuse, how many individuals have experienced abuse, and how such experiences influence psychological, social, and behavioral functioning, as well as physical health. It can be stated confidently that sexual abuse is an issue of serious societal impact, with as many as one in four women and one in six men reporting sexual victimization during childhood.

Despite continual forward progress, a complete epidemiological understanding of CSA remains hindered by issues such as the lack of a cohesive definition, varying research methodologies, delayed disclosure, and non-disclosure. While recent efforts provide valuable information regarding victim and abuse characteristics, investigators should consider conforming to a unified definition of CSA, and collecting information such as age of onset and cessation of abuse as well as the specific abusive acts. Knowledge of CSA is limited to known cases of abuse, and therefore complete comprehension of the issue will not be attained without efforts encouraging public awareness and victim disclosure. It is imperative that future endeavors work toward a unified definition of CSA, aim to improve our understanding of risk factors, and address barriers to disclosure.

## REFERENCES

Arata, C. M. (1998). To tell or not to tell: Current functioning of child sexual abuse survivors who disclosed their victimization. *Child Maltreatment, 3,* 63–71.

Arata, C. M. (2002). Child sexual abuse and sexual revictimization. *Clinical Psychology: Science and Practice, 9*(2), 135–164.

Arriola, K. R. J., Louden, T., Doldren, M. A., & Fortenberry, R. M. (2005). A meta-analysis of the relationship of child sexual abuse to HIV risk behavior among women. *Child Abuse & Neglect, 29,* 725–746.

Bal, S., Crombez, G., Van Oost, P., & Debourdeaudhuij, I. (2003). The role of social support in well being and coping with self-reported stressful events in adolescents. *Child Abuse & Neglect, 27,* 1377–1395.

Barnett, O. W., Miller-Perrin, C. L., & Perrin, R. D. (2011). *Family violence across the lifespan: An introduction* (3rd ed.). Thousand Oaks, CA: Sage.

Bebbington, P., Jonas, S., Brugha, T., Meltzer, H., Jenkins, R., Cooper, C., et al. (2011). Child sexual abuse reported by an English national sample: Characteristics and demography. *Social Psychiatry and Psychiatric Epidemiology, 46,* 255–262.

Briere, J., & Elliott, D. M. (2003). Prevalence and psychological sequelae of self-reported childhood physical and sexual abuse in a general population sample of men and women. *Child Abuse & Neglect, 27,* 1205–1222.

Brown, L. K., Lourie, K. J., Zlotnick, C., & Cohn, J. (2000). Impact of sexual abuse on the HIV-risk-related behavior of adolescents in intensive psychiatric treatment. *American Journal of Psychiatry, 157,* 1413–1415.

Bruck, M., & Ceci, S. J. (1999). The suggestibility of children's memory. *Annual Review of Psychology, 50*(1), 419–439.

Bulik, C. M., Prescott, C. A., & Kendler, K. S. (2001). Features of childhood sexual abuse and the development of psychiatric and substance use disorders. *The British Journal of Psychiatry, 179,* 444–449.

Bybee, D., & Mowbray, C. T. (1993). An analysis of allegations of sexual abuse in a multi-victim day-care center case. *Child Abuse & Neglect, 17,* 767–783.

Canter, D., Hughes, D., & Kirby, S. (1998). Paedophilia: Pathology, criminality, or both? The development of a multivariate model of offence behaviour in child sexual abuse. *The Journal of Forensic Psychiatry, 9,* 532–555.

Carlson, B. E., Maciol, K., & Schneider, J. (2006). Sibling incest: Reports from forty-one survivors. *Journal of Child Sexual Abuse, 15,* 19–34.

Carrion, V. G., Weems, C. F., & Reiss, A. L. (2007). Stress predicts brain changes in children: A pilot longitudinal study on youth stress, posttraumatic stress disorder, and the hippocampus. *Pediatrics, 119,* 509–516.

Centers for Disease Control and Prevention (September 20, 2010). Adverse childhood experiences (ACE) study: Data and statistics. Retrieved November 10, 2010, from <http://www.cdc.gov/ace/prevalence.htm>.

Child Abuse Prevention and Treatment Act, 42 USCA § 5106g (1974).

Child Welfare Information Gateway (2011). Definitions of child abuse and neglect. Retrieved November 10, 2010, from <www.childwelfare.gov/systemwide/laws_policies/statutes/define.cfm>.

Cohen, J. A., Berliner, L., & Mannarino, A. (2010). Trauma focused CBT for children with co-occurring trauma and behavior problems. *Child Abuse & Neglect, 34,* 215–224.

Collings, S. J., Griffiths, S., & Kumalo, M. (2005). Patterns of disclosure in child sexual abuse. *South African Journal of Psychology, 35,* 270–285.

Conklin, J. E. (2003). *Why crime rates fell.* Boston, MA: Allyn and Bacon.

Craven, S., Brown, S., & Gilchrist, E. (2006). Sexual grooming of children: Review of literature and theoretical considerations. *Journal of Sexual Aggression, 12,* 287–299.

Cronch, L. E., Viljoen, J. L., & Hansen, D. J. (2006). Forensic interviewing in child sexual abuse cases: Current techniques and future directions. *Aggression and Violent Behavior, 11,* 195–207.

Cross, T. P., Jones, L. M., Walsh, W. A., Simone, M., & Kolko, D. (2007). Child forensic interviewing in children's advocacy centers: Empirical data on a practice model. *Child Abuse & Neglect, 31,* 1031–1052.

Cuijpers, P., Smit, F., Unger, F., Stikkelbroek, Y., ten Have, M., & de Graaf, R. (2011). The disease burden of childhood adversities in adults: A population-based study. *Child Abuse & Neglect, 35,* 937–945.

De Bellis, M. D., Baum, A. S., Birmaher, B., Keshavan, M. S., Eccard, C. H., Boring, A. M., et al. (1999). Developmental traumatology part I: Biological stress systems. *Biological Psychiatry, 45,* 1259–1270.

Dinwiddie, S., Heath, A. C., Dunne, M. P., Bucholz, K. K., Madden, P. A. F., Slutske, W. S., et al. (2000). Early sexual abuse and lifetime psychopathology: A co-twin-control study. *Psychological Medicine, 30,* 41–52.

DiPietro, E. K., Runyan, D. K., & Fredrickson, D. D. (1997). Predictors of disclosure during medical evaluation for suspected sexual abuse. *Journal of Child Sexual Abuse, 6,* 133–142.

Elliott, D. M., & Briere, J. (1992). Sexual abuse trauma among professional women: Validating the trauma symptom checklist-40 (TSC-40). *Child Abuse & Neglect, 16,* 391–398.

Fergusson, D. M., Horwood, L. J., & Lynskey, M. T. (1996). Childhood sexual abuse and psychiatric disorder in young adulthood: II. Psychiatric outcomes of childhood sexual abuse. *Journal of the American Academy of Child & Adolescent Psychiatry, 35,* 1365–1374.

Finkelhor, D. (1994). The international epidemiology of child sexual abuse. *Child Abuse & Neglect, 18,* 409–417.

Finkelhor, D., & Jones, L. M. (2004). *Explanations for the decline in child sexual abuse cases.* Washington, DC: Office of Juvenile Justice and Delinquency Prevention.

Finkelhor, D., & Jones, L. M. (2006). Why have child maltreatment and child victimization declined? *Journal of Social Issues, 62,* 685–716.

Fortier, M. A., DiLillo, D., Messman-Moore, T. L., Peugh, J., DeNardi, K. A., & Gaffey, K. J. (2009). Severity of child sexual abuse and revictimization: The mediating role of coping and trauma symptoms. *Psychology of Women Quarterly, 33,* 308–320.

Gold, S. N., Swingle, J. M., Hill, E. L., & Elfant, A. S. (1998). Acts of childhood sexual abuse: An empirically derived typology. *Journal of Family Violence, 13,* 233–242.

Gomes-Schwartz, B., Horowitz, J. M., & Cardarelli, A. P. (1990). *Child sexual abuse: The initial effects.* Thousand Oaks, CA: Sage, Inc.

Goodman-Brown, T. B., Edelstein, R. S., Goodman, G. S., Jones, D. P. H., & Gordon, D. S. (2003). Why children tell: A model of children's disclosure of sexual abuse. *Child Abuse & Neglect, 27,* 525–540.

Hall, E. R., & Flannery, P. J. (1984). Prevalence and correlates of sexual assault experiences in adolescents. *Victimology, 9*(3-4), 398–406.

Hammer, H., Finkelhor, D., & Sedlak, A. J. (2002). *Runaway/thrownaway children: National estimates and characteristics.* Washington, DC: Department of Justice, Office of Justice Programs, Office of Juvenile Justice and Delinquency Prevention.

Hanson, R. F., Kievit, L. W., Saunders, B. E., Smith, D. W., Kilpatrick, D. G., Resnick, H. S., et al. (2003). Correlates of adolescent reports of sexual assault: Findings from the national survey of adolescents. *Child Maltreatment, 8,* 261–272.

Haugaard, J. J. (2000). The challenge of defining child sexual abuse. *American Psychologist, 55,* 1036–1039.

Hershkowitz, I., Orbach, Y., Lamb, M. E., Sternberg, K. J., & Horowitz, D. (2001). The effects of mental context reinstatement on children's accounts of sexual abuse. *Applied Cognitive Psychology, 15,* 235–248.

Jones, D. P. H., & McGraw, J. M. (1987). Reliable and fictitious accounts of sexual abuse to children. *Journal of Interpersonal Violence, 2,* 27–45.

Jones, L. M., Cross, T. P., Walsh, W. A., & Simone, M. (2007). Do children's advocacy centers improve families' experiences of child sexual abuse investigations? *Child Abuse & Neglect, 31,* 1069–1085.

Jones, L. M., Finkelhor, D., & Kopiec, K. (2001). Why is sexual abuse declining? A survey of state child protection administrators. *Child Abuse & Neglect, 25,* 1139–1158.

Jonzon, E., & Lindblad, F. (2004). Disclosure, reactions, and social support: Findings from a sample of adult victims of child sexual abuse. *Child Maltreatment, 9,* 190–200.

Kalof, L. (2000). Ethnic differences in female sexual victimization. *Sexuality & Culture, 4,* 75–98.

Kendall-Tackett, K. A., Williams, L. M., & Finkelhor, D. (1993). Impact of sexual abuse on children: A review and synthesis of recent empirical studies. *Psychological Bulletin, 113,* 164–180.

Kendler, K. S., Bulik, C. M., Silberg, J., Hettema, J. M., Myers, J., & Prescott, C. A. (2000). Childhood sexual abuse and adult psychiatric and substance use disorders in women: An epidemiological and cotwin control analysis. *Archives of General Psychiatry, 57,* 953–959.

Kenny, M. C., & McEachern, A. G. (2000). Racial, ethnic, and cultural factors of childhood sexual abuse: A selected review of the literature. *Clinical Psychology Review, 20,* 905–922.

Kierkegaard, S. (2008). Cybering, online grooming and ageplay. *Computer Law & Security Review, 24,* 41–55.

King, G., Trocmé, N., & Thatte, N. (2003). Substantiation as a multitier process: The results of a NIS-3 analysis. *Child Maltreatment, 8,* 173–182.

Kogan, S. M. (2004). Disclosing unwanted sexual experiences: Results from a national sample of adolescent women. *Child Abuse & Neglect, 28,* 147–165.

Leeb, R. T., Poulozzi, L., Melanson, C., Simon, T., & Arias, I. (2008). *Child maltreatment surveillance: Uniform definitions for public health and recommended data elements, Version 1.0.* Atlanta, GA: Centers for Disease Control and Prevention, National Center for Injury Prevention and Control.

Levitt, S. D. (2004). Understanding why crime fell in the 1990s: Four factors that explain the decline and six that do not. *The Journal of Economic Perspectives, 18,* 163–190.

London, K., Bruck, M., Ceci, S. J., & Shuman, D. W. (2005). Disclosure of child sexual abuse: What does the research tell us about the ways that children tell? *Psychology, Public Policy, and Law, 11,* 194–226.

London, K., Bruck, M., Wright, D. B., & Ceci, S. J. (2007). Review of the contemporary literature on how children report sexual abuse to others: Findings, methodological issues, and implications for forensic interviewers. *Memory, 16,* 29–47.

Malloy, L. C., Lyon, T. D., & Quas, J. A. (2007). Filial dependency and recantation of child sexual abuse allegations. *Journal of the American Academy of Child & Adolescent Psychiatry, 46,* 162–170.

Maniglio, R. (2009). The impact of child sexual abuse on health: A systematic review of reviews. *Clinical Psychology Review, 29,* 647–657.

Martin, G., Bergen, H. A., Richardson, A. S., Roeger, L., & Allison, S. (2004). Sexual abuse and suicidality: Gender differences in a large community sample of adolescents. *Child Abuse & Neglect, 28,* 491–503.

Maynes, L. C., & Feinauer, L. L. (1994). Acute and chronic dissociation and somatized anxiety as related to childhood sexual abuse. *American Journal of Family Therapy, 22,* 165–175.

Molnar, B. E., Buka, S. L., & Kessler, R. C. (2001). Child sexual abuse and subsequent psychopathology: Results from the national comorbidity survey. *American Journal of Public Health, 91,* 753–760.

Moore, K. A., Manlove, J., Terry-Humen, E., Williams, S., Papillo, A. R., & Scarpa, J. (2001). *CTS Facts at a Glance.* Washington, DC: Child Trends.

National Children's Alliance (2011). Standards for accredited members. Retrieved December 8, 2011, from <http://www.nationalchildrensalliance.org/index.php?s=76>.

Nelson, E. C., Heath, A. C., Madden, P. A., Cooper, M. L., Dinwiddie, S. H., Bucholz, K. K., et al. (2002). Association between self-reported childhood sexual abuse and adverse psychosocial outcomes: Results from a twin study. *Archives of General Psychiatry, 59,* 139–145.

Paine, M. L., & Hansen, D. J. (2002). Factors influencing children to self-disclose sexual abuse. *Clinical Psychology Review, 22,* 271–295.

Parillo, K. M., Freeman, R. C., Collier, K., & Young, P. (2001). Association between early sexual abuse and adult HIV-risky sexual behaviors among community-recruited women. *Child Abuse & Neglect, 25,* 335–346.

Pereda, N., Guilera, G., Forns, M., & Gumez-Benito, J. (2009). The international epidemiology of child sexual abuse: A continuation of Finkelhor (1994). *Child Abuse & Neglect, 33*, 331–342.

Piper, A. (2008). Investigating child sex abuse allegations: A guide to help legal professionals distinguish valid from invalid claims. *Journal of Psychiatry & Law, 36*, 271–317.

Priebe, G., & Svedin, C. G. (2008). Child sexual abuse is largely hidden from the adult society: An epidemiological study of adolescents' disclosures. *Child Abuse & Neglect, 32*, 1095–1108.

Putnam, F. W. (2003). Ten-year research update review: Child sexual abuse. *Journal of the American Academy of Child and Adolescent Psychiatry, 42*, 269–278.

Romero, G. J., Wyatt, G. E., Loeb, T. B., Carmona, J. V., & Solis, B. M. (1999). The prevalence and circumstances of child sexual abuse among Latina women. *Hispanic Journal of Behavioral Sciences, 21*, 351–365.

Ropelato, J. (2007). Internet pornography statistics. Retrieved December 8, 2011, from <http://internet-filter-review.toptenreviews.com/internet-pornography-statistics.html>.

Rosenfeld, R. (2004). The case of the unsolved crime decline. *Scientific American, 290*, 82–89.

Russell, D. E. H. (1986). *The secret trauma: Incest in the lives of girls and women*. New York, NY: Basic Books.

Sapp, M. V., & Vandeven, A. M. (2005). Update on childhood sexual abuse. *Current Opinion in Pediatrics, 17*, 258–264.

Sas, L. D., & Cunningham, A. H. (1995). *Tipping the balance to tell the secret: The public discovery of child sexual abuse*. London, Ontario, Canada: London Family Court Clinic.

Saywitz, K. J., Mannarino, A. P., Berliner, L., & Cohen, J. A. (2000). Treatment of sexually abused children and adolescents. *American Psychologist, 55*, 1040–1049.

Sedlak, A. J., Mettenburg, J., Basena, M., Petta, I., McPherson, K., Greene, A., et al. (2010). *Fourth national incidence study of child abuse and neglect (NIS-4): Report to Congress*. Washington, DC: US Department of Health and Human Services, Administration for Children and Families.

Sjöberg, R. L., & Lindblad, F. (2002). Limited disclosure of sexual abuse in children whose experiences were documented by videotape. *American Journal of Psychiatry, 159*, 312–314.

Slep, A. M. S., & Heyman, R. E. (2006). Creating and field-testing child maltreatment definitions: Improving the reliability of substantiation determinations. *Child Maltreatment, 11*, 217–236.

Smith, D. W., Letourneau, E. J., Saunders, B. E., Kilpatrick, D. G., Resnick, H. S., & Best, C. L. (2000). Delay in disclosure of childhood rape: Results from a national survey. *Child Abuse & Neglect, 24*, 273–287.

Sorenson, T., & Snow, B. (1990). How children tell: The process of disclosure in child sexual abuse. *Child Welfare, 70*, 3–15.

Steel, J., Sanna, L., Hammond, B., Whipple, J., & Cross, H. (2004). Psychological sequelae of childhood sexual abuse: Abuse-related characteristics, coping strategies, and attributional style. *Child Abuse & Neglect, 28*, 785–801.

Sullivan, J., & Beech, A. (2002). Professional perpetrators: Sex offenders who use their employment to target and sexually abuse the children with whom they work. *Child Abuse Review, 11*, 153–167.

Tavkar, P., & Hansen, D. J. (2011). Interventions for families victimized by child sexual abuse: Clinical issues and approaches for child advocacy center-based services. *Aggression and Violent Behavior, 16*, 188–199.

Ullman, S. E., & Filipas, H. H. (2005). Ethnicity and child sexual abuse experiences of female college students. *Journal of Child Sexual Abuse, 14*, 67–89.

US Department of Health and Human Services. (2011). Administration for children and families, administration on children, youth, and families, Children's Bureau. *Child Maltreatment 2010*. Retrieved from <http://www.acf.hhs.gov/programs/cb/stats_research/index.htm#can>.

Wingenfeld, K., Schaffrath, C., Rullkoetter, N., Mensebach, C., Schlosser, N., Beblo, T., et al. (2011). Associations of childhood trauma, trauma in adulthood and previous-year stress with psychopathology in patients with major depression and borderline personality disorder. *Child Abuse & Neglect, 35*, 647–654.

Wolak, J., Finkelhor, D., Mitchell, K. J., & Ybarra, M. L. (2008). Online "predators" and their victims: Myths, realities, and implications for prevention and treatment. *American Psychologist, 63*, 111–128.

Wyatt, G. E. (1985). The sexual abuse of Afro-American and White-American women in childhood. *Child Abuse & Neglect, 9*, 507–519.

Yancey, C. T., Hansen, D. J., & Naufel, K. Z. (2011). Heterogeneity of individuals with a history of child sexual abuse: An examination of children presenting to treatment. *Journal of Child Sexual Abuse, 20*, 111–127.

Ybarra, M. L., & Mitchell, K. J. (2008). How risky are social networking sites? A comparison of places online where youth sexual solicitation and harassment occurs. *Pediatrics, 121*, e350–e357.

# CHAPTER 13

# Child Sexual Abuse and Adolescent Sexuality

**Christine Wekerle, Terry Bennett, and Karen Francis**
McMaster University, Hamilton, Ontario, Canada[1]

> *Growing up under conditions of child maltreatment constitutes a profound immersion in severe stress that challenges and frequently impairs development across diverse domains of functioning. Not only is psychological development often compromised, but biological consequences also ensue.*
>
> *Cicchetti & Rogosch (2009, p. 48)*

Sexuality is a developmental process that evolves from body awareness as separate from the caregiver, to naming sexual body parts, to understanding procreation, and ultimately to include intimacy expression, behavioral negotiation, protection from sexually transmitted disease, and family planning. Developmentally, sexuality moves into the forefront of the early adolescent with the onset of puberty (around 11 to 12 years of age), which brings visible physical changes (secondary sex characteristics) and reproductive capacity, initiating dramatic changes to the youth's psychological and social life. In the United States, 2011 population-level data on high school students (via self-report) indicates that about half (47.4%) have had intercourse, with about a third (33.7%) reporting recent sexual activity, where a majority were not on birth control pills, Depo-Provera® (76.7%), or used a condom (39.8%) at last intercourse. A minority (15.3%) of high school students had sex with four or more partners (Centers for Disease Control and Prevention [CDC], 2012).

Normatively, developing sexuality is influenced by exploration that is characterized by consent and mutuality. Ideally, sexuality is influenced by positive partnership role models, accurate sexual health education, peer support and knowledge exchange. The youth can be learning about him or herself as a sexual person with the support of stable, secure, and responsive adults and access to a family physician. The caring adult assists

---
[1] Correspondence to: Christine Wekerle, Department of Pediatrics HSC 3A CAAP 3N10, McMaster University, 1280 Main Street W, Hamilton, ON, Canada L8N 3Z5. Email wekerc@mcmaster.ca

*Handbook of Child and Adolescent Sexuality*
DOI: http://dx.doi.org/10.1016/B978-0-12-387759-8.00013-1

in monitoring and providing feedback on adolescent sensation-seeking behaviors that appear to peak alongside pubertal maturation; this important scaffolding for adolescent behavior is in support of reducing the harm potential of normative risk-taking (Blakemore, Barnett, & Dahl, 2010). But what happens if a parent is the highest-risk person to the youth? Or the parent fails to protect the youth from predatory danger? Unfortunately, for many persons, their sexuality is informed also by sexual coercion and attacks on their bodies, as in the case of childhood sexual abuse (CSA). Childhood sexual abuse may be a primary maltreatment, as in the case of incest, or it may be secondary to neglect and the failure to protect the child or adolescent from dangerous persons and situations. With maltreatment being a relationship-based insult, relationship functioning can be expected to be a key concern.

For the sexually abused person, their attention directed to their private parts may be premature, painful, and fraught with threat and fear, associated from the start with something "bad," perhaps even something that cannot be spoken about:

> *Where do I start ... I have never written any of my thoughts down about the sexual abuse I have endured in my lifetime. I am sure, that compared to some, it is not "as bad." To me, it was horrible. It is still with me to this day.... He was always being physically and verbally violent. In high school, he used to come into my room late at night. ... I was so scared of him, I never said a word. My junior high and high school years were horrible. When I was coming out of the bathroom after my shower, he would make me drop my towel and he always wanted "a hug." ... During my life at his house, if I was ever in the bath tub, he would always come in and want to wash me.*
> *http://www.divinecaroline.com/22190/47994-story-sexual-abuse#ixzz1vNHSBit4*

For sexually abused persons, the autonomy, self-pacing, and self-determination to developing sexuality has been robbed from them. The implication is that what ensues may include cognitive distortions in personal rights and responsibilities (i.e., privacy, safety, refusing), impacting negatively relationship expectations and templates (e.g., partners are harmful and untrustworthy) that can create challenged and conflicting emotions (e.g., want and arousal with shame, rage, and fear), and set the stage for power-imbalanced interpersonal behaviors (e.g., victimization, aggression) (Kliewer, Dibble, Goodman, & Sullivan, 2012; Wekerle & Avgoustis, 2003; Wekerle & Wolfe, 2003). CSA-related phobias (e.g., fear of men, fear of women) can produce escape and avoidance patterns, contributing to overall problems in a coherent style of relating and emotional stability (Briere, 2007; Cole, Llera, &

Pemberton, 2009). Maltreatment-related trauma symptoms, such as the dissociation spectrum, can increase the CSA victim's likelihood of challenged sexual behavior negotiation, further hampered by the frequent concomitant of substance abuse that, in the short-term, may be helpful as an anxiolytic for sex-related anxieties. Research on maltreated youth receiving child welfare services indicate that caseworker report of substantiated sexual abuse was associated with both alcohol, cannabis, and other drug use, noting that the majority of CSA victims were female. Post-traumatic stress disorder symptomatology mediated the maltreatment–substance use linkage (Wekerle, Leung, Goldstein, Thornton, & Tonmyr, 2009). Further, child welfare-involved youths do exit this system to become street-involved in young adulthood; these youth continue to experience victimization while living on the street and from boyfriends, as well as having higher rates of both substance and mental health problems (Goldstein et al., 2011). However, substance abuse, in the long-run, will exacerbate the post-traumatic stress symptoms (e.g., Schäfer, Langeland, Hissbach, Luedecke, & Ohlmeier, 2010; Stewart & Israeli, 2002). Such combinations of mental health and substance abuse may undermine sensitivity to danger cues and decisive responding, thereby making revictimization more likely. One exemplar of this comes from a female in residential addiction treatment who was raped by her boyfriend. The sequence was started by his request for a particular sex act, a request she clearly indicated "no" to, explaining that it recalled her CSA experiences to mind. This boyfriend proceeded anyway, and quickly her dissociation was initiated. Her re-entry to conscious awareness was to find herself having been assaulted, feeling distressed, and decompensating. His promises to "not do it again" provided little comfort when her coping was used against her, and constituted vulnerability for revictimization. Thus, for CSA victims, sustained, supportive intimate relating may be more difficult to attain.

The goal of this chapter is to consider CSA victimization and its implication for sexuality, as well as practical strategies in supporting the CSA victim, including mandatory reporting and referencing evidence-based therapeutic practices. A main focus will be the relationship context, considering the adolescent outcomes in terms of sexual victimization and sexual offending.

## CHILD SEXUAL ABUSE STATISTICS

Child sexual abuse (CSA) occurs when a child or adolescent is involved in a sexual situation, with age and context of consent varying by jurisdictions

(Fortin & Jenny, 2012). CSA is defined by the CDC as contact and/or non-contact abuse, perpetrated against a minor by threat, force, intimidation, or manipulation, which does or may cause harm (Leeb, Paulozzi, Melanson, Simon, & Arias, 2008). Non-contact CSA involves such behaviors as threatening sexual attack, "flashing" or exhibitionism, and exposure to pornography; contact CSA involves fondling, penetration, and sexual trafficking (Berliner, 2011). The 2006 United Nations report on violence advanced that between 1% and 21% of women reported sexual victimization prior to age 15 (Pinheiro, 2006). Research on sexually exploited and trafficked children is emergent, highlighting mental health, pregnancy, and HIV infection issues (e.g., Deb, Mukherjee, & Mathews, 2011). The United States CDC study of high school youths, the National 2011 Youth Risk Behavior Survey (YRBS), provides information that 8% of high school youth (11.8% females; 4.5% males) report lifetime sexual maltreatment (i.e., ever physically forced to have sex when they did not want to) (CDC, 2012). There is no significant change from 2001 estimates to 2011 estimates. The YRBS question, though, does not identify the category of perpetrator (i.e., adult, peer, boyfriend, etc.). Sometimes, the CSA perpetrators are the parent(s), but more often non-parental, although they may be known, a relative, or peripherally known (neighbor, babysitter, coach, pastor). That the child or adolescent may not disclose, may recant, not actively "resist," become sexually stimulated due to the manipulation of their physical selves, or show attachment behaviors to the perpetrator is irrelevant to the determination of CSA. Many CSA victims do not disclose until adulthood, or at all (Lyon & Ahern, 2011). CSA rates are more than 30 times higher in self-report than official-report studies (127/1,000 versus 4/1,000) (Stoltenborgh, van IJzendoorn, Euser, & Bakermans-Kranenburg, 2011).

## PROFESSIONAL RESPONSIBILITIES IN CSA

Child-serving professionals are mandated reporters, with most American states thus identifying child daycare providers, substitute caregivers, educators, legal and law enforcement persons, healthcare and social service providers (US Department of Health and Human Services, Administration on Children, Youth, and Families, 2003). Of all the types of maltreatment reported to child welfare, CSA is the lowest frequency category (US Department of Health and Human Services, Administration for Children and Families, Administration on Children, Youth and Families, Children's Bureau, 2010; Trocmé et al., 2010). Adolescents represent the largest sexual assault age category; prior sexual victimization is a risk factor (Kaufman, 2008). Research indicates that medical professionals tend to report younger children more frequently to child welfare, with school-age children more commonly reported by education and social services (Palusci & Ondersma, 2012). Mandatory reporting laws exist to support child protection and protect child well-being: the clinician's reasonable concern, or *suspicion*, that maltreatment may be present prompts a report to the child welfare system to initiate their decision-making to open a file for investigation, on-going services, and so forth. Professionals, as individuals whose reasonable concerns are reported "in good faith" are protected in law. In CSA, the timeliness of reporting is especially important, given the typical lack of CSA-specific medical findings and the sensitivity of the child's disclosure to persuasion and pressure from offenders, especially if the non-offending parent remains aligned primarily with their partner (Asnes & Leventhal, 2010; Faller, 1996). The role of failure to protect of the non-offending parent is a child welfare consideration. Professional duty is the initiation of a report. To protect the child, temporary removal from the home may occur, with some suggestion that it is more frequent for CSA cases (Pence & Wilson, 1994). Ultimately, the intervention of child welfare services is intended to provide safety to the child and contribute to the protection of other children by logging a formal report on a particular perpetrator, who may otherwise establish other relationships where children are at-risk. Without an established consequence, the volitional adult actions can repeat and children's vulnerabilities increase. CSA, like all forms of maltreatment, is not provoked in any way, or deserved. Neither the assault, nor the protection from it, is the child's or adolescent's responsibility. The abuse and neglect of youth is an adult choice. Abuse and neglect should never have happened; the societal safety nets failed; having happened, it should never recur. Sadly, numerous girls and many boys carry the burden of CSA put upon them by perpetrators.

Research shows that children do not predominantly make malicious reports, although details may be subject to memory decay over time (Loftus, Garry, & Feldman, 1994). While CSA accusations by adults occur in custody and access disputes, this is the minority of CSA cases. With credible child disclosure (i.e., behavioral sequences described, sex-related details not commensurate with developmental expectations, coherent story told to different people, etc.), significant child safety concerns are raised when a caretaker is openly and persistently disbelieving of a child's disclosure, and allows further contact between the child (or children) and the suspected or alleged perpetrator (Fortin & Jenny, 2012). Disclosure, though, is not required to consider sexual abuse potentially pertinent. The physical abuse of sexual abuse may not be fully appreciated: injury may occur outside of the anogenital region, and may include injury to the airway, oral cavity, and skin (bruises, bite marks). Further, other health issues (constipation, dental carries, otitis media) may occur at higher frequency in CSA cases. Injuries can be sustained in the act of sexual assault, in restraining the victim, and in enforcing silence and future compliance. Children may show sexualized behavior problems, such as engaging siblings and peers in sexual acts, show persistent self-stimulatory behaviors in public contexts, as well as repeated or persistent sexualized play. Explicitly imitating intercourse or pairing sexuality with violence is uncommon, and warrants comprehensive assessment (Fortin & Jenny, 2012). Research has shown that developmentally appropriate sex-related behaviors occur, such as the preschooler trying to look at others undressing and, when transient and developmentally appropriate, are likely part of the normative sexuality developmental process (Friedrich et al., 1992; Sinclair, Press, Koenig, & Kinnealey, 2005). Medical findings specific to CSA are either from an acute hospital presentation (i.e., sperm taken in a sample from the child's physical examination), or from a pregnancy (Fortin & Jenny, 2012).

It should be noted that, in some jurisdictions, there is no statute of limitations on reporting CSA to child welfare, and wherever minors are present, even if the disclosing victim is no longer a minor, a child welfare report for reasonable suspicion of risk of CSA if the perpetrator has access to children is a consideration. Also, CSA may occur in the context of other types of maltreatment, so if one type of maltreatment is suspected, the other types (physical abuse, emotional abuse, neglect, witnessing domestic violence) need to be assessed. Maltreatment (informal) reporting has already been influenced by the availability of broad communication channels, such as the Internet:

> My sexual predator half-sibling set up my sister, my cousin, and myself in a swimming pool by making us think he was just having fun with us .... After a few times of throwing me up in the air, he slipped his hands down the bottom of my bathing suit touching me up front. I swam away immediately. If he did it to me, I know he did it to my much younger sister and cousin.
> http://www.divinecaroline.com/22190/83919-sexual-predator-grooming-behaviors#ixzz1vNJWbiRG

Mercifully, most individuals will never know child sexual abuse, and many sexual abuse victims live successful lives. This chapter, though, is a consideration in how impairment arises in adolescence from the CSA adverse event. This focus does not negate the contribution of other forms of maltreatment, and that impairment may be broader than sexual functioning issues. The current dominant theoretical mechanism, as Cicchetti & Rogosch (2009) discuss, is severe stress and its impact on the developing brain. CSA may be chronic or may be event-based, and there is evidence emerging on CSA impact on brain structure and functioning, which may link with the time of exposure (Anderson et al., 2008; Tomoda, Navalta, Polcari, Sadato, & Teicher, 2009). While mechanisms are likely multifold, CSA victims are at increased risk for mood and anxiety disorders, suicide attempts, substance abuse, eating disorders, somatization, and repeat victimization, with increasing recent attention to physical disorder and chronic health conditions (Maniglio, 2009; Shenk, Noll, Putnam, & Trickett, 2010; Teicher et al., 2003; Teicher, Tomada, & Andersen, 2006). In the following sections, we consider, in turn, sexual behavior problems (SBPs) and sexual offending.

## SEXUAL BEHAVIOR PROBLEMS

This section will provide an overview of youth sexual acting out of the CSA victim. The harmful effects of CSA emphasize the important interplay between healthy sexual maturation and pathways in physical, cognitive, emotional, and social development. CSA is associated with subversion, threats, manipulation, and "grooming" (a progression of assaultive behavior intended to coerce the child into perceiving some degree of acceptance and engagement in the CSA). For example, the perpetrator may provide special privileges (candy, computer games, concert tickets) first without any behavioral conditions, solely to reinforce the victim's social attention and physical proximity. Next, touching attempts may be passed off as accidental or game-playing, as with swimming, wrestling, etc. This process may span a fair bit of time, and the nature of the force used by the opportunistic perpetrator may be primarily psychological.

The intrusive effects of CSA are often most pronounced and disturbing when sexual behavior problems (SBPs) present in children and adolescents. Children with SBPs have been described as initiating behaviors "involving sexual body parts ... that are developmentally inappropriate or potentially harmful to themselves or others" (Chaffin et al., 2008, p.200). Such behaviors occur in approximately 30% of children who have been sexually abused (Kendall-Tackett, Williams, & Finkelhor, 1993). SBPs deviate from more normative childhood sexual interest or play in that they include: intensely preoccupying sexual activities or interests that interfere with social development; coercive sexual interactions with others; or advanced sexual behaviors such as intercourse or oral sex (Chaffin et al., 2008). They vary widely in their presentation between individuals and across the stages of child and adolescent development, thereby requiring a developmental approach to assessment and treatment (Elkovitch, Latzman, Hansen, & Flood, 2009). For example, one school-age child, with a wide range of toys in a play assessment, first tied "the person" to a chair, then pulled out guns to shoot the doll in their private parts, finally pulling in a road "stop" sign to terminate play.

Youth who have been sexually abused demonstrate considerably higher rates of sexualized behavior compared with community and clinical control groups of nonabused children (effect size, $r=0.66$; see review by Kendall-Tackett, Williams, & Finkelhor, 1993). SBPs are also more common among children who have been exposed to domestic violence or openly sexual adult environments (Friedrich, Fisher, Broughton, Houston, & Shafran, 1998). Behaviors that occur most commonly among children who have been sexually abused include poor physical boundaries, genital self-stimulation, and exhibitionism and voyeurism (Friedrich, 1991). Lower-frequency behaviors include attempted intercourse or oral-genital contact and inserting objects into the vagina or rectum (Friedrich, 1991, 1998), and may be related to characteristics of CSA such as closer relationship to perpetrator, longer duration of abuse, and penetration (Hall, Mathews, & Pearce, 1998). Childhood SBPs appear to decrease over time: parents most commonly raise concerns about preschoolers, and reports diminish progressively thereafter (Elkovitch et al., 2009; Friedrich et al., 1998). This may reflect the eventual extinction of SBPs due to treatment or time, developmental shifts towards expressing other sexual behaviors, children's increasing ability to understand the social context, and observable behaviors becoming more covert (Elkovitch et al., 2009). There is general consensus in the literature that children who exhibit SBPs do not demonstrate increased risk for sexual offending in adolescence or adulthood; later rates of future sexual offense are similar to those of clinical samples of children with emotional and behavior problems, in the range of 2–3% (Chaffin et al., 2008).

Childhood SBPs have been described as "immature and reactive" behaviors that are highly responsive to treatment (particularly cognitive behavior therapy approaches with a parenting component), whereas adolescent SBPs may be mediated by longer-term cognitive self-schemas about sexuality, victimization, and aggression (Kendall-Tackett et al., 1993). Furthermore, during adolescence, the expression of SBPs is shaped by the propensities of the adolescent brain toward risk-taking, reward-seeking behaviors, and peer affiliation (Blakemore et al., 2010; Romer, 2010). Adolescent SBPs may therefore involve more complex trajectories of risk behaviors that are further reinforced by substance abuse, deviant peer groups, unsafe environments, and mental health problems. For example, CSA is associated with earlier age of first intercourse experience, greater number of sexual partners and frequency of intercourse, more frequent unprotected sex, greater risk of adolescent pregnancy, and higher rates of STI, including HIV status (for a review, see Senn, Carey, & Vanable, 2008).

Adolescent sex trade work, or prostitution, is considered to be a particularly high-risk outcome of interest, due to additional health risks of exposure to sexually transmitted infections (STIs), and associated outcomes such as intravenous drug use, interpersonal violence, justice involvement, and homelessness (Miller et al., 2011; Silverman, 2011; Stoltz et al., 2007), and extends to higher prostitution risk in adulthood (Senn et al., 2008). In two cross-sectional Scandinavian studies, researchers surveyed large representative samples of high school students and found that 1–2% of adolescents reported selling sex at least one time, with boys reporting 2–3 times higher rates than girls. Of these, 30–50% endorsed selling sex over 5 or 10 times (Pedersen & Hegna, 2003; Svedin & Priebe, 2007). Adolescents who had exchanged sex for money or goods were significantly more likely to have been sexually abused (adjusted odds ratio (AOR), female = 10.90; AOR, male = 7.52; Svedin & Priebe, 2007), and to have been significantly younger at onset of intercourse (Pedersen & Hegna, 2003; Svedin & Priebe, 2007). Most published studies, however, have focused on high-risk groups such as street-involved youth, or those seeking public healthcare (e.g., for adolescent pregnancy or HIV risk; see review by Senn et al., 2008), and adolescents transitioning out of child welfare may be at risk (NCAW, 2010) due to the sudden drop in financial and case management support that coincides with age-enforced system "graduation" or voluntary exit.

Various individual, family, and contextual factors are also associated with both exposure and outcome, such as family socioeconomic status, negative parenting practices, and child and adolescent addiction, behavioral, and emotional problems (Wilson & Widom, 2010). Using longitudinal studies, researchers have tested hypothetical mechanisms underlying associations between CSA, other child and family variables, and involvement as adolescents or young adults in sex trade work. In one study of predominately African American women that over-sampled children with histories of CSA, involvement in juvenile prostitution demonstrated small ($r = 0.2$)

but significant associations with prior sexual abuse; sexual self- and other-denigrating attitudes mediated the association between child maltreatment (including, but not limited to, CSA) and later involvement in prostitution (Reid, 2011). In a second study, Wilson & Widom (2010) followed up a cohort of children aged 11 and under, with substantiated maltreatment, and found that, as compared with controls, maltreatment (including CSA) was associated with multiple problem behaviors in adolescence such as running away, school difficulties, drug use, and criminality. However, early sexual initiation was the sole mediator in the association between maltreatment and entry into prostitution.

Interventions for children with sexualized behaviors should take into account the child's developmental stage and ecological contexts, including community and culture, family, and individual characteristics. Most importantly, they should rely upon principles of evidence-based practice. Clinicians who provide evidence-based care engage clients in decision-making about services based on the best up-to-date evidence from valid research, and how it fits with the individual client's characteristics, contexts, and needs (Chaffin & Friedrich, 2004; Sackett, Rosenberg, Gray, Haynes, & Richardson, 1996). Chaffin & Friedrich (2004) describe evidence-based practice (EBP) as it pertains to child maltreatment research, describe the interventions that meet EBP criteria, referring readers to the National Child Traumatic Stress Network website, www.NCTSN.org, which lists evidence-based interventions in child maltreatment (http://www.nctsnet.org/resources/topics/treatments-that-work/promising-practices). The Cochrane Collaboration systematic reviews provide advanced summaries of the top-quality primary research studies that focus on the same research question (e.g., efficacy of a particular intervention). Multiple reviews of prevention or treatment interventions for children who have been maltreated are available free on the website: http://www.cochrane.org/about-us/evidence-based-health-care.

Adolescents require different interventions compared with children. For example, SBPs in children appear to improve regardless of treatment chosen, although cognitive behavioral therapy (CBT) is more effective than other treatments for other effects of CSA, such as post-traumatic stress disorder (PTSD) (Macdonald, Higgins, & Ramchandani, 2006). Furthermore, parent training is essential in treating children with sexualized behaviors as well as highly comorbid problems, such as disruptive behavior or anxiety disorders (for a review, see Chaffin & Friedrich, 2004). By contrast, treating adolescents typically involves targeting high-risk sexual behaviors, reducing potential sequelae (e.g., sexually transmissible infections, unintended pregnancies), and treating mental health and addiction issues. Behavioral interventions that address high-risk sexual behaviors and their outcomes often target contraception use, age of sexual initiation, frequency of partners, and sexual negotiation skills (Johnson, Carey, Marsh, Levin, & Scott-Sheldon, 2003). According to a Cochrane review, effective interventions involve non-institutionalized youth and provide condoms together with at least 1 hour of skill demonstration, and general sexual education (Johnson, et al., 2003). These appear to improve condom use and how often youth communicate with partners about sexual risk; however, there is no obvious benefit with respect to frequency of partners. Multi-pronged interventions including contraceptive provision, education, and skill-building are also required to reduce risk of adolescent pregnancy (Oringanje et al., 2009). However, no intervention to date appears to be successful in delaying age of onset of sexual initiation, which is a more consistently reported mediator between CSA and later sexual risk (Johnson et al., 2003; Oringanje et al., 2009). Furthermore, teenagers with high-risk behaviors often require intensive multi-systemic intervention involving educational, vocational, and other skill-building interventions to shift established trajectories and situations such as homelessness, recurrent victimization, antisocial behavior, and sex trading (Wilson & Widom, 2010).

## JUVENILE SEX OFFENDING

About 20% of all sexual assaults are committed by juveniles (Home Office, 2002; Seto & Lalumière, 2010). However, prevalence and incidence estimates of juvenile sexual offending are confounded by the fact that many sexual offenses committed during adolescence do not come to the attention of the criminal justice system, and as many as 47% that do come to the attention of the justice system do not result in formal charges (e.g., Statistics Canada, 2010; Vizard, Hickey, & McCrory, 2007). Juvenile sexual offenders are youth who have been charged and convicted of a sexual offense, which may range from invitation to sexual touching to sexual interference and aggravated sexual assault. They are under the age of majority, but of the age at which they can be held criminally responsible for their actions. Sexual assaults are the most commonly reported offenses in reports of adolescent dating violence made to police by young teenage victims (Statistics Canada, 2010); this is in contrast to community self-reports of dating violence, where physical assault is identified by about 10% of high school youths, with fluctuations by state, and inconsistent significant differences by gender (CDC, 2012; see also http://healthvermont.gov/research/yrbs/2011/index.aspx). In a study of adolescent sexual aggression (rather than sexual offending) in over 70,000 high school students, Borowsky, Hogan, & Ireland (1997) found that almost 5% of male adolescents and 1.3% of female adolescents reported having forced someone into a sexual act. In consideration of sexual aggression rather than sexual offending in particular, identified risk factors include the experience of CSA, witnessing family violence, frequent alcohol and drug use, gang membership, and suicide risk behavior (Borowsky et al., 1997). Protective factors for male adolescents included emotional health, and peer and community connectedness, while academic achievement was a protective factor for females (Borowsky et al., 1997).

Empirically derived research in the area of juvenile sexual offending is limited by a number of factors, including lack of an appropriate comparison group, lack of consistent and psychometrically validated measures, and the reliance on cross-sectional research (Seto & Lalumière, 2010). The American Psychiatric Association (1999) established practice parameters for the assessment of children and youth engaging in sexually abusive behavior. In 2006, "minimal standards of care" were proposed and adopted by the International Association for the Treatment of Sex Offenders regarding the treatment of juvenile sex offenders, including adolescents who have committed a sexual act that could result in a charge (Miner et al., 2006).

Despite challenges, there have been initial clinical and theoretical advances in understanding youth who commit sexual offenses. Research reveals that very few adolescents "specialize" in sexual offending; rather, sexual offending is often part of a general pattern of delinquency. Sexual offenders are more likely to recidivate with nonsexual offenses than with sexual offenses (Nisbet, Wilson, & Smallbone, 2004; Van Wijk, Mali, & Bullens, 2007). Further, adolescents who are convicted of sexual offenses have lower recidivism rates that nonsexual offenders (Burton, Miller, & Shill, 2002), and sexual offenders who have only offended sexually have lower recidivism rates than those who have engaged in sexual and other offending behavior (van Wijk et al., 2007). However, 15–25% of juvenile sexual offenders reoffend sexually (Gretton, Hare, & Catchpole, 2004; Nisbet et al., 2004; Worling & Langstrom, 2006; Worling, Littlejohn, & Bookalam, 2010), and most recidivism happens within the first few years of the initial sexual offense (Worling et al., 2010).

Early age of onset of first criminal offense is often identified as an indicator of chronic offending (Lalumière, Harris, Quinsey, & Rice, 2005).

For example, Vizard, Hickey, & McCrory (2007) found that sexual offenders with an age of onset before 11 years ("early onset") were more antisocial and aggressive earlier in life, and got worse with age. They were also more likely to have experienced childhood physical, sexual, and/or psychological abuse, to have problematic families, as well as many transitions in residence. Late-onset offenders (after age 11 years) were identified as "less pathological," but engaging in higher alcohol and substance use. Age of onset has not been consistently identified across studies, however, with some studies using before age 11 years, others using before age 12 years, and still others using before age 10 years as their definition. Psychopathy has been identified as a risk for recidivism, as has arousal to deviant sexual material as evidenced by penile plethysmographic response (Gretton, McBride, Hare, O'Shaughnessy, & Kumka, 2001). Other identified risk factors include deviant sexual interest, legal sanctions for prior sexual offenses, more than one victim, offending against a stranger, social isolation, and lack of completion of specialized treatment (Worling & Langstrom, 2006).

Also, in their review, Seto & Lalumière (2010) found that adolescent sexual offenders were significantly more likely to be socially isolated. They had less extensive criminal histories than did non-sexual offenders, but more extensive histories than their non-offending peers. Also, they had fewer substance use problems, fewer conduct problems, and fewer antisocial peers. With respect to sexuality, adolescent sex offenders were significantly more likely to have been exposed to sex or pornography, although the effect size was small. There was indication that adolescent sex offenders had earlier age at first intercourse, but it was not clear whether this included intercourse resulting from sexual abuse. These authors found that self-reported anxiety and low self-esteem were significantly higher in adolescent sex offenders than non-sexual offenders, while other areas of psychopathology were not significantly higher. With respect to cognitive abilities, the sex offenders were significantly more likely to have learning problems or disabilities.

## JUVENILE SEX OFFENDING—THE ROLE OF CSA

A multifaceted theory is likely to capture sexual offending best, given the multitude of factors that have been linked to sexual offending, and the significant likelihood that there are diverse pathways to sexual offending. Ward, Polaschek, & Beech (2006) suggest a unified theory encapsulating a number of these explanations, within three factors: (1) biological factors (genetics, temperament); (2) the offender's current and historical context (e.g., CSA, access to victims); and (3) neurological systems involving motivation, emotion, perception, and memory. The inclusion of social skills, and antisocial attitudes and beliefs about women and sexual offending in many theoretical models of sexual offending may not be relevant, but atypical sexual interests, anxiety, low self-esteem, and social isolation may be (Seto & Lalumière, 2010).

The experience of CSA is among the most common variables studied in an attempt to understand adolescent sexual offending, and in a recent meta-analysis was observed to have the second-largest effect size in differentiating between adolescent sexual and non-sexual offenders (Seto & Lalumière, 2010). However, while many children who sexually abuse may have child sexual abuse histories, most individuals with sexual abuse histories do not become sexual abusers in the future. The link between CSA and sexual perpetration has not been clearly delineated, with various explanations postulated including the impact of child sexual abuse in the development of social relationships or atypical sexual interests, re-enactment of CSA, conditioning of sexual arousal, impact on attachment and emotion regulation, and the development of power-related relationship models following the victim–victimizer dyad. The two variables with the largest effect sizes were atypical sexual interests and CSA. Specifically, adolescent sex offenders reported more "atypical sexual fantasies, behaviors, or interests," and greater likelihood of being diagnosed with a paraphilia. The juvenile sexual offenders with child victims were more likely to have a CSA history than the offenders whose victims were peers or adults.

The age at which child sexual abuse occurs may moderate the link between other factors associated with sexual offending in juveniles. For example, Grabell & Knight (2009) explored the link between CSA and juvenile sexual offenders convicted of a serious sexual crime with a victim of any age. They suggested that age 3 to 7 years is a "sensitive period" during which CSA does more damage, and found that the age at which the child sexual abuse occurs may moderate the link between CSA and sexual fantasy, the latter being linked to sexual offending. Burton, Miller, & Shill (2002) compared adolescent male sexual offenders with adolescent non-sexual offenders. Although a sizable proportion of both non-sexual and sexual offenders had experienced sexual victimization, significantly more sexual offenders (79.4%) had sexual abuse histories as compared with non-sexual offenders (46.7%). Of the offenders who had experienced child sexual abuse, sexual offenders were significantly more likely to have experienced physical force during the abuse, and were significantly more likely to have been abused by both male and female perpetrators. Female CSA perpetration, alone or as co-perpetrators with their male partners, is a relatively unstudied area of risk.

In their recent meta-analysis comparing adolescent male sex offenders with adolescent male non-sex offenders, Seto & Lalumière (2010) found many similarities between adolescent sexual and non-sexual offenders. For example, they found no significant difference between adolescent sex offending and non-sex offending males with respect to family communication problems, separation from a parent, familial substance abuse, and familial criminality, or an impact of these problems on victim age. Nor did they find that adolescent sex offenders were more socially incompetent. Both groups were lower in intelligence than non-offending peers. Interestingly, there was no difference between adolescent sexual and non-sexual offenders on general antisocial beliefs and attitudes, or attitudes about sex, females, or sexual offending. Despite the similarities, however, there were also a number of differences, suggesting that treating sexual offenders as equivalent to general delinquents is not sufficient.

The treatment literature suggests that careful assessment and inter-professional collaboration is important to ensure a comprehensive approach to the youth's needs. Treatment is typically directed at risk reduction and risk management, and may be community-based or residential/institutional, with the youth being placed in the least restrictive environment appropriate given his/her risk level. In addition to having the offender monitor his/her own risk factors and skill development, supervision strategies are often employed in the management of juvenile sex offenders. This may take the form of training probation and parole officers about specific factors associated with reoffending, enhancing communication between community treatment providers and supervision officers, establishing community support networks, and other specialized supervision strategies (Center for Sex Offender Management, 2007; Cumming & McGrath, 2000, 2005). Youth may be involved in other therapy (e.g., substance abuse therapy) while receiving sex-offender-specific therapy. Empirical study has not been sufficient to demonstrate which therapy is better than any other, or whether sex-offender-specific therapy is better than general delinquency treatment. In general, research related to treatment of juvenile sex offenders is limited with respect to identifying what treatments work with which offenders (Burton, Smith-Darden, & Frankel, 2006), and no treatments have received strong empirical validation in the literature. Further, the treatment evaluation literature of juvenile sex offenders has many methodological limitations (Langton & Barbaree, 2004). Many treatment programs include components that do not have evidence of being related to recidivism (e.g., empathy for victim; McGrath, Cumming, Burchard, Zeoli, & Ellerby, 2010). Similarly, many treatments for juvenile sex offenders incorporate a component addressing the experience of child sexual abuse. However, as CSA does not appear to be linked to recidivism (Hanson & Morton-Bourgon, 2005), treatment targeting the experience of CSA may not reduce re-offending (Seto & Lalumière, 2010), although maltreatment prevention of all types remains a priority for adolescent health and well-being.

## SUMMARY

The experience of CSA has been tied to a range of impairment, including those in the range of sexuality. However, the myriad of additional adverse experiences obfuscates the specific contribution of CSA, and it would seem that CSA histories are elevated in sexual behavior problems and sexual aggression, although CSA is not a necessary or sufficient condition for these to emerge. Child safety and corrective caregiver guidance can assist in the reduction of inappropriate sexual behaviors; however, once the threshold to sexual offending has been crossed, there is little research to identify what helps prevent the development of sexually aggressive or abusive behaviors in adolescents. Education on healthy sexuality/healthy sexual relationships, programming to improve family, community, and individual functioning, and education about how to interpret mixed media messages about sexuality may be of assistance (Camp et al., 2008). Broader-based impairment targets are helpful for CSA victims, as in trauma-focused cognitive behavior therapy; however, if violence is on-going in the child or adolescent's lives, CSA risk remains (http://tfcbt.musc.edu; Cohen, Mannarino, & Murray, 2011). The primary strategy for supporting healthy sexuality among CSA survivors is the prevention of CSA. When CSA is present, specific support on sexual health is warranted, as in child welfare populations. Sexual health means more than the provision of means for pregnancy and disease prevention, it requires attention to the cognitive, affective, and relational challenges faced by the CSA victim, with focal support in the transitions (to puberty, to dating, to engagement in sex).

Ultimately, the responsibility for minors remains with society, upholding their basic human rights to live in safe environments in all their main domains of the home, school, community, free from sexual harassment, abuse, and assault. Poignantly, CSA often does not support the child's own body as a safe home for their living, and it may never become safe to tell others what is happening or has happened to their bodies. Maltreatment is a clear risk factor for premature death, including suicide, particularly in the child welfare-involved population (Katz et al, 2011; Rhodes & Bethell, 2008). It must always be remembered that CSA is an entirely preventable toxin to a child's body and mind, and we have laws that require us to be alert and act.

## REFERENCES

American Psychiatric Association, (1999). Practice parameters for the assessment and treatment of children and adolescents who are sexually abusive of others. *Journal of the American Academy of Child and Adolescent Psychiatry, 38*(12), 555–765. Available at <http://www.aacap.org/galleries/PracticeParameters/JAACAP_Sexually_Abusive_Children_1998.pdf>.

Anderson, S. L., Tomada, A., Vincow, E. S., Valente, E., Polcari, A., & Teicher, M. H. (2008). Preliminary evidence for sensitive periods in the effect of childhood sexual abuse on regional brain development. *Journal of Neuropsychiatry and Clinical Neurosciences, 20*(3), 292–301.

Asnes, A. G., & Leventhal, J. M. (2010). Managing child abuse: General principles. *Pediatrics In Review, 31*, 47–55.

Berliner, L. (2011). Child sexual abuse. Definitions, prevalence and consequences. In J. E. B. Myers (Ed.), *The APSAC handbook on child maltreatment (pp. 215–232)* (3rd ed.). Thousand Oaks, CA: Sage Publications.

Blakemore, S. J., Burnett, S., & Dahl, R. E. (2010). The role of puberty in the developing adolescent brain. *Human Brain Mapping, 31*(6), 926–933.

Borowsky, I. W., Hogan, M., & Ireland, M. (1997). Adolescent sexual aggression: Risk and protective factors. *Pediatrics, 100*(6), E7.

Briere, J. (2007). Self-awareness, affect regulation, and relatedness: Differential sequels of childhood versus adult victimization experiences. *Journal of Nervous & Mental Disease, 195*(6), 497–503.

Burton, D., Miller, D., & Shill, C. T. (2002). A social learning theory comparison of the sexual victimization of adolescent sexual offenders and non-sexual offending male delinquents. *Child Abuse and Neglect, 26*(9), 893–907.

Burton, D. L., Smith-Darden, J., & Frankel, S. J. (2006). Research on adolescent sexual abuser treatment programs. In H. E. Barbaree, & W. L. Marshall (Eds.), *The juvenile sex offender* (2nd ed.). New York, NY: Guilford.

Camp, C. M. V., Vollmer, T. R., Goh, H., Whitehouse, C. M., Reyes, J., Montgomery, J. L., et al. (2008). Behavioral parent training in child welfare: Evaluations of skills acquisition. *Research on Social Work Practice, 18*(5), 377–391.

CDC (2012). Youth risk behavior surveillance – United States, 2011. Morbidity and Mortality Weekly Report *(MMWR),* <www.cdc.gov/mmwr/> 61 (SS-4).

Center for Sex Offender Management, (2007). *The comprehensive assessment protocol: A systemwide review of adult and juvenile sex offender management strategies.* Washington, DC: US Department of Justice, Office of Justice Programs.

Chaffin, M., Berliner, L., Block, R., Johnson, T. C., Friedrich, W. N., Louis, D. G., et al. (2008). Report of the ATSA task force on children with sexual behavior problems. *Child Maltreatment, 13*(2), 199–218.

Chaffin, M., & Friedrich, B. (2004). Evidence-based treatment in child abuse and neglect. *Child and Youth Services Review, 26*(11), 1097–1113.

Cicchetti, D., & Rogosch, F. A. (2009). Adaptive coping under conditions of extreme stress: Multilevel influences on the determinants of resilience in maltreated children. In E. A. Skinner, & M. J. Zimmer-Gembeck (Eds.), *Coping and the development of regulation. New Directions for Child and Adolescent Development, 124 (pp. 47–59)*. San Francisco, CA: Jossey-Bass.

Cohen, J. A., Mannarino, A. P., & Murrary, L. K. (2011). Trauma-focused CBT for youth who experience ongoing traumas. *Child Abuse & Neglect, 35*(8), 637–646.

Cole, P. M., Llera, S. J., & Pemberton, C. K. (2009). Emotional instability, poor emotional awareness, and the development of borderline personality. *Development & Psychopathology, 21*, 1293–1310.

Cumming, G. F., & McGrath, R. J. (2000). External supervision: How can it increase the effectiveness of relapse prevention?. In D. R. Laws, S. E. Hudson, & T. Ward (Eds.), *Remaking relapse prevention with sex offenders: A sourcebook (pp. 236–253)*. Thousand Oaks, CA: Sage.

Cumming, G., & McGrath, R. J. (2005). *Supervision of the sex offender*. Brandon, VT: Safer Society.

Deb, S., Mukherjee, A., & Mathews, B. (2011). Aggression in sexually abused trafficked girls and efficacy of intervention. *Journal of Interpersonal Violence, 26*(4), 745–768.

Elkovitch, N., Latzman, B. R., Hansen, D. J., & Flood, M. F. (2009). Understanding child sexual behavior problems: A developmental psychopathology framework. *Clinical Psychology Review, 29*(7), 586–598.

Faller, K. C. (1996). Interviewing children who may have been abused: A historical perspective and overview of controversies. *Child Maltreatment, 1*, 83–95.

Fortin, K., & Jenny, C. (2012). Sexual abuse. *Pediatrics in Review, 33*(1), 19–32.

Friedrich, W. N. (1991). Sexual behavior in sexually abused children. *New Directions for Mental Health Services, 51*, 15–27.

Friedrich, W. N., Fisher, J., Broughton, D., Houston, M., & Shafran, C. R. (1998). Normative sexual behavior in children: A contemporary sample. *Pediatrics, 101*(4), E9.

Friedrich, W. N., Grambsch, P., Broughton, D., Kuiper, J., & Beilke, R. L. (1991). Normative sexual behavior in children. *Pediatrics, 88*(3), 456–464.

Friedrich, W. N., Grambsch, P., Damon, L., Hewitt, S. K., Koverola, C., Lang, R. A., et al. (1992). Child sexual behavior inventory: Normative, psychiatric, and sexual abuse comparisons. *Psychological Assessment, 4*(3), 303–311.

Goldstein, A. L., Amiri, T., Vilhena, N., Wekerle, C., Erickson, P., Thornton, T., et al. (2011). *Youth on the street and youth involved with child welfare: Maltreatment, mental health and substance use*. Toronto, ON: University of Toronto.

Grabell, A. S., & Knight, R. A. (2009). Examining childhood abuse patterns and sensitive periods in juvenile sexual offenders. *Sexual Abuse: A Journal of Research and Treatment, 1*(2), 208–222.

Gretton, H., Hare, R., & Catchpole, R. (2004). Psychopathy and offending from adolescent to adulthood: A 10-year follow-up. *Journal of Consulting and Clinical Psychology, 72*(4), 636–645.

Gretton, H. M., McBride, M., Hare, R. D., O'Shaughnessy, R., & Kumka, G. (2001). Psychopathy and recidivism in adolescent sex offenders. *Criminal Justice and Behavior, 28*(4), 427–449.

Hall, D. K., Mathews, F., & Pearce, J. (1998). Factors associated with sexual behavior problems in young sexually abused children. *Child Abuse & Neglect, 22*(10), 1045–1063.

Hanson, R. K., & Morton-Bourgon, K. (2005). The characteristics of persistent sexual offenders: A meta-analysis of recidivism studies. *Journal of Consulting and Clinical Psychology, 73*, 1154–1163.

Home Office, (2002). *The referral order and youth offender panels: Guidance for courts, youth offending teams and youth offender panels*. London, UK: Home Office.

Johnson, B. T., Carey, M. P., Marsh, K. L., Levin, K. D., & Scott-Sheldon, L. A. (2003). Interventions to reduce sexual risk for the human immunodeficiency virus in adolescents, 1985–2000: A research synthesis. *Archives of Pediatrics & Adolescent Medicine, 157*(4), 381–388.

Katz, L. Y., Au, W., Singal, D., Brownell, M., Roos, N., Martens, P. J., et al. (2011). Suicide and suicide attempts in children and adolescents in the child welfare system. *Canadian Medical Association Journal, 183*(17), 1977–1981.

Kaufman, M. (2008). American academy of pediatrics committee on adolescence. Care of the adolescent sexual assault victim. *Pediatrics, 122*(2), 462–470.

Kendall-Tackett, K. A., Williams, L. M., & Finkelhor, D. (1993). Impact of sexual abuse on children: A review and synthesis of recent empirical studies. *Psychological Bulletin, 113*(1), 164–180.

Kliewer, W., Dibble, A. E., Goodman, K. L., & Sullivan, T. N. (2012). Physiological correlates of peer victimization and aggression in African American urban adolescents. *Development and Psychopathology, 24*(2), 637–650.

Lalumière, M. L., Harris, G. T., Quinsey, V. L., & Rice, M. E. (2005). *The causes of rape: Understanding individual differences in the male propensity for sexual aggression*. Washington, DC: American Psychological Association.

Langton, C. M., & Barbaree, H. E. (2004). Ethical and methodological issues in evaluation research with juvenile sexual abusers. In G. O'Reilly, W. L. Marshall, A. Carr, & R. C. Beckett (Eds.), *The handbook of clinical intervention with young people who sexually abuse* (pp. 419–441). Hove, UK: Brunner-Routledge.

Leeb, R. T., Paulozzi, L., Melanson, C., Simon, T. R., & Arias, I. (2008). *Child maltreatment surveillance: Uniform definitions for public health and recommended data elements, version 1.0*. Atlanta, GA: Centers for Disease Control and Prevention, National Center for Injury Prevention and Control. 2008. Available at: <http://www.cdc.gov/violenceprevention/pdf/CM_Surveillance- a.pdf>.

Loftus, E. F., Garry, M., & Feldman, J. (1994). Forgetting sexual trauma: What does it mean when 38% forget? *Journal of Consulting and Clinical Psychology, 62*(6), 1167–1176.

Lyon, T. D., & Ahern, E. C. (2010). Disclosure of child sexual abuse. In J. E. B. Myers (Ed.), *The APSAC handbook on child maltreatment (3d. ed.)* (pp. 233–252). Newbury Park, CA: Sage.

Macdonald, G. M., Higgins, J. P., & Ramchandani, P. (2006). Cognitive-behavioural interventions for children who have been sexually abused. *Cochrane Database of Systematic Reviews*(4), CD001930.

Maniglio, R. (2009). The impact of child sexual abuse on health: A systematic review of reviews. *Child Psychology Review, 29*(7), 647–657.

McGrath, R. J., Cumming, G. F., Burchard, B. L., Zeoli, S., & Ellerby, L. (2010). *Current practices and emerging trends in sexual abuser management: The Safer Society 2009 North American Survey*. Brandon, VT: Safer Society Press.

Miller, C. L., Fielden, S. J., Tyndall, M. W., Zhang, R., Gibson, K., & Shannon, K. (2011). Individual and structural vulnerability among female youth who exchange sex for survival. *The Journal of Adolescent Health: Official Publication of the Society for Adolescent Medicine, 49*(1), 36–41.

Miner, M., Borduin, C., Prescott, D., Bouvensmann, H., Schepker, R., Du Bois, R., et al. (2006). Standards of care for juvenile sexual offenders of the international association for the treatment of sexual offenders. *Sexual Offender Treatment, 1*(3), 1–7.

NCAW Research Group, (2010). The Administration for Children and Families, & US Department of Health and Human Services. *National survey of child and adolescent well-being (NCAW) I - Children involved with child welfare: A transition to adolescence*. Research Triangle Park, NC: RTI International.

Nisbet, I. A., Wilson, P. H., & Smallbone, S. W. (2004). A prospective longitudinal study of sexual recidivism among adolescent sex offenders. *Sexual Abuse: A Journal of Research and Treatment, 16,* 223–234.

Oringanje, C., Meremikwu, M. M., Eko, H., Esu, E., Meremikwu, A., & Ehiri, J. E. (2009). Interventions for preventing unintended pregnancies among adolescents. *Cochrane Database of Systematic Reviews, 2009*(4), CD005215.

Palusci, V., & Ondersma, S. J. (2012). Services and recurrence after psychological maltreatment confirmed by child protective services. *Child Maltreatment, 17*(2), 153–163.

Pedersen, W., & Hegna, K. (2003). Children and adolescents who sell sex: A community study. *Social Science & Medicine, 56*(1), 135–147.

Pence, D. M., & Wilson, C. A. (1994). Reporting and investigating child sexual abuse. *Future of Children, 4*(2), 70–83.

Pinheiro, P. S. (2006). *Report of the independent expert for the United Nations study on violence against children.* New York, NY: WHO. Available at: <http://www.unicef.org/violencestudy/reports/SG_violencestudy_en.pdf>.

Reid, J. A. (2011). An exploratory model of girls' vulnerability to commercial sexual exploitation in prostitution. *Child Maltreatment, 16*(2), 146–157.

Rhodes, A. E., & Bethell, J. (2008). Suicidal ideators without major depression—whom are we not reaching? *The Canadian Journal of Psychiatry, 53*(2), 125–130.

Romer, D. (2010). Adolescent risk taking, impulsivity, and brain development: Implications for prevention. *Developmental Psychobiology, 52*(3), 263–276.

Sackett, D. L., Rosenberg, W. M., Gray, J. A., Haynes, R. B., & Richardson, W. S. (1996). Evidence based medicine: What it is and what it isn't. *BMJ, 312*(7023), 71–72.

Schäfer, I., Langeland, W., Hissbach, J., Luedecke, C., Ohlmeier, M. D., TRAUMAB-Study group. (2010), Childhood trauma and dissociation in patients with alcohol dependence, drug dependence, or both—a multi-center study. *Drug and Alcohol Dependence, 109*(1-3), 84–89.

Senn, T. E., Carey, M. P., & Vanable, P. A. (2008). Childhood and adolescent sexual abuse and subsequent sexual risk behavior: Evidence from controlled studies, methodological critique, and suggestions for research. *Clinical Psychology Review, 28*(5), 711–735.

Seto, M., & Lalumière, M. (2010). What is so special about male adolescent sexual offending? A review and test of explanations through meta-analysis. *Psychological Bulletin, 136*(4), 526–575.

Shenk, C. E., Noll, J. G., Putnam, F. W., & Trickett, P. K. (2010). A prospective examination of the role of childhood sexual abuse and physiological asymmetry in the development of psychopathology. *Child Abuse & Neglect, 34*(10), 752–761.

Silverman, J. G. (2011). Adolescent female sex workers: Invisibility, violence and HIV. *Archives of Disease in Childhood, 96*(5), 478–481.

Sinclair, S., Press, B., Koenig, K. P., & Kinnealey, M. (2005). Effects of sensory integration intervention on self-stimulating and self-injurious behaviors. *American Journal of Occupational Therapy, 59*(4), 418–425.

Statistics Canada, (2010). Study: Police-reported dating violence. *Crime and Justice, and Juristat.* Available at: <http://www.statcan.gc.ca/daily-quotidien/100629/dq100629b-eng.htm>.

Stewart, S. H., & Israeli, A. L. (2002). Substance abuse and co-occurring psychiatric disorders in victims of intimate violence. In C. Wekerle, & A. -M. Wall (Eds.), *The violence and addiction equation: Theoretical and clinical issues in substance abuse and relationship violence* (pp. 98–122). New York, NY: Brunner-Routledge.

Stoltenborgh, M., Van IJzendoorn, M. H., Euser, E. M., & Bakermans-Kranenburg, M. J. (2011). A global perspective on child sexual abuse: Meta-analysis of prevalence around the world. *Child Maltreatment, 16*(2), 79–101.

Stoltz, J. M., Shannon, K., Kerr, T., Zhang, R., Montaner, J. J. S., & Wood, E. (2007). Associations between childhood maltreatment and sex work in a cohort of drug-using youth. *Social Science & Medicine, 65*(6), 1214–1221.

Svedin, C. G., & Priebe, G. (2007). Selling sex in a population-based study of high school seniors in Sweden: Demographic and psychosocial correlates. *Archives of Sexual Behavior, 36*(1), 21–32.

Teicher, M. H., Andersen, S. L., Polcari, A., Anderson, C. M., Navalta, C. P., & Kim, D. M. (2003). The neurobiological consequences of early stress and childhood maltreatment. *Neuroscience and Biobehavioral Reviews, 27*(1-2), 33–44.

Teicher, M. H., Tomoda, A., & Andersen, S. L. (2006). Neurobiological consequences of early stress and childhood maltreatment: Are results from human and animal studies comparable? *Annals of the New York Academy of Sciences, 1071*, 313–323.

Tomoda, A., Navalta, C. P., Polcari, A., Sadato, N., & Teicher, M. H. (2009). Childhood sexual abuse is associated with reduced gray matter volume in visual cortex of young women. *Biological Psychiatry, 66*(7), 642–648.

Trocmé, N., Fallon, B., MacLaurin, B., Sinha, V., Black, T., Public Health Agency of Canada, Minister of Public Works and Government Services Canada et al. (2010). *Canadian incidence study of reported child abuse and neglect 2008 (CIS-2008): Major findings*. Ottawa, ON. Available from: <http://www.phac-aspc.gc.ca/cm-vee/public-eng.php>.

Van Wijk, A. P., Mali, S. R. F., & Bullens, R. A. R. (2007). Juvenile sex-only and sex-plus offenders: an exploratory study on criminal profiles. *International Journal of Offender Therapy and Comparative Criminology, 51*(4), 407–419.

Vizard, E., Hickey, N., & McCrory, E. (2007). Developmental trajectories associated with juvenile sexually abusive behaviour and emerging severe personality disorder in childhood: 3-year study. *The British Journal of Psychiatry, 190*(Suppl. 49), s27–s32.

Ward, T., Polaschek, D., & Beech, A. R. (2006). *Theories of sexual offending*. Chichester, UK: Wiley.

Wekerle, C., & Avgoustis, E. (2003). Child maltreatment, adolescent dating, and adolescent dating violence. In P. Florsheim (Ed.), *Adolescent romantic relations and sexual behavior: Theory, research and practical implications (pp. 213–241)*. Hillsdale, NJ: Erlbaum.

Wekerle, C., & Wolfe, D. A. (2003). Child maltreatment. In E. J. Mash, & R. A. Barkley (Eds.), *Child psychopathology, second edition (pp. 632–684)*. New York, NY: Guilford.

Wekerle, C., Leung, E., Goldstein, A., Thornton, T., & Tonmyr, L. (2009). Up against a wall: Coping with becoming a teen when you have been maltreated as a child. Substance use among adolescents in child welfare versus adolescents in the general population: A comparison of the Maltreatment and Adolescent Pathways (MAP) Longitudinal Study and the Ontario Student Drug Use Survey (OSDUS) datasets. London, ON: University of Western Ontario. Free report copies available from National Clearinghouse on Family Violence <http://www.phac-aspc.gc.ca/ncfv-cnivf/pdfs/nfnts-ado-wallmur-eng.pdf)>.

Wilson, H. W., & Widom, C. S. (2010). The role of youth problem behaviors in the path from child abuse and neglect to prostitution: A prospective examination. *Journal of Research on Adolescence, 20*(1), 26.

Worling, J. R., & Langstrom, N. (2006). Risk of sexual recidivism in adolescents who offend sexually. In H. E. Barbaree, & W. L. Marshall (Eds.), *The juvenile sex offender (pp. 219–247)* (2nd ed.). New York, NY: Guilford Press.

Worling, J. R., Litteljohn, A., & Bookalam, D. (2010). 20-year prospective follow-up study of specialized treatment for adolescents who offended sexually. *Behavioral Sciences and the Law, 28*, 46–57.

# CHAPTER 14

# Memory and Complications to the Interviewing of Suspected Child and Adolescent Victims

### Matthew Fanetti[*], Rachel Fondren-Happel[*], and William T. O'Donohue[†]

[*]Missouri State University, Springfield, Missouri[1], [†]University of Nevada, Reno, Nevada

## INTRODUCTION

The sexual abuse of children is an ongoing problem in most societies. Few societies find adult–child sexual contact to be morally acceptable, and it is a crime with dramatic consequences for the perpetrator. Such consequences often include long prison terms and/or perpetual identification as a perpetrator against children (e.g., Megan's Law). A key problem for the criminal justice and judicial systems is the matter of the reliable discrimination of real cases of abuse from those allegations that are not true. In such cases, children are often the primary witnesses and their testimony is, or can be, the primary evidence. In light of this, it is easy to understand why such testimony is sometimes brought into question during judicial proceedings. Defense attorneys often challenge the evidence used against their clients. These challenges can be directed both toward the child's ability (e.g., cognitive development, linguistic skills) to provide accurate reports of their experiences, as well as to the methods (e.g., the putative use of suggestive questioning) used to generate that testimony. The basic concern is that some of these methods may be either suggestive or may be biased by focusing only on one kind of information (e.g., incriminating against a certain person).

The arguments against allowing children to testify are varied. For example, attorneys may challenge the reliability (accuracy) of a child's memory, suggesting that children, usually due to their immature cognitive processes, may be prone to remember things differently over time or across circumstances. They may challenge a child's ability to participate in court proceedings, suggesting that children may not have the equivalent

---

[1] Correspondence to: Matthew Fanetti, Department of Psychology, Missouri State University, 901 South National Avenue, Springfield, MO 65897. Phone 417-836-6842; email MFanetti@MissouriState.edu

information-processing capacity or cognitive sophistication of adults to understand questions presented to them, to understand the oath taken before testimony, etc. Challenges may also be that children are less able to distinguish fact from fantasy, or that children may be likely to fabricate details, either purposefully or accidentally. Fortunately, we now have a growing database from well-designed research studies to address some of these concerns.

Arguments for allowing children to testify are also varied and may also be based upon assumptions rather than scientific evidence. For example, one common belief is that children who verbalize sexual statements probably have been sexually abused. The assumption is that the probable pathway for them to have this precocious sexual knowledge is from an abusive experience. This, of course, ignores the huge potential impact that ubiquitous technology such as the Internet, or even cable television, has on the experiences and sexual knowledge of children. If the child has not directly experienced this kind of sexual material, perhaps peers have and have shared this knowledge with the child. Thus, this sort of technology has indirectly impacted the child. Thus, precocious sexual knowledge or behavior may indicate some sort of problematic pathway, but is by no means diagnostic of sexual abuse. People also may believe that children have no reason to fabricate details of sexual abuse. Such a claim assumes intentionality on the part of the child (i.e., the child is intentionally and knowingly stating a falsehood). As we shall see, false memories can be created without the child's awareness and without intentionality coming into play. Children can and do lie about sexual abuse, although this is relatively rare (O'Donohue, Cirlugea, & Benuto, in preparation). In addition, it is well established that children may deny abuse when abuse has occurred (Cederborg, Lamb, & Laurell, 2007). Reasons may include fear of the perpetrator, fear of upsetting family structure, etc. In summary, a child may have motives for disclosing or not disclosing abuse, and may experience a set of contingencies not readily apparent to outside observers. Acknowledging such possibilities highlights the need to consider multiple hypotheses in each specific case. Gathering information to confirm or rule out such possibilities can help to disambiguate a case.

The problems associated with the foregoing issues were dramatically revealed during a flush of large-scale and infamous daycare child abuse scandals in the 1980s and 1990s. These cases include the McMartin (Eberle & Eberle, 1993) and the Kelly Michaels (Schreiber et al., 2006) and Edenton child sexual abuse (CSA) cases, as well as numerous others around the United States and the world. In each of those cases, children were interviewed and asked to provide details of (what was thought to be) systematic and vicious sexual abuse, often involving dozens or hundreds of instances. These were heavily covered by the media and became national phenomena, which also sparked the rising fear of satanic cults that collected children to use for sacrifice. However, accusations of poor or contaminating, and sometimes abusive, interviewing practices led to a new fear of the interviewing process itself (Rabinowitz, 2003).

Fortunately, memory researchers had already begun to systematically explore the malleability of human memory (e.g., Braine, 1965; Broadbent, 1957; Hasher & Griffin, 1978; Loftus, 1974; Loftus & Palmer, 1974; Oldfield, 1954). While this early memory research was often focused on adults, it provided useful paradigms for studying and understanding children's memory abilities as well. For these reasons, the rise of these large-scale cases saw a complementary rise in the formal scientific scrutiny of such matters. Most of the claims in these infamous cases did not survive scientific scrutiny; though whether that was justified continues to be an issue for debate. In any event, the success of the scientific examination of the investigative process yielded a subsequent flurry of research regarding children's memory and the factors that influence memory. Three decades later, we are now better able to answer questions about children's memory. The purpose of this chapter is to briefly explore several important issues related to interviewing alleged victims of sexual abuse.

## GENERAL MEMORY ISSUES
### Atkinson and Shiffrin

Early modern memory research sought to establish basic models through which psychology can understand the mechanisms of memory. Perhaps the best-known or most-often utilized model was proposed by Atkinson and Shiffrin (1968; Shiffrin and Atkinson, 1971). Their model proposed the now familiar differentiations between Sensory Memory (SM), Short-Term Memory (STM), and Long-Term Memory (LTM).

Sensory memory is essentially the neural after-effects of interactions with environmental stimuli. We are often unaware of this because we continually "refill" our senses with new information, and stop attending to the old. Consider an example of sensory memory in the visual system. If you are looking at this chapter on white paper or (better yet) on a computer screen, simply close your eyes. If you notice the outline of the place the paper was in your visual field, you are detecting your visual sensory (i.e., Iconic) memory.

Short-term memory is that which we use while consciously working on a task, thus it is called our "working memory." It is short in duration (e.g., about 20 seconds if left alone) and small in capacity (e.g., 5–9 "items"). Generally, phone numbers are seven digits long. This allows STM to maintain the number while one fumbles with the phone for a few seconds.

Long-term memory is any memory that can be utilized after fading from STM, whether that duration is several minutes or many years. LTM is thought to have unlimited duration and capacity, but might be better described as being functionally unlimited. As long as there is no physiological disease process, humans are able to remember some things from early in their lives, and are able to build new and lasting memories. However, the brain filters which memories are kept, though all of the mechanisms for this selection are not yet completely understood.

According to Atkinson and Shiffrin, the main mechanism that allows events to progress through these stages of memory (i.e., SM to STM to LTM) is rehearsal. Rehearsal is the voluntary or automatic mental repetition of an experience. This repetition allows the longer-term storage of the experience and eases the process of recall.

## Depth of Processing Model

Although the Atkinson and Shiffrin model is widely accepted, it does not explain one important problem: what about memories that are immediately shuffled to long-term memory, even though we have not gone through any rehearsal processes?

Craik & Lockhart (1972) proposed a supplemental theory, referred to as the "Depth of Processing Model" (DOP). This model suggests that it is the effectiveness (or depth) of processing, not the amount of rehearsal, that allows memories to be shifted to LTM and allows them to be buffered from filtered removal. The model seeks to explain why some experiences can be easily remembered, even if there was no time for analysis. For example, we often have no trouble remembering a television show we watch. As we watch, we quickly interpret the behaviors of familiar characters and contrast these behaviors with our expectations. If someone were to ask us what "happened," we would have little trouble recalling it in detail. However, if we watch a new show, our ability to remember the details will be hampered, though we may remember more basic things, such as our own emotional responses to it. Each event would be new, and would need to be understood on its own merit.

The DOP model also allows for the use of effortful processing, such as that used in difficult college courses—not completely dissimilar to the Atkinson and Shiffrin approach. That is, with greater time spent on difficult events, we will commit them to LTM to the extent that we understand them. Thus, the student's "cram-session" or rote memorization yields some LTM usage, but not much buffer from quick decay. Understanding what happened is the key to the stability of the memory.

## Reconstructive Memory

Although models of reconstructive memory began to surface in scientific research in the 1960s and early 1970s (Braine, 1965; Pollio & Foote, 1971), Elizabeth Loftus has worked to apply basic memory research to help understand some of the key controversies in forensics. Through basic (now considered classic) experiments, she was able to establish that simple alterations to interview questions can yield significant and (sometimes) lasting alterations to reported memory (Dale, Loftus, & Rathburn, 1978; Loftus & Palmer, 1974, Loftus & Pickrell, 1995). Examples of these studies will be described later in this chapter.

The reconstructive model (Braine, 1965; Pollio & Foote, 1971) posits that memories are not stored in LTM as intact units of experience (e.g., like a video recording), but rather as individual details with varying degrees of association to each other. In addition to these loosely connected details, we also store a script of the experience—a kind of story we use to narrate the memory. Together, they form the building blocks of memory (the details) and the assembly manual (the script). The likelihood of reliably recalling experienced events would then depend upon the completeness of the script and the degree to which the details "stick together" (or are recalled at all).

When an event is recalled, we essentially pull up components (i.e., the script and the details) to report the memory. There may be a bidirectional flow of influence between the nature of the script and the nature of the recalled details. If we have an especially vivid script of the events we believe happened, we may be more likely to omit details that don't seem highly related, and we may unwittingly alter others in a way that better fits with the script. If the script of the events is incorrect, consider how this might change the details that are recalled. Thus, "details" may not be completely stable or intransigent, given that our own scripts may be wrong or inadequate. Furthermore, imagine if this script were provided by an interviewer, rather than by a child's own experience. This possibility underlies some iconic child memory research.

## Classic Memory Research

Dale et al. (1978) studied the potential effects of very subtle question alterations on children's recollections of events that they had seen in a film. They allowed preschool children to watch four short films, and then asked questions about them. The questions were varied in several ways: (1) by the actual presence or absence of the item being asked; (2) by the affirmative or negative nature of the question (i.e., "Did you…" vs. "Didn't you…"); and (3) by the use of single vs. plural quantifiers (e.g., some, a, any). They presented questions such as the following:

- Did you see the little girl?
- Did you see a bridge?
- Did you see any planes?
- Didn't you see the elephant?
- Didn't you see some orange juice?
- Didn't you see a man fall?
- Did you see some flowers?
- Didn't you see any watermelon?

They concluded that the actual form of the question had no impact on the accuracy of the child's recollection, if the event in the question actually occurred. The probability of responding correctly was 73–90% (an accuracy ratio that we now know is fairly standard). However, if the event being questioned did *not* actually occur in the film, then the way the question was asked had a significant impact on accuracy. For example, when asked about singular events that did not happen, children were less likely to answer incorrectly (e.g., "yes") when the question was phased as "Did you see a…," (22% incorrect), "Didn't you see a …," (27% incorrect) or "Didn't you see the … (33% incorrect). However, when the question was phrased as, "Did you see the …," children were significantly more likely to answer incorrectly (56% incorrect). Furthermore, when asked about multiple events that did not occur, the form of the question also played a role in the accuracy of the child's answers. For example, questions phased as, "Did you see any …" (35% incorrect) or "Didn't you see some …" (34% incorrect) yielded a greater percentage of incorrect responses than did questions phrased as, "Did you see some …" (22% incorrect) or "Didn't you see any…" (27% incorrect). The authors concluded that, when children have no actual memory of the event(s) in question, children may pick up verbal cues—that may be quite subtle—from the interviewer to determine the "correct" answer. In actual forensic cases in which a young child has no or few details, either because they did not actually experience the events in question or because they have more errors of omission than do adults, the child may pick up unintentional cues regarding the interviewer's beliefs about the events, and their answers may reflect these subtle and misleading cues.

In another classic experiment, Leichtman & Ceci (1995) studied the effect of stereotypes on the way that children remember an experienced event. They allowed children to witness a man, Sam Stone, who came into their preschool classroom. He came into the room, commented on a story being read, waved, and left. Children in experimental conditions received either a pre-event suggestion about his clumsiness or no suggestion, and either a post-event suggestion during the interview or no post-event suggestion.

Researchers found that young children who had no pre-event or post-event suggestion provided the most accurate accounts and were right 90% of the time. Young children who were given only post-event suggestion (i.e., that Sam Stone had ripped a book or soiled a teddy bear) were more likely to give incorrect positive statements (21%). Children given pre-event stereotype induction (i.e., a story about how Sam Stone was clumsy, but good-natured) were more likely to incorrectly endorse misdeeds (37%). Finally, children who were given both pre-event stereotype information and post-event suggestion were the most likely to falsely accuse Sam Stone (72%). These numbers were slightly lower for older children, and the percentages dropped when children were asked if they actually witnessed the event. However, findings indicate that children may respond not only to misleading information in interviews, but also to stereotypes or pre-interview beliefs they hold about a certain aspect of their memory. Essentially, children in experimental conditions were given a different "script" than the children in the control group and subsequently provided different details in their recall.

Thompson, Clarke-Stewart, & Lepore (1997) examined the effect that more aggressive interviewing styles may have on children's recollections of experienced events. Five- to six-year-old children were asked to participate in a memory task, during which they were left alone in a laboratory. While working on their tasks, a janitor, Chester, came into the room and engaged in one of three activities: (1) simple cleaning; (2) cleaning and playing with toys; or (3) cleaning and playing and then asking children to keep it a secret. Children were then interviewed by three adults: the janitor's "boss;" the adult who had been in the original memory task; and their own parent. The first two adults engaged in one of three interviewing styles: accusatory (e.g., that Chester had been "playing"); non-accusatory (e.g., that Chester had been cleaning); and neutral. The parents were coached to ask open-ended questions in a neutral fashion.

Results indicated that suggestive interviews can powerfully affect the way that children report the witnessed behaviors of others, even when the suggestion is in contrast to what children actually saw. Furthermore, children continued to report the suggested events (rather than actual observations) even when asked neutral questions by their own parents, both immediately after the first interviews and after a week's delay. Additionally, according to the authors, the request for secrecy had a greater effect in the neutral condition than the incriminating or exculpating conditions, when the style of questioning was open-ended. When asked a direct question about the janitor's behavior, children quickly revealed the "secret." However, when asked open-ended questions, the valence of the question affected the child's responses. If the interviewer was neutral (vs. incriminating or exculpating), the child was likely to resist revealing the "secret" for a longer period of time.

That the subsequent reports of the children to their parents continued to support the valence of the suggestions over that of the observations is particularly problematic. It could indicate that children do not simply alter the way that they report events in the face of coercive interviews, but that they also alter the way that they remember them. So, in terms of reconstructive memory, these children have altered the script of their experience, and then details that seem to support that script are more easily reported. For forensic interviewers, this has been the concern about repeated unstructured interviews—especially when the exact nature of those interviews is not available for observation (i.e., was not video recorded).

Garven, Wood, Malpass, & Shaw (1998) connected the laboratory studies of coercive interviewing to the real world by utilizing interviewing strategies that were actually used by child interviewers in the McMartin daycare case. Researchers identified several problematic interviewing techniques in the McMartin interviews. "Suggestive questions" are those that include new information not yet verbalized by the child. The "other people" technique involves telling the child that others have already provided some information, or even specific information. "Positive and negative consequences" involves providing actual contingencies for a child's provision of certain types of answers. "Asked-and-answered" involves repeating questions to which children have already given clear answers. "Inviting speculation" involves asking the child to make guesses about what happened, especially after they have indicated uncertainty or lack of knowledge.

Preschool children were read a story, during which the reader (i.e., "Manny Morales"), read the story of *The Hunchback of Notre Dame* in a way the researchers described as "engaging." They were subsequently interviewed using suggestive techniques derived from those used in the McMartin interviews, including social comparison and reward techniques. Researchers concluded that children in the suggestion plus social coercion group were significantly more likely to generate incorrect responses than those in the simple suggestion group. For example, when children in the simple suggestion group were asked about whether a bad word was said, the percentage of "yes" answers (which was incorrect) was 3.3%. However, when the same suggestion was made in the context of "social incentive," the percentage jumped to 55.6%. When a simple suggestive question was asked about whether a crayon was thrown, the percentage of incorrect "yes" answers was 6.7%. When those questions were asked in the context of "social incentive" the percentage jumped to 66.7%. What this means is that, even if suggestion has deleterious effect on memory accuracy, the inclusion of such things as reward and social comparison can dramatically magnify that effect.

These research studies represent only some of the classic research that has set a stage for subsequent studies of memory. In the decade that followed, an increasing depth and breadth of research was conducted to further explore children's event recall and limitations.

Gilstrap & Ceci (2005), in a novel type of study, examined the relationship of child behaviors and interviewer behaviors during forensic interviews. That is, they examined the extent to which the child's behaviors may generate suggestive questions from the interviewer, rather than the traditional exploration of how interviewer behavior affects child responses. Using lag-sequential analyses of interviews, they also studied the degree to which prior child behavior (vs. adult suggestive questions) predicts a child's denial or incorrect acquiescence. Their results indicate that suggestive questions were likely to be followed by denials, rather than acquiescence. However, when the suggestion included new and misleading suggestions, this pathway predicted incorrect acquiescence. More importantly, prior child behavior in the interview tended to be both more predictive of responses to questions, and may have a more direct impact on the question choices of interviewers. The authors discuss the limitations of the design (e.g., level of coercion, perception of contingency for interviewers), and caution against interpreting this as contradicting volumes of previous research. However, the interactions between child behavior and interviewer behavior promise to be a rewarding avenue for future study.

Bruck, Ceci, Francoeur, & Barr (1995) examined the degree to which pain in an experienced event affects the ability of suggestive questions to alter reported recall. They followed 75 5-year-old children after they received an immunization. Children were interviewed one week after the injection, and then again one year after the injection. Immediately after the injection, children were given pain-affirming, pain-denying, or neutral feedback. One week later, they did not differ in their reports of their experience of pain ($p > 0.96$) or how much they cried ($p > 0.25$).

However, one year later, they were again interviewed. At this point, they were given either pain-denying or neutral information (pain-affirming was not utilized); and they were given either incorrect or correct information about the behaviors of the physician during the injection. According to the authors, when assessing pain, there was both a main effect for time ($F(1,61) = 35.32$, $p < 0.001$), and an interaction between time and group ($F(1,61) = 6.04, p < 0.02$). This means that children in these two groups were significantly less likely to remember feeling pain, but also that the children in the one-year, pain-denying group were significantly less likely to remember pain than those in the neutral group. After one year, suggestion had a significant impact on the memory of pain. There was also a time-by-group interaction for their memory of crying ($F(1,60) = 9.04$, $p < 0.04$). Finally, Bruck et al. assessed the degree to which the correct or incorrect, one-year, post-event suggestions were reflected by the children. For example, some children were given false information to suggest that the physician's assistant had given them the shot, while other children were not given this false information. Those who were given this false suggestion were significantly more likely to mistakenly report that the PA had administered the injection than those who did not receive the false suggestion ($F(3) = 13.41, p < 0.003$).

Taken together, the Bruck et al. (1995) findings support the notion that, immediately after events, children may have memories that are fairly stable and resistant to suggestion. However, after a significant time delay (a time delay not uncommon in forensic interviewing), children may be significantly more prone to post-event suggestion related to both personal experience and to observed events.

Berliner, Hyman, Thomas, & Fitzgerald (2003) examined the characteristics of children's memories for "traumatic" and "positive" experiences with children that were confirmed to have been victims of abuse. The idea of "positive" experiences relates only to the idea that some children, especially older male children, may interpret the sexual activity differently from others. It did not imply that the activity was beneficial to their development in any way. Utilizing the Children's Memory Characteristics Questionnaire, Therapist Version (Hyman & Loftus, 1998) and the Trauma Symptoms Checklist for Children (TSCC; Briere, 1996), they found that traumatic memories were significantly less detailed and coherent ($t(29) = -3.06, p < 0.01$; means not provided) than positive memories, but had significantly more emotional impact ($t(29) = 2.39, p < 0.05$; means not provided). The foregoing may be interpreted to mean that the clarity of a memory is not a useful indicator of the validity of the memory. More precisely, it provides no support for the idea that traumatic memories have greater clarity or completeness than other memories. However, it does support the idea that traumatic memories may have somewhat greater emotional impact. Alternatively, positive experiences may be clearer, but have less emotional impact. In this study, differences between traumatic and positive experiences were greater for younger children and decreased with age.

Berliner et al. (2003) suggested two alternative theoretical explanations for the observed differences. First, children may not be attending to the traumatic events in the same way that they attend to the positive events. They may try to think about other things, focus on different stimuli, or even dissociate. They may not understand what is happening to them, or may be confused by the events. This leads to a difference in the way that traumatic and positive events are encoded and perhaps stored. Second, they suggest that the same results might be caused by the way that children recall traumatic experiences. Specifically, they may have a long pattern of avoiding the emotional events, and thus no longer have intact details to report. When considered in the context of reconstructive memory, these findings are consistent with existing research, and support the notion that children's recall of the details of traumatic events is not clearer, or more resistant to suggestion, than the details of memories of non-traumatic events. However, Berliner et al.'s findings should be considered with caution, because the psychometric properties of the instruments utilized have not been well established.

## GENERAL TRENDS IN CHILD MEMORY

Ceci & Bruck (1993; and Bruck & Ceci, 1999) examined the then-current state of children's memory research in an important review that drew some interesting conclusions which we will discuss. These conclusions continue to generate empirical support. In order to understand "accuracy" in children's recollections, we must first understand what it means to be considered accurate.

Human memory is not perfect. We make mistakes and we get things wrong. Adults being asked to serve as eye-witnesses have imperfect memories, as well (Davis & Loftus, 2007). Even so, eye-witness testimony of adults is often considered important in judicial proceedings. Furthermore, examinations of a witness' motivations may sometimes be considered more than a witness' memory ability.

Therefore, it is not as relevant to consider the accuracy of children in an absolute sense (i.e., directly compared with the state of reality), but rather, it is more relevant to compare children's memory capabilities with those of adults whose testimony is often considered sufficiently accurate to be admitted into evidence. For the purposes of most research, the concept of memory is defined as follows: an accurate statement is one correctly reflecting something that actually happened; an error of commission is an inaccurate statement about something that happened or a verbalized statement about something that did not occur; an error of omission is a failure to report an event that happened (usually thought to be relevant to the case); and a correct rejection is the lack of report of an event that did not occur. Correct rejections are relevant to forensic studies, but are impossible to measure because the scope of things that did not occur is infinite. However, distinguishing a correct rejection from an error of omission can be an important task for an interviewer, especially one who has a set of pre-existing beliefs about the nature of an alleged crime.

For most purposes, the remaining three possibilities can be utilized to understand memory accuracy. Accuracy can be defined as the ratio of correct statements to errors of commission. According to Ceci & Bruck (1993) and Bruck & Ceci (1999), the accuracy of child statements about experienced events is approximately 3:1, or 75%. What this means is that about 75% of the details provided will be correct, and about 25% will be incorrect in some fashion. If this sounds like a high or low number, then consider that this same ratio is also shared by both adolescents and adults, in free recall tasks (Ackil & Zaragoza, 1995; Ceci & Bruck, 1993). This suggests that children, in free recall, can be every bit as accurate as adults. But this is only part of the picture. The remaining analysis pertains to errors of omission. They suggest that the area that differentiates children's recollections from those of adults is the number of items they do not provide in free recall (Ackil & Zaragoza, 1995; Ceci & Bruck, 1993). Overall, young children report fewer details than do older children, who utter fewer than adolescents. Adolescents report fewer than adults. Stated differently, the older the individual, the more details (s)he is likely to report. While this is a general trend and may be impacted by other factors—such as rapport, intelligence, motivation, and reward—it does illuminate one problem with forensic interviews of children.

The problems with these interviews lie not with children's basic accuracy in non-suggestive free-recall, but with how many details they can provide and how interviewers are expected to proceed when there are few details provided. If a child's report about an alleged event included few or impoverished details, do we conclude that this is due to a lack of actual experience with the alleged event (i.e., it did not occur), or do we attribute this to the general nature of young children's rates of errors of omission? If you assume the former, you risk neglecting to gather evidence of "true" cases of abuse and allowing abuse to continue. If you assume the latter, you must decide how to proceed in collecting those details. This choice of interpretation is at the heart of many disagreements between the purist memory researcher and the real-world interviewer.

If the latter assumption is applied, then the interviewer must engage in something more structured than genuine free-recall or narrative answers. Such questions may start out as simple queries for more information, though often focusing on specific things. These foci can be (legitimate or illegitimate) cues for the child. Follow-up questions can also develop into much more direct forms, such as multiple-choice or yes-no queries. The problem is that each subsequent step toward providing more information to guide the child's responses also risks revealing to a child the pre-held beliefs (or suspicions) of the interviewer. When these direct questions don't yield more responses, interviewers may be tempted to engage in more coercive or leading styles, sometimes including information that the child has not provided.

Research has indicated that these more coercive and directive styles, especially if they happen to be related to things that the child did not experience, may yield more incorrect statements from the child (Garven et al. 1998). In other words, a leading style has a tendency to shift the ratio of accuracy mentioned above away from the 3:1 we might hope to achieve. Directly stated, children have the capacity to recall experiences as well as adults, although not as completely. Attempts to help them fill-in the "holes" of their memory can yield mixed results that include a decrease in accuracy, depending on the child's actual experiences.

As mentioned in the section of this chapter on memory models, it might be that children have less well-developed explanations of the events that unfold around them, which provides a kind of incomplete script of events. The incomplete script may prevent them from efficiently storing details (that they later do not provide). But as they subsequently reappraise those events (perhaps with the aid of the gleaned interpretations of the forensic process), the newly developing script may introduce the possibility of incorporating details (perhaps brought up in interviews) which seem to fit (i.e., confirmation bias) or may generate their own as they retell the events with the new or more-full script.

## EVALUATING INTERVIEWS FOR POTENTIAL BIAS

Memory experts were an important part of the resolution of cases such as the McMartin and Kelly Michaels scandals (Eberle & Eberle, 1993; Schreiber et al., 2006). With the development of research and a more complete understanding of variables that can affect a child's report, more psychologists are being called on to evaluate interviews conducted in the forensic investigation process.

Fanetti, O'Donohue, & Bradley (2006) attempted to organize the extant research related to children's memory into a prototype assessment tool for use when evaluating interviews of children that have already been conducted. The Protocol for Evaluating Forensic Interviews of Children (PEFIC) is an observational rating scale designed to assess for the most often identified threats to the accuracy of child event recall. It is based on a hypothesis-testing model. The assumptions of the PEFIC are that if you can explicate the most common threats to child memory accuracy, and if you can reliably identify the presence of these threats in an interview, then you should be able to identify the rough potential for (interview-based) contamination within the interview. In other words, if you can identify that the interview did not make the known mistakes, then the interview can be said to be free from those effects. However, the authors caution that this does not translate to the veracity of the child's iterations (which cannot be known without some external verification or hard evidence).

The enumerated "biasing factors" are (Fanetti et al., 2006):
1. Rapport Problems
2. Leading Questions
3. Disconfirmations
4. Inappropriate Reinforcement
5. Repetitive Questions
6. Total Response Considerations—including non-verbal communication (e.g., body-language), para-verbal communication (e.g., tone of voice or rate of speech), and verbal communication (e.g., actual words used)
7. Encouraging Speculation
8. Conformity Press
9. Outside Contamination
10. Child Role & Purpose
11. External Threats and Bribes
12. Truth Knowledge
13. Truth Importance
14. Freedom for "I don't know" responses
15. Authority Pleasing.

Authors evaluated both the reliability and content validity of rater identifications with a mean, pairwise kappa calculated against a "gold-standard" set of agreed-upon interview samples. Results indicated that overall kappas were 0.97 for items 1–8 (i.e., intra-interview influences), and 0.95 for items 9–15 (i.e., extra-interview influences). This indicates a basic ability to identify occurrences of each type of behavior and assessment. It does not identify whether a child's report was actually affected by the presence of the factor.

A follow-up (O'Donohue, Benuto, & Fanetti, 2010) suggests that other considerations also be made in addition to PEFIC rating. They include consideration of these 18 factors:

1. The child, due to rapport problems, may not have been comfortable and therefore may not have answered in a complete and accurate manner.
2. The child did not know that she could say, "I don't know" when she did not know the truth.
3. The child did not understand what it means to tell the truth.
4. The child did not know the importance of telling the truth.
5. The child did not understand her role in the interview or the purpose of the interview, and therefore her answers may have been distorted.
6. The child might have felt uncomfortable discussing certain topics with the interviewer, therefore may not have answered in a complete and accurate manner.

7. The child had experienced some sort of externally derived threatening experience, which may have served to distort answers (e.g., fear of threats to self, loved-ones, or property).
8. The child did not feel as though she had a choice in the type of responses she provided.
9. The child answered in a certain way in an attempt to please an authority figure.
10. There were leading questions.
11. The child's verbalizations at times were disconfirmed.
12. The interviewer inappropriately reinforced certain types of answers.
13. There were repetitive and perhaps coercive questions.
14. There were aspects of the child's total response (e.g., body posture, facial expressions, etc.) that gave a different interpretation to the child's answer.
15. The interviewer encouraged the child to speculate about important details, after the child has indicated that she was not sure about an answer or did not have the information.
16. The interviewer referenced the fact that other individuals (e.g., peers) had been interviewed regarding the interview topic and/or indicated what the other individuals' responses were.
17. The interviewer focused or redirected the child toward information about a specific detail or individual.
18. The child's report has been contaminated by some outside source, such as experience with another professional (e.g., retroactive interference from some other interviews).

In addition, O'Donohue et al. (2010) recommend the context of the child's allegation also be examined along the following dimensions:

1. A possible history of lying by the child.
2. The emergence of "fantastical" details in the allegation by the child.
3. Allegations with logistical implausibilities (e.g., the abuse occurred on the front lawn during the day when cars were driving by).
4. Impoverished descriptions of abuse (e.g., "he abused me").
5. Inconsistency of allegations (regarding core details, e.g., inconsistent statements regarding what happened or how many times abuse occurred).
6. "Stake" analysis (i.e., whether the child or another has a stake in a certain outcome).
7. "Outcry" analysis (i.e., the circumstances of the first disclosure).

Taken together, the PEFIC and the follow-up assessment points lay out a fairly comprehensive method to evaluate the process by which a child's memories are gathered, as well as the usual characteristics of reports that were derived through problematic means. It is not meant as a way to attack child interviews, but rather as a way to ensure that they are conducted and interpreted in the most effective way possible. If each point is considered separately, an interview that fails one or several of them might be worth a second examination.

## CHILD ADVOCACY CENTERS

Child advocacy centers (CACs) were introduced in the 1990s as a way to offer "child-friendly" options for forensic child-abuse investigations. Currently, over 800 CACs are in operation in the United States (National Children's Advocacy Center, 2012). Child advocacy centers vary on the specific services they provide, but the most common service provided by these agencies is forensic interviews by professionals trained in child interviewing. The idea of the CAC is to limit interviewing and investigative exposure of children to as few people as possible. Essentially, this allows the "trail of evidence" to be more accurately understood. Furthermore, this (in theory) also allows for these fewer people to be more highly trained in the collection of that evidence. While staff turnover and lack of funding may limit that reality, the goal still exists. One positive aspect of CACs is the development of standardized interviewing procedures. Standardization allows for better evaluation of procedures, and the gradual improvement of evidence collection.

## HOW CACs INTERVIEW

It is important for psychologists to understand how most CACs conduct interviews, not because they are all equally effective, but so that we can understand some of the strengths and weaknesses of the state of the field. After all, psychologists rarely do these interviews in CACs, unless they happen to be part of a CAC or law enforcement agency. There are several protocols that are available to CACs for forensic interviews (Anderson et al., 2010; Lamb, Orbach, Hershkowitz, Esplin, & Horowitz, 2007; Steele, 2003). These protocols are usually guidelines, rather than structured interviews, and have more similarities than differences. Rather than discussing all such interview protocols, the most widely adopted will be the focus here. There are several nationally recognized forensic-interviewing protocols available for questioning children. Some research has been conducted regarding their characteristics. Three common variants of available forensic-interviewing protocols are the National Children's Advocacy Center (NCAC) protocol (Steele, 2003), CornerHouse (RATAC) protocol (Anderson et al., 2010), and National Institute of Child Health and Human Development (NICHD) protocol (Lamb et al., 2007). While the available protocols have more similarities than differences, especially with the phases/stages involved, each can be more or less appropriate based on various factors, including jurisdictional preference, age of the child, and development.

## National Children's Advocacy Center (NCAC) Forensic Interviewing Protocol

The National Children's Advocacy Center (NCAC) opened in 1985 in Huntsville, Alabama, to look for a more effective way to interact with child victims. Its mission was to develop a more systematic approach to child abuse investigations (to reduce error), and to reduce unintended trauma by involving them in the criminal justice system. The National Children's Advocacy Center also trains working professionals in a multidisciplinary team approach to investigating alleged crimes against children. The NCAC protocol is semi-structured and flexible, which allows the child's responses to provide direction to the interview.

The NCAC protocol cautions against leading questions, like many other interviewing protocols. According to Steele (2003), the most important aspect of training is to operationally define what a "leading question" is, and to instruct interviewers regarding what they are and how they work, not simply to be told to avoid them.

The "stages" in the NCAC protocol include the following: introductions; rapport building; developmental screening; question formation guidelines; transition question; abuse-specific inquiry guidelines (which are tailored to the child based on how "active" the disclosure is); gathering details of any disclosure using open-ended narrative or narrative inquiries; and interview closure (Steele, 2003). While each interview can be markedly different (these are not structured interviews), the protocol is an attempt to control the most problematic styles of interview, and provides basic guidance in the interview process to encourage practices informed by the empirical literature. It is important to note that no validity studies of this interview or effectiveness studies (e.g., fidelity) of the training process have been conducted.

## CornerHouse Forensic Interview Protocol (RATAC)

CornerHouse, a private, non-profit child advocacy center opened in 1989 in Minneapolis, Minnesota. Soon after came the development of the CornerHouse Forensic Interview Protocol, also known as RATAC. RATAC stands for the stages of their forensic interview protocol: Rapport; Anatomy Identification; Touch Inquiry; Abuse Scenario; and Closure. It is also a semi-structured protocol that allows for flexibility and developmental differences. CornerHouse partnered with the National Child Protection Training Center (NCPTC), and has reportedly trained over 23,000 professionals from 48 states and nine foreign countries under the name ChildFirst (Anderson et al., 2010). ChildFirst is a five-day training program available to law enforcement officers, attorneys, forensic interviewers, child advocates, therapists, and other professionals who work with alleged child victims.

For example, CornerHouse suggests using the "Process of Inquiry" as a means of understanding and using the different types of questions available in forensic interviews (Anderson et al. 2010). The typical question types available, according to the "Process of Inquiry," are free-recall, focused-recall, multiple-choice, yes/no, and leading (or misleading). Ultimately, CornerHouse leaves the decision of which types of questions to ask during a forensic interview to the interviewer, though they suggest it is dependent on many factors including age, ability, and developmental or cognitive concerns. They recommend a "balanced" use of open-ended and "focused" questions to minimize suggestibility. What is important is that CornerHouse attempts to help interviewers understand the dangers of "focused" questions, although it allows their use. Again, there are no studies of the validity of the interview protocol, nor are there studies of the effectiveness of the training.

## National Institute of Child Health and Human Development (NICHD) Protocol

Another available protocol for forensic interviewing was developed by the Eunice Shriver National Institute of Child Health and Human Development. This protocol is structured, meaning there are specific questions and interactions that are intended to take place during each stage of the forensic interview. Some argue that a structured protocol may reduce the likelihood of the use of leading questions (since specific question wording is provided to the interviewer), which may be true; however, one pitfall of structured protocols is a lack of flexibility. Essentially, this protocol is similar to a decision-tree, in that the interviewer determines which question to ask next dependent upon the response the child gives. An example of this type of question, according to Lamb et al. (2007) is:

> 8. "Did somebody [briefly summarize allegations or suspicions without specifying names of alleged perpetrator or providing too many details]." (For example, "Did somebody hit you?" or "Did somebody touch your wee-pee [private parts of your body]?")
> [Wait for an answer.]
> [If the child confirms or makes an allegation, go to question 10.]
> [If the child gives a detailed description, go to question 10a.]
> [If the child does not confirm or does not make an allegation, proceed to question 9.]

These types of questions provide interviewers with specific instructions on how to proceed during the forensic interview and, because of this, extensive training is necessary to master appropriate use of this protocol.

This protocol, along with many others, acknowledges the importance of rapport-building during the forensic interview. This protocol suggests that a truth–lie discussion takes place during the Introduction stage, and provides a script for engaging in this discussion. Additional stages include: training in episodic memory; transition to substantive issues; investigating the incidents; and eliciting information that has not been mentioned by the child. Like many other protocols, NICHD sees the value of narrative dialogue from the child throughout the interview to elicit as many details as possible.

The actual frequency of use of this protocol compared with others is unknown, but is anecdotally presumed to be lower than the others mentioned in this chapter. Again, no studies of the validity of the protocol have been reported.

## Extended Forensic Interview Model (NCAC)

There is growing popularity of the use of the extended forensic interview model (formerly known as the forensic evaluation model) when allegations of abuse arise. This "multi-interview" model allows children more than one opportunity to disclose abuse, and may be used if there are concerns regarding the children's willingness to disclose. The thought behind this model is that some children may be unable or unprepared to disclose their abusive experience(s) in a single forensic interview. Even though the dangers of the stereotypic repeated interview are still a matter of debate, there is some support for the notion that children who have been abused may not be willing to disclose this given the short-term nature of the relationship presented in a one-interview model (Olafson & Lederman, 2006; Sorenson & Snow, 1991).

The intention is not to have a "repeated" interview, but to spread the interview process over a greater amount of time and reduce rapport-barriers such as lack of trust. Persons who conduct these extended interviews are intended to be mental health professionals with training in child forensics, linguistics, suggestibility research, and other developmental considerations (Carnes, Nelson-Gardell, Wilson, & Orgassa, 2001). The stages in the extended forensic interview model are designed to be similar to those that take place during single forensic interviews. Extended interviews are susceptible to the same criticisms as other forensic interviews. Multiple interviews are not inherently more suggestive, but it is important to consider the possibilities of an increased use or impact of contaminating techniques that could take place during multiple contacts with children (Rooy, Lamb, & Pipe, 2009).

To be clear, such interviews represent what is currently being used at CACs across the country. We are not reviewing the best interviews available, simply the styles of interviews evaluators will likely see when consulting or providing expert evaluation. However, there is a general lack of empirical, published psychometric evaluation of the most commonly used interviews. In addition, there has been little empirical examination of the effectiveness of the training methods to generate interviewers who refrain from the types of problematic questions and styles the interview designers purport to control.

## OTHER TRAINING

One final consideration in the pursuit of cases of alleged child sexual abuse is the chain of evidence. Most research focuses on the impact of interviews and interviewer behaviors on child memory or child reports. Logistically, much has already happened (or may have happened) prior to any formal interviewing. Namely, a child has had to make some kind of initial statement, which is often known as the "outcry." Since those statements may have been somewhat ambiguous, those first-line professionals may have had to make decisions about reporting the statement, following up to clarify, providing safety, etc. In fact, rarely are forensic interviewers the first to explore the allegations in a degree of detail (Anderson et al., 2010). In addition, it is an all too common (and regrettable) practice that these initial information recipients do not record their interviews with the child. This raises the specter of biasing factors at this stage. Thus, even before we can control the interview environment, the child may have been exposed to the types of contaminating factors that forensic interviewers are taught to avoid. Neither parents nor non-forensic professionals may have the knowledge or experience to understand either the questions to avoid, or the importance of avoiding them.

Missouri State University has advocated a system of training not just for forensic interviewers, but also for all child health and welfare professionals. In that pursuit, professionals complete a short (four-course) certificate program that covers: (1) general child forensic psychology; (2) detailed issues in child abuse and exploitation; (3) child law and judicial experiences; and (4) applied experience in child forensics. To teach these courses, qualified community experts are utilized, and the university system provides an opportunity for academic review and evaluation. Although data are still being collected, anecdotal evidence suggests that these graduate level certificate recipients are valued as information disseminators in their varied places of employment. Specifically, in an environment where "mandated reporting" and child abuse issues have become increasingly important, agencies have realized how little training is available. Involving community members has the benefit of making the training relevant to current problems and issues in a community. In addition, training becomes accessible to agencies that trust other community members (sometimes more than they trust the "Ivory Tower" of the academy).

## REFERENCES

Ackil, J., & Zaragoza, M. (1995). Developmental differences in eyewitness suggestibility and memory for source. *Journal of Experimental Child Psychology*, 60, 57–83.

Anderson, J., Ellefson, J., Lashley, J., Lukas-Miller, A., Olinger, S., Russell, A., et al. (2010). The CornerHouse forensic interview protocol: RATAC. *T.M. Cooley Journal of Practical & Clinical Law*, 12, 194–331.

Atkinson, R., & Shiffrin, R. (1968). Human memory: A proposed system and its control processes. In K. Spence, & J. Spence (Eds.), The Psychology of Learning and Motivation: II. Oxford, UK: Academic Press.

Berliner, L., Hyman, I., Thomas, A., & Fitzgerald, M. (2003). Children's memory for trauma and positive experiences. *Journal of Traumatic Stress*, 16(3), 229–236.

Braine, M. (1965). The insufficiency of a finite state model for verbal reconstructive memory. *Psychonomic Science*, 2(10), 291–292.

Briere, J. (1996). *Trauma symptoms checklist for children (TSCC): Professional manual*. Odessa, FL: Psychological Assessment Resources.

Broadbent, D. (1957). A mechanical model for human attention and immediate memory. *Psychological Review*, 64(3), 205–215.

Bruck, M., & Ceci, S. (1999). The suggestibility of children's memory. *Annual Review of Psychology*, 50, 419–439.

Bruck, M., Ceci, S., Francoeur, E., & Barr, R. (1995). "I hardly cried when I got my shot!" Influencing children's reports about a visit to their pediatrician. *Child Development*, 66, 193–208.

Carnes, C., Nelson-Gardell, D., Wilson, C., & Orgassa, C. (2001). Extended forensic evaluation when sexual abuse is suspected: A multisite field study. *Child Maltreatment, 6*(3), 230–242.

Ceci, S., & Bruck, M. (1993). Suggestibility of the child witness: A historical review and synthesis. *Psychological Bulletin, 113*(3), 403–439.

Cederborg, Ann-Christin, Lamb, M. E., & Laurell, O. (2007). In M. -E. Pipe, M. E. Lamb, Y. Orbach, & A. -C. Cederborg (Eds.), *Child sexual abuse: Disclosure, delay, and denial (pp. 159–173)*. Mahwah, NJ: Lawrence Erlbaum Associates.

Craik, F., & Lockhart, R. (1972). Levels of processing: A framework for memory research. *Journal of Verbal Learning and Verbal Behavior, 11*(6), 671–684.

Dale, P., Loftus, E., & Rathburn, L. (1978). The influence of the form of the question on the eyewitness testimony of preschool children. *Journal of Psycholinguistic Research, 7*(4), 269–277.

Davis, D., & Loftus, E. (2007). Internal and external sources of misinformation in adult witness memory. In M. Toglia, J. Read, D. Ross, F. David, & R. Lindsay (Eds.), *The handbook of eyewitness psychology, Volume I: Memory for events*. Mahwah, NJ: Lawrence Erlbaum.

Eberle, P., & Eberle, S. (1993). *The abuse of innocence: The McMartin preschool trial*. New York, NY: Prometheus Books.

Fanetti, M., O'Donohue, W., & Bradley, A. (2006). A method for evaluating child forensic interviews. *American Journal of Forensic Psychology, 24*(3), 5–27.

Garven, S., Wood, J., Malpass, R., & Shaw, J. (1998). More than suggestion: The effect of interviewing techniques from the McMartin preschool case. *Journal of Applied Psychology, 83*(3), 347–359.

Gillstrap, L., & Ceci, S. (2005). Reconceptualizing children's suggestibility: Bidirectional and temporal properties. *Child Development, 76*(1), 40–53.

Hasher, L., & Griffin, M. (1978). Reconstructive and reproductive processes in memory. *Journal of Experimental Psychology, 4*(4), 318–330.

Hyman, I., & Loftus, E. (1998). Memory for trauma: The intersection of clinical psychology and cognitive science. *Clinical Psychology Review, 18*(8), 933–947.

Lamb, M., Orbach, Y., Hershkowitz, I., Esplin, P., & Horowitz, D. (2007). Structured forensic interview protocols improve the quality and informativeness of investigative interviews with children: A review of research using the NICHD Investigative Interview Protocol. *Child Abuse and Neglect, 31*(11-12), 1201–1231.

Leichtman, L., & Ceci, S. (1995). The effects of stereotypes and suggestions on preschoolers' reports. *Developmental Psychology, 31*(4), 568–578.

Loftus, E. (1974). *Eyewitness testimony*. Cambridge, MA: Harvard University Press.

Loftus, E., & Pickrell, J. (1995). The formation of false memories. *Psychiatric Annals, 25*(12), 720–725.

Loftus, E., & Palmer, J. (1974). Reconstruction of automobile destruction: An example of the interaction between language and memory. *Journal of Verbal Learning and Verbal Behavior, 13*, 585–589.

National Children's Advocacy Center (2012). The National Children's Advocacy Center History. Retrieved February 5, 2012, from The National Children's Advocacy Center website, <http://www.nationalcac.org/history/history.html>.

O'Donohue, W., Benuto, L., & Fanetti, M. (2010). Children's allegations of sexual abuse: A model for forensic assessment. *Psychological Injury and Law, 3*, 148–154.

O'Donohue, W., Cirlugea, O., & Benuto, L. Manuscript in preparation.

Olafson, E., & Lederman, Judge C. (2006). The state of the debate about children's disclosure patterns in child sexual abuse cases. *Journal and Family Court Journal, 57*(1), 27–40.

Oldfield, R. (1954). Memory mechanisms and the theory of the schemata. *British Journal of Psychology, 45*, 14–23.

Pollio, H., & Foote, R. (1971). Memory as a reconstructive process. *British Journal of Psychology, 62*(1), 53–58.

Rabinowitz, D. (2003). *No crueler tyrannies: Accusation, false witness, and other terrors of our times*. New York, NY: Free Press.

Rooy, D., Lamb, M., & Pipe, M. (2009). Repeated interviewing: A critical evaluation of the risks and potential benefits. In K. Kuehnle, & M. Connell (Eds.), *The evaluation of child sexual abuse allegations*. Hoboken, NJ: Wiley.

Schreiber, N., Bellah, L., Martinez, Y., McLaurin, K., Stok, R., Garven, S., et al. (2006). Suggestive interviewing in the McMartin preschool and Kelly Michaels daycare abuse cases: A case study. *Social Influence, 1*(1), 16–46.

Shiffrin, R., & Atkinson, R. (1971). Storage and retrieval processes in long-term memory. *Psychological Review, 76*(2), 179–193.

Sorenson and Snow, (1991). How children tell: The process of disclosure in child sexual abuse. *Child Welfare, 70*(1), 3–15.

Steele (2003) Child forensic interview structure, national children's advocacy center. APSAC Advisor, Fall 2003.

Thompson, W., Clarke-Stewart, K., & Lepore, S. (1997). What did the janitor do? Suggestive interviewing and the accuracy of children's accounts. *Law and Human Behavior, 21*(4), 404–426.

# CHAPTER 15

# Treating Children and Adolescents in the Aftermath of Sexual Abuse

**Elisabeth Pollio, Alissa Glickman, Leah Behl, and Esther Deblinger**
University of Medicine and Dentistry of New Jersey, Stratford, New Jersey[1]

## INTRODUCTION

The difficulties that can occur in the wake of child sexual abuse are numerous and varied, and the impact is potentially long-term. Emotional and behavioral sequelae include depression, anxiety, suicidal ideation and attempts, poor self-esteem, sleep difficulties, dissociation, aggression, interpersonal difficulties, substance use, and sexualized behaviors (e.g., Hornor, 2010; Maniglio, 2009; Paolucci, Genuis, & Violato, 2001). Extensive research has been conducted with children who have been sexually abused, as well as with adults with a history of child sexual abuse. Many studies have documented a wide range of responses to child sexual abuse, from no to minimal symptom reactions to a host of mild to severe psychosocial difficulties (e.g., Jumper, 1995; Kendall-Tackett, Williams, & Finkelhor, 1993). While some children appear to be resilient and may bounce back from the experience of sexual abuse without professional intervention, others may suffer difficulties that, if gone untreated, create an unfortunate negative life trajectory that may impact the child's overall development and functioning.

Research, in fact, has documented associations between child sexual abuse and numerous psychiatric disorders, including post-traumatic stress disorder (PTSD), panic disorder, major depressive disorder, dissociative identity disorder, alcohol and drug dependence, and borderline personality disorder (e.g., Deblinger, McLeer, Atkins, Ralphe, & Foa, 1989; Kendler et al., 2000; Putnam, 2003.) The sequelae are not limited to psychiatric

---

[1] Correspondence to: Elisabeth Pollio, PhD, Child Abuse Research Education and Service (CARES) Institute, University of Medicine and Dentistry of New Jersey, School of Osteopathic Medicine, 42 East Laurel Road, Stratford, NJ 08084. Phone 856-566-7036; fax 856-566-6108; email pollioes@umdnj.edu

symptoms, as physical health difficulties, including abdominal pain, gastrointestinal symptoms, pelvic pain, cardiopulmonary symptoms, and obesity have been linked to child sexual abuse, even years after the abuse (e.g., Irish, Kobayashi, & Delahanty, 2010; Leserman, 2005). Further, neurobiological changes have been associated with child sexual abuse (e.g., Cohen, Perel, DeBellis, Friedman, & Putnam, 2002; Putnam, 2003).

In addition to psychiatric disorders and physical health difficulties, other potential long-term effects of sexual abuse have been documented. Research conducted as part of the well-known Adverse Childhood Experiences (ACE) Study found that a history of child sexual abuse was associated with an increased risk of alcohol problems, illicit drug use, suicide attempts, marrying an alcoholic, and current marital and family problems for both men and women (Dube et al., 2005). In addition, older adolescents and adults, particularly women, with a history of child sexual abuse have been shown to be at an increased risk for revictimization (e.g., Hornor, 2010; Maniglio, 2009; Nelson et al., 2002). Given the wide-ranging difficulties and potential long-lasting impact of child sexual abuse, it is critical to provide early, effective treatment to ameliorate symptoms, lessen the risk of developing psychiatric disorders and other difficulties into adulthood, and help reduce the risk of revictimization. It is also essential that the treatment utilized has demonstrated efficacy to provide children with the best possible opportunity to heal.

## REVIEW OF EVIDENCE-BASED TREATMENTS FOR CHILD SEXUAL ABUSE

Although there have been numerous clinical descriptions of potentially valuable interventions for children who have experienced sexual abuse dating back decades (e.g., Friedrich, Berliner, Urquiza, & Beilke, 1988; Gil, 1991; James & Nasjleti, 1983; MacFarlane & Waterman, 1986; Sgroi, 1982), empirical evaluations examining the efficacy of therapies designed for this population only began to appear in the scientific literature in the 1990s (e.g., Berliner & Saunders, 1996; Celano, Hazzard, Webb, & McCall, 1996; Cohen & Mannarino, 1996b; Deblinger, Lippmann, & Steer, 1996; Deblinger, McLeer, & Henry, 1990;). The early scientific investigations tended to be pre–post and quasi-experimental studies with more recent investigations utilizing randomized controlled designs. This chapter will review a sampling of treatments for child sexual abuse that have demonstrated their efficacy in at least one randomized controlled trial, the "gold standard" of treatment outcome research. Effect sizes will be noted when available using Cohen's (1992) guidelines for effect size interpretation. Although several promising therapies exist, there are few treatment models that have been tested to such a rigorous extent. Further, treatments that have been tested via this gold standard typically average only one randomized controlled trial. Trauma-Focused Cognitive Behavioral Therapy (TF-CBT), however, has demonstrated its efficacy in over 12 randomized controlled trials. This model has the strongest empirical base among the treatments that address trauma symptoms in children, and therefore TF-CBT will be reviewed in greater detail later in this chapter.

Berliner & Saunders (1996) randomly assigned 80 sexually abused children aged 4 to 13 to a 10-week sexual abuse-specific therapy group, with or without stress inoculation training and gradual exposure. Participants in both groups demonstrated significant reductions in symptoms of anxiety and depression, internalizing and externalizing symptoms, sexual behaviors, and fears commonly held among children who have been sexually abused. Although there were not significant reductions in the total score of a more general measure of children's fear, three factor scores (fear of unknown, fear of injury and small animals, and fear of danger and death) showed significant improvement. As hypothesized, there were no significant differences over time between the groups on measures of depression, behavior problems, and sexual behavior problems. However, contrary to the expected outcome, there were also no significant differences between groups on measures of fear and anxiety. The authors describe possible explanations for this lack of difference between groups, including that the majority of children did not have clinically significant fear and anxiety symptoms at pretreatment, the treatments may not have been meaningfully different as some stress inoculation training and gradual exposure elements were present in both groups, and the sexual abuse-specific treatment without the added components may have been sufficient to significantly reduce the non-clinical fear and anxiety symptoms in their sample.

In a study of 32 sexually abused girls ages 8 to 13, Celano et al. (1996) randomly assigned children and their non-offending caregivers to one of two short-term individual treatments. The treatment as usual condition consisted of supportive, unstructured psychotherapy, and the experimental condition utilized a structured therapy based on Finkelhor & Browne's (1985) theoretical model of the four traumagenic dynamics intrinsic to sexual abuse. Significant decreases were found within both conditions in caregiver-reported internalizing and externalizing symptoms, child and caregiver-reported PTSD symptoms, and child-reported self-blame and powerlessness beliefs. Children assigned to both conditions also demonstrated significant increases in overall functioning. Differences between conditions, including greater increases in caregiver supportiveness and optimism, and greater decreases in caregiver self-blame, favored the experimental condition.

Trowell et al. (2002) randomly assigned 71 girls who had experienced sexual abuse (aged 6 to 14) to focused psychoanalytic individual psychotherapy or psychoeducational group therapy. Children in both conditions demonstrated a decrease in psychiatric symptoms, as measured by a semi-structured interview and improvement in overall functioning. Although there was not a significant difference between groups on these measures, significant improvement in symptoms of PTSD favored the individual therapy condition, with effect sizes generally falling within the medium range. This difference, however, may have been a function of the longer duration of the individualized treatment as compared with the group treatment.

Another study randomly assigned 14 Iranian girls aged 12 to 13, who had been sexually abused, to a Cognitive Behavioral Therapy (CBT) condition or an Eye Movement Desensitization and Reprocessing (EMDR) condition (Jaberghaderi, Greenwald, Rubin, Zand, & Dolatabadi, 2004). Participants received the assigned treatment for up to 12 sessions, with a 10-session minimum for the CBT group (no minimum for the EMDR group). Significant decreases in parent-reported PTSD symptoms with large effect sizes and teacher-reported behavioral difficulties with medium effect sizes were found within both conditions, with no significant differences between the conditions. Child-reported PTSD symptoms decreased significantly within the EMDR group, but not within the CBT condition; however, the difference between conditions was not significant. The difference in mean number of sessions per treatment condition, 6.1 for the EMDR group and 11.6 for the CBT group, was significant. However, as noted above, the CBT group had a 10-session minimum, whereas the EMDR group had no minimum.

Other studies have investigated treatment effects on children with mixed trauma histories. Below is a sampling of studies utilizing random assignment in which sexual abuse was among the traumas experienced by the participants. Najavits, Gallop, & Weiss (2006) compared Seeking Safety with treatment as usual in a randomized controlled trial among a sample of 33 adolescent females (average age was 16) with a dual diagnosis of PTSD and Substance Use Disorder. Seeking Safety is designed to enhance coping skills within the cognitive, behavioral, and interpersonal domains. In this study, sexual abuse was the most common trauma category (87.9% of the sample). Results indicated that participants in the Seeking Safety condition demonstrated significantly greater improvements than those in the treatment as usual condition on measures related to substance abuse symptoms, cognitions related to substance abuse and PTSD, and psychopathology. In addition, significant differences favoring Seeking Safety were found on two subscales of the trauma symptom measure (sexual concerns and sexual distress). Between-group effect sizes were medium to large.

The Structured Sensory Intervention for Traumatized Children, Adolescents and Parents—At-risk Adjudicated Treatment Program (SITCAP-ART) was compared with a waitlist list control group in a randomized controlled study of 20 adjudicated adolescents with varying trauma histories in residential treatment (Raider, Steele, Delillo-Storey, Jacobs, & Kuban, 2008). Sexual maltreatment was listed among the most frequently documented traumas of the participants. SITCAP-ART is a structured treatment approach that emphasizes the importance of experiencing traumatic memories at a sensory level in a safe environment. To that end, drawing tasks and treatment-specific questions are used to elicit sensations associated with trauma. Cognitive reframing and processing then follow the sensory-based processing. The program lasts 10 to 11 sessions, consisting of seven group sessions, one individual debriefing session, one individual processing session, and one parent and adolescent session. In the present study, participants in the SITCAP-ART condition demonstrated significant improvements in trauma symptoms and a variety of internalizing and externalizing symptoms, including rule-breaking and aggressive behaviors. No significant improvements were found among the control group. Of note, a modification of SITCAP has also been developed for at-risk traumatized children aged 6 to 12.

## REVIEW OF TRAUMA-FOCUSED COGNITIVE BEHAVIORAL THERAPY RESEARCH

Trauma-Focused Cognitive Behavioral Therapy (TF-CBT) was originally designed for children, adolescents, and non-offending caregivers facing the crisis of child sexual abuse. Early investigations evaluating the potential benefits of this model in individual and group formats were conducted via pre–post and quasi-experimental designs (Deblinger et al., 1990;

Stauffer & Deblinger, 1996). Later, at independent sites in Pennsylvania (Cohen and Mannarino) and New Jersey (Deblinger and colleagues) very similar TF-CBT models were scientifically evaluated via randomized controlled trials. In a study evaluating the efficacy of TF-CBT as compared with non-directive supportive therapy for 67 preschool children with a history of child sexual abuse, Cohen & Mannarino (1996b) found that preschool children (2 to 7 years) randomly assigned to TF-CBT exhibited significantly greater improvements with respect to inappropriate sexual behaviors, as well as general behavior problems, than did children assigned to non-directive supportive therapy. The results of a similar investigation, examining the treatment responses of 49 older children who had experienced child sexual abuse, demonstrated that children (7 to 14 years) assigned to TF-CBT exhibited significantly greater improvement with respect to social competence and depression than did those assigned to the non-directive supportive condition (Cohen & Mannarino, 1998). Deblinger, Lippmann, & Steer (1996) conducted a randomized trial for 90 children (7 to 13 years) with a history of child sexual abuse in which the specific effects of the parent and child interventions associated with TF-CBT were examined. In this investigation children and their caregivers were randomly assigned to one of three TF-CBT conditions (i.e., child only; parent only; parent and child), or a community referral condition. The results of this study demonstrated that children randomly assigned to participate in the TF-CBT child intervention (i.e., child only or parent and child) showed significantly greater improvement with respect to PTSD than did children assigned to the community referral and/or parent only conditions. The non-offending parent's participation in one of the TF-CBT conditions (i.e., parent only or parent and child), on the other hand, was associated with significantly greater improvements with respect to parenting practices, children's levels of externalizing behavior problems, and child-reported depression. A randomized controlled trial also examined TF-CBT in the context of group treatment (Deblinger, Stauffer, & Steer, 2001). TF-CBT provided in group format in the aftermath of child sexual abuse led to significantly greater benefits for 44 young children (2 to 8 years) and their caregivers when compared with less structured support/educational groups. Within-group effect sizes were generally medium to large for the TF-CBT group as compared with small to medium within-group effect sizes for the support group. Caregivers in the TF-CBT groups as compared with those in the support groups demonstrated significantly greater improvement with respect to abuse-related emotional distress. Young children in the TF-CBT groups showed greater improvement with respect to body safety skills than did those assigned to the children's support/educational groups. However, no differences were noted between the conditions with respect to children's PTSD symptoms, potentially because young children in both conditions experienced exposure to child sexual abuse educational information, and the narrative component was not incorporated into the children's TF-CBT groups due to the young age of the children and the group format.

In more recent years, the above researchers collaborated in refining the TF-CBT model for children and further evaluating its efficacy in multisite investigations. In their initial multisite investigation, 229 children (aged 8 to 14) were randomly assigned to TF-CBT or a child/client-centered approach. Children in the TF-CBT condition exhibited significantly greater improvement with respect to PTSD, depression, feelings of shame, dysfunctional attributions, and behavior problems (Cohen, Deblinger, Mannarino, & Steer, 2004). Likewise, non-offending caregivers participating in this study reported greater improvements with respect to their self-reported abuse-related distress, depression, parenting practices, and parental support of the child when they were assigned to TF-CBT compared with the client-centered condition (Cohen et al., 2004). Between-group effect sizes were generally within the medium range. In a recent multisite dismantling study, 210 children aged 4 to 11 were randomly assigned to one of four conditions in which TF-CBT was delivered in 8 versus 16 sessions, with and without the narrative component (Deblinger, Mannarino, Cohen, Runyon, & Steer, 2011). The results of this investigation indicated that TF-CBT delivered with the narrative component in 8 sessions, appeared to be the most efficient and effective in helping children overcome abuse-related fear and generalized anxiety, whereas the 16-session skills-focused condition without the narrative seemed to be most effective in helping parents improve their parenting practices and in turn assisting their children in overcoming externalizing behavior problems. Effect sizes were large within the various conditions. It should also be noted that the clinical improvements reported in several of the above treatment outcome investigations have been maintained over 1- and 2-year follow-up periods (e.g., Cohen & Mannarino, 1997; Cohen, Mannarino, & Knudsen, 2005; Deblinger, Mannarino, Cohen, & Steer, 2006; Deblinger, Steer, & Lippmann, 1999). Finally, the results of the above studies by the original TF-CBT developers have been replicated by other researchers, further documenting the efficacy of TF-CBT with children who have experienced sexual abuse, as well as youngsters exposed to other traumas (i.e., Dorsey, Kerns, Trupin, Conover, & Berliner, 2011; King et al., 2000; Lyons, Weiner, & Scheider, 2006). In summary, TF-CBT has been evaluated in numerous scientific investigations, including over a dozen completed randomized controlled trials. Moreover, this treatment approach has received the highest ratings for its efficacy based on extensive reviews of the treatment outcome literature sponsored by the Department of Justice (Saunders, Berliner, & Hanson, 2004; www.musc/edu/cvc), the US Department of Health and Human Services (www.nrepp.samhsa.gov), and the California Evidence-Based Clearinghouse for Child Welfare (www.cebc4cw.org).

## DESCRIPTION OF TRAUMA-FOCUSED COGNITIVE BEHAVIORAL THERAPY

An outline and case example of the TF-CBT approach for children and their families in the aftermath of child sexual abuse is provided below. However, the original treatment manuals provide a more in-depth description of the TF-CBT approach (Cohen, Mannarino, & Deblinger, 2006; Deblinger & Heflin, 1996), as do the free-of-charge introductory TF-CBT training and consultation sites available via the internet (www.musc.edu/tfcbt; www.musc.edu/ctg; www.musc.edu/tfcbtconsult).

The components of TF-CBT incorporate psychoeducation and skills that progressively build on one another with an increasing focus on the affective and cognitive processing of the sexual abuse and related experiences. The therapy is provided to family members during separate individual child and caregiver sessions, with the ultimate goal of the caregiver taking on an increasingly active and supportive role in conjoint parent–child sessions. Therapists are encouraged to be flexible and creative when implementing TF-CBT, using careful clinical judgment to tailor the approach and the timing of the implementation of the components to the needs of the family.

It is very important to involve the caregiver in treatment if at all possible. Often when a child experiences a trauma the caregivers also have great difficulty coping with the aftermath of the traumatic experience(s). Involvement in treatment helps caregivers in many ways to work through these difficulties and to be able to provide support to their child, which is a key factor in a child's recovery from trauma such as sexual abuse (e.g., Cohen & Mannarino, 1996a; Deblinger et al., 1996). In addition, TF-CBT provides guidance to caregivers so they may address children's behavioral difficulties in the aftermath of trauma effectively and consistently outside the therapy session. The following is a description of the TF-CBT components, which can be summarized by the acronym **PRACTICE**: **P**arenting; **P**sychoeducation; **R**elaxation; **A**ffective Expression and Modulation; **C**ognitive Coping; **T**rauma Narrative and Processing; *In Vivo* Mastery of Trauma Reminders; **C**onjoint Child—Parent Sessions; **E**nhancing Future Safety and Development (Cohen et al., 2006). Given the important role of the caregiver, the parenting component will be discussed in detail, followed by the remaining components as implemented with both children and their caregivers.

**P**arenting is a treatment component that is critical all throughout therapy. When children have experienced sexual abuse or other traumas, caregivers often experience a wide array of emotions that can interfere with their ability to be responsive to their children's needs. For example, some caregivers think that they did not protect their child sufficiently. These thoughts may lead to feelings of guilt and self blame, as well as exaggerated fears for their child's safety and well-being. Unfortunately these thoughts, if not corrected through education and cognitive coping, can lead to maladaptive parenting in the form of overindulgence and/or over-protectiveness.

When children experience a trauma, often their emotional distress is shown through problematic behaviors. Even excellent caregivers, thus, can benefit from support and guidance in responding to their child's emotional and behavioral difficulties. General behavior management techniques can be utilized to help caregivers manage any type of behavioral issue from aggression to sexual behavior problems. The first steps to being able to manage behaviors include understanding how children learn both positive and negative behaviors, while also learning to uncover the function of the problem behavior for the child.

Explaining how children learn behaviors can help caregivers understand how their children's problematic behaviors developed, and how these behaviors may be replaced with healthier positive behaviors. Children often learn through observations, associations, and consequences (Deblinger & Heflin, 1996). First, children learn through observing others, especially their caregivers. Therefore, caregivers are encouraged to learn and model the same healthy coping behaviors their children are learning in therapy, while minimizing behaviors they would prefer their children not to imitate. Second, children learn through associating experiences and feelings. For example, when children learn to associate pain with touching a hot stove and thereafter avoid hot stoves, they have learned a healthy avoidant behavior. In the context of traumatic experiences, associations between negative feelings and the actual trauma may generalize to innocuous trauma reminders, leading to problematic avoidant behaviors. However, these generalized associations can be corrected and new associations may be created through exposure and processing such that children learn to associate traumatic memories with feelings of confidence and strength. Finally, children learn through both positive and negative consequences. Thus, when caregivers effectively and consistently provide positive consequences for healthy coping behaviors and negative consequences for problematic behaviors, their children's overall adjustment improves.

A functional analysis consists of looking at the antecedents and the consequences of the problem behaviors in the different situations that they occur. Through a functional analysis it can be determined under what circumstances the child exhibits the behavior, and whether there is a trigger, either situational or emotional, for that behavior. Identifying the triggers can help caregivers change the antecedents that are resulting in the undesirable behaviors. For example, a child who becomes aggressive due to the anger he or she feels when reminded of the sexual abuse may benefit from using basic coping skills such as deep breathing. The parent may then learn to coach the child to use healthy coping behaviors to deal with his or her anger, consequently decreasing the aggressive behavior. The analysis may also reveal what the child is getting from the problematic behavior (e.g., attention, control). For example, the behavior may be inadvertently reinforced by negative parental attention. The identification of this pattern of behavior can lead to a discussion with the caregivers about minimizing their tendency to yell or lecture in response to their child's aggressive or angry behavior. Caregivers may then be encouraged to refocus their efforts on noticing and praising their child when he or she uses appropriate coping skills to manage anger-provoking cues or reminders. Functional analysis can also identify what the child is getting from the behavior, so the therapist can work with the parent to help the child achieve the desired consequence in an appropriate way. For example, a child's non-compliant behavior in response to parental requests may be motivated by an increased desire for control. In such a case, parents may help children achieve feelings of control by learning to give children a choice of two alternative ways to comply with a request.

A core feature of the parenting component involves providing guidance and motivation for caregivers to utilize basic behavior management principles to encourage healthy coping skills and prosocial behaviors, while discouraging problematic behaviors. Global and specific praise, for example, uses the reinforcement of caregivers' positive attention to help children feel good about themselves and learn what specific behaviors are desired of them. When children are left feeling good about their behavior through the positive attention of their caregiver, they are more likely to repeat that behavior.

Caregivers are also taught to actively ignore behavior that is annoying but not harmful by removing the attention children want when they are engaging in undesirable behaviors. Behaviors such as whining would fall into this category. Not giving children attention when they are involved in these types of behaviors, while praising them when they perform appropriate alternative behaviors, can be a very powerful combination to change children's behavior.

It is very important for children to have clear rules and guidelines. Continuing to adhere to the rules and guidelines that were in place prior to the trauma helps children feel that life is continuing as before. Caregivers are provided guidance in developing rules, giving children instructions, and administering negative consequences, such as time-outs for problematic behaviors. For older children and adolescents, other non-attention-based negative consequences are recommended, such as giving short work chores to complete or the temporary removal of privileges. It is important that negative consequences be administered without long lectures or explanations. Discussions of the problematic behavior, if necessary, can take place at a later time when the child is behaving appropriately. This is important so that children do not receive reinforcement in the form of attention when they misbehave.

Identifying what is at the root of the behavior can help the caregiver remove the environmental reinforcers of the problematic behavior and identify replacement behaviors. Helping caregivers understand how children learn, and how to use attention to discourage the problematic behavior and encourage appropriate replacement behaviors is very effective in managing behavioral problems. Educating caregivers about the basics of behavior management can go a long way towards helping establish a healthy home environment for children who have experienced trauma.

**P**sychoeducation, which is provided to both the child and caregiver, begins at session one and is interwoven throughout the treatment. Information and education about the assessment findings and treatment model are provided, highlighting the structure and the collaborative nature of the treatment model from the start. The objectives are to actively engage the family, normalize the family's response to the sexual abuse or other trauma experienced, and to provide important and relevant trauma-related educational information. These objectives are accomplished through providing information about the trauma and related experiences (e.g., investigation, medical exam, assessment, and treatment course), while also explaining the symptoms the child is experiencing in relation to the trauma and the course of treatment planned. This process begins to instill hope as families learn that their reactions are not atypical, and that effective treatment exists. Providing psychoeducation about child sexual abuse and encouraging open discussion begins the process of gradual exposure, demonstrating to the child and family that they need not fear discussing the issue with their therapist.

**R**elaxation assists children and their caregivers with managing the physical symptoms related to stress. Children are taught about their bodies' physical reactions to stress and in particular trauma, and then strategies to manage these reactions, such as deep breathing, imagery, and progressive muscle relaxation, are practiced. It is also beneficial to teach these skills to caregivers and encourage them to utilize these strategies themselves, as well as to reinforce their children's use of the skills. Children can demonstrate and teach their caregivers these skills in the conjoint portion of the session. Mindfulness may also be taught as a method of relaxing the mind and focusing on the present moment. Mindfulness can be particularly helpful for clients who feel stuck in the past because of intrusive recollections of the sexual abuse and/or those clients who have frequent worries about the impact of the sexual abuse on the future.

**A**ffective Expression and Modulation involves helping children and caregivers identify, express, and manage their feelings more effectively. Children are initially encouraged to identify a wide array of feelings and provide examples of situations in which they have felt those emotions. This can often be accomplished through various games that enhance rapport in addition to building skills. Encouraging the development and use of a more expansive emotional vocabulary can help children more effectively express and manage their emotions. Appropriate means of expressing emotions are practiced and reinforced. Feelings specific to the trauma experienced are also elicited during this component as a beginning step toward personalizing the discussion of the sexual abuse. This component also provides the caregiver with the opportunity to share with the therapist the many feelings he or she has been experiencing in the wake of the trauma. During the conjoint portion of the session, caregiver–child communication can be enhanced through the child's sharing his or her feelings with the caregiver, and the caregiver's praising the child for the emotional expression.

**C**ognitive Coping involves first educating clients about automatic thought processes so that they can ultimately effectively share and explore thoughts related to the traumatic experiences. Initially, however, the focus is on teaching clients to capture non-trauma-related automatic thoughts that often go by so quickly they may be unaware of them. In the context of this component, many children learn for the first time that we all talk to ourselves almost all the time. Next, therapists may help their clients understand the interrelationships between thoughts, feelings, and behaviors through the presentation of the cognitive triad; that is, using the depiction of a triangle to demonstrate how thoughts influence feelings, which influence behaviors. Examples are offered as to how thinking differently about a situation can lead to more or less positive feelings and more or less productive behaviors. Children are taught the distinction between thoughts and feelings, and they begin to identify their thoughts in different situations. Children are encouraged through examples and role-plays to dispute inaccurate and unhelpful thoughts and in turn generate more helpful, accurate thoughts with respect to common social situations. However, the focus on more actively eliciting and disputing dysfunctional trauma-related thoughts is not initiated with children until they have completed much of their trauma narrative, as described in the next component. Since caregivers, on the other hand, typically do not write a trauma narrative, therapists may begin eliciting and validating the caregiver's abuse-related feelings and thoughts earlier in treatment. In fact, therapists generally begin to help caregivers during this component to identify times when they are feeling particularly distressed, in order to capture the abuse-related feelings and associated underlying thoughts with the goal of utilizing cognitive coping skills to dispute inaccurate and negative sexual abuse-related thoughts (for example, as noted in the parenting section above, that they did not sufficiently protect their child). Therapists often utilize the Socratic Method to help caregivers correct inaccurate thoughts and replace them with more accurate and more positive coping statements.

Creating the **T**rauma Narrative and Processing (also known as gradual exposure) involves encouraging children to describe details of the trauma in a graduated manner in an effort to desensitize them to innocuous trauma reminders and memories. After explaining the rationale, children share what occurred prior to, during, and after the sexual abuse or other trauma(s) experienced, including their thoughts, feelings, behaviors, and physical sensations. The repetition of this process allows the children to eventually tolerate memories and reminders without significant distress. Not only are the painful emotions associated with the trauma lessened and therefore avoidance is decreased, but also inaccurate or unhelpful thoughts (such as the child thinking the abuse was his/her fault) can be challenged and corrected when the narrative is completed and processed. Depending on the individual child, the narrative may take the form of a book, a poem, a song, or other such media. The rationale for the trauma narrative is also explained to the caregivers. If clinically appropriate, the trauma narrative is gradually shared with the caregiver, initially with the therapist alone and then, if indicated, in a conjoint session in which the child shares the narrative with the caregiver. It is essential that the caregiver is adequately prepared for these conjoint sessions later in treatment so that he or she can respond to the child's narrative in a therapeutic manner. This component provides the caregiver with the opportunity to decrease his/her own distress associated with the trauma in individual sessions, model for the child sharing thoughts and feelings about the trauma rather than avoiding them, and promotes effective open discussion of the trauma in which the child feels safe and supported by the caregiver. Of note, gradual exposure is interwoven throughout the treatment, such as through psychoeducation about sexual abuse and identifying feelings associated with being sexually abused, thereby preparing the child for the trauma narrative component which is then experienced as a natural step in the gradual exposure process.

The *In Vivo* Mastery of Trauma Reminders component assists children to overcome their avoidance of innocuous reminders of the trauma in the environment. Avoidance is a powerful reinforcer, in that the child does not experience distress when avoiding the feared stimuli and therefore continues to avoid in an effort to minimize distress. In order to break this cycle of avoidance, the child is gradually exposed to the feared stimuli. When the dreaded consequences of such an exposure do not occur, the anxiety associated with the trauma reminder lessens. This component may not be a necessary part of every treatment, as the trauma narrative exposure may be sufficient. However, its utilization may be helpful when a specific stimulus continues to be avoided, even after the completion of the narrative. *In vivo* exposure is most commonly utilized when children remain fearful and avoidant of specific places or stimuli (e.g., darkness, school, public bathrooms, etc.) that interfere with their adaptive functioning.

As described throughout, Conjoint Child–Parent Sessions enhance communication between the child and caregiver, and provide the opportunity, as clinically appropriate, to review psychoeducation material, practice skills, and eventually read the child's trauma narrative. In addition, these sessions provide the opportunity for a discussion of age-appropriate sex education and healthy sexuality, which is particularly beneficial for children who have been sexually abused. As noted above, children and caregivers should be well prepared by the therapist for these sessions, particularly when reading the trauma narrative.

Enhancing Future Safety and Development involves teaching children safety skills to help them feel efficacious and prepared as much as possible should a potentially dangerous situation arise. Children are praised for the effective safety skills they have already used, including telling about the abuse, in an effort to minimize self-blame. Additional safety skills are then identified and practiced with an emphasis placed on communicating with trusted adults. Practicing these skills in specific scenarios, particularly through role-plays, enhances the child's ability to use these skills in real-world situations. In addition, these exercises can be utilized in the conjoint portion of the session to allow the child to practice telling the caregiver about the potentially dangerous situation being role-played, thus again enhancing child–caregiver communication.

## A CASE STUDY OF TF-CBT FOR CHILD SEXUAL ABUSE WITH SEXUALLY REACTIVE BEHAVIORS

The following case study is provided to illustrate how TF-CBT works in practice with a child who was sexually abused and is also exhibiting sexually reactive behaviors. Robert (not his real name) is a 7-year-old boy attending treatment with his mother following Robert's disclosure of sexual abuse by his 20-year-old male babysitter, Luke, who was a friend of the family. Robert's parents were close friends with Luke's parents, the children had attended many outings together, and Luke had always gotten along well with Robert. Robert's parents asked Luke to babysit a couple of times a month. On the Sunday morning following a night when Luke was babysitting, Robert's mother noticed a hickey on Robert's neck. Robert lied at first and said that he fell. Robert's mother remained concerned, and she had her husband ask Robert about it. Robert disclosed to his father that Luke had been sexually abusing him nearly every time he watched him. Robert disclosed that, specifically, Luke had kissed him on the mouth and neck, and engaged Robert in mutual genital touching. Robert's parents took him to the police station, where he reported the details to a detective. The detective called child protective services, and an investigation followed that resulted in Luke being charged with sexual assault of a minor.

Prior to initiating treatment, an assessment was conducted that included interview and self-report measures completed by both Robert and his mother. Though encouraged to participate, Robert's father was unable to attend, but agreed to review sessions and participate in homework assignments with his wife as much as possible. Assessment measures included the PTSD module of the Schedule for Affective Disorders and Schizophrenia for School-Age Children (Kaufman et al., 1997) to assess PTSD symptoms from Robert's and his mother's perspective, The Shame Questionnaire (Feiring, Taska, & Lewis, 1999) to assess Robert's feelings of shame related to the sexual abuse, the Children's Depression Inventory (Kovacs, 1992) to assess Robert's self-reported symptoms of depression, the Children's Sexual Behavior Inventory (Friedrich et al., 1992) to assess parent-reported sexual behaviors, and the Child Behavior Checklist (Achenbach, 1991) to assess Robert's emotional and behavioral functioning more broadly from his mother's perspective. In addition, Robert's mother's level of distress was assessed by such self-report measures as the Beck Depression Inventory–Second Edition (Beck, Steer, & Brown, 1996) and the Parent Emotional Reaction Questionnaire (Cohen & Mannarino, 1996b). Results of the assessment indicated that, although Robert did not meet the full criteria for PTSD, Robert and his mother reported several symptoms of PTSD, including frequent thoughts of the sexual abuse, avoidance of discussing the abuse, distress when presented with reminders of the abuse, difficulty falling asleep, nightmares, sexual behaviors including excessively masturbating at home and in public and acting out sexually with other children, and decreased interest in activities. Robert reported feeling shame related to the sexual abuse, as well as some symptoms of depression. His mother reported that Robert had shown increased anxiety, withdrawal, and depression, as well as somatic complaints. Robert was doing well academically and he had many friends. Robert's mother noted that behaviorally, she had observed him touching his penis over and under his clothes, both at home and in public. She also noted that she had recently caught him touching his 4-year-old brother's penis while his brother was taking a nap. His mother had been responding to these behaviors by yelling at Robert to stop and lecturing him on how "That is not a nice thing to do."

Treatment with Robert's mother began with a review of the results of the assessment and psychoeducation about responses to trauma. She expressed concern that Robert was damaged and would never be able to function normally. She also feared that he was going to become a sex offender, because of his inability to control his impulses. Robert's mother said she felt helpless and overwhelmed. The therapist listened empathetically and then provided her with education about children's responses to trauma, highlighting that the imitation of sexualized behaviors is not uncommon among young children. The therapist also provided education about how children learn behaviors through observation, association, and consequences, and emphasized that just as behaviors are learned, they can also be unlearned. Robert's mother felt calmer when the therapist praised her for her dedication to her son, and reaffirmed that she is doing the right thing by bringing him to treatment. In addition, the therapist helped her to understand that she will be learning parenting skills that will help to change Robert's behaviors, thereby giving her more hope and empowerment. A discussion ensued about the importance of line-of-sight supervision of Robert and other children, including his brother, to reduce opportunities for inappropriate touching of other children. She wanted to know if she was going to have to do this forever, and she was reassured by the therapist that eventually Robert would learn the rules for touching in treatment and after a period of time in which there were no inappropriate behaviors, she would be able to relax her supervision of him.

The structure of treatment was then explained to Robert's mother, helping her to understand that Robert would initially be learning basic safety rules about OK and not OK touches due to his sexually reactive behaviors, while she would begin with parenting skills. She was told that then they would both move into learning coping skills, eventually discussing the sexual abuse and processing thoughts and emotions related to it, followed by sex education and additional safety skills to reduce the risk of victimization in the future. Robert's mother left the session feeling more confident and optimistic.

At the onset of treatment, Robert was asked to give two baseline narratives, one about a neutral, positive topic and another about the sexual abuse. The purpose of this was to encourage spontaneous narratives to assess Robert's ability to express himself, as well as to assess for abuse-related avoidance. Robert's neutral narrative focused on a recent visit to a local amusement park. Robert was asked to describe everything that happened from the time he got to the amusement park until the time he ate lunch with his family there, as well as his feelings, his bodily sensations, and what his brain was saying to him (thoughts). His description of the events was concrete, as expected, with some details about the different rides he went on. In addition, it was noted that his ability to share thoughts, feelings, and sensations was limited. Next, Robert was asked to share why he was coming for therapy. Robert acknowledged it was because of what Luke did to him. Robert was then provided with the same instructions to share all of the details to make the therapist feel as though she was there. Robert's description consisted of a single sentence, and when asked for thoughts, feelings, and bodily sensations, Robert indicated he felt sad and mad when his mother found out, but then stated he did not want to talk about it anymore. He was given a lot of praise from the therapist for what he had shared. The therapist also reviewed what she learned about Robert's strengths, and how therapy would help Robert and his family. The therapist then spent some time getting to know Robert, including learning about his favorite activities and interests, and generally building rapport.

Next, Robert's treatment focused on acknowledgement of his experience of sexual abuse and providing basic child sexual abuse education, as well as teaching him about OK and not OK touches. While in most cases therapy would initially focus on coping skills, given the concerns about Robert's sexual acting out with his younger brother, therapy sexual behavior rules were reviewed. The therapist reassured Robert that many children who have been sexually abused do not know the rules about private parts because someone like Luke broke the rules with them, and they may not have been taught the rules in the first place. Robert was informed that many children are curious about private parts, and if they did not learn the rules, it does not mean that they are bad, it just means that they need to learn the rules and once they have learned the rules, it is important to follow them or there will be consequences when they forget so that they will remember better in the future. Robert responded well to this introduction to body safety skills, and he and the therapist made a list of OK touches (e.g., handshakes, high fives, taps on the shoulder, and hugs from family) and not OK touches (e.g., hitting, kicking, biting, and touching private parts) that were to be posted in the therapy room during Robert's sessions. In addition, Robert was provided with sexual behavior rules

(Swisher, Silovsky, Stewart, & Pierce, 2008), which he named "Touching Rules." These included: it's OK to touch your private parts when you are alone; it's not OK to touch other people's private parts; it's not OK for other people to touch your private parts (the therapist was clear about exceptions); it's not OK to show your private parts to other people (or for other people to show their private parts to you); and it's not OK to make other people uncomfortable with your sexual words or behavior. Robert was informed that this list would be copied and shared with his mother so that she could post them at home and use them to teach his brother about OK and not OK touches as well. Robert took great pride in decorating his list of rules, which gave him the opportunity to feel ownership of these new rules.

The next few sessions focused on reviewing the body safety guidelines presented in the first session, as well as developing a sense of boundaries and personal space. Robert read the book *Personal Space Camp* (Cook, 2007) to help him understand the concept of personal space, and then the therapist had him stand up and put his arms out in front of himself, to see if he was far enough away from the therapist or if he was invading personal space. He was taught that personal space means "arms length away," and he role-played how to ask someone to please back up if he or she was in his personal space, as well as how to listen to others asking him to please back up if he was in their personal space. Elements of assertiveness were incorporated into these role-plays, and this led into a natural progression of discussing feelings he might experience when someone is in his personal space.

Affective expression skill-building activities were next incorporated into sessions using feelings posters, feelings faces cards, and feelings games. During these exercises, Robert identified different times he felt different ways. He very much enjoyed the games and became more outgoing and talkative as each session progressed. Robert then learned cognitive coping skills. The therapist read the book *The Hyena Who Lost her Laugh* (Lamb-Shapiro, 2000), and through this they discussed helpful versus hurtful thoughts. Robert was educated about the connection between thoughts, feelings, and behaviors using the book, and later using drawings of people with blank faces and thought bubbles above their heads. Robert was asked what the child might be thinking in a given situation (e.g., if a friend doesn't want to play with him/her) and then Robert would state the thought to the therapist, who would write it in the thought bubble. Next, Robert would draw the face on the drawing to represent what the child might be feeling if he or she is having that thought. Then the therapist asked Robert what the child might do if he had that thought and feeling, and they discussed this. Robert seemed to work hard evaluating whether the thought was helpful or hurtful, and if it was hurtful he was challenged to help the child think of a more helpful thought. As this process was repeated, Robert seemed to become more skilled in differentiating accurate and helpful thoughts from inaccurate and/or unhelpful thoughts.

During Robert's mother's sessions, she learned the same coping skills as Robert, only they were introduced in a more adult manner. For example, she made a list of as many feelings as she could think of and then she identified the feelings she felt when she first found out about the abuse, when she has observed her son engaging in sexual behaviors, and how she feels now about the sexual abuse. She was then introduced to the cognitive triangle, and the relationship between thoughts, feelings, and behaviors was explained to her.

Robert's mother also began learning parenting skills that are taught to every parent participating in TF-CBT. However, the therapist discussed with her how to apply these skills to sexualized behaviors. Robert's mother was informed that sexual behaviors are best managed when they are treated like any other challenging behavior, as making a bigger deal about them provides added attention that is likely to increase rather than decrease the sexualized behavior. She was encouraged to remain calm when addressing sexualized behaviors, and to address them the same way as she would aggressive or other problem behaviors.

Over the next several sessions, Robert's mother was introduced to praise, active ignoring, giving effective instructions, and consequences such as time-out. She was encouraged to praise appropriate behaviors that could replace the inappropriate sexualized behaviors, such as healthy affectionate behaviors or OK touches. She also focused on finding other appropriate behaviors to praise, so that Robert would be getting more positive attention than negative attention. When active ignoring was introduced, it was explained to Robert's mother that obviously she could not ignore public or abusive sexualized behaviors, as it is never appropriate to ignore any behavior that can be harmful, but she learned that she can minimize her discussions and avoid lecturing and overreacting when she sees him masturbating or trying to touch another child, as that provides him with more attention and is therefore likely to increase the inappropriate behaviors. She learned that she should simply tell him which rule he is breaking, and then she should provide a consequence. Giving effective instructions was an important parenting skill for her so that she could begin to be clear with Robert about expectations both at home and in public. For example, after discussing and developing a treatment plan in an individual parent session, during a conjoint session, Robert's mother was able to clearly explain to Robert that he may touch his private parts only when he is in the bathroom or in private, and not when other people are around. Consequences for inappropriate behaviors were also discussed with Robert's mother, and she was given specific guidance on how to use time-out so that it would be most effective. Robert's mother determined that time-out would be used only for harmful behaviors Robert might exhibit such as hitting or kicking others, touching others' private parts, and touching his own private parts in public. She found this to be very effective, as Robert understood when he received a time-out that he had broken an important safety rule. Each of these skills was practiced during joint sessions, and Robert's mother was assigned homework each week to target specific behaviors to praise, and skills to practice with Robert.

Robert and his mother both discussed the concept of redirection when Robert feels the urge to touch his private parts in front of other people or touch another child's private parts. It was discussed that Robert could benefit from another activity that he could do to keep his hands busy, and during a joint session, he and his mother came up with playing with a small "koosh ball" at home and having a piece of soft fabric in his pocket when he is outside of the house. Robert really liked the soft fabric and would play with it when he felt the urge to act out sexually, as it would soothe him as well as provide an activity to keep his hands occupied with an appropriate action. Robert also learned relaxation skills such as how to blow his belly up like a big balloon (deep breathing), guided imagery, and an exercise called "Tin Soldier-Wet Noodle" that focuses on tensing and then relaxing the body, as it became clear through a functional analysis that Robert's masturbatory behaviors were exacerbated when he was feeling anxious.

Meanwhile, Robert began psychoeducation about sexual abuse. He read the book *Please Tell* (Jessie, 1991), and played the "What Do You Know?" card game (Deblinger, Neubauer, Runyon, & Baker, 2006) with the therapist to learn more information about sexual abuse at an age-appropriate level. Robert then began his trauma narrative about the sexual abuse. He was given a choice as to how he wanted to tell about the sexual abuse, and he chose to make a book and draw pictures, just like

Jessie in the book *Please Tell*. Robert was excited to make the cover to his book and he called it, *My Story About Sexual Abuse*. Each session, Robert was given two choices as to what relevant topic he wanted to discuss or write about related to the sexual abuse. The therapist had in mind a list of potential topics, including the first incident of sexual abuse, the most distressing sexual abuse experience, telling his parents, talking to the police, receiving a sexual abuse-focused medical exam, when he touched his brother, and coming to therapy. The therapist chose two of these to present as choices for Robert to incorporate into his narrative each session. Over the course of a handful of sessions, Robert drew pictures and told about each of these experiences. While he talked, the therapist acted as his secretary and typed what Robert said word for word. When the therapist read the narrative back to Robert, she encouraged him to add thoughts and feelings to each page prior to moving on to the next chapter. Then the typed words for each chapter were cut out and pasted onto the associated page with his picture.

Concurrently, Robert's mother received education about facts related to sexual abuse. She then began processing her own thoughts and feelings about the sexual abuse Robert experienced, as well as her concerns about his current and future behaviors. She was prepared for the fact that Robert might not want to come to treatment during this phase of therapy, or that he might have transient increases in traumatic stress symptoms as he discussed his memories in detail. The therapist assured Robert's mother that this is normal, she should continue to bring him to treatment even if he does not want to come, and that she should continue to treat all challenging behaviors with the parenting skills she had learned in treatment.

Robert's mother discussed her concerns that Robert may have enjoyed the sexual abuse and may become a perpetrator as he gets older. She was provided education about how the human body, particularly the private parts, responds to touch and it is common for children to feel a nice sensation if their private parts are touched gently. However, it was emphasized to her that the fact that she brought him to treatment to address the sexual abuse was wonderful, because Robert was learning the rules about OK and not OK touches and was utilizing other more appropriate behaviors. The therapist also discussed with her how the vast majority of children who have experienced sexual abuse and/or have sexual behavior problems do not become adult offenders, particularly those who have received therapy, and most importantly have the parental support Robert has. Robert's mother expressed guilt over having left him with a male babysitter, but with processing and using the cognitive triangle, she was able to see how she could not have predicted this, as she trusted her friend's son and had no reason not to trust him. She was able to name many males that had never inappropriately touched a child, and ultimately this helped her to realize that there was nothing wrong with leaving Robert with a male babysitter; it was just that Luke had a problem that she could not have anticipated.

Around the holiday season, Robert's mother indicated that Robert was acting more aggressively and she was concerned it was somehow related to the therapy focusing on the sexual abuse. After conducting a functional analysis, it became clear that Robert's mother was distracted by the stressors of the season, and was yelling more and praising Robert less. She was encouraged to continue using the parenting skills she had learned, including differential attention and time-out for inappropriate sexual and aggressive behavior. More specifically, Robert's mother was encouraged to identify specific behaviors to praise, and she identified playing nicely, sharing, and using OK touches. The following week, Robert's mother came into session distressed because she had turned her back on Robert and his brother for just a minute to get something from another room, and when she returned she caught Robert pulling his brother's pants down. When the therapist asked how she responded, Robert's mother reported that she remained outwardly calm (although "freaking out" inwardly) and she sent him to time-out for breaking the safety rule of using not OK touches. She was praised extensively by the therapist for maintaining her cool and following through on the plan. Despite her initial increase in anxiety about Robert's potential for inappropriate behaviors, her consistency with discipline paid off, as she did not see another recurrence of age-inappropriate sexual behavior. This was also addressed in Robert's session that day. Robert was encouraged to process how his brother may have felt when Robert pulled down his pants. Moreover, he was reminded that his brother looks up to him and imitates him. With that in mind, the therapist collaborated with Robert to identify other ways he could playfully engage his brother, offer appropriate affection, and/or redirect his own impulses with acceptable activities. With the help of the therapist, Robert made a list with pictures of all the possible replacement behaviors, such as rubbing his fabric, playing with the "koosh ball," taking deep breaths, doing the tin-soldier–wet-noodle exercise, playing with his cars, coloring, talking to his mom or dad, or doing jumping jacks to release built up energy.

This list was sent home and posted in the house for Robert as a reminder of positive activities that could help him manage feelings of anxiety and anger, or desires to engage in inappropriate sexual behaviors.

When Robert completed most of his narrative, the therapist sat with him and helped him put the chapters into chronological order to help consolidate his memories in an organized manner. Then the therapist began cognitive processing by reviewing each page with Robert and challenging any distorted thoughts. Robert's primary distorted thought was that he "let" Luke touch him because he didn't say no or try to stop him. He shared that Luke said it was a game and he went along with it because he thought it was fun, as Luke was acting silly and making him laugh. The therapist helped Robert to process this thought by pointing out that Luke did not give Robert a choice as to whether he wanted him to touch his private parts, and that Luke just did it to Robert even though he was older and knew it was wrong. In addition, Robert was educated about how, when someone wants to sexually abuse a child, he or she often makes the inappropriate interactions fun so that the child willingly goes along with it. Robert was reassured that he had not done anything wrong, as he did what most children would do when a trusted babysitter asks them to do something. Robert began to understand that Luke had "tricked him" by making it fun, and that Luke was bigger and knew the body safety rules, including that touching kids' private parts was not okay. As Robert internalized these beliefs, his affect improved and he began enjoying therapy more. His mother reported that he seemed happier and less anxious at home.

When the processing was completed, Robert was very proud of his book and excited to share it with his mother. However, prior to sharing the narrative, Robert and his mother had a conjoint session in which they played the "What Do You Know?" card game (Deblinger et al., 2006) together. This provided an opportunity for Robert and his mother to show that they had learned a lot about sexual abuse. It also gave Robert the opportunity to feel comfortable talking about sexual abuse in general, in order to help him become more comfortable with the idea of sharing his narrative with his mother. Robert was quieter at first during the game, but once he saw his mother answer a few questions correctly, he became much more involved and answered most of the rest of the questions. His mother praised him for every effort at answering questions, and they had a lot of fun with this activity. After the conjoint session, the therapist processed Robert's reactions to the game, and he appeared quite impressed that his mother knew as much information as she did about sexual abuse.

The therapist had been sharing Robert's narrative with his mother during her individual sessions, and helping her to process her thoughts and feelings about the abuse. She became successful at using cognitive coping skills to reframe her thoughts about the information she was hearing in the narrative. As the time for Robert to share his narrative approached, Robert's mother prepared to respond to his narrative during a conjoint session. She prepared to praise Robert for talking about the abuse and expressing his feelings, and to reinforce to him that Luke was the one who did something wrong, not Robert. Robert's mother rehearsed exactly what she was going to say with the therapist so that she felt prepared for the conjoint session. During the conjoint sessions in which Robert shared his narrative with his mother, he had the therapist read the chapters out loud and then his mother responded directly to Robert. Robert's mother used active listening to reflect back what she heard in the narrative and provided much empathy, and Robert beamed when his mother praised his work. He spontaneously asked if she was mad at him, and his mother responded appropriately by saying that she was not mad at him, rather she was mad at Luke. Robert chose to read the final page of his narrative to his mom in which he wrote a summary of his experiences in therapy, as well as all the skills he had learned, and he reflected what he learned about himself, his mom, and his family. He ended his narrative with what he would tell other children about sexual abuse. Robert's mother was delighted to hear this final chapter, which incorporated what he had learned about sexual behavior rules, and she praised Robert for all his hard work.

The final phase of therapy focused on age-appropriate sex education and enhanced body safety skills exercises. Robert's mother prepared for sex education by reading some books and deciding which was most consistent with her belief system. She decided to read *Where Did I Come From?* (Mayle, 1977), a book that gives a detailed overview about body parts, their uses, and how babies are made, through the development of a fetus and its birth. Robert's mother discussed with the therapist that she would like to add in that sex is only for people who are both adults who are in love and married. During a conjoint session, Robert's mother and the therapist together provided Robert with sex education, with Robert's mother reading the book and inserting information about her values and the therapist serving as a support and coach to Robert's mother as needed.

During the final sessions, Robert learned body safety skills. He and the therapist discussed what to do if someone tries to touch his private parts. Robert learned, "No-Go-Tell," which is an easily remembered method for helping young children remember to yell no, go and run, and tell an adult (just like he did) if someone gives them any not OK touches (Deblinger & Heflin, 1996). Robert role-played many situations in which he might need to use No-Go-Tell, including everything from "stranger danger" to familiar figures such as a teacher or a relative trying to engage him in sexual behaviors, to peers using aggressive or sexual not OK touches. Robert was shy at first with the role-plays but became more confident with practice. His mother was learning during her sessions how to respond to any disclosures Robert might make. She practiced active listening, and learned how to elicit a narrative of what happened by asking open-ended questions. She was also encouraged to praise Robert for coming to her with any potential disclosures. She role-played this process several times in individual parent sessions with the therapist, which helped her to confidently role-play body safety scenarios with her son in conjoint session. The therapist pretended to be someone doing something not OK to Robert and Robert practiced yelling no, running, and telling his mother, who in turn responded appropriately. Doing these role-plays gave Robert the opportunity to see how his mother would respond should he ever need to make a disclosure about not OK touches in the future.

After 15 sessions, Robert and his mother completed the TF-CBT protocol and they felt comfortable with the level of skills learned in treatment. Robert had not exhibited any sexualized behaviors in over two months, and his mother felt prepared with how to handle any that might emerge. His symptoms of depression, PTSD, and behavior problems, as assessed by the standardized measures described earlier, had decreased significantly and he was functioning well with his peers. Robert did not report any shame with regard to the sexual abuse any more, and he felt proud of the book he had written about his experience of sexual abuse.

For the final session, a graduation celebration was planned with Robert, his mother, and the therapist, in which they reviewed their accomplishments. Robert made a graduation hat out of construction paper with the therapist, and Robert and his mother once again reviewed all of the changes they both had made since beginning treatment. Robert's mother was reassured that she could call any time with questions, and they could always return for booster sessions should any concerns arise, but it was also emphasized that she could call to share positive accomplishments as well. They concluded with balloons and snacks to celebrate how much they had learned in treatment and to leave them with a positive feeling regarding all of their accomplishments.

## CONCLUSION

Child sexual abuse is a widespread public health problem that has the potential to severely undermine the healthy psychosocial development of children and adolescents. In recent years, however, interventions have been developed to address the therapeutic needs of youth and their families in the aftermath of child sexual abuse. This chapter reviewed clinical interventions that have demonstrated efficacy in at least one randomized controlled trial, highlighting in greater detail the intervention that has garnered the most empirical support for its efficacy with this population: Trauma-Focused Cognitive Behavioral Therapy (TF-CBT; Cohen, Mannarino, & Deblinger, 2006; Deblinger & Heflin, 1996). Several rigorous reviews of the scientific literature have led to TF-CBT receiving the highest ratings for its efficacy and practicality with respect to its clinical implementation and dissemination. Thus, this chapter outlines the PRACTICE components of TF-CBT, and the utilization of this approach is described in the context of a case history. In sum, early effective intervention appears critical to disrupting the highly negative trajectory often associated with child sexual abuse (i.e., chronic PTSD, depression, interpersonal and substance abuse difficulties). The available evidence suggests that children and their non-offending caregivers can greatly benefit from participation in an evidence-based intervention designed to specifically address the common negative psychosocial sequelae of child sexual abuse.

## REFERENCES

Achenbach, T. M. (1991). *Integrative guide for the 1991 CBCL/4-18 YSR and TRF profiles*. Burlington, VT: University of Vermont, Department of Psychiatry.

Beck, A. T., Steer, R. A., & Brown, G. K. (1996). *Manual for beck depression inventory 2nd edition*. San Antonio, TX: The Psychological Corporation.

Berliner, L., & Saunders, B. E. (1996). Treating fear and anxiety in sexually abused children: Results of a controlled 2-year follow-up study. *Child Maltreatment, 1*, 294–309.

Celano, M., Hazzard, A., Webb, C., & McCall, C. (1996). Treatment of traumagenic beliefs among sexually abused girls and their mothers: An evaluation study. *Journal of Abnormal Child Psychology, 24*, 1–17.

Cohen, J. (1992). A power primer. *Psychological Bulletin, 112*, 155–159.

Cohen, J., Deblinger, E., Mannarino, A., & Steer, R. (2004). A multisite, randomized controlled trial for children with sexual abuse-related PTSD symptoms. *Journal of the American Academy of Child & Adolescent Psychiatry, 43*, 393–402.

Cohen, J. A., & Mannarino, A. P. (1996a). Factors that mediate treatment outcome of sexually abused preschool children. *Journal of the American Academy of Child & Adolescent Psychiatry, 35*, 1402–1410.

Cohen, J. A., & Mannarino, A. P. (1996b). A treatment outcome study for sexually abused preschool children: Initial findings. *Journal of the American Academy of Child & Adolescent Psychiatry, 35*, 42–50.

Cohen, J. A., & Mannarino, A. P. (1997). A treatment study for sexually abused preschool children: Outcome during a one-year follow-up. *Journal of the American Academy of Child & Adolescent Psychiatry, 36*, 1228–1235.

Cohen, J. A., & Mannarino, A. P. (1998). Interventions for sexually abused children: Initial treatment outcome findings. *Child Maltreatment, 3*, 17–26.

Cohen, J. A., Mannarino, A. P., & Deblinger, E. (2006). *Treating trauma and traumatic grief in children and adolescents.* New York, NY: The Guilford Press.

Cohen, J. A., Mannarino, A. P., & Knudsen, K. (2005). Treating sexually abused children: One year follow-up of a randomized controlled trial. *Child Abuse & Neglect, 29*, 135–145.

Cohen, J. A., Perel, J. M., DeBellis, M. D., Friedman, M. J., & Putnam, F. W. (2002). Treating traumatized children: Clinical implications of the psychobiology of posttraumatic stress disorder. *Trauma, Violence, & Abuse, 3*, 91–108.

Cook, J. (2007). *Personal space camp.* Chattanooga, TN: National Center for Youth Issues.

Deblinger, E., & Heflin, A. H. (1996). *Treating sexually abused children and their nonoffending parents: A cognitive behavioral approach.* Newbury Park, CA: Sage Publications.

Deblinger, E., Lippmann, J., & Steer, R. (1996). Sexually abused children suffering post-traumatic stress symptoms: Initial treatment outcome findings. *Child Maltreatment, 1*, 310–321.

Deblinger, E., Mannarino, A. P., Cohen, J. A., Runyon, M. K., & Steer, R. A. (2011). Trauma-focused cognitive behavioral therapy for children: Impact of the trauma narrative and treatment length. *Depression and Anxiety, 28*, 67–75.

Deblinger, E., Mannarino, A. P., Cohen, J. A., & Steer, R. A. (2006). A follow-up study of a multisite, randomized, controlled trial for children with sexual abuse-related PTSD symptoms. *Journal of the American Academy of Child & Adolescent Psychiatry, 45*, 1474–1484.

Deblinger, E., McLeer, S., Atkins, M. S., Ralphe, D., & Foa, E. (1989). Post-traumatic stress in sexually abused, physically abused, and non-abused children. *Child Abuse & Neglect, 13*, 403–408.

Deblinger, E., McLeer, S. V., & Henry, D. (1990). Cognitive behavioral treatment for sexually abused children suffering post-traumatic stress: Preliminary findings. *Journal of the American Academy of Child & Adolescent Psychiatry, 29*, 747–752.

Deblinger, E., Neubauer, F., Runyon, M., & Baker, D. (2006). *What do you know?* Stratford, NJ: CARES Institute.

Deblinger, E., Stauffer, L., & Steer, R. (2001). Comparative efficacies of supportive and cognitive behavioral group therapies for young children who have been sexually abused and their nonoffending mothers. *Child Maltreatment, 6*, 332–343.

Deblinger, E., Steer, R. A., & Lippmann, J. (1999). Two-year follow-up study of cognitive behavioral therapy for sexually abused children suffering post-traumatic stress symptoms. *Child Abuse & Neglect, 23*, 1371–1378.

Dorsey, S., Kerns, S. E., Trupin, E., Conover, K. A., & Berliner, L. (2011). Child welfare social workers as service brokers for youth in foster care: Findings from project focus. *Manuscript under review.*

Dube, S. R., Anda, R. F., Whitfield, C. L., Brown, D. W., Felitti, V. J., Dong, M., et al. (2005). Long-term consequences of childhood sexual abuse by gender of victim. *American Journal of Preventive Medicine, 28*, 430–438.

Feiring, C., Taska, L., & Lewis, M. (1999). Age and gender differences in children's and adolescents' adaptation to sexual abuse. *Child Abuse & Neglect, 23*, 115–128.

Finkelhor, D., & Browne, A. (1985). The traumatic impact of child sexual abuse: A conceptualization. *American Journal of Orthopsychiatry, 55*, 530–541.

Friedrich, W. N., Berliner, L., Urquiza, A. J., & Beilke, R. L. (1988). Brief diagnostic group treatment of sexually abused boys. *Journal of Interpersonal Violence, 3*, 331–343.

Friedrich, W. N., Grambsch, P., Damon, L., Hewitt, S. K., Koverola, C., Lang, R. A., et al. (1992). Child sexual behavior inventory: Normative and clinical comparisons. *Psychological Assessment, 4*, 303–311.

Gil, E. (1991). *The healing power of play: Working with abused children.* New York, NY: The Guilford Press.

Hornor, G. (2010). Child sexual abuse: Consequences and implications. *Journal of Pediatric Health Care, 24*, 358–364.

Irish, L., Kobayashi, I., & Delahanty, D. L. (2010). Long-term consequences of childhood sexual abuse: A meta-analytic review. *Journal of Pediatric Psychology, 35*, 450–461.

Jaberghaderi, N., Greenwald, R., Rubin, A., Zand, S. O., & Dolatabadi, S. (2004). A comparison of CBT and EMDR for sexually-abused Iranian girls. *Clinical Psychology and Psychotherapy, 11*, 358–368.

James, B., & Nasjleti, M. (1983). *Treating sexually abused children and their families.* Palo Alto, CA: Consulting Psychologists Press.

Jessie. (1991). *Please tell!* Center City, MN: Hazelden Foundation.

Jumper, S. A. (1995). A meta-analysis of the relationship of child sexual abuse to adult psychological adjustment. *Child Abuse & Neglect, 19*, 715–728.

Kaufman, J., Birmaher, B., Brent, D., Rao, U., Flynn, C., Moreci, P., et al. (1997). Schedule for affective disorders and schizophrenia for school-age children-present and lifetime version (K-SADS-PL): Initial reliability and validity data. *Journal of the American Academy of Child & Adolescent Psychiatry, 36*, 980–988.

Kendall-Tackett, K. A., Williams, L. M., & Finkelhor, D. (1993). Impact of sexual abuse on children: A review and synthesis of recent empirical studies. *Psychological Bulletin, 113*, 164–180.

Kendler, K. S., Bulik, C. M., Silberg, J., Hettema, J. M., Myers, J., & Prescott, C. A. (2000). Childhood sexual abuse and adult psychiatric and substance use disorders in women. *Archives of General Psychiatry, 57*, 953–959.

King, N. J., Tonge, B. J., Mullen, P., Myerson, N., Heyne, D., Rollings, S., et al. (2000). Treating sexually abused children with posttraumatic stress symptoms: A randomized clinical trial. *Journal of the American Academy of Child & Adolescent Psychiatry, 39*, 1347–1355.

Kovacs, M. (1992). *Children's depression inventory.* North Tonawanda, NY: Multi-Health Systems.

Lamb-Shapiro, J. (2000). *The hyena who lost her laugh.* New York, NY: Childswork/Childsplay.

Leserman, J. (2005). Sexual abuse history: Prevalence, health effects, mediators, and psychological treatment. *Psychosomatic Medicine, 67*, 906–915.

Lyons, J. S., Weiner, D. A., & Scheider, A. (2006). A field trial of three evidence-based practices for trauma with children in state custody: *Report to the Illinois Department of Children and Family Services.* Evanston, IL: Mental Health Resources Services and Policy Program; Northwestern University.

MacFarlane, K., & Waterman, J. (1986). *Sexual abuse of young children.* New York, NY: The Guilford Press.

Maniglio, R. (2009). The impact of child sexual abuse on health: A systematic review of reviews. *Clinical Psychology Review, 29*, 647–657.

Mayle, P. (1977). *Where did I come from?* New York, NY: Kensington Publishing.

Najavits, L. M., Gallop, R. J., & Weiss, R. D. (2006). Seeking safety therapy for adolescent girls with PTSD and substance use disorder: A randomized controlled trial. *Journal of Behavioral Health Services & Research, 33*, 453–463.

Nelson, E. C., Heath, A. C., Madden, P. A. F., Cooper, M. L., Dinwiddie, S. H., Bucholz, K. K., et al. (2002). Association between self-reported childhood sexual abuse and adverse psychosocial outcomes. *Archives of General Psychiatry, 59*, 139–145.

Paolucci, E. O., Genuis, M. L., & Violato, C. (2001). A meta-analysis of the published research on the effects of child sexual abuse. *The Journal of Psychology, 135*, 17–36.

Putnam, F. W. (2003). Ten-year research update review: Child sexual abuse. *Journal of the American Academy of Child & Adolescent Psychiatry, 42*, 269–278.

Raider, M. C., Steele, W., Delillo-Storey, M., Jacobs, J., & Kuban, C. (2008). Structured sensory therapy (SITCAP-ART) for traumatized adjudicated adolescents in residential treatment. *Residential Treatment for Children and Youth, 25*, 167–185.

Saunders, B. E., Berliner, L., & Hanson, R. F. (2004). *Child physical and sexual abuse: Guidelines for treatment.* Charleston, SC: National Crime Victims Research and Treatment Center. *[Revised Report: April 26, 2004].*

Sgroi, S. M. (1982). *Handbook of clinical intervention in child sexual abuse.* Lexington, MA: Lexington Books.

Stauffer, L. B., & Deblinger, E. (1996). Cognitive behavioral groups for nonoffending mothers and their young sexually abused children: A preliminary treatment outcome study. *Child Maltreatment, 1*, 65–76.

Swisher, L., Silovsky, J. F., Stewart, J., & Pierce, K. (2008). Children with sexual behavior problems. *Juvenile and Family Court Journal, 59*, 49–69.

Trowell, J., Kolvin, I., Weeramanthri, T., Sadowski, H., Berelowitz, M., Glasser, D., et al. (2002). Psychotherapy for sexually abused girls: Psychopathological outcome findings and patterns of change. *British Journal of Psychiatry, 180*, 234–247.

# CHAPTER 16

# Medical Assessment and Treatment of Suspected Child and Adolescent Victims of Sexual Abuse

Reena Isaac and Angelo P. Giardino
Baylor College of Medicine and Texas Children's Hospital, Houston, Texas[1]

## INTRODUCTION

The medical evaluation for suspected child sexual abuse can be a daunting consideration for parents, caretakers, patients, and non-medical professionals. Such evaluations serve to provide comprehensive medical assessments of potential victims, to provide possible testing and treatment of possible infections and other physical or psychological sequelae of the abuse or assault, and to provide forensic information and collection of such evidence when needed. A thorough medical assessment of potential child victims when conducted sensitively and responsibly can provide important information regarding the child's body and health. With this in mind, the medical assessment has important therapeutic value and serves as a powerful tool in the total evaluation and recovery of the child.

Child sexual abuse is most often times cloaked in secrecy, and a high level of suspicion may be required to identify and recognize the problem (Kempe, 1978). The diagnosis of sexual abuse and the protection of the child and siblings from further harm is dependent upon the physician's consideration of the possibility of such a diagnosis. When such a concern for a child's safety and health arises, a prompt report to law enforcement and/or child protective services should be made so that investigations can be conducted. Sexual abuse occurs when a child is engaged in sexual activities that (s)he cannot comprehend, for which

---

[1] Correspondence to: Angelo P. Giardino, MD, PhD, Chief Medical Officer, Texas Children's Health Plan; Chief Quality Officer, Medicine, Texas Children's Hospital; Clinical Professor, Baylor College of Medicine, 2450 Holcombe, Suite 34L, Houston, TX 77021. Phone 832-828-1216; fax 832-825-8765; email apgiardi@texaschildrens.org

(s)he is developmentally unprepared and is unable to give informed consent, and/or when there is violation of the laws or social mores of society (American Academy of Pediatrics , 1999). In this chapter, we use the term "child" to mean an individual under 18 years of age. Sexual abuse includes a full spectrum of activities ranging from oral-genital, genital, anal contact, and fondling, by or of the child, to non-contact forms of abuse, such as exhibitionism and voyeurism, and various methods of abuse may occur in isolation, occur simultaneously, or progress from less invasive to more invasive forms of abuse.

The medical evaluation and diagnosis of child sexual abuse are the sum of its separate parts. Formulating an accurate medical diagnosis of sexual abuse requires an understanding of the value of each component of the medical evaluation. The components are as follows: (1) obtaining a thorough medical history; (2) performing and understanding the limitations of the physical examination; and (3) understanding the clinical and forensic value of the presence of various sexually transmitted infections (STIs).

## OVERVIEW AND APPROACH TO THE MEDICAL EVALUATION

The medical evaluation serves to assess the physical and emotional health of a child after an allegation of sexual abuse has been made. It also provides documentation of injuries and provides an opportunity to gather evidence that may support such a diagnosis. Prior to the physical examination, time should be taken to build rapport with the child and family by making proper introductions, and by detailing in clear language the purpose of the medical examination. The medical evaluator should also dispel inaccurate notions regarding said examination. To produce a more comforting environment for clear and accurate dialogue, it is often beneficial to engage in non-threatening conversation separate from discussion of the allegations for a few minutes. Progressing on to the child's medical history portion of the interview begins to establish the child's purpose for a medical evaluation and a quest for the determination of the child's health status and needs. If the child is old enough to accurately provide information regarding his or her health, then the child may be asked such questions either alone or with a caretaker present. Finkel (2008) discussed the special relationship that patients, including pediatric patients, have with their physician, and noted that this relationship provides a unique opportunity for sharing sensitive information. If it is assessed that a minor's parent is likely to be very emotional, it is prudent to have the parent interviewed alone so that the child is not also affected prior to the examination. The following information should be obtained while taking a medical history (Finkelhor, 1993):

- a past medical history;
- a medical-psychological review of systems for abuse-related problems;
- a family history;
- a social history;
- a developmental history.

It is recommended that the abuse allegations not be discussed with the historians/caretakers while the child is present.

Although most symptoms are not specific to sexual abuse, as they can be present in other medical conditions, there are several signs and symptoms that may raise concerns of possible sexual abuse. Nightmares, trouble sleeping, school problems, enuresis, discharge or bleeding, or other behavioral or physical changes, while in isolation may not necessarily dictate a concern for possible sexual abuse (Friedrich, 2001; Hunter, 1985; Krugman, 1986). However, a combination of symptoms and/or a sign or symptom coupled with a disclosure can further support the concern. It is important to acknowledge also that a child may not display such behavioral or physical signs or symptoms related to such trauma.

When children are able to explain the reason for their presentation in the medical setting, it is preferable to interview them alone. An extensive history is not required from a child who has previously disclosed, but enough information should be obtained to aid the physician in determining the child's medical condition and to generate a treatment plan. Disclosure of sexual abuse is a dynamic process. Children may initially provide a history of minimal sexual contact. As time progresses, there may be further and more detailed disclosures regarding the abuse. This may occur because the child realizes that (s)he is being believed, and that possible threats made by the alleged perpetrator are now perceived as empty. Other children may disclose completely on an initial interview. Regardless, thorough examinations need to be performed with any history of possible sexual abuse. In studies of legally confirmed cases of child sexual abuse, a majority of victims had no diagnostic physical findings, or had normal physical examinations (Adams, Harper, Knudson, & Revilla, 1994). Heger, Ticson, Velasquez, & Bernier (2002) analyzed their data from a large child abuse referral center and estimated the presence of physical findings in sexual abuse cases to be in the single digits of percentage and no higher than 8% of the children evaluated. Therefore, obtaining a clear medical history from the child is one of the most important parts of the child's sexual abuse evaluation. Open-ended, non-leading questions should be used to obtain the medical history. Table 16.1 provides examples of the types of questions used in interviewing children.

A history of sexual abuse obtained during the course of medical diagnosis and treatment may be admissible in court as an exception to the laws restricting hearsay testimony. Such information should be carefully recorded. The use and documentation of the child's own words in quotes is important to include in such documentation. Salient areas of information to document in the child's record include:

- the person(s) (if known) who had abused him/her and the age(s) of the person(s);
- the areas of the child's body that were touched by the assailant;
- the extent of the abuse (forms of contact, types of abuse);
- the presence of a possible exchange of blood and secretions between the child and assailant;
- the time-frame of the abuse (e.g., when it first occurred, when it last occurred);
- possible exposure to pornography;
- if other children may have been abused or were at risk of having been abused.

During the history–taking portion of the medical evaluation, the clinician should consider the risk of physical injury, risk of infection transmission, risk of pregnancy, risk of psychological sequelae, and the risk to the safety of others.

It is not unusual after an initial disclosure for a child to recant his or her allegations (Sorenson, 1991). Recantation may occur for several reasons. The child may have been pressured to recant, may have become fearful of the possibility of being removed from home and family, or may be overwhelmed by the consequences of the disclosure (e.g., removal from the home, doubt and suspicion by others) (Sorenson & Snow, 1991). Nevertheless, the child's initial disclosure should not be discounted. When closing the interview, it is important to reassure the child that (s)he was brave to make an outcry. This reassurance and validation may be the most important message the patient will hear during the entire medical evaluation.

**Table 16.1 Types of Interview Questions.** A Continuum of Types of Questions used in Interviewing Children Alleged to have been Sexually Abused and Confidence in Responses -by Kathleen Coulborn Faller*

| | Question Type | Example | Child Response |
|---|---|---|---|
| Open-Ended | A. General | How are you? | Sad, *cause my dad poked me in the pee-pee. |
| | B. Focused | How do you get along with your dad? | OK, except when he pokes me in the pee-pee. |
| | | Did anything happen to your pee-pee? | My daddy poked me there. |
| | | What did he poke you with? | He poked me with his ding-dong. |
| | C. Multiple Choice | Did he poke you with his finger, his ding-dong, or something else? | He used his ding-dong. |
| | | Did this happen in the daytime or nighttime? | In the day night. |
| | D. Yes-No Questions | Did he tell you not to tell? | No, he didn't say anything like that. |
| | | Did you have your clothes off? | No, just my panties. |
| | E. Leading Questions | He took your clothes didn't he? | Yes. |
| Closed-Ended | | Didn't he make you suck his penis? | Yes. |

More Confidence → Less Confidence

*Source:* Faller (1990). Reprinted by permission of the American Professional Society on the Abuse of Children, 350 Poplar Avenue, Elmhurst, IL 60126. Email apsac@apsac.org; web www.apsac.org; phone 877-402-7722.

## TIMING OF PHYSICAL EXAMINATION

The time-frame of the last incident is important information that should be obtained on a child's initial presentation for alleged sexual abuse. The determination of where and when the child should be evaluated can be made by knowing the child's last possible sexual contact with the assailant.

If the incident occurred more than 72 hours prior to presentation, an appointment for an evaluation can be scheduled at a later time in a less stressful setting, such as an advocacy center or outpatient clinic familiar with these medical evaluations (in contrast to a busy emergency center). If an assault of a child has occurred less than 72 hours before the child's presentation, and/or the history reveals the likelihood of transfer of biological evidence from the perpetrator or likely resultant physical trauma, a timely examination and forensic evidence collection is indicated. In this instance, possible acute injuries and/or other physical findings should be appropriately documented, and biologic trace materials preserved.

Some jurisdictions may have extended time allowances for forensic evidence collection, such as within 96 or even 120 hours of the last sexual contact. It is important to know of such protocols in one's own community. However, studies on prepubertal children suggest that such guidelines do not suit this population, as no collected swabs were positive for sperm/semen more than 9 hours after an alleged assault (Christian et al., 2000). Most forensic evidence in these studies was found in either the children's clothing or in bed linens taken from the home by the police (Christian et al., 2000; Young, Jones, Worthington, Simpson, & Casey, 2006). More recent studies utilizing DNA amplification techniques in assessing such cases further demonstrate the very low rates of detection of biological transfer on the prepubertal body beyond 24 hours of suspected sexual assault (Girardet et al, 2011; Thackeray, Hornor, Benzinger, & Scribano, 2011). Collection of evidence in a timely manner in acute sexual assault cases is therefore recommended. Clinical judgment and state statutes should guide the physician's decisions regarding the collection of forensic evidence. The immediate assessment for potential life-threatening physical trauma, as well as the physical health and welfare of the child, take precedence over any forensic investigation. When the last alleged sexual contact/abuse has occurred less than 72 hours before presentation in a medical setting, protocols for child sexual assault victims should be followed to secure biological trace evidence such as epithelial cells, semen, saliva, and blood. Maintenance of the "chain of custody" is also paramount.

If there is physical evidence (e.g., clothing, bedding) that is not in police custody or present at the time of the child's medical evaluation, retrieval and submission of these items to authorities is important. It has been found that there is greatest likelihood of retrieving forensic evidence from such items (Christian et al., 2000). If the child's contaminated clothing/linens are at home, caretakers should be instructed to place these items in a paper bag, and the caretaker should be instructed to provide this bag and its contents to law enforcement authorities.

An evaluation should be performed immediately if: (1) the child complains of pain in the genital or anal area; or (2) there is evidence or complaint of anogenital bleeding or injury. Such injuries should be both treated and documented. Genital and anal injuries in children heal quickly, and may not be evident if an examination is delayed. If the alleged assault has occurred within the previous 72 hours, a medical assessment of the child must be performed immediately and the collection of possible biological transfer evidence from the child obtained for later forensic analysis. Emergent medical intervention is also recommended when the child is experiencing significant behavioral or emotional problems and needs evaluation for possible suicidal ideation/plan (Adams et al, 2007).

The person taking the report must determine whether the child is in immediate danger of further abuse or reprisal by the perpetrator. The child can be brought to the emergency department for safety until the authorities have been contacted.

## PREPARATION OF THE CHILD FOR EXAMINATION

The examiner should anticipate that the child and/or caretaker may have an inaccurate preconception of what the physical examination will entail. Such preconceptions can serve as barriers to conducting the examination comfortably, and should be anticipated and addressed before proceeding. Taking the time to explain the importance of the examination helps to earn the child's trust and sets the stage for the physical examination and the collection of laboratory specimens. The rapport developed with the child while taking the medical history will serve the examiner well as the examination proceeds. No coercion, deceit, or force should be used, either directly or indirectly, to convince a child to submit to an examination of his or her body. The child must be fully informed and cooperative. Physical restraint of an uncooperative child is not acceptable, as child victims may have previously experienced physical restraint and control by their perpetrator(s). Such experiences may serve to further traumatize the child. Therefore a child should not be subjected to such experiences during a medical examination. If an emergent evaluation is essential for the child's well-being and health determination and the child is unable to cooperate with the examination, use of anesthesia or conscious sedation may be warranted (Parker, Mahan, Giugliano, & Parker, 1997; Yaster & Maxwell, 1999).

Children who have been engaged in sexually inappropriate activities have had little or no control over what they have experienced. Once disclosure occurs, it is important for children to begin to feel as if they will now have some measure of control about what happens to their bodies. Allowing the child to have some choices, such as where to sit during the examination or what color gown to wear may provide the child with some sense of control over their environment, and demonstrates respect for his or her decisions. Such gestures are likely to enhance the physician–patient relationship, enhance the child-patient's degree of cooperation with medical evaluation procedures, and may have considerable therapeutic value. The examiner should answer any questions that the child or caretaker has as they arise during the evaluation.

## Relaxation and Distraction Techniques

Carefully preparing the child for physical and anogenital examinations may decrease the level of anxiety and stress the child experiences before the evaluation. Techniques to decrease the child's anxiety include establishing familiarity with the setting, and telling the child in a friendly way what he or she can expect during the evaluation. The Genital Examination Distress Scale (GEDS) may be used to assess the emotional distress of a child during the anogenital component of the sexual abuse evaluation (Fischer, 1999). The GEDS is used while the child undergoes the examination and may help compare different approaches to the examination. Generally, children respond well to the examination when someone talks with them about the purpose of the procedures and what to expect during the evaluation (Lawson, 1990). The examiner should anticipate age-appropriate anxieties associated with a visit to the doctor and address them with the child before the examination. Young children should have a parent or trusted guardian present throughout the physical examination. Adolescents should be given the choice of whether a guardian will be present in the examination. The equipment used during the anogenital examination (i.e., a colposcope) can appear intimidating to the family and child. A colposcope is a magnification and lighting tool often used to inspect, evaluate, and photodocument the anogenital region. Steward, Schmitz, Steward, Joye, & Reinhart (1995) found that children were not generally retraumatized by the colposcopic examination of the genital area, and the child's anxiety was lessened after completion of the examination. Few data support the examination as a form of revictimization to the child (Britton, 1998). The child will often be less fearful if (s)he has the opportunity to look through the colposcope and have the light shined on the skin of the hand to demonstrate that the procedure is not a painful one, or see an image in a book that is magnified when viewing a monitor. Children often respond best when they are informed about the examination and what they are to expect during and after the evaluation.

Distracting the child during the examination can also help to reduce anxiety and stress. Singing, counting, reciting nursery rhymes, identifying objects in a book or poster, or talking about pleasant experiences may help the child relax and cooperate during the examination.

## EXAMINATION

The medical examination of the child should proceed in a head-to-toe manner, beginning at the top of the body but completing the physical examination with the anogenital examination. Such a comprehensive physical exam promotes an environment of trust and safety, because it relays to the child that every part of his or her body is important, not just their genitalia. The assessment needs to be executed competently. The purpose of the physical examination is to identify signs of physical trauma—including ligature marks, defensive wounds, and contusions, as well as self-inflicted trauma such as cutting—or neglect, and to address previously unmet or undiagnosed healthcare needs (Girardet, Giacobbe, Bolton, Lahoti, & McNeese, 2006). Photodocumentation, measurements, and keen descriptions of signs and areas of trauma to the child's body are necessary for clear documentation of the child's injuries. It is recommended that discussion of the anogenital examination occurs before proceeding with this portion of the examination. The physician should be competent and comfortable in identifying anatomical structures and normal variations of these structures, as well as with identifying conditions that may mimic sexual abuse. It is prudent for the examiner to have a chaperone in the room during the examination. The child may be uncomfortable with, or embarrassed by, the anogenital examination. The connections and rapport developed during the initial components of the medical evaluations should help ease the transition to the anogenital examination.

The Tanner stages are a sexual maturity rating system that tracks the normal appearance and pattern of pubic hair in the male and female; breast development in the female; and testicle size, scrotum, and phallus development in the male. These physical characteristics noted on inspection of children of both genders have been shown to correlate with the hormonal changes occurring during adolescent development (Tanner, 1962). The Tanner stages are as follows.

Pubic hair:
- Stage 1: Preadolescent. No pubic hair. Fine vellus type hair similar to that over the abdomen.
- Stage 2: There is the appearance of sparse, long, and slightly pigmented hair. Straight or slightly curled hair develops at the base of the penis or along the labia.
- Stage 3: Hair darkens and becomes more coarse and curled. It increases in density.
- Stage 4: Hair is of adult type, but the area covered by it is considerably less than in the adult. No hair spread to the surfaces of the thighs.
- Stage 5: Adult hair characteristics in quantity and type. There is hair spread to the medial surface of the thighs.

Breast development:
- Stage 1: Preadolescent. Elevation of papilla.
- Stage 2: Breast bud stage. Elevation of breast bud and papilla only, due to recession of the areola to the general contour of the breast.
- Stage 3: The breast and areola continue to enlarge. There is no separation in the contour of the breast and areola. Continuous, rounded contour.
- Stage 4: The areola and nipple increase in size. They form a secondary mound of tissue projecting above the contour of the breast.
- Stage 5: The breast shows adult configuration with prominent nipple and a smooth, rounded contour.

Male genitalia:
- Stage 1: Preadolescent. Testes, scrotum, and penis are small. Size and proportion as that in early childhood.
- Stage 2: Enlargement of scrotum and testes. Skin of scrotum reddens and changes in texture. Little or no change in size of penis.
- Stage 3: Further growth of testes and scrotum, with lengthening of penis.

- Stage 4: Growth in breadth and development of the glans, with increased size of the penis.
- Stage 5: Adult size and shape of penis.

Puberty begins when the brain disperses hormonal signals that trigger a series of changes in the child's body. In the United States, girls enter puberty between 10 and 11 years of age, on average, and boys begin to develop between 11 and 13 years of age, on average. The National Health and Nutrition Examination Survey III (NHANES, 1988–1994) provides data on the sexual maturation of American boys and girls of different ethnic groups. Many factors can affect the timing of the onset and duration of puberty, including: genetic variables; nutrition; geographic conditions; and excessive exercise (Wu, Medola, & Buck, 2002).

When examining the anogenital area, an examination position may be selected that is comfortable for both child and examiner. The examination position should also allow for the best visualization of the anatomical structures with the least discomfort to the patient. The examination position should take the child's modesty into account. Young female children are examined in the frog-leg position on the examination table. This position has the child lying supine (face up) on the examination table with the legs of the child bent and allowed to fall to either side of the body. This position can be described to the child and caretaker also as a "butterfly" position. Young children, to further allow for comfort and ease of examination, may also be examined in this position while lying or sitting in a caretaker's lap while the adult sits or lies on the examination table. Adolescent females may be examined in the lithotomy position, or in "stirrups." When examining the female genitalia with the child in the frog-leg position, two techniques assist in observing the internal aspects of the genitalia. (1) Labial separation is accomplished by gently placing the examiner's thumb and index finger at the 10 and 2 o'clock positions on the labia majora. With gentle splaying of the thumb and finger laterally, the labia major will separate to enhance visualization of the labia minora and the superior portions of the vestibule. When using (2) labial traction, the examiner gently grasps the left and right labia with the thumb and index finger of each hand and applies downward and lateral traction on the labia majora. Traction will open the vestibule for visual inspection of its integral parts. When the child is in the prone knee-chest position, upward and lateral pressure applied with the thumbs at the 3 and 9 o'clock positions will accomplish the same goal.

The confirmation of injuries secondary to trauma include: (1) examining the patient in a second position (e.g., prone knee-chest); or (2) the use of swabs or foley catheter to indicate interruption of the hymenal tissue. These techniques provide additional assistance in allowing direct manipulation of the hymenal tissue (by swab and/or foley catheter) or by indirect manipulation (such as the use of gravity or the child's production of internal pressure (as in producing a cough) that allows for full visualization of the tissues. When using the foley catheter (which is more often used for the extraction of urine when placed in the urethra for medical purposes) in the sexual abuse evaluation, the deflated foley is inserted into the vaginal opening beyond the hymenal ring. The foley's tip is then inflated with either water or air, and the small balloon tip is then slowly extracted and gently pulled out of the orifice, thereby stretching the hymenal ring. Interruptions of the ring may then be more accurately seen. Signs of trauma should be carefully documented by detailed diagrams illustrating the findings or by photodocumentation. It is essential to have an adequate strong light source and magnification tool for a proper examination. A colposcope is ideal, but not necessary, for assessing and photodocumenting the anogenital area. Colposcopy does not significantly increase the recognition of physical findings that are diagnostic of sexual abuse; however, it is an excellent tool for magnification of the anatomy, and may provide excellent photodocumention of the examination (Adams, Girardin, & Faugno, 2001). Additionally, photodocumentation of the anogenital examination allows for peer review of concerning or questionable examinations without having the child return for repeat examinations. In addition to allowing images of forensically abnormal examinations to be captured, photodocumentation of subsequent examinations may aid in the chronicling of healing injuries. A speculum examination is not recommended for prepubertal children unless there is severe bleeding and intravaginal lacerations are of concern. For cases in which one suspects severe vaginal lacerations, surgery or gynecology consultations should be sought, and the child should be examined under sedation. When the child is unable to cooperate and the examination must be performed because of the likelihood of trauma, infection, and/or the need to collect forensic samples, the use of sedation must be considered. When examining boys for possible sexual abuse, the penis should be carefully inspected for inflammation, bleeding, or discharge. The male genitalia may be examined with the patient lying supine or standing. To examine the anus, the child may be placed in the lateral decubitus (lying on the side) position or the supine, knee-chest position (face up with the patient's knees drawn to the abdomen).

Findings that are diagnostic of trauma and/or sexual contact include the following: lacerations, abrasions, or scars of the anogenital area; bleeding; discharge; or the presence of semen. An acutely assaulted child or adolescent may have fresh lacerations, bruising, hymenal tears with or without bleeding, and discharge. Physical signs of chronic abuse may include missing or interrupted hymenal tissue, scarring, and discharge. The size of the hymenal opening is of negligible forensic value (McCann, 1990). The hymen varies with age, the extent of relaxation of the child, the amount of labial traction applied, and the shape of the hymen itself. Pregnancy and the identification of sperm found in specimens taken directly from the child's body are diagnostic of sexual contact. Most often the physical examination will be normal, even with a clear history of sexual abuse given by the child (Adams, Harper, Knudson, & Revilla, 1994; Heger, Ticson, Velasquez, & Bernier, 2002). A normal physical examination should not discount a clear disclosure of sexual abuse. Alternatively, a child may present with clear evidence of anogenital trauma without providing an adequate history of abuse. It is important to note that an abused child may initially deny having experienced abuse. A report to child protective services is necessary in such situations, given the strong indications.

The evaluation and exploration of the presence and/or treatment of sexually transmitted infection (STI) of child victims of sexual abuse is assessed by the elements of the history and physical examination. These elements include the following: reported events of the assault; the child's age; the signs and symptoms reported; the prevalence of an STI in the community; and the available information of the risk status of the perpetrator. There are exceptions to the general rule that STIs beyond the neonatal period are evidence of sexual abuse. Chlamydial infections in young children might be the result of perinatally acquired infection, which has, in some cases, persisted for as long as two to three years (Bell, Stamm, & Wang, 1992). Genital warts have been diagnosed in children who have been sexually abused, but also in children who have no other evidence of sexual abuse. All sexually transmitted organisms can be transmitted via direct sexual contact. A few, such as human papillomavirus (HPV) and herpes simplex virus (HSV), can be transmitted by nonsexual means or by autoinoculation—transmission of the virus from one part of the body to another by the patient alone (such as finger to the mouth).

Laboratory techniques that best identify specific STIs have medicolegal implications. The techniques should have the highest positive predictive value, as well as optimal specificity. It is important to minimize false-positive results. Studies have highlighted the potential utilization of nucleic acid amplification tests (NAATs) for the diagnosis of certain sexually transmitted pathogens. Such methods include polymerase chain reaction (PCR) and transcription-mediated amplification (TMA). These tests are considered to require less intrusive sampling methods. Given the low prevalence rates of infection in the child population, continued study into the diagnosis and management of such infections are ongoing (Hammerschlag, 1998; Kellogg, Baillargeon, Lukefahr, Lawless, & Menard, 2004; Palmer, Mallinson, Wood, & Herring, 2003; Black et al., 2009).

## DOCUMENTATION

All healthcare professionals who evaluate children alleged to have been sexually abused must maintain written and visual documentation of their medical evaluations consistent with acceptable medical records standards. The patient's record must accurately reflect the history and physical examination obtained in the course of the medical evaluation. Diagrams and photographs are essential tools for documenting physical findings of trauma. The preservation of such documentation is essential for legal proceedings.

### Interpretation of Medical Findings

The clinician should be familiar with the body of research on abused and nonabused children when interpreting the physical and laboratory findings suspected to have been sexually abused. Criteria that have been subjected to peer review delineate appropriate approaches to interpreting findings (Adams et al., 2007). Adams' approach to interpreting medical findings in suspected child sexual abuse cases has gained wide acceptance and categorizes findings on physical examinations in sexual abuse evaluations as being normal variants, indeterminate, or diagnostic of trauma that may be related to sexual contact (Adams, 2010).

### Documentation of the Medical Assessment

It is important to maintain a meticulous medical record to preserve evidence and factual information in sexual abuse cases. Description on the child's affect, language skills, and reaction to the examination is essential. When a case is heard in court months or years after the child was first seen, a detailed medical chart can help the physician be an effective witness.

Examples of documentation (impressions of the medical evaluation) are the following.
- A 6-year-old boy gives a clear, consistent disclosure of fondling (e.g., "he touched my cookie and it hurt") of genitals. (2) Normal physical and anogenital examination. A normal examination neither rules out nor confirms sexual abuse.
- A 9-month-old boy presents with perianal warts. (2) Mother reports no concerns of sexual abuse. Mother with known history of genital warts. (3) Physical and anogenital examination reveal perianal warts. No other physical injuries or concerns noted. (4) Such lesions may be considered to be of indeterminate specificity for sexual transmission, and may have been transmitted vertically in this patient given the maternal history.
- A 16-year-old girl discloses acute sexual assault. Patient reports genital-genital penetration at knifepoint by unknown assailant. (2) Physical examination reveals bruises to right cheek, and bite mark to left breast. Anogenital examination reveals localized bruising from 3–5 o'clock of the hymenal ring, transaction down to the vaginal wall at 7 o'clock with scant bleeding, and surrounding redness and tenderness to palpation. (3) These physical findings are evidence of blunt force penetrating trauma, and are consistent with the adolescent's report of acute sexual assault. (4) Sexual assault examination and forensic evidence collection completed. (5) STI prophylaxis provided. (6) Urine pregnancy test is negative. (7) Pregnancy prophylaxis offered. Patient accepted. (8) HIV Post-Exposure Prophylaxis (HIV PEP) offered, and family and patient counseled. Patient and family accepted HIV PEP.

## MULTIDISCIPLINARY TEAMS

It is essential to understand that the medical perspective is a relatively small yet significant portion of investigations into child sexual abuse cases. The physician's role is to safeguard the health and welfare of the child, but added responsibilities lie in the education and communication of sexual abuse-related information to other agencies. In many situations, law enforcement officers may be unfamiliar or unaware of the assortment of factors involved in assessing the mental and medical health of victims of child sexual abuse (Scribano & Giardino, 2009). Children sometimes minimize their experiences or are embarrassed to disclose penetrating injury. Therefore, first responders may forego or delay a child's medical examination because it may be seen as unnecessary.

Of note, studies in recent decades have shown that most forensic medical examinations do not yield abnormal findings. For example, a study of 2,384 children seen at a tertiary referral center for alleged sexual assault found that less than 4% yielded forensic evidence and only 0.6% had a sexually transmissible disease, even though approximately two-thirds of the sample reported penetration of the vagina or anus (Heger et al., 2002). In a study of 36 pregnant adolescents seen for sexual abuse evaluations, only two (6%) had definitive findings of penetration. Four girls (8%) had findings suggestive of penetration (Kellogg, Menard, & Santos, 2004). Berenson et al. (2000) compared 192 prepubertal girls with a history of sexual abuse to 200 girls with no known history of sexual abuse. The study revealed that examination results of abuse victims rarely differed from those of nonabused children.

The foregoing information reveals that the physical examination itself is rarely diagnostic of abuse. A medical history and medical interview of the child is necessary for the purpose of diagnosis. It is important to determine the type of contact the child has described, and how recently this may have occurred.

Although the physical examination maintains an important place in the evaluation, it cannot stand alone. Persons who investigate child sexual abuse cases or work with children who may be victims should understand the process by which children disclose (Sorenson & Snow, 1991). Some children may disclose all events at once, while others may reveal the extent of the abuse in segments.

In the spirit of the multidisciplinary team model, physicians, law enforcement officers, prosecutors, and social service workers should work to coordinate services in each community, to minimize trauma to the child, while working to benefit children's health and safety. Enhanced communication and coordination with the other multidisciplinary team members can further assist in the protection of the child and the formulation of the case.

## REFERENCES

Adams, J. A. (2010). Medical evaluation of suspected child sexual abuse: 2009 update. *APSAC Advisor*, 3–4, Winter.

Adams, J. A., Girardin, B., & Faugno, D. (2001). Adolescent sexual assault: Documentation of acute injuries using photocolposcopy. *Journal of Pediatric and Adolescent Gynecology, 14*, 175–180. doi:10.1016/S1083-3188(01)00126-7.

Adams, J. A., Harper, K., Knudson, S., & Revilla, J. (1994). Examination findings in legally confirmed child sexual abuse: It's normal to be normal. *Pediatrics, 94*, 310–317. Retrieved from <http://pediatrics.aappublications.org.ezproxyhost.library.tmc.edu/content/94/3/310.full.pdf+html>.

Adams, J. A., Kaplan, R. A., Starling, S. P., Mehta, N. H., Finkel, M. A., Botash, A. S., et al. (2007). Guidelines for medical care of children who may have been sexually abused. *Journal of Pediatric and Adolescent Gynecology, 20,* 163–172. doi:10.1016/j.jpag.2006.10.001.

American Academy of Pediatrics Committee on Child Abuse and Neglect. (1999). Guidelines for the evaluation of sexual abuse of children: Subject review. *Pediatrics, 103,* 186.

Bell, T. A., Stamm, W. E., & Wang, S. P. (1992). Chronic *chlamydia trachomatis* infection in infants. *The Journal of the American Medical Association, 267*(16), 2188. doi:10.1001/jama.1992.03480030078041.

Berenson, A. B., Chacko, M. R., Wienmann, C. M., Mitshaw, C. O., Friedrich, W. N., & Grady, J. J. (2000). A case-control study of anatomic changes resulting from sexual abuse. *American Journal of Obstetrics and Gynecology, 184*(5), 830–831. doi:10.1016/S0002-9378(00)70331-0. Apr.

Black, C. M., Driebe, E. M., Howard, L. A., Fajman, N. N., Sawyer, M. K., Girardet, R. G., et al. (2009). Multicenter study of nucleic acid amplification tests for detection of *chlamydia trachomatis* and *Neisseria gonorrhoeae* in children being evaluated for sexual abuse. *Pediatric Infectious Disease Journal, 28*(7), 608–613. doi:10.1097/INF.0b013e31819b592e.

Britton, H. (1998). Emotional impact of the medical examination for child sexual abuse. *Child Abuse and Neglect, 22,* 573–579. doi:10.1016/S0145-2134(98)00029-5.

Christian, C. W., Lavelle, J. M., De John, A. R., Loiselle, J., Brenner, L., & Joffe, M. (2000). Forensic evidence findings in prepubertal victims of sexual assault. *Pediatrics, 106*(1), 100–104. doi:10.1542/peds.106.1.100.

Faller, K. C. (1990). Types of questions for children alleged to have been sexually abused. *The APSAC Advisor, 3*(2), 3–5.

Finkel, M. S. (2008). "I can tell you because you're a doctor." *Pediatrics, 122*(2), 442. doi:10.1542/peds.2008-1416.

Finkelhor, D. (1993). Epidemiological factors in the clinical identification of child sexual abuse. *Child Abuse and Neglect, 17,* 67–70.

Fischer, H. (1999). The Genital Examination Distress Scale (GEDS). *Child Abuse and Neglect, 23*(12), 1205.

Friedrich, W. N., Dittner, C. A., Action, R., et al. (2001). Child sexual behavior inventory: Normative, psychiatric and sexual abuse comparisons. *Child Maltreatment, 6,* 37–49. doi:10.1177/1077559501006001004.

Girardet, R., Bolton, K., Lahoti, S., Mobray, H., Giardino, A. P., Isaac, R., et al. (2011). Collection of forensic evidence from pediatric victims of sexual assault. *Pediatrics, 128*(2), 233–238. doi:10.1542/peds.2010-3037.

Girardet, R. G., Giacobbe, L., Bolton, K., Lahoti, S., & McNeese, M. C. (2006). Unmet health care needs among children evaluated for sexual assault. *Archives of Pediatric Adolescent Medicine, 160,* 70–73. doi:10.1001/archpedi.160.1.70.

Hammerschlag, M. R. (1998). Sexually transmitted diseases in sexually abused children: Medical and legal implications. *Sexually Transmitted Infections, 74,* 167–174. doi:10.1136/sti.74.3.167.

Heger, A., Ticson, L., Velasquez, O., & Bernier, R. (2002). Children referred for possible sexual abuse: Medical findings in 2384 children. *Child Abuse & Neglect, 26,* 645–659. doi:10.1016/S0145-2134(02)00339-3.

Hunter, R. S., Kilstrom, N., & Loda, F. (1985). Sexually abused children identifying masked presentations in a medical setting. *Child Abuse and Neglect, 9,* 17–25. doi:10.1016/0145-2134(85)90087-0.

Kellogg, N. D., Baillargeon, J., Lukefahr, J. L., Lawless, K., & Menard, S. W. (2004). Comparison of nucleic acid amplification tests and culture techniques in the detection of *neisseria gonorrhoeae* and *chlamydia trachomatis* in victims of suspected child sexual abuse. *Journal of Pediatric and Adolescent Gynecology, 17*(5), 331–339. doi:10.1016/j.jpag.2004.07.006.

Kellogg, N. D., Menard, S. W., & Santos, A. (2004). Genital anatomy in pregnant adolescents: "Normal does not mean 'nothing happened'." *Pediatrics, 113*, e67–e69. Retrieved from <http://pediatrics.aappublications.org/content/113/1/e67.long>.

Kempe, C. H. (1978). Sexual abuse, another hidden pediatric problem: The 1977 C. Anderson Aldrich Lecture. *Pediatrics, 62*(3), 382–389.

Krugman, R. D. (1986). Recognition of sexual abuse in children. *Pediatric Review, 8*, 25–30. doi:10.1542/pir.8-1-25.

Lawson, L. (1990). Preparing sexually abused girls for genital evaluation. *Issues in Comprehensive Pediatric Nursing, 13*, 155–164. doi:10.3109/01460869009009033.

McCann, J., Wells, R., Simon, M., et al. (1990). Genital findings in prepubertal girls selected for nonabuse: A descriptive study. *Pediatrics, 86*, 428–439.

NHANES, III. (1997). *Analytic and reporting guidelines: The Third National Health and Nutrition Examination Survey (1988-94)*. Hyatsville, MD: National Center for Health Statistics, Center for Disease Control and Prevention. Retrieved from <http://www.cdc.gov/nchs/nhanes/nh3data.htm>.

Palmer, H. M., Mallinson, H., Wood, R. L., & Herring, A. J. (2003). Evaluation of the specificities of five DNA amplification methods for the detection of *Neisseria gonorrhoeae*. *Journal of Clinical Microbiology, 41*, 835. doi:10.1128/JCM.41.2.835-837.2003.

Parker, R. I., Mahan, R. A., Giugliano, D., & Parker, M. M. (1997). Efficacy and safety of intravenous midazolam and ketamine as sedation for therapeutic and diagnostic procedures in children. *Pediatrics, 99*, 427–431. doi:10.1542/peds.99.3.427.

Scribano, P. V., & Giardino, A. P. (2009). Interdisciplinary approaches to child maltreatment: Assessing community resources. In M. Finkel, & A. P. Giardino (Eds.), *Medical evaluation of child sexual abuse: A practical guide, 3ed* (pp. 289–311). Elk Grove, IL: American Academy of Pediatrics.

Sorenson, T., & Snow, B. (1991). How children tell: The process of disclosure in child sexual abuse. *Child Welfare, 70*, 3–15.

Steward, M., Schmitz, M., Steward, D., Joye, N., & Reinhart., M. (1995). Children's anticipation of and response to colposcopic examination. *Child Abuse and Neglect, 19*, 997–1005. doi:10.1016/0145-2134(95)00061-C.

Tanner, J. (1962). *Growth at Adolescence (2nd ed)*. Oxford, UK: Blackwell Scientific Publications.

Thackeray, J. C., Hornor, G., Benzinger, E. A., & Scribano, P. V. (2011). Forensic evidence collection and DNA identification in acute child sexual assault. *Pediatrics, 128*(2), 227–232. doi:10.1542/peds.2010-3498.

Yaster, M., & Maxwell, L. (1999). The pediatric sedation unit: A mechanism for safe pediatric sedation. *Pediatrics, 103*, 198–201.

Young, K. L., Jones, J. G., Worthington, T., Simpson, P., & Casey, P. H. (2006). Forensic laboratory evidence in sexually abused children and adolescents. *Archives of Pediatric Adolescent Medicine, 160*, 585–588. doi:10.1001/archpedi.160.6.585.

Wu, T., Medola, P., & Buck, G. M. (2002). Ethnic differences in the presence of secondary sex characteristics and menarche among U.S. girls: The third national health and nutrition examination survey, 1988-1994. *Pediatrics, 110*, 752–757. doi:10.1542/peds.110.4.752.

# CHAPTER 17

# Teaching Sexual Abuse Prevention Skills to Children

**Raymond G. Miltenberger and Laura Hanratty**
University of South Florida, Tampa, Florida[1]

Children are exposed to a number of threats to their personal safety as they grow up. These safety threats may come from their interaction with others (e.g., sexual abuse, abduction, violence), or from their interaction with the physical environment (accidents, poisoning, drowning, self-inflicted firearm injuries). Safety threats may be low incidence, but highly dangerous events that a child might never experience, such as an abduction lure or sexual abuse lure, or safety threats may come from events that occur with regularity such as riding a bike, crossing a street, or living in a home with a swimming pool (e.g., Miltenberger & Gross, 2011). Reoccurring safety threats often are predictable, afford the child frequent opportunities to practice safety skills, and provide parents opportunities to prompt and reinforce skills. For example, wearing a bike helmet each time the child rides a bike, using a safety belt each time a child rides in a vehicle, or waiting for the signal and looking both ways each time a child crosses a street. With repeated opportunities for practice and reinforcement from parents, these safety skills often are well learned and consistently executed.

On the other hand, low incidence or low probability safety threats are not predictable, and the child does not have a chance to practice safety skills on a regular basis. In fact, because of their low probability of occurrence, the child may never have the opportunity to practice the skills unless he or she participates in a safety skills training program. Furthermore, this class of safety threats typically occurs when an adult is not present, so an adult cannot prompt the use of safety skills or exert stimulus control over the emission of the safety skills. Thus, low incidence safety threats pose the greatest challenge for children to learn and execute the safety skills when the threat arises.

[1] Correspondence to: Raymond G. Miltenberger, University of South Florida, Department of Child and Family Studies, MHC2113A, Tampa, FL 33612. Phone 813-974-5079; fax 813-974-6115; email miltenbe@usf.edu

Handbook of Child and Adolescent Sexuality
DOI: http://dx.doi.org/10.1016/B978-0-12-387759-8.00017-9

Child sexual abuse is one of the dangerous, but low incidence, safety threats that a child might face at some point before adulthood. Child sexual abuse can consist of sexual contact from an adult or adolescent perpetrator (e.g., fondling, oral sex, or intercourse), or it can consist of exploitation by a perpetrator where there is no physical contact (e.g., a child being subjected to pornography or being observed, photographed, or video recorded while undressed or in sexual poses) (e.g., Finkelhor, Hotaling, Lewis, & Smith, 1990). Sexual abuse is a serious problem, because it places children who experience it at increased risk for precocious sexual behavior, academic problems, maladaptive behavior, sexually transmitted diseases, eating disorders, sexual revictimization, and psychological problems such as depression and anxiety as they progress through childhood into adolescence and adulthood (e.g., Arias, 2004; Browne & Finkelhor, 1986; Chen et al., 2010; Kilpatrick et al., 2003; Tyler, 2002; Wonderlich, Brewerton, Jocic, Dansky, & Abbott, 1997). It is estimated that 25% of girls and 17% of boys experience sexual abuse (e.g., Dube et al., 2005). Although sexual abuse is much too prevalent in society, it is still a low-incidence safety threat that most children will not experience. Thus, the absence of repeated practice with reinforcement over time decreases the probability that the child will execute the skills should a sexual abuse situation arise. Yet, for those children who are exposed to a sexual abuse situation, the safety threat is serious and execution of the appropriate prevention skills is critical. Therefore, all children should participate in sexual abuse prevention skills training to increase the likelihood that they will use the skills if they ever experience a sexual abuse lure.

Child sexual abuse typically is perpetrated by a known adult, most often through a process of positive inducement where the child is "groomed" by the perpetrator, and the nature of the physical contact evolves from innocuous to sexual over time (e.g., Budin & Johnson, 1989; Conte, Wolf, & Smith, 1989; Dube & Herbert, 1988; Elliott, Browne, & Kilcoyne, 1995). Contrary to popular belief, sexual abuse typically is not perpetrated by a stranger (as is often the case with abduction; Poche, Brouwer, & Swearingen, 1981), but by an individual, typically a male, who has a relationship with the child or the child's parents, and thus has established some trust with the child (e.g., Conte et al., 1989; Finkelhor et al., 1990; Saunders, Kilpatrick, Hanson, Resnick, & Walker, 1999). Because children are taught to be compliant with requests from adults in positions of authority (parents, teachers, babysitters, coaches, etc.), children also are likely to comply with the seemingly innocuous requests from a perpetrator. Once the perpetrator has developed a history of compliance with a child victim, the requests become more sexual in nature, until the child is engaging in (or acquiescing to) sexual activity. Over time the child may come to recognize the inappropriateness of the interaction with the perpetrator, but may be persuaded, bribed, or threatened to continue interacting with the perpetrator and keep the sexual activity with the perpetrator a secret (e.g., Budin & Johnson, 1989; Conte et al., 1989). For children to be safe from sexual abuse, they need to be able to discriminate the occurrence of an inappropriate interaction or request (i.e., a sexual abuse lure) and respond with the appropriate safety skills.

## SEXUAL ABUSE PREVENTION SKILLS

The sexual abuse prevention skills a child must exhibit to stay safe consist of: (1) saying "no" in response to a sexual abuse lure; (2) getting away from the perpetrator; and (3) telling a trusted adult about the incident. These skills are targeted in sexual abuse prevention skills training programs (Wurtele, 2008, 2009). Saying "no" is important, because it allows the child to avoid inappropriate contact with the perpetrator by assertively refusing to engage in the requested behavior. Getting away is important because it removes the child from the perpetrator and makes it less likely that the perpetrator can use force or other coercive actions (e.g., verbal persuasion, bribes, or threats) to get the child to comply. Informing a trusted adult about the incident is important so the adult can take action to make sure the perpetrator is never again in a position to lure the child or engage in abusive actions.

In order to execute these safety skills in the presence of the safety threat (the sexual abuse lure from the adult), the child must be able to discriminate circumstances under which an adult's behavior constitutes a safety threat (e.g., Boyle & Lutzker, 2005; Kenny & Wurtele, 2010; Miltenberger & Thiesse-Duffy, 1988; Wurtele, 1993). That is to say, the child must recognize that the sexual abuse lure is an inappropriate request from an adult; the sexual abuse lure must function as a discriminative stimulus ($S^D$) for engaging in the safety skills (an $S^D$ is a stimulus or event that evokes a behavior because the behavior has been reinforced consistently in its presence). Therefore, the goal of sexual abuse prevention skills training is to teach the child to discriminate the safety threat and immediately execute the safety skills (e.g., Miltenberger & Thiesse-Duffy, 1988; Miltenberger, Thiesse-Duffy, Suda, Kozak, & Bruellman, 1990). To discriminate the safety threat and execute the safety skills, the behavior must be in the child's repertoire, and the sexual abuse lure must function as an $S^D$ and have stimulus control over the behavior. For the lure to function as an $S^D$ and have stimulus control over the safety skills, the child has to have a history of practicing the safety skills with reinforcement in the presence of simulated sexual abuse lures during training sessions.

These safety skills (say "no," get away, and tell) share common features with the safety skills children learn to use in response to other safety threats, such as an abduction lure from a stranger (e.g. Johnson et al., 2005; Johnson et al., 2006), an unsecured container of poison in the home (Dancho, Thompson, & Rhoades, 2008), or an accessible firearm found in the home (Himle, Miltenberger, Flessner, & Gatheridge, 2004; Miltenberger et al., 2004; Miltenberger et al., 2005). The essential features of safety skills across safety threats are to: (1) recognize or discriminate the presence of the safety threat and take action to avoid contact with the safety threat; (2) escape from the safety threat; and (3) tell a trusted adult immediately about the safety threat (recognize, avoid, escape, and report). Wurtele (2008) similarly categorized the safety skills into three essential steps: recognize, resist, and report. In the case of abduction, a child learns to engage in the same skills in response to an abduction lure as a child would use in response to a sexual abuse lure: say "no;" get away; and tell an adult (e.g., Carroll-Rowan & Miltenberger, 1994; Johnson et al., 2005, 2006; Olsen-Woods, Miltenberger, & Foreman, 1998). In response to finding a firearm or poison, the child is taught to refrain from touching it, leave the room or area where the safety threat is located, and tell an adult (e.g., Dancho, Thompson, & Rhoades, 2008; Himle, Miltenberger, Flessner, & Gatheridge 2004; Himle, Miltenberger, Gatheridge, & Flessner, 2004). Although the $S^D$s to which the child must safely respond are different, the safety skills are virtually the same across safety threats, except for the behavior involved in avoiding the safety threat. With sexual abuse prevention skills or abduction prevention skills, the behavior involved in avoiding the threat is to say "no," because the safety threat is a lure (a request to engage in unsafe behavior) that comes from an older person. With poisons or found firearms (or other dangers in the physical environment such as matches, lighters, open gate to a swimming pool, or unexploded ordinance in a war zone), the behavior involved in avoiding the threat is to refrain from touching it. In both cases, after the child recognizes and avoids the safety threat, the child must immediately execute the remaining two skills (get away and tell) in order to escape from the presence of the threat so it cannot harm him or her in the moment, and to get an adult to eliminate the safety threat so it cannot harm him or her in the future.

## ASSESSMENT OF SAFETY SKILLS

Three types of assessment have been used in the research on safety skills training: verbal or self-report assessment (e.g., Wurtele, 1990; Wurtele, Currier, Gillispie, & Franklin, 1991; Wurtele, Marrs, & Miller-Perrin, 1987); role-play or skills assessment; and naturalistic or in situ assessment (Gatheridge et al., 2004; Himle, Miltenberger, Gatheridge, & Flessner 2004; Kelso, Miltenberger, Waters, Egemo-Helm, & Bagne, 2007: Lumley, Miltenberger, Long, Rapp, & Roberts, 1998; Miltenberger et al., 1999). These assessment procedures are discussed next.

### Verbal Report Assessment

In a verbal report assessment a researcher describes a safety threat situation and asks the child to report what he or she would do in the situation. Gatheridge et al. (2004) and Himle, Miltenberger, Gatheridge, & Flessner (2004) utilized self-report assessment as one measure of firearm injury prevention skills. The researchers described a situation in which a child finds a handgun in a room in the home, and asked the child what he or she would do in that situation. The child's response was rated on a 4 point scale (0 = child said she would touch the gun, 1 = child said she would not touch the gun, 2 = child said she would not touch the gun and would get away from the gun, 3 = child said she would not touch the gun, would get away from the gun, and would tell an adult about finding the gun). Similar verbal report assessments have been used in research on abduction prevention skills training (Carroll-Rowan & Miltenberger, 1994; Olsen-Woods et al., 1998) and sexual abuse prevention skills training (Lumley et al., 1998; Miltenberger et al., 1999). In research on sexual abuse prevention skills training with women with intellectual disabilities, Lumley et al. (1998) described a scenario in which a staff member presented a sexual abuse lure and asked the participant what she would do in the situation. Lumley et al. rated the woman's response on a 5 point scale (0 = said she would agree to the requested behavior, 1 = said she would do nothing, 2 = said she would say "no," 3 = said she would say "no" and leave the room, and 4 = said she would say "no," leave the room, and tell another staff member about the incident).

Verbal report is the form of assessment primarily utilized in child sexual abuse prevention skills training research (e.g., Harvey, Forehand, Brown, & Holmes, 1988; Saslawsky & Wurtele, 1986; Wurtele, 1990, 1993; Wurtele, Gillispie, Currier, & Franklin, 1992; Wurtele, Kast, Miller-Perrin,

& Kondrick, 1989). Sexual abuse prevention researchers have developed a number of self-report instruments for assessing sexual abuse prevention knowledge (the term knowledge is used instead of skills, because these verbal report assessments measure the child's description of sexual abuse prevention skills rather than the execution of the skills). For example, Tutty (1995) developed the "Children's Knowledge of Abuse Questionnaire-Revised," Hazzard, Webb, Kleemeier, Angert, & Pohl (1991) developed the "What I Know About Touching Scale," and Saslawsky and Wurtele (1986) developed the "Personal Safety Questionnaire" and the "What If Situations Test" (WIST), and used these instruments to evaluate sexual abuse prevention programs.

The WIST presents six scenarios involving appropriate and inappropriate touch, and measures the child's verbal responses to questions asked about the scenarios. These scenarios include three appropriate requests and three inappropriate requests (sexual abuse lures). The appropriate requests include a parent or doctor touching the child's private parts when the private parts are injured on a tricycle, and a request from a nurse to put medicine on a child's private parts in the presence of a parent. The three inappropriate requests include a request by a neighbor for the child to undress and submit to being photographed, a request by a babysitter for the child to touch the babysitter's private parts, and a request by a man at a park for the child to undress so the man can touch the child's private parts. The WIST provides an appropriate request recognition score and an inappropriate request recognition score, based on whether the child can discriminate between the innocuous scenarios and the sexual abuse scenarios. The WIST also provides a Total Skill Score based on the child's responses to the questions about the three sexual abuse items. Responses earn points if they indicate the child would: (1) refuse to go along with the request; (2) immediately leave the situation; (3) report the incident to one or more adults; and (4) describe the person and situation involved in the sexual abuse lure when reporting the incident. Higher scores on the WIST (up to 8 points for responses to each of three sexual abuse scenarios for a Total Skill Score of 24 points) are taken as a measure of the child's ability to recognize a sexual abuse lure and engage in the safety skills.

The WIST has good test-retest reliability for the appropriate and inappropriate request recognition scores and for the Total Skill Score (Wurtele, 1993), so it is a psychometrically sound instrument. The WIST has been used to assess sexual abuse prevention knowledge in a number of studies (e.g., Wurtele et al., 1987, 1989, 1991, 1992). However, even though the

WIST is psychometrically sound and widely used, it and other self-report measures used in sexual abuse prevention skills training research are limited by the fact that they only measure a child's verbal responses. These verbal report assessments measure a child's knowledge about sexual abuse situations and sexual abuse prevention skills. However, the child's verbal statements discriminating sexual abuse lures in scenarios and identifying the appropriate safety skills provide no evidence that the skills are in the child's repertoire, or that the child would execute the skills in a real sexual abuse situation. Therefore, verbal report assessments have limited utility for measuring the behavioral outcomes of child sexual abuse prevention programs (e.g., Carroll, Miltenberger, & O'Neill, 1992; Roberts & Miltenberger 1999).

## Role-Play Assessment

In a role-play assessment, the researcher creates a scenario in which a safety threat is present and asks the child to "show me what you would do" in the situation. For example, in research on firearm injury prevention, the researchers put a handgun (a real but disabled firearm) on a table and told the child to pretend the gun was on a table in a room in the child's house (e.g., on the night stand next to the parents' bed). The researcher then asked the child to do what he would do if he saw the gun there (Gatheridge et al., 2004; Himle, Miltenberger, Gatheridge, & Flessner, 2004). In the assessment, another researcher in an adjoining room was identified as playing the role of the child's parent so the researchers could determine if the child would execute all three safety skills (refrain from touching the gun, leave the room, and tell the parent). The child's performance in the role-play was rated on the same 0–3 point scale as used in the verbal report assessment. Role-play assessments also have been used in two studies evaluating sexual abuse prevention skills training for women with intellectual disabilities (Lumley et al., 1998; Miltenberger et al., 1999), scored with the same 0–4 point scale.

Unlike a verbal report assessment, the role-play assessment requires the child to *demonstrate* the safety skills, not simply *describe* the safety skills. The results of a role-play assessment indicate whether the safety skills are in the child's repertoire. Whereas the verbal report assessment demonstrates knowledge acquisition, the role-play assessment demonstrates skill acquisition. Unfortunately, research on firearm injury prevention skills training with children and sexual abuse prevention skills training with women with intellectual disabilities has shown that the results of verbal report assessments and role-play assessments do not correspond (Gatheridge et al., 2004; Himle, Miltenberger, Gatheridge, & Flessner, 2004; Lumley et al., 1998; Miltenberger et al., 1999). For example, Himle, Miltenberger, Gatheridge, & Flessner (2004) showed that following training with the Eddie Eagle GunSafe Program, 4- and 5-year-old children could describe the prevention skills during a verbal report assessment, but could not demonstrate those same skills in a role-play assessment. Gatheridge et al. (2004) found a similar lack of correspondence between verbal report and role-play assessments with 6- and 7-year-olds. The lack of correspondence between the results of the verbal report assessment and the role-play assessment of the child's skills calls into question the value of a verbal report assessment of safety skills (Miltenberger, 2008; Miltenberger & Gross, 2011).

## In Situ Assessment

During an in situ assessment or naturalistic assessment (e.g., Lumley et al., 1998; Miltenberger et al., 2004, 2005; Poche et al., 1981; Poche, Yoder, & Miltenberger, 1988) the researcher creates a situation in which a child is exposed to a simulated safety threat without knowledge that an assessment is taking place. In situ assessment occurs in the child's natural environment as part of a normal routine without an adult present. To the child, the situation is "real." In research on teaching abduction prevention skills to children, Johnson et al. (2005) had a research assistant approach a child while the child was alone in a public place (e.g., playground, store, front yard) and ask the child to leave with him. The research assistant recorded the child's responses to the abduction lure. (It should be noted that the parent, who consented to the assessment and helped arrange it with the researchers, was always nearby but out of sight, and the researcher assistant never left with the child.) In research on teaching firearm injury prevention skills to children, Gross, Miltenberger, Knudson, Bosch, & Brower-Breitwieser (2007) had the parents of 4- to 7-year-olds place a gun (disabled handgun) in a location in the home without the child's knowledge and ask the child to go to that room for some reason (e.g., to get a snack). A hidden video camera recorded the child's behavior so the researchers could assess the use of the safety skills as a child found a gun alone at home without an adult present. This same in situ assessment method has been used in all studies evaluating the effects of firearm injury prevention skills training and abduction prevention skills training (Miltenberger, 2008; Miltenberger & Gross, 2009), thus measuring the actual use of the skills in the presence of the (simulated) safety threat.

The results of in situ assessments identify the behavior the child will exhibit in the actual safety threat situation, because the assessment simulates the actual safety threat situation. It involves: (1) contact with the simulated safety threat in the natural environment; (2) no knowledge of the assessment; (3) no adult presence. On the other hand, the role-play assessment assesses the use of the safety skills in a contrived situation (the classroom or training room) under the stimulus control of the researcher's presence (the researcher is a likely $S^D$ for the safety skills). Because the role-play assessment occurs in the presence of the researcher, it will allow the researcher to determine whether the child has acquired the skills, but not whether the child will use the skills in the "real" situation. Only an in situ assessment can accomplish the latter goal.

Research on safety skills training with children has demonstrated that there is a lack of correspondence between the results of role-play assessments and in situ assessments; what children do in front of the researcher is not what they do alone in the presence of a safety threat (e.g., Gatheridge et al., 2004; Himle, Miltenberger, Gatheridge, et al., 2004). Furthermore, research shows there is a lack of correspondence between the results of verbal report assessments and in situ assessments; what children say they will do in response to a safety threat is not what they actually do when alone in the presence of the safety threat (e.g., Carroll-Rowan & Miltenberger, 1994; Gatheridge et al., 2004; Himle, Miltenberger, Gatheridge, & Flessner, 2004; Olsen-Woods et al., 1998). This same lack of correspondence between verbal report and in situ assessment results, and between role-play and in situ assessment results also has been found in research on teaching sexual abuse prevention skills to women with intellectual disabilities (Lumley et al., 1998; Miltenberger et al., 1999). However, in situ assessments have never been used in research on sexual abuse prevention skills training with children. Therefore, without in situ assessments, there is no evidence that safety skills taught in training sessions will be used in an actual sexual abuse situation. However, given the lack of correspondence between verbal report and in situ assessment in studies with women with intellectual disabilities (Lumley et al., 1998; Miltenberger et al., 1999), and in studies teaching other safety skills to children (e.g., Gatheridge et al., 2004; Himle, Miltenberger, Gatheridge, & Flessner, 2004; Olsen-Woods et al., 1998) there is reason to be skeptical that the results of verbal report assessments would predict actual use of the skills in response to a sexual abuse lure. Clearly, researchers need to investigate this issue.

## Conclusions

Valid assessment of safety skills is critical for determining the effectiveness of a sexual abuse prevention skills-training program or any other child safety skills-training program. A valid assessment is one that measures the skills when the simulated safety threat is presented in the natural environment, when an adult is not present, to the child who has no knowledge that an assessment is taking place. Research demonstrates that in situ assessment is the only valid assessment of safety skills. This finding has been demonstrated with firearm injury prevention skills (e.g., Gatheridge et al., 2004; Himle, Miltenberger, Gatheridge, & Flessner, 2004), abduction prevention skills (Carroll-Rowan & Miltenberger, 1994; Olsen-Woods et al., 1998), and sexual abuse prevention skills with women with intellectual disabilities (Lumley et al., 1998; Miltenberger et al., 1999). The fact that in situ assessments have not been used to evaluate the effectiveness of child sexual abuse prevention skills-training programs makes it difficult to draw conclusions about the effectiveness of these programs. It is clear from the research that children do acquire knowledge about sexual abuse and prevention skills as a result of participating in these programs (Harvey et al., 1988; Miltenberger & Thiesse-Duffy, 1988; Wurtele, 2008, 2009; Wurtele et al., 1987, 1989; Wurtele, Saslawsky, Miller, Marrs, & Britcher, 1986). However, researchers have not demonstrated that the skills will be used in seemingly real sexual abuse situations following training. When in situ assessment has been used to evaluate child sexual abuse prevention skills training, the researchers measured children's responses to the lures of strangers, thus assessing abduction prevention skills rather than sexual abuse prevention skills (Fryer, Kraizer, & Miyoshi, 1987; Miltenberger & Thiesse-Duffy, 1988; Miltenberger et al., 1990). Although researchers later recognized this limitation (e.g., Lumley et al., 1998; Miltenberger et al., 1999; Roberts & Miltenberger, 1999), in situ assessments involving sexual abuse lures have yet to be used to evaluate sexual abuse prevention programs for children. This issue and recommendations for future research utilizing in situ assessments will be discussed in the conclusions at the end of the chapter.

## TRAINING APPROACHES

Two major training approaches have been evaluated for teaching sexual abuse prevention skills and other safety skills to children. These two approaches are an informational approach and an active learning approach (Miltenberger, 2008; Miltenberger & Gross, 2011). In an informational or passive learning approach, instructions and/or modeling of safety skills are provided in a variety of ways, such as lecture or discussion (e.g., Conte, Rosen, Saperstein, & Shermack, 1985; Fryer et al., 1987; Poche et al., 1988), written materials (e.g., Himle, Miltenberger, Gatheridge, & Flessner, 2004; Kolko, Moser, Litz, & Hughes, 1987; Miltenberger & Thiesse-Duffy, 1988), film or video (e.g., Beck & Miltenberger, 2009; Byers, 1986; Gatheridge et al., 2004; Poche et al., 1988), or theatrical presentations (e.g., Borkin & Frank, 1986; Swan, Press, & Briggs, 1985). The defining feature of an informational approach is that information about the safety threat and the safety skills appropriate to the threat is provided without the opportunity to practice the skills in response to a simulation or role-play of the safety threat. This approach stands in contrast to an active learning approach, in which information is provided through instructions and modeling and, in addition, the child is provided the opportunity to practice the skills in response to simulated or role-played safety threats, and receive praise for successful performance and corrective feedback when necessary (e.g., Himle, Miltenberger, Flessner, & Gatheridge, 2004; Johnson et al., 2005, 2006; Miltenberger et al., 2004, 2005; Wurtele et al., 1986, 1987).

## Informational Approaches

Informational approaches provide information about a specific safety threat (e.g., sexual abuse, abduction, loaded firearms) and the safety skills a child needs to use in response to the threat (recognize, avoid, escape, report). Informational approaches have appeal because they can be used to educate large numbers of children efficiently, as in a classroom, and may be accessible to parents and teachers to provide training to their own children or students. Furthermore, some prevention programs are commercially available for purchase, such as the Red Flag Green Flag sexual abuse prevention program (Kolko et al., 1987; Miltenberger & Thiesse-Duffy, 1988; Miltenberger et al., 1990), the Safe Side abduction prevention program (Beck & Miltenberger, 2009), and the Eddie Eagle Gunsafe program (Gatheridge et al., 2004; Himle, Miltenberger, Gatheridge, et al., 2004).

The appeal and accessibility of informational approaches to safety skills training notwithstanding, research suggests that these approaches are not as effective as active learning approaches involving repeated rehearsals of the skills with praise and feedback (e.g., Beck & Miltenberger, 2009; Gatheridge et al., 2004; Himle, Miltenberger, Gatheridge, & Flessner, 2004; Wurtele et al., 1986, 1987, 1989). Research shows that active learning approaches are more effective than informational approaches in producing knowledge gains following sexual abuse prevention training (Wurtele et al., 1986, 1987, 1989). Furthermore, active learning approaches are more effective than informational approaches in producing skill acquisition and generalization during in situ assessments in research on abduction prevention skills (Beck & Miltenberger, 2009) and firearm injury prevention skills (Gatheridge et al., 2004; Himle, Miltenberger, Gatheridge, & Flessner, 2004).

Wurtele and colleagues conducted a number of studies showing that active learning approaches produced greater gains in knowledge of sexual abuse prevention skills than did informational approaches. Wurtele et al. (1986) compared the effectiveness of behavioral skills training (BST), a film about sexual abuse, the combination of BST and film, and an attention control with kindergarten/first grade students and 5th/6th grade students. Training with BST consisted of instructions about appropriate and inappropriate touch, discussion of the appropriate safety skills, modeling of the skills, and the opportunity to rehearse the skills with reinforcement and corrective feedback. The film (Touch; Illusion Theater, 1984) discussed and modeled four safety skills (say "no," yell for help, get away, and tell someone) in response to various abusive scenarios. Although a 15 minute discussion followed the film, there was no active rehearsal component. Wurtele et al. showed that knowledge scores were significantly higher in the two BST groups than in the control group, whereas the scores in the film group were not significantly higher than controls. Wurtele et al. (1987) showed similar results comparing participant modeling (an active learning condition) with symbolic modeling (an informational condition) for teaching sexual abuse prevention knowledge to kindergarten age children. In this study, children learned significantly more in the active learning condition. In another comparison of active versus passive learning procedures for teaching sexual abuse prevention skills, Wurtele et al. (1989) showed, through self-report assessments, that preschoolers who received BST performed better than those who received a feelings-based curriculum (an informational approach) and those in an attention-control group.

In addition to the research on informational approaches to teaching sexual abuse prevention skills to children, other research has compared informational approaches and active learning approaches for teaching other safety skills, specifically, firearm injury prevention skills and abduction prevention skills. Poche et al. (1988) evaluated two informational approaches for teaching abduction prevention skills to kindergarten and first grade students: (1) a lecture and brief film that a police officer presented in the local schools about the dangers of abduction and the safety skills a child should use in response to an abduction lure (standard presentation); and (2) a modeling video developed by the researchers that showed children successfully engaging in safety skills in response to multiple exemplars of abduction lures (modeling group). In addition, Poche et al. evaluated an active learning condition in which children viewed the video and then practiced the skills with praise and feedback (rehearsal group). Poche et al. showed that the rehearsal group performed significantly better during in situ assessments than did the other groups. In addition, the video group performed significantly better than the standard presentation group. The standard presentation group did not perform better than controls. This study was one of the first to show the superiority of an active learning approach over an informational approach to teaching safety skills as measured by in situ assessments.

Other research produced findings consistent with Poche et al. (1988), demonstrating the superiority of an active learning approach for teaching other safety skills as measured through in situ assessments. Gatheridge et al. (2004) showed that behavioral skills training was more effective than the Eddie Eagle GunSafe program (an informational approach) for teaching 6- and 7-year-old children to react safely when they found a gun (don't touch it, get away, and tell an adult). The Eddie Eagle program consisted of instructions and modeling using coloring books, discussion, and a video. An instructor, guided by an instructor's manual, presented the Eddie Eagle program to a small group of children in 10 minute sessions conducted over five consecutive days. The BST condition included instructions and modeling with rehearsal of the skills with feedback, also presented in 10 minute sessions across five days to small groups of children. Gatheridge et al. found that significantly more children in the BST group than in the Eddie Eagle or control groups exhibited the safety skills during role-play and in situ assessments following training. Similarly, Himle, Miltenberger, Gatheridge, & Flessner (2004) showed the superiority of BST over the Eddie Eagle program with 4- and 5-year-olds.

Beck & Miltenberger (2009) evaluated the Safe Side abduction prevention program, a commercially available 40 minute video that discusses abduction lures and safe responses to abduction lures (say "no," get away, and tell), and provides multiple models of children using the safety skills in response to a variety of abduction lures. The Safe Side program is available for purchase over the Internet, and is touted as an award-winning program (www.thesafeside.com). Beck and Miltenberger used in situ assessments to measure the abduction prevention skills of 6- to 8-year-olds at baseline and following their viewing of the Safe Side video. The results showed that the abduction prevention skills did not improve for any of the 6 participants after watching the video. However, after participating in a training procedure involving rehearsal of the safety skills with feedback implemented by the parents in the public location where the assessment took place, all children exhibited the safety skills in subsequent in situ assessments. This active learning procedure (in situ training) demonstrated as effective by Beck and Miltenberger is described in the next section.

A consistent finding in the research on informational approaches to teaching safety skills to children is that an informational approach does not result in the acquisition or generalization of safety skills as measured with in situ assessments (e.g., Beck & Miltenberger, 2009; Gatheridge et al., 2004). Although children might successfully describe the safety skills following an informational training procedure (e.g., Gatheridge et al., 2004: Himle, Miltenberger, Gatheridge, & Flessner, 2004), they do not successfully use the skills when faced with a simulated safety threat in a naturalistic situation without the knowledge that they are being assessed (e.g., Beck & Miltenberger, 2009; Gatheridge et al., 2004). Thus, following participation in a safety skills training program that did not include active rehearsal, reinforcement, and feedback, it is unlikely that children would use the skills if faced with an actual safety threat. This research questions the value of an informational approach to training, with the clear implication that active learning is the preferred training approach. However, in research on sexual abuse prevention skills training, when active learning approaches were implemented and shown to be superior to informational approaches, the results were assessed only with self-report measures. Thus, although there is evidence for the superiority of an active learning approach for teaching abduction prevention skills and firearm injury prevention skills, there is no similar evidence for the effectiveness of an active learning approach for teaching sexual abuse prevention skills. The following section describes the research demonstrating the effectiveness of an active learning approach for teaching safety skills to children.

## Active Learning Approaches

As described earlier, active learning approaches to teaching safety skills involve not only information giving (instructions and modeling), but the opportunity for the child to practice the skills under the stimulus control of simulated safety threats with reinforcement and corrective feedback until the skills are executed consistently across learning trials. Two active learning approaches have been evaluated in the child safety skills-training research:

behavioral skills training (BST) and in situ training (IST). Whereas BST involves instructions, modeling, rehearsal, and feedback with simulated safety threats in a training session apart from the child's normal routine, IST involves repeated practice of the safety skills with feedback following an in situ assessment when a safety threat is simulated in the child's natural environment. In essence, IST consists of turning an in situ assessment into a training session. To conduct IST, the trainer first arranges an in situ assessment and, if the child does not execute the safety skills correctly, the trainer (previously unseen by the child) enters the situation and requires the child to practice the safety skills a number of times with feedback in the situation. Practicing the skills with reinforcement in the situation promotes generalization of the skills to similar situations. Because the child learns to emit the safety skills in the context of a safety threat experienced in the natural environment while no adult is present, the safety threat rather than the presence of the trainer or other adult develops stimulus control over the safety skills (Miltenberger, 2008; Miltenberger & Gross, 2009).

BST has been evaluated for teaching sexual abuse prevention skills (Harvey et al., 1988; Miltenberger & Thiesse-Duffy, 1988; Miltenberger et al., 1990; Wurtele et al., 1986, 1987, 1989), abduction prevention skills (Poche et al., 1981, 1988; Johnson et al., 2005, 2006), and firearm injury prevention skills (Gatheridge et al., 2004; Himle, Miltenberger, Gatheridge, & Flessner, 2004; Himle, Miltenberger, Flessner, & Gatheridge, 2004; Miltenberger et al., 2004). In addition, IST has been evaluated for teaching abduction prevention skills (Beck & Miltenberger, 2009; Johnson et al., 2005, 2006) and firearm injury prevention skills to children (Gatheridge et al., 2004; Himle, Miltenberger, Flessner, & Gatheridge, 2004; Miltenberger et al., 2004, 2005). Although IST has not been evaluated for teaching sexual abuse prevention skills to children, perhaps because researchers are hesitant to conduct in situ assessments of sexual abuse prevention skills with children (e.g., Leventhal & Conte, 1987; Roberts & Miltenberger, 1999; Carroll et al., 1994), IST has been evaluated for teaching sexual abuse prevention skills to women with intellectual disabilities (Lumley et al., 1998; Miltenberger et al., 1999).

## *Behavioral Skills Training (BST)*

Research by Wurtele, as described earlier (Wurtele et al., 1986, 1987, 1989), demonstrated that BST was superior to informational approaches to teaching sexual abuse prevention skills to children. However, the primary limitation of this work and other research evaluating BST for teaching sexual abuse prevention skills (e.g., Harvey et al., 1988) is that assessment relied on verbal report rather than assessment of actual skills when presented with a simulated sexual abuse lure. As a result, the conclusions that can be drawn from these studies are limited; it just is not known whether children who demonstrated increased sexual abuse prevention *knowledge* in these studies would use sexual abuse prevention *skills* if ever faced with a sexual abuse lure. Without in situ assessments, actual benefit to the children participating in the studies cannot be measured.

Other research evaluating BST to teach sexual abuse prevention skills used verbal report assessment and in situ assessment (Miltenberger & Thiesse-Duffy, 1988; Miltenberger et al., 1990) to evaluate the effectiveness of the program. However, the in situ assessment evaluated the children's responses to an abduction lure from a stranger in a public place, rather than a sexual abuse lure from a known individual. Therefore, the authors did not evaluate sexual abuse prevention skills in their in situ assessment and, as a result, no conclusions can be drawn about the effectiveness of the training program for teaching actual sexual abuse prevention skills. Similarly, Haseltine & Miltenberger (1990) evaluated a BST program for teaching sexual abuse prevention skills to women with mild intellectual disabilities, but assessed abduction prevention skills (responses to a lure to leave with a stranger) rather than sexual abuse prevention skills. Again, no conclusions could be drawn about the effectiveness of the BST program for teaching the women to respond to sexual abuse lures.

Researchers evaluating BST for teaching other safety skills have used in situ assessments to evaluate the training programs (e.g., Gatheridge et al., 2004; Himle, Miltenberger, Gatheridge, et al., 2004; Miltenberger et al., 2004, 2005). Considering the similarity of safety skills taught in this research to sexual abuse prevention skills (recognize, avoid, escape, report), the results of this research have direct relevance for teaching sexual abuse prevention skills. This research has produced mixed findings regarding the effectiveness of BST for promoting the use of safety skills when children are faced with a simulated safety threat during an in situ assessment. Himle, Miltenberger, Gatheridge, & Flessner (2004) showed that 4- and 5-year-olds demonstrated firearm injury prevention skills in role-play assessments following a BST program, but that the same children did not use the skills when they found a gun during in situ assessments. On the other hand, Gatheridge et al. (2004) found that many of the 6- and 7-year-olds who participated in the same BST program did use the firearm injury prevention skills during in situ assessments following training.

In follow-up to these studies, Himle, Miltenberger, Flessner, & Gatheridge (2004) and Miltenberger et al. (2004) evaluated individual BST with booster sessions for teaching firearm injury prevention skills to 4–5-year-olds and 6–7-year-olds, respectively. Himle, Miltenberger, Flessner, & Gatheridge found that 3 out of 8 participants engaged in the safety skills during in situ assessments following BST, and Miltenberger et al. found that 3 out of 6 children engaged in the safety skills upon finding a gun during an in situ assessment following BST. These studies and others (e.g., Jostad, Miltenberger, Kelso, & Knudson, 2008) suggest that BST for teaching safety skills for firearm injury prevention is effective for about half of the participants. Other research evaluating BST for teaching abduction prevention skills showed it was effective (as measured with in situ assessments) for most, but not all, participants (Poche et al., 1981, 1988). Unfortunately, researchers have not identified any methods to determine which children will benefit from BST and which children will need additional training. Across the studies in which BST was not entirely effective, IST was the additional training method found to be effective for children who did not benefit from BST.

### *In Situ Training (IST)*

A number of studies evaluated the effectiveness of IST for teaching safety skills to children. Research on IST has shown it to be effective following BST (Gatheridge et al., 2004; Himle, Miltenberger, Flessner, & Gatheridge 2004; Miltenberger et al., 2004), in conjunction with BST (Johnson et al., 2005, 2005), following an informational program (Gatheridge et al., 2004; Beck & Miltenberger, 2009), and following no training (Miltenberger et al., 2012). Gatheridge et al. (2004) used in situ assessments to evaluate BST and the Eddie Eagle program for teaching firearm injury prevention skills to 6- and 7-year-olds. When the children failed to exhibit the safety skills following training, Gatheridge et al. implemented one IST session. The previously unseen trainer entered the room while the child was in the presence of the gun and required the child to rehearse the safety skills in the situation a number of times. In a subsequent in situ assessment, most children in the BST and Eddie Eagle groups engaged in the correct safety skills. Similarly, Beck & Miltenberger (2009) used in situ assessments to evaluate abduction prevention skills after 5–8-year-olds watched the Safe Side video. When a child did not exhibit the skills, the parent (who was out of sight during the assessment) immediately walked up to the child and implemented IST in the public location where the assessment occurred. If the assessment occurred in the aisle of a department store, the child practiced running from that location to the parent in the next aisle and reporting the event. One or more IST sessions were required for all children to perform the safety skills correctly in subsequent in situ assessments. In another study evaluating the Safe Side program, Miltenberger et al. (2012) showed that children who watched the Safe Side video performed no better than children in the control group when abduction prevention skills were evaluated with in situ assessments. However, when the children received one IST session following their failure to use the skills during the assessment, the performance of children in both groups significantly improved; most children exhibited the skills in a second in situ assessment.

Other researchers evaluated the effectiveness of IST after BST was not completely effective for teaching firearm injury prevention skills to children. Himle, Miltenberger, Flessner, & Gatheridge (2004) and Miltenberger et al. (2004) used in situ assessments to evaluate safety skills and showed that BST was effective with half of the participants. For the children who did not benefit from BST, the researchers implemented IST and all children subsequently demonstrated the safety skills consistently during in situ assessments.

Following these demonstrations of the effectiveness of IST conducted after BST was found to be only partially effective for teaching safety skills to children, researchers evaluated IST combined with BST for teaching abduction prevention skills (Johnson et al., 2005) and firearm injury prevention skills (Miltenberger et al., 2005). In both studies, the researchers implemented two BST sessions across 2 or 3 days and, 30 minutes following the second BST session, conducted an in situ assessment and implemented IST. If children performed correctly during the in situ assessment, they received praise. However, if the child did not perform the safety skills correctly, the trainer showed up and required the child to repeatedly practice the skills. For example, if the child did not say "no," run away, and tell when presented with an abduction lure, the researcher who was previously unseen, walked up to the child (as the confederate who presented the lure walked away) and made the child practice the skills on the spot (Johnson et al., 2005).

The essence of IST is that the adult (researcher, parent) catches the child in the act of engaging in unsafe behavior in the presence of the safety threat and requires the child to practice the skills on the spot. This procedure is the most consistently successful approach to teaching safety skills; it greatly increases the likelihood that the child will execute the skills the next time the safety threat is present in a similar situation (Miltenberger, 2008; Miltenberger & Gross, 2011). It is thought that both positive and negative reinforcement and positive punishment (the addition of an aversive stimulus or event following the behavior that decreases the likelihood of the behavior in the future) may play a role in the effectiveness of IST (e.g., Miltenberger et al., 2005). During IST, the adult (researcher, teacher, parent) catches the child engaging in unsafe behavior in the presence of the safety threat and requires the child to rehearse the skills a number of times. The adult's praise for the child's correct rehearsal of the skills in the situation may positively reinforce the use of the skills in the presence of the safety threat. In addition, getting caught may punish the unsafe behavior in the presence of the safety threat, and avoidance of getting caught engaging in unsafe behavior in the presence of the safety threat in subsequent assessments may negatively reinforce the use of the safety skills. Regardless of the basic principles that underlie the effectiveness of IST, research suggests it is effective with or without prior exposure to BST or other training procedures.

To date, IST has not been evaluated for teaching sexual abuse prevention skills to children, probably because in situ assessments have not been used to evaluate child sexual abuse prevention programs. However, IST has been evaluated for teaching sexual abuse prevention skills to women with mild and moderate intellectual disabilities (Egemo-Helm et al., 2007; Miltenberger et al., 1999). Miltenberger et al. (1999) evaluated a 10 week BST program for teaching sexual abuse prevention skills to 5 women with intellectual disabilities. They showed that the women acquired the skills as assessed through verbal report and role-play assessments. However, the women did not execute the skills during in situ assessments. During in situ assessments, a male confederate was introduced to the women as a new staff member. After building rapport with the participant for about 15 min, the confederate presented a sexual abuse lure to the participant while the two of them were alone in a room in the group home. If the participant did not engage in the sexual abuse prevention skills, the trainer (previously unseen by the participant) entered the room and, along with the confederate, provided instructions and modeling and required the participant to practice the skills until she executed the skills two times without prompts.

Miltenberger et al. (1999) showed that, following 2 to 6 IST sessions, the women executed the safety skills correctly in subsequent in situ assessments. This study is one of the first to use in situ assessments to evaluate sexual abuse prevention skills. The first was conducted by Lumley et al. (1998) who also showed that, following 10 BST sessions, women with intellectual disabilities did not correctly execute the sexual abuse prevention skills when a male confederate posing as a staff member presented a sexual abuse lure. Lumley et al. documented that the skills demonstrated in role-play assessments did not generalize to in situ assessments. Miltenberger et al. subsequently demonstrated that IST was effective for promoting generalization of sexual abuse prevention skills to in situ assessments. In a follow up study, Egemo-Helm et al. (2007) also demonstrated that BST combined with IST was effective, as measured with in situ assessments, for teaching sexual abuse prevention skills to women with mild and moderate intellectual disabilities.

## Conclusions

There is a fairly large literature evaluating child sexual abuse prevention-training programs (e.g., Wurtele, 2008, 2009). Across numerous studies there is a consistent finding that these training programs, especially those involving active learning approaches, result in increased knowledge about sexual abuse and sexual abuse prevention skills (e.g., Harvey et al., 1988; Miltenberger & Thiesse-Duffy, 1988; Wurtele et al., 1986, 1987, 1989). However, the major limitation of every published study evaluating child sexual abuse prevention programs is the absence of assessment of the child's actual behavior when presented with a seemingly real but simulated sexual abuse prevention lure following training (in situ assessment). Without in situ assessments to evaluate program effectiveness, researchers and trainers can only presume that what children say they would do is what they would actually do when faced with a sexual abuse lure. Unfortunately, research that utilizes in situ assessment to evaluate safety skills training programs for other safety threats shows consistently that verbal reports do not correspond to actual behavior when the child is exposed to the simulated safety threat; children do not do what they say they would do (e.g., Carroll-Rowan & Miltenberger, 1994; Gatheridge et al., 2004; Himle, Miltenberger, Gatheridge, & Flessner, 2004; Olsen-Woods et al., 1998). Although there is some indirect evidence from interviews with adults that participation in child sexual abuse prevention programs makes it: (1) more likely that children will use the sexual abuse prevention skills when victimized or threatened (Finkelhor, Asdigian, & Dziuba-Leatherman, 1995); and (2) less likely that children will be victims of sexual abuse (e.g., Gibson & Leitenberg, 2000), there is no direct evidence through valid skills assessments that sexual abuse prevention programs result in the use of sexual abuse prevention skills.

Although there is no direct evidence that sexual abuse prevention skills training programs are effective, there is evidence that other child safety skills training programs consisting of active learning approaches are effective (e.g., Himle, Miltenberger, Flessner, & Gatheridge, 2004; Johnson et al., 2005, 2006; Miltenberger et al., 2004, 2005; Poche et al., 1981, 1988). As documented through the results of in situ assessments, BST and IST are effective for teaching abduction prevention skills and firearm injury skills to children (Miltenberger, 2008; Miltenberger & Gross, 2011). The problem with BS and IST is that they often are implemented with individual children, require substantial time and trainer expertise, and must be conducted in the context of in situ assessments. As a result, these procedures are not easily utilized by parents and teachers for efficiently teaching large groups of children. Nonetheless, these approaches are empirically validated, and researchers will need to consider adapting these assessment and training procedures for teaching sexual abuse prevention skills.

## Recommendations

Based on the findings from research on teaching safety skills to children and women with intellectual disabilities, a number of recommendations are offered for further development and evaluation of programs for teaching sexual abuse prevention skills to children.

### *Development and Social Validation of in Situ Assessments*

Because the research on sexual abuse prevention skills training is limited by the use of self-report assessments, and in situ assessments are likely to be controversial, researchers might consider working on the development and social validation of in situ assessment measures for evaluating child sexual abuse prevention skills training. Taking direction from research on sexual abuse prevention with women with intellectual disabilities in which in situ assessments were utilized successfully (Lumley et al., 1988; Miltenberger et al., 1989), researchers could develop in situ assessment scenarios for use with children and evaluate the social validity of the scenarios. To be valid simulations of sexual abuse scenarios a child might actually experience, the assessment scenarios would need to include individuals the child knows presenting sexual abuse lures to the child. However, having an adult in the child's life present a sexual abuse lure for the purposes of assessment is likely to be highly unacceptable to those involved, and possibly unethical. Lumley et al. (1988) and Miltenberger et al. (1989) addressed these concerns by utilizing a confederate who established rapport with the participant after being introduced as a new staff member. As a result, the individual was no longer a stranger, but did not have an established relationship with the participant that might be damaged by presenting a sexual abuse lure.

A similar strategy might be used to develop in situ assessment scenarios for use with children. Perhaps a confederate could be introduced as a friend of the parents and, after spending some time in the home, the confederate could deliver a lure to the child. This scenario would have to be arranged with the agreement and cooperation of the parents. Furthermore, the assessment situation and sexual abuse lure would have to be chosen with care. Similarly, a confederate might present a lure to a child at school after being introduced as a new "teacher's aide." Again, utilizing an assessment such as this would only be done with the full cooperation of the parents and school personnel, and would have to be highly structured and supervised. The common feature of the in situ assessment scenarios that could be used to assess child sexual abuse prevention skills training programs is that the scenarios would involve a confederate introduced to the child as someone in authority or known to the family. The confederate would spend some time getting to know the child (and thus, would no longer be a stranger) before delivering the sexual abuse lure.

If researchers planned to pursue this strategy of developing and socially validating a pool of sexual abuse lures to use during in situ assessments with children, they would need to do so knowing that the research might be highly controversial to some individuals. University institutional review boards (IRBs) would have to carefully consider and approve such research. As such, researchers would have to convince IRB members that the need for valid assessment of sexual abuse prevention skills outweighs the potential problems that could result from the research. If researchers do conduct studies to socially validate scenarios for in situ assessments of child sexual abuse prevention skills, and the social validity results show that parents and teachers find such an approach unacceptable, then the research would not proceed further. However, if researchers identified a pool of scenarios that parents and teachers rated as acceptable, then this social validation of the assessment would permit the researchers to proceed to use these assessments to evaluate the effectiveness of child sexual abuse prevention programs.

Kopp & Miltenberger (2008) evaluated the acceptability and social validity of scenarios depicting sexual abuse lures. Staff from a local rape and abuse crisis center helped the researchers develop 35 scenarios. Each scenario identified a known individual (family friend, neighbor, relative) presenting an inappropriate request to a child. Child protective service workers completed a survey asking how socially valid the scenarios were as depictions of sexual abuse lures, and how acceptable the scenarios would be when used as role-plays for assessing sexual abuse prevention skills with 10-year-old children. The child protection workers rated all the scenarios as: (1) accurate depictions of sexual abuse lures; and as (2) acceptable for use as role-plays to evaluate sexual abuse prevention training. Similar research might be pursued to assess the social validity of scenarios to be included in in situ assessments.

### *Evaluation of BST and IST for Child Sexual Abuse Prevention Skills Training*

If a pool of scenarios can be socially validated for use in the in situ assessment of sexual abuse prevention skills, then researchers could proceed to develop BST and IST training programs for teaching child sexual abuse prevention skills. However, before proceeding it would be important for researchers to socially validate the training program that focuses on teaching children to resist sexual abuse lures from known individuals, to be certain that parents and teachers found it acceptable (e.g., Kopp & Miltenberger, 2009). Such training would involve instructions and modeling of the skills with the opportunity to rehearse the skills in response to realistic sexual abuse scenarios from the pool of approved scenarios (e.g., Kopp & Miltenberger, 2008). Furthermore, such training would require in situ assessment using approved scenarios for valid assessment of the training procedures, and the implementation of IST if the child did not exhibit the safety skills during the assessment. This research would parallel the successful safety skills training research conducted to teach abduction prevention skills to children (e.g., Johnson et al., 2005, 2006), firearm injury prevention skills to children (e.g., Himle, Miltenberger, Flessner, & Gatheridge, 2004; Miltenberger et al., 2004, 2005), and sexual abuse prevention skills with women with intellectual disabilities (Lumley et al., 1998; Miltenberger et al., 1999). If BST and IST proved successful (as assessed with in situ assessments) when used in individual training sessions for teaching sexual abuse prevention skills to children, the next step would be to evaluate the procedures implemented with groups of children to increase efficiency.

## Adapting BST and IST for Training Children in Groups

Training children in groups is clearly a more efficient use of trainer time and resources than training one child at a time. Although safety skills training research demonstrates the effectiveness of individual training with BST and IST (Himle, Miltenberger, Flessner, & Gatheridge, 2004; Johnson et al., 2005; Miltenberger et al., 2004, 2005), there is some evidence that training children in groups also is effective. Poche et al. (1988), Carroll-Rowan & Miltenberger (1994), and Olsen-Woods et al. (1998) used BST to teach abduction prevention skills to children in preschool, kindergarten, and first grade classrooms. In each study, the children received group instruction and modeling, and then each student in the class had the opportunity to practice the skills with feedback in simulated abduction situations role-played in front of the class. Gatheridge et al. (2004) used a similar procedure implementing BST to teach firearm injury prevention skills to a small group of 6- and 7-year-old children. In all of these studies, in situ assessments demonstrated the procedures to be effective, with over half of the children exhibiting all of the safety skills, and a large majority of the children showing improvements in safety skills.

Researchers could apply this same group training model to teach child sexual abuse prevention skills. The teacher would provide information about sexual abuse and sexual abuse prevention skills, and then use live or video modeling to demonstrate the sexual abuse prevention skills in response to a variety of scenarios in which known adults delivered a variety of sexual abuse lures (chosen from a pool of approved training lures). During the modeling component, after the lure is delivered, the teacher could stop the action (pause the video) and quiz the students about what the child ought to do in the situation. For example, the video model might show an adult family friend asking to take a shower with the child after playing soccer and, before the child in the video responds, the teacher could pause the video and ask the class, "What should the child do?" At this point, the children would have an opportunity to recite the safety skills and receive praise (or corrective feedback) from the teacher. The teacher would then restart the video so the children could see the child in the video engage in the correct safety skills. This type of interactive video modeling was combined with active student rehearsal by Poche et al. (1988) and Carroll-Rowan & Miltenberger (1994) to teach abduction prevention skills to children. This same type of interactive modeling could be conducted live in front of the class as well.

Once children in the class receive instructions and modeling, each child would take a turn practicing the sexual abuse prevention skills. First the teacher would describe the concept of role-playing as pretending that the situation described by the teacher is real, and that the child is to act as he or she would really act in the situation. The teacher then would describe in detail a scenario in which an adult presents a sexual abuse lure, set up the scenario in front of the class, and initiate the role-play. It would be best to have a second teacher or teacher's aide pretend to be the adult who presents the lure to the student so the teacher conducting the session would not have to switch roles to provide feedback. When the child demonstrates the sexual abuse prevention skills in the role-play, the teacher would provide descriptive praise for successful use of the safety skills and corrective feedback for any aspect of the child's behavior that needed improvement. For example, if the child did not say "no" loudly enough, or if the child did not run away immediately, or if the child did not tell an adult after running away or tell immediately, the teacher would tell the child how to improve the performance and have the child practice the skills again in the same role-play until the child exhibited the skills correctly. Each child would participate in rehearsal with feedback until every child exhibited the skills fluently. As a result of participating in such a group BST program, every child practices the skills with feedback, and sees all the other children practice the skills with feedback in a wide variety of role-plays. The teacher could also encourage children to give each other feedback so the observing children would have to be actively involved in other children's rehearsals.

To be able to evaluate the effectiveness of such a group-training program, each child's parents would have to consent to having their child participate in one or more in situ assessments, depending on the nature of the research design. In situ assessment would be an essential aspect of the research to document the effectiveness of BST for teaching sexual abuse prevention skills in the classroom. Although IST has been demonstrated consistently as the most successful procedure for teaching other safety skills, there would be little utility in evaluating IST for teaching sexual abuse prevention skills, because it is highly unlikely that it would be adopted for classroom use. IST is a time-intensive training procedure that can only be conducted on an individual basis, therefore, researchers' time and resources are best devoted to evaluating the success of BST. In this regard, researchers could evaluate the parameters of BST to determine which parameters make it most effective when conducted at the classroom level. These parameters might include the number and types of sexual abuse lures to include in training, the number and types of behavioral rehearsals, the number of sessions, the timing of sessions, the content of sessions, and the need for booster sessions that produce the best results for the most children. Researchers might also evaluate the characteristics of the children least likely to benefit from training so additional resources or alternative training approaches can be identified and utilized.

If research shows sexual abuse prevention-training programs to be acceptable for implementation in schools, research to evaluate the effectiveness of BST programs could begin in earnest. If this research then consistently shows class wide BST programs to be effective, BST for teaching child sexual abuse prevention skills would join the ranks of evidence-based educational practices, and researchers could switch their focus to promoting the dissemination and large-scale adoption of BST. With the transition from research to routine educational practice, there would no longer be a need for continued use of in situ assessments, which may increase the acceptability and thus the adoption of sexual abuse prevention training on a large scale.

## REFERENCES

Arias, I. (2004). The legacy of child maltreatment: Long-term health consequences for women. *Journal of Women's Health, 13*, 468–473.

Beck, K., & Miltenberger, R. (2009). Evaluation of a commercially-available abduction prevention program and in situ training by parents to teach abduction prevention skills to children. *Journal of Applied Behavior Analysis, 42*, 761–772.

Borkin, J., & Frank, L. (1986). Sexual abuse prevention for preschoolers: A pilot program. *Child Welfare, 65*, 75–81.

Boyle, C. L., & Lutzker, J. R. (2005). Teaching young children to discriminate abusive from nonabusive situations using multiple exemplars in a modified discrete trial teaching format. *Journal of Family Violence, 20*, 55–69.

Browne, A., & Finkelhor, D. (1986). Impact of child sexual abuse: A review of the research. *Psychological Bulletin, 99*, 66–77.

Budin, L. E., & Johnson, C. F. (1989). Sex abuse prevention programs: Offenders' attitudes about their efficacy. *Child Abuse & Neglect, 13*, 77–87.

Byers, J. (1986). Films for child sexual prevention and treatment: A review. *Child Abuse & Neglect, 10*, 541–546.

Carroll, L., Miltenberger, R., & O'Neill, K. (1992). A review and critique of research evaluating child sexual abuse prevention programs. *Education and Treatment of Children, 15*, 335–354.

Carroll-Rowan, L., & Miltenberger, R. (1994). A comparison of procedures for teaching abduction prevention to preschoolers. *Education and Treatment of Children, 17*, 113–128.

Chen, L. P., Murad, M. H., Paras, M. L., Colbenson, K. M., Sattler, A. L., Goranson, E. N., et al. (2010). Sexual abuse and lifetime diagnosis of psychiatric disorders: Systematic review and meta-analysis. *Mayo Clinic Proceedings, 85*, 618–629.

Conte, J. R., Wolf, S., & Smith, T. (1989). What sexual offenders tell us about prevention strategies. *Child Abuse & Neglect, 13,* 293–301.

Conte, J. R., Rosen, C., Saperstein, L., & Shermack, R. (1985). An evaluation of a program to prevent the sexual victimization of young children. *Child Abuse & Neglect, 9,* 319–328.

Dancho, K., Thompson, R., & Rhoades, M. (2008). Teaching preschool children to avoid poison hazards. *Journal of Applied Behavior Analysis, 41,* 267–271.

Dube, R., & Herbert, M. (1988). Sexual abuse of children under 12 years of age: A review of 511 cases. *Child Abuse & Neglect, 12,* 321–330.

Dube, S. R., Anda, R. F., Whitfield, C. L., Brown, D. W., Felitti, V. J., Doug, M., et al. (2005). Long-term consequences of childhood sexual abuse by gender of the victim. *American Journal of Preventive Medicine, 28,* 430–438.

Egemo-Helm, K. R., Miltenberger, R. G., Knudson, P., Finstrom, N., Jostad, C., & Johnson, B. (2007). An evaluation of in situ training to teach sexual abuse prevention skills to women with mental retardation. *Behavioral Interventions, 22,* 99–119.

Elliott, M., Browne, K. D., & Kilcoyne, J. (1995). Child sexual abuse prevention: What offenders tell us. *Child Abuse & Neglect, 19,* 579–594.

Finkelhor, D., Asdigian, N., & Dziuba-Leatherman, J. (1995). The effectiveness of victimization prevention instruction: An evaluation of children's responses to actual threats and assaults. *Child Abuse & Neglect, 19,* 141–153.

Finkelhor, D., Hotaling, G., Lewis, I. A., & Smith, C. (1990). Sexual abuse in a national sample of adult men and women: Prevalence, characteristics, and risk factors. *Child Abuse & Neglect, 14,* 19–28.

Fryer, G. E., Krazier, S., & Miyoshi, T. (1987). Measuring actual reduction of risk to child abuse: A new approach. *Child Abuse & Neglect, 11,* 173–179.

Gatheridge, B. J., Miltenberger, R., Huneke, D. F., Satterlund, M. J., Mattern, A. R., Johnson, B. M., et al. (2004). A comparison of two programs to teach firearm injury prevention skills to 6 and 7 year old children. *Pediatrics, 114,* e294–e299.

Gibson, L. E., & Leitenberg, H. (2000). Child sexual abuse prevention programs: Do they decrease the occurrence of child sexual abuse? *Child Abuse & Neglect, 24,* 1115–1125.

Gross, A., Miltenberger, R., Knudson, P., Bosch, A., & Brower-Breitwieser, C. (2007). Preliminary evaluation of a parent training program to prevent gun play. *Journal of Applied Behavior Analysis, 40,* 691–695.

Harvey, P., Forehand, R., Brown, C., & Holmes, T. (1988). The prevention of sexual abuse: Examination of the effectiveness of a program with kindergarten-age children. *Behavior Therapy, 19,* 429–435.

Haseltine, B., & Miltenberger, R. (1990). Teaching self-protection skills to persons with mental retardation. *American Journal on Mental Retardation, 95,* 188–197.

Hazzard, A., Webb, C., Kleemeier, C., Angert, L., & Pohl, J. (1991). Child sexual abuse prevention: Evaluation and one-year follow-up. *Child Abuse & Neglect, 15,* 123–138.

Himle, M., Miltenberger, R., Gatheridge, B., & Flessner, C. (2004). An evaluation of two procedures for training skills to prevent gun play in children. *Pediatrics, 113,* 70–77.

Himle, M. B., Miltenberger, R. G., Flessner, C., & Gatheridge, B. (2004). Teaching safety skills to children to prevent gun play. *Journal of Applied Behavior Analysis, 37,* 1–9.

Johnson, B. M., Miltenberger, R. G., Egemo-Helm, K., Jostad, C. M., Flessner, C., & Gatheridge, B. (2005). Evaluation of behavioral skills training for teaching abduction prevention skills to young children. *Journal of Applied Behavior Analysis, 38,* 67–78.

Johnson, B. M., Miltenberger, R. G., Knudson, P., Egemo-Helm, K., Kelso, P., Jostad, C., et al. (2006). A preliminary evaluation of two behavioral skills training procedures for teaching abduction prevention skills to school children. *Journal of Applied Behavior Analysis, 39,* 25–34.

Jostad, C., Miltenberger, R., Kelso, P., & Knudson, P. (2008). Peer tutoring to prevent gun play: Acquisition, generalization, and maintenance of safety skills. *Journal of Applied Behavior Analysis, 41,* 117–123.

Kelso, P., Miltenberger, R., Waters, M., Egemo-Helm, K., & Bagne, A. (2007). Teaching skills to second and third grade children to prevent gun play: A comparison of procedures. *Education and Treatment of Children, 30*, 29–48.

Kenny, M. C., & Wurtele, S. K. (2010). Children's abilities to recognize a "good" person as a potential perpetrator of childhood sexual abuse. *Child Abuse & Neglect, 34*, 490–495.

Kilpatrick, D. G., Ruggerio, K. J., Acierno, R., Saunders, B. E., Resnick, H. S., & Best, C. L. (2003). Violence and risk of PTSD, major depression, substance abuse/dependence, and comorbidity: Results from the national survey of adolescents. *Journal of Consulting and Clinical Psychology, 71*, 692–700.

Kolko, D. J., Moser, J. T., Litz, J., & Hughes, J. (1987). Promoting awareness and prevention of child sexual victimization using the Red Flag/Green Flag Program: An evaluation with follow-up. *Journal of Family Violence, 2*, 11–35.

Kopp, B., & Miltenberger, R. (2008). Evaluating the validity and social acceptability of child sexual abuse prevention skills measures. *Child & Family Behavior Therapy, 30*, 1–11.

Kopp, B., & Miltenberger, R. (2009). Evaluating the acceptability of four versions of a child sexual abuse prevention program. *Child & Family Behavior Therapy, 31*, 192–202.

Leventhal, J. M., & Conte, J. R. (1987). Programs to prevent sexual abuse: What outcomes should be measured? *Child Abuse & Neglect, 11*, 169–172.

Lumley, V., Miltenberger, R., Long, E., Rapp, J., & Roberts, J. (1998). Evaluation of a sexual abuse prevention program for adults with mental retardation. *Journal of Applied Behavior Analysis, 31*, 91–101.

Miltenberger, R. (2008). Teaching safety skills to children: Prevention of firearm injury as an exemplar of best practice in assessment, training, and generalization of safety skills. *Behavior Analysis in Practice, 1*, 30–36.

Miltenberger, R. G., & Gross, A. (2011). Teaching safety skills to children. In W. Fisher, C. Piazza, & H. Roane (Eds.), *Handbook of applied behavior analysis (pp. 417–432)*. New York, NY: Guilford.

Miltenberger, R. G., Flessner, C. A., Gatheridge, B. J., Johnson, B. M., Satterlund, M. J., & Egemo, K. (2004). Evaluation of behavioral skills training procedures to prevent gun play in children. *Journal of Applied Behavior Analysis, 37*, 513–516.

Miltenberger, R. G., Gatheridge, B. J., Satterlund, M., Egemo-Helm, K., Johnson, B. M., Jostad, C., et al. (2005). Teaching safety skills to children to prevent gun play: An evaluation of in situ training. *Journal of Applied Behavior Analysis, 38*, 395–398.

Miltenberger, R., & Thiesse-Duffy, E. (1988). Evaluation of home-based programs for teaching personal safety skills to children. *Journal of Applied Behavior Analysis, 21*, 81–88.

Miltenberger, R., Fogel, V., Beck, K., Koehler, S., Graves, R., Noah, J., et al. (2012). Examining the efficacy of the Safe Side abduction prevention program and parent conducted in-situation training. Manuscript submitted for publication.

Miltenberger, R., Roberts, J., Ellingson, S., Galensky, T., Rapp, J., Long, E., et al. (1999). Training and generalization of sexual abuse prevention skills for women with mental retardation. *Journal of Applied Behavior Analysis, 32*, 385–388.

Miltenberger, R., Thiesse-Duffy, E., Suda, K., Kozak, C., & Bruellman, J. (1990). Teaching prevention skills to children: The use of multiple measures to evaluate parent versus expert instruction. *Child & Family Behavior Therapy, 12*, 65–87.

Olsen-Woods, L., Miltenberger, R., & Foreman, G. (1998). The effects of correspondence training in an abduction prevention training program. *Child & Family Behavior Therapy, 20*, 15–34.

Poche, C., Brouwer, R., & Swearingen, M. (1981). Teaching self-protection skills to young children. *Journal of Applied Behavior Analysis, 14*, 169–176.

Poche, C., Yoder, P., & Miltenberger, R. (1988). Teaching self-protection to children using television techniques. *Journal of Applied Behavior Analysis, 21*, 253–261.

Roberts, J., & Miltenberger, R. (1999). Emerging issues in the research on child sexual abuse prevention. *Education and Treatment of Children, 22,* 84–102.

Saslawsky, D. A., & Wurtele, S. K. (1986). Educating children about sexual abuse: Implications for pediatric intervention and possible prevention. *Journal of Pediatric Psychology, 11,* 235–245.

Saunders, B. E., Kilpatrick, D. G., Hanson, R. F., Resnick, H. S., & Walker, M. E. (1999). Prevalence, case characteristics, and long-term psychological correlates of child rape among women: A national survey. *Child Maltreatment, 4,* 187–200.

Swan, H. L., Press, A. N., & Briggs, S. L. (1985). Child sexual abuse prevention: Does it work? *Child Welfare, 65,* 395–405.

Tutty, L. M. (1995). The revised children's knowledge of abuse questionnaire: Development of a measure of children's understanding of sexual abuse prevention concepts. *Social Work Research, 19,* 112–120.

Tyler, K. A. (2002). Social and emotional outcomes of childhood sexual abuse: A review of recent research. *Aggression and Violent Behavior, 7,* 567–589.

Wonderlich, S. A., Brewerton, T. D., Jocic, Z., Dansky, B. S., & Abbott, D. W. (1997). Relationship of child sexual abuse and eating disorders. *Journal of the American Academy of Child and Adolescent Psychiatry, 36,* 1107–1115.

Wurtele, S. K. (1990). Teaching personal safety skills to four-year-old children: A behavioral approach. *Behavior Therapy, 21,* 25–32.

Wurtele, S. K. (1993). The role of maintaining telephone contact with parents during the teaching of a personal safety program. *Journal of Child Sexual Abuse, 2,* 65–82.

Wurtele, S. K. (2008). Behavioral approaches to educating young children and their parents about child sexual abuse prevention. *Journal of Behavior Analysis of Offender and Victim Treatment and Prevention, 1,* 52–54.

Wurtele, S. K. (2009). Preventing sexual abuse of children in the twenty-first century: Preparing for challenges and opportunities. *Journal of Child Sexual Abuse, 18,* 1–18.

Wurtele, S. K., Currier, L. O., Gillispie, E. I., & Franklin, C. F. (1991). The efficacy of a parent-implemented program for teaching preschoolers personal safety skills. *Behavior Therapy, 21,* 25–32.

Wurtele, S. K., Gillispie, E. I., Currier, L. L., & Franklin, C. F. (1992). A comparison of teachers vs. parents as instructors of a personal safety program for preschoolers. *Child Abuse & Neglect, 16,* 127–137.

Wurtele, S. K., Kast, L. C., Miller-Perrin, C. L., & Kondrick, P. A. (1989). A comparison of programs for teaching personal safety skills to preschoolers. *Journal of Consulting and Clinical Psychology, 57,* 505–511.

Wurtele, S. K., Marrs, S. R., & Miller-Perrin, C. L. (1987). Practice makes perfect? The role of participant modeling in sexual abuse prevention programs. *Journal of Consulting and Clinical Psychology, 55,* 599–602.

Wurtele, S. K., Saslawsky, D. A., Miller, C. L., Marrs, S. R., & Britcher, J. C. (1986). Teaching personal safety skills for potential prevention of sexual abuse: A comparison of treatments. *Journal of Consulting and Clinical Psychology, 54,* 688–692.

# CHAPTER 18

# Adolescence and Commercial Sexual Exploitation

## Prostituted Girls in the US

**Linda M. Williams**
University of Massachusetts Lowell, Lowell, Massachusetts[1]

## INTRODUCTION

Conflicting images and conceptual frameworks are evoked by the words "prostitution" and "commercial sexual exploitation" when used in relation to children and youth. For adults, it has been suggested that "prostitution" could be reframed as "sex work" (Agustin, 2008), although research suggests that even when prostitution is legalized for adults it involves harm, violence, and coercion that go beyond the average "job" (Farley, 2004a,b; Raymond, 1998; Sullivan, 2005). There are convincing arguments that prostitution legitimizes violence against women (Bristol Feminist Network, n.d.) by contributing to the sexualization of women and girls, and to societal tolerance of sexual violence and exploitation. Child and teen prostitutes are victims of sexual exploitation. While the debate about adult prostitution and its position as "sex work" is not the focus of this chapter, review and discussion of prostituted[2] teens and their commercial

---

[1] Correspondence to: Linda M. Williams, PhD, Professor, Department of Criminal Justice and Criminology, University of Massachusetts Lowell, Lowell, MA 01854. Phone 978-934-4118; fax 978-934-3077; email linda_williams@uml.edu

[2] Discussion of this issue is fraught with language problems. As was the case with the first years of addressing the problem of child sexual abuse in the 1970s and 1980s, understanding of CSE is changing and evolving as we learn more about the victims and offenders. We have learned that the language we use to describe the behaviors is critical and nuances in terms (prostitute vs. prostituted, for example) are critical. With adolescents, we face the difficulty of trying to find language that recognizes the vulnerability and victimization of those who are prostituted, along with acknowledgment of the agency, volition, and desires of the adolescent girl or boy (Williams, 2010). Writing the words "teen involved in prostitution" may suggest to some a willingness or voluntary involvement on the part of the minor. Some prefer the term prostituted teen that makes more clear that the prostitution is at the hands of someone else—the customer, client (or some would call this person the rapist, john, or trick) or the third party exploiter (also called the pimp, panderer, or procurer) who benefits from the acts and takes the money.

*Handbook of Child and Adolescent Sexuality*
DOI: http://dx.doi.org/10.1016/B978-0-12-387759-8.00018-0

© 2013 Elsevier Inc.
All rights reserved.

sexual exploitation (CSE) can provide some grounding for consideration of adult experiences with prostitution.

One might wonder, as CSE is violence, why is a chapter on CSE included in a book on adolescent sexuality? Undoubtedly, CSE impacts adolescent sexual development in ways that have not been thoroughly researched. We also need to learn more about adolescent males and prostitution, both from the point of view of prostituted and prostituting adolescent males as well as boys who pay for sex and participate in the demand for prostitution. Beyond knowledge of the dynamics and consequences of CSE of adolescents there is also a need to challenge arguments that blame the victim, and to clarify the role of the adolescents in CSE. Despite documentation of harm in regard to the prostitution of children, many of the rationalizations offered 30 years ago to deflect attention from the harms and the criminal aspects of intra-familial child sexual abuse are employed in regard to CSE today. Arguments are made that the teen (male or female) "asked for" it, "volunteered," or willingly agreed to it, "enjoyed it" or "seduced" the "client," or that this "john" did not know the teen was under the age of consent. These views serve to defend policies that focus on arrest and control of the prostituted juvenile and release without charges the customers or "johns," who instead could be charged with rape of a minor (Williams & Frederick, 2009). These approaches reflect justifications that rationalize and neutralize the culpability of the person who pays to have sexual intercourse with a child or underage teen (Estes & Weiner, 2001; Flowers, 2001) and blame the victims. Although there has been some important research on CSE, the commercial sexual victimization of youth has been understudied. As was also the case with intra-familial child sexual abuse decades ago, CSE may have escaped attention in large part because of the secrecy of the behaviors, the youth and vulnerability of the victims, and the use of a variety of tactics by the perpetrators (including violence, fear, force, and "grooming") (Williams & Fredrick, 2009). In CSE, the youth is engaged, solicited, or forced to engage in sexual conduct in return for a fee, food, or clothing. Further contributing to the neglect of this crime is the fact that often the children who are prostituted are throwaways, or are poor, minority, runaway, or drug-involved, and garner little sustained public concern or attention because they are not empowered constituencies (Estes & Weiner, 2001).

This chapter will provide background on CSE of female adolescents and its dynamics, and discuss harms to teens while taking the perspective that minors involved in the sex trade or trafficking, whether internationally or domestically, are best viewed as victims and not offenders.[3] United Nations proclamations and recent trafficking legislation around the globe assert that persons under 18 engaged in commercial sex are victims, and that those who are underage cannot be seen as volunteering to be trafficked. There is scant research on adolescent male victims of CSE, and the topic deserves its own chapter. While some of the issues may be the same for male and female victims and this chapter will refer to some data recently collected about CSE males, the focus is on female adolescent victims.

Our social and legal responses to prostituted children and youth in the United States often challenge this assertion that the teens are victims. Although the approach has changed in some states, in many jurisdictions teens who are found to have traded sex for money and who have attained a certain age (for example, 17) can be and often are arrested and charged in criminal courts. Recent research suggests that United States law enforcement personnel are inconsistent in their treatment of prostituted juveniles (Finkelhor & Ormrod, 2004; Halter, 2007). This inconsistency may reflect the conflict between law enforcement-driven criminalization of prostituted youth and other statutes and regulations, including child welfare provisions that define sexual contact by an adult with a 17-year-old as a reportable act of child maltreatment. Indeed, these child welfare agencies would likely place responsibility on the offending adults or on other adults who failed to protect the youth and recognize prostituted juveniles as victims in need of protection. More attention has recently been paid to CSE of youth (Albanese, 2007; Cooper, Estes, Giardino, Kellog, & Vieth, 2005; Curtis et al., 2008; Estes & Weiner, 2001; Friedman, 2005; Gragg, Petta, Bernstein, Eisen, & Quinn, 2007), and the victimization is more likely today to be challenged on the local, national, and international levels in an attempt to reduce the numbers of victimized children, and the manner and severity of the harm inflicted on them. On the other hand, even in the child welfare system, because of their demeanor and behavior, prostituted girls and boys are often held in distain by social service providers and the community in general (Friedman, 2005), and they may be seen as offenders even by those operating outside of the justice system.

---

[3] It is interesting that the term "victim" is also fraught with problems. In a recent governmental document in the United States it was stated: "although the term 'victim' is used throughout this solicitation as the one used by the legal system for the wronged party, applicants should demonstrate their understanding of and respect for the resiliency and perseverance of youth affected by CSEC."

Evidence has been mounting that commercially sexually exploited girls have been repeatedly victimized in a variety of destructive and damaging ways, including: physical (Widom & Kuhns 1996); emotional (Kidd & Krall 2002); sexual abuse (Brannigan & Gibbs Van Brunschot, 1997; Forst, 1994; Simons & Whitbeck, 1991); drug abuse (Inciardi, Pottieger, Forney, Chitwood, & McBride, 1991); and social marginalization (Farrow, Deisher, Brown, Kulig, & Kipke, 1992; Inciardi et al., 1991). This view of the teens as victims and documentation of the negative consequences (Farley, 2004a; Cooper et al., 2005) may be seen by some as directly contradicted by statements adolescent girls may make about the "attractions" associated with prostitution. These teens may assert that they are "doing what they want" or (for girls) that they love their pimp or "daddy." They may assert that they do not view themselves as the victims. While it has been reported that girls are insidiously drawn to "the life" by the deceits and outright lies of those who recruit them, the lures of parties, drugs, or even the simple shelter and food that they may also get as part of the payment barter, these notions that teens are attracted to this "life" not only contribute to the assessment by others that they control their fate (Friedman, 2005), but also to the ambivalence with which they are viewed by the criminal justice system and the community (see for example, Weitzer, 2007). Questions are raised: is prostitution of teens a matter of choice or coercion? Who can consent? Friedman (2005) and many others present evidence that prostituted girls are victims of pimps and johns who exploit them, and that there is usually little individual choice involved. The victim discourse presents evidence that teens usually turn to prostitution as a result of desperation, or due to manipulation by adults (Priebe & Suhr, 2005). As a result, discussion of this topic as part of adolescent sexuality presents challenges. The first challenge is not to permit such discussions to be used to either dogmatically attempt to control adolescent sexuality or to justify adult–teen sexual contact. Second, the scant scientific and mostly exploratory and descriptive research on this topic tells us little about the correlates and long-term consequences of CSE, and reflects little concern for issues of adolescent sexuality. No doubt the challenges of conducting research on matters of child exposure to CSE are many, but such research is needed.

Based on what we know, if we wish to understand more about adolescents' experiences with sexual victimization in general, especially in regard to CSE, and to frame future research questions, it is important to place the experience in a broader social context.

# SOCIAL CONTEXT OF COMMERCIAL SEX AND ADOLESCENCE

## Incidence and Prevalence

Commercial sexual exploitation of children is a crime that has only recently received significant attention in the United States and around the globe. While the US Department of Justice estimates that the number of children (those under the age of 18) currently involved in prostitution, child pornography, and trafficking may be anywhere between 100,000 and 3 million (Friedman, 2005), we find that knowledge of CSE and our public response to the problem is still evolving (Farrell, McDevitt, & Fahy, 2008). There is a growing and compelling literature on domestic sex trafficking of girls in the United States (Clawson & Grace, 2007; Albanese, 2007; Gragg et al., 2007; Lloyd, 2005; Friedman, 2005; Priebe & Suhr, 2005), and some about CSE of girls and boys (Curtis et al., 2008). In addition, we have also begun to hear directly from female survivors of CSE themselves (GEMS, 2008; Lloyd, 2011). To date it has been difficult to get national estimates and descriptions of the breadth, scope, and nature of CSE (Estes & Weiner, 2001; Curtis et al., 2008; Friedman, 2005). Studies of its incidence and prevalence are underway.

While jurisdictions vary on the specific age, the most widely used definitions state that CSE of youth occurs when a person 17 years of age or younger is engaged, solicited, or forced to engage in sexual conduct or performance of sexual acts in return for a fee, food, drugs, shelter, clothing, gifts, or other goods. The sexual conduct may include any direct sexual contact or live, filmed, or photographed display or other performances (e.g., stripping) involving sexual acts or for the sexual gratification of others. Domestically trafficked youth comprise the majority of CSE victims in the US Federal legislation (Trafficking Victims Protection Act – TVPA 2000, revised in 2008), funding, and US Department of Justice supported task force activity continues to bring the domestic sex trafficking of children into focus in the United States although most of that focus has been on CSE of girls. This activity includes attention to traffickers who coerce children and youth to enter the commercial sex "industry" through a variety of recruitment and control mechanisms, and who engage the children in exploitation in strip clubs, street-based prostitution, escort services, and brothels. There is evidence from the field that domestic sex traffickers target vulnerable youth, such as runaway and homeless youth, and it is often reported that for females the average entrant into prostitution in the United States is a 12- to 13-year-old victim of CSE.

While there has been some attempt to count the number of youth victimized by CSE, for numerous reasons reliable estimates for this crime have been elusive. Getting counts from police is not only difficult because of the ways in which the crimes may be classified, but also because much CSE does not come to the attention of the police. While studies have found that about 25% of homeless youth have exchanged sex for money, food, or a place to stay (Tyler, Whitbeck, Hoyt, & Cauce, 2004), many agencies (such as shelters for homeless youth, drop-in centers for runaways, and drug abuse treatment programs) do not seek to identify CSE victims among those youth they encounter. In some cases this is because they are not knowledgeable about the potential risk for CSE among the youth they serve or in their geographic location, they have limited resources to address this issue in their community, or they do not ask because they do not want to have to report CSE to the authorities against the wishes of the youth they are attempting to serve. In addition, the victims of CSE are often unwilling or reluctant to disclose this experience. We have inadequate data about whether CSE is more common in some areas of the United States, if patterns differ by race, ethnicity, or gender, and how to properly count the incidence and prevalence for youth who are likely to be highly transient and move around the country (Williams & Frederick, 2009).

In 2008, using an application of respondent driven sampling (RDS) statistical techniques, Curtis & colleagues (2008) estimated that there were 3,946 CSEC victims in New York City. This number does not include those youth that could not be referred via RDS methods (e.g., girls trafficked into the country, or who are tightly controlled by adults indoors or who do not socialize with other youth). Curtis and colleagues now have been funded to develop estimates of the number of victims nationwide.

In their New York City sample of 249 there were 48% female, 45% male, and 8% transgender youth; and the average age of entry into CSE was 15 years of age. In this New York City sample, African American and mixed race youth comprised 48% of the youth, and just over a quarter were white (24%) or Hispanic (23%). While over one-half of the youth reported that they were from New York City (56%), many were from other jurisdictions, with only 8% reporting that they were born outside of the United States. Many of the youth were currently homeless, with 32% characterizing their housing situation as living in the street. (Curtis et al., 2008, p. 3).

Thus, the best evidence we have is that where CSE is most common is among youth living in extreme poverty, often without significant family support and who find themselves living "life on the streets" as a homeless, runaway, or thrown away youth. It is in these situations that vulnerability to CSE increases (Tyler et al., 2004).

## Framing the Issue Among Homeless or Runaway Teens

The number of the homeless youth under the age of 18 who lack parental, foster, or institutional care is difficult to assess. The best governmental statistics suggest that in the United States there are from 1.6 to 2.5 million homeless and runaway youth under the age of 18. Recent research mapping and documenting the lives of homeless youth (Williams & Frederick, 2009), and communications with colleagues engaged in similar research in other nations, suggest a need to frame our understanding of these youth as "internal migrants"—youth who live at the margins of the jurisdictions and daily cross boundaries that govern much of the way services in the United States are organized. As such, they are displaced persons who have traveled outside their home communities, and who find themselves stigmatized, disenfranchised, and unwelcome in their current locations.

Many adolescent female victims of CSE report prior experiences of sexual victimization by family members, acquaintances, peers, and strangers (Williams & Frederick, 2009). Many have experienced physical violence and also the numbing of feelings about it. In recent research on pathways to CSE, when the teens talked about important events in their lives that shaped them into who they are today, they often mentioned experiences with family violence, including: a long history of physical, sexual, and emotional abuse; a history of attempting to protect siblings from abuse; and witnessing violence between adults.

While some had serial foster care placements, the low status of the youth and their weak voice in our social system often leave them in dire straits. For girls, their invisibility, poverty, cold, hunger, and duress are taken advantage of by the pimps.

Many of the homeless teens and adolescents involved in CSE have fled family conflict, abuse, and community violence, and all face serious economic problems and residential instability. They have found themselves on the streets, couch surfing, or in inadequate shelters hampered by social policies and social inequalities that often provide them little safe recourse and keep them "hidden in plain sight." They may adopt "survival strategies" such as theft, trading sex for food or a place to stay, involvement in CSE, and/or other coping mechanisms such as the use of drugs and alcohol. The multiple oppressions of gender, race, class, and commoditization of sex affect their lives dramatically and, although in some places in the United

States there have been notable advances in services, there is a profoundly inadequate system response in health services, educational services, housing, safety, and security, as well as an absence of knowledge about or concern for homeless youth, their victimization, or their sexuality. While these youth confront issues of STDs/HIV, pregnancy, criminal victimization, and mental health problems, the social and community response is often focused on behavioral control, and ignores the youths' strengths, sexuality, and capabilities. These problems of unhelpful responses are compounded when youth represent minority racial or ethnic groups, or are gay, lesbian, or transsexual.

While adolescence is typically a broad developmental period encompassing many stages of growth, among homeless youth age and stage demarcations are more fluid. Outside of the socially and developmentally structured United States educational system, homeless or runaway youth aged 14 to 24 often have similar life experiences and may associate freely, together seeking shelter, sustenance, services, and community. Their associations and connections challenge social, community, and jurisdictional responses and our notions of adolescent sexuality. Beginning to address these issues requires innovative social science research, with a focus on adolescent health and sexuality and provisions for incorporating the perspectives of the youth into the study questions, design, data collection, and interpretation of findings.

## HOW YOUTH GET INVOLVED IN CSE
### Abandonment and Survival

When we endeavor to discuss the sexuality and functioning of youth who live in the streets, we have to start with an understanding of their day-to-day lives and the level of hardship they encounter. In the author's research on Pathways to Commercial Sexual Exploitation (Williams & Frederick, 2009), a youth told the interviewer:

> *Well I had blankets but they threw 'em away yesterday.... When I went to squat at the park people cleaned everything up ... threw it all away.*
> *...you know, food is like the only really necessity.... I usually like, eat [out] of the garbage. I just think it's a lot easier. It's a lot cleaner than people think it is. ... a lot of the time like if people throw away leftovers, you know, it's still in that box, you know. ... I wouldn't, you know, just like ... reach into the bottom of the trash can, [where] gunk builds up and like, you know, take something off there but ...*
> *[I usually sleep] by the [she mentions the doorway of a trendy youth-oriented national chain] ... you don't get bothered.*
> *Sometimes I would just like sleep in a stairwell or like, sit in one until um, a library opened and then I could go read and sleep in the library.*

Those youth who became victims of CSE have frequently had to survive life on the streets and spend time searching for a safe place to stay, food, and positive supports.

*I mean, in my case survival is trying to find a place to sleep every night ... or trying to find, make sure that I'm, you know, that I'm not going hungry.*

They are aware of the grim realities of their lives and social position:

*I'm at the, I'm at the bottom, you know? ... The only place I could really go is up.*

The adjustments youth make when they have no place to stay include walking miles each day and sleeping in doorways, eating from the trash, and finding drop-in centers where they can do laundry. After weeks of sleeping in train stations, one young woman spoke of her entry into prostitution as a teen:

*Well, um, I got involved with a friend who had been talking to me about it, and .... said you can make enough money, you know, to support yourself for a while. He said that he would be the person that would help me out, help me manage my money and everything like that. So I mean it was basically a pimp ... you know what I mean? (Williams & Frederick, 2009).*

In this environment it is of little surprise that children who are impoverished, alone and find no stable place to stay are victimized by CSE. While some accounts of entrance into the life of being prostituted, of CSE, reflect extreme force, violence, and threats, many young women interviewed (Williams & Frederick, 2009) describe a gradual introduction to "the life." Runaways (or children who were pushed out or moved out of their families) with no place to stay may be given shelter by people who eventually turn them out on the streets or advertise them online to exchange sex for money. While in some cases the prostitution of the vulnerable youth occurs nearly overnight, for some a gradual process of grooming takes place. For example, one former teen runaway said:

*I spent the night over their house and then they took me to this other man's house and then that's when .. um .. we was over there and I had sex with that man and then he let me stay in his house for the rest of three weeks or whatever ... he was really nice .. he .. he didn't ask me for nothin' else or whatever. He was just like whatever I want to do I can do it and then that was it. (Williams & Frederick, 2009).*

In a common scenario, after a short time being "sheltered" by an older male, the demand for sex becomes more frequent and more uncomfortable for the teen, then she is asked and eventually is required to have sex with others.

For teens on the street, survival is an everyday task, the *key element* of daily life. The dangers of violence, lack of shelter, and lack of nutritious food are basic and require daily work. Notably, at times survival may involve balancing competing risks. The streets are unsafe, so where does a teen who has either run away or been pushed out of his or her home stay? And survival can lead to more risks, and to a vulnerability to CSE such as the survival strategy (staying with seemingly "nice" strangers) who may take her to a more safe and secure place away from knife fights at a shelter or exposure to the elements she would encounter if she stays on the street. But this strategy may lead to being forced into prostitution. The concept of "survival-focused coping" (Goodman, Smyth, Borges, & Singer, 2009) applies to the experiences of these young women. They know that the basics they need for safety and survival are uncertain and, as a result, clearly devote a significant portion of their emotional, cognitive, and social resources to navigating daily life. But, as Goodman and her colleagues point out in their application of the notion of survival-based coping to impoverished victims of intimate partner violence, the teens living on the streets also know that the fallout of negative decisions or mistakes can be catastrophic. For example as one victim stated:

> I mean when you get the money it feels good ... but at the point in time when you're jumpin' in and out of cars, sleepin' with this guy and then goin' to sleep with that guy you feel nasty ... (Williams & Frederick, 2009).

## Gender Relations

A major contributor to entry into CSE appears to be perceptions about male–female relationships that place females in a role of passive acceptance of male dominance, as well as reflect an extreme focus on the physical attributes of the male, his desirability to other females, his possessions, his older age, and the flattering nature of his attention and control. This focus is revealed by Williams & Frederick (2009), who report that a 16-year-old with a family history characterized by absent, incarcerated, drug abusing, and mentally ill adults was asked: "And how did you, how did you meet him?" The teen replied:

> Uh, it was about 12 o'clock at night. I'm .. walking across like a big parking lot to my house ... He pulls up/no, he blows the horn from across the street. "Bla, bla, bla". I'm like, "who's that?" And just keep on goin'. I look back and I see him pulling into the parking lot where I'm walking and I say "oh." He pulls up in this big, cute little truck, or whatever. He's cute so I'm like, "Oh what's goin' on?" I'm on the phone.

*I said, "I'm going to call you back." So he's in the car [and says], "Yo ma, you're real cute." So I'm like, "How ya doin?" You know, he, he's a tad bit older than me but he's cute. <How old?> He's got a car. I'm not sure, but he's like 20, late twenties or early thirties but he's older than me. <Okay> So I'm like "oh he's cute, he's got a car." So, the first thing I come up and say "you got a wife?" Big old truck, fancy truck, "You got a wife?"... He said, "No, I don't got no wife, you know." So I'm like, oh, he's real cute, you know? And so I got in the car. (Williams & Frederick, 2009).*

A recurrent theme for girls victimized by CSE is the way in which the attention of a desirable older male overwhelmed all caution they might have otherwise experienced. While their family lives may have placed them at risk for the approaches of such men, the culturally supported appeal of a cool, cute, male when combined with neglect or abuse by family makes his approach likely to be successful in pulling her into "the life." Some young women, even after they were exploited by such a man in the past, maintained a conviction that the cute and cool older guys are the ones you want to attract and perhaps get to be "real" with. If such a man sought her attention or wished to have sexual relations, in many instances the young girls would respond positively.

*Um, like the strangest thing happened ... I'm in the car and like he wanted somethin' but that's just all dudes. So I wasn't really, you know, surprised about that one. He wanted something from me and I was like, "no, no, no!" ... He wanted to have sex ... And it was the first time with him and I'm like, "wow." You know.... I wanted to do it. Because, I don't know, I guess I liked him. And he was real cute so, I wanted to do it.*

Some of the young women learned from past experiences: one who had been hurt before and had "only" one prior CSE incident told the interviewer:

*and people always say, "A boy will tell you anything," and now I see that it's true. Mmm .. Yes, don't believe nothing boys say.*

For other young women, the seduction by the pimp was enabled by notions of his behavior as part of a repertoire of appropriate male–female relationships:

*He came to pick me up. And the weirdest thing is, when he got there / just listen to everything how I'm saying it. When he got there, there was a lady in the car, in the front seat ... She was just real pretty, little heels, nice little dress, skirt all the way up here to half of her legs. She was looking real pretty and icy, diamonds and everything. Okay. He told her to get in the back and let me sit in the front. And I'm like, "wow." .... So she gets in the back. (Williams & Frederick, 2009).*

In a short time, however, for some teens, the attentions of an older, cute, possessive male turn to coercion into prostitution.

A cultural and societal frame surrounds the CSE of girls in the United States and contributes to this problem. The methods used by pimps and others to control and exploit female adolescents exist in a context of a larger culture that normalizes the "pimp" and "ho" terminology and roles. In the United States, for example, there is a market for baby clothing that displays the word "pimp" on a toddler's blue shirt and "ho" on a pink shirt. Recently stores were found to stock panties for pre-adolescent girls with the phrase written on the front "who needs credit cards?" The notion of a child as a "ho" and other cultural messages that girls receive in music and the media normalizes the propositions made by pimps.

On the demand side of prostitution of teens, the "john" and the societal response to individuals who pay a female adolescent for sex is an important element of CSE. Prostituting adolescent girls is a booming commercial enterprise with great demand. That these perpetrators and rapists are released, or fined, or sent to school so they can have their records expunged reinforces the message to victimized girls that what happened to them (the CSE) is not a big deal.

## Force and Control by the Exploiters

Exploitation and control are a major aspect of CSE, although there may be some in the community who still would suggest that this life is the "choice" of teens rather than a survival strategy. The reality is that CSE involves adults having sex with children and teens in exchange for money or goods. For those girls "in the life" it often involves, and usually could not continue without, a third-party exploiter—the "pimp" or "daddy." This person, usually a male, procures the girls for the "customer-exploiter-john" and benefits from the exchange. The primary feature of CSE is the status of the exploited person as a child with whom sexual acts occur through coercion, manipulation, grooming, or force.

In addition to the power and authority that comes with the older age of the pimp (in relation to the victim), the narratives of the teens interviewed for the Pathways Study reveal extensive evidence of force and violence. Interestingly, the violence may not be used to force the teen into "the life," but may be more commonly relied upon to keep her there, to make her stay. Extreme violence by a pimp in some cases may have the impact of leading to teens' exiting "the life;" however, violence directed at others but executed before an audience of other CSE victims may be used by pimps to keep these victims in "the life." Accounts of violence reported by Williams & Frederick (2009) were often about violence perpetrated by a pimp against another female.

> *I mean sometimes you get some pimps that are nice but then you get other pimps, like the pimp ... He whooped this girl's ass right in front of me.*
> *I've seen people get shot in the head in front of me over it. ... I've seen girls get shot ... And I was just like "what am I gonna do?" I had nobody so that's the only thing I knew how to do to make good money.*
> *And when you come out your mouth wrong for your daddy you get slapped. Um, I don't remember what she said but she said somethin' and ... he picked her up by her ponytail off her feet and it was just like, pow!, slapped the s___ out of her.*
> *He had other friends that were pimps. And I seen them do some things to some of the girls that work for them. ... Beat 'em. Um, just embarrassing, like humiliating things in public. Slap 'em in public ... stripped their clothes off and throw 'em out if they didn't have their money.*
> *... she [another young girl who was controlled by the same pimp] was in the tub and I went in the bathroom; ... She was bleeding from her eyes ... she was bleeding from her lips. She was bleeding from her nose. She had scratches on her neck.*

## Psychological Manipulation and Isolation

It is likely that the psychological manipulation the pimp employs is the most common tool he uses to bring a teen into "the life" and keep her there. We have heard how pimps "romance" teens, starting off as a "boyfriend" who showers her with gifts and attention. This works, especially with young women who have received little from their families or foster families (Williams & Frederick, 2009).

> *He treated me nice. Spent a thousand dollars on me. Got my nails done, my eyebrows arched. My hair, I had weaves. He just spent a whole lot of money on me. And I felt like a queen. Everything I needed he'd get it for me.*
> *I felt like a Queen.... I never felt like a queen before.*
> *I went shopping all the time ... but it was on his terms, when he wanted to go.*

Once the child was in "the life" and experienced its traumatic consequences, the pimp appeared to know exactly when to reel her back in:

> *when you're jumpin' in and out of cars, sleepin' with this guy and then goin'... to sleep with that guy, you feel nasty ... You feel like ... like you're not wanted ... and that's when the pimp comes in to make you feel like you're wanted. ... You know what I mean?*

But pimps also used more than affection and attention to keep the teen trapped in "the life." They appear to be masters of psychological manipulation.

> He would always just remind me, "you have nowhere else to go, if you go back home you're gonna go to jail. I take care of you, ain't nobody else gonna take care of you like that."

## Sexual and Physical Violence

In CSE, sexual victimization is continuous and on-going, not a single and solitary, discrete event. Hundreds of men have sexual intercourse, oral sexual penetration, or anal penetration with an adolescent victim in the course of a few weeks. The teens also are sexually victimized by the pimps (directly through rape by the pimp and also through the CSE they purvey), and they are sexually victimized by the "clients" who pay or otherwise arrange for sex acts over which the teen has little control. The victims describe rapes, beatings with objects such as baseball bats and cords, being stabbed, shot, burned and tied up, and also spoke about becoming numbed to the pain (Williams & Frederick, 2009):

> I got in the car. I charged him $200 … We do what we had to do … he was driving down this dirt road and … he pulled out a knife and he grabbed me by my hair and [during a rape] held the knife to my throat … he told me to get out of the car and wait and … I was standing there for like two seconds … And I ran like a bat out of hell. I ended up cutting most of my toe off that day … I was running so fast I didn't feel it.
> Cause I could have been dead … like I don't know … like with different people and then … like I could have died. … I was like gettin' into cars and they could have killed me and stuff.

## RESEARCH ON COMMON FEATURES OF COMMERCIAL SEXUAL EXPLOITATION

As Albanese (2007) reported, there are common features of CSE that include minors being exploited for monetary gain and the sexual gratification of the exploiters and their clients, the constant seeking of new "recruits," false promises of a "better life" as a central recruitment tool, and the fact that, once exploited, children are often threatened or assaulted to ensure obedience and prevent escape. Indeed, according to those who work with victims of CSE and researchers who have investigated this problem, recruitment and sexual exploitation primarily is directed at runaway, homeless, and transient or unemployed youth who may trade sex as a means of survival, or who are vulnerable to adults who manipulate them for profit (Tyler et al., 2004).

In the study by Curtis and colleagues in New York City, many girls, boys, and transgender youth reported their friends were responsible for their entry into CSE (46%, 44%, and 68%, respectively), although some of these "friends" were acting as surrogate recruiters for pimps (Curtis et al., 2008, p. 3). Whether "pimp-involved" or not, exploitation and control are a major aspect of CSE, although there may be some who still would suggest that this life is a "choice" of teens rather than a survival strategy. The reality is that CSE involves adults (mostly men) having sex with children and teens in exchange for money or goods.

## Failure of Care Systems and CSE

Coy (2008) examined young women's life-story narratives on routes from foster care to prostitution in the United Kingdom, and demonstrated the psychosocial legacies of their care experiences—how they defined themselves and placed themselves in the world. These were instrumental in their entry into selling sex. According to Coy, research has also uncovered a correlation between boys in and leaving local authority care, and their vulnerability to sexually exploitative environments and selling sex (Gibson, 1995; Davies, 1998).

While comparable studies are not available on United States populations, in the United Kingdom and elsewhere around the globe one finds that many of the women who are prostituted have been in the foster care system. Moss & King (2001) and O'Neill & Campbell (2002) found that 39% and 51% of prostituted females had been in foster care. Estes & Weiner (2001) identified youth in foster care as being at high risk for CSE.

While the focus of existing explanations of young women's involvement in commercial sex is on grooming and coercion, according to Coy (2008) this denies not only the complex ways in which some young women exercise their own agency (see also Williams, 2010), but also neglects the role of peer introduction and association (Curtis et al. 2008). In Coy's research women reflected that the failure of the care system to meet their wider needs also precipitated their involvement in prostitution—that if they had not come to feel that prostitution fitted with their sense of self and relationship with the body, they would not have considered selling sex as a means of generating income. Coy argues that experiences in foster care, along with the females' personal histories (of maltreatment and abuse), created what she has labeled "psychosexual vulnerabilities" and that the multiple placements that characterized life in foster care instilled in the girls a feeling of insecurity. Coy argues that young women without a web of relationships in their lives felt that they were invisible, and described how this was reinforced with each move and placement breakdown. Based on their narratives, Coy describes their "troubled sense of ownership of their bodies" that came from how they were treated by others. Others used them for violence and sexual release, leaving them with little sense of clear ownership or a feeling of bodily integrity. Indeed, the women Coy interviewed expressed feelings of hostility towards their bodies as a result of physical and sexual abuse, and described developing a range of dissociative mechanisms. In addition, the young women were acutely aware of their social alienation. Similarly Williams & Frederick (2009) found youth reflected acute awareness of their social status and the extreme challenges before them. More research is needed to develop a better understanding of the psychosexual vulnerability described by Coy, and to design and test strategies for ameliorating these consequences.

## COMMUNITY RESPONSE

Children and youth exposed to the cumulative destructive factors of child maltreatment and CSE have been found to have many and deep harms and coincident needs. Both the anecdotal and, increasingly, the more systematic or empirically-based profiles of these prostituted teens (Curtis et al., 2008; Cooper et al., 2005; Friedman 2005; Gragg et al., 2007) show patterns of involvement in multiple service-based systems (children and youth or child protective services, mental/behavioral health, juvenile/criminal justice, and physical health) because of their multiple, cumulative, and long-lasting needs. The best evidence we have to date is that, with a few notable exceptions, these agency involvements are usually not tailored to the needs of CSE youth, and are usually short-lived, uncoordinated, and unsupported by professional best practices, whether expert- or evidence-based models (Clawson & Grace, 2007; Estes & Weiner, 2001).

Substantial gaps exist in both the conceptual reach and the range of services provided to at-risk female adolescents, and to CSE youth and their families by government and nongovernmental organizations (Estes & Weiner, 2001). Few governmental or nongovernmental organizations have begun to confront the policy and service implications of CSE in even the simplest terms. Despite increased attention to this issue by federal authorities, few local jurisdictions have defined what is meant by CSE, and fewer still have integrated their definitions into formal policies and procedures.

In order to advance efforts to respond to the needs of victims of CSE, a paradigm shift is needed.

There is a significant gap in services to victims of CSE, and a lack of coordination and collaboration between the complex of local, county, and state law enforcement, human service, and other agencies serving children and youth. Recovery from prostitution is multifaceted and complicated, and as such must include more than one service provider (MacInnes, 1998). Effective programs engage multidisciplinary allies in order to develop efficacious partnerships on behalf of these victims (NCMEC, 2002).

To escape CSE, teens need a safe place to stay, with nutritious food and services that respect their "survivor" status and foster resilience. But often there are no services that meet their needs, and teens may see the streets as less harmful and more likely to help them "survive" than the programs offered in their communities. Teens may be understandably reluctant to turn themselves over to adults, especially when they have found so many adults they have encountered to be untrustworthy (Williams, 2010).

Older teens need places to stay where they may be able to maintain some (appropriate) levels of autonomy and be empowered to make the situation work. Williams & Frederick's (2009) and Coy's (2008) interviews with prostituted females reveal a long history of highly destructive families fraught with violence and dysfunction. Many of the teens have been in numerous foster care settings, or have lived on the streets or with no permanent home for months and even years. They often have little trust in the child welfare systems that they have encountered in the past. Their experiences, their psychosexual vulnerabilities, along with their survival-based coping skills, suggest a need for the development of meaningful partnerships between youth and skilled social service providers and systems of care. Without such partnerships that provide the youth with pathways to achieve freedom from the life of prostitution and the control of the pimp, and without some meaningful control over their lives (including in many cases freedom from their families) (Bittle, 2002), there is little likelihood of success. Service providers need to understand that, while victimization via CSE is damaging, for some throwaway youth it can be part of their survival-focused coping/micro-control (Goodman et al., 2009).

Implementing an approach that would meet the needs of prostituted teens requires a shift in the way we understand social control of youth, and a major cognitive shift in how we view the relationship between the states, teens, and their families. The narratives of teens who have been prostituted underscore the urgency of this need, along with the complexity of making this policy change, and putting the appropriate empowering and psychotherapeutic supports in place.

In general, Williams (2009) observed that, while the community can muster concern for pre-pubescent sexually abused children, this concerned response is less often forthcoming when the victims are adolescents. Perhaps this is because of the challenges of dealing with adolescents who have begun to more clearly form their own identities and desires and because, when compared with younger children, they have a greater level of integration into the community. This makes societal responses necessarily more complex, and requires the involvement and coordination of more individuals, community groups, and institutions. Seldom has the child sexual abuse literature addressed these special issues of interventions with adolescents (Williams, 2009).

Based on findings from the Pathways Study (Williams, 2008, 2009), the inability to meet the needs of these youth can be attributed, in part, to failure to develop ways to reach, build, and maintain connections with and support for youth on the streets; lack of coordination of, and training for, services across multiple jurisdictions; reluctance to provide means by which youth can be free of destructive families; and failure to provide appropriate interventions for those with complex trauma.

## REFERENCES

Agustin, L. M. (2008). *Sex at the margins: Migration, labour markets and the rescue industry.* London, UK: Zed Books.

Albanese, J. (2007). *Commercial sexual exploitation of children: What do we know and what do we do about it?* Washington, DC: National Institute of Justice.

Bittle, S. (2002). When protection is punishment: Neo-liberalism and secure care approaches to youth prostitution. *Canadian Journal of Criminology, 44,* 317–350.

Brannigan, A., & Gibbs Van Brunschot, E. (1997). Youthful prostitution and child sexual trauma. *International Journal of Law and Psychiatry, 20,* 337–354.

Bristol Feminist network (n.d.). Retrieved 2.1.12. <http://www.bristolfeministnetwork.com/uploads/6/1/7/7/9/617942/bfn_position_paper_the_sex_industry.pdf>.

Clawson, H., & Grace, L. G. (2007). *Finding a path to recovery: Residential facilities for minor victims of domestic sex trafficking.* Washington, DC: U.S. Department of Health and Human Services.

Cooper, S. W., Estes, R. J., Giardino, A. P., Kellog, N. D., & Vieth, V. I. (Eds.). (2005). *Medical, legal, and social science aspects of child sexual exploitation: A comprehensive review of pornography, prostitution, and internet crimes, vols. 1 and 2.* Saint Louis, MI: G.W. Medical Publishing, Inc.

Coy, M. (2008). Young women, local authority, care and selling sex. *British Journal of Social Work, 38*(7), 1408–1424.

Curtis, R., Terry, K., Dank, M., Dombrowski, K., Khan, B., Muslim, A., et al. (2008). *The commercial sexual exploitation of children in New York City.* New York, NY: Center for

Court Innovation and John Jay College of Criminal Justice. [Report to the national institute of justice].
Davies, N. (1998). *Dark heart: The truth about hidden Britain.* London, UK: Virago.
Estes, R. J., & Weiner, N. A. (2001). *The commercial sexual exploitation of children in the U.S., Canada, and Mexico.* Philadelphia, PA: University of Pennsylvania, Center for the Study of Youth Policy.
Farley, M. (2004a). Prostitution is sexual violence. *Psychiatric Times, Special Edition,* 7–10.
Farley, M. (2004b). "Bad for the body, bad for the heart:" Prostitution harms women even if legalized or decriminalized. *Violence Against Women, 10*(10), 1087–1125.
Farrell, A., McDevitt, J., & Fahy, S. (2008). *Understanding and improving law enforcement responses to human trafficking.* Northeastern University. [Final report submitted to National Institute of Justice, US Department of Justice].
Farrow, J. A., Deisher, R. W., Brown, R., Kulig, J. W., & Kipke, M. D. (1992). Health and health needs of homeless and runaway youth. *Journal of Adolescent Health, 13,* 717–726.
Finkelhor, D., & Ormrod, R. (2004). Prostitution of juveniles: Patterns from NIBRS office of juvenile justice and delinquency prevention. *U.S. Department of Justice* [(June) 12 pages].
Flowers, R. B. (2001). *Runaway kids and teenage prostitution.* Westport, CT: Greenwood Press.
Forst, M. L. (1994). Sexual risk profiles of delinquents and homeless youths. *Journal of Community Health, 19,* 101–114.
Friedman, S. (2005). *Who is there to help us: How the system fails sexually exploited girls in the United States.* New York, NY: EPCAT-USA, Inc.
GEMS (Girls Educations and Mentoring Service). (2008). *The GEMS art book: Breaking the silence.* New York, NY: GEMS.
Gibson, B. (1995). *Male order: Life stories from boys who sell sex.* London, UK: Cassell.
Goodman, L. A., Smyth, K. F., Borges, A. M., & Singer, R. (2009). When crises collide: How intimate partner violence and poverty intersect to shape women's mental health and coping. *Trauma, Violence and Abuse: Special Issue on the Mental Health Implications of Violence Against Women, 10*(4), 306–329.
Gragg, F., Petta, I., Bernstein, H., Eisen, K., & Quinn, L. (2007). *New York prevalence study of commercially sexually exploited children final report.* Rockville, MD: WESTAT.
Halter, S.. (2007), Youth engaging in prostitution: The social construction of the child sexual abuse victim by law enforcement. Paper presented at the annual meeting of the american society of criminology. Atlanta, GA: 14–17 November 2007.
Inciardi, J. A., Pottieger, A. E., Forney, M., Chitwood, D., & McBride, D. (1991). Prostitution, IV drug use, and sex-for-crack exchanges among serious delinquents: Risks for HIV infection. *Criminology, 29,* 221–235.
Kidd, S., & Krall, M. J. (2002). Suicide and prostitution among street youth: A qualitative analysis. *Adolescence, 37,* 411–430.
Lloyd, R. (2005). Acceptable victims? Sexually exploited youth in the U.S. *Encounter: Education for Meaning and Social Justice, 18,* 3.
Lloyd, R. (2011). *Girls like us: Fighting for a world where girls are not for sale, an activist finds her calling and heals herself.* New York, NY: Harper.
MacInnes, R. (1998). *Children in the game.* Calgary, AB: Street Teams.
Moss, J., & King, S. (2001). *Prostitution: How women sleep rough.* Stoke-on-Trent, UK: Potteries Housing Association.
NCMEC, (2002). *Female juvenile prostitution: Problem and response.* Alexandria, VA: National Center for Missing and Exploited Children.
O'Neill, M., & Campbell, R. (2002). Working together to create change: Walsall prostitution consultation research. *Walsall: Staffordshire University/Liverpool Hope University/Walsall Health Authority*
Priebe, A., & Suhr, C. (2005). *Hidden in plain view: The commercial sexual exploitation of girls in Atlanta.* Atlanta, GA: The Atlanta Women's Agenda. *[September].*

Raymond, J. (1998). Prostitution as violence against women: NGO stonewalling in Beijing and elsewhere. *Women's Studies International Forum, 21*, 1–9.

Simons, R. L., & Whitbeck, L. B. (1991). Sexual abuse as a precursor to prostitution and victimization among adolescent and adult homeless women. *Journal of Family Issues, 12*, 361–379.

Sullivan, M. (2005). *What happens when prostitution becomes work?* Amherst, MA: Coalition Against Trafficking in Women.

Tyler, K. A., Whitbeck, L. B., Hoyt, D. R., & Cauce, A. M. (2004). Risk factors for sexual victimization among male and female homeless and runaway youth. *Journal of Interpersonal Violence, 19*, 503–520.

Weitzer, R. (2007). The social construction of sex trafficking: Ideology and institutionalization of a moral crusade. *Politics and Society, 3*, 447–475.

Williams, L. M. (2008). *Terror and trauma for homeless and prostituted street youth: How can mental health and societal response be improved?* Paper presented at the annual meeting of the International Society for Traumatic Stress. Chicago, IL.

Williams, L. M. (2009). Provide justice for prostituted teens: Stop arresting and prosecuting girls. In Natasha A. Frost, Joshua D. Freilich, & Todd R. Clear (Eds.), *Contemporary issues in criminal justice policy: Policy proposals from the American Society of Criminology conference* (pp. 227–306). Belmont, CA: Cengage/Wadsworth.

Williams, L. M., & Frederick, M. E. (2009). *Pathways into and out of commercial sexual victimization of children: Understanding and responding to sexually exploited teens.* Lowell, MA: University of Massachusetts Lowell.

Williams, L. M. (2010). Harm and resilience among prostituted teens: Broadening our understanding of victimization and survival. *Social Policy and Society, 9*(2), 243–254.

Widom, C. S., & Kuhns, J. B. (1996). Childhood victimization and subsequent risk for promiscuity, prostitution, and teenage pregnancy: A prospective study. *American Journal of Public Health, 86*, 1607–1612.

# CHAPTER 19

# Legal Responses to Adolescent Victims of Sexual Violence

**Roger J.R. Levesque**
Indiana University, Bloomington, Indiana[1]

The legal machinery addressing sexual violence against adolescents is nothing short of massive, and massively complex. It involves the criminal justice system and child welfare system, as well as numerous other systems regulated by special legal rules to address sexual victimization, such as laws relating to medical, health, and educational institutions (see Levesque, 2011). Indeed, no major social institution is immune from special rules relating to the protection of adolescent victims from sexual violence. A fundamental reason for these special protections is that the legal system pervasively views juveniles as peculiarly vulnerable to sexual violence. Juveniles are perceived as so inherently vulnerable that some criteria for sexual offences use their age as a proxy for violence. For example, even when juveniles engage in what could be deemed as voluntary sexual activity, the legal system may define those actions as inherently abusive through statutory rape and other laws that create strict liability offenses for groups of individuals who would engage in sexual activity with juveniles (Levesque, 2008). The strong prohibitions against engaging in sexual activity with minors, and the existence of multiple systems that do respond to violence against minors, contribute to the perception that our legal system moves aggressively to ensure adolescent victims' rights, and punish severely those who offend against them. Yet, the reality is that neither is likely to happen in the vast majority of cases involving sexual violence against adolescents.

The legal system's general failure to move aggressively against those who victimize adolescents generally derives from two sources: the nature of offenses against minors; and the nature of our legal system's responses

[1] Correspondence to: Roger J.R. Levesque, JD, PhD, Chair and Professor of Criminal Justice, 302 Sycamore Hall, Indiana University, Bloomington, IN 47405. Phone 812 856 1210 or 812 855 9325; fax 812 855 5522; email rlevesqu@indiana.edu

to violence against minors. In terms of the nature of the offenses, much of the sexual violence against minors is perpetrated by other minors, and family members perpetrate much of the sexual offenses against those who are very young (Levesque, 1999, 2000a). The nature of those relationships hampers efforts to respond to victimization, including even whether reports are made to law enforcement. Similarly, even when violence is perpetrated by adults who are strangers to victims, the nature of the violence hampers disclosure. Research repeatedly reveals that few adolescents disclose their sexual victimization to professionals, and even fewer report to authorities (see e.g., Priebe & Svedin, 2008). In terms of the legal system's overall responses to the victimization of minors, difficulties arise from the extent to which our legal system remains fragmented and relies on multiple response systems (controlled by different legal rules) that can vary from one state to the next, and even from one community to the next (Levesque, 2011). Further complicating matters is our legal system's pervasive concern with the rights of offenders rather than the rights of victims, so much so that there is no general jurisprudence of victim's rights (Levesque, 2008). Although the legal system does seek to offer extra protections to children involved in legal proceedings (such as when or how they might provide testimony), those types of protections do not necessarily transfer well to adolescent victims, and those protections may not be relevant to the vast majority of victims because their cases never involve formal legal proceedings (Levesque, 2002). In many ways, then, the legal machinery dedicated to assisting victimized adolescents certainly has an important role to play in addressing sexual violence against adolescents, but that machinery is subject to considerable practical and legal challenges that strain systems, hamper their overall effectiveness, and may not serve adolescents as well as expected.

This chapter explores some of the key legal systems' responses to the sexual victimization of adolescents. The discussion particularly focuses on the child welfare and criminal justice systems, as both have different legal rules and embrace different missions, and both are the dominant systems that devote considerable resources to addressing victimization. That analysis also focuses on highlighting some of the challenges that the systems tackle, both due to the implementation and the very nature of the legal rules that bind them. The chapter also examines the challenges faced by reform efforts aiming to counter limitations in the legal system's responses to the sexual victimization of adolescents. The conclusion emphasizes the peculiar place of adolescents in the law, and how their status influences legal responses that necessarily will be limited due to the complexities of sexual offenses against youth, youth's developing capabilities, and youth's place in families, law, and society.

## DOMINANT LEGAL RESPONSES TO THE SEXUAL VICTIMIZATION OF ADOLESCENTS: THEIR PROCESSES AND INHERENT LIMITATIONS

Although we may tend to think that the criminal justice system responds to the victimization of youth, the reality is that two general systems constitute the juvenile victim justice system: the criminal justice system and child welfare (sometimes referred to as "child protection" or "dependency") system. These systems can overlap, and they also can be separate and compete with each other when responding to victimization (Levesque, 2011). Understanding legal responses to juveniles' sexual victimization requires understanding how both of these systems function, how they can function together, how they can end up competing against each other, and how they perhaps should remain separate. Our analysis reveals that the systems have similar yet often competing goals, and that neither system can fully meet their respective goals without the existence of the other. Our analysis further concludes that, if their goals include preventing, responding to, and protecting adolescents from sexual victimizations, then both systems cannot operate effectively without the assistance of other socializing institutions and the laws that regulate them. Thus, although we focus on two dominant systems, those two are only part of a much broader and complex legal system that regulates society's responses to the sexual victimization of youth. In addition, even though we note that there are two dominant systems, those systems are reified concepts that refer to multiple subsystems, because each state implements their own system under the guidance of minimal standards set by federal statutes, policy mandates, and Constitutional interpretations.

### Child Welfare Systems

The child welfare system generally limits itself to offenses typically viewed as child maltreatment, which can include physical and sexual abuse, neglect, and emotional maltreatment (Levesque, 2008). It generally focuses on the entire family as it responds to the victimization of minors. As a result, the victimization that concerns child welfare systems the most is the type involving perpetrators who are caretakers—usually adult family members, but sometimes siblings and others living in a household. With notable exceptions, the system seeks to ensure that families remain intact, and assumes that children are better off with their families. As a result, much of child welfare law involves the regulation of resources that would go to families, when those resources are to be provided, and what types of procedures are in place to ensure the safety of children and the rights of parents, as well as those of their children (Levesque, 2008). As a legal system, child welfare law necessarily involves the balancing of sometimes competing rights and interests, which necessarily complicate efforts to protect adolescents from sexual victimization and respond to those who have been victimized.

The child welfare system devotes considerable resources and attention to uncovering abuse, a necessarily well-placed focus given the hidden nature of maltreatment (especially sexual maltreatment; see Levesque, 1999). Generally, victims come to the attention of child welfare systems through a variety of sources that report suspected maltreatment. Indeed, the system has come considerably adept at uncovering instances of maltreatment, as the number of reports has increased dramatically as a result of requiring reports from certain professionals (e.g., teachers and physicians) and sometimes anyone who knows of victimizations (see Flaherty, 2006). All legal systems require that these reports be screened to determine the state's appropriate level of response. Thus, the reports often are made through hotlines that triage calls and determine whether to investigate allegations. This screening process is necessary, in that well-meaning reporters may not have sufficient evidence or may not present reliable information; the screening also is necessary in that the reported situations need to fall within the child welfare system's jurisdiction that gives the state the power to act. In a real sense, then, the child welfare system's overall response to sexual victimization remains a reactive one; the system relies on reports to initiate interventions. While it is true that the system itself may more generally embrace prevention, its prevention efforts relate more to other forms of maltreatment, especially neglect. Indeed, prevention programs relating to the sexual victimization of youth primarily are school-based (Finkelhor, 2009), and those programs also generally aim to increase the reporting of abuse (especially reporting to mandated reporters), and have produced mixed results, in that studies are inconclusive as to whether such programs actually reduce victimizations. This example of prevention efforts reveals but one instance in which the child welfare system relies on other systems; the system itself does not actively seek out victims. Rather, it mandates that other systems report to it.

Mandated reporting laws nicely exemplify an effort by the legal system to take victimization seriously, but they also exemplify the challenges of aggressively pursuing the uncovering of maltreatment. Mandated reporting laws certainly have contributed to a significant rise in the uncovering of maltreatment, but important commentaries have pointed out that, while these laws are well-intentioned, they do not come without costs. For example, mandatory reporting may hinder families from seeking the needed assistance on their own or may contribute to overburdening legal systems, as interpretations of what constitutes sufficient evidence can vary from individual to individual, and a reasonable system cannot ignore allegations reported to it (see Levi & Brown, 2005). Also problematically, while it is reasonable to seek to uncover and respond to abusive situations, the reality is that families and individuals retain a right to privacy, and those privacy rights include the right to be free from unnecessary intrusions in their relationships (see Levesque, 2008). Even disregarding those important rights, child welfare systems (and any other system that would investigate allegations) have limited resources that constrain their investigative reach. Not surprisingly, the entire child welfare system's approach has been criticized for focusing too much on sleuthing and not enough on remedying the negative effects of maltreatment and its prevention (see Lukens, 2007; Melton, 2005). Despite these criticisms, evidence does point to the benefits of interventions (Finkelhor & Jones, 2004), and strong arguments could be made that efforts to uncover abuse are important given that sexual abuse often can leave no mark and can occur within the privacy of relationships, as well as the privacy of dwellings. In the end, then, uncovering abuse remains considerably challenging, both because of legal mandates and the realities of practice, and the nature of the offenses. These challenges are difficult to overstate given that the foundation of legal responses to victimization necessarily rests on uncovering abusive situations and, even when not intervening directly, on determining the extent to which these situations exist.

Cases that are screened as indicating maltreatment undergo an investigation that involves assessing the steps deemed necessary to protect victims and remedy their circumstances. Generally, child welfare systems concern themselves with assessing safety, risk, needs for services, child protection, and maintaining family relationships (Pence & Wilson, 1992). During the investigation, staff may authorize medical examinations, mental health evaluations, or other services. In cases involving emergencies, investigators have the authority to take the child into custody; otherwise they can leave the child in the home or with other trusted adults (Levesque, 2008). The typical factors considered in these situations include the offender's potential recidivism, the attitude of the non-offending caregiver, the presence of other children in the home, the extent to which the family has other problems, and the nature of the offenses. As expected (and much like any state intervention in families and people's lives), considerable variation exists in responses to allegations, and most responses are determined on situation-specific grounds, rather than on rules that require automatic, predetermined responses. Efforts have been made to identify risk factors for maltreatment, develop risk assessment tools, and enact guidelines for responding to cases (D'Andrade, Austin, & Benton, 2008; Dubowitz, et al., 2011), but the child welfare system remains marked by considerable discretionary decision-making. Indeed, that discretion in responding to allegations of victimization remains a distinguishing feature of child welfare systems and the criminal justice system (Levesque, 2002, 2006). The major exception to these rules fostering discretion is the controversial mandatory arrest laws relating to adults engaged in domestic violence (see Goodman & Epstein, 2011). Still, and even despite considerable discretion, child welfare systems are under the mandate to consider seriously reports and allegations.

Assessments that eventually determine appropriate legal responses typically involve interviewing victims. Indeed, victims typically are interviewed multiple times (Faller, 1993). Given that law enforcement may have jurisdiction over some of the offenses against juveniles, child welfare officials who investigate allegations of maltreatment may decide (and in some instances may be required) to involve police and prosecutors' offices. That involvement may occur before, during, or after the interviewing stage. That variation exists because of the nature of how cases are uncovered; for example, sometimes allegations are made that initially do not involve sexual victimization. The variation also exists, however, because states vary between automatic referral and discretionary referral from one agency to another; but even when systems permit, child welfare investigations refer to law enforcement when they need investigative assistance, or when it becomes clear that criminal laws have been broken. Once law enforcement agencies are involved, interviewing tactics can range from conjoint investigation by both agencies to a coordinated investigation as part of multi-agency team efforts. Where interagency coordination is poor, both agencies may conduct separate interviews. Importantly, the relative success of coordination may be due as much to the personalities of individuals responding to allegations as to the legal and policy mandates regulating coordinated responses.

Although the process of investigation can be delineated easily, it actually constitutes an exceedingly complex legal process. Exemplary of the complexities is the interviewing of victims. Child protection professionals necessarily engage in forensic interviewing, with psychological research strongly indicating the benefits of obtaining the maximum information in one interview and limiting multiple interviews (see Gilstrap & Ceci, 2005). Researchers offer that suggestion based on the finding that real potential exists for suggestibility, and they caution that investigators must keep in mind that false allegations are a major concern for all cases, but are deemed especially more problematic when dealing with children (Bruck, Ceci, & Hembrooke, 1998; Ceci & Bruck, 1995). Despite this long line of research, another line of research now indicates that law enforcement actually may need to conduct multiple interviews, since victims of sexual victimization are highly resistant to reporting about abuse to law enforcement; research indicates that initial interviews produce more avoidance and denials of sexual acts, and more complete and informative reports may require two or three interviews (see Leander, 2010). Yet another important line of research reveals that not all interviewing professionals are trained in best-practices (Herman, 2005; Vieth, 2006), which eventually can create problems for the appropriate disposition of cases. And, even when victims are not interviewed repeatedly, their reports may well be contaminated, given that they likely have told their experiences to others before having been interviewed by professionals (see Priebe & Svedin, 2008). Importantly, the potential for problematic interviewing and investigations may be real, but the reality also is that cases of maltreatment vary widely, with some types occurring multiple times over long periods of time, which as a result vitiate many of the major concerns raised by researchers. In addition, problems that arise from multiple interviews are not inherent only to cases involving youth; multiple interviewing (and especially leading interviewing) can be problematic for the eventual disposition of any dispute involving victims and witnesses, especially if uncontaminated evidence will be needed for prosecutions, and witnesses will be required to testify at later court processes (Levesque, 2006). Not surprisingly, research on the negative effects of multiple and other problematic aspects of interviewing reveals the importance of how and when children are interviewed (see Goodman & Quas, 2008).

Although it would seem that thorough investigations are critical and absolutely necessary, the accumulation of evidence cannot proceed as freely as might be thought. An obvious limitation is the ability of investigators to access and examine child victims, as both victims and their families have fundamental rights that limit what investigators can do. The classic examples in this area are the right to privacy, as well as the rights of parents to raise their children as they deem fit (Levesque, 2008). Thus, for example, children cannot be too easily removed from their homes, nor can searches of their bodies be conducted without proper grounds for doing so. Inappropriate searches, removals from homes, and other infringements on alleged victims and offenders leaves the state (and those who carried out its work) vulnerable to legal actions and penalties (Levesque, 2002).

Yet another important limitation on the state's investigation, as noted above, concerns the potential contamination of evidence that might be necessary for the successful prosecution of offenders, or even the successful accumulation of evidence to permit interventions. Even interventions that might be deemed necessary and benign, such as medical examinations, could be problematic. For example, medical examinations can provide evidence, assess medical needs, and facilitate recovery. In addition, examinations can illuminate a history of similar or related injuries, verify historical consistency, and sometimes identify inflicted injuries. Evidence also may sometimes be collected to identify a perpetrator. Yet, victimization often cannot be confirmed nor disconfirmed through medical examinations, and there may not be a need to identify perpetrators, or doing so through physical evidence may not be possible given the nature of abuse. Even if medical findings indicate abuse (e.g., abnormal anogenital findings), those physical findings actually have been shown not to relate to important legal outcomes such as appearing in court and gaining a conviction (see, e.g., Hansen, Mikkelsen, Sabroe, & Charles, 2010). Thus, great concern attaches to whether medical examinations will be beneficial or will be stressful and further traumatize victims (Pence & Wilson, 1992; Waibel-Duncan, 2001). Some also have questioned whether the medical examination or the forensic interview should be done first during an investigation, while others report that physical examinations actually are not reliable indicators of maltreatment (noting that the victims' reports are the most reliable and helpful) (see e.g., Piper, 2008). Thus, much thought needs to be given to what can be done, when it should be done, and whether it should be done. Importantly, not conducting certain examinations may lead to criticism (from victims, parents, other professionals, and the public), but concern for the welfare and fundamental rights of victims may militate against aggressive interviewing techniques, as well as those that would be commonly expected.

Investigators in the child welfare system determine whether child maltreatment has occurred based on evidence that can meet a predetermined standard of proof, with that standard often being reasonable grounds that the allegations can be substantiated, not whether (unlike the criminal justice system) abuse occurred beyond a reasonable doubt. Importantly, the child welfare system's standard to substantiate risk to a child or that abuse has occurred varies throughout the processing of cases, with, for example, less certainty being needed for temporarily removing children from their homes than the level of certainty needed for terminating the rights of parents to their children (Levesque, 2008). The failure to substantiate claims of child maltreatment often occurs due to insufficient evidence, lack of cooperation, or inadequate agency performance. This point is of significance in that it highlights how instances involving victimization may end up without further legal responses. This is even the case despite the child welfare system's use of a low burden of proof that victimization has occurred before it can initiate responses (Levesque, 2002). Unlike other systems, however, the child welfare system does permit the allocation of resources to help prevent future maltreatment by using preventive or remedial services such as counseling, psychoeducation, and family support. The system permits the use of such resources even when abuse has not been substantiated formally, as its legal mandate generally includes addressing the needs of children deemed at risk of harm (Levesque, 2008). These resources may not have been able to prevent the victimization, but they clearly can play important roles in mediating their negative effects. Unfortunately, resources are limited and many families do not receive the care they need, even when abuse has been substantiated (Levesque, 2002).

Child maltreatment cases that do end up substantiated move through either informal or formal resolutions. Informal resolutions involve agreements between parties that need not involve full court proceedings; rather, they make use of family conferencing and other negotiation alternatives. When the state and parents disagree about suggested outcomes, full court proceedings are more likely. They are needed, for example and especially, when children will be permanently removed from their families. In such instances, several states explicitly permit the appointment of a guardian *ad litem* or other representative to serve as the child's advocate in court proceedings. In addition, parents have considerable rights to the custody and care of their children. The rights of family members, although appropriately highly protected by legal systems, have the potential for negative repercussions for maltreated children. Those negative repercussions can include the long wait that youth experience in foster care, as well as the severing of ties from family members who could be appropriate caretakers (Levesque, 1995a). These challenges have been the subject of considerable legal developments over the past few decades, with the result that laws increasingly aim to speed the resolution of cases (Levesque, 2008), which also happens to increase the challenges that families face when time is necessary to rebuild bonds and establish more secure homes. The balance between the firm commitment that society gives to the rights of parents and families, and the need to protect vulnerable individuals within them, remains one of the most challenging policy and legal issues facing efforts to address the victimization of youth (see Levesque, 2001; Levesque, 2008). Importantly, these challenges relate even to sexual victimization by non-family members, as seen in the families' need to assure that they are able to protect adolescent victims from future harm and able to respond appropriately to their needs, which could include more effective supervision. Regardless of whether offenders were from within or outside of the victims' families, families can be deemed in need of assistance, and addressing these needs can raise important issues.

## Criminal Justice Systems

Criminal justice systems potentially relate directly to sexual violence against adolescents. The systems, for example, can address a variety of sex crimes, such as physical and sexual assaults, as well as statutory rape and criminal neglect. Unlike child welfare systems, criminal justice systems can respond to all types of perpetrators, including family members, strangers, adults, or juveniles (Levesque, 2011). And, also unlike child welfare systems, criminal justice systems can respond much more aggressively and punish offenders quite severely, including controlling them once released to society (Levesque, 2006). Overall, it is difficult to overestimate the potential power of the criminal justice system in responding to victimization. Yet, it is important to not overstate the system's actual effectiveness and ability to address sexual victimization. Generally, our legal system permits criminal justice systems to retain much power precisely because, in order to ensure justice, its responses have more robust protections against their use.

The criminal justice system is mandated to respond to crimes such as child sexual abuse and other sex offenses against minors. Police investigate reports of juvenile victimization, and if suspicion of child maltreatment (abuse within the family) is found, police typically are mandated to report their suspicion to child welfare services. If police find probable cause that children were harmed in a manner that falls within sexual offense statutes, they are empowered to make arrests. Generally, sexual contact between an adult and a juvenile under the age of 16 is considered a criminal offense, although it is important to note that prohibitions related to the age of juveniles and perpetrators, as well as the types of sexual contact, can vary considerably across jurisdictions (see Levesque, 2000a). Importantly, the system explicitly aims to identify perpetrators, and to seek ways to either punish or control them, an aim that is quite different from the child welfare system that places its focus explicitly on the victim and remedying their situations. The distinction is of considerable significance, as concern focuses on offenders and, in a real sense, victims play a secondary role, as illustrated by the names of cases being prosecuted on behalf of the state, not victims (e.g., it is the "State v." the name of the offender, the victim's name is not part of the name of the case); and the same is true for cases involving minors as witnesses (their being witnesses is a matter of state interest, not a matter of the minors' own subjective interests; see Cooper, 2011). This is not to say that the criminal justice system does not work on behalf of victims and does not seek to address their needs and concerns; it is to say that the system is formally designed to focus on offenders, as it is a system of public prosecution where victims are not party to cases. That focus can become quite problematic when dealing with minors, but it comes with the need to protect defendants' basic, constitutional rights (see Levesque, 1995b). Thus, in responding to sexual violence against adolescents, both police and prosecutors actually have no clients; instead, they represent the state and are beholden to society at large; their obligation is to do what is best for society, which includes fairness to defendants as well as victims.

The criminal justice system has an adjudicatory process (from the identification of a case to its ultimate resolution) that mirrors that of the child welfare system, tries to address similar concerns, and seeks to address similar challenges. The fundamental difference between both systems is that law enforcement actually is, in important ways, more limited in what it can do to address victims' needs, given that police and others who would intervene to accumulate evidence and prosecute cases operate in a system that seeks to uphold higher constitutional standards by giving increased protections to those it would bring into the system. Unlike the civil system (which is the basis of the child welfare system), the criminal justice system must be much more careful and certain in its execution. For example, compared with searches by child welfare officials, the searches and seizures conducted by police generally must be done only with a higher level of certainty that they will find what they seek, their actions will receive greater scrutiny, and the remedy for their errors is the dismissal of cases (Levesque, 2002). The major rationale for the difference is that the criminal justice system is deemed punitive, and thus it must confer more robust constitutional protections to suspects and defendants so that they can fairly defend themselves against the state; and the child welfare system is deemed rehabilitative and remedial, and thus can be more free to intrude in people's lives. In a real sense, one system seeks to accuse and adjudicate an appropriate penalty, while the other system is deemed as one that seeks to offer assistance and is in less need of creating protections against the system's potential errors. Although reasonable arguments could be made that removing one's children and terminating relationships with them could be extremely punitive, and worse than incarceration, the systems simply are not framed to recognize that possibility. Thus, a state's child welfare system could commit several errors in its efforts to find a parent unfit, but the parent still could have their rights terminated if the state has sufficient grounds to prove the parent unfit. If the criminal justice system commits errors that violate, for example, offender's rights in the accumulation of evidence against them, then the system generally forgoes the use of that evidence, even if it means not prosecuting offenders and forfeiting their punishment (Levesque, 2006). These general differences clearly have important repercussions throughout the criminal justice system's processing of allegations, from the initial identification of suspects to the prosecution and disposition of their cases.

Given how the different systems have fundamentally different orientations to dealing with victimization, but still need to address similar issues, it is not surprising that the criminal justice system, just like the child welfare system, faces important challenges in identifying cases of victimization. Indeed, one of the most important research findings that sheds considerable light on the legal identification and response to sex crimes involving minors (as well as adults) is the pervasive under-reporting and, as a result, low arrest and even lower prosecution rates. The overall low arrest rate can be seen as demonstrating the limited resources of police, absence of appropriate evidence, and the perceived nature of sexual offenses. The low rates also are attributable to the hesitancy of victims to report and press charges.

The failure to report likely is due to a variety of reasons, and those reasons have to do with the perception of the criminal justice system's effectiveness (with some victims not coming forward for fear that nothing much will happen and others, ironically, not coming forward for fear that too much will happen), as well as fear of intimidation from offenders (see Finkelhor, Ormrod, Turner, & Hamby, 2011). The failure to not even know about victimizations remains one of the criminal justice system's fundamental limitations.

The criminal justice system's low rates of processing cases involving adolescent victims (low compared with the actual number of offenses) also likely come from other important sources. Some types of sexual victimization simply are not processed by the criminal justice system. For example, research now well supports claims that over half of all offenders against juveniles are other juveniles (Finkelhor & Ormrod, 2000). This is a significant finding for at least two important reasons. First, victimizations between same-age peers remain less likely to be reported and, equally importantly, laws give similar-aged peers fewer protections from victimization. For example, strict liability sex offenses tend to permit sexual activity among peers, as long as there was no overt force, and some offenses that would require evidence of force are problematic to pursue because force between similar-aged peers may be difficult to discern and prove (as is often associated with date rape cases) (see Levesque, 1999, 2000a). Second, juvenile status means the potential circumvention of criminal court systems in favor of using juvenile courts. It is true, however, that crimes deemed more violent generally are more likely to be transferred to adult court (the traditional criminal justice system) for processing (including prosecution and sentencing) (see Cauffman et al., 2007) and actually may require automatic transfers (see Levesque, 2000a). When dealing with sex crimes, juvenile court systems increasingly take on characteristics of adult courts that have a greater capacity to control offenders (such as through sex offender registration laws; see Levesque, 2006); and this continues even though juvenile courts retain different goals (such as rehabilitating offenders). Also true is the manner in which the juvenile court system increasingly follows similar processes, and that juvenile offenders in juvenile courts increasingly have rights similar to those processed in adult courts. Despite the juvenile courts' increasingly taking on characteristics of adult courts and the transfer of juveniles to adult systems, offenders in juvenile courts are treated differently, and their offenses generally are not subject to the same penalties that could arise from prosecutions in the traditional criminal justice system.

Equally importantly, criminal justice systems and child welfare systems have widely documented "crime reports." No such systematic and popularized system relates to the juvenile justice system. As a result, the nature and extent of the problem remains considerably much more hidden. In the end, it is clear that victimization by juveniles poses important issues for legal efforts to recognize and respond effectively to the sexual victimization of adolescents.

Prosecutors become involved in cases either in conjunction with an investigation or after an arrest. Decisions regarding prosecution vary depending on the jurisdiction and, equally likely, the prosecutor. In virtually all cases, prosecutors evaluate a case's potential before determining whether or how to proceed with the prosecution. Those evaluations include considering the potential negative consequences for victims. Regardless of what offenders were arrested for, the prosecutors decide the nature of the charges to file, as well as whether to offer plea bargains (and thus avoid trials). In those determinations, prosecutors often bring the cases before a judge or a grand jury to determine whether the proffered evidence supports probable cause to press formal charges. While in both cases a child may testify, cases are dismissed upon the failure to establish probable cause. In addition, cases that are plead rather than tried avoid the need for the victim to testify at trials and other related hearings (although sentencing hearings can include victims' testimonies, either formally in court or through statements made and presented to the sentencing court by the staff members who prepare sentencing reports). Just as police and others involved in investigations interview victims and must weigh several factors when they work with minors, then, so do prosecutors and others who work with the court systems to determine appropriate dispositions.

Given the importance of victims' statements and testimony in prosecuting cases (coupled with the increased recognition that victimizations deserve legal responses), victims' roles in prosecutions have led to important legal developments. For example, to protect vulnerable witnesses from potential harms associated with testifying in open court, they may be able to deliver testimony through closed-circuit television, or from a witness allowed to testify regarding what the child said or otherwise reported to them (Levesque, 2002). Importantly, however, the rules guiding efforts to protect victims from the potential harms of testifying in court are undergoing significant challenges, with the result that the use of these special protections is becoming increasingly limited (Levesque, 2008). Most notably, in Crawford v. Washington (2004), the Supreme Court made child abuse prosecutions much more difficult as it banned "testimonial" hearsay of an unavailable witness unless the defendant had a prior opportunity to cross-examine the declarant. Juveniles' statements in forensic interviews within abuse litigation are now considered largely testimonial. This becomes problematic, in that forensic interviews had proven useful in detecting abuse, and the Court's current stance threatens research and practice that had developed more effective ways of eliciting statements from child witnesses (see Fox, 2009). More concretely, it means that courts must exclude from consideration previously routinely admitted statements against offenders. The results of these developments have yet to be appreciated fully. But, it is reasonable to expect that there might be a decrease in prosecutions due to the failure to obtain admissible evidence, an increase in pressure to have vulnerable victims and witnesses testify in court proceedings, and, given the difficulties of obtaining evidence, a decrease in prosecutions and plea agreements when they would otherwise have been routinely obtained. The laws regulating how victims are to be treated have clear effects on prosecutions and their outcomes.

Concerns about victims' statements, including the need to reduce traumas associated with interviews and testimony, as well as the need to provide reliable testimony, have led to the development of important efforts to coordinate multiple agencies and the different systems that respond to allegations of abuse. The most notable examples are the development of child advocacy centers, such as Child Abuse Assessment Centers (CAAC) and Child Advocacy Centers (CAC). CAACs seek to determine whether abuse occurred, while CACs support and advocate for the child and family (see Joa & Edelson, 2004). For example, CACs focus on providing child-friendly facilities, using multidisciplinary teams to interview children, as well as on providing medical examinations, mental health services, victim advocacy, case reviews, and tracking (Jackson, 2004). Importantly, they also assist in coordinating interactions between child welfare and law enforcement personnel, including prosecutors (Cross, Finkelhor, & Ormrod, 2005; Perona, Bottoms, & Sorenson, 2006). Although these efforts have provided important examples of success, they nevertheless have been subjected to significant criticisms, such as their potentially complicating matters by adding to an already bureaucratic process (Newman, Dannenfelser, & Pendleon, 2005). They also have been criticized to the extent that important differences remain in caseloads, professional influence, and agency goals (see Pence & Wilson, 1992). Despite these criticisms, these developments reveal well how legal systems recognize the importance of addressing young victims' needs, both for the victims' own sake and for the proper resolution of cases.

As expected, once cases are referred to prosecution, instances where cases actually are prosecuted vary widely. Rates differ based on resources and the priority given to juvenile victim cases, but also because of screening procedures and the types of cases referred. Prosecution is less likely when victims are very young, when they are related to the perpetrator, are female, or when they suffer less severe offenses (see e.g., Stroud, Martens, & Barker, 2000). If the victim's story is inconsistent or the family opposes prosecution efforts, cases are also less likely to be prosecuted (Gray, 1993). Charges are also much less likely to be filed by prosecutors if they lack corroborating witnesses (see Walsh, Jones, Cross, & Lippert, 2010). These generalities, however, mask a complex reality. For example, it may be assumed that the system discriminates against female victims, which may well be the case. But research does show that male victims of sexual abuse may be more likely to be abused by perpetrators who abuse multiple victims and are not related to them (see Levesque, 1994), and these cases may be more likely to be stronger. Importantly, even if cases are prosecuted, they still may be dismissed by the jury, judge, or even the prosecutor. As with most other crimes, those involving sexual offenses against minors are likely to not be tried; they likely are resolved through guilty pleas. Research, not surprisingly, suggests that prosecutors move forward with cases they believe are strong, and in which they can exert leverage in negotiating charges and sentences (see Cross, Walsh, Jones, & Simone, 2002).

Research relating to the sentences for sex crimes remains rare, as research in this area tends to lump together all forms of maltreatment, and tends to center on whether there were convictions rather than focus on the nature of the sentence. One study that examined the sentencing patterns of prosecuted sex crimes against minors did find, however, that individual victims' experiences generally are less predictive of sentencing outcomes than perpetrators' characteristics, that sentences generally tend to be lenient, that intra-family and stranger abuse seem to be taken equally seriously, and that the criminal justice system does seem to incarcerate those society is most worried about: the persistent predators who abuse several children (see Levesque, 2000b). Despite that study, and given the considerable lack of robust research in this area, it remains difficult to draw firm conclusions about the sentencing patterns of cases involving adolescents' sexual victimization. Perhaps the best conclusion that can be reached draws from other areas of research to conclude: (1) that the vast majority of those who offend against adolescents do not get punished; and (2) that, once involved in the legal system and responding to charges, the majority of offenders are found responsible (e.g., plead guilty to some offense) (Cross, Walsh, Jones, & Simone, 2002); but (3) how severe their penalties actually are remains a matter in need of further investigation.

After they have served their sentences (or perhaps upon conviction), offenders still can be subjected to considerable legal control. Offenders, both juvenile and adult, can be required to comply with multiple measures to decrease their likelihood of reoffending. Most notably, they can be civilly committed, required to undergo therapy, mandated to register their locations when released from commitment, and required to notify communities of their presence (La Fond & Winick, 1998; Marques, Wiederanders, Day, Nelson, & van Ommeren, 2005). These measures have attracted considerable public support, but they also have attracted considerable controversy. Among concerns expressed by researchers are the reform's potential lack of effectiveness in terms of preventing sexual assaults as well as, especially for juvenile offenders, hampering their effective rehabilitation and reintegration into communities (see Petznick, 2011; Stine, 2011). Other criticisms include their being based on overly stereotyped characterizations of sexual offenders when the reality is that offenders constitute a diverse group, with the majority actually falling outside of effective management efforts (see Finkelhor, 2009). Despite those concerns, the management approach to dealing with offenders continues, because the legal system permits the types of responses that have gained popularity. The legal system can accommodate these reforms because offenders have considerably reduced rights after they have been adjudicated guilty. Adding to those reduced rights is the manner that some laws regulating the control of those deemed sex offenders are framed as civil laws (rather than criminal laws), a framing that is of significance given, as we have seen above, that the civil justice system retains considerably more freedom to intervene in people's lives.

## THE VICTIM'S RIGHTS MOVEMENT

One of the most important developments in legal responses to adolescents' sexual victimization is the manner in which youth have benefitted from the general victims' rights movement. This development is of significance for two reasons. First, the victimization of children did not become a staple for legal interventions until the 1980s, when reporting requirements began to identify large numbers of cases in which children's testimony would be important to determine whether criminal defendants were guilty of child abuse or endangerment, or whether children were maltreated and should be placed under the supervision of the state. As a result, even young children now testify regularly about their own abuse in both criminal and child welfare cases. Indeed, juveniles who testify in criminal court overwhelmingly appear as victims, rather than bystanders, with sexual assault and incest being the most common cases in which they testify (see Goodman, Quas, Bulkley, & Shapiro, 1999). Second, youth are a potentially large group of witnesses and victims of sex crimes, as evidenced by numerous areas of research. For example, estimates reveal that children constitute approximately 71% of all reported sex crime victims (Finkelhor & Ormrod, 2000). Likewise, the most recently published, comprehensive survey of adolescents and caretakers of young children revealed that nearly one in five girls aged 14 to 17 had been the victim of a sexual assault or attempted sexual assault at some previous time (Finkelhor, Ormrod, Turner, & Hamby, 2011). Further, recent federal statistics presenting yearly national reports identified over 65,000 child victims of sexual abuse after investigation by child protective services agencies (US Department of Health and Human Services, 2010). Importantly, these figures are understated, because they do not include victims sexually assaulted by strangers as well as the large percentage of cases currently not reported to the authorities (Olafson & Lederman, 2006). Juveniles, then, are likely to be involved in the legal system and become witnesses, and that involvement has a high chance of being due to their sexual victimization. The legal system has sought to address their needs, and it has done so as part of a broader recognition of victims' rights.

The legal system, particularly the criminal justice system, now recognizes broad and specific rights for both adult and juvenile victims, and those rights include the rights to protection, privacy, and participation. Following constitutional mandates, criminal justice systems' legal processes traditionally have focused on defendants and on ensuring that their rights were protected. Given that focus, the new victim-centered protections signify a discernible and foundational shift in the law. Particularly when dealing with juveniles, Congress, federal courts, the Supreme Court, and over half the states now specifically identify child witness' interests as important in the administration of criminal justice (see Beloof, 2007). Given the relatively recent emergence of systematic efforts to recognize the rights of victims, these can be viewed as quite dramatic developments.

The breadth and depth of these developments can be understood by highlighting two federal statutes, as they codified many of the cases that had been decided before them, and lay a foundation for state jurisdictions to follow. The first important statute to emphasize is the Victims of Child Abuse Act of 1990 (2006). Through that statute, Congress enabled child victims and witnesses in federal courts to request protection from directly confronting defendants, and judges hold the power to order testimony to be taken in rooms outside the trial courtrooms and televised by two-way closed circuit television. The second statute, the Crime Victims' Rights Act (2005), provides another set of rights and is a broader one that applies to all victims. That statute affords crime victims many participation rights, including: the right to timely and accurate notice of public court proceedings; the right not to be excluded from public court proceedings; the right to be heard at public court proceedings involving release, plea, sentencing, and parole proceedings; the right to full and timely restitution; the right to proceedings free from unreasonable delay; the right to confer with the prosecutor; the right to be protected from the accused; and the right to be treated with fairness and respect. These are considerably significant and expansive developments that recognize and seek to respond to what have been identified as the secondary harms that victims can suffer when their cases are adjudicated (for a history of these developments, see Aaronson, 2008). Indeed, the recognized rights and remedies are so expansive that they have been construed as potentially infringing on the public prosecution model by undermining prosecutorial and judicial discretion, and threatening the rights of those accused of criminal offenses (see e.g., Levine, 2010). These concerns underscore the remarkable extent to which the newly developed rights can go to the very foundation of our justice system and the challenges faced by efforts to address victims' legitimate concerns.

As a culmination of the above developments, the American Bar Association (2009) directly examined the rights of juvenile victims and witnesses, and announced a list of rights for child witnesses and their guardians. Those rights include the right to know what is happening in the court case that came about from the child's report; the right to be in court whenever the judge and the prosecutor are there to discuss the case (before a trial starts); the right to request to speak to the judge anytime the judge makes a major decision in the case; the right to ask the judge to provide reasonable protection before, during, and after the trial if the child feels scared or threatened; the right to request services and people to talk to outside of the courtroom about their feelings; the right to ask a judge to appoint a guardian or attorney to represent them if they would like to talk to someone privately without their parents or legal guardian knowing; the right to ask the judge to allow a parent, guardian, or another adult whom the child trusts to be present during their testimony; and whether or not there is a trial, the right to know if the defendant is sent to jail or prison and, if so, when the defendant is expected to be released. Given how the rights of victims historically have been played down by the legal system, especially the criminal justice system, these enumerations are, without doubt, considerably significant.

Although pronouncements of victims' rights reflect important developments, they remain marked by significant limitations. Fundamentally, as we have seen, the victimization of juveniles may well involve the child welfare system, and the above rights concern themselves with the criminal justice system. Even when responses enlist the criminal justice system, important limitations remain. Most notably, although a victim and witness may make requests, those requests need not necessarily be granted. For example, the right to not deliver testimony in the presence of defendants has been recognized through Supreme Court cases, and essentially codified in the federal Victims of Child Abuse Act of 1990 (2006). But, to grant an order permitting the use of closed-circuit television, the court must make a case-specific finding that a child witness would suffer substantial fear or trauma and be unable to testify or communicate reasonably because of the physical presence of the defendant. The reason for these important caveats is that Constitutional mandates that still focus on and protect the rights of the accused considerably limit developments (see Levesque, 2008). Thus, although the system may seek to protect victims and involve them in less harmful ways, concerns about the reliability of evidence continue to influence those efforts, and such concerns end up having very broad ramifications for how witnesses can be treated. In addition to those limitations, there also remains considerable diversity in the juvenile victims' right to representation, in both the child welfare system and the criminal justice system (Levesque, 2008). And it is difficult to argue that the majority of victims are well represented. For example, the most recent federal reports (for 2009) reveal that even in the child welfare system, which remains theoretically more focused on the child, over three million children receive preventive services per year, one-fifth of them are placed in foster care, but only 16% have court-appointed representatives assigned to them (US Department of Health and Human Services, 2010). Neither last nor least, the developments also remain significantly limited in that the state retains the right to pursue allegations, and regardless of what victims may wish, they are not likely to even become witnesses if the state decides not to pursue cases. This is of significance in that it underscores how the victims' rights movement focuses on legal processes and how its major influence, at least for now, emerges when legal processes are involved. As we have seen, in reality, legal systems tend not to be involved in responses to sexual victimization. Most victimizations simply are not reported, and the vast majority of cases that are pursued do not go to trial (Levesque, 2006). As a result, it is important not to overstate the potential effect of these protections for the vast majority of victims, as it is important not to assume that legal systems even respond to victimizations. These criticisms, however, should not detract from the real, positive effects that the victims' rights movement has had for victims who do become involved in the legal system, especially the criminal justice system.

## CONCLUSIONS

Several conclusions may be drawn from our brief review of legal responses to adolescents' sexual victimization. First, adolescents occupy a peculiar place in law, and that place means that multiple systems respond to their victimization. Regrettably, those systems are not tightly connected, and several practical and jurisprudential concerns challenge efforts for a more unified, streamlined system. The separation of the two dominant systems addressing victimization is likely to continue, given their goals and the nature of the rights that undergird them. But there continues to be a need for more scholarship and research focusing on their greater integration, at least in terms of better determining which ones could better serve victims (such as revisiting the legal understanding of privacy and confidentiality so as to address the ability to share information across multiple systems and agencies). Second, adolescent victims benefit from professionals and others who can assist them through legal proceedings, as actually has been recognized as important for adults and for young children by victim advocates; but that assistance would benefit from being more comprehensive and include, most notably, assistance outside of court proceedings not only for the victims, but also for their natural support systems (e.g., non-abusive parents). Third, and relatedly, a focus on helping the largest number of victims also is of importance, as revealed by the reality that much research has focused on court proceedings' effects on victims, when most do not go through them; it would seem that more research would be needed to understand stresses associated with being interviewed by case workers and other investigators, with family members being subjected to investigations, and with being separated from family members and other support systems. Fourth, research relating to adolescents' sexual victimization often does not offer relevant findings that can be used to enhance legal responses, as they may not be getting to the core of the legal issues that need to be addressed if reforms are to be effective. Multiple reasons account for limitations in research, with the most notable one being that the legal system is exceedingly complex, varied, and must deal simultaneously with a wide range of concerns. Lastly, the potentially vast differences in how different systems and communities treat victims also are worth much closer examination. Sound reasons exist for permitting differences in how communities respond to victimization. But the nature of those differences deserves increasing scrutiny as researchers continue to examine legal responses to victimization and the nature of victimization itself; and the permissibility of those differences also continues to gain appropriately increased scrutiny as legal systems move toward better recognizing the important role victims play in legal responses. In the end, a close look at how legal systems respond to the sexual victimization of adolescents reveals truly foundational and expansive developments, and a close look at those impressive developments reveals fundamental limitations in addressing adolescents' victimization.

## REFERENCES

Aaronson, D. E. (2008). New rights and remedies: The federal crime victims' rights act of 2004. *Pace Law Review, 28*, 623–682.

American Bar Association (2009). Child victim rights, American Bar Association Criminal Justice Section Newsletter, Winter 2009. Available at <http://new.abanet.org/sections/criminaljustice/PublicDocuments/childvictimrights.pdf>.

Beloof, D. E. (2007). Weighing crime victims' interests in judicially crafted criminal procedure. *Catholic University Law Review, 56*, 1135–1170.

Bruck, M., Ceci, S., & Hembrooke, H. (1998). Reliability and credibility of young children's reports: From research to policy and practice. *American Psychologist, 53*, 136–151.

Cauffman, E., Piquero, A. R., Kimonis, E., Steinberg, L., Chassin, L., & Fagan, J. (2007). Legal, individual, and contextual predictors of court disposition in a sample of serious adolescent offenders. *Law and Human Behavior, 31*, 519–535.

Ceci, S. J., & Bruck, M. (1995). *Jeopardy in the courtroom: A scientific analysis of children's testimony*. Washington, DC: American Psychological Association.

Cooper, T. A. (2011). Sacrificing the child to convict the defendant: Secondary traumatization of child witnesses by prosecutors, their inherent conflict of interest, and the need for child witness counsel. *Cardozo Public Law, Policy & Ethics Journal, 9*, 239–286.

Crawford v. Washington (2004). 541 U.S. 36.

Crime Victims' Rights Act (2005). Pub. L. No. 108-405, 118 Stat. 2261 (2004) (codified at 18 U.S.C.A. § 3771.
Cross, T. P., Finkelhor, D., & Ormrod, R. (2005). Police involvement in child protective services investigations: Literature review and secondary data analysis. *Child Maltreatment*, *10*, 224–244.
Cross, T. P., Walsh, W., Jones, L. M., & Simone, M. (2002). Prosecution of child abuse: A meta-analysis of rates of criminal justice decisions. *Trauma, Violence, & Abuse*, *4*, 323–340.
D'Andrade, A., Austin, M., & Benton, A. (2008). Risk and safety assessment in child welfare: Instrument comparisons. *Journal of Evidence-Based Social Work*, *5*, 31–56.
Dubowitz, H., Kim, J., Black, M. M., Weisbart, C., Semiatin, J., & Magde, L. S. (2011). Identifying children at high risk for a child maltreatment report. *Child Abuse and Neglect*, *35*, 96–104.
Faller, K. C. (1993). *Child sexual abuse: Intervention and treatment issues*. Washington, DC: US Department of Health and Human Services.
Finkelhor, D. (2009). The prevention of childhood sexual abuse. *Future of Children*, *19*, 169–194.
Finkelhor, D., & Jones, L. M. (2004). *Explanations for the decline in child sexual abuse cases*. Washington, DC: US Department of Justice, Office of Juvenile and Delinquency Prevention. Available at <http://www.ncjrs.gov/pdffiles1/ojjdp/199298.pdf>.
Finkelhor, D., & Ormrod, R. (2000). Characteristics of crimes against juveniles. *Juvenile Justice Bulletin – NCJ179034*. Washington, DC: US Government Printing Office. pp. 1–11.
Finkelhor, D., Ormrod, R., Turner, H., & Hamby, S. (2011). School, police, and medical authority involvement with children who have experienced victimization. *Archives of Pediatric and Adolescent Medicine*, *165*, 9–15.
Flaherty, E. G. (2006). Does the wording of the mandate to report suspected child abuse serve as another barrier to child abuse reporting? *Child Abuse & Neglect*, *30*, 341–343.
Fox, B. (2009). Crawford at its limits: Hearsay and forfeiture in child abuse cases. *American Criminal Law Review*, *46*, 1245–1265.
Gilstrap, L. L., & Ceci, S. J. (2005). Reconceptualizing children's suggestibility: Bidirectional and temporal properties. *Child Development*, *76*, 40–53.
Goodman, G. S., & Quas, J. A. (2008). Repeated interviews and children's memory: It's more than just how many. *Psychological Science*, *7*, 386–390.
Goodman, G. S., Quas, J. A., Bulkley, J., & Shapiro, C. (1999). Innovations in child witnesses: A national survey. *Psychology, Public Policy, and Law*, *5*, 225–281.
Goodman, L., & Epstein, D. (2011). The justice system response to domestic violence. In Mary P. Koss, Jacquelyn W. White, & Alan E. Kazdin (Eds.), *Violence against women and children, Vol. 2: Navigating solutions (pp. 215–235)*. Washington, DC: American Psychological Association.
Gray, E. (1993). *Unequal justice: The prosecution of child sexual abuse*. New York, NY: Free Press.
Hansen, L. A., Mikkelsen, S. J., Sabroe, S., & Charles, A. V. (2010). Medical findings and legal outcomes in sexually abused children. *Journal of Forensic Sciences*, *55*, 104–109.
Herman, S. (2005). Improving decision making in forensic child sexual abuse evaluations. *Law and Human Behavior*, *29*, 87–120.
Jackson, S. L. (2004). A USA national survey of program services provided by child advocacy centers. *Child Abuse and Neglect*, *28*, 411–421.
Joa, D., & Edelson, M. G. (2004). Legal outcomes for children who have been sexually abused: The impact of child abuse assessment center evaluations. *Child Maltreatment*, *9*, 263–276.
La Fond, J. Q., & Winick, B. (1998). Sex offenders and the law. *Psychology, Public Policy, and Law*, *4*, 3–24.
Leander, L. (2010). Police interviews with child sexual abuse victims: Patterns of reporting, avoidance and denial. *Child Abuse & Neglect*, *34*, 192–205.

Levesque, R. J. R. (1994). Sex differences in the experience of child sexual victimization. *Journal of Family Violence, 9,* 357–369.

Levesque, R. J. R. (1995a). The failures of foster care reform: Revolutionizing the most radical blueprint. *Maryland Journal of Contemporary Legal Issues, 6,* 1–35.

Levesque, R. J. R. (1995b). Prosecuting sex crimes against children: Time for "outrageous" proposals? *Law & Psychology Review,* 59–91.

Levesque, R. J. R. (1999). *Child sexual abuse: A human rights perspective.* Bloomington, IN: Indiana University Press.

Levesque, R. J. R. (2000a). *Adolescents, sex, and the law: Preparing adolescents for responsible citizenship.* Washington, DC: American Psychological Association. [(Series in Law, Psychology and Public Policy)].

Levesque, R. J. R. (2000b). Sentencing sex crimes against children: An empirical and policy analysis. *Behavioral Sciences & the Law, 18,* 331–341.

Levesque, R. J. R. (2001). *Culture and family violence: Fostering change through human rights law.* Washington, DC: American Psychological Association. [(Series in Law, Psychology and Public Policy)].

Levesque, R. J. R. (2002). *Child maltreatment and the law: Foundations in science, policy and practice.* Durham, NC: Carolina Academic Press.

Levesque, R. J. R. (2006). *The psychology and law of criminal justice processes.* Hauppauge, NY: Nova Science Publishers.

Levesque, R. J. R. (2008). *Rethinking child maltreatment law: Returning to first principles.* New York, NY: Springer.

Levesque, R. J. R. (2011). The law's response to child maltreatment. In Mary P. Koss, Jacquelyn W. White, & Alan Kazdin (Eds.), *Handbook of violence against women and children, Vol. 2: Navigating solutions* (pp. 47–69). Washington, DC: American Psychological Association.

Levi, B. H., & Brown, G. (2005). Reasonable suspicion: A study of Pennsylvania pediatricians regarding child abuse. *American Academy of Pediatrics, 116,* 5–12.

Levine, D. (2010). Public wrongs and private rights: Limiting the victim's role in a system of public prosecution. *Northwestern University Law Review, 104,* 335–362.

Lukens, R. J. (2007). The impact of mandatory reporting requirements on the child welfare system. *Rutgers Journal of Law & Public Policy, 5,* 177–233.

Marques, J. K., Wiederanders, M., Day, D. M., Nelson, C., & van Ommeren, A. (2005). Effects of a relapse prevention program on sexual recidivism: Final results from California's sex offender treatment and evaluation project. *Sexual Abuse: A Journal of Research and Treatment, 17,* 79–107.

Melton, G. B. (2005). Mandated reporting: A policy without reason. *Child Abuse & Neglect, 29,* 9–18.

Newman, B. S., Dannenfelser, P. L., & Pendleon, D. (2005). Child abuse investigations: Reasons for using child advocacy centers and suggestions for improvement. *Child and Adolescent Social Work Journal, 22,* 165–181.

Olafson, E., & Lederman, C. (2006). State of debate about children's disclosure patterns in child sexual abuse cases. *Juvenile and Family Court Journal, 57,* 27–40.

Pence, D., & Wilson, C. (1992). *The role of law enforcement in the response to child abuse and neglect.* Washington, DC: US Department of Health and Human Services.

Perona, A. R., Bottoms, B. L., & Sorenson, E. (2006). Research-based guidelines for child forensic interviews. In V. I. Vieth, B. L. Bottoms, & A. R. Perona (Eds.), *Ending child abuse* (pp. 81–130). Binghamton, NY: The Haworth Press.

Petznick, T. (2011). Only young once, but a registered sex offender for life: A case for reforming California's juvenile sex offender registration system through the use of risk assessments. *Berkeley Journal of Criminal Law, 16,* 228–263.

Piper, A. (2008). Investigating child sex abuse allegations: A guide to help legal professionals distinguish valid from invalid claims. *Journal of Psychiatry & Law, 36,* 271–317.

Priebe, G., & Svedin, C. G. (2008). Child sexual abuse is largely hidden from the adult society: An epidemiological study of adolescents' disclosures. *Child Abuse & Neglect, 32,* 1095–1108.

Stine, E. J. (2011). When yes means no, legally: An eighth amendment challenge to classifying consenting teenagers as sex offenders. *DePaul Law Review, 60,* 1169–1227.

Stroud, D. D., Martens, S. L., & Barker, J. (2000). Criminal investigation of child sexual abuse: A comparison of cases referred to the prosecutor to those not referred. *Child Abuse and Neglect, 24,* 689–700.

US Department of Health and Human Services. (2010). *Child maltreatment 2009.* Washington, DC: US Government Printing Office. Available from <http://www.acf.hhs.gov/programs/cb/stats_research/index.htm#can>.

Victims of Child Abuse Act of 1990 (2006). Pub. L. No. 101-647, tit. II, § 225(a), 104 Stat. 4792, 4798 (1990) (codified as amended at 18 U.S.C. § 3509(h).

Vieth, V. I. (2006). Unto the third generation: A call to end child abuse in the United States within 120 years. In V. I. Vieth, B. L. Bottoms, & A. R. Perona (Eds.), *Ending child abuse (pp. 5–54).* Binghamton, NY: The Haworth Press.

Waibel-Duncan, M. K. (2001). Medical fears following alleged child abuse. *Journal of Child and Adolescent Psychiatric Nursing, 14,* 179–185.

Walsh, W. A., Jones, L. M., Cross, T. P., & Lippert, T. (2010). Prosecuting child sexual abuse: The importance of evidence type. *Crime & Delinquency, 56,* 436–454.

# PART Five

# Children with Sexual Behavior Problems and Adolescent Sexual Offenders

# CHAPTER 20

# Children with Sexual Behavior Problems

Jane F. Silovsky, Lisa M. Swisher, Jimmy Widdifield, Jr., and Vicky L. Turner

University of Oklahoma Health Sciences Center, Oklahoma City, Oklahoma[1]

## INTRODUCTION

In the course of growing up, children will choose a variety of behaviors out of curiosity and self-interest which may lead to behaviors that break societal rules about appropriate behavior. A child wants a piece of candy and takes it from a store, or is curious about fire and lights paper with a lighter, or wants to play with a toy and grabs it from another child. Responses from the environment, including parents and other caregivers, impact the course of a child's development and how they gain the knowledge and skills needed to follow society's rules, such as do not steal or set fires, and how to negotiate with others. Multiple pathways could lead to learning to follow rules or to more severe conduct behavior problems.

This pattern of behaviors and responses also occur with sexual development. Children may be motivated to try out new behavior by curiosity, such as looking at each other's genitals. Much of this behavior is typical; however, some children demonstrate sexual behaviors that are outside of the typical range, in frequency, duration, types of behavior, and impact on themselves and others. Sometimes the behavior is triggered by traumatic experiences, from seeing sexual activity of others, or through the media. How the environment responds impacts future thoughts and behaviors. This is true of a wide range of conduct problems; however, when children's behaviors are perceived as "sexual," complications arise regarding the interpretation and response to them, due to the sensitive and taboo nature of the topic of sex and children, strongly held beliefs about what

---

[1] Correspondence to: Jane Silovsky, PhD, University of Oklahoma Health Sciences Center, Department of Pediatrics, Center on Child Abuse & Neglect, 940 NE 13th Street, 4th Floor Nicholson Tower Suite 4900, Oklahoma City, OK 73104. Phone 405-271-8858; fax 405-271-2931; email Jane-Silovsky@ouhsc.edu

is appropriate and inappropriate, and mixed messages children receive through the media and other aspects of society.

This chapter will address problematic sexual behaviors in children. Sexual development occurs throughout infancy, childhood, and adolescence, and is best understood in the context of children's physical, motor, language, cognitive, social, emotional, and moral development. A wide range of knowledge and behaviors are considered to be part of normal or typical sexual development, as described in Chapter 5. Sexual behavior occurs on a continuum from typical, to concerning, to problematic (Johnson, 1990), and guidelines for determining where a behavior falls on this continuum will be provided in this chapter. There appear to be multiple pathways to the development of sexual behavior problems in childhood which will be discussed, as well as what is known for best practices in assessment and treatment for these children. This chapter will focus on problematic sexual behavior of children, aged 12 and younger. Chapter 21 will address problematic and illegal sexual behavior of adolescents.

## DEFINITIONS

For children, we define behaviors as "sexual" by the behaviors shown, rather than the underlying intentions and motivations. The specific intent and motivations are wide ranging and often difficult to determine in young children. Sexual behavior problems (SBP) are child initiated behaviors related to physical boundaries or sexual body parts (e.g., breasts, vagina, vulva, penis, mouth, scrotum, anus, and buttocks) that are developmentally inappropriate or potentially physically or emotionally harmful to the child or others (Silovsky & Bonner, 2003). Typical sexual behaviors can become problematic when such behaviors do not respond to parental intervention and continue to occur at greater frequency/duration than normally occur (Araji, 1997; Chaffin et al., 2008; Hall, Matthews, & Pearce, 1998; Johnson, 1990). Sexual behaviors in children can also be considered problematic when participation in day-to-day activities, such as school, doing chores, and spending time with family and friends, is disrupted. The ages and developmental abilities of the children involved and the emotional responses are important to consider when evaluating the behaviors. Some jurisdictions give specific age differences (such as 5 years) to define sexual behaviors between children as abusive. In clinical practices it is recommended to examine not only the children's chronological ages, but also abilities and areas of development when assessing potentially problematic sexual behavior. Sexual behaviors characterized by coercion, intimidation, force, or aggression are rare, do not occur in normative, non-clinical samples, and are of serious concern (Friedrich, 2002).

Types of problematic sexual behavior are diverse and wide ranging. Some children repeatedly try to watch their siblings or parents change clothes or bathe, even after provided clear privacy rules in the home and given consequences for breaking these rules. Other children may touch the private parts of schoolmates in the bathroom. Others spend too much time touching their own genitals, and cause physical harm. Children may also engage in SBP of sexual language, poor physical boundaries, and use of "provocative" clothing, style, and dance. In today's fast-paced technological world, children may engage in SBP by gaining access to pornographic pictures and videos, or taking pictures of their own private parts to text or email to friends. Rarer SBP include oral-genital contact and penetration, and any use of force or coercion. Children with SBP may initiate any of these behaviors with other children, adults, or animals. Jurisdictions vary regarding what behaviors are considered illegal, delinquent, or criminal, and the age ranges for law enforcement response.

Most SBP occur among children who know each other and are playing together already (Chaffin et al., 2008; Friedrich & Trane, 2002; Lamb & Coakley, 1993; Larsson, 2001; Rutter, 1971). Young children often choose to interact socially with children of the same sex. Therefore, SBP can commonly include same-sex interactions. Caution should be used with the terms "homosexual" and "heterosexual" as descriptors of interactions in children, as these terms are used to describe adult sexual orientation. SBP, regardless of the sex of the child and others involved in the behavior, does not predict sexual orientation in adolescence or adulthood.

## DIFFERENTIATING TYPICAL SEXUAL DEVELOPMENT FROM PROBLEMATIC SEXUAL BEHAVIOR

Typical sexual development in children is best understood in the context of other areas of child development. For detailed information regarding typical child sexual development and behavior, please refer to Chapters 6 and 8 in this book. In summary, typical sexual development includes a range of behaviors including self-touch, looking and showing private parts, and touching others' private parts. Young children, including infants, may touch and play with their own genitalia (Martinson, 1981; Rutter, 1971). This behavior appears related to curiosity and pleasure seeking (Gordon &

Schroeder, 1995). Preschool age children are curious, impulsive, and pleasure seekers. At least a third of a normative sample of children between the ages of 2 and 5 years were found to undress in front of others, try to look at people undressing, and touch adult's breasts (Friedrich, Grambsch, Broughton, Kuiper, & Beilke, 1991). Normative sexual behaviors of school-age children include self-touch behaviors, interest in media content that contains nudity, and increasing interest in the opposite sex for children at the end of this developmental stage (Friedrich, 1997; Rutter, 1971).

When determining where sexual behavior falls on the continuum of typical, concerning, and problematic, consider the types of behavior, frequency, duration, emotional responses, and ages/abilities of the children. Normative sexual behaviors may occur intermittently, and are responsive to parental feedback and supervision. Normative data from research by Friedrich and colleagues (e.g., Friedrich, 1997; Friedrich et al., 1992, 2001; Friedrich, Fisher, Broughton, Houston, & Shafran, 1998; Friedrich, Sandfort, Oostveen, & Cohen-Kettenis, 2000) and the Child Sexual Behavior Inventory provides guidance in examining the frequency and types of behaviors (see the section on assessment, below, for more details).

Parents and professionals may have difficulty distinguishing typical sex play from problematic sexual behavior when the behavior occurs among children (e.g., children looking at, showing, or touching each other's genitals). Sexual play among children is not an uncommon occurrence (Lamb & Coakley, 1993; Larsson, 2001; Reynolds, Herbenick, & Bancroft, 2003). Guidelines indicate that sexual play among children occurs spontaneously and intermittently, is mutual and exploratory in nature, does not involve coercion or aggression, and is not associated with physical or emotional harm (Chaffin et al., 2008; Silovsky & Bonner, 2003). Children can't legally consent. In sex play, the children are mutually agreeing on the behavior, with no coercion or control issues. In contrast, sexual behaviors that are planned, frequent, interfere with daily functioning, coerced, and/or cause distress or harm are problematic. Problematic sexual behavior may also include specific types of behavior that are rare. From research with a variety of cultures, sexual acts that are intrusive (e.g., insertion of finger or object in another child's vagina or rectum), planned, or involved aggression were not reported to occur in normative, nonclinical samples (Friedrich, 2002).

There is not a set age difference that differentiates sex play from problematic sexual behavior, as the children's abilities and skills impact the assessment. Two children can be the same chronological age, but be quite disparate in cognitive skills, experience, power, size, and capabilities.

Developmental disabilities or delays are present when functional aspects of a child's development in one or more areas (e.g., gross/fine motor, speech/language, cognition, social personal, and activities of daily living) are significantly delayed compared with the expected level for their age. This can include such disabilities as autism spectrum disorders, mental retardation, Down Syndrome, cerebral palsy, and fetal alcohol spectrum disorders (American Academy of Pediatrics (AAP), 2001, 2007; Neef, 2001). It can be difficult to determine typical versus problematic sexual behaviors in children with developmental disabilities, due to differences between actual chronological age and cognitive ability/maturity (Gillham, Carter, Volkmar, & Sparrow, 2000).

Children with developmental disabilities may be functionally and cognitively delayed, and their "true" or mental age peer group may be considerably younger than their chronological age (Gillham et al., 2000; Joseph, Tager-Flusberg, & Lord, 2002). Closely assessing the antecedents, intentions, motivations, and potential use of coercion may be needed when examining sexual behaviors that occur among same-age peers, including a child with a disability. Further, when a child with a developmental disability initiates sexual behavior with a younger child who has commensurate social development, the behaviors may be more characteristic of sex play (e.g., spontaneous, motivated by curiosity, intermittent, with no use of coercion or force), but are defined as problematic because of the age difference and potential impact on the younger child. This sexual behavior would still require parental response and correction, to teach appropriate knowledge and skills, and to address the child's curiosity. Problematic sexual behavior in individuals with developmental disabilities may be related to: poor boundaries/social skills; lack of impulse control; tendency toward repetitive/perseverative behaviors; lack of opportunity for social relationships; and difficulty understanding abstract concepts like private versus public and social cues (Volkmar, Lord, Bailey, Schultz, & Klin, 2004; Willemsen-Swinkels & Buitelaar, 2002). Therefore, conceptualization of sexual behavior in children with developmental disabilities should be made in the context of the child's mental age (Klin, 2000).

## PREVALENCE, ORIGINS, AND CONCEPTUALIZATION OF PROBLEMATIC SEXUAL BEHAVIOR

Accurate rates of incidence and the prevalence of SBP in children are unknown, and are impacted by inconsistent definitions of the behaviors, limited epidemiological and longitudinal research, and fragmented professional responses. In the early 1990s, there were significant increases in cases involving children with SBP reported to child protection services, juvenile justice, and treatment providers (Butts & Snyder, 1997; Vermont Social Services and Rehabilitative Services, 1996—cited in Gray, Pithers, Busconi, & Houchens, 1999). The cause of the increase is unknown, although it is possible that public awareness of SBP in children, changes in child maltreatment reporting laws, changing definitions of SBP, or of a combination of factors are responsible for the increase (Chaffin et al., 2008). Research on related behaviors and factors would suggest some optimism for improvements in sexual behavior of youth. For example, the arrest rate for forcible rape committed by youth 10–17 years of age has decreased by 27% since 1999 (Puzzanchera, 2009), as have national rates of child sexual and physical abuse (Finkelhor & Jones, 2006; US Department of Health and Human Services, 2011).

Children with SBP are children who made poor choices and engaged in a behavior that carries a significant amount of emotional weight within our culture. Certainly, it is concerning when a child engages in SBP, particularly those who have been aggressive and coercive. However, it is inappropriate to label or classify them as pedophiles, perpetrators, deviants, or child molesters. Such labels stigmatize children for behaviors that are not indicative of long-term pathology. Extreme responses to children with SBP have been found by the family, schools, child welfare, and courts, including children beaten by distressed parents, placed in adult lock-up facilities, or placed in long-term residential care (Chaffin & Bonner, 1998; Chaffin, 2008). Given what is known about the origins of the behaviors and responsivity to short-term outpatient treatment, such responses are unwarranted.

Problematic sexual behaviors can be found in children from all walks of life (Chaffin, Letourneau, & Silovsky, 2002). Children with SBP are boys and girls, preschool to adolescent in age, and from all socioeconomic levels and cultures. Preschool-age (aged 3–6) girls are more likely to be referred for treatment for SBP than are preschool boys, while school-age (aged 7–12) boys tend to be more likely to be referred than are school-age girls (Bonner, Walker, & Berliner, 1999; Gray, Busconi, Houchens, & Pithers, 1997; Silovsky & Niec, 2002). Preschool-age children with SBP tend to have a more overt (less hidden) and a higher frequency of the sexual behaviors than older children (Friedrich et al., 1992; Friedrich et al., 2001; Silovsky & Niec, 2002). Children's SBP typically become more concealed as they get older and are adjusting to cultural and societal mores and norms around modesty, privacy, and relation to adults (Friedrich et al., 1992, 2001; Lamb & Coakley, 1993; Larsson, 2001; Reynolds, Herbenick, & Bancroft, 2003).

The motivations and intentions of children when they engage in SBP are as varied as the types of behaviors. It is important to be clear that the use of the word "sexual" within the SBP term describes the nature of the behavior: that is, the behavior involves sexual body parts or other behavior in a way that is generally considered as sexual. "Sexual" does not infer that children's intention and motivation were related to sexual gratification. For most children, sexual arousal and gratification does not appear to be the primary motivation, but rather attention seeking, imitation, curiosity, anxiety reduction, distraction, self-soothing, and other coping strategies appear more common (Silovsky & Bonner, 2003). Sexual behaviors in children may resemble adult sexual behaviors. However, the behaviors of children and adults are quite disparate in terms of motives, meaning, understanding of impact and consequences, purposes, and emotional implications.

While SBP describes a set of behaviors, it is not in and of itself a syndrome or psychological diagnosis (Chaffin et al., 2008). SBP are clinically concerning behaviors that may or may not be related to a pattern of other behaviors, or clinical diagnoses. Some children's SBP may be a part of a larger or overall pattern of disruptive behavior (Friedrich, Davies, Fehrer, & Wright, 2003; Pithers, Gray, Busconi, & Houchens, 1998b, c). Children with SBP are often found to have co-occurring diagnoses, particularly disruptive behavior disorders, trauma related disorder, other internalizing disorder, and learning and language delays, with preschool-aged children perhaps presenting with a higher rate of co-occurring concerns (Pithers et al., 1998b, c; Silovsky & Niec, 2002).

Problematic sexual behaviors often have negative impacts on the family and social environments. Families with children with SBP tend to demonstrate higher levels of general parental stress, difficult relationships between parent and child, as well as challenges in peer relationships (Bonner et al., 1999; Pithers, Gray, Busconi, & Houchens, 1998a; Silovsky & Niec, 2002). Parents of children with SBP may struggle with disbelief, shame, negative perception of their child, guilt, anger, sadness, reminders of their own trauma histories, and the social isolation that can occur due to difficulty in discussing SBP of their child with others (Friedrich, 2002; Silovsky, 2009).

A commonly held historical assumption was that SBP were exclusively sexually reactive behavior of children who had been sexually abused. Early research on SBP were based on this assumption, and examined what types of sexual behaviors were indicative of a history of sexual abuse. Although sexually abused children do show higher rates of sexual behaviors than other clinically referred children (Friedrich, 1993; Friedrich et al., 2001), with as much as 30% of young children and 6% of older children demonstrating SBP (Kendall-Tackett, Williams, & Finkelhor, 1991), most sexually abused children do not develop SBP. Sexual behaviors in and of themselves are not a valid indicator of abuse history (Friedrich, 2002). Many children with SBP do not have childhood sexual victimization histories (Bonner et al., 1999; Friedrich et al., 2003; Silovsky & Niec, 2002). Thus, displaying SBP does not automatically imply previous child sexual abuse, although sexual abuse can have an impact on the development of SBP, particularly with preschool-aged children.

In contrast to the belief of sexual abuse as the single cause, a developmental psychopathology framework has been a better approach in understanding the complexity of the development, effects, maintenance, and treatment of problematic sexual behaviors in children (Elkovitch, Latzman, Hansen, & Flood, 2009). It is useful to understand these children in the context of both their individual characteristics and social ecology, and how experiences and individual factors interact throughout the course of their development. The etiology of children with SBP is multifaceted, influenced by a variety of cultural and societal factors (Chaffin et al., 2008; Friedrich et al., 2001; Thigpen, 2009; Friedrich et al., 2000). The origins of SBP in children are most likely a combination of individual child factors (developmental delays, language delays, impulsivity, poor coping skills), family adversity (lack of guidance and supervision, stress, trauma, parental depression, substance abuse), modeling of coercion (harsh discipline, physical abuse, domestic violence, peer and community violence), and modeling of sexuality (child sexual abuse that is influenced by type of abuse, relationship and number of perpetrators, age of abuse, duration, and exposure to adult sexual behavior) (Chaffin et al., 2008; Friedrich et al., 2003; Silovsky, Swisher, Widdifield, & Burris, 2011). Genetics may also be a contributing factor to childhood sexual behavior (Langstrom, Grann, & Lichtenstein, 2002).

Multiple pathways can lead to problematic sexual behavior in children (Chaffin et al., 2008). It can be useful to group these pathways into those related to a general pattern of disruptive behaviors, reactions to traumatic experiences, imitative behaviors, or a combination of these factors. Often, children with SBP present with a range of sexual and nonsexual disruptive behaviors (Bonner et al., 1999; Chaffin et al., 2008; Pithers et al., 1998b, c; Silovsky & Niec, 2002). These children have problems following rules at home, at school, and/or in the community. They may be physically aggressive with other children, defiant, hyperactive, disruptive, and may frequently lie, take things from others, and have temper tantrums. Some children present with inattentiveness, suggesting ADHD. Thus, in these cases the sexual behavior problems are part of a spectrum of behavior problems of the child, or in DSM terms, a disruptive behavior disorder. The origins of the sexual behavior likely correspond with general behavior problems, including coercive parent–child interactions, poor supervision, exposure to violence, parental depression, child learning and attention problems, and genetic factors.

Other children with SBP present with a trauma history and corresponding post-traumatic stress disorder symptoms (Bonner et al., 1999; Pithers et al., 1998b, c; Silovsky & Niec, 2002). In children presenting with trauma-related symptoms (PTSD, Adjustment Disorder), the sexual behavior problems may be conceptualized as re-experiencing symptoms of PTSD. In addition to the sexual behavior problems, these children present with a combination of nightmares, hypervigilance, startle responses, distress associated with memories about the traumatic event, as well as arousal and avoidance symptoms. At times, these children may present with other internalizing symptoms, such as of separation anxiety or depression. SBP may be more likely to co-occur with PTSD when the sexual abuse was pervasive, involved penetration, or multiple perpetrators (Friedrich et al., 2003; Pithers et al., 1998b). It is important to note that, while SBP can be a symptom of PTSD, children who have been sexually abused may demonstrate SBP without PTSD symptoms.

Some children present with both significant disruptive behavior disorder and symptoms of PTSD. Often these children have had multiple adverse life experiences, including living in poverty, neglect, exposure to substance abuse, witnessing violence, and experiencing abuse. Sexualized home environments lead some children to develop a sexualized pattern of interacting with others, such as siblings, peers, and adults, perceiving this as normative. It is not unusual for children with SBP, behavior problems, and trauma histories to be in the care of the state. These children often have experienced multiple placement changes as they are moved among foster homes, relative's homes, and the parents' home.

Another significant group, perhaps about a fifth of children with SBP depending on the community served by the clinical agency (Bonner et al., 1999; Pithers et al., 1998b), present with sexual behavior problems as the primary and only concern. These children often have no premorbid issues and have been functioning well at home and school; they have no other problematic behavior or significant internalizing symptoms. These children may have seen sexual media or exposure to sexual behavior or material that caused confusion, curiosity, or otherwise prompted sexual behavior deemed inappropriate. These children may have experienced sexual abuse, such as an older youth may have touched their private parts. The sexual abuse may not have been scary for the young child, but instead confusing and awkward. Not able to understand the ramifications of the behavior, these young children repeat the experiences with other children in their lives.

The long-term prognosis of children with SBP, including children with aggressive sexual behavior, is very good. Research on treatment outcomes indicates that when children receive cognitive behavioral interventions with their caregivers, the rates of future SBP were low (2%) and similar to those of a comparison group of children with no known previous SBPs (Carpentier, Silovsky, & Chaffin, 2006).

## CLINICAL ASSESSMENT

Clinical assessment of SBP in children is the first step to determining and implementing effective services to reduce or eliminate SBP. This section will focus on clinical assessments with these goals, and not forensic evaluations designed for official legal investigations. Clarification of goals and purposes of the assessment should begin during the referral and screening process. Caution is warranted to avoid mixing clinical and forensic (e.g., forensic investigation for child sexual abuse) roles.

The clinical assessment begins at referral; when warranted, it continues with formal clinical evaluation and remains ongoing, both formally and informally, throughout services. The assessment process facilitates safety planning, and determines when and what treatment services are best suited for the child with SBP and their family. When warranted, assessment tools should be adapted for use with children who have developmental or learning disabilities. Further, ongoing assessment provides guidance to professionals involved with the child and family when considering discharge from services.

It is important that professionals involved in the assessment process possess a number of qualifications. Assessors should at minimum have a

Master's degree and be licensed by the appropriate agency or organization for their degree and profession (or in training for such license). Further, specific education in child development and behavior (sexual and broadly), etiology and evidence-based treatment of childhood mental health diagnoses, and individual and social-ecological risk and protective factors for SBP and general behavior problems is needed. It is important that assessors be well versed in cultural norms, values, and beliefs, as well as cultural differences, regarding parenting and child sexual behaviors (Chaffin et al., 2008).

A focused clinical assessment can facilitate determining if sexual behaviors are, indeed, problematic and developing treatment recommendations. A multisource (e.g., caregiver, teacher, caseworker, other adult, child) and multimethod (e.g., semistructured interviews, standardized normed questionnaires, review of background documents) approach is recommended for gathering information about the child's sexual behaviors, overall social-ecological functioning (individual, family, school, peers, community), and risk and protective factors. In developing conclusions and recommendations, examine the best interests of the child along with the interests of other children, family, and the community (Chaffin et al., 2008).

Functional assessment can be used to assess contributing factors to SBP. A comprehensive functional assessment identifies the SBPs of concern, stimuli correlated with the onset and maintenance of the SBP, specific environmental features of the SBP, and behaviors that may serve to replace the SBP. Treatment plans developed from the perspective of a functional assessment can help to ensure that the child's subjective level of functioning is represented (Gresham, Bebe-Frankenberger, & MacMillan, 1999; Lonigan, Elbert, & Johnson, 1998; Luiselli et al., 2001).

Types, frequency, duration, antecedents, responses, consequences, and factors contributing to the amelioration and maintenance of the sexual behavior problems are areas to assess. Safety planning for the home, school, and community will be guided by details regarding interpersonal sexual behavior problems, including the extent of planning and coercion, frequency, duration, relationship with the other children involved, caregiver interventions, supervision and guidance, and responsiveness of the sexual behaviors to corrective actions (Chaffin et al., 2008). When changes in placement are anticipated (e.g., child is in foster care and the plan is reunification or adoption), protective and risk factors both in the temporary living environment and in the anticipated future living environment will need to be examined. Environmental factors weigh heavily in safety and treatment planning. Examining individual factors (e.g., impulsivity, learning skills, and challenges) help identify supports needed to help the child learn and follow privacy and safety rules. Often children will fail to admit past SBP during the assessment for a variety of reasons (e.g., events are distal and memory has faded, children have difficulty admitting mistakes, shame related to the topic, confusion about events, questions used, or other aspects) that are unrelated to prognosis or treatment responsiveness.

*The Child Sexual Behavior Inventory 3rd Edition* (CSBI; Friedrich, 1997) can be a useful tool as part of the overall evaluation of the child with SBP. The CSBI is administered to caregivers, and assesses the frequency of sexual behaviors over the preceding six months. The measure has standardized norms according to gender and age. Since the third revision (published version) of the CSBI, four additional items have been added to assess aggressive and coercive sexual behaviors. In the normative sample, none of the aggressive or coercive items were endorsed (Friedrich, 2002). Including these items provides the assessor with an additional set of critical items related to sexual behaviors.

Other measures of sexual behaviors include the *Child Sexual Behavior Checklist* (CSBCL, 2nd Revision), which assesses a wide range of sexual behaviors, environmental risk and protective factors, and problematic characteristics of children with SBP, but has no published norms (Johnson & Friend, 1995). The Weekly Behavior Report is a short instrument designed for preschool-aged children and tracks week-to-week changes in sexual behaviors, as well as other emotional and behavior symptoms, and is useful not only in the initial assessment, but also to track weekly treatment progress (Cohen & Mannarino, 1996).

When conducting assessment of SBP in children, consider assessing common co-occurring clinical concerns of: (1) disruptive behavior disorder symptoms (e.g., attention-deficit hyperactivity disorder, oppositional defiant disorder); (2) trauma-related symptoms for children who have experienced a trauma; (3) other internalizing symptoms; (4) social skills deficits; and (5) learning and sensorimotor strengths and concerns. For children who have a trauma history and related symptoms are reported, the Trauma Symptom Checklist for Children and the Trauma Symptom Checklist for Young children (child and caregiver report, respectively) can facilitate examining symptoms of PTSD. These instruments also have subscales related to sexual concerns (Briere, 1996; Briere et al., 2001). The UCLA PTSD Index is also a useful instrument for assessing PTSD symptoms in children (Pynoos, Rodriguez, Steinberg, Stuber, & Frederick, 1998).

Official investigations of suspected sexual abuse, particularly any forensic interviews, are ideally completed prior to clinical assessments. Disclosures of possible sexual abuse not previously investigated often require reports to authorities. Many children with SBP have no known history of sexual abuse. The child's sexual behavior problems may raise concerns about possible sexual abuse history, but no disclosure or other evidence is noted. Origins of problematic sexual behavior tend to be multifaceted, and thus no clear single cause may be applicable. With current safety clearly established, efficacious treatment can follow, even with vague understandings of the origins of the SBP. Repeated questioning regarding abuse history is not fruitful and can interfere with future investigations if these are warranted (Chaffin et al., 2008).

Ideally, when possible, assessment tools should be adapted specifically for use with children who have developmental delays. Currently, the known measures of sexual behavior of children have not been adapted, and as such results must be interpreted in the context of the developmental disability in conjunction with life history, appropriate psychological and psychiatric measures, and cognitive and functional assessments (Cooper, 2009; Luiselli et al., 2001; Volkmar, Cook, Pomeroy, Realmuto, & Tanguay, 1999; Volkmar, Klin, Marans, & Cohen, 1996). It is important that those professionals involved in both the assessment and treatment process have clinical training and experience in working with children who have developmental delays and disabilities (Cooper, 2009).

## TREATMENT PLANNING

As noted above, sexual behavior problems are behaviors, and not a disorder in and of itself. SBP may be an isolated concern, part of a pattern of disruptive behavior disorder symptoms, related to a trauma disorder (e.g., PTSD), a combination of these, or something else. Treatment planning to address problematic sexual behavior should be based on an examination of the range of presenting problems and the results of the initial assessment.

Treatment outcome research on sexual behavior problems in children can be grouped into two categories: (1) sexual behavior problem focused treatments; and (2) sexual abuse focused treatments that include components designed to target sexual behavior problems. Research on SBP focused treatments have primarily examined group treatments, with two randomized clinical trials having been conducted with school-aged children (Bonner et al., 1999; Pithers, Gray, Busconi, & Houchens, 1998b).

Bonner and colleagues (1999) compared a cognitive behavior group (SBP-CBT) to play therapy (PT). Both programs were 12 sessions in length, with therapists first seeing the children as a group and then meeting with the caregivers as a group. Short-term reductions in SBP were found in both groups. At 10-year follow-up, children randomized to the SBP-CBT had significantly lower reports of sex offenses (2%) compared with the PT group (11%) (Carpentier et al., 2006). SBP-CBT rate was commensurate to the comparison clinical group with no known previous SBP (3%). The California Evidence Based Clearinghouse for Child Welfare (CEBC) recently rated this treatment as a 2 "supported by research evidence" (http://www.cebc4cw.org/topic/sexual-behavior-problems-in-children-treatment-of/).

In SBP-CBT, children learn rules about private parts and sexual behaviors, abuse prevention skills, sex education, appropriate boundaries, coping and self-control strategies, and how to apply the skills to facilitate keeping these rules in the future (Bonner et al., 1999; Silovsky et al., 2011). Caregivers were taught how to supervise the children, teach and implement rules in the home, communicate about sex education, and reduce behavior problems by utilizing behavior parent training strategies.

Trauma-Focused Cognitive Behavior Therapy (TF-CBT) has evidence, including randomized clinical trials with follow-ups of 1 to 2 years, of reducing sexual behavior problems in children who have been sexually abused and present with PTSD symptoms (CEBC http://www.cebc4cw.org/program/trauma-focused-cognitive-behavioral-therapy-tf-cbt-sexual-behavior-problems-in-children-treatment-of/; Cohen & Mannarino, 1997, 1998; Stauffer & Deblinger, 1996). For children who do have SBP *and* have related trauma symptoms, TF-CBT has strong support for treating both sets of symptoms. Focus on behavior parent training with additional work on safety planning, boundaries, and sexual behavior rules may be beneficial. A recent study examining duration of TF-CBT and inclusion/exclusion of the trauma narrative component found longer treatment with more focus on behavior parent training (rather than the trauma narrative) to be more effective in reducing child behavior problems and improving parenting practices (Deblinger, Mannarino, Cohen, Runyon, & Steer, 2011).

A meta-analysis was conducted a few years ago examining all treatment outcome studies available at that time in which treatment of SBP was a primary or secondary (sexual abuse treatment studies) outcome (St. Amand, Bard, & Silovsky, 2008). The manuals for each treatment were coded for the presence of a range of components, including approach (CBT, Play Therapy), modality (family, group, individual), and topics (e.g., relaxation, sexual behavior rules, sex education) addressed with the child and with the caregiver. Results examining 11 studies of 18 treatments found that the overall degree of change over the course of treatment was estimated at a 0.46 standard deviation decline in SBP. Four parent practice elements (i.e., Behavior Parent Training, Rules about Sexual Behavior, Sex Education, and Abuse Prevention Skills), one child practice element (i.e., Self-Control Skills), family involvement, and preschool age group had significant impact on the effect size variability across treatments when practice elements and sample characteristics were examined individually. Behavior Parent Training and preschool age group were the strongest predictors of reduction of SBP when multiple covariates were examined simultaneously.

Thus, active caregiver involvement in treatment is essential for progress. Individual, family, and systems barriers can interfere with caregiver participation. Creating an environment within and across service agencies supporting caregiver engagement in service provision is critical for progress (Silovsky et al., 2011).

These results of treatment outcome research on SBP are consistent with what we know about treatment of nonsexual behavior problems in children. Numerous randomized clinical trials have demonstrated that short-term behavior parent training (such as Parent Child Interaction Therapy (pcit.phhp.ufl.edu), the Incredible Years (www.incredibleyears.com), Multidimensional Treatment Foster Care (www.mtfc.com), and Barkley's Defiant Child protocol (www.russellbarkley.org)) effectively treat externalizing behavior problems, including aggression, noncompliance, and other rule-breaking behavior (Brestan & Eyberg, 1998; Chamberlain et al., 2008; Hembree-Kigin & McNeil, 1995; Webster-Stratton, 2005; Westermark, Hansson, Olsson, 2010). In general, these treatments have in common teaching caregivers: (1) relationship-building skills; (2) strategies to increase prosocial behavior such as with praise and reinforcements; and (3) strategies to decrease inappropriate behavior, such as use of clear, immediate, developmentally appropriate consequences (Patterson, Reid, & Eddy, 2002). These behavior parent training treatments are particularly effective with overt behavior problems characteristic of Oppositional Defiant Disorder.

Significant improvements in covert behavior problems severe enough to involve juvenile services and legal charges have been consistently found with Multisystem Therapy (MST; www.mstservices.com), a home and community-based intensive treatment addressing parenting, supervision, monitoring, and youth engagement in pro-social behaviors with non-delinquent peers (Borduin, Henggeler, Blaske, & Stein,1990; Henggeler, Schoenwald, Borduin, Rowland, & Cunningham, 2009; Letourneau, Chapman, & Schoenwald, 2008; Letourneau et al., 2009). MST has been augmented to address illegal sexual behavior in youth (MST-SB), and has been found to reduce SBP in older youth and adolescents (Letourneau et al., 2008, 2009).

## Special Issues: Children with Developmental Disabilities

A child with a developmental disability will likely need more concrete education and directed support to understand and manage the thoughts, feelings, desires, and even physical changes to follow rules about sexual behavior and privacy (Joseph et al., 2002). Children with DD tend to learn at a slower rate; have unique communication needs; have limited literary skills; need concrete presentation of information due to difficulty with abstract thinking and comprehension; and have trouble relating information to their own life experience without in vivo practice of skills (Joseph et al., 2002; Klin, 2000). Methods found useful include providing the child with simple strategies to engage others in social interactions, as well as discussing and helping youth practice appropriate affection, including with whom and where (Gresham et al., 1999). For example, if someone hugs a child with an intellectual disability but does not explain the purpose, the child may believe that it is okay to hug lots of people without a specific reason or social cue. Overall, role-playing relationship/social skills with feedback and encouragement may be useful (Gresham et al., 1999; Joseph et al., 2002). A related idea would be to teach typical peers as "social interaction coaches" who can supportively model for the identified child how to initiate social interactions (Joseph et al., 2002; Taubman, Brierley, Wishner, Baker, McEachin, & Leaf, 2001). Private vs. public behaviors is an important distinction, but it is an abstract concept so it may be difficult to understand. Children with significant developmental delays are likely to need support to generalize skills that they have learned in a particular therapeutic setting to other settings or situations (Lonigan et al., 1998; Scheeringa, 2001).

## SYSTEMS BARRIERS AND SUPPORTS

Children and youth with sexual behavior problems often have multiple systems involved in their lives that can provide significant supports, but more often are barriers to progress. Myths and misunderstandings of these children too often lead to labeling, isolation of the children, and decision-making that is not guided by the actual risk and protective factors found in the child, family, and larger community. Schools will expel or insist on home-bound educational programming. Children will be placed in long-term corrective or residential institutions. Treatments in these institutions are too often developmentally inappropriate, and based on approaches for adults with pedophilias or sex offenders. Public policy may require these children to register as "sex offenders," perhaps for life. When the sexual behavior problems occur among siblings, the systems response can lead to long-term separation of families members, fragmented services, and failure to account for individual strengths and wishes. These systems barriers complicate progress and provision of evidence-based treatments for children with SBP and their families. Recognizing these challenges, efforts are being made by the Office of Juvenile Justice and Delinquency Prevention (OJJDP) to develop community-based, coordinated care for youth with SBP, the child victims, and the families utilizing evidence-based treatments and multidisciplinary community change teams to improve systems' responses (Silovsky & Bonner, 2011).

## SUMMARY AND CONCLUSIONS

Sexual behavior problems of children are clinically concerning behaviors that involve private parts or physical boundaries. The children who demonstrate problematic sexual behaviors are diverse. Multiple pathways involving combinations of individual and social-ecological factors contribute to the development and maintenance of the sexual behaviors, as well as the co-occurring conditions. Assessment and treatment planning can be facilitated by examining the role of a pattern of disruptive behavior symptoms, trauma and trauma symptoms, learning and developmental supports needed, exposure to sexualized material, and a combination of these factors. SBP have been responsive to short-term outpatient cognitive-behavioral approaches to treatment that actively involve the caregivers in behavior parent training, with positive long-term prognosis.

## REFERENCES

American Academy of Pediatrics. (2001). Committee on children with disabilities: Developmental surveillance and screening of infants and young children. *Pediatrics, 108,* 192–195.

American Academy of Pediatrics. (2007). Committee on children with disabilities : Identification and evaluation of children with autism spectrum disorders. *Pediatrics, 120*, 1183–1215.

Araji, S. K. (1997). *Sexually aggressive children: Coming to understand them.* Thousand Oaks, CA: Sage.

Bonner, B. L., Walker, C. E., & Berliner, L. (1999). *Children with sexual behavior problems: Assessment and treatment.* Washington, DC: Administration of Children, Youth, and Families, DHHS. (Final Report, Grant No. 90-CA-1469).

Borduin, C. M., Henggeler, S. W., Blaske, D. M., & Stein, R. J. (1990). Multisystemic treatment of adolescent sexual offenders. *International Journal of Offender Therapy and Comparative Criminology, 34*, 105–113.

Brestan, E. V., & Eyberg, S. M. (1998). Effective psychosocial treatments of conduct-disordered children and adolescents: 29 years, 82 studies, and 5,272 kids. *Journal of Clinical Child Psychology, 27*, 180–189.

Briere, J. (1996). *Trauma symptom checklist for children: Professional manual.* Odessa, FL: Psychological Assessment Resources, Inc.

Briere, J., Johnson, K., Bissada, A., Damon, L., Crouch, J., Gil, E., & Ernst, V. (2001). The Trauma Symptom Checklist for Young Children (TSCYC): Reliability and association with abuse exposure in a multi-site study. *Child Abuse and Neglect, 25*, 1001–1014.

Butts, J. A., & Snyder, H. N. (1997). The youngest delinquents: Offenders under age 15. *Juvenile Justice Bulletin.* Washington, DC: US Department of Justice, Office of Justice Programs, Office of Justice and Delinquency Prevention.

Carpentier, M., Silovsky, J. F., & Chaffin, M. (2006). Randomized trial of treatment for children with sexual behavior problems: Ten year follow-up. *Journal of Consulting and Clinical Psychology, 74*, 482–488.

Chaffin, M. (2008). Our minds are made up – don't confuse us with the facts: Commentary on policies concerning teen and preteen juvenile sex offenders. *Child Maltreatment, 13*, 110–121.

Chaffin, M., & Bonner, B. (1998). "Don't shoot, we're your children;" Have we gone too far in our response to adolescent sexual abusers and children with sexual behavior problems? *Child Maltreatment, 3*, 314–316.

Chaffin, M., Berliner, L., Block, R., Cavanaugh Johnson, T., Friedrich, W. N., Garza Lewis, D., et al. (2008). Report of the ATSA task force on children with sexual behavior problems. *Child Maltreatment, 13*, 199–218.

Chaffin, M., Letourneau, E., & Silovsky, J. F. (2002). Adults, adolescents and children who sexually abuse children. In L. Berliner, J. Myers, J. Briere, C. T. Hendrix, C. Jenny, & T. A. Reid (Eds.), *The APSAC handbook on child maltreatment.* Thousand Oaks, CA: Sage.

Chamberlain, P., Price, J., Leve, L. D., Laurent, H., Landsverk, J. A., & Reid, J. B. (2008). Prevention of behavior problems for children in foster care: Outcomes and mediation effects. *Prevention Science, 9*, 17–27.

Cohen, J. A., & Mannarino, A. P. (1996). A treatment outcome study for sexually abused preschool children: Initial findings. *Journal of the American Academy of Child & Adolescent Psychiatry, 35*, 42–50.

Cohen, J. A., & Mannarino, A. P. (1997). A treatment study for sexually abused preschool children: Outcome during a one-year follow-up. *Journal of the American Academy of Child and Adolescent Psychiatry, 36*, 1228–1235.

Cohen, J. A., & Mannarino, A. P. (1998). Factors that mediate treatment outcome in sexually abused preschool children: Six- and 12-month follow-up. *Journal of the American Academy of Child and Adolescent Psychiatry, 37*(1), 44–51.

Cooper, C. (2009). Assessment of autism spectrum disorders [Review of the book *Assessment of autism spectrum disorders,* by S. Goldstein, J. A. Naglieri, & S. Ozonoff]. *Journal of Child and Family Studies, 18*, 491–493. doi:10.1007/S10826-009-9270-1.

Deblinger, E., Mannarino, A. P., Cohen, J. A., Runyon, M. K., & Steer, R. A. (2011). Trauma-focused cognitive behavioral therapy for children: Impact of the trauma narrative and treatment length. *Depression and Anxiety, 28*, 67–75.

Elkovitch, N., Latzman, R., Hansen, D. J., & Flood, M. F. (2009). Understanding child sexual behavior problems: A developmental psychopathology framework. *Clinical Psychology Review, 29,* 586–598.

Finkelhor, D., & Jones, L. M. (2006). Why have child maltreatment and child victimization declined? *Journal of Social Issues, 62,* 685–716.

Friedrich, W. N. (1993). Sexual victimization and sexual behavior in children: A review of recent literature. *Child Abuse and Neglect, 17,* 59–66.

Friedrich, W. N. (1997). *Child sexual behavior inventory: Professional manual.* Odessa, FL: Psychological Assessment Resources, Inc.

Friedrich, W. N. (2002). *Psychological assessment of sexually abused children and their families.* Thousand Oaks, CA: Sage.

Friedrich, W. N., Davies, W., Fehrer, E., & Wright, J. (2003). Sexual behavior problems in preteen children: Developmental, ecological, and behavioral correlates. *Annals of the New York Academy of Sciences, 989,* 95–104.

Friedrich, W. N., Fisher, J., Broughton, D., Houston, M., & Shafran, C. (1998). Normative sexual behavior in children: A contemporary sample. *Pediatrics, 101,* 1–8.

Friedrich, W. N., Grambsch, P., Broughton, D., Kuiper, J., & Beilke, R. L. (1991). Normative sexual behavior in children. *Pediatrics, 88,* 456–464.

Friedrich, W. N., Grambsch, P., Damon, L., Hewitt, S. K., Koverola, C., Lang, R. A., et al. (1992). Child sexual behavior inventory: Normative and clinical comparisons. *Psychological Assessment, 4,* 303–311.

Friedrich, W. N., Sandfort, T. G., Oostveen, M., & Cohen-Kettenis, J. (2000). Cultural differences in sexual behavior: 2-6 year old Dutch and American Children. *Journal of Psychology and Human Sexuality, 12,* 117–129.

Friedrich, W. N., Fisher, J. L., Dittner, C., Acton, R., Berliner, L., Butler, J., et al. (2001). Child sexual behavior inventory: Normative, psychiatric, and sexual abuse comparisons. *Child Maltreatment, 6*(1), 37–49.

Friedrich, W. N., & Trane, S. T. (2002). Sexual behavior in children across multiple settings. *Child Abuse & Neglect, 26,* 243–245.

Gillham, J. E., Carter, A. S., Volkmar, F. R., & Sparrow, S. S. (2000). Toward a developmental operational definition of autism. *Journal of Autism and Developmental Disorders, 30,* 269–278. doi:10.1023/A:1005571115268.

Gordon, B. N., & Schroeder, C. (1995). *Sexuality: A developmental approach to problems.* New York, NY: Plenum Publishing Corp.

Gray, A., Busconi, A., Houchens, P., & Pithers, W. D. (1997). Children with sexual behavior problems and their caregivers: Demographics, functioning, and clinical patterns. *Sexual Abuse: A Journal of Research and Treatment, 9*(4), 267–290.

Gray, A., Pithers, W. D., Busconi, A., & Houchens, P. (1999). Developmental and etiological characteristics of children with sexual behavior problems: Treatment implications. *Child Abuse & Neglect, 23*(6), 601–621.

Gresham, F. M., Bebe-Frankenberger, M. E., & MacMillan, D. L. (1999). A selective review of treatments for children with autism: Description and methodological considerations. *School Psychology Review, 28,* 559–575. Retrieved from <http://www.nasponline.org>.

Hall, D. K., Mathews, F., & Pearce, J. (1998). Factors associated with sexual behavior problems in young sexually abused children. *Child Abuse & Neglect, 22,* 1045–1063.

Hembree-Kigin, T. L., & McNeil, C. B. (1995). *Parent-child interaction therapy.* New York, NY: Plenum.

Henggeler, S. W., Schoenwald, S. K., Borduin, C. M., Rowland, M. D., & Cunningham, P. (2009). *Multisystemic therapy for antisocial behavior in children and adolescents* (2nd ed.). New York, NY: Guilford Press.

Johnson, T. C., & Friend, C. (1995). Assessing young children's sexual behaviors in the context of child sexual abuse evaluations. In T. Ney (Ed.), *True and false allegations of child sexual abuse: Assessment and case management (pp. 49–72).* Philadelphia, PA: Brunner/Mazel.

Johnson, T. C. (1990). Children who act out sexually. In J. McNamara, & B. H. McNamara (Eds.), *Adoption and sexually abused child (pp. 63–73)*. Portland, ME: University of S. Maine.

Joseph, R. M., Tager-Flusberg, H., & Lord, C. (2002). Cognitive profiles and social communicative functioning in children with autism spectrum disorder. *Journal of Child Psychology and Psychiatry, 43*, 807–821. doi:10.1111/1469-7610.00092.

Kendall-Tackett, K., Williams, L. M., & Finkelhor, D. (1993). Impact of sexual abuse on children: A review and synthesis of recent empirical studies. *Psychological Bulletin, 113*, 164–180.

Klin, A. (2000). Attributing social meaning to ambiguous visual stimuli in higher-functioning autism and asperger syndrome: The social attribution task. *Journal of Child Psychology, Psychiatry, and Allied Discplines, 41*, 831–846. doi:10.1111/1469-7610.00671.

Lamb, S., & Coakley, M. (1993). "Normal" childhood play and games: Differentiating play from abuse. *Child Abuse and Neglect, 17*, 515–526.

Langstrom, N., Grann, M., & Lichtenstein, P. (2002). Genetic and environmental influences on problematic masturbatory behavior in children: A study of same-sex twins. *Archives of Sexual Behavior, 31*, 343–350.

Larsson, I. (2001). *Children and sexuality: "Normal" sexual behavior and experiences in childhood*. Department of Health and Environment, Division of Child and Adolescent Psychiatry.

Letourneau, E. J., Chapman, J. E., & Schoenwald, S. K. (2008). Treatment outcome and criminal offending by youth with sexual behavior problems. *Child Maltreatment, 13*, 133–144.

Letourneau, E. J., Henggeler, S. W., Borduin, C. M., Schewe, P. A., McCart, M. R., Chapman, J. E., et al. (2009). Multisystemic therapy for juvenile sexual offenders: 1-year results from a randomized effectiveness trial. *Journal of Family Psychology, 23*(1), 89–102.

Lonigan, C., Elbert, J., & Johnson, S. (1998). Empirically supported psychosocial interventions for children: An overview. *Journal of Clinical Child Psychology, 27*, 138–145. doi:10.1207/s15374424jccp2702-1.

Luiselli, J. K., Campbell, S., Cannon, B., DiPietro, E., Ellis, J. T., Taras, M., et al. (2001). Assessment instruments used in the education and treatment of persons with autism: Brief report of a survey of national service centers. *Research in Developmental Disabilities, 2*(2001), 389–398. doi:10.1016/S0891-42229(01)00079-8.

Martinson, F. M. (1981). Eroticism in infancy and childhood. In L. L. Constantine, & F. M. Martinson (Eds.), *Children and sex: New finding, new perspectives (pp. 23–35)*. Boston, MA: Little, Brown.

Neef, N. A. (2001). The past and future of behavior analysis in developmental disabilities: When good news is bad and bad news is good. *The Behavior Analyst Today, 2*(4), 336–343.

Patterson, G. R., Reid, J. B., & Eddy, J. M. (2002). A brief history of the Oregon model. In J. B. Reid, G. R. Patterson, & J. Snyder (Eds.), *Antisocial behavior in children and adolescents: A developmental analysis and model for intervention (pp. 3–21)*. Washington, DC: American Psychological Association.

Pithers, W. D., Gray, A., Busconi, A., & Houchens, P. (1998a). Caregivers of children with sexual behavior problems: Psychological and familial functioning. *Child Abuse & Neglect, 22*(2), 129–141.

Pithers, W. D., Gray, A., Busconi, A., & Houchens, P. (1998b). Children with sexual behavior problems: Identification of five distinct child types and related treatment considerations. *Child Maltreatment, 3*(4), 384–406.

Pithers, W. D., Gray, A., Busconi, A., & Houchens, P. (1998c). Five empirically-derived subtypes of children with sexual behavior problems: Characteristics potentially related to juvenile delinquency and adult criminality. *The Irish Journal of Psychology, 19*(1), 49–67.

Puzzanchera, C. (2009). *Juvenile arrests 2008*. Washington DC: US Department of Justice, OJJDP, NCJ. [228479].

Pynoos, R. S., Rodriguez, N., Steinberg, A., Stuber, M., & Frederick, C. (1998). *UCLA PTSD index for DSM-IV*. Los Angeles, CA: UCLA.

Reynolds, M., Herbenick, D., & Bancroft, J. (2003). The nature of childhood sexual experiences: Two studies 50 years apart. In J. Bancroft (Ed.), *Sexual development*. Bloomington, IN: Indiana University Press.

Rutter, M. (1971). Normal psychosexual development. *Journal of Child Psychology and Psychiatry, 11*, 259–283.

Scheeringa, M. S. (2001). The differential diagnosis of impaired reciprocal social interaction in children: A review of disorders. *Child Psychiatry and Human Development, 32*, 71–89. doi:10.1023/A:1017511714145.

Silovsky, J. F. (2009). *Taking action: Support for families of children with sexual behavior problems*. Brandon, VT: Safer Society Press.

Silovsky, J. F., & Bonner, B. L. (2003). Sexual behavior problems. In T. H. Ollendick, & C. S. Schroeder (Eds.), *Encyclopedia of clinical child and pediatric psychology (pp. 589–591)*. New York, NY: Kluwer Press.

Silovsky, J. F., & Niec, L. (2002). Characteristics of young children with sexual behavior problems: A pilot study. *Child Maltreatment, 7*, 187–197.

Silovsky, J. F., & Bonner, B. L. (2011, October). Falling through the cracks: Serving youth with sexual behavior problems. Presented at OJJDP Children's Justice and Safety Conference, Washington DC.

Silovsky, J. F., Swisher, L., Widdifield, J. Jr., & Burris, L. (2011). Children with sexual behavior problems. In P. Goodyear-Brown (Ed.), *The handbook of child sexual abuse: Prevention, assessment and treatment (pp. 401–429)*. Hoboken, NJ: John Wiley & Sons.

St. Amand, A., Bard, D., & Silovsky, J. F. (2008). Meta-analysis of treatment for child sexual behavior problems: Practice elements and outcomes. *Child Maltreatment, 13*(2), 145–166.

Stauffer, L. B., & Deblinger, E. (1996). Cognitive behavioral groups for nonoffending mothers and their young sexually abused children: A preliminary treatment outcome study. *Child Maltreatment, 1*, 65–76.

Taubman, M., Brierley, S., Wishner, J., Baker, D., McEachin, J., & Leaf, R. B. (2001). The effectiveness of a group discrete trial instructional approach for preschoolers with developmental disabilities. *Research in Developmental Disabilities, 22*(2001), 205–219. doi:10.1016/S0891-4222(01)00068-3.

Thigpen, J. W. (2009). Early sexual behavior in a sample of low-income, African American children. *Journal of Sex Research, 46*(1), 67–79. doi:10.1080/00224490802645286.

US Department of Health and Human Services, Administration for Children and Families, Administration on Children, Youth and Families Children's Bureau. (2011). Child maltreatment 2010. Available from <http://www.acf.hhs.gov/programs/cb/stats_research/index.htm#can>.

Volkmar, F. R., Cook, E. H., Pomeroy, J., Realmuto, G., & Tanguay, P. (1999). Practice parameters for the assessment and treatment of children, adolescents, and adults with autism and other pervasive developmental disorders [Supplemental Issue]. *Journal of the American Academy of Child and Adolescent Psychiatry, 38*, 32s–54s. doi:10.1097/00004583-199912001-00003.

Volkmar, F. R., Klin, A., Marans, W., & Cohen, D. J. (1996). The pervasive developmental disorders: Diagnosis and assessment. *Mental Retardation, 5*, 963–977. doi:10.1352/0895-8017(1996)109<267:TCOTET>2.0.CO;2.

Volkmar, F. R., Lord, C., Bailey, A., Schultz, R. T., & Klin, A. (2004). Autism and pervasive developmental disorders. *Journal of Psychology and Psychiatry, 45*, 135–170. doi:10.1046/j.0021-9630.2004.003.7.X.

Webster-Stratton, C. (2005). The incredible years: A training series for the prevention and treatment of conduct problems in young children. In E. D. Hibbs, & P. S. Jensen (Eds.),

*Psychosocial treatments for child and adolescent disorders: Empirically based strategies for clinical practice (pp. 507–555)* (2nd ed.). Washington, DC: American Psychological Association.

Westermark, P. K., Hansson, K., & Olsson, M. (2010). Multidimensional treatment foster care (MTFC): Results from an independent replication. *Journal of Family Therapy, 33,* 20–41.

Willemsen-Swinkels, S. H., & Buitelaar, J. K. (2002). The autistic spectrum: Subgroups, boundaries, and treatment. *Psychiatric Clinics of North America, 25,* 811–836. doi:10.1016/SO193-953X(02)00020-5.

# CHAPTER 21

# Adolescents Adjudicated for Sexual Offenses

### Amanda M. Fanniff[*] and Judith V. Becker[†]
[*]Palo Alto University, Palo Alto, California[1], [†]University of Arizona, Tucson, Arizona

Adolescents adjudicated for sexual offenses have been the focus of increasing attention for the past several decades. While sexual offenses committed by male adolescents were often not taken seriously, nor considered to be an indication of deviant sexual interest during most of the twentieth century (Zimring, 2004), research in the 1980s indicating that many adult sex offenders' deviant sexual interests and/or behaviors started during adolescence (e.g., Abel, Mittelman, & Becker, 1985; Groth, Longo, & McFadin, 1982) led to a rapid growth in treatment programs designed for adolescents (National Adolescent Perpetrator Network, 1993). Additionally, public policy reforms in the 1990s and 2000s have included specialized social control policies targeting adolescents adjudicated for sexual offenses, including registration, community notification, and indefinite civil commitment (e.g., Becker & Hicks, 2003; Chaffin, 2008; Letourneau & Miner, 2005). Adolescents adjudicated for sexual offenses are commonly court-ordered into treatment (Becker & Hicks, 2003), and treatment providers working with this population have long sought out useful assessment techniques and efficacious interventions. Unfortunately, the public policy imperative to intervene with this population resulted in clinical developments outpacing research to determine empirically supported practice. Early efforts often assumed that adolescents who committed sexual offenses were very similar to adult sex offenders, an assumption that was not supported by subsequent research (Letourneau & Miner, 2005), yet some of the practices developed on the basis of this assumption remain in use today.

This chapter will review the empirical support for assessment measures and interventions developed for or used with adolescents adjudicated for

---

[1] Correspondence to: Amanda M. Fanniff, PhD, Pacific Graduate School of Psychology, Palo Alto University, 1791 Arastradero Rd, Palo Alto, CA 94304. Phone 650-961-7503 ext 36; fax 650-433-3888; email afanniff@paloaltou.edu

sexual offenses, after a brief review of research on characteristics of this population. The review of assessment measures focuses on sexual interest measures, polygraph, amenability measures, risk assessment instruments, and treatment progress measures. The review of interventions focuses on cognitive behavioral and multisystemic therapy, with some discussion of potentially promising new approaches that have not yet been the subject of rigorous outcome research. Recommendations for both assessment and treatment practices are offered for clinicians working with male adolescents adjudicated for sexual offenses.

The focus of this chapter is specifically limited to assessment and treatment for male adolescents. Males are more commonly arrested for sexual offenses, with females comprising 8.84% of arrests of individuals under age 18 for sexual crimes (excluding prostitution and commercialized vice) in 2010 (US Department of Justice, 2011). Female adolescent offenders are an important population that has historically been understudied, but given the unique needs of this subpopulation, they are outside the scope of the current review. Fortunately, the body of literature regarding this subpopulation is growing, leading to advances in the understanding of the prevalence, etiology, and appropriate treatment for female adolescents (Frey, 2010; McCartan, Law, Murphy, & Bailey, 2011; Slotboom, Hendriks, & Verbruggen, 2011; Vandiver, 2010). Additionally, children with sexual behavior problems (CSBPs: children under age 12 who have engaged in problematic sexual behaviors) are also outside the scope of the current chapter, as this group is also quite different from adolescent males adjudicated for sexual offenses. Readers are referred to recent qualitative and quantitative reviews for information about etiology, assessment, and treatment for CSBPs (Chaffin et al., 2008; Elkovitch, Latzman, Hansen, & Flood, 2009; St. Amand, Bard, & Silovsky, 2008).

## CHARACTERISTICS OF ADOLESCENT MALES ADJUDICATED FOR SEXUAL OFFENSES

Adolescents adjudicated for sexual offenses are a heterogeneous population. They come from all racial, ethnic, and cultural backgrounds. Their offenses comprise the full range of sexual offenses, including hands-on offenses (e.g., molestation) and hands-off offenses (e.g., exhibitionism), with varying degrees of coercion against victims of all ages. An early critical review of the research on juveniles who committed sexual offenses indicated that many of these youth lacked social skills, and presented with conduct disorder, learning problems, depression, and/or impulse control difficulties (Becker, Harris, & Sales, 1993). Research has also indicated many of these youth have histories of maltreatment, such as physical and sexual abuse, and many have witnessed intimate partner violence in the home (e.g., 22%, 14%, and 41%, respectively; Fanniff & Kolko, 2012). Seto & Lalumière (2010) completed a large meta-analysis of research comparing juveniles adjudicated for sexual offenses to other delinquents on a variety of theory-relevant characteristics, with results indicating that juveniles adjudicated for sexual offenses had higher rates of sexual, physical, and emotional abuse, higher rates of violence in the family, greater social isolation (but were not higher on other indications of social skills deficits), and more mental health problems (particularly anxiety). Juveniles adjudicated for sexual offenses were similar to other delinquents, in having somewhat below average intellectual functioning, problematic family relationships, and conduct problems; however, juveniles adjudicated for sexual offenses were less likely to have delinquent peers and had less extensive criminal histories (Seto & Lalumière, 2010).

Attempts have been made to identify homogeneous subtypes of adolescents adjudicated for sexual offenses. Various subtyping schemes have been suggested, including distinguishing juveniles who have committed only sex offenses from those with a variety of offense types (e.g., Butler & Seto, 2002) or distinguishing subtypes based on the age of the victims (e.g., Fanniff & Kolko, 2012). The distinction between youth with only sex offenses and those with a variety of offenses may be more meaningful (Rajlic & Gretton, 2010) than distinctions based on victim age (Fanniff & Kolko, 2012). Hunter (2006) described research indicating that sexually offending youth could be classified into one of three groups: adolescent onset, non-paraphilic (youth who were experimenting or engaged in sexually abusive behaviors in a transient manner due to difficulties establishing age-appropriate relationships with peers); early adolescent onset, paraphilic (youth who may be developing pedophilia and are more likely to select male child victims); and life course persistent (youth who engage in a variety of conduct-disordered and oppositional behaviors). It is clear that this is a heterogeneous population and, although there are some promising subtyping schemes available, additional research is needed.

## ASSESSMENT OF ADOLESCENTS ADJUDICATED FOR SEXUAL OFFENSES

Comprehensive assessment with this population should include a thorough clinical interview and developmentally appropriate measures designed to assess the youth's individual characteristics, as well as his ecological context (Fanniff & Becker, 2006a). One treatment program's assessment protocol, for example, includes measures of general psychopathology, trauma symptoms, parenting practices and discipline, and other domains in addition to sexual behavior and cognition measures (Kolko, Noel, Thomas, & Torres, 2004). Such comprehensive assessments are strongly recommended, but the focus for this chapter is on specialized instruments designed for or commonly used with adolescents adjudicated for sexual offenses. Additionally, given the lack of updated research, self-report measures such as the Adolescent Cognitions Scale and the Adolescent Sexual Interest Card Sort are not discussed (see Fanniff & Becker, 2006b for a review).

## Assessment of Sexual Interest
### Plethysmograph

The plethysmograph has long been utilized as a means to assess sexual interest on the part of adults (e.g., Freund & Watson, 1991) and adolescents (e.g., Becker, Kaplan, & Tenke, 1992) who have committed sexual offenses. This technique assesses changes in either penile circumference or volume in response to stimuli that vary on dimensions of interest (e.g., age and gender of target, degree of coercion; Seto, 2001). Among adult offenders, plethysmography has demonstrated concurrent validity, particularly regarding assessment of pedophilic interests (e.g., Stinson & Becker, 2008), and deviant sexual interest has been shown to be significantly associated with recidivism (Hanson & Morton-Bourgon, 2005). The validity and utility of the plethysmograph when used with juvenile offenders has been more controversial (e.g., Seto, 2001), although survey research suggests it is used by at least 9% of treatment programs for male adolescents in the United States and 20% of programs in Canada (McGrath, Cumming, Burchard, Zeoli, & Ellerby, 2010). Only one study has examined the test-retest reliability of the plethysmograph when used with adolescents; adequate test-retest reliability was found for most of the 19 categories of stimuli investigated (Becker, Hunter, Goodwin, Kaplan, & Martinez, 1992). A variety of research has demonstrated greater deviant sexual arousal in juveniles with male child victims (Clift, Rajlic, & Gretton, 2009; Murphy, DiLillo, Haynes, & Steere, 2001; Rice, Harris, Lang, & Chaplin, 2012; Seto, Lalumière, & Blanchard, 2000), juveniles with male child victims who were also victims of sexual abuse (Becker, Hunter, Stein, & Kaplan, 1989), or juveniles who offended exclusively against males (Hunter, Goodwin, &

Becker, 1994). Juveniles who demonstrate arousal to child stimuli have also been found to have a greater number of victims than other youth (Blanchard & Barbaree, 2005; Seto et al., 2000), and to score higher on a brief measure of pedophilic interests scored on the basis of offense history (Seto, Murphy, Page, & Ennis, 2003).

While these results are promising, studies that have attempted to use results of plethysmography to discriminate between youth with different types of victims have produced unimpressive sensitivity and specificity (e.g., sensitivity of 61.5% and specificity of 67.8% for juveniles who offended against male children, Clift et al., 2009; at cut-score of 0, sensitivity 28.6% for juveniles with only male child victims, specificity 92%, Seto et al., 2000). Additionally, factors unrelated to offense characteristics have been found to be associated with erectile responding, such as having been a victim of sexual and/or physical abuse (Becker et al., 1992; Murphy et al., 2001); the effect of such confounds makes interpretation of assessment profiles more complicated. Also, evidence that some juveniles can successfully suppress their sexual response (Clift et al., 2009), and that denial of the offense is associated with different response profiles (Becker et al., 1992), suggests that plethysmography has limited utility in assessing youth who deny their offense. Evidence regarding the predictive validity of phallometrically assessed deviant arousal is also mixed. Juveniles who demonstrated arousal to children have been found to be significantly more likely to sexually recidivate in some research (Clift et al., 2009; Rice et al., 2012), but this finding is not consistent (Gretton, McBride, Hare, O'Shaughnessy, & Kumka, 2001). Of interest, sexual interest in children was a particularly powerful predictor when juveniles demonstrated deviant responding even when instructed to suppress arousal (Clift et al., 2009). Overall, there are concerns about the utility of the plethysmograph to provide information to inform treatment that is not otherwise available to the evaluator (e.g., through self-report, victim selection), but additional research on the connection with recidivism is warranted.

### *Viewing Time Measures*
Several measures designed to subtly record the amount of time that individuals spend looking at males and females of varying ages have been developed as an alternative means of assessing sexual interest. Viewing time has been found to be associated with sexual interest and/or arousal in non-offending adults (e.g., Quinsey, Ketsetzis, Earls, & Karamanoukian, 1996; Rullo, Strassberg, & Israel, 2010) and adult sex offenders (e.g., Abel,

Huffman, Warberg, & Holland, 1998; Letourneau, 2002). Viewing time measures thus represent a less intrusive way to assess sexual interest than plethysmography, and are being employed by more than a third of treatment programs for adolescent males who have engaged in sexually abusive behaviors (McGrath et al., 2010).

The Abel Assessment *for sexual interest*™ (AASI) is one such measure that has been studied in adolescent male offenders, and is comprised of subjective ratings of sexual interest, viewing time for slides representing 22 categories of sexual stimuli, and a questionnaire about sexual history and interests (Abel et al., 2004). An early study of the AASI found test-retest correlations were too low to suggest strong stability of scores in a sample of 81 adolescent males, 41 of whom had committed sexual offenses against children (Smith & Fischer, 1999). Regarding screening validity, one scoring method demonstrated high specificity (98% of non-offenders were classified as uninterested in children) but low sensitivity (15% of offenders were classified as interested in children; Smith & Fischer, 1999), and an alternative scoring method was associated with improved sensitivity but decreased specificity (Smith & Fischer, 1999). Abel (2000) articulated several flaws in the Smith & Fischer (1999) study, including the conflation of offending against a child with sexual interest in children, and the failure to ensure members of the control group were not interested in children. In a large study of adolescent males who had engaged in problematic sexual behaviors, those who had child victims looked at slides of children significantly longer than did adolescents who did not have child victims (Abel et al., 2004); however, the authors acknowledged that the relationship was not strong enough to use viewing time alone to identify male adolescents who have offended against or are specifically interested in children.

An alternative viewing time measure, the Affinity Measure of Sexual Interest, has been studied in a sample of 78 adolescent males who acknowledged a contact sexual offense (Worling, 2006). The Affinity visual stimuli include males and females in four age categories which participants rate on sexual attractiveness while their viewing time is recorded. Worling (2006) found all measures (sexual attractiveness ratings, self-report sexual arousal graphs, and viewing time) had at least adequate internal consistency, and found a significant correlation between sexual attractiveness ratings and viewing time for most stimulus categories. There was an unexpected significant negative correlation between attractiveness ratings and viewing time for the slides of adult females, with higher attractiveness ratings being made more quickly for this subset of stimuli. The viewing time measure, attractiveness ratings, and the self-report sexual arousal graph were all able to identify adolescents with male child victims at a rate significantly better than chance, but no measures could correctly identify adolescents with female child victims (Worling, 2006). Given the accuracy of self-report, it is not clear that the viewing time component of the Affinity Measure is necessary for accurate assessment.

Only one study to date has investigated another visual reaction-based assessment of sexual interest: the "attentional blink" response to rapid serial visual presentation of images (Crooks, Rostill-Brookes, Beech, & Bickley, 2009). There is preliminary evidence that individuals' accuracy is reduced when responding to images that quickly follow after a particularly attractive or salient image; however, in a sample of 25 adolescent offenders against children and 26 adolescent non-sexual offenders, both groups demonstrated reduced accuracy after viewing pictures of animals, but not after viewing pictures of children (Crooks et al., 2009).

There is no research as yet investigating the validity of any viewing time measure when used to assess adolescents who deny their offenses, and no large normative (i.e., non-offending) sample, limiting the conclusions that can be drawn about the validity of these measures. Additionally, the research is frequently limited by using victim choice as an indicator of sexual preference. An offender may choose a younger victim for a variety of reasons (e.g., opportunity, experimentation, impulsivity; Abel, 2000), and the inclusion of juveniles who committed offenses against children but do not have persistent pedophilic interest may have resulted in weaker between-group differences than would be found if juveniles with persistent attraction to children could be separated into one group (e.g., Crooks et al., 2009; Smith & Fischer, 1999). There is also a reasonable concern that offenders can easily manipulate their response times if they learn that this is the measure of interest (Seto, 2001). Nonetheless, the results available to date suggest that, at best, the use of the viewing time measures in assessing sexual interest in children among male adolescents adjudicated for sexual offenses is not harmful (as indicated by self-report of the degree to which the Affinity Measure was upsetting; Worling, 2004), although self-report may not be as distorted as originally presumed and may provide essentially the same information as a viewing time measure.

## *Multiphasic Sex Inventory-II (MSI-II)*

The MSI-II (Nichols & Molinder, 2001) is a self-report measure developed to assess a variety of psychosexual characteristics in individuals charged with or convicted of sexual offenses, including sexually deviant interests, cognitive distortions, sexual knowledge, and response style (Arbisi, 2010). The measure includes scales developed through rational item selection (e.g., scales reflecting paraphilias), as well as scales developed through a criterion-related procedure (Molester Comparison and Rapist Comparison; Arbisi, 2010). There are some concerns regarding the representativeness of the normative sample and internal consistency (Arbisi, 2010), and there is controversy regarding the validity of the measure (Arbisi, 2010; Bugaj, 2010; Kalichman, Henderson, Shealy, & Dwyer, 1992). The MSI has been used as a measure of treatment progress in adult sex offenders (e.g., Miner, Marques, Day, & Nelson, 1990), and has been shown to be related to sexual recidivism in adult sex offenders (Craig, Browne, Beech, & Stringer, 2006). There is a form of the MSI-II designed for use with males ages 12-19, with most of the scales demonstrating acceptable internal consistency (Nichols & Molinder Assessments, Inc., 2010); however, there is no peer-reviewed research available for review regarding this measure as used to assess adolescent males, and reliability is not sufficient to establish validity.

## Polygraph

While not a measure specifically related to sexual offending, polygraphy is commonly used with adolescents adjudicated for sexual offenses. A comprehensive review of the evidence regarding the validity of polygraphy indicated that specific-incident polygraph tests have been shown to discriminate deception from truth with better than chance (although far from perfect) accuracy among the types of examinees represented in the research literature (National Research Council, 2003). The NRC (2003) also concluded that these estimates of accuracy are likely overestimates, due to measurement bias in observational studies and given that the research participants are under much less stress than individuals being interrogated. Nonetheless, polygraphy is used by about 50% of both community and residential treatment programs for adolescent males in the United States, including full disclosure examinations (to determine if the offender has disclosed his full offending history), specific issue examinations (e.g., to determine if the individual committed the offense for which he was convicted), and maintenance examinations (to determine if the offender has been compliant with treatment and supervision conditions; McGrath et al., 2010). Full disclosure and maintenance examinations are more similar to screening tests (Grubin, 2008), which have less empirical support than specific-issue tests (Meijer, Verschuere, Merckelbach, & Crombez, 2008; NRC, 2003). Programs likely continue to use the polygraph despite the lackluster evidence for validity because there is research demonstrating that juveniles disclose more victims, offenses, and/or use of force when they undergo a polygraph examination (Emerick & Dutton, 1993; Hindman & Peters, 2001). The accuracy of the additional disclosures made when juveniles undergo a polygraph examination is unknown. Proponents of the use of polygraph suggest that treatment may be incomplete and less effective if providers do not know the offender's entire history, and that the risks associated with inaccurate results are lower when polygraph is used for treatment purposes with a convicted offender rather than for an investigation of a crime (e.g., Grubin, 2008; Emerick & Dutton, 1993). Given that denial is not associated with recidivism (Hanson & Morton-Bourgon, 2005), that there is no evidence that more complete disclosure during therapy is associated with reduced recidivism, and that juveniles can be successfully treated without the use of polygraphy (Chaffin, 2011), this basis for inclusion of the polygraph is not well supported. Additionally, there is evidence that a proportion of adult offenders will make false disclosures after a "deceptive" polygraph (e.g., Kokish, Levenson, & Blasingame, 2005); while this issue has not been studied in juveniles, there is reason to be concerned that juveniles will be more likely to make false disclosures than adults (Owen-Kostelnik, Reppucci, & Meyer, 2006). Chaffin (2011) noted the ethical concerns that result from the inadequate research base demonstrating the benefits of this technique, stating: "it is less than responsible when a field embraces unusual, coercive, and intrusive practices with minors without simultaneously undertaking the rigorous testing needed to judge whether intended benefits actually exist" (p. 12). Becker & Harris (2004) conclude that "what appears to be important to facilitate disclosure is creating a safe environment in which a youth is willing to disclose his sexual history" (p. 200). Establishing such therapeutic conditions is likely sufficient to gather adequate information about the youth's history for successful treatment.

## Amenability to Treatment

Amenability to treatment has been defined as the capacity to engage in and/or benefit from available treatment (Kent v. United States, 1966; Loving & Patapis, 2007; McGrath, 1991). In making recommendations to the juvenile court, particularly regarding disposition, mental health professionals must balance risk to the community against the juvenile's amenability to treatment (Mulvey & Iselin, 2008). Such judgments are best conducted with the use of structured assessment instruments, either actuarial or structured professional judgment measures (Mulvey & Iselin, 2008). An interview-based measure designed to inform transfer evaluations, the Risk-Sophistication-Treatment Inventory (RST-I; Salekin, 2001), includes a treatment amenability scale, and may prove useful in assessing juveniles adjudicated for sexual offenses. There is some initial evidence for the reliability, concurrent validity, and criterion validity of this measure (Leistico & Salekin, 2003; Salekin et al., 2005), but it has not yet been studied in juveniles adjudicated for sexual offenses, and does not address factors that may be unique to sex offender specific treatment (Kimonis, Fanniff, Borum, & Elliott, 2011). The development of a tool to assess amenability in juveniles adjudicated for sexual offenses would enable evaluators to provide a more complete picture of relevant factors to judges making disposition decisions, and may improve treatment by identifying youth (and families) in need of a pretreatment intervention such as motivational interviewing.

## Risk Assessment
### Sexual Recidivism Risk Assessment Measures
There is a large and growing body of literature regarding the assessment of sexual recidivism risk in juveniles adjudicated for sexual offenses, with some promising signs, but there is also clear reason for caution. There are several specialized instruments that have been developed, with varying evidence for their reliability and validity.

The most commonly studied instrument to date is the Juvenile Sex Offender Assessment Protocol-II[2] (J-SOAP-II; Prentky & Righthand, 2003). The original J-SOAP was developed based on a review of research regarding juveniles who sexually offend, general delinquents, and adult sex offenders (Prentky, Harris, Frizell, & Righthand, 2000), and the revised J-SOAP-II was informed by research regarding the reliability and factor structure of the measure (Righthand et al., 2005), and included changes to add potentially relevant items and improve the reliability of coding (Prentky & Righthand, 2003). There are four scales: Sexual Drive/Preoccupation (Scale 1), Impulsive/Antisocial Behavior (Scale 2), Intervention (Scale 3), and Community Stability/Adjustment (Scale 4). Overall, the evidence regarding the reliability of the J-SOAP-II suggests at least adequate internal consistency and inter-rater reliability for most

---

[2] The authors are limiting their review to peer-reviewed, published research for the J-SOAP-II, as for all assessments and treatments covered in this chapter.

scales (see Fanniff & Letourneau (2012), for a review). Several studies have found inadequate inter-rater reliability for Scale 4, although this may be indicative of the need for a clinical interview to reliably score this scale, rather than an indication that the scale is inherently problematic (Aebi, Plattner, Steinhausen, & Bessler, 2011; Martinez, Flores, & Rosenfeld, 2007; Fanniff & Letourneau, 2012). The evidence regarding the predictive validity of the J-SOAP-II is mixed. Scale 1 has been shown to have a positive predictive relationship with sexual recidivism in three studies (Chu, Ng, Fong, & Teoh, 2012; Prentky et al., 2010; Rajlic & Gretton, 2010), but was unrelated or negatively related to sexual recidivism in seven studies (Aebi et al., 2011; Caldwell & Dickinson, 2009; Caldwell, Ziemke, & Vitacco, 2008; Martinez et al., 2007; Parks & Bard, 2006; Powers-Sawyer & Miner, 2009; Viljoen et al., 2008). There is mixed evidence regarding the relationship between Scale 2 and sexual recidivism (e.g., Aebi et al., 2011; Viljoen et al., 2008), as is expected given the focus of this scale on general criminogenic risk factors. Scale 3 has been found to have a positive predictive relationship with sexual recidivism in four studies (Caldwell et al., 2008; Martinez et al., 2007; Prentky et al., 2010; Rajlic & Gretton, 2010), although an equal number of studies have failed to find this relationship (Aebi et al., 2011; Chu et al., 2012; Parks & Bard, 2006; Viljoen et al., 2008). The results are more generally positive for Scale 4, with four studies finding a significant positive predictive relationship (Aebi et al., 2011; Martinez et al., 2007; Prentky et al., 2010; Rajlic & Gretton, 2010), and two studies failing to identify a significant relationship (Chu et al., 2012; Viljoen et al., 2008); however, Scale 4 has been included in fewer studies than all other scales because the youth must have been in the community for a minimum amount of time prior to scoring the measure (Prentky & Righthand, 2003). For the same reason, studies have varied in their definition of the J-SOAP-II Total Score (as some studies use only Scales 1–3 to calculate this score), and again studies are evenly split between those that found a significant positive relationship (Aebi et al., 2011; Martinez et al., 2007; Prentky et al., 2010; Rajlic & Gretton, 2010) and those that did not (Caldwell et al., 2008; Chu et al., 2012; Parks & Bard, 2006; Viljoen et al., 2008). The J-SOAP-II does not yet have cut-off scores, and in its current form is intended to structure evaluators' assessments to ensure inclusion of relevant risk factors (Prentky & Righthand, 2003). The only study to investigate the accuracy of clinical judgments informed by the J-SOAP-II found that raters did not identify recidivists above chance level accuracy (Elkovitch, Viljoen, Scalora, & Ullman, 2008). A recent meta-analysis found that the total score and individual scales were significantly associated with sexual recidivism (aggregated correlations ranging from 0.09 to 0.19), although there was significant heterogeneity across studies (Viljoen, Mordell, & Beneteau, 2012) and the aggregated areas under the curve (AUCs) (ranging from 0.60 to 0.70) did not indicate large effects (Rice & Harris, 2005). Given the inconsistency of the results to date, caution is required when using the J-SOAP-II to inform opinions delivered to the courts and to inform treatment-related decisions.

Another sexual recidivism risk assessment tool with some promising research support is the Estimate of Risk of Adolescent Sexual Offense Recidivism (ERASOR; Worling & Curwen, 2001), a measure designed to be used as a structured professional judgment tool. The items on the ERASOR were selected based on research on adolescent sexual recidivism, checklists and guidelines for assessing risk and protective factors in adolescents who sexually offend, and studies of adult sexual recidivism. There are five categories of risk factors included: Sexual Interests, Attitudes, and Behaviors; Historical Sexual Assaults; Psychosocial Functioning; Family/Environmental Functioning; and Treatment (Worling & Curwen, 2001). The coding manual suggests rating factors as present, possibly/partially present, not present, or unknown, and evaluators are instructed to use their clinical judgment to combine the risk factors into an overall rating of low, moderate, or high risk. For research purposes, numerical scores are typically assigned to each item, and they are summed to produce scale scores for each category of risk factors as well as a total score. The internal consistency of the ERASOR is acceptable (Worling, 2004) and its inter-rater reliability is generally good to excellent (Viljoen, Elkovitch, Scalora, & Ullman, 2009; Worling, 2004; Worling, Bookalam, & Litteljohn, 2012), although one study found less than adequate inter-rater reliability (Chu et al., 2012). There is a small but growing body of evidence demonstrating that the ERASOR total score and/or sum of risk factors rated as "present" has a positive predictive relationship with sexual recidivism (Chu et al., 2012; Rajlic & Gretton, 2010; Worling et al., 2012), with only one of these studies failing to find a similar effect for the clinical rating (Worling et al., 2012). One additional study found neither the total score nor the clinical rating to be a significant predictor of sexual recidivism (Viljoen et al., 2009). The accuracy of the clinical rating and total score are both greater when predicting sexual recidivism over a shorter follow-up (2.5 years; Worling et al., 2012). The total score, structured professional judgment rating, and two out of five individual scales were significantly associated with sexual recidivism in a recent meta-analysis (significant aggregated correlations ranging from 0.11 to 0.21), although there was significant heterogeneity across studies, and the aggregated AUCs (significant results ranging from 0.60 to 0.66) were not indicative of a strong relationship (Viljoen et al., 2012). In summary, the evidence to date regarding the ERASOR is promising, but additional research conducted on independent samples by different research groups would provide greater confidence in the predictive validity of the measure.

There are additional risk assessment tools developed for the assessment of sexual recidivism risk in juvenile offenders that have been included in only one peer-reviewed empirical study each: the Juvenile Sexual Offense Recidivism Risk Assessment Tool – II (J-SORRAT-II; Epperson, Ralston, Fowers, & DeWitt, 2005) and the Juvenile Risk Assessment Scale (JRAS; Office of the Attorney General, 2006). The initial research regarding these instruments is not promising (Caldwell et al., 2008; Viljoen et al., 2008), but additional research is needed to clarify their psychometric properties.

## *General Delinquency Risk Assessment Measures*

Although there is some evidence that the J-SOAP-II (e.g., Aebi et al., 2011; Martinez et al., 2007) and the ERASOR (e.g., Chu et al., 2012; Worling et al., 2012) may predict general recidivism, these results are not consistent across studies, and there are a variety of well-validated general delinquency risk assessment tools available for this purpose. Three commonly used measures that have also been studied in juveniles adjudicated for sexual offenses are the Youth Level of Service/Case Management Inventory 2.0 (YLS/CMI 2.0; Hoge & Andrews, 2011), the Structured Assessment of Violence Risk in Youth (SAVRY; Borum, Bartel, & Forth, 2006), and the Psychopathy Checklist: Youth Version (PCL:YV; Forth, Kosson, & Hare, 2003). There is consistent evidence for the predictive accuracy of these measures across meta-analyses, with moderate effect sizes comparable to those found for risk assessment in adult populations (Edens, Campbell, & Weir, 2007; Olver, Stockdale, & Wormith, 2009; Schwalbe, 2007), and some evidence to suggest greater incremental validity for the SAVRY and PCL:YV than the YLS/CMI (Welsh, Schmidt, McKinnon, Chattha, & Meyers, 2008). The PCL:YV (Caldwell et al., 2008; Gretton et al., 2001; Parks & Bard, 2006; Viljoen et al., 2009), SAVRY (Viljoen et al., 2008), and YLS/CMI (Caldwell & Dickinson, 2009; Chu et al., 2012; Viljoen et al., 2009) have also consistently been demonstrated to predict general and/or violent recidivism in juveniles adjudicated for sexual offenses. Contrary to research regarding general delinquents, the YLS/CMI has been found to provide incremental validity over the PCL:YV in predicting violent and general reoffending among juveniles adjudicated for sexual offenses (Viljoen et al., 2009). There is mixed evidence regarding the relationship between general delinquency risk measures and sexual recidivism (e.g., Parks & Bard, 2006; Viljoen et al., 2009), but there is a solid research foundation for using these measures with this population to predict general recidivism risk.

## Assessment of Treatment Progress

Clinicians often want to have a means to assess an individual's progress through treatment in order to inform ongoing interventions. The Treatment Progress Inventory for Adolescents who Sexually Abuse (TPI-ASA; Oneal, Burns, Kahn, Rich, & Worling, 2008) is a tool designed for treatment planning and assessment of progress in sex offense-specific treatment. The TPI-ASA is comprised of nine dimensions reflecting common treatment targets: inappropriate sexual behavior; healthy sexuality; social competency; cognitions supportive of sexual abuse; attitudes supportive of sexual abuse; victim awareness; affective/behavioral regulation; risk prevention awareness; and positive family caregiver dynamics. Initial research has demonstrated adequate to excellent internal consistency (with the expected exception of the inappropriate sexual behavior dimension; Oneal et al., 2008). Additionally, the dimensions indicative of more positive response to treatment (e.g., healthy sexuality, social competency) were significantly positively correlated with each other, and were negatively correlated with cognitions supportive of sexual abuse (Oneal et al., 2008). These initial results are promising, but additional research regarding the reliability and validity of this measure is needed. Another treatment progress measure, the Juvenile Sex Offense Specific Treatment Needs and Progress Scale (Righthand, 2005), has been developed, but has not yet been investigated in peer-reviewed studies.

## Recommendations for Practitioners

The evidence is mixed regarding many of the specialized assessment instruments developed for use with adolescents adjudicated for sexual offenses, and the demand for techniques for use with this population is high; together these conditions put clinicians in a difficult position. Although clinicians may want to uncover all aspects of a juvenile's offense history or arousal patterns, there is no evidence that such practices improve treatment outcome. Additionally, there is no information regarding how youth who deny their offenses respond on plethysmograph or viewing time measures; if these measures are only valid with youth who admit their offense, it seems that the measures would provide limited advantages above and beyond the information provided by the youth's self-report. Attempts to verify all aspects of the youth's self-reported history through polygraph may also be problematic, given the ethical concerns related to using a coercive technique that hasn't been proven to lead to greater benefit, and given the possibility that youth will be more likely to offer false disclosures subsequent to an examination considered deceptive. Perhaps the best way to prepare for successful treatment is as simple as establishing a strong therapeutic alliance to provide an environment that feels safe. Clinicians may gather enough information for successful treatment in this manner, will be modeling how to have a respectful and non-coercive relationship, and will be able to build on this relationship when implementing interventions. Clinicians may also find assessments designed to measure amenability or treatment progress to be useful to assist treatment planning. While more research is needed regarding these measures, there appears to be minimal risk of harm from using such measures, as long as they are not employed to determine which juveniles are eligible for treatment.

Risk assessment is perhaps the area most fraught with concern for clinicians working with adolescents adjudicated for sexual offenses. Clinicians are increasingly likely to face requests for risk assessment with this population, and refusal to conduct such evaluations due to the inadequate research base may result in courts relying exclusively on the recommendations of prosecutors or decisions influenced by general or sex offender instruments, without information regarding the need for caution in their interpretation (Vitacco, Caldwell, Ryba, Malesky, & Kurus, 2009). Evaluators can be more confident in their use of general delinquency risk measures to predict general recidivism than in the identification of which youth present the greatest risk for sexual reoffense. Perhaps future research will identify existing or new risk tools that are consistently strongly related to sexual recidivism. For now, the recommendations offered by Vitacco & colleagues (2009) are sound: focus on short-term risk; use a comprehensive and empirically informed assessment approach; consider the low base rates of sexual recidivism and that risk can be decreased through maturation and treatment; and assess peer, family, and community factors in addition to individual risk factors. Additionally, research suggests that evaluators should be particularly cautious in using the J-SOAP-II and ERASOR with adolescents who have engaged in a variety of delinquent acts (Rajlic & Gretton, 2010), and in making risk determinations in youth under age 16 (Viljoen et al., 2008, 2009).

## TREATMENT FOR ADOLESCENTS ADJUDICATED FOR SEXUAL OFFENSES

There is a growing body of evidence suggesting that treatment for adolescents adjudicated for sexual offenses is effective. Two meta-analyses have demonstrated a significant effect of treatment, with the largest effect sizes found for cognitive behavioral treatment and multisystemic therapy (Reitzel & Carbonell, 2006; Walker, McGovern, Poey, & Otis, 2005). The majority of treatment programs for male adolescents who have engaged in sexual offending identify cognitive behavioral as the primary theory of their program (63.8% of community programs, 69.8% of residential programs; McGrath et al., 2010). Multisystemic therapy is less commonly implemented, with 18.7% of community programs identifying this as one of the top three theories influencing the program (McGrath et al., 2010). The nature of these two treatment approaches and the evidence of their efficacy is reviewed below, followed by a brief description of promising new approaches.

### Cognitive Behavioral Therapy (CBT)

Cognitive behavioral therapy for adolescents adjudicated for sexual offenses is typically a multi-component treatment informed by cognitive theories as well as classical and operant conditioning principles. The vast majority of treatment programs identify beliefs and attitudes that may have led to the inappropriate sexual behaviors or may serve to reinforce them as a target of treatment for this population (McGrath et al., 2010). Restructuring any "permission-giving statements" or other problematic beliefs is a major goal of CBT (Becker, 1990, p. 364). Behavioral aspects of CBT include techniques designed to help the adolescent identify precursors that led to him committing an offense, and to develop skills to assist in refraining from the inappropriate behavior. This may take the form of covert sensitization (in which the client focuses on highly aversive images of the negative consequences of sexual behavior to control such interests), verbal satiation (in which offenders use deviant thoughts in a repetitive manner to satiate themselves and reduce interest), and/or relapse prevention (Becker, 1990). CBT programs also typically provide training to address any skills deficits that may have served as precursors to the inappropriate behavior. Common skills training components include social skills training, sexual education, and emotion regulation. CBT also often includes treatment components focused on offender responsibility/accountability and victim empathy, including techniques designed to assist in developing an appreciation for the negative effects experienced by victims. Additionally, given the high rates of traumatic experiences in this population, trauma-focused CBT or other approaches to address trauma are also commonly utilized (McGrath et al., 2010). Inpatient and outpatient programs both commonly identify CBT as their primary theoretical orientation (McGrath et al., 2010), and programs vary considerably in length. The vast majority of treatment programs report providing individual, group, and (to a somewhat lesser extent) family therapy, although there seems to be a greater emphasis on delivery of services in group therapy in both types of programs (McGrath et al., 2010). The majority of service providers are Master's level clinicians in community programs and Bachelor's level providers in residential programs (McGrath et al., 2010). This data is not specific to programs specializing in CBT, but given the proportion of programs involved in the survey that identified CBT as one of their primary theoretical approaches, the data is considered likely representative of CBT delivered to adolescents adjudicated for sexual offenses.

As indicated above, CBT has been found to be an effective approach for this population in two meta-analyses. Verbal satiation appears to be associated with decreased deviant arousal as assessed by plethysmography (Hunter & Goodwin, 1992; Kaplan, Morales, & Becker, 1993), although extensive treatment may result in decreased arousal to consensual stimuli as well (Hunter & Goodwin, 1992). Additionally, younger juveniles (Hunter & Goodwin, 1992; Kaplan et al., 1993), juveniles with a more extensive offending history (Hunter & Goodwin, 1992), and juveniles with peer victims (Kaplan et al., 1993) may be less responsive to verbal satiation. Studies of full CBT treatment packages with multiple components have also demonstrated reduced deviant sexual arousal in juveniles with male child victims (Becker, Kaplan, & Kavoussi, 1988), or juveniles with either gender victim (Hunter & Santos, 1990). While these results are promising, not all studies of CBT have demonstrated decreased deviant arousal. Covert sensitization has not been shown to significantly reduce deviant sexual arousal or self-reported masturbation to deviant fantasies (Aylwin, Reddon, & Burke, 2005; Weinrott, Riggan, & Frothingham, 1997). Additionally, the use of covert sensitization and fantasy logs may even temporarily increase deviant fantasies (Aylwin et al., 2005). Furthermore, given that decreased deviant sexual arousal has not been shown to be associated with decreased sexual recidivism in adults (e.g., Rice, Quinsey, & Harris, 1991), studies demonstrating an effect on recidivism are necessary. An initial effectiveness study and a long-term follow-up regarding a comprehensive CBT and relapse prevention program has demonstrated such effects (Worling & Curwen, 2000; Worling, Litteljohn, & Bookalam, 2010). The Sexual Abuse, Family Education, and Treatment (SAFE-T) program includes individual, group, and family treatment modalities with both sexual specific (e.g., denial and accountability, deviant sexual interest) and more general (e.g., anger, social skills) treatment targets. The initial study compared offenders who completed treatment to those who received only assessment, received treatment elsewhere, refused treatment, or dropped out of treatment. Those who completed the SAFE-T program demonstrated significantly lower sexual (5% vs. 18%), violent non-sexual (19% vs. 32%), and non-violent (21% vs. 50%) recidivism over an average follow-up of 6.23 years (Worling & Curwen, 2000). These results have recently been extended by an additional 10 years of follow-up data, with findings still indicating that juveniles who completed the SAFE-T program had lower recidivism rates for sexual (9% vs. 21%), violent non-sexual (22% vs. 39%), and non-violent rearrest (28% vs. 52%; Worling et al., 2010). These results are certainly encouraging, although some caution is necessary given the inclusion of treatment refusers and dropouts in the comparison group (Letourneau, 2004).

## Multisystemic Therapy

The treatment approach with the best evidence of effectiveness to date is multisystemic therapy (MST). MST was developed as an intervention for serious juvenile offenders, targeting the multiple interacting systems (including individual, family, peer, school, and community factors) that impact involvement in delinquency through community- and home-based services designed to build upon the natural strengths within the systems surrounding the youth (Henggeler, Schoenwald, Borduin, Rowland, & Cunningham, 1998). Treatment is driven by nine principles of MST, and key goals are to provide parents with the skills and resources needed to address problem behaviors in their children, and to provide adolescents the skills needed to cope with familial and extra-familial problems (Letourneau et al., 2009). Adaptations for use with juveniles who have engaged in sexual offenses include techniques to address denial of the offense, safety planning, and promotion of age-appropriate peer relationships (Letourneau et al., 2009). As noted, MST is provided in home and community settings, and thus is utilized in outpatient treatment. Therapists are available to clients 24 hours a day, maintain small case loads to enable such intensive service provision, and are provided supervision to ensure adherence to the treatment model (Henggeler, 2011). Clinicians from a variety of disciplines are able to learn and adhere to the principles of MST (Henggeler, 2011), and MST is commonly delivered by Master's level clinicians (e.g., Curtis, Ronan, & Borduin, 2004). Treatment is designed to be present-focused and brief, with treatment usually lasting 15–24 weeks (Curtis et al., 2004). MST has been shown to be a cost-effective approach, with savings over the long term of $6,000 to $12,000 per youth despite up-front costs (Klietz, Borduin, & Schaeffer, 2010).

In general delinquency populations, MST has been shown to create greater reductions in offending, as well as greater improvements in other domains (e.g., family functioning) compared with control treatments in a meta-analysis of 11 studies (Curtis et al., 2004), as well as more recent effectiveness studies (e.g., Timmons-Mitchell, Bender, Kishna, & Mitchell, 2006). Additionally, there are now three randomized controlled trials investigating the impact of MST on juveniles who engaged in sexual offenses (Borduin, Henggeler, Blaske, & Stein, 1990; Borduin, Schaeffer, & Heiblum, 2009; Letourneau et al., 2009). While conclusions that could be drawn from the earliest study were limited by the very small sample ($n=16$), there was a significant difference in both sexual and nonsexual recidivism rates (Borduin et al., 1990). At one year post-treatment, Letourneau and colleagues (2009) found that juveniles who received MST showed greater reductions than juveniles who received treatment as usual in problematic sexual behaviors, self-reported delinquency, substance use, and externalizing symptoms. Borduin & colleagues (2009) followed youth for an average of 8.9 years, and found that juveniles who received MST were significantly less likely to reoffend either sexually (8.3% vs. 45.8%) or non-sexually (29.2% vs. 45.8%) than the control group. Additionally, juveniles who received MST showed greater improvements in other domains as well (e.g., psychiatric symptoms, peer bonding and social maturity, academic performance; Borduin et al., 2009). This promising line of research suggests that MST is an efficacious intervention for adolescents adjudicated for sexual offenses.

## Other Promising Approaches

There are several therapeutic approaches that have not yet been the subject of outcome research, but may prove to be effective interventions.

Hunter, Gilbertson, Vedros, & Morton (2004) described two innovative approaches to treatment that provide comprehensive, community-based care emphasizing highly individualized treatment delivered within a social-ecological treatment model, targeting broad treatment goals beyond sexual behavior, and fostering close collaboration between legal and clinical professionals. Such approaches appear likely to be beneficial, given some overlap with MST (e.g., the focus on the social-ecological context and community-based service delivery). Another approach that may prove useful with this population is the Good Lives Model (Thakker, Ward, & Tidmarsh, 2006). This approach uses a strong, positive therapeutic alliance to help clients identify and achieve realistic and positive goals; this may more readily engage juveniles than more punitive, avoidance-based approaches like CBT (Thakker et al., 2006). A strengths-based, developmentally sensitive integrative approach has been outlined for use with adolescents adjudicated for sexual offenses by Longo (2005). Finally, motivational interviewing (Miller & Rollnick, 2002) or other motivation-based approaches (Patel, Lambie, & Glover, 2008) may prove useful as either a standalone treatment or a pretreatment intervention, given that adolescents are often court-ordered into treatment, and may not be intrinsically motivated for change. For all of these promising approaches, controlled outcome research is necessary to determine whether these interventions are effective with this particular population.

## Recommendations for Practitioners

Overall, treatment for adolescents adjudicated for sexual offenses appears to be effective in reducing recidivism rates (e.g., Reitzel & Carbonell, 2006). CBT and MST have the best empirical support to date, with MST being the only treatment approach to demonstrate its effectiveness in multiple randomized controlled trials. Given the success of MST and the SAFE-T program, family involvement in treatment seems to be an important ingredient for success. Additionally, treatment goals that are substantially broader than the sex offense focused goals of traditional CBT are likely to produce better treatment outcomes. It is also reasonable to hypothesize that treatment provided in the community will lead to greater change that is more sustainable (Fanniff & Becker, 2006a; Hunter et al., 2004), and that interventions developed for use with general delinquents will be effective (Fanniff & Becker, 2006a) given similarities between adolescents adjudicated for sexual offenses and other delinquents (e.g., Ronis & Borduin, 2007). The current authors continue to believe that the most effective treatment interventions will: (1) be community-based; (2) be heavily influenced by empirically supported treatment of delinquents; (3) be informed by risk-need-responsivity principles (Andrews & Bonta, 2010); (4) include broad treatment goals beyond deviant sexuality; and (5) be delivered more often in individual than group format (Kirsch, Fanniff, & Becker, 2011). Readers are also referred to the Standards of Care established by the International Association for the Treatment of Sexual Offenders (Miner et al., 2006) which similarly emphasizes developmentally-sensitive assessment and intervention, a social-ecological understanding of problem behaviors, and identification of broad treatment goals, among other useful recommendations.

## CONCLUSIONS

The science and practice of clinical work with adolescents adjudicated for sexual offenses continue to develop at a rapid pace. New assessment techniques and innovative intervention approaches are promising but require additional research. Techniques that are based in adult models of the etiology and treatment of sexual offending are still influential, but new developmentally sensitive approaches are gaining ground. The field should continue to move in this positive direction, developing assessment tools and interventions for this population not based on techniques used with adults, but by drawing from the broader fields of normative child development, developmental psychopathology, and the rich literature regarding the etiology and treatment of other delinquents. Further research should also focus on the impact that specialized social control policies such as community notification have on these youth and their families.

## REFERENCES

Abel, G. G. (2000). The importance of meeting research standards: A reply to Fischer and Smith's articles on the Abel Assessment for Sexual Interest™. *Sexual Abuse: A Journal of Research and Treatment, 12*(2), 155–161. doi:10.1177/107906320001200206.

Abel, G. G., Huffman, J., Warberg, B., & Holland, C. L. (1998). Visual reaction time and plethysmography as measures of sexual interest in child molesters. *Sexual Abuse: A Journal of Research and Treatment, 10*(2), 81–95. doi: 0.1177/107906329801000202.

Abel, G. G., Jordan, A., Rouleau, J. L., Emerick, R., Barboza-Whitehead, S., & Osborn, C. (2004). Use of visual reaction time to assess male adolescents who molest children. *Sexual Abuse: A Journal of Research and Treatment, 16*(3), 255–265. doi:10.1177/107906320401600306.

Abel, G. G., Mittelman, M., & Becker, J. V. (1985). Sexual offenders: Results of assessment and recommendations for treatment. In H. H. Ben-Aron, S. I. Huckers, & C. D. Webster (Eds.), *Clinical criminology: Current concepts (pp. 191–205).* Toronto: M & M Graphics.

Aebi, M., Plattner, B., Steinhausen, H.-C., & Bessler, C. (2011). Predicting sexual and nonsexual recidivism in a consecutive sample of juveniles convicted of sexual offences. *Sexual Abuse: A Journal of Research and Treatment, 23*(4), 456–473. doi:10.1177/1079063210384634.

Andrews, D. A., & Bonta, J. (2010). *The psychology of criminal conduct, Fifth edition.* New Providence, NJ: Matthew Bender & Company, Inc.

Arbisi, P. A. (2010). Review of the Multiphasic Sex Inventory II. Mental Measurements Yearbook, 16. Retrieved on 1/25/12.

Aylwin, A. S., Reddon, J. R., & Burke, A. R. (2005). Sexual fantasies of adolescent male sex offenders in residential treatment: A descriptive study. *Archives of Sexual Behavior, 34*(2), 231–239. doi:10.1007/s10508-005-1800-3.

Becker, J. V. (1990). Treating adolescent sexual offenders. *Professional Psychology: Research and Practice, 21*(5), 362–365. doi:10.1037/0735-7028.21.5.362.

Becker, J. V., & Harris, C. (2004). The psychophysiological assessment of juvenile offenders. In G. O'Reilly, W. L. Marshall, A. Carr, & R. C. Beckett (Eds.), *The handbook of clinical intervention with young people who sexually abuse* (pp. 191–202). New York, NY: Psychology Press, Taylor and Francis Group.

Becker, J. V., Harris, C. D., & Sales, B. D. (1993). Juveniles who commit sexual offenses: A critical review of research. In G. C. Nagayama Hall, R. Hirschman, J. R. Graham, & M. S. Zaragoza (Eds.), *Sexual aggression* (pp. 215–228). Washington, DC: Taylor & Francis.

Becker, J. V., & Hicks, S. J. (2003). Juvenile sexual offenders: Characteristics, interventions, and policy issues. *Annals of the New York Academy of Sciences, 989*(1), 397–410. doi:10.1111/j.1749-6632.2003.tb07321.x.

Becker, J. V., Hunter, J. A., Goodwin, D., Kaplan, M. S., & Martinez, D. (1992). Test-retest reliability of audio-taped phallometric stimuli with adolescent sex offenders. *Annals of Sex Research, 5*(1), 45–51. doi:10.1007/BF00849876.

Becker, J. V., Hunter, J. A., Stein, R. M., & Kaplan, M. S. (1989). Factors associated with erection in adolescent sex offenders. *Journal of Psychopathology and Behavioral Assessment, 11*(4), 353–362. doi:10.1007/BF00961533.

Becker, J. V., Kaplan, M. S., & Kavoussi, R. (1988). Measuring the effectiveness of treatment for the aggressive adolescent sexual offender. *Annals of the New York Academy of Sciences, 528*(1), 215–222. doi:10.1111/j.1749-6632.1988.tb50865.x.

Becker, J. V., Kaplan, M. S., & Tenke, C. E. (1992). The relationship of abuse history, denial and erectile response profiles of adolescent sexual perpetrators. *Behavior Therapy, 23*(1), 87–97. doi:10.1016/S0005-7894(05)80310-7.

Blanchard, R., & Barbaree, H. E. (2005). The strength of sexual arousal as a function of the age of the sex offender: Comparisons among pedophiles, hebephiles, and teleiophiles. *Sexual Abuse: A Journal of Research and Treatment, 17*(4), 441–456. doi:10.1177/107906320501700407.

Borduin, C. M., Henggeler, S. W., Blaske, D. M., & Stein, R. J. (1990). Multisystemic treatment of adolescent sexual offenders. *International Journal of Offender Therapy and Comparative Criminology, 34*(2), 105–113. doi:10.1177/0306624X9003400204.

Borduin, C. M., Schaeffer, C. M., & Heiblum, N. (2009). A randomized clinical trial of multisystemic therapy with juvenile sexual offenders: Effects on youth social ecology and criminal activity. *Journal of Consulting and Clinical Psychology, 77*(1), 26–37. doi:10.1037/a0013035.

Borum, R., Bartel, P., & Forth, A. (2006). *Structured Assessment of Violence Risk in Youth (SAVRY).* Lutz, FL: Psychological Assessment Resources.

Bugaj, A. (2010). Review of the Multiphasic Sex Inventory II. Mental Measurements Yearbook, 16.

Butler, S. M., & Seto, M. C. (2002). Distinguishing two types of adolescent sex offenders. *Journal of the American Academy of Child & Adolescent Psychiatry, 41*(1), 83–90. doi:10.1097/00004583-200201000-00015.

Caldwell, M. F., & Dickinson, C. (2009). Sex offender registration and recidivism risk in juvenile sexual offenders. *Behavioral Sciences & the Law, 27*, 941–956. doi:10.1002/bsl.907.

Caldwell, M. F., Ziemke, M. H., & Vitacco, M. J. (2008). An examination of the sex offender registration and notification act as applied to juveniles: Evaluating the ability to predict sexual recidivism. *Psychology, Public Policy, and Law, 14*(2), 89–114. doi:10.1037/a0013241.

Chaffin, M. (2008). Our minds are made up–Don't confuse us with the facts: Commentary on policies concerning children with sexual behavior problems and juvenile sex offenders. *Child Maltreatment, 13*(2), 110–121. doi:10.1177/1077559508314510.

Chaffin, M. (2011). The case of juvenile polygraphy as a clinical ethics dilemma. *Sexual Abuse: A Journal of Research and Treatment, 23*(3), 314–328. doi:10.1177/1079063210382046.

Chaffin, M., Berliner, L., Block, R., Cavanagh Johnson, T., Friedrich, W. N., Garza Louis, D., et al. (2008). Report of the ATSA task force on children with sexual behavior problems. *Child Maltreatment, 13*(2), 199–218. doi:10.1177/1077559507306718.

Chu, C. M., Ng, K., Fong, J., & Teoh, J. (2012). Assessing youth who sexually offended: The predictive validity of the ERASOR, J-SOAP-II, and YLS/CMI in a non-Western context. *Sexual Abuse: A Journal of Research and Treatment, 24*(2), 153–174. doi: 10.1177/1079063211404250.

Clift, R. J. W., Rajlic, G., & Gretton, H. M. (2009). Discriminative and predictive validity of the penile plethysmograph in adolescent sex offenders. *Sexual Abuse: A Journal of Research and Treatment, 21*(3), 335–362. doi:10.1177/1079063209338491.

Craig, L. A., Browne, K. D., Beech, A., & Stringer, I. (2006). Psychosexual characteristics of sexual offenders and the relationship to sexual reconviction. *Psychology, Crime, & Law, 12*(3), 231–243. doi:10.1080/10683160500151084.

Crooks, V. L., Rostill-Brookes, H., Beech, A. R., & Bickley, J. A. (2009). Applying rapid serial visual presentation to adolescent sexual offenders: Attentional bias as a measure of deviant sexual interest? *Sexual Abuse: A Journal of Research and Treatment, 21*(2), 135–148. doi:10.1177/1079063208328677.

Curtis, N. M., Ronan, K. R., & Borduin, C. M. (2004). Multisystemic treatment: A meta-analysis of outcome studies. *Journal of Family Psychology, 18*(3), 411–419. doi:10.1037/0893-3200.18.3.411.

Edens, J. R., Campbell, J. S., & Weir, J. M. (2007). Youth psychopathy and criminal recidivism: A meta-analysis of the Psychopathy Checklist measures. *Law and Human Behavior, 31*(1), 53–75. doi:10.1007/s10979-006-9019-y.

Elkovitch, N., Latzman, R. D., Hansen, D. J., & Flood, M. F. (2009). Understanding child sexual behavior problems: A developmental psychopathology framework. *Clinical Psychology Review, 29*(7), 586–598. doi:10.1016/j.cpr.2009.06.006.

Elkovitch, N., Viljoen, J. L., Scalora, M. J., & Ullman, D. (2008). Assessing risk of reoffending in adolescents who have committed a sexual offense: The accuracy of clinical judgments after completion of risk assessment instruments. *Behavioral Sciences & the Law, 26*(4), 511–528. doi:10.1002/bsl.832.

Emerick, R. L., & Dutton, W. A. (1993). The effect of polygraphy on the self report of adolescent sex offenders: Implications for risk assessment. *Annals of Sex Research, 6*(2), 83–103. doi:10.1177/107906329300600201.

Epperson, D. L., Ralston, C. A., Fowers, D., & DeWitt, J. (2005). *Scoring guidelines for the Juvenile Sexual Offense Recidivism Risk Assessment Tool - II (JSORRAT-II)*. Ames, IA: Authors.

Fanniff, A. M., & Becker, J. V. (2006a). Developmental considerations in working with juvenile sex offenders. In R. Longo, & D. Prescott (Eds.), *Current perspectives on working with sexually aggressive youth and youth with sexual behavior problems* (pp. 119–141). Holyoke, MA: NEARI Press.

Fanniff, A. M., & Becker, J. V. (2006b). Specialized assessment and treatment of adolescent sex offenders. *Aggression and Violent Behavior, 11*(3), 265–282. doi:10.1016/j.avb.2005.08.003.

Fanniff, A. M., & Kolko, D. J. (2012). Victim age based subtypes of juveniles adjudicated for sexual offenses: Comparisons across domains in an outpatient sample. *Sexual Abuse: A Journal of Research and Treatment, 24*(3), 224–264. doi:10.1177/1079063211416516.

Fanniff, A. M. & Letourneau, E. J. (2012). Another piece of the puzzle: Psychometric properties of the J-SOAP-II. *Sexual Abuse: A Journal of Research and Treatment 24*(4), 378–408. doi: 10/1177/1079063211431842.

Forth, A., Kosson, D., & Hare, R. D. (2003). *Psychopathy Checklist: Youth Version (PCL:YV)*. North Tonawanda, NY: Multi-Health Systems, Inc.

Freund, K., & Watson, R. J. (1991). Assessment of the sensitivity and specificity of a phallometric test: An update of the phallometric diagnosis of pedophilia. *Psychological Assessment, 3*(2), 254–260. doi:10.1037/1040-3590.3.2.254.

Frey, L. L. (2010). The juvenile female sexual offender: Characteristics, treatment and research. In T. A. Gannon, & F. Cortoni (Eds.), *Female sexual offenders: Theory, assessment, and treatment (pp. 53–71)*. New York, NY: John Wiley & Sons Ltd.

Gretton, H. M., McBride, M., Hare, R. D., O'Shaughnessy, R., & Kumka, G. (2001). Psychopathy and recidivism in adolescent sex offenders. *Criminal Justice and Behavior, 28*(4), 427–449. doi:10.1177/009385480102800403.

Groth, A. N., Longo, R. E., & McFadin, J. B. (1982). Undetected recidivism among rapists and child molesters. *Crime & Delinquency, 28*(3), 450–458. doi:10.1177/001112878202800305.

Grubin, D. (2008). The case for polygraph testing of sex offenders. *Legal and Criminological Psychology, 13*(2), 177–189. doi:10.1348/135532508X295165.

Hanson, R. K., & Morton-Bourgon, K. E. (2005). The characteristics of persistent sexual offenders: A meta-analysis of recidivism studies. *Journal of Consulting and Clinical Psychology, 73*(6), 1154–1163. doi: 10.1037/0022-006X.73.6.1154.

Henggeler, S. W. (2011). Efficacy studies to large-scale transport: The development and validation of multisystemic therapy programs. *Annual Review of Clinical Psychology, 7*, 351–381. doi:10.1146/annurev-clinpsy-032210-104615.

Henggeler, S. W., Schoenwald, S. K., Borduin, C. M., Rowland, M. D., & Cunningham, P. B. (1998). *Multisystemic treatment of antisocial behavior in children and adolescents*. New York, NY: Guilford Press.

Hindman, J., & Peters, J. M. (2001). Polygraph testing leads to better understanding adult and juvenile sex offenders. *Federal Probation, 65*(3), 8–15.

Hoge, R. D., & Andrews, D. A. (2011). *Youth Level of Service/Case Management Inventory 2.0 (YLS/CMI 2.0)*. North Tonawanda, NY: Multi-Health Systems, Inc.

Hunter, J. A. (2006). Understanding diversity in juvenile sexual offenders: Implications for assessment, treatment, and legal management. In R. E. Longo, & D. S. Prescott (Eds.), *Current perspectives: Working with sexually aggressive youth and youth with sexual behavior problems (pp. 63–77)*. Holyoke, MA: NEARI Press.

Hunter, J. A., Gilbertson, S. A., Vedros, D., & Morton, M. (2004). Strengthening community-based programming for juvenile sexual offenders: Key concepts and paradigm shifts. *Child Maltreatment, 9*(2), 177–189. doi:10.1177/1077559504264261.

Hunter, J. A., & Goodwin, D. W. (1992). The clinical utility of satiation therapy with juvenile sexual offenders: Variations and efficacy. *Annals of Sex Research, 5*(2), 71–80. doi:10.1007/BF00849732.

Hunter, J. A., Goodwin, D. W., & Becker, J. V. (1994). The relationship between phallometrically measured deviant sexual arousal and clinical characteristics in juvenile sexual offenders. *Behaviour Research and Therapy, 32*(5), 533–538. doi:10.1016/0005-7967(94)90142-2.

Hunter, J., & Santos, D. (1990). The use of specialized cognitive-behavioral therapies in the treatment of adolescent sexual offenders. *International Journal of Offender Therapy and Comparative Criminology, 34*(3), 239–247. doi:10.1177/0306624X9003400307.

Kalichman, S. C., Henderson, M. C., Shealy, L. S., & Dwyer, M. (1992). Psychometric properties of the Multiphasic Sex Inventory in assessing sex offenders. *Criminal Justice and Behavior, 19*(4), 384–396. doi:10.1177/0093854892019004003.

Kaplan, M. S., Morales, M., & Becker, J. V. (1993). The impact of verbal satiation on adolescent sex offenders: A preliminary report. *Journal of Child Sexual Abuse, 2*, 81–88. doi:10.1300/J070v02n03_06.

Kent V. United States, 383 U.S. 541 (1966).

Kimonis, E. R., Fanniff, A. M., Borum, R., & Elliott, K. (2011). Clinicians' perceptions of indicators of amenability to sex offender specific treatment in juveniles. *Sexual Abuse: A Journal of Research and Treatment, 23*(2), 193–211. doi:10.1177/1079063210384278.

Kirsch, L. G., Fanniff, A. M., & Becker, J. V. (2011). Treatment of adolescent and adult sex offenders. In J. E. B. Myers (Ed.), *The APSAC handbook on child maltreatment (pp. 289–306)* (3rd ed.). Thousand Oaks, CA: Sage Publications.

Klietz, S. J., Borduin, C. M., & Schaeffer, C. M. (2010). Cost-benefit analysis of mulitsystemic therapy with serious and violent juvenile offenders. *Journal of Family Psychology, 24*(5), 657–666. doi:10.1037/a0020838.

Kokish, R., Levenson, J. S., & Blasingame, G. D. (2005). Post-conviction sex offender polygraph examination: Client-reported perceptions of utility and accuracy. *Sexual Abuse: A Journal of Research and Treatment, 17*(2), 211–221. doi:10.1007/S1I194-005-4606-X.

Kolko, D. J., Noel, C., Thomas, G., & Torres, E. (2004). Cognitive-behavioral treatment for adolescents who sexually offend and their families: Individual and family applications in a collaborative outpatient program. *Journal of Child Sexual Abuse, 13*(3), 157–192. doi:10.1300/J070v13n03_09.

Leistico, A. -M. R., & Salekin, R. T. (2003). Testing the reliability and validity of the Risk, Sophistication-Maturity, and Treatment Amenability Instrument (RST-i): An assessment tool for juvenile offenders. *The International Journal of Forensic Mental Health, 2*(2), 101–117.

Letourneau, E. J. (2002). A comparison of objective measures of sexual arousal and interest: Visual reaction time and penile plethysmography. *Sexual Abuse: A Journal of Research and Treatment, 14*(3), 207–223. doi:10.1177/107906320201400302.

Letourneau, E. J. (Ed.). (2004). *Sexual Abuse: A Journal of Research and Treatment, 16*, 77–81.

Letourneau, E. J., Henggeler, S. W., Borduin, C. M., Schewe, P. A., McCart, M. R., Chapman, J. E., et al. (2009). Multisystemic therapy for juvenile sexual offenders: 1-year results from a randomized effectiveness trial. *Journal of Family Psychology, 23*(1), 89–102. doi:10.1037/a0014352.

Letourneau, E. J., & Miner, M. H. (2005). Juvenile sex offenders: A case against the legal and clinical status quo. *Sexual Abuse: Journal of Research and Treatment, 17*(3), 293–312. doi:10.1177/107906320501700304.

Longo, R. E. (2005). An integrated experiential approach to treating young people who sexually abuse. *Journal of Child Sexual Abuse, 13*(3), 1930213. doi:10.1300/J070v13n03_10.

Loving, J. L., & Patapis, N. S. (2007). Evaluating juvenile amenability to treatment: Integrating statutes and case law into clinical practice. *Journal of Forensic Psychology Practice, 7*(1), 67–78. doi:10.1300/J158v07n01_07.

Martinez, R., Flores, J., & Rosenfeld, B. (2007). Validity of the juvenile sex offender assessment protocol-II (J-SOAP-II) in a sample of urban minority youth. *Criminal Justice and Behavior, 34*(10), 1284–1295. doi:10.1177/0093854807301791.

McCartan, F. M., Law, H., Murphy, M., & Bailey, S. (2011). Child and adolescent females who present with sexually abusive behaviours: A 10-year UK prevalence study. *Journal of Sexual Aggression, 17*(1), 4–14. doi:10.1080/13552600.2010.488302.

McGrath, R. J. (1991). Sex-offender risk assessment and disposition planning: A review of empirical and clinical findings. *International Journal of Offender Therapy and Comparative Criminology, 35*(4), 329–351.

McGrath, R., Cumming, G., Burchard, B., Zeoli, S., & Ellerby, L. (2010). *Current practices and emerging trends in sexual abuser management: The Safer Society 2009 North American survey.* Brandon, VT: Safer Society Press.

Meijer, E. H., Verschuere, B., Merckelbach, H. L. G. L., & Crombez, G. (2008). Sex offender management using the polygraph: A critical review. *International Journal of Law and Psychiatry, 31*(5), 423–429. doi:10.1016/j.ijlp.2008.08.007.

Miller, W. R., & Rollnick, S. (2002). *Motivational interviewing: Preparing people for change, Second edition.* New York, NY: Guilford Press.

Miner, M., Borduin, C., Prescott, D., Bovensmann, H., Schepker, R., DuBois, R., et al. (2006). Standards of care for juvenile sexual offenders of the International Association for the Treatment of Sexual Offenders. *Sexual Offender Treatment, 1*(3), 1–7.

Miner, M. H., Marques, J. K., Day, D. M., & Nelson, C. (1990). Impact of relapse prevention in treating sex offenders: Preliminary findings. *Annals of Sex Research*, *3*(2), 165–185. doi:10.1007/BF00850869.

Mulvey, E. P., & Iselin, A. R. (2008). Improving professional judgments of risk and amenability in juvenile justice. *The Future of Children*, *18*(2), 35–57. doi:10.1353/foc.0.0012.

Murphy, W. D., DiLillo, D., Haynes, M. R., & Steere, E. (2001). An exploration of factors related to deviant sexual arousal among juvenile sex offenders. *Sexual Abuse: A Journal of Research and Treatment*, *13*(2), 91–103. doi:10.1177/107906320101300203.

National Adolescent Perpetrator Network, (1993). The revised report from the National task force on juvenile sexual offending. *Juvenile and Family Court Journal*, *44*(4), 1–155.

National Research Council. (2003). *The polygraph and lie detection*. Washington, DC: The National Academies Press.

Nichols and Molinder Assessments, Inc.. (2010). Multiphasic Sex Inventory II – Adolescent Male Form. Downloaded on 1/25/12 from <http://www.nicholsandmolinder.com/sex-offender-assessment-msi-ii-jm.php>.

Nichols, H. R., & Molinder, I. (2001). *Multiphasic sex inventory-II, adolescent male form*. Fircrest, WA: Nichols & Molinder Assessments, Inc.

Office of the Attorney General of New Jersey (2006). *Juvenile risk assessment scale manual*. Retrieved from. <http://www.state.nj.us/lps/dcj/megan/jras-manual-scale-606.pdf> 27.01.12.

Olver, M. E., Stockdale, K. C., & Wormith, J. S. (2009). Risk assessment with young offenders: A meta-analysis of three assessment measures. *Criminal Justice and Behavior*, *36*(4), 329–353. doi:10.1177/0093854809331457.

Oneal, B. J., Burns, G. L., Kahn, T. J., Rich, P., & Worling, J. R. (2008). Initial psychometric properties of a treatment planning and progress inventory for adolescents who sexually abuse. *Sexual Abuse: A Journal of Research and Treatment*, *20*(2), 161–187. doi:10.1177/1079063208317465.

Owen-Kostelnik, J., Reppucci, N. D., & Meyer, J. R. (2006). Testimony and interrogation of minors: Assumptions about maturity and morality. *American Psychologist*, *61*(4), 286–304. doi:10.1037/0003-066X.61.4.286.

Parks, G. A., & Bard, D. E. (2006). Risk factors for adolescent sex offender recidivism: Evaluation of predictive factors and comparison of three groups based upon victim type. *Sexual Abuse: Journal of Research and Treatment*, *18*(4), 319–342. doi:10.1177/107906320601800402.

Patel, S. H., Lambie, G. W., & Glover, M. M. (2008). Motivational counseling: Implications for counseling male juvenile sex offenders. *Journal of Additions and Offender Counseling*, *28*(2), 86–100. doi:10.1002/j.2161-1874.2008.tb00035.x.

Powers-Sawyer, A. B., & Miner, M. H. (2009). Actuarial prediction of juvenile recidivism: The static variables of the Juvenile Sex Offender Assessment Protocol-II (J-SOAP-II). *Sexual Offender Treatment*, *4*(2), 1–11.

Prentky, R., Harris, B., Frizell, K., & Righthand, S. (2000). An actuarial procedure for assessing risk with juvenile sex offenders. *Sexual Abuse: Journal of Research and Treatment*, *12*(2), 71–93. doi:10.1177/107906320001200201.

Prentky, R. A., Li, N. -C., Righthand, S., Schuler, A., Cavanaugh, D., & Lee, A. F. (2010). Assessing risk of sexually abusive behavior among youth in a child welfare sample. *Behavioral Sciences & the Law*, *28*(1), 24–45. doi:10.1002/bsl.920.

Prentky, R., & Righthand, S. (2003). *Juvenile sex offender assessment protocol-II (J-SOAP-II) manual*. Bridgewater, MA: Justice Resource Institute.

Quinsey, V. L., Ketsetzis, M., Earls, C., & Karamanoukian, A. (1996). Viewing time as a measure of sexual interest. *Ethology and Sociobiology*, *17*(5), 341–354. doi:10.1016/S0162-3095(96)00060-X.

Rajlic, G., & Gretton, H. M. (2010). An examination of two sexual recidivism risk measures in adolescent offenders: The moderating effect of offender type. *Criminal Justice and Behavior*, *37*(10), 1066–1085. doi:10.1177/0093854810376354.

Reitzel, L. R., & Carbonell, J. L. (2006). The effectiveness of sexual offender treatment for juveniles as measured by recidivism: A meta-analysis. *Sexual Abuse: A Journal of Research and Treatment*, *18*(4), 401–421. doi:10.1177/107906320601800407.

Rice, M. E., & Harris, G. T. (2005). Comparing effect sizes in follow-up studies: ROC Area, Cohen's d, and r. *Law and Human Behavior, 29*(5), 615–620. doi:10.1007/s10979-005-6832-7.

Rice, M. E., Harris, G. T., Lang, C., & Chaplin, T. C. (2012). Adolescents who have sexually offended: Is phallometry valid? *Sexual Abuse: A Journal of Research and Treatment, 24*(2), 133–152. doi: 10.1177/1079063211404249.

Rice, M. E., Quinsey, V. L., & Harris, G. T. (1991). Sexual recidivism among child molesters released from a maximum security psychiatric institution. *Journal of Consulting and Clinical Psychology, 59*(3), 381–386. doi:10.1037/0022-006X.59.3.381.

Righthand, S. (2005, November). Juvenile Sex Offense Specific Treatment Needs & Progress Scale. Downloaded from: <http://www.csom.org/pubs/JSOProgressScale.pdf>.

Righthand, S., Prentky, R., Knight, R., Carpenter, E., Hecker, J. E., & Nangle, D. (2005). Factor structure and validation of the juvenile sex offender assessment protocol (J-SOAP). *Sexual Abuse: Journal of Research and Treatment, 17*(1), 13–30. doi:10.1177/107906320501700103.

Ronis, S. T., & Borduin, C. M. (2007). Individual, family, peer, and academic characteristics of male juvenile sexual offenders. *Journal of Abnormal Child Psychology, 35*(2), 153–163. doi:10.1007/s10802-006-9058-3.

Rullo, J. E., Strassberg, D. S., & Israel, E. (2010). Category-specificity in sexual interest in gay men and lesbians. *Archives of Sexual Behavior, 39*(4), 874–879. doi:10.1007/s10508-009-9497-3.

Salekin, R. (2001). *Manual for the risk, sophistication, and treatment inventory*. Lutz, FL: Psychological Assessment Resources.

Salekin, R. T., Salekin, K. L., Clements, C. B., Leistico, A. -M. R., Grisso, T., Vincent, G., et al. (2005). *Risk-sophistication-treatment inventory mental health screening and assessment in juvenile justice. (pp. 341–356)*. New York, NY: Guilford Press.

Schwalbe, C. S. (2007). Risk assessment for juvenile justice: A meta-analysis. *Law and Human Behavior, 31*(5), 449–462. doi:10.1007/s10979-006-9071-7.

Seto, M. C. (2001). The value of phallometry in the assessment of male sex offenders. *Journal of Forensic Psychology Practice, 1*(2), 65–75. doi:10.1300/J158v01n02_05.

Seto, M. C., & Lalumière, M. L. (2010). What is so special about male adolescent sexual offending? A review and test of explanations through meta-analysis. *Psychological Bulletin, 136*(4), 526–575. doi:10.1037/a0019700.

Seto, M. C., Lalumière, M. L., & Blanchard, R. (2000). The discriminative validity of a phallometric test for pedophilic interests among adolescent sex offenders against children. *Psychological Assessment, 12*(3), 319–327. doi:10.1037//1040-3590.12.3.319.

Seto, M. C., Murphy, W. D., Page, J., & Ennis, L. (2003). Detecting anomalous sexual interests in juvenile sex offenders. *Annals of the New York Academy of Sciences, 989*(1), 118–130. doi:10.1111/j.1749-6632.2003.tb07298.x.

Slotboom, A. -M., Hendriks, J., & Verbruggen, J. (2011). Contrasting adolescent female and male sexual aggression: A self-report study on prevalence and predictors of sexual aggression. *Journal of Sexual Aggression, 17*(1), 15–33. doi:10.1080/13552600.2010.544413.

Smith, G., & Fischer, L. (1999). Assessment of juvenile sexual offenders: Reliability and validity of the Abel assessment for interest in paraphilias. *Sexual Abuse: A Journal of Research and Treatment, 11*(3), 207–216. doi:10.1177/107906329901100304.

St. Amand, A., Bard, D. E., & Silovsky, J. F. (2008). Meta-analysis of treatment for child sexual behavior problems: Practice elements and outcomes. *Child Maltreatment, 13*(2), 145–166. doi:10.1177/1077559508315353.

Stinson, J. D., & Becker, J. V. (2008). Assessing sexual deviance: A comparison of physiological, historical, and self-report measures. *Journal of Psychiatric Practice, 14*(6), 379–388. doi:10.1097/01.pra.0000341892.51124.85.

Thakker, J., Ward, T., & Tidmarsh, P. (2006). A reevaluation of relapse prevention with adolescents who sexually offend: A Good-Lives Model. In H. E. Barbaree, & W. L. Marshall (Eds.), *The juvenile sex offender (pp. 313–335)* (2nd ed.). New York, NY: Guilford Press.

Timmons-Mitchell, J., Bender, M. B., Kishna, M. A., & Mitchell, C. C. (2006). An independent effectiveness trial of multisystemic therapy with juvenile justice youth. *Journal of Clinical Child and Adolescent Psychology, 35*(2), 227–236. doi:10.1207/s15374424jccp3502_6.

US Department of Justice, Federal Bureau of Investigation (2011, September). Crime in the United States, 2010. Retrieved December 27, 2011, from <http://www.fbi.gov/about-us/cjis/ucr/crime-in-the-u.s/2010/crime-in-the-u.s.-2010/index-page>.

Vandiver, D. M. (2010). Assessing gender differences and co-offending patterns of a predominantly "male-oriented" crime: A comparison of a cross-national sample of juvenile boys and girls arrested for a sexual offense. *Violence & Victims, 25*(2), 243–264. doi:10.1891/0886-6708.25.2.243.

Viljoen, J. L., Elkovitch, N., Scalora, M. J., & Ullman, D. (2009). Assessment of reoffense risk in adolescents who have committed sexual offenses: Predictive validity of the ERASOR, PCL:YV, YLS/CMI, and Static-99. *Criminal Justice and Behavior, 36*(10), 981–1000. doi:10.1177/0093854809340991.

Viljoen, J. L., Mordell, S., & Beneteau, J. L. (2012). Prediction of adolescent sexual reoffending: A meta-analysis of the J-SOAP-II, ERASOR, J-SORRAT-II, and Static-99. *Law and Human Behavior, 36*(5), 423–438. doi: 10.1037/h0093938.

Viljoen, J. L., Scalora, M., Cuadra, L., Bader, S., Chávez, V. N., Ullman, D., et al. (2008). Assessing risk for violence in adolescents who have sexually offended: A comparison of the J-SOAP-II, J-SORRAT-II, and SAVRY. *Criminal Justice and Behavior, 35*(1), 5–23. doi:10.1177/0093854807307521.

Vitacco, M. J., Caldwell, M., Ryba, N. L., Malesky, A., & Kurus, S. J. (2009). Assessing risk in adolescent sexual offenders: Recommendations for clinical practice. *Behavioral Sciences & the Law, 27*, 929–940. doi:10.1002/bsl.909.

Walker, D. F., McGovern, S. K., Poey, E. L., & Otis, K. E. (2005). Treatment effectiveness for male adolescent sexual offenders: A meta-analysis and review. *Journal of Child Sexual Abuse, 13*(3), 281–293. doi:10.1300/J070v13n03_14.

Weinrott, M. R., Riggan, M., & Frothingham, S. (1997). Reducing deviant arousal in juvenile sex offenders using vicarious sensitization. *Journal of Interpersonal Violence, 12*(5), 704–728. doi:10.1177/088626097012005007.

Welsh, J. L., Schmidt, F., McKinnon, L., Chattha, H. K., & Meyers, J. R. (2008). A comparative study of adolescent risk assessment instruments: Predictive and incremental validity. *Assessment, 15*(1), 104–115. doi:10.1177/1073191107307966.

Worling, J. R., & Curwen, T. (2000). Adolescent sexual offender recidivism: Success of specialized treatment and implications for risk prediction. *Child Abuse & Neglect, 24*(7), 965–982. doi:10.1016/S0145-2134(00)00147-2.

Worling, J. R., & Curwen, T. (2001). Estimate of risk of adolescent sexual offense recidivism (ERASOR; Version 2.0). In M. C. Calder (Ed.), *Juveniles and children who sexually abuse: Frameworks for assessment (pp. 372–397)*. Lyme Regis, UK: Russell House.

Worling, J. R. (2004). The estimate of risk of adolescent sexual offense recidivism (ERASOR): Preliminary psychometric data. *Sexual Abuse: A Journal of Research and Treatment, 16*(3), 235–254. doi:10.1177/107906320401600305.

Worling, J. R. (2006). Assessing sexual arousal with adolescent males who have offended sexually: Self-report and unobtrusively measured viewing time. *Sexual Abuse: A Journal of Research and Treatment, 18*(4), 383–400. doi:10.1007/s11194-006-9024-1.

Worling, J. R., Bookalam, D., & Litteljohn, A. (2012). Prospective validity of the estimate of risk of adolescent sexual offense recidivism (ERASOR). *Sexual Abuse: A Journal of Research and Treatment, 24*(2), 203–223. doi: 10.1177/1079063211407080.

Worling, J. R., Litteljohn, A., & Bookalam, D. (2010). 20-year prospective follow-up study of specialized treatment for adolescents who offend sexually. *Behavioral Sciences and the Law, 28*(1), 46–57. doi:10.1002/bsl.912.

Zimring, F. E. (2004). *An American travesty: Legal responses to adolescent sexual offending*. Chicago, IL: University of Chicago Press.

# CHAPTER 22

# Legal Responses to Adolescents' Sexual Offending

Roger J.R. Levesque
Indiana University, Bloomington, Indiana[1]

## INTRODUCTION

Adolescents who offend against others pose important challenges for legal systems. Those challenges range from determining whether they can be held culpable, whether they are culpable in specific situations, how to deal with those who are deemed culpable, what to do with those who have committed offenses but are not culpable, to settling on how to redress harms and prevent future ones. These difficult challenges have led legal systems to develop two dominant ways to respond to offenders, including those accused of offending, as well as those deemed at risk for doing so. The first system is a long-standing one, the criminal justice system. Generally, that system seeks to identify those who have offended, prosecute them, and then punish or otherwise control them. The system does so not only to incapacitate, deter, and rehabilitate offenders, but also to protect society. The second system, which is much more recent but still well established, is the juvenile justice system. That system seeks to identify those who have committed offenses or who are at risk of offending, and then seeks to rehabilitate or otherwise find ways to reintegrate them into their communities so that they will not continue offending. That system also considers the need to protect society, but not the need to punish. Despite deep differences in the two systems' missions, the latter system increasingly is undergoing transformations that make it less distinguishable from the former, and it increasingly turns offenders to criminal courts and their sanctions. Still, both systems retain different characteristics that, together, allow for responding quite comprehensively to juveniles deemed to have committed a wide variety of sex offenses, as well as those deemed at risk of offending.

[1] Correspondence to: Roger J.R. Levesque, JD, PhD, Chair and Professor of Criminal Justice, 302 Sycamore Hall, Indiana University, Bloomington, IN 47405. Phone 812 856 1210 or 812 855 9325; fax 812 855 5522; email: rlevesqu@indiana.edu

Given the importance of these two systems, this chapter examines both. We begin by detailing the key components of both systems and their undergirding goals and rationales. We also examine criticisms of both systems, as well as emerging reforms and efforts aiming to counter criticisms of the systems' relative effectiveness. The general theme emerging from our discussion highlights the legal system's general failure to take fuller advantage of empirical findings relating to adolescents' sexual offending and the challenges of responding to the vast majority of offenses. The chapter ends with a brief look at potential legal and policy reforms that can embrace research on both adolescents' sexual offending and on current legal responses to their offenses. The conclusion emphasizes the continued need for a broad range of approaches to adolescents' sexual offending and for better ensuring that some goals do not come at the expense of foreclosing others if justice systems ever are going to address the wide range of offending behaviors and situations that foster them more effectively.

## JUVENILE JUSTICE SYSTEM RESPONSES

Juvenile justice systems were envisioned to protect youth from the harsh punishments and related consequences associated with being involved in the adult criminal justice system. In a real sense, the system removed young offenders from the criminal court's processing and sought to rehabilitate and reintegrate them into society. The foundational rationale for that differential treatment (both then and now) is that youth are different from adults in two important ways: youth are less culpable and they possess greater capacity for rehabilitation. As expected, juvenile offenders constitute a varied group, and not all exhibit those two characteristics differently from most adults. As a result, the system devotes considerable resources to efforts that seek to determine which juveniles are different, and how to respond to those characteristics. Although the juvenile court system clearly has focused on offenders' characteristics, those necessarily remain balanced against the need to address victims' needs, including those of broader society, for protection from harm. This balancing between protecting offenders and society has emerged as a key concern that shapes the legal systems' responses to adolescent sex offenders.

A primary consideration in juvenile court systems' responses relates to the manner in which they gain jurisdiction over juvenile offenders. Currently, courts make use of two primary modalities to gain jurisdiction over adolescents who sexually offend. First, age is a key qualifier, with many states granting juvenile courts jurisdiction over those 17 years of age and younger. Importantly, the age range can vary from state to state, and can range from the age of 15 to 18, and often 21 if the offense was committed prior to the lower jurisdictional age. Minimum ages are not often recognized, and, if they are, it is often only for presumptions of capacity. The second, often ignored modality through which juvenile courts gain jurisdiction over offenders is by using the immaturity defense, whereby defendants claim an inability to appreciate the consequences of their actions due to immature mental capacities. This approach requires states to have a juvenile court system with no absolute age-based minimum, and with mandates that grant discretionary jurisdictions for adolescents. Together, these two ways provide courts with a very broad reach over a wide variety of offenders and types of offenses.

In multiple jurisdictions, juvenile courts actually also serve as a family court system, and even if they do not, juveniles' cases can involve the family court system (sometimes referred to as dependency court or child welfare system). This is of significance in that courts, regardless of what the system finds for the specific juvenile, may initiate child protection actions. These systems can be enlisted to provide family-based interventions for perpetrators as well as victims (see Levesque, 2008). These systems are in place to assist families, for example, in better managing youth, ensuring their rehabilitation, and offering needed services. Importantly, however, individual rights (including the family's right to privacy), as well as federal mandates regulating the implementation of child protection services, restrict the use of some of these potential interventions (Levesque, 2002, 2011). Still, the place of child welfare/family court systems in intervening to address the needs of offenders cannot be underestimated, as we will see again below.

Juvenile courts that deal with adolescent sex offenders typically gain jurisdiction after they confirm the violation of a penal code. This can take several forms. First, juvenile courts gain jurisdiction over sex offenders to the extent that statutes analogize adolescent misconduct to that of adults, and the courts use the corresponding adult penal statutes to determine legal responses. In this regard, adolescents' sexual offenses may fall into any or all categories of sexual offenses, depending on how sexual assault is described in the statutes: e.g., mandatory; repeat; violent; or aggravated juvenile offenses. In this instance, several laws regulate, for example, sexual interactions with minors, and those regulations can have quite a broad range. Second, juvenile courts also gain jurisdiction over sex offenders through specialized statutes relating specifically to juveniles. Although status offenses are thought to have been abolished by federal mandate, several laws specifically regulate minors' conduct when their actions would not constitute an offense if conducted by an adult. The clear example of these mandates is laws that aim to control youth's moral development, such as their engaging in sexual activity and other disobedient, incorrigible, and unruly behavior. This type of control is found, for example, in efforts to control girls' sexual activity, especially what can be deemed promiscuous or otherwise sexually inappropriate behavior (see Dalby, 1994; Humphrey, 2004). Thus, the legal system envisions two types of sexual offenses that can be perpetrated by juveniles: offenses that are similar to those of adults; and those that apply specifically and only to youth.

Determining whether a violation of a penal statute has occurred is not as straightforward as it might seem. This difficulty is expressed even in the ways that the juvenile court can gain jurisdiction over juveniles through laws regulating sexual assault. The juvenile court can gain jurisdiction over sexual assault cases in two major ways: through the presence of coercion or its proxy, age. Thus, if the defendant used force to attempt or complete sexual contact without consent, then adult penal codes apply. The only complication relating to jurisdiction arises when a need emerges to consider waiving the alleged offender to adult court. If that happens, then the juvenile court system loses jurisdiction over the case, and that loss continues unless the adult court "decertifies" its jurisdiction and returns the case to the juvenile court system. Still, juvenile offenders generally fall under the juvenile court's jurisdiction, either because their sexual acts involved coercion, or their partners were under age. As shown below, other sexually related offenses can lead to juvenile court jurisdiction, but those no longer figure as prominently in reports of offending. For now, then, we focus on the actions deemed dominant in court responses, and those tend to be cases involving the victimization of others, due to either force or inappropriate age.

The use of age as a proxy creates considerable complexities and nuances, and those vary from one jurisdiction to the next. Juvenile court systems may define sexual assault through age as a proxy by using two approaches. The first approach to defining sexual assault combines minimum ages and maximum separation of ages among offenders and victims. This approach can become complicated when juveniles are within statutory age limits that permit sexual activity and their actions involved no threat or use of force. Only when the law deems a victim as unable to give consent does the perpetrator become culpable. The second approach makes use of child molestation statutes, wherein the victim's age establishes criminal culpability. Most states have statutes that criminalize child sexual abuse, and minors may be prosecuted by courts even if they fall within those age limitations. If they were not allowed to be prosecuted, some minors essentially would have a license to molest others. Minors must demonstrate capacity and knowledge of wrongfulness in order for courts to gain jurisdiction. And, as noted above, if they do not demonstrate that culpability by having the requisite capacity and knowledge, then other legal systems can be enlisted, such as the child welfare system, to assist families in better managing and socializing those who offended or, if needed, to remove children from their problem-inducing environments.

The multiple ways juvenile courts gain jurisdiction over adolescents deemed sex offenders reflect an increasing interest in controlling adolescents' sexual behavior, although the actual effectiveness of these controls remains to be determined. Historically, sex offenses that were of keen interest to juvenile court systems focused on girls, and the court systems particularly focused on girls' promiscuity. Much has been written, for example, about how the legal system has sought to control girls' sexual behavior, and how it has framed it as acting out and used it as grounds, for example, to institutionalize them (see Humphrey, 2004; Moore & Padavic, 2010). This tendency to control girls' sexual activity remains, most notably, even after statutory offenses were deemed inappropriate and efforts were made to abolish them as a response to the need to still assist youth who were experiencing problems (including having parents who were unable to respond properly to their needs). Courts developed equally effective mechanisms to achieve the ends of categorizing youth and bringing adolescents within the courts' control. The central way courts have done so is through the use of "valid court orders." These orders permit courts to bring girls to court and impose sanctions on them, including secure detention when they, for example, engage in activity not sanctioned by the court or their parents (see Dalby, 1994). These new mechanisms not only reflect society's interest in controlling youth's sexual behavior, but also reveal how court systems can resist explicit policy changes that seek to exclude youth from their control.

Over the past few decades, the law's reach over adolescents' sexual activity has widened considerably to include boys, but even these more expansive efforts leave a broad swath of sexual offenses outside of the legal system. This widening has been seen as due to both society's recognition that children's victimization needs to be taken more seriously, and to the recognition that juveniles can be perpetrators of serious crimes that need to be taken much more seriously in the name of protecting victims as well as broader societal interests. These two recognitions resulted from an emerging rejection of the view that adolescents' problematic sex acts were a by-product of normal aggressiveness of sexually maturing boys, and of rejecting "boys-will-be-boys" attitudes that viewed acts of sexual aggression more as nuisances than the sexual assaults they actually were. Despite the juvenile justice system's increasing focus on boys as well as girls who commit sexual offenses, broadly defined, it is important to keep in mind that the vast majority of sexual offenses involving youth tend not to lead to the involvement of legal systems. Sexual offenses committed by and against youth tend not to be reported, with a small percentage (less than 15%) resulting in the arrest of offenders (see Stein & Nofziger, 2008). It certainly would be disingenuous to argue that adolescents' sex offenses remain as unrecognized by justice and mental health systems and that interventions, if at all, wait until offenders become adults. Yet, sex offenses still remain largely hidden, and the need to uncover them plays a key role in shaping legal responses, especially in terms of fostering a more punitive approach to sex offenses in the hopes of deterring and preventing future offenses. Whether these measures are effective may well remain to be determined, but policies clearly reflect that trend.

Once a juvenile justice system has gained jurisdiction over an alleged offender, the system is notable for the manner it bestows considerable rights on the accused, as well as the way it grants courts extensive discretion to adjudicate cases brought to them. Without doubt, those empowered to enforce statutory mandates relating to adolescents are given considerable discretion. For prosecutors discretionary power is far from unusual, in that they retain considerable power to determine which cases to pursue, charges to consider, and penalties to seek (see Levesque, 2006). Prosecutors also hold substantial authority to determine which cases they wish to adjudicate leniently or harshly. Even as efforts increasingly seek to control prosecutors' discretion, such as through mandatory transfers to adult court (see below) for specific offenses, prosecutors retain the power over transfers to the extent that they may not charge those offenses. Importantly, so long as the age requirement and other statutory provisions for gaining jurisdiction are met, nothing bars the state from pursuing a juvenile. Also importantly, juvenile court judges also retain significant power. Most notably, they control transfer hearings that would determine where juveniles could be tried (adult or juvenile court, or sometimes not at all), and they maintain control throughout the adjudication of cases heard before them as well as over the imposition of dispositions. A look at the power of prosecutors and judges leads to the conclusion that the potential application of statutes may be clear, but how they are implemented, as well as used at all, remains a matter of considerable discretion by those entrusted with enforcing them.

The discretion of juvenile court personnel, although still remarkably broad, has met clear opposition in the form of Supreme Court mandates as well as laws that increasingly aim to provide juveniles with protections from unfettered discretion. Commentators attribute a rise in protections against discretion to a 1967 Supreme Court case, *In re Gault* (1967). That case, arguably the leading Supreme Court case recognizing the rights of juveniles against state actions, actually involved an alleged sex offender, Gault, who was a 15-year-old when accused of making an obscene phone call "of the irritatingly offensive, adolescent, sex variety" to an older lady (In re Gault, 1967, p. 1432). His actions, although rather tame by today's standards, were enough to support a potential six-year period of incarceration. The potential deprivation was considered quite dramatic, especially given that, had he been an adult, the allegations would have supported a misdemeanor offense carrying a maximum punishment of a small fine and two months imprisonment. Although the Supreme Court was troubled with the juvenile court's result, its real concern was not necessarily with the outcome but the process. Gault's parents had not, for example, been given meaningful notice of the allegations, the neighbor who had been offended by the phone call had not appeared in court to testify against Gault, Gault did not have legal representation, and the trial court had appeared less than judicious in examining the case closely and in providing grounds for its decision. Given how Gault and his parents had been treated, the case was a particularly strong one to argue against the reduced recognition of juveniles' rights in judicial proceedings, and for the need to increase protections from excessive punishments.

The Supreme Court took Gault's case as an opportunity to provide juveniles with a wide variety of rights, as it found that the juvenile court system had failed to provide the youth with appropriate safeguards against arbitrary court actions. As a result, the Court granted juveniles a panoply of basic rights, such as the right to notice of charges, right to counsel, and right to confront and cross-examine accusers. These basic constitutional protections have been expanded by state courts and other constitutional cases that have granted juveniles the right against self-incrimination, right to transcript recordings of hearings, and right to appeal (in some circumstances) their adjudications. In turn, these developments have turned the juvenile court away from being one marked by enormous discretion (deemed necessary for individualized, tailored, rehabilitative resolutions) toward one that generally grants adolescents rights similar to, but clearly not coterminous with, those that adults gain in criminal courts (see e.g., Birckhead, 2009).

*Gault*'s recognition that juveniles deserve constitutional protections from arbitrary state action in the context of juvenile court systems may have been quite dramatic and transformative, but the actual nature of and effects of changes have been debatable. Some find the changes to be critical to ensuring justice, and others find them to be essentially seeking to replicate the adult court system, doing it wrongly, and then leaving juveniles open to more retributional punishment rather than rehabilitative dispositions (see Feld, 1995). Although the negative effects of recognizing the rights of adolescents have yet to be fully evaluated and recognized, the case is of significance for the manner it not only recognized the right to basic due process protections, but also acknowledged the danger of juvenile courts' giving youth the worst of both worlds. The Court bottomed its decision on the proposition that youth in juvenile courts received neither the solicitous care and rehabilitative treatment postulated for youth, nor the fuller protections accorded to adults in criminal courts. Despite enduring controversies, there is no doubt that the original goal of a rehabilitative juvenile court takes a second seat to one that gives youth basic rights. Indeed, *Gault* is very much a case demonstrating concern about processes rather than their outcomes.

Not surprisingly, a remarkable limitation of the juvenile rights revolution, which *Gault* has been credited as launching, is its failure to address the outcomes of adjudications. *Gault* itself was quite clear: it limited itself to the actual adjudicatory hearing, not to what happened before it, or even to the judicial proceedings that could happen after it, such as appeals, as well as, equally importantly, the implementation of the cases' eventual disposition (the equivalent of what would be a sentence in adult court). *Gault*, then, did nothing to limit juvenile courts' considerable discretion in devising dispositions. This is of considerable significance, in that dispositions may range from no legal response to extreme legal consequences, and a very wide continuum of possibilities exists between those two poles. For particularly or potentially violent adolescents, programs aim to remove them from their homes and communities. In addition to incarceration, institutionalization in detention centers, psychiatric hospitals, and boot camps may be warranted. For the less violent, non-institutional programs may be utilized, including excursion programs or community supervision. Adolescents also may participate in a variety of alternatives; and both those who are considered more and those considered less violent may be subjected to important control measures in community settings, such as by registering with law enforcement (so that policing agencies and sometimes the public know where they live), as well as announcing to neighbors and others that they have been adjudicated sex offenders. As described in greater depth below, these developments directly contradict the juvenile court's original mandate that focused on the need to preserve delinquent adolescents' privacy, treatment, confidentiality, and reintegration. But, nevertheless, they are important legal developments in response to adolescent offenders. And these developments currently proceed with few limitations that would control the immense discretion held by juvenile courts.

Another key limitation with the *Gault* decision, a limitation that often goes ignored, is the extent to which the juvenile justice system's shift towards affording more rights and greater autonomy to delinquent youth has not extended to all classes of juvenile offenders. *Gault* expressly limited its holding to the adjudicatory hearing for youth who could be determined delinquent, which means that they have committed an offense deemed illegal regardless of the offender's age. And those cases needed to be the type serious enough that they potentially could lead to institutionalization. As a result, the case essentially ignored status offenses. But the juvenile court system did not, even despite federal mandates meant to abolish them (see Arthur & Waugh, 2009). These offenses are classifications of transgressions committed by juveniles that would not be a crime if committed by an adult, such as truancy, running away, curfew violations, and ungovernability. Notably, different jurisdictions use different labels for what essentially are status offenders, such as Children in Need of Protection or Services (CHIPS), Children in Need of Supervision (CHINS), or Persons in Need of Supervision (PINS) (see e.g., Levesque, 2002, 2008). These different labels and systems are of significance. The systems in which these "offenses" can be heard may not provide offenders with procedural due process rights or other opportunities to voice their interests. Instead, the nature of these statutory categories grants courts discretion to determine appropriate dispositions, and it does so by denying youth, for example, basic rights against self-incrimination and the right to counsel identified in *Gault*. As noted above, many "status offense" statutes contain general catch-all provisions that refer to "disobedient," "incorrigible," or "ungovernable" youth who are beyond their parents' control. These criteria are particularly vague and likely to remain so to provide courts with the ability to use discretion to assist youth. Although youth may have some forms of representation (e.g., guardian *ad litems*), the system continues to resist the development of basic due process rights (Levesque, 2008), a resistance that several commentators have taken to be a root cause of paternalistic attitudes and efforts to control girls' sexual behaviors (see Humphrey, 2004; Kim, 2010) as well as those from minority groups (see Freiburger & Burke, 2011). In a real sense, the continued ability of juvenile courts to use their discretion to control status offenders has resulted in what some appropriately have viewed as an exception that has swallowed the rule announced in *Gault* that juveniles have basic, constitutional rights in court proceedings that could deprive them of basic liberties (see Arthur & Waugh, 2009).

Importantly, whether dealing with status offenders, delinquents, or other categories of children in need of services, there remains a focus on rehabilitation and reintegration. There has been a rapid development of young-offender programs, and juveniles who are neither repeat offenders nor violent, and who have supportive environments, tend to remain in the court system and receive rehabilitative services (Bishop & Frazier, 2000), especially when compared with youth prosecuted in adult courts. Particularly noteworthy are community-based therapeutic models, most notably intensive probation supervision that uses more frequent contact between the officers, adolescents, and parents. These models permit taking advantage of the one critical factor that emerges from the wide range of rehabilitative alternatives: an ecological focus. Programs that focus on the multidetermined nature of violent behavior appear particularly effective, with essentially promising services being those offered during adolescence and before the establishment of chronic patterns (Henggeler et al., 2009; Borduin, Schaeffer, & Heiblum, 2009). Despite the wide range of service options that exist in theory and even when part of statutory mandates, and despite our knowing the type of program that can respond to juveniles effectively, appropriate service options are not always available in practice. Dispositions stemming from juvenile court adjudications, then, remain an area ripe for important legal developments to take advantage of what we know about the nature of adolescents' sexual offending. And those developments will reach effectiveness only to the extent that they can foster systems that can be tailored appropriately to offenders' needs as well as those of broader society.

## CRIMINAL JUSTICE RESPONSES

As noted above, the Supreme Court has created extensive procedural rights for adolescents when they are faced with deprivation of their liberties. When focusing on the rights of juveniles relating to the criminal courts, attention necessarily centers on two points: how the courts gain jurisdiction over juveniles; and the courts' disposition of their cases (e.g., the type of sentences and other controls). What happens in the middle of those two points tends not to be of interest for the simple reason that, once transferred to adult courts, juveniles are considered "adults," and they enjoy the same trial rights of adults. Concerns for potentially treating juveniles differently once they have been found guilty arise because sentences and other controls tend to be individualized as they consider the characteristics of the offenders as well as the offense (Levesque, 2006). At this juncture, in legal proceedings, the key concern involves the extent to which the juvenile should, indeed, be treated differently because of their developmental status. Given how criminal courts potentially distinguish juveniles from adults at the beginning and end of court processes, the following discussion centers on these two endpoints and their significance for juveniles' rights.

The year before the Supreme Court announced its landmark decision in *Gault*, it had decided an equally important case that addressed the rights of juveniles who essentially would be caught between juvenile and criminal courts. That case, *Kent v. United States* (1966) 383 U.S. 541, addressed the rights an alleged offender retains when the state seeks to move them to criminal courts. This issue is of considerable significance, in that juveniles transferred to adult court necessarily miss out on the benefits of being processed in juvenile court, such as the court's rehabilitative orientation as well as the clear limit on the age of offenders over whom the court can exert control. The court recognized that significance, as it found that juveniles had a right to increased protections from arbitrary transfers. The court did so by finding the informality in waiver hearings constitutionally deficient, and it did so in a case that arguably seemed to be best served in adult court. Like Gault, Kent was an alleged sex offender, but his offenses were much more problematic and the type that would attract considerable scrutiny and penalties. Kent, at 16, came into police custody for allegedly entering a woman's home and raping her. The evidence against Kent was quite strong, and he had a long history of offenses. The prosecution filed a motion to waive juvenile court jurisdiction, and the court, without a formal hearing and without conferring with Kent or his representatives, transferred him to adult court. Kent was found guilty of housebreaking and robbery, but not guilty of rape by reason of insanity. He was sentenced to from 30 to 90 years in prison; had he been tried in juvenile court, the maximum time commitment would have been 5 years, until he would have turned 21. The Supreme Court reversed, citing a failure to provide basic due process protections at transfer hearings. Among other protections, the court agreed that juveniles were entitled to a hearing before a judicial waiver, a statement of reasoning for the judicial determination, and access to court documentation used in the transfer determination. While doing so, the court listed factors that may be considered at transfer hearings, including the seriousness of the offense, the complaint's prosecutorial merit, the juvenile's sophistication and maturity, the juvenile's history of offenses, the potential to protect the public, and the likelihood of reasonable rehabilitation through the juvenile court. These and similar factors have become the "*Kent* factors" that typically govern judicial decisions regarding juveniles' transfers to adult court (see Levesque, 2000).

By approximately two decades after *Kent*, the vast majority of states had enacted legislation altering the criteria for waivers to adult court. These changes expanded the number and types of juveniles eligible for waiver, and sexual offenses figured prominently in those revisions. The reforms permitted some types of offenses to lead to automatic waiver to adult court, while some combined the offenses with the emotional maturity of juveniles. These presumptive transfer provisions are of significance since they avoid the need for *Kent*-type hearings and, rather than allowing a focus on the offender's characteristics, they focus on the nature of the offenses. Still, it may be that prosecutors can charge cases differently to avoid automatic waivers, but the goal of reforms addressing waivers to adult court has been to reduce prosecutorial or judicial control and influence over decisions relating to transfers. Even if there are hearings, it may be that youth who engage in sexual offenses are deemed more mature, less amenable to rehabilitation, more dangerous to others, more likely to repeat sexual transgressions, and more sophisticated (and therefore more adult-like and more worthy of criminal court jurisdiction). Thus, in a vast majority of states, decisions to transfer certain sex offenders to adult court are automatic and, if not, then the nature of some offenses increases the chances that they will be tried in adult court. Research examining transfers to adult court supports claims that sex offenses, while a small minority of all delinquency petitions, are overrepresented among cases leading to a motion to seek a waiver, as well as the total number of cases transferred to adult court (see Dawson, 1992). Juveniles who commit sex offenses that come to the attention of justice systems, then, are disproportionately likely to find themselves in adult court.

The other end of criminal court processes—the sentencing of offenders and devising of ways to control them—is notable for important legal developments that aim to control offenders. Juveniles treated as adults may be sentenced to one of several innovative measures that fall under the rubric of sexual predator laws that seek to further society's broad interest in community protection. First, registration statutes effective in all states require offenders to supply law enforcement officials with their social security numbers, home addresses, photographs, fingerprints, and information related to past sexual crimes. Second, community notification statutes enacted in the majority of states mandate the distribution of registration information to the community or some form of public disclosure. Third, civil commitment statutes may be used to confine potentially dangerous, involuntary sex offenders, with some states permitting the confinement of sexual offenders after they have served their prison sentences. These three methods serve to restrict the freedom of convicted offenders, with the ones being deemed most at risk of offending subjected to the most restrictions. Legally, these restrictions rest on the rationale that they deter offenders from repeating their crimes, by limiting their access to potential victims and by allowing families and individuals to protect themselves.

Beyond state statutes, there has been a recent slew of federal mandates. Federal legislation now provides funding contingent on the enactment of more aggressive legislative responses to sexual offenders. The Jacob Wetterling Crimes Against Children and Sexually Violent Offender Registration Act (1994) requires states to enact laws governing the registration of sexual offenders, including the creation of a database, and the sharing of information with the FBI, to government agencies, and the public if necessary for protection. The law has been amended and now mandates community notification as to the presence of a sexual predator (Megan's Law, 1996); and law enforcement now may disclose registry information to residents about sex offenders who live in their proximity. Equally importantly, the Adam Walsh Child Protection and Safety Act of 2006 (2006) now obligates states to submit to registration and community notification of juveniles adjudicated delinquent of aggravated sexual abuse when they were 14 or older at the time of the offense, with these new databases permitting online searches beyond states' borders (for a discussion of these laws, see Bowater, 2008). It would be difficult to overestimate the federal government's interest in shaping states' responses to sex crimes, including those committed by juveniles.

The federal statutes and trends are impressive for several reasons. The speed at which they have been enacted across jurisdictions has been phenomenal. The legislative changes affecting all states also have been made without the typical state experimentation that serves to guide the development of effective policies. Equally importantly, they have been enacted and have required states to follow them, even in the absence of social science evidence to support their use (see Trivits & Reppucci, 2002). They also demonstrate the effort and extent to which the federal government and states will go to protect society. Commitment laws protect public safety through the immediate and long-term removal of sexually violent predators; other methods devised to control sex offenders essentially serve to protect the community and demonstrate the broad powers in states' arsenals to combat sexual violence. Finally, they are impressive in that they continue to spread in breadth and depth, despite persistent controversies and growing evidence challenging their effectiveness.

The above developments are not only impressive, but also considerably important in that, as it turns out, even delinquency adjudications are sufficient for constituting the underlying basis or entry point for petitions for sexually dangerous persons to be controlled by them. That is the case since these new provisions are civil in nature, and they tend not to be seen as punishment (Levesque, 2006). The reality is that they likely are experienced as punishment and, equally importantly, they reveal how the promise of the juvenile court's original mandate to remove juveniles from criminal courts has lost its appeal, and how justice systems further collapsed the juvenile court within the criminal court's approaches to problem behavior and offenders. As even a minority of the states recognize juveniles' rights to trial (see Birckhead, 2009), for example, protections automatically afforded adults accused of sexual offenses are not necessarily available to those adjudicated delinquent. Also important to consider are how confidentiality constituted a defining feature of juvenile courts, on the rationale that offenders needed guidance and assistance, rather than retribution and punishment, so that they could better reintegrate successfully into society and not have a future inappropriately tarnished by mistakes. Thus, delinquency adjudications increasingly hold the potential for exposing juveniles to controls reserved for adults (including juveniles tried as adults).

The effectiveness of these responses depends on their actual use. Regrettably, research evaluating them tends to be quite sparse, but important findings continue to emerge. For example, the most established and studied reform, the transfer to adult courts, gains considerable popularity. Advocates of the aggressive use of waivers assert that they satisfy the public's desire for tougher consequences, adequately respond to unrehabilitatable adolescents, and provide longer sentencing unavailable in the juvenile courts. In practice, this orientation lends itself to a punitive and incapacitating judicial system. In fact, studies have found that sentencing becomes harsher (at least for sex offenders) once adolescents have been transferred. Adolescents convicted of rape and transferred to adult court are sentenced, on average, to nearly 17 years in adult correctional facilities (see Brown & Langan, 1998). That average reaches far beyond what they would have received had they been adjudicated in juvenile courts. Importantly, though, the nature of sex offenses varies considerably, as do their penalties. Still, punishment is not the only goal of intervention, which leads us to consider the effectiveness of these measures as they relate to other goals.

Whether other goals of intervention are met remains debatable, or at least not readily established given the current state of the research. It may well be, as the courts are able to achieve punishment goals, that those goals may be met at the expense of other critical goals. Research specifically relating to transfers' collateral effects on sex offenders remains essentially nonexistent, but we can draw from social science research relating more generally to transfers. Reviews reveal at least five points of concern related to the long-term effects of transfers, as well as the actual transfer itself (see Levesque, 2000). First, prosecutorial waivers allow prosecutors to choose criminal or juvenile justice forums; it places more value on the safety of the community than on the best interests of the community, and lacks procedural protections that judicial waivers otherwise afforded. Second, automatic waivers remove the individualization of the justice system and reject the possibility that the juvenile is rehabilitatable in juvenile court. Third, judicial transfers may not ensure justice, as young adolescents may not understand their rights, and clinicians may be unable to inform the court of the efficaciousness of treatment and rehabilitation. Fourth, juveniles may be less culpable and lose their rehabilitative opportunities in adult court. Fifth, transfers negatively effect recidivism rates. Recidivism has been shown to increase and occur sooner in those who are transferred, and transferred adolescents are more likely to commit subsequent felony offenses. Thus, while transfers may quickly incapacitate and permit harsh responses, their consequences are not uniformly positive.

Once waived to adult court, adolescents may have sex-perpetrator statutes applied to them, unless the relevant statutes state otherwise. These laws, meant to fill gaps in the ability of criminal justice systems to control offenders, have been criticized by commentators and researchers who conclude that these methods once may have been valuable, but they may have expanded to the point of diluting their effectiveness even to the point of being counterproductive (see Bowater, 2008; Caldwell, Ziemke, & Vitacco, 2008; Garfinkle, 2003; Letourneau, Bandyopadhyay, Sinha, & Armstrong, 2009a, 2009b). Despite these claims, it is important to emphasize that research has yet to answer even basic questions about the collateral consequences of control mechanisms for adolescent sex offenders. There appears to be a sense that these laws increasingly are being applied to adolescents, given statutory reforms and a sputtering of state cases challenging them, such as mandatory sex offender registering and community notification (see e.g., In re J.W., 2003; In re S.M.M., 1997) and for the civil commitment of violent juvenile predators (In re the Commitment of Tremaine Y., 2005). Yet, no national data reveals how they have had an impact on juvenile sex offenders, such as how many have been subjected to civil commitments due to being found sexually dangerous or violent predators; nor is there data on adolescents subjected to the need to register with local (and national) law enforcement and notify communities of their presence. Thus, in a real sense, we do not have a firm grip on the extent and actual nature of these controlling mechanisms.

Despite important limitations in research, several studies now have examined the effectiveness of these mandates, and those studies that have focused on juvenile sex offenders do challenge claims of their effectiveness. Notably, registration and control has been deemed problematic (and even counterproductive), given that so few adolescent sex offenders reoffend, with one study showing that offenders who meet criteria for registration do not reoffend (either sexually or nonsexually) at rates significantly higher than those who do not meet criteria for registration—a finding that seriously challenges the appropriateness of risk assessment and the management of youthful sexual offenders (Batastini, Hunt, Present-Koller, & DeMatteo, 2011). That study has reinforced others indicating that policies requiring registration fail to deter future sex crimes or reduce juveniles' recidivism, in that registered offenders are as likely to commit other sexual offenses as are juvenile offenders who are not registered (see Caldwell & Dickenson, 2009; Caldwell, Ziemke, & Vitacco, 2008; Letourneau & Armstrong, 2008; Letourneau et al., 2009b). This area of research suggests that efforts to control juveniles, such as through public notification and increased surveillance, tend to target those who are at relatively low risk of offending, and who actually might not benefit from enhanced surveillance.

That the surveillance may not be reaching the offenders most in need, and reaching those who do not need it, is not surprising in light of the challenges facing efforts to predict offending behaviors (see Levesque, 2006). Still, the most recent evidence actually indicates considerable flaws in the classifications of risk found in legal mandates requiring surveillance. The risk assessment tools developed by researchers, which continue to increase in effectiveness, do not relate well to the legal mandates classifying risks of offending. For example, an important study examined how legislative mandates classified offenders' risk (through a tiered system) with well-established sex offender assessment protocols (Caldwell, Ziemke, & Vitacco, 2008). The study followed participants for an average of over 5½ years and found significant inconsistencies in risk designations, with none of the states' risk protocols and only one clinical assessment tool significantly predicting new general, violent, or sexual offense charges. Equally importantly, some of the state protocols captured offenders into high tier designations (deemed at highest risk) when those offenders actually had lower rates of new violent offense charges than their nontiered counterparts. At best, studies like these demonstrate a lack of construct validity among assessment approaches, and a general failure to significantly and reliably predict sexual or other reoffending charges among adolescent sex offenders.

The above findings are expected when viewed in light of research on juvenile sex offending. Research has long shown and increasingly confirmed that sexual offenses committed by juveniles actually are not correlated with adult offending, suggesting a general aging out of sexual offenses, as there is an aging out of the vast majority of offenses (see Nisbet, Wilson, & Smallbone, 2004; Zimring, Piquero, & Jennings, 2007). Similarly, research also indicates that juveniles considered sex offenders do not reveal higher rates of recidivism for sex crimes than do juveniles who are arrested for crimes not related to sex offenses (see, Caldwell, 2007; Kahn & Chambers, 1991). Equally importantly, adults' sex offending relates closely to their offending as juveniles, but the offending as juveniles need not relate to sexual offenses; and, importantly, individuals with a juvenile record of sexual offending, while juveniles actually are less likely to have adult criminal records (see Zimring et al., 2007). Policies focused on deterring juvenile sex offenders' recidivism miss 90% of individuals who grow up to commit sex crimes as adults, a finding that translates into legal systems' potentially misidentifying 90% of offenders who become adult offenders (Zimring et al., 2007). Thus, males engaging in juvenile sexual offenses are not more likely to engage in future sexual offenses than males who have committed nonsexual offenses. These findings comport with those from other longitudinal studies indicating that a significant proportion of adolescents who sexually offended do go on to pursue criminal activity beyond adolescence, but few actually specialize in sexual offending (Carpentier, Leclerc, & Proulx, 2011). Lastly, meta-analyses reveal that sexual recidivism rates for juvenile sex offenders do not relate to levels of secure placement, such as those in the community, in residential care, or in secured custody (Caldwell, 2010). These findings again are not surprising, given that studies consistently show that the rate of sexual reoffending is very low, even among juveniles who have not received treatment (Parks & Bard, 2006). If anything, these studies question the current use of controlling mechanisms, as the reality of juvenile sexual recidivism is very different from the myth.

Despite considerable research challenging the effectiveness of recent management efforts increasingly applied to juveniles, reforms continue to focus on them, arguably because others are potentially problematic. Responses to adolescents' sexual offending always seem to face important challenges. One example of reforms that seems reasonable but potentially problematic in practice relates to the need to focus on interagency collaboration. Being able to keep better track of youth and offer appropriate assistance certainly seems like a worthy and even necessary endeavor. It already has resulted in a variety of initiatives that focus on promoting more effective communication among key agencies working with youth, including schools, law enforcement, child welfare or juvenile courts, and even public housing (see Henning, 2004). It may be difficult to argue against the importance of sharing information about high-risk offenders. But these control methods raise important practical issues, such as those relating to their increasing the stigmatic effects of interventions and eliminating supportive social networks. These are significant in that they are the very types of supports that are linked to the most successful treatment programs for juvenile offenders: the only empirically supported treatment of adolescent sex offenders deemed to be effective is multisystemic treatment (see Borduin & Schaeffer, 2001; Borduin et al., 2009; Henggeler et al., 2009). Thus, even if theory and a thoughtful look at issues suggest a need for broad responses, those may not work well in practice without a close consideration of other factors that may, in the end, replace potential benefits with considerable harms. Legal responses to adolescents necessarily remain complex and require careful examinations of how they influence the multiple systems that respond to youth.

## FURTHERING LEGAL REFORMS

Without doubt, the dominant policy responses to the increased recognition of adolescents' sexual offending involve a move toward more punitive and controlling sanctions. Given the real harms that victims can suffer, it remains difficult to argue against these trends. Considerable problems arise, however, when considering the wide variety of sexual acts that may fall under the umbrella of sexual offending. These actions can range from voluntary sexual actions with similar-aged peers, which research largely depicts as normative and rampant (Levesque, 2000), to sexual actions that even society becomes increasingly uncomfortable with the criminal justice system's harsh responses to them, such as some situations involving "sexting" (see Leary, 2010). Yet, there have not been systematic efforts detailing more precisely how the legal system can support more nuanced approaches to situations involving adolescents' potentially offending sexual behavior. Still, a close look at our understanding of adolescents' place in law and society offers important suggestions that can support recommendations emerging from research.

As long recognized, and as confirmed by even recent Supreme Court cases, adolescents are not analogous to adults and they may not benefit from the same treatment. The legal system has recognized as much with the founding of the juvenile court system. That system now has been transformed radically in the manner it treats certain groups of offenses and offenders. Few now doubt, for example, that giving juveniles adult-like procedural rights arguably resulted in increasing the punitiveness of the juvenile court, what leading researchers have viewed as a criminalization of the juvenile justice system (Feld, 1993), and even a greater exclusion of youth from the juvenile court itself. This has resulted in a shift away from the court's rehabilitative and reintegrative mission, even when the most difficult cases are removed from it. Recently, however, even the Supreme Court has called for treating youth differently and has drawn sharp lines categorically requiring their exclusion from the harsh treatment of criminal courts. This categorical exclusion of juveniles from adult-like punishments has been most notably revealed in jurisprudence involving the death penalty (Roper v. Simmons, 2005) and life imprisonment (Graham v. Florida, 2010). These cases explicitly recognize the need for legal systems to take seriously youth's potential for growth and reintegration, even in instances involving extremely serious offending. Equally importantly, these cases considerably relied on scientific evidence supporting claims of a unique developmental stage of juvenile offenders, particularly regarding their capacity to increase their impulse control and decision-making capacity as they mature. The court's line of reasoning further affirmed the view that, in addition to being capable of reforming themselves, some adolescents are deemed less culpable of their crimes. Creating systems that run counter to the ability of offenders to demonstrate their rehabilitation (and be less culpable and worthy of severe punishment) would run counter to these new jurisprudential understandings of adolescents as redeemable.

Importantly, the law remains enormously complex; it is not clear how age would control in other situations than the ones that the court recently has announced, but social science evidence can shed light on whether existing directions support assumptions. This is particularly the case because the Eighth Amendment has been interpreted as applying to punishments in the criminal justice system (Levesque, 2006), and much of the new sex offender control mechanisms are civil in nature, are not deemed punitive, and are considered appropriate consequences of a legitimate regulatory system. Still, the above jurisprudential developments embracing substantial neurological, psychological, and sociological evidence may show that the youthfulness of offenders can be a concern in the criminal justice systems' responses. As we have seen, despite an increasingly national concern supported by federal mandates that sexual offenders are different, little empirical evidence supports that concern for a juvenile population. That lack of empirical evidence reduces the justification for a system that classifies these youth among the worst offenders. For example, registration and other control policies appear bottomed on flawed assumptions relating to juvenile offenders, to the extent that the policies do not reach their intended goals of identifying the highest-risk offenders and deterring future offending. Indeed, research not only questions the effectiveness of these policies, but also suggests detrimental effects, for missing high-risk individuals and falsely categorizing those at risk does not lead to effective public safety, the rehabilitation of offenders, and a sense that the system is fair. These findings suggest the need to revisit the use of policies aimed at controlling juvenile sex offenders in their communities.

Several recommendations can be made to encourage a re-examination of policies applied to juveniles and to prevent risky changes in the legal treatment of juvenile offenders. Legal controls that apply adult sanctions without the benefit of adult proceedings to youthful offenders are problematic. They are problematic both because they do not provide youth with sufficient legal protections, and also because they are inconsistent with the traditional goals of how the legal system should treat youth. Federal mandates now remove, for example, judicial discretion in deciding which juveniles should be placed on national registries. Most notably, the new laws ignore potentially relevant factors that may influence deviant sexual offending. To the extent to which youth receive adult punishments and are subjected to control measures designed for adults, they arguably should retain the rights adults have to protect themselves from inappropriately being held accountable to sanctions originally tailored for adults.

Without doubt, society and potential victims have an interest in safety. Concerns for public safety need not be ignored and can benefit from social science findings. Legal mandates that seek to control sex offenders increasingly use a very wide net, including efforts to reduce discretion that would by-pass strict mandates. The best available evidence indicates that such efforts are problematic, and that reasonable alternatives exist that have been shown to be more effective. Empirically validated clinical and actuarial violence risk assessments could serve as better foundations for controlling mechanisms such as registration. These methods consider individual and situational factors relevant to adolescents, rather than relying on specific adjudications and a uniform list of offenses. These methods have the added benefit of potentially enhancing the effectiveness of treatments and playing a greater role in ensuring public safety. Identifying dynamic treatment needs and determining the appropriate intensity of supervision and services are best achieved through careful, individualized evaluations. Such evaluations are consistent with not only the goals of the juvenile court, but also the fundamentals of due process on which our legal system rests. It is true that individualized standards move us toward increased discretion, and the dangers associated with it, but existing evidence indicates that current trends, although well intentioned, are somewhat misguided and place society at risk.

Laws also could be revised in ways that make more sense when applied to juveniles. This would include, for example, devising more appropriate classifications of offenders such that their risk would consider their ages, appraised levels of risk, and sexual offense histories. Determining high risk of reoffending based on a victim's young age, for example, makes sense for adult offenders, but not necessarily for young offenders who are engaging in similar-age relationships, some of which may be consensual. Such efforts would help reduce the risk of disproportionately including offenders who engage in low-risk, normative sexual behaviors. Another example would include limiting the time for which the legal system could exert control over young offenders. This consideration is consistent with not only the jurisprudential foundation of juvenile justice systems, but also the above-noted Supreme Court's admonition that those who offend as juveniles be given opportunities to demonstrate that they have reformed themselves. And this recommendation also would parallel some that would limit full notifications given that they become permanent records that, again, could stifle reintegration efforts as they heighten long-term stigmatic effects. It also would parallel the implications of research highlighting the failure of registration and notification policies to identify juvenile recidivists and improve public safety. That failure actually suggests that the best policy may well be to remove juveniles from their reach.

Appropriately removing juveniles from the more extreme focus on control designed for adults may make sense to the extent that opportunities for treatment, education, employment, and normative relationships increase (much as future misconduct decreases) when reducing the chances of prolonged stigmatic effects from past behavior. No one is well served by scientifically unfounded policies that potentially have adverse effects on society, as well as on those who offend. This is not to say that offenders should not be held accountable; rather, it is to say that they perhaps should be held accountable differently than current trends require. Control mechanisms still can continue, but their use could be enhanced if they consider the developmental state of offenders and tailor their approaches. The availability of these assessment tools, and their already mandated application to juvenile offenders, could enable juvenile courts and even criminal courts to spare reformed juveniles from stigma that could be lifelong and incompatible with the recognized need to rehabilitate juvenile offenders when appropriate.

Legal mandates already seek to enhance the integration of multiple service systems, and research indicates that such policies make considerable sense. Although full integration may raise important legal and practical concerns (see above), juvenile sex offenders' dispositions reflect an interdependence between legal and mental health systems. These systems rely on each other for partial solutions to the problems presented by offenders. Juvenile sex offenders, for example, generally exhibit a need for greater self-control. Greater control can come from both the judicial systems' imposition of external controls as well as, equally importantly, mental health systems' assisting offenders to develop internal controls. Neither form of control is sufficient in and of itself, and each system can reach greater effectiveness when they work together. Despite this need, juveniles still have limited rights to reintegrative services. The Supreme Court has stated that "[a]s a general matter, a State is under no constitutional duty to provide substantive services for those within its border" (Youngberg v. Romeo, 1982, p. 317). That lack of obligation has not been met with efforts to impose them. States continue to disagree as to whether an adolescent has a right to rehabilitative services, and many instead highlight safety, punishment, and individual accountability (Levesque, 2000). The narrowly focused interventions that currently dominate juvenile justice services continue to be challenged by research indicating that family-based and community-based interventions present the most promising outcomes for adolescents with problem behaviors, and earlier intervention for young adolescents may be integral to rehabilitating those who would otherwise continue offending into adulthood, as well as those who offend only during the adolescent period (see Levesque, 2000; Carpentier et al., 2011; Ronis & Borduin, 2007). As a result, the enduring necessity to focus on offenders' needs returns to much of what the juvenile court was supposed to be about as it recognized that the social welfare of adolescents ultimately remains a broad societal responsibility rather than a narrow judicial one. Judicial systems can assist, such as by helping to ensure access to services. But addressing violence requires a host of social programs and policies aimed at the basic needs of adolescents, children, families, and their communities.

## CONCLUSION

Juveniles who commit sexual offenses, especially violent ones, pose considerable challenges for justice systems. Legal responses necessarily address debates about how to balance the rights of individuals with the need for public decency and safety, and those debates are marked by images of youth's vulnerability contrasted with notions of their culpability. Those notions tend not to reflect the realities that continue to emerge from our best evidence relating to the nature of adolescents' sexual offending, as well as legal responses to it. Given how some recent policies tend to be going against the best available evidence, there should be no doubt that cases involving juvenile sex offenders will continue to pose important challenges and present truly difficult cases for both juvenile and criminal courts.

Responses to juvenile sex offending have changed quite dramatically over the past few decades, as have responses to juvenile crime in general. Increasingly, criminal courts and adult sanctions and control mechanisms are being enlisted to address juveniles' problem behaviors. These developments clearly go against the rehabilitative mission of the justice system, particularly the juvenile justice system that was envisioned to suit the peculiar social and developmental status of adolescents. Tougher sentencing, registration, and public notification now exemplify the criminalization of justice system responses to juvenile sexual offending. This philosophy directly contradicts the prior concern for focusing on delinquent adolescents' privacy, treatment, confidentiality, and reintegration. Some of these changes have been attributed to the effects of two leading Supreme Court cases dealing with juveniles, *Gault* and *Kent*, that transformed the juvenile court from one with a long history of unchecked powers to one that has become another rights-based institution seeking to limit the court's discretion. The cases established the basic rights of juveniles accused of crimes, as they focused on the due process rights of offenders. By doing so, however, the cases and responses to them initiated a shift in responses to juvenile offenders, a shift from rehabilitation to retribution and deterrence, from benevolent guidance to harsh punishment.

Just as *Kent* and *Gault* may have hastened a more retributive response to offenders as they recognized youth's basic due process rights, recent Supreme Court cases concerning substantive rights may move legal responses in the opposite direction. Those cases, most notably *Roper* and *Graham*, have centered on the types of punishments and sanctions states may impose on juvenile offenders. These cases recognize the need for legal systems to take seriously youth's potential for growth and reintegration, even in instances involving extremely serious offending. How these cases will impact other areas of laws relating to juveniles remains to be seen, but they certainly provide strong jurisprudential bases for re-examining recent trends in responses to juvenile sex offenders, and they do so in ways that affirm the appropriateness of engaging empirical research to shed misconceptions and foster more realistic approaches to addressing the realities of adolescents' place in law and society.

Empirical research on youth's sexual offending and emerging policies may well discredit current directions in responding to juvenile sex offenders, but returning to policies that ignore serious offending also would be misguided. Equally misguided would be efforts that run counter to those aiming to assist sexual assault victims by ensuring that their victimizations are recognized and subject to appropriate responses. Currently, the vast majority of adolescent victims do not have their victimizations addressed by justice systems. They deserve a better response. Without doubt, those responses must include a focus on accountability and community protection. But, we now know that those measures can be implemented in ways that respect the rights of juveniles, recognize their developmental needs, and shape justice systems in ways so that they do not pursue punishment and control at the expense of making other important aims difficult to achieve. Among those critical aims undoubtedly would be assisting offenders' rehabilitation and reintegration, as well as addressing victims' needs and acting in society's overall best interests.

## REFERENCES

Adam Walsh Child Protection and Safety Act. (2006). Pub. L. No. 109-248, 120 Stat. 587.

Arthur, P. J., & Waugh, R. (2009). Status offenses and the juvenile justice and delinquency prevention act: The exception that swallowed the rule. *Seattle Journal for Social Justice, 7*, 550–570.

Batastini, A. B., Hunt, E., Present-Koller, J., & DeMatteo, D. (2011). Federal standards for community registration of juvenile sex offenders: An evaluation of risk prediction and future implications. *Psychology, Public Policy, and Law, 17*, 451–474.

Birckhead, T. R. (2009). Toward a theory of procedural justice for juveniles. *Buffalo Law Review, 57*, 1447–1513.

Bishop, D. M., & Frazier, C. E. (2000). Consequences of transfer. In J. Fagan, & F. E. Zimring (Eds.), *The changing borders of juvenile justice: Transfer of adolescents to the criminal court* (pp. 227–276). Chicago, IL: University of Chicago Press.

Borduin, C. M., & Schaeffer, C. M. (2001). Multisystemic treatment of juvenile offenders: A progress report. *Journal of Psychology and Human Sexuality, 13*, 25–42.

Borduin, C. M., Schaeffer, C. M., & Heiblum, N. (2009). A randomized clinical trial of multisystemic therapy with juvenile sexual offenders: Effects on youth social ecology and criminal activity. *Journal of Consulting and Clinical Psychology, 77*, 26–37.

Bowater, B. M. (2008). Adam Walsh child protection and safety act of 2006: Is there a better way to tailor the sentences of juvenile sex offenders? *Catholic University Law Review, 57*, 817–851.

Brown, J. M., & Langan, P. A. (1998). *State court sentencing of convicted felons, 1994.* Washington, DC: US Department of Justice, Bureau of Justice Statistics.
Caldwell, M. F. (2007). Sexual offense adjudication and recidivism among juvenile offenders. *Sexual Abuse: A Journal of Research and Treatment, 19,* 107–113.
Caldwell, M. F. (2010). Study characteristics and recidivism base rates in juvenile sex offender recidivism. *International Journal of Offender Therapy and Comparative Criminology, 54,* 197–212.
Caldwell, M. F., & Dickinson, C. (2009). Sex offender registration and recidivism risk in juvenile sexual offenders. *Behavioral Sciences and the Law, 27,* 941–956.
Caldwell, M. F., Ziemke, M. H., & Vitacco, M. J. (2008). An examination of the sex offender registration and notification act as applied to juveniles: Evaluating the ability to predict sexual recidivism. *Psychology, Public Policy, and Law, 14,* 89–114.
Carpentier, J., Leclerc, J., & Proulx, J. (2011). Correlates of recidivism among adolescents who have sexually offended. *Sexual Abuse: A Journal of Research and Treatment, 23,* 434–455.
Dalby, C. (1994). Gender bias toward status offenders: A parternalistic agenda carried out through the JJDPA. *Law and Inequality, 12,* 429–456.
Dawson, R. O. (1992). An empirical study of Kent style juvenile transfers to criminal court. *St. Mary's Law Journal, 23,* 975–1054.
Feld, B. C. (1993). Criminalizing the American juvenile court. In M. Tonry (Ed.), *Crime and justice: A review of research,* 17, pp. 197–280.
Feld, B. C. (1995). Violent youth and public policy: A case study of juvenile justice law reform. *Minnesota Law Review, 79,* 965–1128.
Freiburger, T. L., & Burke, A. S. (2011). Status offenders in the juvenile court: The effects of gender, race, and ethnicity on the adjudication decision. *Youth Violence and Juvenile Justice, 9,* 352–365.
Garfinkle, E. (2003). Coming of age in America: The misapplication of sex-offender registration and community notification laws to juveniles. *California Law Review, 93,* 183–208.
Graham v. Florida (2010). 130 S. Ct. 2011.
Henggeler, S. W., Letourneau, E. J., Chapman, J. E., Borduin, C. M., Schewe, P. A., & McCart, M. R. (2009). Mediators of change for multisystemic therapy with juvenile sexual offenders. *Journal of Consulting and Clinical Psychology, 77,* 451–462.
Henning, K. (2004). Eroding confidentiality in delinquency proceedings: Should schools and public housing officials be notified? *New York University Law Review, 79,* 520–611.
Humphrey, A. (2004). The criminalization of survival attempts: Locking up female runaways and other status offenders. *Hastings Women's Law Journal, 15,* 165–184.
In re Gault (1967). 387 U.S. 1.
In re J. W. (2003). 204 Ill 3d 50.
In re S.M.M. (1997). 558 58 N.W.2d 405 (Iowa).
In re the Commitment of Tremaine Y. (2005). 279 Wis. 2d 448.
Jacob Wetterling Crimes Against Children and Sexually Violent Offender Registration Act. (1994). Pub. L. 103-322, Title XVII, Subtitle A, §170101, Sept. 13, 1994, 108 Stat. 2038, 42 USC. §14071.
Kahn, T., & Chambers, H. (1991). Assessing reoffense risk with juvenile sexual offenders. *Child Welfare, 70,* 333–346.
Kent v. United States (1966). 383 U.S. 541.
Kim, J. J. (2010). Left behind: The paternalistic treatment of status offenders within the juvenile justice system. *Washington University Law Review, 87,* 843–867.
Leary, M. G. (2010). Sexting or self-produced child pornography? The dialog continues – structured prosecutorial discretion within a multidisciplinary response. *Virginia Journal of Social Policy & the Law, 13,* 486–566.

Letourneau, E. J., & Armstrong, K. S. (2008). Recidivism rates for registered and nonregistered juvenile sexual offenders. *Sexual Abuse: A Journal of Research and Treatment, 20*, 393–408.

Letourneau, E. J., Bandyopadhyay, D., Sinha, D., & Armstrong, K. (2009a). Effects of sex offender registration policies on juvenile justice decision making. *Sexual Abuse: A Journal of Research and Treatment, 21*, 149–165.

Letourneau, E. J., Bandyopadhyay, D., Sinha, D., & Armstrong, K. S. (2009b). The influence of sex offender registration on juvenile sexual recidivism. *Criminal Justice Policy Review, 20*, 136–153.

Levesque, R. J. R. (2000). *Adolescents, sex, and the law: Preparing adolescents for responsible citizenship*. Washington, DC: American Psychological Association.

Levesque, R. J. R. (2002). *Child maltreatment and the law: Foundations in science, policy and practice*. Durham, NC: Carolina Academic Press.

Levesque, R. J. R. (2006). *The psychology and law of criminal justice processes*. Hauppauge, NY: Nova Science Publishers.

Levesque, R. J. R. (2008). *Rethinking child maltreatment law: Returning to first principles*. New York, NY: Springer.

Levesque, R. J. R. (2011). The law's response to child maltreatment. In Mary P. Koss, Jacquelyn White, & Alan Kazdin, (Eds.), *Handbook of violence against women and children* (Vol. 2, pp. 47–69). Washington, DC: American Psychological Association. [Navigating Solutions].

Megan's Law. (1996). Pub. L. No. 104-145, 110 Stat. 1345.

Moore, L. D., & Padavic, I. (2010). Racial and ethnic disparities in girls' sentencing in the juvenile justice system. *Feminist Criminology, 5*, 263–285.

Nisbet, I. A., Wilson, P. H., & Smallbone, S. W. (2004). A prospective longitudinal study of sexual recidivism among adolescent sex offenders. *Sexual Abuse, A Journal of Research & Treatment, 16*, 223–234.

Parks, G. A., & Bard, D. E. (2006). Risk factors for adolescent sex offender recidivism: Evaluation of predictive factors and comparison of three groups based upon victim type. *Sexual Abuse: A Journal of Research and Treatment, 18*, 319–342.

Ronis, S., & Borduin, C. B. (2007). Individual, family, peer, and academic characteristics of male juvenile sexual offenders. *Journal of Abnormal Child Psychology, 35*, 153–163.

Roper v. Simmons (2005). 543 U.S. 551.

Stein, R. E., & Nofziger, S. D. (2008). Adolescent sexual victimization: Choice of confidant and the failure of authorities. *Youth Violence and Juvenile Justice, 6*, 158–177.

Trivits, L. C., & Reppucci, N. D. (2002). Application of Megan's Law to juveniles. *American Psychologist, 57*, 690–704.

Youngberg v Romeo. (1982). 457 U.S. 307.

Zimring, F. E., Piquero, A. R., & Jennings, W. G. (2007). Sexual delinquency in Racine: Does early sex offending predict later sex offending in youth and adulthood? *Criminology and Public Policy, 6*, 507–534.

# INDEX

## A

Abduction prevention skills, 422–423, 429–431
  of 6- to 8-year-olds, 431–432
  teaching, 426, 430–431, 433–436, 439, 441–442
Abel Assessment for sexual interest™ (AASI), 524
Abnormal sexuality, defining, 202–204
Abstinence, 178–180, 225–226
Abstinence-only programs, 43, 240–241
Abstinence-plus programs, 43
Abused-abuser hypothesis, 208–209
Accuracy, defined, 358–359
Active learning approaches, 429–431
  Behavioral Skills Training (BST), 433–435
  In Situ Training (IST), 435–438
  for teaching sexual abuse prevention skills, 432–438
*Adam Walsh Child Protection and Safety Act of 2006* (2006), 559–560
Adolescence and commercial sexual exploitation (CSE), 449, 453–455
  abandonment and survival, 456–458
  community response, 464–466
  failure of care systems and, 463–464
  force and control by exploiters, 460–461
  gender relations, 458–460
  psychological manipulation and isolation, 461–462
  research on common features of, 462–464
  social context of, among homeless/runaway teens, 455–456
Adolescent sex offenders, 98, 337–339, 549–550, 562, 564–565
Adolescent sex trade work, 333
Adolescent sexual abuse, incidence and prevalence of, 307–308
Adolescent sexual behavior problems (SBPs), 332–333
Adolescent victims of sexual violence, legal responses to, 469

  processes and inherent limitations, 471–485
  child welfare systems, 471–478
  criminal justice systems, 478–485
  victim's rights movement, 485–489
Adolescents adjudicated for sexual offenses, 519
  amenability to treatment, 527–528
  assessment of sexual interest, 521–534
    Multiphasic Sex Inventory-II (MSI-II), 525–526
    plethysmograph, 522–523
    viewing-time measures, 523–525
  characteristics of, 520–521
  legal responses, 547
    criminal justice responses, 557–565
    furthering legal reforms, 565–569
    juvenile justice system responses, 548–557
  polygraph, 526–527
  recommendations for practitioners, 532–534
  risk assessment, 528–532
    general delinquency measures, 531–532
    sexual recidivism measures, 528–531
  treatment for, 534–539
    cognitive behavioral therapy (CBT), 534–536
    multisystemic therapy (MST), 536–537
    recommendations for practitioners, 538–539
  treatment progress, assessment of, 532
Adrenarche, 147
  premature, 160
Adult–child sexual contact, 347
Adult prostitution. *See* Prostitution
Adult sex offenders, 519, 525–526
Adverse Childhood Experiences (ACE) Survey, 308
Affective Expression and Modulation, 382–383
Affective expression skill-building activities, 389–390

Affinity Measure of Sexual Interest, 524–525
Age-appropriate sex education, 395
Aggressive behavior of children, 380
Alcohol and illicit drug use, influence of, 253
  childhood sexual abuse (CSA) and, 263
  dating violence and, 263–264
  descriptive epidemiology, 254–263
  future directions, 269–270
  selective findings from prevention and intervention studies, 266–269
  and sexual intercourse patterns, 254–260
  and sexual risk outcomes, 260–262
  STD/HIV prevention
    among youth in treatment, 267–268
    for youth not in treatment programs, 268–269
  theories and common mechanisms of, 264–266
Amenability to treatment, 527–528
American Bar Association (2009), 487–488
American Psychological Association (APA), guidelines for, 8
AMH, 117–118
AMSTAR questionnaire, 58–62
AMSTAR$_{CAS}$ items, 59–62, 59t–61t
  adolescents and child sexuality, judged by, 85t–87t
  analysis and interpretation, 61
  a priori design, 59
  literature search, 59
  studies, coding of, 60
Anal sex, 185
ANOVA, 52–53
Antecedents, 115–116, 380
"Asked-and-answered,", 354–355
Attachment theory, 208–209
Autonomy, of child, 16–17
Avoidance, 384–385

**B**

"Bad me", 119
Barkley's Defiant Child protocol, 511
Barrier methods, 227, 239–240
Baseline measurement, 101

Behavior of children, 380
  aggressive behavior, 380
  noncompliant behavior, 380
Behavioral change theories, 236–237
Behavioral interventions to increase contraceptive use, 237–239
Behavioral learning theory, 208–209
Behavioral skills training (BST), 267–268, 433–435
  adapting, 442–444
  evaluation of, 441
Behavior-rating scale, 24
Behaviors and partnerships, sexual milestones in, 199–201
Best Interest Standard, 4
Bisexuality, 280–282
Body-to-body contact, 119
Boys
  aware of genital differences, 122, 152–153
  developmental implications, 125–126
  earlier pubertal onset in, 150–151
  exhibitionism in, 211–212
  expectations, 6–7
  expression of sexuality, 208
  gender- appropriate behaviors, 121
  gender role behavior, 161
  masturbatory behaviors, 155–156
  normative sexual behaviors of, 34–35
  playground scripts for, 130–131
  precocious puberty, 160
  pubertal progression in, 147
  and sexual offenses, 551–552
  sexually explicit media among, 176
  with sexual behavior problems, 502–503
Broad index, 59–62
Browne's theoretical model, 373–374

**C**

California Evidence Based Clearinghouse for Child Welfare (CEBC), 377–378, 509–510
CAPTA Reauthorization Act of 2010, 304–305
Caregivers' attitudes on children's sexuality, 159
Case studies, 23
Case studies and interviews with minors, 23

Categorical models, 55
Centers for Disease Control (CDC), 224, 305
Child Abuse Assessment Centers (CAAC), 483–484
Child Advocacy Center (CAC), 315–316, 363, 483–484
  CornerHouse Forensic Interview Protocol (RATAC), 365
  extended forensic interview model, 366–367
  interviews in, 363–367
  National Children's Advocacy Center (NCAC), 364
  National Institute of Child Health and Human Development (NICHD) protocol, 365–366
Child memory, general trends in, 358–360
Child protection system. See Child welfare system
Child Protective Services (CPS) data, 307–308
Child sexual abuse (CSA), 325, 371–372, 401–402, 415, 420–421
  and alcohol and drug use, 263
  case study of TF-CBT for, 385–396
  defining, 304–307
  disclosure and allegations of, 313–316
  evidence-based treatments for, 372–377
  incidence and prevalence of, 307–308
  juvenile sex offending, 335–340
  outcomes of, 316–319
  prevention skills training, 441
  professional responsibilities in, 328–331
  -related phobias, 326–327
  sexual behavior problems, 331–335
  statistics, 327–328
  victim and abuse characteristics, 309–313
    sexual abuse experiences, characteristics of, 311–313
    sexual abuse victims, characteristics of, 309–311
  victims of, 401
Child Sexual Behavior Checklist (CSBCL), 508
Child Sexual Behavior Inventory (CSBI), 24, 124, 154–155, 508

Child welfare system, 328–329, 471–478, 549
Child's sexual abuse evaluation
  interview questions, types of, 403–404, 405*t*
ChildFirst, 365
Childhood obesity, 148–149
Childhood sexual behavior
  direct, systematic observational methodology, 32–34
  meta-analytic techniques, 25
  self-monitoring of, 31–32
  single-case experimental designs for, 30–31
Childhood sexual behavior problems (SBPs), 331–333
Childhood sexuality research, ethical constraints in, 33–34
Children in Need of Protection or Services (CHIPS), 555–556
Children in Need of Supervision (CHINS), 555–556
Children with sexual behavior problems (CSBPs), 520
Children's Depression Inventory, 386–387
Children's Memory Characteristics Questionnaire, Therapist Version, 357
Children's Sexual Behavior Inventory, 386–387
Children's treatment for sexual disorder/behavior, 3–6
  best interests for, 10–15
  consent, rudiments for, 3–6
  hot button case, 6–10
  large issues, 16–18
  moral disagreement, 15–16
  parents role in, 3–4
Chlamydial infections, in young children, 413
Coercion, 135–136, 306
Cognitive behavioral therapy (CBT), 334–335, 374, 534–536
Cognitive coping, 383, 395
Cognitive social learning theory, 121, 126–127
Coitus, 178, 183, 185

Colposcope, 408–409, 411–412
Commercial sex and adolescence, social context of
  framing the issue among homeless or runaway teens, 455–456
  incidence and prevalence, 453–455
Commercial sexual exploitation (CSE), 453–455. *See also* Prostitution
  abandonment and survival, 456–458
  failure of care systems and, 463–464
  force and control by the exploiters, 460–461
  gender relations, 458–460
  psychological manipulation and isolation, 461–462
  research on common features of, 462–464
Commercially sexually exploited girls, 452
Communities and adolescents' sexual and contraceptive behavior, 233
Competence, of adults, 3
Condom use, 228
  adolescent substance abusers and, 261, 334–335
  and ethnicity, 229
  religiosity and, 233–234
  sensation-seeking and, 230
  and sexual and alcohol risk reduction condition, 268–269
  at sexual debut, 227–229, 241–242
  within relationships, 232–233
Conjoint Child–Parent Sessions, 385
Consent, rudiments of, 3–6
Continuous models, 55
Contraceptives, 225–228
  access to reproductive health and contraceptive services, 239–240
  barrier methods, 227
  behavioral change theories, 236–237
  behavioral interventions to increase the use of, 237–239
  hormonal methods, 226–227
  promotion and provision of, among US adolescents, 240–241
  use and non-use, predictors of, 228–236

  biological and developmental factors, 228–229
  communities, 233
  family, 231–232
  media, 234–235
  new research on intrapersonal factors, 231
  peers, 232
  personality characteristics, 230
  psychological and behavioral factors, 229–230
  relationships and partner characteristics, 232–233
  religious beliefs, 233–234
CornerHouse Forensic Interview Protocol (RATAC), 363–365
Correct rejections, 358
Correlation coefficient, 52
Crime Victims' Rights Act (2005), 487
Criminal justice system, 471, 478–485, 548, 562
Criminal responses, 557–565
Cross-gender behaviors, 161
Cultural beliefs, in child's treatment, 10–12
Cultural factors impacting sexual development and behavior, 158–159
Curiosity, in children
  learning bases, 120

# D

Dating scripts, 131–132
Dating violence, 224–225, 335–336
  and alcohol and drug use, 263–264
Decisional capacity, of child, 3, 7
Dehydroepiandrosterone (DHEA), 147
Dehydroepiandrosterone sulfate (DHEAS), 147
Depo-Provera®, 227, 325
Depth of Processing Model (DOP), 350–351
Developing child, sexual cognitions in, 197–199
Developmental disability, children with, 500–501
  sexual behavior problems of, 512
Developmental Implications, of gender schema theory, 125–126

"Developmental readiness,", 180
Developmentally related sexual behaviors, 124
Diagnostic and Statistical Manual of Mental Disorders, 203
Dihydrotestosterone (DHT), 117–118
Direct, systematic observations, of childhood sexual behavior, 32–34
Disclosure process, 314–315
Discriminative stimulus, 421–422
Dissociation spectrum, 326–327
Domestic sex trafficking of children, 453

# E

Early-onset substance use, 255–257, 270
Eddie Eagle GunSafe Program, 425–426, 429, 431
Effect sizes, 55, 238–239
  averaging, 53–54
  inconsistency, determining, 54
  potential moderators of, 55
Endocrine-disrupting compounds (EDCs), 149–150
Enhancing Future Safety and Development, 385
Error of commission, 358
Error of omission, 358
Estimate of Risk of Adolescent Sexual Offense Recidivism (ERASOR), 530–534
Estrogen, from fat cells, 149
Ethnicity and condom use, 229
Eunice Shriver National Institute of Child Health and Human Development, 365–366
Evidence-based practice (EBP), 334
Evidence-based treatments
  for children with sexual behavior problems, 512–513
  for child sexual abuse, 372–375
Evolutionary theories, 209
Exhibitionism, 211–212, 332, 520–521
Extended forensic interview model, 366–367
Eye Movement Desensitization and Reprocessing (EMDR) condition, 374
Eye-witness testimony of adults, 358

# F

Facebook©, 313
Family
  role, in sexual health of adolescents, 231–232
  sexual culture, 173–175
Female. *See also* Girls
  adolescent offenders, 520
  alcohol use in, 255*t*
  fetus, sexual development in, 117–118
  first intercourse of, 126
  HIV in, 260
  juvenile sexual offenders, 206–208
  marijuana use in, 255*t*
  prostitution, 465
  puberty in, 147
  same-sex sexual contact, 278
  as sexual abuse victims, 309
  sexual behavior, 256*t*
    for 14–17-year-old, 179*f*, 183–184
    for 18–19-year-old, 278
  sexually transmitted disease (STD) in, 260
  Tanner stages, of sexual maturity system, 146–147
Finkelhor and Browne's theoretical model, 373–374
Firearm injury prevention skills, 425–426
Functional magnetic resonance imaging (fMRI), 35

# G

Gay/lesbian identities, 282–283, 293
Gay-related stress, 258
Gender Identity Disorder (GID), 161–162
  prepubertal children and, 160
Gender identity, 286–287, 289–290
Gender schema theory, 121–127
  developmental Implications, 125–126
  learning from each other, 123–125
  sexual double standard, 126–127
Gender segregation, 123, 130–131
Gender socialization, 124
Gender-based value system, 122
Gendered sexual scripts, softening of, 132–133

Gender-nonconforming youths, 275–276, 286–288
Gender-related socialization, 123
General delinquency risk assessment measures, 531–532
Genetic testing, for childhood sexual behavior, 36–37
Genital Examination Distress Scale (GEDS), 408–409
Girls. *See also* Female
  adrenarche in, 147
  alcohol/drug use by, 258
  menarche in, 147
  "normative" sexual development, understanding, 193–202
    behaviors and partnerships, sexual milestones in, 199–201
    developing child, sexual cognitions in, 197–199
    physiological responses and sexual maturation, 195–197
  paraphilias and sexual offending, 202–212
    abnormal sexuality, defining, 202–204
    characteristics of, 205–208
    gaps in the literature, 211–212
    prevalence of, 204–205
    theoretical perspectives, 208–209
    treatment approaches, 209–211
  precocious puberty in, 160–161
  premature adrenarche in, 147
  prostitution in US, 449
  pubertal progression in, 147
  same-sex attractions in, 278
  sex trafficking in US, 453
  sexual development in, 193
  thelarche in, 147
Good Lives Model, 537–538
"Good me,", 119
Graham v. Florida, 2010, 565–566
Group psychotherapy, 210

# H

Healthy sexual development, 137–138
Herpes simplex virus (HSV), 261–262, 413
Human immunodeficiency virus (HIV) prevention, 238–239, 258
Human papillomavirus (HPV), 221–222, 413

Hypothalamic–pituitary–adrenal (HPA) axis, 317
Hypothalamic–pituitary–gonadal (HPG) hormone axis, 145–146, 146*f*
Hypothetical *versus* actual dating scenarios, 131–132

# I

Illicit drug use, influence of. *See* Alcohol and illicit drug use, influence of
Implanon®, 226–227
*In re Gault* (1967), 553
In Situ training (IST), 435–438
  adapting, 442–444
  development of, 439–441
  evaluation of, 441
  social validation of, 439–441
*In Vivo* Mastery of Trauma Reminders, 378–379, 384–385
Incredible Years, 511
Influence technique, in children, 125–126
Informant reports and rating scales, 24–25
Informational approaches, for teaching sexual abuse prevention skills, 429–432
Information-motivation-behavioral skills model (IMB) of AIDS-prevention behavior, 268
Informed consent, theory of, 6
Intention–behavior relations, 230
Internet, sexual victimization via, 313
Interpersonal context, 128–129
Interpersonal violence (IPV), 263–264
Interview question
  evaluating, for potential bias, 360–363
  for sexually abused children, 405*t*
"Inviting speculation,", 354–355

# J

Jacob Wetterling Crimes Against Children and Sexually Violent Offender Registration Act (1994), 559–560
Juvenile
  court system, 481–482, 548–550
  justice samples, 204–205
  justice system responses, 548–557
  nonsexual offenders, 211
  prostitution, 333–334
    treatment of, 451

sex offenders, 43–44, 206, 210
sex offending, 204–205, 335–340
victim justice system, 471
Juvenile justice system responses, 548–557
Juvenile Risk Assessment Scale (JRAS), 531
Juvenile Sex Offender Assessment Protocol-II (J-SOAP-II), 528–530
Juvenile sex offending, 335–340
Juvenile Sex Offense Specific Treatment Needs and Progress Scale, 532
Juvenile Sexual Offense Recidivism Risk Assessment Tool – II (J-SORRAT-II), 531

## K

*Kent v. United States* (1966), 527–528, 557–558

## L

*The Lancet*, 46–47
Large-group experimental designs, 98
Learning about sex, 123–125
Learning bases, 118–127
  cognitive social learning theory, 121
  gender schema theory, 121–127
    developmental Implications, 125–126
    learning from each other, 123–125
    sexual double standard, 126–127
  motivation, 118–121
Legal reforms, furthering, 565–569
Legal responses
  to adolescents' sexual offending, 547
  to adolescent victims of sexual violence, 469
  criminal justice responses, 557–565
  furthering legal reforms, 565–569
  juvenile justice system responses, 548–557
  processes and inherent limitations, 471–485
    child welfare systems, 471–478
    criminal justice systems, 478–485
    victim's rights movement, 485–489
Leptin, 149
Life Skills Training (LST) prevention intervention, 269
Long-term memory (LTM), 349–351

## M

Magnetic resonance imaging (MRI), 35
Male
  adolescents offenders, 520
    treatment for, 522–523
  alcohol use in, 255*t*
  condoms, 239–240
  fetus, sexual development in, 117–118
  juvenile sexual offenders, 210
  marijuana use in, 255*t*
  non-sex offenders, 339
  same-sex sexual contact, 278
  as sexual abuse victims, 309
  sexual behavior, 256*t*
    for 14–17-year-old, 179*f*, 183–184
    for 18–19-year-old, 278
  sexual offenders, 339
  Tanner stages, of sexual maturity system, 146–147
Male adolescents offenders, 520
Maltreatment-related trauma symptoms, 326–327
Masturbation, 181–182, 391
  in childhood years, 195–196
  in school-age children, 155–156
McMartin interviews, 354–355
Media, 134–135
  impact of, on sexual behavior, 157–158
  pubertal onset and, 151–152
  and sexual healthy behavior, 234–235
Medical evaluation for suspected child sexual abuse, 401
  documentation, 414–415
    medical assessment, 414–415
    medical findings, interpretation of, 414
  examination of, 409–414
  medical assessment and treatment
    approach to, 402–404
    multidisciplinary teams, 415–416
    overview of, 402–404
    physical exam, timing of, 406–407
  preparation of child for examination, 407–409
    distraction techniques, 408–409
    relaxation techniques, 408–409
Medline databases, 21

Memory
  Atkinson and Shiffrin model, 349–350
  of child, 347–348
  classic memory research, 352–357
  defined, 358
  Depth of Processing Model (DOP), 350–351
  general trends in, 358–360
  reconstructive memory, 351–352
Menarche, 147
Meta-analysis techniques
  of childhood and adolescent sexuality (CAS), 42–47
  for childhood sexual behavior, 25
Methodological quality
  AMSTAR questionnaire for, 58–59
  of systematic review and meta-analysis, 58–59, 85*t*–87*t*
Mindfulness, 382
Minority stress, 258, 284
Minors, case studies and interviews with, 23
Minors, sexuality of, 3–6
"Missing discourse of desire,", 200
Missouri State University, 368
Moral disagreement, 15–16
Motivation, 118–121
Multidimensional Treatment Foster Care, 511
Multiphasic Sex Inventory-II (MSI-II), 525–526
Multiple-baseline (MBL) designs, 104–110
  across behaviors, 108
  across settings, 108–109
  across subjects, 105–108
Multisystem Therapy (MST), 210–211, 511–512, 536–537

# N

Narrative reviewing, 45
National 2011 Youth Risk Behavior Survey (YRBS), 327–328
National Child Abuse and Neglect Data System (NCANDS), 307–308
National Child Protection Training Center (NCPTC), 365
National Children's Advocacy Center (NCAC), 363–364, 366–367
National Children's Alliance (NCA), 315–316
National Health and Nutrition Examination Survey III, 411
National Incidence Study of Child Abuse and Neglect (NIS-4) data, 307–310
National Institute of Child Health and Human Development (NICHD) protocol, 363–366
*National Survey of Family Growth*, 225
Negative feedback mechanisms, 145–146
Network- Individual-Resource (NIR) theory, 236–237
Neuroimaging studies, for childhood sexual behavior, 35–36
Non-behavioral negative sexual outcomes, 135
Noncompliant behavior of children, 380
Non-consensual intercourse, 310
Non-contact child sexual abuse (CSA), 326–327
Nonexclusive patterns of attraction, 282–283
Non-suggestive free-recall, 359
Non-Western nations
  normative sexual development in, 37
Non-White child population
  normative sexual development in, 37
Normative sexual behaviors, 500
"Normative" sexual development, understanding, 193–202
  behaviors and partnerships, sexual milestones in, 199–201
  developing child, sexual cognitions in, 197–199
  physiological responses and sexual maturation, 195–197
Not OK touches, 387–389, 392–393, 395–396
Nucleic acid amplification tests (NAATs), 413–414
NuvaRing®, 227

# O

Obesity
  in children, 148–149
  and pubertal onset, 148–149

Objectification, 306
Odds ratios (OR), 52
Office of Juvenile Justice and Delinquency Prevention (OJJDP), 512–513
OK touches, 388–391, 393–396
Online environments
  media researchers for, 135
Oral contraceptive pills (OCPs), 225–226
Oral-genital sexual behaviors, 183–184
Orgasm, in adolescents, 186
Ortho Evra®, 227
"Outcry,", 367–368
Outliers, analysis of, 55
Overweight children and early puberty, 149

# P

Paraphilias and sexual offending, in girls, 202–212
  abnormal sexuality, defining, 202–204
  characteristics of, 205–208
  gaps in the literature, 211–212
  prevalence of, 204–205
  theoretical perspectives, 208–209
  treatment approaches, 209–211
Parent Child Interaction Therapy, 511
Parent Emotional Reaction Questionnaire, 386–387
Parents, 379
  and child sexual behaviors, 506–507
  influence, in child's sexual behavior, 173–175
  monitoring, 231
  as proxy decision makers, 17
  skills, 265, 387
  treatment methods, role in, 3–4
    choosing for children, 3–6
Partnered sexual behaviors, 172–173, 177–178, 182–186
  and sexual relationships, 182–183
  subjective sexual experiences, 185–186
Peers, 23–24, 199
  and friends, in sexual socialization, 175–176
  sexual health information from, 232
Permissive societies, 159
"Personal Safety Questionnaire,", 423–424
Personal safety, of children, 419

Persons in Need of Supervision (PINS), 555–556
Physiological responses and sexual maturation, in girls, 195–197
Plan B One-Step®, 239–240
Playground scripts, 130–131
Plethysmograph, 100, 522–523
Polygraph, 526–527
Polymerase chain reaction (PCR), 413–414
Pornography, 34, 135–136, 176–177, 206–207, 311–312, 337, 453
Positive health, 253, 270
Post-traumatic stress disorder (PTSD), 317–318, 326–327, 334–335
Precocious puberty, 160–161
"Pre-coital" sexual experiences, 199
Pregnancy, 413
  prevention, 45
  sexual risk behaviors, 43
  teenage, 223–224, 228, 308
  unintended, 223–224
  unplanned, 178–179
  unwanted, 222–223, 240–241
Premarital sex, 223
Premature adrenarche, 147, 160
Prepubertal children, sexual behavior of, 21, 147
  cultural factors impacting sexual development and behavior, 158–159
  defining prepubertal, 145–147
  early childhood, 152–155
    sexual behavior, 153–155
    sexual knowledge, 152–153
  and gender identity disorder, 160
  precocious puberty, 160–161
  premature adrenarche, 160
  reasons for, 148–152
    endocrine-disrupting compounds (EDCs), 149–150
    obesity, 148–149
    social environment, 150–152
  school-age children, 155–158
    sexual behavior, 155–158
    sexual knowledge, 155
Prepubertal, defining, 145–147
Pre-pubescent sexually abused children, 466

584  Index

Preschoolers, 152, 355
  classic memory research with, 352
  sexual behavior in, 153–155
  sexual knowledge in, 152–153
Prevention skills, of sexual abuse. *See*
    Teaching sexual abuse prevention
    skills to children
Privacy, sexual activities and, 198–199
Problem behavior theory (PBT), 265
Problematic sexual behaviors, in children, 317
  clinical assessment, 506–509
  conceptualization of, 501–506
  definitions, 498–499
  origin of, 501–506
  prevalence of, 501–506
  systems barriers and supports, 512–513
  treatment planning, 509–512
    special issues, 512
  typical sexual development,
    differentiating, 499–501
Professional responsibilities, in child sexual
    abuse, 328–331
Prostitution, 333, 449–450, 452–453
  adolescent girls, 460
  in juvenile, 333–334, 450
    treatment of, 451
  legalization of, 449–450
  for money, 261
  in teenage, 460
  in UK, 463
  in US girls, 449–450
Protocol for Evaluating Forensic Interviews
    of Children (PEFIC), 360
Proximate antecedents, 115–116
PsychINFO, 21
Psychoeducation, 381–382
  about sexual abuse, 391–392
Psychopathy Checklist: Youth Version
    (PCL:YV), 531–532
"Psychosexual vulnerabilities,", 463–464
Puberty, 145–146
  at earlier ages. *See* Prepubertal children,
    sexual behavior of
Publication Bias, 56–57

**R**

Randomized controlled trials (RCTs), 84, 98
Reconstructive memory, 351–352

Redirection, concept of, 391
Relaxation, 382, 391
Religion's role, in Child's treatment,
    10–12
Religious beliefs and sexual behavior,
    233–234
Remote antecedents, 115–116
Reproductive health and contraceptive
    services, access to, 239–240
Research methods, 21
  on child and adolescent sexuality, 22
  in childhood behavior
    direct, systematic observations of,
      32–34
    meta-analytic techniques, 25
    sexual thoughts and behavior, self-
      monitoring of, 31–32
    single-case experimental designs, 25
  dilemmas impeding, 37–38
  future research, directions for, 34–37
    genetic testing, 36–37
    neuroimaging studies, 34–35
    non-White US samples, 37–38
    systematic observational methodology,
      34–35
  informant reports and rating scales,
    24–25
  minors, case studies and interviews, 23
  shortcomings of, 22–25
  strengths of, 22–25
  young adults, retrospective recall of,
    23–24
Research on child and adolescent sexuality,
  22
Research strategies, strengths and
    shortcomings of, 22–25
Research syntheses related to childhood
    and adolescent sexuality (CAS), 41
  discussion, 88–90
  evidence-based resources, 42–47
  reviews addressing, 63*t*–69*t*
    characteristics of, 70*t*–83*t*
  systematic reviews and meta-analysis,
    42–47
    analysis, 53–57
    boundaries setting, 48–49
    coding studies, 50–51
    defining question, 48

interpreting and presenting results, 56–57
literature, 49–50
magnitude, estimating, 51–53
procedures, 47–57
publication bias, 56–57
temporal trends in, 90*f*
systematic reviews survey, 57–91
method, 58–62
Respondent driven sampling (RDS) statistical techniques, 454
Restrictive societies, 159
Results, interpreting and presenting, 57
Reversal and withdrawal designs, 101–104
Revictimization, risk of, 318, 372
Reviews, characteristics of, 70*t*–83*t*
Risk assessment measures
general delinquency, 531–532
sexual recidivism, 528–531
Risk-taking behaviors, 230
Role play assessment, 425–427

## S

Safe Side abduction prevention program, 431–432
Safety skills, assessment of, 423–428
in situ assessment, 426–427
role play assessment, 425–426
verbal report assessment, 423–425
Safety threats, to children, 419
Same-gender models, 121
Same-sex attractions, 279–283, 286
Same-sex peer interactions, 123, 131
Same-sex sexuality, 277–278
School-age children
sexual behavior in, 155–157
sexual knowledge in, 155
Scripts
dating, 131–132
playground, 130–131
sexual, 132–134
social, 129–134
Sedentary media usage and puberty onset, 151–152
Seeking Safety, 374–375
Self-concept, 119, 123, 177
Self-exploration, 153
Self-monitoring, 31–32

Self-touch/self-rubbing behaviors, 153
Sensation-seeking, 230
Sensory memory (SM), 349–350
Sex education, 395
Sex for money, 454, 457
Sex offenders, 337, 339–340, 512–513, 549–550, 559–560, 562
Sex offending, 563–564, 570
Sex trade worker. *See* Prostitution
"Sex work,", 449–450
Sex, defining, 115–116
Sex-offender-specific therapy, 339–340
Sexting, 157–158, 176–177, 203–204
Sexual abuse experiences, characteristics of, 311–313
Sexual abuse prevention skills, teaching, 421–422
educating child, 421
recommendations, 439–444
BST, adapting, 442–444
BST, evaluation of, 441
in situ assessments, development and social validation of, 439–441
IST, adapting, 442–444
IST, evaluation of, 441
safety skills assessment, 423–428
in situ assessment, 426–427
role play assessment, 425–426
verbal report assessment, 423–425
training approaches, 428–444
active learning approaches, 432–438
informational approaches, 429–432
"What If Situations Test" (WIST), 424–425
Sexual abuse victims, characteristics of, 309–311
Sexual abuse, 305, 348–349
by known adult, 420–421
history of, 404
Sexual Abuse, Family Education, and Treatment (SAFE-T) program, 535–536
Sexual assaults, 335–336
Sexual behavior problems (SBP), in children, 497
clinical assessment, 506–509
conceptualization of, 501–506
definitions, 498–499
origin of, 501–506

Sexual behavior problems (*Continued*)
  prevalence of, 501–506
  systems barriers and supports, 512–513
  treatment planning, 509–512
    special issues, 512
  typical sexual development, differentiating, 499–501
Sexual behavior problems (SBPs), in adolescent, 332–333
Sexual behavior
  in childhood. *See* Childhood sexual behavior
  cultural factors impacting, 158–159
  in early childhood, 153–155
  in prepubertal children, 152–160
  problems. *See* Sexual behavior problems (SBP), in children
  rules, 388–389
  in school-age children, 155–157
    impact of media/technology on, 157–158
Sexual coercion, 224–225
Sexual cognitions, in developing child, 197–199
Sexual development in adolescents, 171
  conceptual organization of, 172–173
  sexual repertoire, 178–186
    abstinence, 178–180
    masturbation, 181–182
    partnered sex, 182–186
  sexual selfhood, 177–178
    sexual anxiety, 178
    sexual openness, 177
    sexual self-esteem, 177–178
  sexual socialization, 173–177
    family sexual culture and parents' influence, 173–175
    peers and friends in, 175–176
    sexually explicit media and, 176–177
Sexual development, 115–118
  cultural factors impacting, 158–159
  differentiating, 499–501
  healthy sexual development, 137–138
  learning bases, 118–127
    cognitive social learning theory, 121
    gender schema theory, 121–127
    motivation, 118–121

  social bases, 127–137
    culture, 127–128
    interpersonal context, 128–129
    media, 134–135
    pornography, coercion, and sexual violence, 135–136
    sexual double standard, 136–137
    social scripts, 129–134
Sexual differentiation, 117–118
Sexual disorder/behavior, children's treatment for. *See* Children's treatment for sexual disorder/behavior
Sexual double standard, 126–127, 136–137
Sexual education, 209–210, 240–241
Sexual grooming, 312–313
Sexual health of adolescents, 221
  contraceptives, 225–228
    access to reproductive health and contraceptive services, 239–240
    barrier methods, 227
    behavioral change theories, 236–237
    behavioral interventions to increase contraceptive use, 237–239
    hormonal methods, 226–227
    promotion and provision of, 240–241
    use and non-use, predictors of, 228–236
  sexual behavior, 222–223
  sexual coercion, 224–225
  sexually transmitted infections, 224
  unintended pregnancy, 223–224
Sexual ill-health, 221–222
Sexual interaction, initiating, 132–133
Sexual intercourse patterns
  alcohol and other substance use and, 254–260
Sexual interest, assessment of, 521–534
  Multiphasic Sex Inventory-II (MSI-II), 525–526
  plethysmograph, 522–523
  viewing-time measures, 523–525
Sexual knowledge
  of children, 348
  in early childhood, 152–153
  in school-age children, 155
Sexual maturity rating system, 410

Sexual media messages, 157
Sexual norm transmission, 174–175
Sexual offenses, adolescents adjudicated for. *See* Adolescents adjudicated for sexual offenses
Sexual orientation, 276–277
Sexual play, 154–155, 196
 with siblings, 156
Sexual recidivism risk assessment measures, 528–531
Sexual repertoire, 172–173, 178–186
 abstinence, 178–180
 masturbation, 181–182
 partnered sex, 182–186
Sexual risk behaviors
 alcohol use and, 258, 260–261
Sexual selfhood, 172–173, 177–178
 sexual anxiety, 178
 sexual openness, 177
 sexual self-esteem, 177–178
Sexual socialization, 172–177
 family sexual culture and parents' influence, 173–175
 peers and friends in, 175–176
 sexually explicit media and, 176–177
Sexual talk, 310
 unwanted, 310
Sexual thoughts and behaviors, self-monitoring of, 31–32
Sexual touch, 310–312
 unwanted, 310
Sexual victimization, of adolescents, 471–485
Sexual violence, 135–136
 legal responses of, to adolescents
  child welfare systems, 471–478
  criminal justice systems, 478–485
  processes and inherent limitations, 471–485
  victim's rights movement, 485–489
Sexuality, 325
 of minors, 3–6
  treatment methods, 3–6
Sexually explicit media and adolescent sex, 176–177
Sexually transmitted disease (STD)
 alcohol and other substance use and, 260–262

 STD/HIV prevention. *See* STD/HIV prevention
Sexually transmitted infections (STIs), 221–222, 224, 227, 240–241, 333, 413
Sexual-minority youths, 275–276
 defining, 278–279
 mental health of, 283–286
 substance use and sexual behaviors of, 258
The Shame Questionnaire, 386–387
Short-term memory (STM), 349–350
Single-case experimental designs, 30–31
"Small-n designs", 30
Small-n research designs, 30–31
Small-n research design, in child and adolescent sexuality, 97
 baseline measurement, 101
 measurement, 99–101
 multiple-baseline designs, 104–110
 reversal and withdrawal designs, 101–104
Social bases, 127–137
 culture, 127–128
 interpersonal context, 128–129
 media, 134–135
 pornography, coercion, and sexual violence, 135–136
 sexual double standard, 136–137
 social scripts, 129–134
  dating scripts, 131–132
  playground scripts, 130–131
  sexual scripts, 132–134
Social Cognitive Theory (SCT), 236
Social Development Model (SDM), 265
Social environment, puberty onset and, 150–152
Social learning theory, 208–209
 cognitive, 121
Social SciSearch databases, 21
Social stigmatization, 290–291
Socio-religious statuses, 173
Spermarche, 147
*SRY*, 117–118
Standardized mean difference, 52
STD/HIV prevention
 among youth in treatment for substance use problems, 267–268
 for youth not in treatment programs, 268–269

Stigmatization
  exposure to, 290–293
  social, 290–291
Structured Assessment of Violence Risk in Youth (SAVRY), 531–532
Structured Sensory Intervention for Traumatized Children, Adolescents and Parents—At-risk Adjudicated Treatment Program (SITCAP-ART), 374–375
Subjugation, 306
"Suggestive questions,", 354–356
Suspected child sexual abuse, medical evaluation for, 401
  documentation of, 414–415
    interpretation of medical findings, 414
    medical assessment, 414–415
  examination of, 409–414
    distraction techniques, 408–409
    preparation of child for, 407–409
    relaxation techniques, 408–409
  medical assessment and treatment of, 401
    overview approach to, 402–404
    physical exam, timing of, 406–407
  multidisciplinary teams, 415–416
Systematic observation, of childhood sexual behavior, 32–34

## T

Tanner stages, of sexual maturity system, 410
Tanner Staging, 146–147
Teaching sexual abuse prevention skills to children, 419
  recommendations, 439–444
    BST, adapting, 442–444
    BST, evaluation of, 441
    in situ assessments, development and social validation of, 439–441
    IST, adapting, 442–444
    IST, evaluation of, 441
  safety skills assessment, 423–428
    in situ assessment, 426–427
    role play assessment, 425–426
    verbal report assessment, 423–425
  sexual abuse prevention skills, 421–422
  training approaches, 428–444
    active learning approaches, 432–438
    informational approaches, 429–432
Technology, impact of
  on sexual behavior, 157–158
Teenage pregnancy, 223–224
  alcohol use and, 262
Testosterone, 117–118
Thelarche, 147
Theories and common mechanisms of influence among alcohol, drugs, and sexual behaviors, 264–266
Theories of planned behavior (TPB), 229–230, 236
Theories of reasoned action (TRA), 229–230, 236
Toddlers
  sexual behavior in, 153–155
  sexual knowledge of, 152–153
Traditional sexual script, 199
Training approaches, for teaching sexual abuse prevention skills. *See* Teaching sexual abuse prevention skills to children
Transcription-mediated amplification (TMA), 413–414
Transgender youths, 275–276, 288–290
Transsexual individuals, 286–287
Trauma Narrative and Processing, 383–384
Trauma Symptoms Checklist for Children (TSCC), 357
Trauma-Focused Cognitive Behavioral Therapy (TF-CBT), 372–373, 510
  case study of, 385–396
  research, 375–378
  therapy, 378–385
Treatment of children, for sexual disorder/behavior. *See* Children's treatment for sexual disorder/behavior
Treatment Progress Inventory for Adolescents who Sexually Abuse (TPI-ASA), 532
Typical child sexual development, 499–500

## U

UCLA PTSD Index, 508
Unintended pregnancy, 223–224, 262. *See also* Teenage pregnancy

United States, sexuality of children in, 325
Unsafe sexual practices, substance use and, 254–257

## V
Verbal report assessment, 423–425
Victim and abuse characteristics, 309–313
   sexual abuse experiences, 311–313
   sexual abuse victims, 309–311
Victims of Child Abuse Act of 1990 (2006), 487–489
Victim's rights movement, 485–489

## W
"Warmth," feelings of, 119
"What If Situations Test" (WIST), 423–425
Withdrawal and reversal designs, 101–104
"Working memory,", 350

## Y
Young adults, retrospective recall of, 23
Youth Level of Service/Case Management Inventory (YLS/CMI), 531–532
Youth Risk Behavior Survey (YRBS), 254, 327–328